W9-BCU-022

The Other American

THE OTHER AMERICAN

The Life of Michael Harrington

MAURICE ISSERMAN

PublicAffairs
NEW YORK

Published in the United States by PublicAffairs™, a member of the Perseus Books Group.

Printed in the United States of America.

Photo credits: "Neddie" Harrington courtesy of Stephanie Harrington. "Ned" Harrington courtesy of St. Louis University High School Yearbook. "Ed" Harrington courtesy of the Holy Cross Archives. Edward Harrington courtesy of the Holy Cross Yearbook. Cartoon courtesy of the Catholic Worker. Dorothy Day courtesy of the Marquette University Archives. Bogdan Denitch courtesy of Carol Sydney Marshall. Norman Thomas courtesy of the Tamiment Library, New York University. Michael Harrington at a Socialist Party conference courtesy Peter Graham. Michael Harrington in Paris courtesy Stephanie Harrington. Harrington marriage announcement courtesy of *The Village Voice.* Max Schactman courtesy of Peter Graham. Book covers courtesy of the author. Lyndon Johnson © Magnum Photo, Inc./René Burri. Sargent Shriver © Black Star. The march on Montgomery © Black Star. Photo of Irving Howe courtesy of the City University of New York. Michael Harrington and family © Bob Adelman. Stephanie, Alex, and Teddy Harrington courtesy of Harry Fleischman. Michael Harrington, Marjorie Phyfe Gellerman and William Winpisinger courtesy of the author. Michael Harrington speaking in Atlanta courtesy of Matt Mancini.

Book design by Jenny Dossin.

LIBRARY OF CONGRESS CATALOGING-IN-PUBLICATION DATA

Isserman, Maurice.

The other American : the life of Michael Harrington/Maurice Isserman.

p. cm.

Includes bibliographical references and index.

ISBN 1-891620-30-4

1. Harrington, Michael, 1928–1989 2. Social scientists—United States—Biography. 3. Political scientists—United States—Biography. 4. Socialists—United States—Biography. I. Title.

H59. H36 I85 2000

300'.92—dc21

[B] 99-056654

CONTENTS

PREFACE

Just over a year before he died of cancer in 1989 at the age of sixty-one, Michael Harrington remarked to an interviewer, "It's almost as if my life has been a well-plotted story. Almost."[1] It was certainly in keeping with the larger contours of this "plot" that a copy of E.M. Forster's great novel of Edwardian England, *Howard's End*, was found on Michael's bedside table when he died at home the following summer.

Howard's End revolves around the complications that arise when its well-intentioned and well-to-do heroines, the Schlegel sisters, involve themselves, somewhat disastrously, in the lives of the English poor. Though Helen and Margaret Schlegel are naifs, Forster is clearly in their camp in the ensuing confrontation between the values of culture and commerce. In a passage which, under less dire circumstances, would likely have appealed to Michael's puckish sense of humor, a fatuous bourgeois villain warns the idealistic sisters to avoid getting "carried away by absurd schemes of social reform . . . You can take it from me that there is no Social Question—except for a few journalists who try to get a living out of the phrase."[2]

It was the "social question" upon which Michael Harrington would make his own reputation—and a living of sorts—by drawing the attention of Americans to the existence of what he called "The Other America." Michael's book of the same title, published at the start of the 1960s, challenged the then all-but-universal opinion (at least among the opinion-forming classes) that the United States had helped all but a tiny minority of its citizens to a fair share of the astonishing economic abundance of its affluent society. *The Other America* went on to inspire the most ambitious "scheme of social reform" of the later twentieth century in the United States, the war on poverty launched during the administration of President Lyndon Johnson. Some historians of the 1960s have compared the significance of *The*

Other America to that of *Uncle Tom's Cabin* for the 1860s.[3] And on the eve of the new millennium, *Time* magazine described *The Other America* as one of the ten most influential nonfiction books of the 20th century to be published anywhere in the world, putting Michael's writings on poverty in such distinguished company as Sigmund Freud's *Civilization and its Discontents* and Alexander Solzhenitsyn's *The Gulag Archipelago*.[4]

There is another passage in Forster's novel that may have caught Michael's eye in those last days, if he were in the mood and condition to reflect upon his own almost-well-plotted life story:

> "Looking back on the past six months, Margaret [Schlegel] realized the chaotic nature of our daily life, and its difference from the orderly sequence that has been fabricated by historians. Actual life is full of false clues and sign-posts that lead nowhere. With infinite effort we nerve ourselves for a crisis that never comes. The most successful career must show a waste of strength that might have removed mountains, and the most unsuccessful is not that of the man who is taken unprepared, but of him who has prepared and is never taken."[5]

In the pages to follow I will be following Michael Harrington's life through three overlapping and interrelated stories. There is, first of all, the story of Michael Harrington, the "man who discovered poverty," and the consequences of that discovery for Michael and for the nation. Secondly, there is the story of Michael Harrington, the heir to Eugene Debs and Norman Thomas as America's foremost socialist and the decidedly mixed success of his efforts of over a quarter-century to create a "left-wing of the possible." And, finally, there is the story of Michael Harrington's personal transformation from golden youth to a kind of secular Saint Francis of Assissi—a legend that Michael helped create, and yet at the same time at whose restrictions he chafed. These three sequences in Michael's almost-well-plotted life are as "orderly" as I could make them, but bearing in mind Miss Schlegel's injunction, I have tried to avoid the temptation of making them too orderly. I have been on the lookout for those false clues and signposts that lead nowhere—including those occasional instances when the clues were deposited and the signposts erected by Michael himself.

I knew Michael Harrington, but not well. Nor were we contemporaries. He was born in 1928. I was born in 1951, about the same time that he moved into the Catholic Worker House of Hospitality on the Lower East Side of New York. He was part of what he would call the "missing generation" on the American Left, those who came of political age in the 1950s; I was part of the succeeding generation who came of age in the 1960s, the New Left that Michael hoped to influence. "Only Connect" is the famous epigraph to

Howard's End. That didn't happen with Michael and my generation, at least not in the 1960s.

I knew about him, of course. In the mid–1960s when I was sixteen years old, and a volunteer on an American Friends Service Committee (AFSC) summer work project in a poor and racially mixed neighborhood of Indianapolis, I was given a reading list that included *The Other America*. I read it and admired it, but not as much as I admired another book on the list, *The Autobiography of Malcolm X*. Given the timing, Michael never had a chance. We arrived in Indianapolis in June of 1967, at the beginning of what turned into the bloodiest of the "long hot summers" of racial unrest. Detroit and Newark exploded. Although racial tensions weren't as bad where we found ourselves (in fact the only real hostility our motley crew of teenaged idealists encountered was from some local white toughs who objected to the fact that some of the black volunteers on the project had white girlfriends), the AFSC subsequently scrapped its urban volunteer programs, fearing the worst. I reread Malcolm X's autobiography several times over the next few years. I did not pick up another book by Michael Harrington for the next ten.

However, Malcolm (or at least his would-be ideological successors) did not wear that well. An eventful decade or so later I encountered Michael again, this time in person when he was giving a speech at Harvard University. He was making a pitch that evening for Edward Kennedy's candidacy for the Democratic presidential nomination in 1980. In the question and answer period that followed I predicted, in a belligerent tone left over from an earlier period of militant certainty, that he would no doubt go on to endorse Jimmy Carter in the event that Kennedy failed to wrest the nomination from the Democratic incumbent. "Well, of course," Michael replied mildly, and then proceeded to lay out a very thoughtful justification for the politics of the lesser evil. Although I wasn't completely persuaded, within a year I wound up voting for that very same lesser evil. I also joined the Democratic Socialist Organizing Committee (DSOC), the political organization of which Michael was founder and chairman.

Over the next few years, I encountered Michael on a number of occasions. I heard him speak a good half dozen times (including once when I brought him to the college where I was then teaching, thus gaining the chance to participate in one of the classic Harrington rituals, drinking beer with him afterwards while he told stories of past political wars and debacles). I also interviewed him on two occasions for my book *If I Had a Hammer: The Death of the Old Left and the Birth of the New Left*, which was published in 1982.

I encountered Michael for the final time at a speech he delivered in western Massachusetts in the spring of 1987. Since the last time I had heard him speak, he had undergone treatment for a cancerous growth in his throat. He seemed much older to me until he started speaking; the familiar power and cadence of his speech was reassuring. But late that fall I learned that he was again battling cancer, and this time there was little hope that he could beat it. I remember sitting down to Thanksgiving dinner with an old friend and comrade of Michael's, and the two of us agreeing that someone—maybe me—should get in touch with him and arrange to tape his reminiscences. Only Connect. But for various reasons I didn't; the chance was lost.

The Other American is not the first book about the life of Michael Harrington (among others, Michael wrote two of his own); I doubt if it will be the last.[6] For those who will explore Michael's life and legacy in future years, I have arranged to deposit the interviews I did for this book, along with other research materials, at the Tamiment Library at New York University, which is already home to the Michael Harrington papers. The list of debts I incurred in writing this book is extremely long, and my gratitude as deep. The reference librarians at Hamilton College deserve first mention, along with the many archivists with whom I was privileged to work in collections across the country. Eugene Tobin, first as dean of faculty and then as president of Hamilton College, was supportive throughout the period it took to bring this book to completion. I was extremely fortunate to be selected as an Andrew E. Mellon Faculty Fellow at Harvard University for the year 1992–1993; the fellowship theme that year at Harvard was biography, and I learned a great deal from the project directors, Richard Hunt, William S. McFeely, Marjorie Garber, and Henry Louis Gates, Jr., as well as from my fellow Fellows, Jeffery Decker, Mary Rhiel, David Suchoff, and Dennis Trout. The Michael Harrington Foundation provided funds for the transcription of the interviews for this book. Most of the transcriptions were done by Jan Pieroni, who also conducted one of the interviews for me on a trip she took to Stockholm, Sweden.

I am grateful to the following individuals who shared their memories of Michael in personal conversations with me: Jean Arthur, Betty Bartelme, Jules Bernstein, Heather Booth, Peggy Brennan, Ed Brungard, William F. Buckley, Jim Chapin, Ed Clark, Jack Clark, Eldon Clingon, Marty Corbin, John Cort, Richard Dempsey, Bogdan Denitch, Norman Dorsen, Peter Dreier, Ed Egan, Father William Faherty, S.J., Ed Fancher, Eileen Fantino-Diaz, Jim Finn, Molly Finn, Peggy FitzGibbon, Richard Fitzsimmons, Harry Fleischman, Joan S. Franklin, John Kenneth Galbraith, Liz Gallin, Herb Gans, Todd Gitlin, Alec Harrington, Stephanie Harrington, Ted Harrington, Richard Healey, Bill Hegarty, Father Robert Henle, S.J., Stuart Holland, Irving Howe, Ruth Jordan, Steve Kelman, Irving Kristol, David Kusnet, Bob Kuttner, Pat Lacefield, Dinah Leventhal, Mark Levinson, Frank Llewelyn, Art Lipow, Bill Loftus, Roberta Lynch, Peter Mandler, Steve Max, Senator George McGovern, Neil McLaughlin, David

McReynolds, Debbie Meier, Harold Meyerson, Arthur Moore, Jo-Ann Mort, Senator Daniel Patrick Moynihan, Joe Murphy, Jack Newfield, Mary Perot Nichols, Peter Novick, Dave O'Brien, Ned O'Gorman, Roger O'Neill, Father John Padberg, S.J., Father Paul Reinert, S.J., Victor Reuther, Nancy Rice, Skip Roberts, Eugene Rostow, Joe Schwartz, Stanley Sheinbaum, Carl Shier, Marian Shier, Nancy Shier, Jim Shoch, Steve Silbiger, John Stanley, Peter Steinfels, Don Stillman, Jack Stuart, Irwin Suall, Bill Thomas, Martin Towey, Diana Trilling, Dan Wakefield, Jane Warwick, Msgr. Jerome Wilkerson, and Father Fred Zimmerman. Diana Trilling, Dave Garrow, Todd Gitlin, and David Hacker generously provided me copies of interviews they had done with Michael for their own projects. I also spoke with a number of other people over the telephone or had letters from them about Michael; these contributions are acknowledged in the endnotes. I had very helpful conversations about the Catholic Church, of which I knew virtually nothing when I started this project, with my fellow historians Dave O'Brien, Martin Towey, James Fisher, Fred McGinness, and Maureen Miller. I thought I knew more about the history of the American Left, but I am very grateful to fellow specialists in the field Nick Salvatore, Mike Kazin, Joe Schwartz, and Peter Mandler, all of whom read the manuscript in its entirety, and saved me from some world-class "what-was-I-thinking?" blunders.

This book has had a strenuous publishing history. I initially signed to do it under the justly celebrated editorial direction of Joyce Seltzer at a publishing house with which she is no longer associated and that, seeing as I have no good to say of it, shall go nameless. Things being what they were in the publishing world of the 1990s, the project wound up orphaned. Though I couldn't continue my work with Joyce, I was blessed with having Geoff Shandler of PublicAffairs press step in as her most able successor. Editorial assistant Mary-Claire Flynn made her own heroic contributions in the final stages of production.

Only Connect. The most important connection in my own life is with my wife Marcia, and my children Ruth and David. Marcia lived with this project for ten years; Ruth and David have lived with it for their entire lives. This book is dedicated to them.

Clinton, New York
December 1999

The Other American

CHAPTER ONE

Community, Family, and Faith, 1928–1944

That you are going to America is bad, but I really don't know what other advice to give you. . . . Outside of New York, the only endurable place is St. Louis.

Frederick Engels to Joseph Weydemeyer
August 7, 1851[1]

Catherine Harrington gave birth to her first and only child in St. Louis Maternity Hospital at 5:10 P.M. on the cold and cloudy afternoon of February 24, 1928. The baby, a boy, was named for his father, Edward Michael Harrington Sr., and was received into the Catholic fold three weeks later, when he was baptized by the Reverend William J. Glynn in St. Roch's Church, located just down the street from his parents' apartment. St. Roch's was named for a fourteenth-century French aristocrat who, at the age of twenty, gave away all his possessions to the poor and cared for the victims of the plague. The red brick church had been built in 1911 to serve the needs of the Irish-American parishioners who were moving westward into more prosperous suburbs from the decaying city center of St. Louis.[2]

Edward Michael the younger would be known to his childhood friends as Ned, to college friends as Ed, and later, and to a wider world, as Michael or Mike. In the late winter of 1928, when Michael was born, John F. Kennedy was attending the fifth grade at the socially exclusive Riverdale Country Day School in the Bronx. Lyndon Baines Johnson was completing his first year at Southwest Texas State Teacher's College in San Marcos. Dorothy Day, a radical journalist two years older than Michael's mother, was living in Greenwich Village and rethinking her life's mission after her recent conversion to Catholicism. And eleven months after Michael's birth, in Atlanta, Georgia, the wife of a prominent black minister, bore a son they would name Martin Luther King Jr.

The issues of poverty, equality, and social justice that John Kennedy, Lyndon Johnson, Dorothy Day, Martin Luther King Jr.—and Michael Harrington—came to be identified with were not much on the minds of the residents of St. Louis in February 1928, at least not according to the pages of the local newspapers. On the day Michael was born, the editors of the *St. Louis Post Dispatch* filled their front page with stories of regional crime and scandals. On the sports page, St. Louis Cardinals' batting star and manager Rogers Hornsby predicted that the Boston Braves would emerge as the "dark horse" candidate to win the 1928 National League pennant—a generous judgment, since it was the Cardinals who went on to clinch the pennant that fall. The economic news was good, if unremarkable, in a generally prosperous decade; on the St. Louis Merchant's Exchange wheat closed a cent ahead of the previous day, and on the New York Stock Exchange, General Motors stock closed fractionally higher.[3]

In the months that followed, election news came to dominate the headlines. In St. Louis, as in a number of the nation's largest cities, the Democratic presidential contender, Governor Al Smith of New York, ran a strong race. By calling for the repeal of Prohibition—a popular position in St. Louis, as in other cities with large immigrant populations—Smith (the first Catholic nominated as a major party presidential candidate) challenged his opponent on a highly charged cultural and social issue. But "Coolidge prosperity" was a compelling argument for maintaining Republican control of the White House. Accepting the Republican presidential nomination that summer of 1928, Herbert Hoover declared, "We in America today are nearer to the final triumph of poverty than ever before in the history of any land. The poorhouse is vanishing from among us." It was a reassuring message and a belief that most Americans apparently shared.[4]

There was another candidate that year who ran against both Hoover and Smith. Norman Thomas, a tall, patrician forty-three-year-old former Presbyterian minister with a booming voice, was launching the first of six bids for the presidency as the candidate of the Socialist Party. It had been eight years since the Socialists had run their last presidential campaign. In 1920, in the midst of the postwar "Red Scare," their imprisoned leader, Eugene Debs, had attracted a million votes. Since then the Socialist Party's strength had dwindled, a victim of wartime intolerance and internal factionalism. Hoping to revive his party's fortunes, Thomas boldly challenged the notion that the rising tide of national prosperity in the 1920s was lifting all boats equally: "By comparison with Europe," Thomas conceded in a speech quoted in the *St. Louis Globe Democrat,* "our workers are prosperous." But given the vast natural resources of the United States, and the fact that the nation had been spared the physical destruction that the world war had wreaked on Europe, why did so many working-class Americans have so little to show for their hard work? "The misery of the textile towns, the tragedy of the coal fields, the justified discontent of the farmers—these things are but the more dramatic proofs of our failure to end poverty." Thomas's eloquence and obvious sincerity won him devoted admirers but relatively few votes; on election day, Thomas received just over a quarter million ballots.[5]

A year later, with the crash of the stock market and the onset of the Great Depression, Thomas's concerns would suddenly seem more relevant to the nation. But in 1928, aside from grumbling over Prohibition, the citizens of St. Louis were enjoying an unprecedented era of civic good feelings. The Cardinals' upset victory over the New York Yankees in the 1926 World Series and the reflected glory of Charles Lindbergh's daring transatlantic flight aboard the "Spirit of St. Louis" in May 1927 did much to assuage the sense of civic inferiority that had beset the city since it had been upstaged by Chicago, its midwestern rival, in the late nineteenth century. In the 1920s St. Louis had nearly 800,000 residents, making it the nation's sixth largest city. It boasted communities of solid brick homes and lush greenery, as well as estimable universities, libraries, opera companies, and symphonies.

St. Louis residents were proud of their city's history, especially its frontier heritage. As the "gateway to the west," the city's early years had been shaped by the clash of colonial ambitions and were redolent of the romance of fur trapping and mountain men, the overland trail, and the Mississippi river boat. A decade after the upstart Chicago beat out St. Louis for the honor of staging the Columbia Exposition (marking the 400th anniversary of the discovery of the New World), the city fathers retaliated by hosting a world's fair in 1904 to celebrate the centenary of the Louisiana Purchase. Attracting millions of visitors, the fair proved a boon to the city's reputation and economy. The fair also left the city the physical legacy of a handsome park and a stately art museum, as well as the popular song "Meet Me in St. Louis."[6]

St. Louis was a city that had long been welcoming to youthful talent, beginning with the French merchant-explorer Auguste Chouteau, who was just fourteen years old when he traveled up the Mississippi by bateau with a party of workmen to establish a fur post on the west bank of the river in 1764. Before he died, he became a wealthy man, while the city he helped found passed under the control of the Spanish, back to the French, and, in 1804, on to the United States.[7]

As the city's economy shifted in the nineteenth century from frontier trading post to industrial manufacturing center, and as new immigrant groups arrived to supplant the original French settlers, other ambitious young men found avenues toward wealth. John Mullanphy, an Irish immigrant who arrived in St. Louis in 1804, built a vast fortune in the cotton market and in real estate and was St. Louis's first millionaire; his son Bryan was elected the city's mayor in 1847 on the Democratic ticket. Mullanphy left a lasting legacy through his funding of hospitals, orphanages, and schools in the city. He also gave his name to Mullanphy Street in "Kerry Patch," a neighborhood on the city's near north side that would become the center of a rapidly expanding Irish-American community in the 1840s.[8]

In 1881 another young Irish immigrant, this one named Patrick R. FitzGibbon, found his way to St. Louis and settled in Kerry Patch. His life too would prove a tale of immigrant success, albeit on a more modest scale than Chouteau or Mullanphy.

Patrick had been born on May 4, 1861, in a thatched roof cottage on his parents' small rented farm in Ballylegan, Glanworth, in County Cork, Ireland, the second of Richard and Margaret Fitzgibbon's eight children.[9] (The Irish Fitzgibbons spelled their name without the capitalized "G" adopted by the American wing of the family.) Family lore asserts that the Fitzgibbons left Ballingaddy in County Limerick to settle in Ballylegan in 1622, having obtained a large grant of land from the abbey in Glanworth, thanks to family ties with the local abbot.[10] Glanworth is located on a bend in the River Blackwater, about twenty-six miles north of the city of Cork. In earlier centuries the village had been Glanore, or "the golden glen," and was known for the fertility of its fields. A narrow old stone bridge, reputed to be over 600 years old, spans the river that runs past the village. The ruins of an old castle and a thirteenth-century Dominican priory, the latter destroyed by Cromwell's soldiers in the seventeenth century, testify to its former glories.[11]

But Glanworth was no golden glen in the mid-nineteenth century. Like most of their compatriots in Ireland's western counties, Patrick's parents were subsistence farmers in a region burdened by British rule, overpopulation, and, most disastrously, a blight on their staple crop, the potato. Travelers visiting County Cork in the "hungry 40s" left stark accounts of the destitution they witnessed. Dogs and rats feasted on the human corpses that lined the roads.[12] Local authorities insisted that to be eligible for relief, the poor had to enter the county's workhouses rather than receive the supposedly character-sapping, non-custodial "outdoor relief." Many poor people were reluctant to do so because of the harsh discipline and overcrowding associated with the workhouses and because of the danger of cholera epidemics. In response to their plight, crowds of men, women, and children, armed with spades and shovels, terrified the local gentry by marching through the streets chanting "work or food." Some ransacked flour and bread shops. Others hijacked grain deliveries and stole livestock. Those caught by the authorities were sentenced to transportation to the penal colonies in Australia for terms as long as fifteen years.[13] All told, over 100,000 people are estimated to have died of disease or starvation in County Cork during the famine years of 1846–1850. Nearly 100,000 more emigrated.[14]

Despite a gradual improvement in conditions for the farmers of County Cork in subsequent decades, life remained hard and uncertain. The potato blight recurred for three years running in the mid-1860s. The outbreak of the

American Civil War temporarily interrupted the flow of Irish immigrants to the United States; but when the war ended, emigration again picked up. In 1872, a year when heavy rainfalls again threatened the potato crop, eleven-year-old Patrick FitzGibbon left his ancestral home in Glanworth for the United States.[15]

FitzGibbon family legends offer various explanations for young Patrick's departure, including political trouble with the British authorities and horse theft.[16] In any case, it was by no means uncommon in nineteenth-century Ireland for children to choose, or be forced, to leave their families behind when they emigrated. One of Patrick's brothers and two of his sisters would also leave for America over the next several years.[17] Traveling to the United States on board the *Dresden* from Queenstown (now the city of Cobh), Patrick reportedly obtained boat fare by selling two of his father's sheep.[18]

After arriving in New York, Patrick took a job shoveling snow. He was also able to attend several years of grade school before setting out in 1878 to seek his fortune in the American west. In 1881, after some transient years in Iowa, the Dakotas, and Montana, he made his way to St. Louis. There he was joined by his younger brother John, who became a city policeman, and his younger sister Margaret, a nurse.[19]

For the first four decades of his life in St. Louis, Patrick lived on Mullanphy Street, or on nearby O'Fallon and Cass Streets. This neighborhood, a densely settled warren of tenements, groceries, saloons, and churches, was the center of the Irish immigrant community. Few native-born outsiders ever ventured into Kerry Patch, which was known to the police as the "Bloody Third District" for its street brawls. (A St. Louis guide book described the residents of Kerry Patch in 1878 as a population whose "chief amusements consist of punching each other's eyes.")[20] Despite the hostility of outsiders toward their community, which in early years included occasional assaults on the district by armed bands of nativist "Know-Nothings," Patrick and other Irish immigrants could feel secure in their growing numbers. Like many other American communities of the era, St. Louis was an immigrant town. According to the 1880 census, nearly 30,000 St. Louisans were Irish immigrants; along with a much more sizable German population and other immigrant groups, two-thirds of the city's 350,000 residents in 1880 consisted of immigrants and their children.[21]

St. Louis was also a city with a strong tradition of working-class radicalism. Thousands of German socialists had fled their homeland in the aftermath of the failed revolution of 1848; some, like Karl Marx and Frederick Engels, settled in England; others, like Joseph Weydemeyer, a veteran of the Prussian army and a radical journalist, made their way to the United States.

Taking Engels's advice, Weydemeyer settled first in New York, where he published Marx's writings in a short-lived German-language newspaper and founded the first explicitly Marxist political group in the New World. Meanwhile, hundreds of his compatriots had arrived in St. Louis, where they organized fraternal organizations and trade unions. The St. Louis '48ers were also drawn into the struggle against slavery; in 1861, members of the German-American community's turnverein (paramilitary gymnastic clubs), who were hastily recruited into federal service, tipped the military balance in the city against the secessionists. Weydemeyer himself finally arrived in St. Louis as a colonel in the Union Army. When he wasn't occupied with military duties, he corresponded with Engels and handed out copies of Marx's inaugural address to the International Workingmen's Association in London. After the war, Weydemeyer edited a labor newspaper and was elected auditor of St. Louis County on the Republican ticket. His political career was cut short by his death in the cholera epidemic of 1866.[22]

The socialist movement retained a modest following among St. Louis's German-Americans in the postwar era. Four years before Patrick FitzGibbon's arrival in the city, St. Louis socialists even enjoyed a brief, exhilarating moment of power. In response to wage cuts, a strike broke out among railroad workers in West Virginia in mid-July 1877; within days the strike had spread north and westward, drawing in hundreds of thousands of workers and paralyzing the nation's rail system. In St. Louis, under the leadership of the socialist Workingmen's Party, the railroad strike turned into a general strike of the city's workers—not just the radically inclined Germans but also the Irish and, to the particular horror of the authorities, blacks. Acting under the strike committee's directive to "Keep sober and orderly . . . and don't plunder," thousands of strikers marched through the city's streets, while a brass band played the "Marseillaise." For several days, while red flags fluttered over the city, the local police hid inside their stations. However, it soon became apparent that the revolution was not at hand. As strike sentiment began to ebb, the St. Louis police emerged from their hiding places. The first city-wide general strike in the history of the United States was brought to an end by the mass arrest of its leaders.[23]

Many viewed the St. Louis "Commune" as the harbinger of escalating class warfare, and authorities in St. Louis, as in many other cities, hastened to build fortress-like national guard armories to keep the immigrant population in check. About a third of the workers who had gone out on strike against the railroads in 1877 were Irish-Americans, and the conservatively inclined hierarchy of the Catholic Church was appalled. The Catholic prelate of Peoria, Bishop J. L. Spalding, warned in 1880 that it would be "almost impossible" for the church to keep its Irish working-class parishioners "out of trades-unions and other societies, the tendency of which in the United States will be more and more in the direction of communism."[24]

Some Irish-Americans, like Patrick FitzGibbon's fellow immigrant from

County Cork, mine organizer "Mother" Mary Jones, were drawn to radical doctrines and organizations.[25] But most were not. Irish-Americans became devoted trade unionists, providing the leaders for nearly half of the 100-odd unions represented in the American Federation of Labor (AFL) at the turn of the century. In St. Louis, the Irish were the backbone of the local craft, utilities, and building trade unions. These unions were often militant, sometimes even violent, in defense of their members' bread-and-butter interests, but they usually opposed involvement in socialist or independent labor politics. For most Irish immigrant workers, the strong pulls of ethnic identity, religious affiliation, and loyalty to the Democratic Party undermined the potential for the kind of broad class-conscious radicalism that came to the fore briefly in the 1877 strike. Seven decades after the St. Louis general strike, in the midst of the Great Depression, a group of St. Louis socialists showed up on a picket line to support a strike by gashouse workers. They wound up being beaten up by the predominantly Irish-American strikers for their gesture of labor solidarity.[26]

Patrick FitzGibbon made his first appearance in the city directory in 1885 as a bartender; by the next year he had advanced to saloonkeeper. He held onto the saloon for years, while trying his hand at a variety of other pursuits. From 1889 to 1893 he served as inspector of streets and superintendent of street sprinkling. For the next four years he was a copyist for the city recorder of deeds. In 1902 he was elected as the city register, a post he held for four years. He had been a partner in the FitzGibbon Brothers (nature unknown) in 1894 and was president of the Catalpa Gold and Copper Mining Company in 1909. (Before arriving in St. Louis, Patrick's brother John had worked as a gold prospector in California and at a smelter in the lead mines in Leadville, Colorado; the two brothers' business enterprises may have grown out of John's connections and experiences.[27]) Patrick also ran an undertaking establishment at one point. By 1915, he was the St. Louis agent for the Reliance Life Insurance Company of Pittsburgh, Pennsylvania. Patrick did not become a rich man, but he and his family enjoyed a level of material well-being that far exceeded what he had known as a child in County Cork.[28]

Throughout his years in St. Louis, Patrick remained a loyal and passionate supporter of the city's Irish-dominated Democratic machine. Naturalized as an American citizen on June 27, 1884, he voted for Democrat Grover Cleveland in that fall's presidential election. By 1888, FitzGibbon was leader of the Jacksonian Democratic Club of St. Louis's fourteenth ward. He attended the Democratic national conventions of 1888, 1892, and 1896 as a delegate, was vice chairman of the Missouri delegation to the 1904 convention, and was a delegate to the 1912 and 1916 conventions.

Even when his active involvement in politics waned, his partisanship remained undiminished. His granddaughter Peggy remembers him sitting in a lawn chair in the summer of 1940 listening to every word broadcast over the radio from the Democratic convention. (When the Republican convention came on the radio, he snapped, "Turn that damn thing off.") Four years later, too ill to leave his house to attend mass, he refused to take Communion from the local priest because he suspected the man of harboring Republican sympathies. On election day 1944, Patrick insisted that he be carried out of the house and down to the polling place, so he could cast a final ballot for Franklin Delano Roosevelt. (He died on April 17, 1945, just five days after the death of his beloved FDR.)[29]

The arrival of large numbers of Jews and Poles in St. Louis at the end of the nineteenth and the start of the twentieth century led the city's more established ethnic communities to resettle in newer and less crowded neighborhoods. The Germans moved in a widening triangle westward from south St. Louis, the Irish in a similar pattern westward from north St. Louis. Inevitably the two overlapped, and as they did so, the ethnic character of newer Catholic parishes grew more dilute. Intermarriage among Catholic ethnic groups became more frequent, as Irish- and German-Americans, and eventually Poles and others, shared churches, parochial schools, and membership in Knights of Columbus chapters. Patrick FitzGibbon held out in Kerry Patch longer than many of his compatriots; finally in 1920 he purchased a comfortable, three-story, single-family house with a wide lawn and backyard on Bartmer Avenue, in Saint Rose of Lima Parish on St. Louis's west side.

FitzGibbon had known little stability in his own childhood, but he was able to offer his own children both a secure home and a step-up in life. Patrick had married the twenty-one-year-old Nellie Dillon on November 13, 1889; like her husband, she was an Irish immigrant, born in Tipperary.[30] Large families were the norm among the Irish, both in Ireland and in the United States, in the nineteenth century, and Nellie would eventually bear fourteen children, nine of whom lived to adulthood.[31] A largely self-taught man who loved to read literature and history, FitzGibbon was sensitive about his own lack of formal education beyond grade school. In an era when most adults didn't graduate from high school, the expectation in the FitzGibbon family was that Patrick's children, including the daughters, would go to college. An impressive glass bookcase in Patrick's study served as a material symbol to his offspring of his devotion to the written word. In addition to the local newspapers, he read the *Manchester Guardian* and Irish newspapers. His granddaughter Peggy recalled him quoting "Gray's Elegy in a Country Churchyard" when she was a young child; he was disappointed to discover that she didn't know the poem.[32] FitzGibbon's attempts to instill in his children a respect for learning were successful: Of his four male offspring who survived to adulthood, three became lawyers, and of the five surviving daughters, two, including Michael's mother Catherine, became school teachers.[33]

Catherine, born on April 27, 1899, was the fifth of Patrick and Nellie's fourteen children. She seems to have been a prissy child, unhappy with the fate that had made her the daughter of a saloonkeeper in a disreputable neighborhood. A childhood acquaintance would recall Catherine, in pigtails and pinafore, sitting on the stone steps of her father's saloon, bristling in indignation when the neighborhood children greeted her by her hated nickname, "Katchoo."[34] After graduating from Central High School in 1917, she enrolled in Harris Teachers College, from which she received a teaching degree in 1920.

Catherine grew into a tall and attractive young woman, with pale skin and dark hair combed back into a tight bun. She craved respectability but also felt the conflicting tug of the new freedoms that young women were claiming in the 1920s. Although no flapper, she favored bright lipsticks and matching nail polish, smoked cigarettes, and drank hard liquor, behavior that in proper circles at the time was considered at least a little risqué. She had a competitive streak, expressed most successfully in playing bridge; along with her close friend and bridge partner, Virginia Brungard, she would win the first Missouri state tournament competition for women.[35] She and Brungard would in time become two of the most influential women in the city's politics.[36]

A Jesuit educator, Father Frederick "Fritz" Zimmerman, got to know Catherine well in later years, when Michael was attending the high school where he was principal. She was, he recalled, "a very vivacious person, talkative. She expressed what she thought." John Padberg, a high school classmate of Michael's, also remembered her from those years: "She was a forceful, vigorous woman. I don't mean a harridan or a shrew or anything like that. You knew that she was intelligent, that she was determined."[37]

Zimmerman's praise and Padberg's disclaimers notwithstanding, there were many people who did find Catherine hard to take; within Michael's circle, his mother was variously referred to as "Madame Harrington," "Catherine the Great," and "The Czarina."[38] Catherine displayed a drivenness that, though it might have been appreciated in a man, for most of her adult life was deemed inappropriate for a woman. Catherine could get an education and a job; she taught at the Mark Twain School in St. Louis for two years after her graduation. But she did so with the knowledge that the moment she married, Missouri state law made her ineligible for continued employment as a public school teacher. Furthermore, Catholic teachings on marriage emphasized the wife's duty to subordinate her own interests and desires to the needs of her husband and her children; a woman entering matrimony was encouraged to display a saintly spirit of self-abnegation.[39] Catherine was never consciously a rebel; a graduate student who interviewed her in the 1970s noted with apparent approval that she was "not the strident, women's rights [type]." [40] But Catherine was not passive either, though her willfulness could take eccentric forms; she was famous for arriving at social occasions ten minutes early, sitting in the car at the curb watching her wristwatch, and then appearing at the door at exactly the moment the invitation specified.[41]

Friends of the Harrington family remember Catherine's husband, if they remember him at all, as being about as meek and unassuming as his wife was outgoing and assertive. No photograph of Edward Harrington Sr. seems to have survived, either in the public domain or in family papers. Peggy FitzGibbon remembered "Uncle Eddie" as "an awfully nice guy, with a funny sense of humor." But he was also "quiet, very quiet. Catherine had more to say about everything than Uncle Eddie. Uncle Eddie would just sit there, kind of quietly." Another boyhood friend of Michael's, Bill Loftus, described the elder Mr. Harrington as "a very nice, quiet, henpecked man who never spoke unless you asked him to, and he knew his place, which was down at the office making money."[42]

The documentation that survives for the St. Louis Harringtons is scarce compared to that for the FitzGibbons. Edward Michael Harrington Sr. was born in 1889, one of a family of at least five children raised in St. Louis. His father was born in Ohio; his mother in Ireland. By the age of sixteen, according to the St. Louis city directory, Edward was working as a draftsman, a job he held until his military service in the American Expeditionary Force in 1917–1918. He briefly harbored the ambition to become a cartoonist but after the war decided on the more prosaic but financially reliable field of law.[43] Edward attended evening classes at St. Louis University law school and was admitted to the Missouri bar in 1923.[44] After several years of general practice, he settled into a specialty of patent law. His biggest account was with the Maloney Electric Company, a St. Louis manufacturer of generators and transformers for large electrical equipment. At the start of the 1920s, apparently a confirmed bachelor, he was living with two unmarried younger sisters.[45]

But Edward's bachelor days were numbered once he met Catherine. Harrington belonged to a club of young men known as the Chicks, who owned a cabin on the Meramec River. Despite Prohibition, the younger set of St. Louis gathered on warm days on the banks of the Meramec to drink bathtub gin and homemade beer. It was on an outing to the Chicks's cabin early in the 1920s that Edward and Catherine's romance began. Catherine was visiting the cabin that day as the guest of her friend Virginia and Virginia's soon-to-be husband, Edward Brungard. Virginia's upcoming nuptials may have given Catherine a sense that time and opportunity were slipping away from her; in any case, she decided Edward was going to be her husband that first day, and on June 17, 1922, she succeeded in bringing him to the altar.[46]

Once married, Catherine had no intention of sitting home and changing diapers. She bore only one child, and he was conceived a full five years after her marriage to Edward. Given Catherine's strong religious views, it seems unlikely that she strayed so far from church teachings as to use artificial birth control; more likely, the results were achieved through a rigorous abstinence.[47] In 1928, when Michael was born, his parents lived in an apartment on Waterman Avenue on St. Louis's west side, in the Kingsbury neighborhood. They moved soon after to another apartment in Kingsbury on Maple Avenue. This was a desirable and only recently developed neighborhood, inhabited by the professional middle classes. It was close to the zoo, opera, and art museum, with movie theaters, an ice skating rink, and the locally celebrated Doerr and Zeller ice cream parlor nearby.[48]

By 1935, Michael's father was doing well enough to buy the family a comfortable three-bedroom house on quiet tree-lined Harvard Street in University City. University City was a planned, ready-made miniature city of about 60,000 residents bordering St. Louis's prosperous western edge. The community was completely residential, and every winding road was named for a college or university. In 1942, the Harringtons moved back to the west end of St. Louis, to a house on McPherson Avenue, where Michael lived for his last two years before leaving for college.

The Harrington homes were comfortable, unpretentious houses. The backyards were spacious. The Harvard Street house backed onto the River Desperes, and Michael and his friends played out watery adventures along its shore.[49] The census may have classified the Harringtons as urban dwellers, but Michael's surroundings as a child combined the spaciousness and relaxed pace of the small town with an easy access to the city's amenities. As an only child, Michael always had his own room. The living room of the Harrington household, one frequent visitor recalled, was the kind of place "where you could entertain eight or ten friends without anybody stepping on anybody else's toes." A grand piano stood in the center of the living room, covered with a fringe shawl and family pictures.[50] In that setting, it was easy to learn the amenities of social conversation. Throughout Michael's childhood, the Harringtons frequently entertained family and friends. The atmosphere was informal; cocktails ("highballs" of bourbon and soda) would be served before and after dinner. When the Brungards and Harringtons got together, the radio would be tuned to Jack Benny, Charlie McCarthy, or Fred Allen during dinner. Afterwards the adults would gather in the living room to talk politics and play bridge.[51]

This was not the life that a lot of their fellow citizens were living in those years. During the depression, St. Louis enjoyed the dubious distinction of being home to the largest Hooverville in the United States; by 1933 nearly one in three workers in the city was unemployed.[52] Although Michael would later "vaguely recall breadlines" from the 1930s, they made little impression on him at the time.[53] The Harringtons were well enough off to send their son to private schools, keep a car, have a maid, and take family summer vacations. Still, Michael's father never felt as though he earned enough money. At one point, Edward had been taken advantage of in a business deal, losing a large sum of money in the process, and the memory of the loss rankled. And Catherine pushed her husband to do better, comparing their financial situation with that of better-off friends.[54]

Barred by law from pursuing her teaching career, Catherine did not let marriage or motherhood prevent her from continuing her education. A year after giving birth she returned to school, this time to Washington University, where she took a course on "Ancient and Modern Conceptions of Man" and a three semester Western civilization sequence. In 1933, when Michael started kindergarten, she enrolled at Fontbonne College, a local Catholic women's college, and majored in economics, getting A's in most of her courses. She received her B.A. from Fontbonne in June 1937 and then went on to graduate study at St. Louis University, receiving an M.A. in economics in 1940. Catherine thrived in her studies, while keeping up a demanding schedule of volunteer work: During the years Michael was growing up, she served as president of Mother's Club at St. Louis University High School, as a member of the Archdiocesan Council of Catholic Women, and as one of the board of directors of the Catholic Women's League Nursery. She also entertained frequently at her home. One visitor to the Harrington home recalled occasions when Catherine would sit in the living room with her guests after dinner, an economics textbook on her lap, taking part in the general conversation but studying at the same time. In 1944, the year that Michael left for college, she returned to Fontbonne, this time as director of personnel and student guidance.[55]

As a boy, Michael very much wanted to please his loving, formidable, and difficult mother. He was inspired by her example. And he learned to do and say the things that she valued. "Once, when Michael was 7 years old, we were both reading in bed," she told an interviewer after her son became famous. "He was reading Dickens and he turned to me and said, 'My, this author expresses himself well.'"[56] In his books, in later life, Michael praised his mother, if somewhat formally; it was from her, he wrote in the acknowledgments to *The Other America,* that he "first learned of justice." In his memoir *Fragments of the Century,* he described her with the single adjective "idealistic."[57] One interviewer detected a more ambivalent note. A *New York Herald Tribune* reporter wrote in a 1964 profile of Michael that his mother "is an ex-school teacher who is still active in community causes." And then, noting Michael's facial expression, she quoted his description of Catherine as "'public spirited, you could say, . . . I suppose she exerted a great influence in my life.' (Post-Freudian smile)."[58]

If Michael did harbor ambivalent feelings for his mother, such feelings were not in evidence when he spoke of his other parent. In both *Fragments of the Century* and in his acknowledgments to *The Other America,* Michael used an adjective to describe Edward Harrington Sr. that is conventionally reserved by sons to describe their mothers—"gentle." In a letter written five years before his father's death in 1955, Michael elevated his father to the level of a tragic and selfless hero. "He is a wondrous gentle man," Michael wrote to a girlfriend, "but one who was once poor. Had he not been, he might have become anything—the gentle things, perhaps an artist. But as it is, he has spent much of his life tortured by the thought of insecurity and willing one thing, that the son he loved so much would not face what he did."[59] The only evidence that Michael may have been troubled by his father's meek demeanor or by the general tenor of his parents' relationship lies in the acid portraits that he offered in short stories he wrote as a teenager, stories in which a series of middle-aged male Caspar Milquetoastish characters appear. "At the ripe age of forty years," Michael wrote of one of them, "he had just received permission from his wife to smoke . . . and his high life consisted of quaffing a little 3.2% ale in the cellar. . . . He still lived in the racy past of a three day Banking Clerks' Convention at Atlantic City."[60]

One way in which Edward's gentleness expressed itself was an unwillingness to lay a hand on his son. He also taught Michael to avoid conflict with his strong-willed mother. Although rarely a disobedient child, Michael once did something to enrage Catherine (the exact nature of the transgression is no longer remembered by those who heard Michael's retelling of the story). Catherine responded by sending her son off to his bedroom to await a spanking from his absent father. When Edward returned, Catherine informed him of Michael's misdeed and sent him upstairs, armed with a hairbrush, to settle accounts. Instead of delivering the spanking, Edward and Michael conspired to deceive Catherine; the father hit the side of the bed with the hairbrush, while the son cried out convincingly. Michael's mother was satisfied that justice had been done, while the male Harringtons enjoyed their victory over maternal law and order.[61]

Michael absorbed other lessons at Catherine's parents' house on Bartmer street, where the Harringtons would go for Sunday dinners and holidays. As loyal Democrats, the FitzGibbons had much to celebrate in the 1930s. When the newly elected president Franklin Roosevelt ended Prohibition in 1933, sixteen St. Louis breweries reopened for business. As a result, FDR secured the loyalty of the city's German-American brewery owners and workers alike; together with Irish-Americans and blacks they made St. Louis a fervently Democratic city in the 1930s.[62] The Democrats were able to elect their first mayor in St. Louis in a quarter-century. And in 1940 Michael's uncle David was elected as judge of the St. Louis Court of Criminal Corrections, a post he would fill for the next thirty-four years. (Judge FitzGibbon was known for his humane treatment of those brought before him in criminal proceedings, on occasion personally paying the fines he levied on poorer defendants.)[63]

Many children would have found the endless talk about politics boring. Michael did not. By the time he was eight, he was chiming in with his own opinions about Franklin Roosevelt and Father Coughlin. "I can see him in our living room on a Sunday afternoon," his cousin Peggy FitzGibbon would recall, "talking politics with the adults. The adults would be amused. They egged him on."[64]

Boyhood in St. Louis did not make Michael a radical. But the imprint of his earliest experiences could be seen in the kind of radical he turned out to be. From his grandfather, Michael acquired a fascination with politics, a love of rhetoric, and a sense that words had meaning and consequence. From his uncle David, he learned that laws were not abstractions but were, or should be, about how people deserve to be treated. From his father, he learned ways of defusing or avoiding personal conflict and also acquired a resentment against the values of a world in which "nice guys" tended to be overlooked or pushed around or cheated. And finally, from his mother, he acquired a respect for intellectual accomplishment, a sense of self-respect and self-discipline, and an authority figure whose firm standards of right and wrong he alternately hoped to fulfill and rebelled against.

Apart from family, the presence that loomed largest in Michael's life in his years growing up in St. Louis was that of the Catholic Church. From the time Michael's parents sent him off to kindergarten to the day he graduated from high school, he received an intense schooling, both in the religious doctrines of Catholicism, and, more importantly, in habits of thought. Michael would later depart from the formal teachings of the church but, as he would be the first to acknowledge, never shed their influence.

In 1932, at the age of four, Michael was enrolled by his parents in the parochial kindergarten sponsored by St. Rose's parish. The school was located on Goodfellow Street, just around the corner from his grandfather's house on Bartmer Avenue. He started kindergarten a year earlier than usual, so that he could accompany his five-year-old cousin and close companion Peggy to school. The two children absorbed their lessons well. Peggy would grow up to become a nun. And Michael seemed destined for a religious vocation himself. He would willingly go hungry so that he could put his lunch money in the missionary donation box at St. Rose's, happy in the assurance that his contribution would help "save a baby in China for Christ."[65] By the time he was nine, he was serving as an altar boy in the parish church and had memorized the Latin responses so well that he "could recite the Confiteor at absolutely breakneck speed," though he did so "without the least suspicion that I was thereby summoning the hosts of heaven to hear my sins." Michael was reminded one day that religion should be more than ritual incantation.

After he proudly recited his Latin phrases for his grandfather, Patrick asked him to translate them and then reprimanded the boy sharply when he proved incapable of doing so.[66]

Although Michael's close relationship with his grandfather provided a living link to the country of his forebears, he grew up "without serious memory of British oppression on the old sod." The wave of enthusiasm for Irish independence that had swept through St. Louis's Irish-American community during and immediately after the world war had subsided by the time Michael was born.[67] Nor had he ever personally felt the sting of anti-Catholic discrimination. St. Louis's Irish-Catholics "were not born wounded" by vivid memories of discrimination. To be sure, the city had witnessed episodes of nativist violence in the nineteenth century. But unlike their brethren in Boston, the St. Louis Irish "shared a religion with the aristocracy of the city," the descendants of the original French settlers. It was the city's white, Anglo-Saxon Protestants, Michael later noted, who were "somewhat arriviste."[68]

Although the feeling of being part of an embattled ethnic and religious minority lingered among many Irish-Americans in the 1930s and 1940s, it did not affect Michael. Of course, as the child of avidly Democratic Irish-Catholics, Michael could not have avoided hearing the story of how Al Smith had been victimized by anti-Catholicism in the 1928 presidential election. But that probably seemed ancient history to a boy growing up in the 1930s and 1940s. President Roosevelt was doing his best to salve the wounded feelings of his Catholic constituents through the strategic use of high-level appointments, such as sending Joseph Kennedy as ambassador to Great Britain.[69]

At the same time, in popular culture, Irish-Catholics found themselves embraced as America's favorite ethnic subculture. With an eye on winning the favor of the Legion of Decency, the Catholic pressure group that monitored the movies, the Hollywood studios in the 1930s and 1940s served up a regular fare of tales in which hearty and engaging Irish-American Catholic priests were the heroes. These ranged from Pat O'Brien's depiction of the "battling two-fisted clergyman of the lower East Side"—Father Connolly in *Angels with Dirty Faces*—in 1938 to Barry Fitzgerald's cantankerous but good-hearted Father Fitzgibbon in *Going My Way* in 1944. The latter movie was reportedly a favorite of both Al Smith and Pope Pius XII; Michael saw it soon after it opened in St. Louis.[70]

Of course, Michael did not have to go to the movies to see priests. He grew up surrounded by them. He saw them not only at mass on Sundays and in school on a daily basis but also as frequent guests to his house. Catherine counted a number of Jesuit priests as friends and bridge partners. These were not the simple parish priests of Hollywood legend. She preferred the company of politically savvy and intellectually acute men of the cloth. Influential figures such as Father Paul Reinert (president of St. Louis University) and Father Robert Henle (dean of the Graduate School at St. Louis University, who would later serve as president of Georgetown University) were among those welcomed as guests in the Harrington home.[71]

Michael remained at St. Rose's parish school through the third grade. In the fall of 1936, his parents enrolled him in Chaminade College Prep School, an exclusive boy's school run by the Marianist religious order. At Chaminade, students were expected to tend their souls as well as their studies. Daily attendance at mass was required.[72] The students put in a long school day, from 8:45 in the morning until 3:45 in the afternoon, with classes in religion, English, reading, arithmetic, history, and geography. Mandatory sports kept Michael after classes every day until 5:00 P.M. Michael, whose IQ test in the fifth grade stood at an estimable 146, had no trouble at all meeting the academic challenge. Only once in his four years at the school did he rank below the top half of his class, and he graduated first among the twenty-one students in his seventh grade class.[73]

Catherine's decision to enroll Michael at Chaminade may have been motivated by a desire to have him attend the same school as Virginia Brungard's son Ed. Michael and Ed grew up to be as inseparable as their mothers were. The two boys were constantly in and out of each other's houses and backyards. They spent several summers together when their families rented summer places in Kimmswick, Missouri, about twenty miles south of St. Louis on the Mississippi River. One day in the summer of 1933—in an adventure worthy of those fictional Missourians Tom Sawyer, Huck Finn, and Becky Thatcher—Ed, Mike, and Peggy constructed a raft. They were poling it down Rock Creek toward the open waters of the Mississippi when they were apprehended in mid-stream by the Brungard family maid.[74]

Ed Brungard, a year older than Michael, saw to it that his younger companion was included in school and neighborhood activities with the other boys. Although Michael found a place for himself in the rough and tumble of boyhood society, he always kept himself a little apart. Brungard remembered how Michael would "be in the middle of playing outside and excuse himself and go upstairs and read a book. He was more interested in reading than in playing ball."[75]

If Ed played the role of big brother to Michael, his cousin Peggy, also a year older, proved a substitute older sister. She was the one he went to when he wanted to discuss feelings and ideas that would not have found sympathy from his male companions or his parents. Peggy was the first to learn that Michael wanted to be a poet when he grew up. He recited snatches of T. S. Eliot and other poetry to her. He knew she wouldn't laugh when he told her that he had chosen "Sir Michael John" as the nom de plume under which he intended to publish his work. Well aware of the derision that his secret identity and aspirations would have provoked had they been known on the playing fields of Chaminade, Michael shared his confidences frugally.[76]

In the spring of 1940, when Michael was completing seventh grade and Ed Brungard was completing eighth grade, they were both personally recruited to attend St. Louis University High School. "We understand you have a boy here," a priest said when he knocked on the door of the Brungard house. "We would like to have him go to our school." Catherine Harrington and Virginia Brungard consulted, and Catherine decided that Michael would skip eighth grade and go on with Ed to high school.[77]

Catherine took her religion seriously, but there was also an element of social calculation at work when she entrusted her son to the Jesuits. The Jesuits were a particularly influential order in St. Louis, having founded a university, a medical school, and a host of other educational and charitable institutions. Alumni of Jesuit schools were well represented among the city's professional, business, and political classes. Catherine knew she was providing him with the personal network he would need to make his mark in St. Louis society, as well as with the opportunity to gain a first rate education.

St. Louis University High was widely regarded as the best Catholic school in St. Louis, and by some as the best school, private or public, in the city. It drew its students from the most distinguished families of the city's Catholic aristocracy, as well as from ambitious middle-class families. (Its yearly tuition of $120 set it out of the price range of most working-class Catholics in those depression years.)[78]

Just as there were distinctions between Catholic high schools in St. Louis, so, too, were there distinctions among St. Louis University High School students. Michael was part of an elite group of about thirty students out of his entering class of two hundred who were enrolled in the "Classical Course." These students were tracked together in most of their classes for the next four years, taking Latin for all four years and Greek for at least two years. St. Louis University High School students were encouraged to think of themselves as part of a spiritually militant and classically trained elite. "Forth from Jesuit Schools," Michael's freshman yearbook proclaimed in a headline, "Joining the Chivalry of Christ, the Ranks of Youth Emerge." In an extended analogy that must have had particular resonance for young men coming of age in those war years, Michael's classmates were told they were "a trained, formidable army of youth . . . joined in serried, marching ranks in the Mystical Body of Christ."[79]

As advisers to Catholic princes in the wars of religion of the seventeenth century, the Jesuits had earned a reputation for ruthlessness. They were the shock troops of the Counter-Reformation. They were also known for their courage and spirit of self-sacrifice. By the late sixteenth century, Jesuit missionaries had set out for Africa, Asia, and the New World. This was dangerous work; the Jesuits counted eight martyrs in French Canada alone. Spiritual ardor was not enough; Jesuit leaders emphasized the importance of unquestioning obedience to the orders received from superiors.[80] Leon Trotsky, who knew a thing or two about the functioning of centralized, disciplined organizations, liked to compare the Jesuits to the Bolsheviks.[81]

Some of Michael's teachers were Jesuit priests; others were "scholastics" (a term used to designate members of the order who were selected for the course of studies that would lead to the priesthood. Jesuit scholastics ordinarily took three years out from their studies to teach in a Jesuit high school).[82] All together, it took fifteen years to be trained as a Jesuit priest. The order attracted men of great zeal, and often of equal gifts as teachers. Some, like Father Bill Wade, were legendary.

A scholastic at St. Louis University High School in the early 1930s, and from 1939 through 1966 a leading member of the philosophy department of St. Louis University, Father Wade provoked his students by challenging their facile acceptance of Catholic teachings. As Robert Henle recalled, "He could take either side of an argument and maintain it. He would come in on Tuesday and he would say, now here's Kant's argument against the existence of God. I want you to refute it in the next class. Then he would take them on in the next class. The students got so angry that very often you would hear shouting in his classroom. They would forget that he was playing a part. He would cut them to pieces and then they would run back to the library and read more books and come back with better arguments."[83] Although Father Wade had left the high school for his position at the university before Michael enrolled, Michael fell under his influence (he was one of the priests Catherine regularly invited to dinner). Michael admired Father Wade's style of tough-minded and unsentimental defense of the faith, as well as his liberal political sympathies. It was to Wade that Michael would go when he first developed doubts about Catholicism.[84]

Of course, not every Jesuit priest or scholastic was a Bill Wade, but the Jesuit teachers were bearers of an educational tradition and philosophy that was supposed to eliminate the need for individual inspiration. The *Ratio Studiorum,* a collection of rules adopted in 1599 for teachers and students in Jesuit schools, laid out a curriculum in which courses in Latin and Greek and in philosophy, theology, literature, and the arts were designed to promote learning in graduated steps. The emphasis was on hard work and on a discipline instilled through memorization, drill, and exercises. The purpose of the *Ratio Studiorum* was to develop supple minds capable of a spirited defense of a fixed system of ideas. The graduate of a Jesuit school would ideally write Latin like Cicero, think like Aristotle—and remain content with theology as prescribed by St. Thomas Aquinas.[85]

Yearbook prose as a rule runs to the high-minded and inspirational; at Michael's high school the platitudes carried more of a punch. The most important benefit of a Jesuit education, the 1942 St. Louis University High School yearbook proclaimed, was that it instilled "the necessary fortitude and enthusiasm to step forth into battlefield, college or workaday world, and strive towards the urgent conversion of a perverted, pagan universe."[86]

Even allowing for yearbook hyperbole, there is no question that St. Louis University High managed to instill in its students a genuine sense of élan and community. John Padberg, one of Michael's classmates, remembered that during their years at the high school "the kids were wildly in love with the place. It was hard to get us to come home in the evening. My mother said at times she didn't know why I didn't keep a bed down at the school."[87]

Of course, no one, faculty or students, seriously expected that St. Louis University High School graduates were actually going to convert the entire world, let alone the United States, to Roman Catholicism. Michael's classmates were destined to become lawyers, doctors, and dentists, not soldiers in a religious war. And the boys did, in fact, go home at the end of the day, returning for better or worse to the influences of the secular world and the company of family and friends. Few students entered the school with the intention of pursuing a religious vocation (Padberg was one of only three members of the class of 1944 who went on to join the Jesuits). While incipient religious heretics in their number were even fewer, nonetheless, as one of Michael's classmates recalled, "piety doesn't come naturally to adolescents."[88]

Michael was only twelve years old at the start of his freshman year in high school. A yearbook photograph taken the following spring shows him with a round face and a slightly anxious expression, towered over by his fellow staffers on the school newspaper. Classmate Richard Dempsey remembered him being "a little chubbier, a little more of a boy" than the other freshmen. Even in his senior year, Michael was still being ribbed in the school newspaper's gossip column (which was written by Dempsey) as "our little pal, Neddie Harrington": "What prominent senior (last name—Harrington) slinks and cowers 'neath the dread menace of the curfew," the newspaper joked in April 1944; "seems that our Ned is underage."[89]

Because of the disparity in age and size, Michael couldn't compete on the playing fields; he never went out for any of the school's sports teams. He also displayed a studied indifference to the standards of dress maintained by his peers. Jerome Wilkerson, two years ahead of Michael at the high school, recalled that the student body included "some of the wealthiest kids in St. Louis." They were the kids who set the tone that most of the other students aspired to match. But not Michael. "Some of them looked like the cover of *Esquire,* with matching argyle sweaters and socks. Ned was never like that. He was always a little slovenly. He didn't care about a lot of things that other kids cared about."[90]

Catherine Harrington did her best to spruce up her son's appearance; after all, for her the point of sending Michael to this particular school was to ease his assimilation into the best circles in St. Louis Catholic society. It could not have been easy for her to tolerate Michael's affectation of ill-fitting clothes, unshined shoes, and a black navy watch cap, as if he were some character off the streets from her childhood in Kerry Patch. But Michael fended off his mother's efforts to dress up his image. He would not compete with his classmates on any terrain on which he felt at a disadvantage. Instead, he formed a high-minded rationale for ignoring conventional grooming expectations. Asked by classmate Bill Loftus why he didn't bother to wash his face, Michael replied placidly, "Poets don't."[91]

Michael was sensitive about the difference in his age and tried unsuccessfully to shed the nickname "Ned," preferring the less boyish-sounding "Ed." But in general he seems to have taken the ribbing that came his way in good humor. His classmates remember him as quick and funny: a "wise-cracker," a "gentle scoffer." His freshman yearbook labeled him "class comedian."[92] Despite his social disadvantages, Michael was not, it seems, unpopular or picked on. He created an identity for himself that allowed him to stand a little apart from the crowd, but also to make his mark within the community. He was fortunate enough to be enrolled in a school where brains as well as brawn were admired. If it wasn't acceptable to plan a lifetime career as a poet, it was still within the realm of acceptable behavior to read, write, and appreciate poetry. Michael would later recall, marveling, how as a freshman member of the school newspaper staff "I heard the sports editor discussing—freely, voluntarily, naturally—his sonnets with his friends."[93]

Frequent and lengthy writing assignments were among the hallmarks of Jesuit education. Father John Divine, who as English department chairman directed the school newspaper and the literary group, was a particularly strong influence on Michael. Divine oversaw the Dauphin Room, where the school's newspaper and yearbook writers congregated after school. There was a whiff of what passed for adult sophistication that accompanied hanging out in the Dauphin Room. (Apart from the quality of literary conversation, one of the room's attractions to Michael was that it was the only place in the school building where non-seniors were allowed to smoke. Since his freshman year Michael had been a heavy smoker; classmates remember the nicotine stains on his fingers as part of the bedraggled appearance he cultivated.)[94]

Father Divine's students would remember him as a cantankerous hypochondriac, with a bad case of dandruff; he was also one of the most demanding and inspiring teachers in the school.[95] In Michael's senior English class, Divine assigned six Shakespeare plays, as well as novels by Dickens,

Thackeray, and George Eliot. According to John Padberg: "Ned was more influenced by John Divine than anybody else. He learned literature. He learned rigor in writing. He learned to ask very acute questions. Divine never let you get by with a sloppy thought." Michael, like other students, was a little in awe of Divine. But he stood up to him on occasion, as he began to develop his own literary tastes. Students in Divine's senior class were allowed to choose a contemporary novel to read and report on to the class. Michael's choice, Padberg recalled, was *A Tree Grows in Brooklyn,* which was regarded as a "very dirty novel" at the time. "His choice both outraged and amused John Divine," but in the end he allowed Michael to report on the book.[96]

Michael earned academic honors his first two years at St. Louis University High School, then let his grades slip his last two years in courses that didn't hold his interest. He consistently received his highest marks in English and history, his lowest in the sciences, mathematics, and physical education. He graduated a respectable, if not outstanding, thirty-second in a class of one hundred and seventeen. In Divine's class, however, he got straight A's.[97]

Michael found other ways to stand out. He served on the newspaper for all four years at the school, rising to news editor his senior year. When he became sports editor, his weekly column, full of school boy in-jokes, was the first item that many readers turned to when they picked up the paper.[98] The 1941 yearbook commented that freshman Harrington "seems to be in about every organization he could find at school." He joined the debate team, the yearbook, the Latin club, the library club, and the radio club. He even marched with the band one year, carrying a French horn, although he couldn't play any musical instrument. A "Senior Spotlight" column in the student newspaper in 1944 called him a "stellar member of almost every [school] organization" during his "four outstanding years at the school." His activities made "Ed Harrington one of the most famous and popular '44 graduates."[99]

In debate, Michael found an arena of competition in which he won particular distinction. Debate was taken very seriously at the high school: The debate team's tournament records took up three pages in the yearbook. Debaters prepared rigorously for competition. Each year a topic would be assigned for all high school debate teams, usually bearing on some question of public policy, and the debaters would head for the libraries to research the arguments for and against proposals for world government, universal military service, or government ownership of the railroads. The boys assembled boxes of notes and statistics to buttress their arguments. But a really inspired debater brought something more than careful preparation to the contest. As Bill Loftus, one of Michael's debate teammates, recalled: "Many a time in high school, I saw Mike win a debate by standing there with his open Irish face, blinking at the judges, quoting brilliantly from a purely fictitious authority to prove his point. In one debate he even had the nerve to quote from

'Dr. Dingbat Fu,' and they bought it. He was very, very good."[100]

The pudgy twelve-year-old who entered St. Louis University High School as a freshman grew into a gangling sixteen-year-old senior in 1944. Like most adolescents, Michael and his classmates spent a good deal of time preoccupied with the mysterious changes going on in their bodies. The Jesuits, knowing what they were up against, preached hard and often on the evils of masturbation, promiscuity, and divorce. The official line on sex was faithfully echoed in an editorial in the student newspaper in the spring of Michael's senior year. The United States was doomed to repeat the cycle of decline and fall suffered by ancient Greece and Rome, and by modern France, "if we do not safeguard the only thing worth fighting for: the sanctity of the home."[101] The all-male school environment, a rigorous regimen of sports, and the companionship and supervision of celibate adults, were all intended to reinforce the boys' respect for sexual abstinence. The absence of the opposite sex helped considerably in this endeavor. Girls were invited to St. Louis University High School only on rare and carefully chaperoned occasions.

It was thus a memorable occasion for Michael when, on his first date, he double-dated with classmate Tom Dooley (one of the wealthiest boys in the school, later to win fame as an anticommunist medical missionary in Indochina).[102] The two young couples were driven to the movies in the Dooley family's chauffeur-driven limousine; the senior Mr. Dooley's prominence in St. Louis's war industry provided ready access to scarce gas ration coupons. (Although the Church fathers warned of the dangers of lax morality in wartime, rubber and gasoline rationing effectively limited the opportunities for sexual exploration represented by automobiles, which ever since the 1920s had garnered notoriety as rolling bedrooms.) The actual incidence of sexual transgressions was rare, as Ed Brungard remembered: "It was considered sexually a major event if you got to squeeze a girl's breast." Michael graduated high school a virgin. Some of Michael's classmates, Tom Dooley among them, had other sexual inclinations, but homosexuality was considered such an abhorrent practice that the Jesuits didn't bother preaching against it.[103]

But neither the teachings of the Catholic Church nor the lack of available young women kept Harrington and his classmates from thinking a great deal about forbidden fruits. At school-sponsored religious retreats, the students discussed sex "endlessly and scholastically" and, according to Michael, were unimpressed when one of the Jesuits defined an erection as "nature's stop sign, an interpretation that seemed to us to be at direct odds with our experience."[104]

In addition to the normal anxieties and preoccupations of adolescence, Michael and his classmates could hardly forget that the war raging in Europe and Asia had a claim on their future. For two and a half years leading up to their graduation in 1944, Michael's classmates had followed the news of distant combat with understandable interest, thrilled by the drama, heroism, and sacrifice of war as it was portrayed in American newspapers and movies. They also knew that if the Germans and Japanese had not surrendered by the time they graduated, they would soon be joining their older brothers in the Pacific, Italy, and France. That lent a sense of moral gravity not ordinarily possessed by most eighteen-year-olds to Michael's classmates. Half of the class of 1944, those who had already turned eighteen, graduated early in January of that year so they could join the war effort. By the spring of that year, fourteen of the school's alumni had already been killed or were listed as missing in action in the war; students were required to attend a requiem high mass for every alumnus who died.[105] For most of Michael's classmates, plans for college and careers had to be postponed indefinitely. Michael would have been happy to join them. But since he was still two years under draft age upon graduation, he was not destined to serve in this particular "Good War." Instead, he applied to and was accepted by the College of the Holy Cross in Worcester, Massachusetts, another Jesuit institution.[106]

Michael was always grateful for the training he received from the Jesuits. He was not alone in appreciating its virtues. "I feel that creating habits of discipline and study was good," one of Michael's contemporaries declared, reflecting on his own education. "I am not against that kind of life, Spartan to some degree. And I think that, as a rule, the Jesuits formed people of character." The fact that the graduate in question was Cuban revolutionary leader Fidel Castro suggests that it was not always entirely predictable to what ends those who were products of the Jesuit *Ratio Studiorum* would apply their education.[107]

In fact, despite the Jesuits' four-centuries-old reputation as defenders of altar and throne, the political message offered students at St. Louis University High School in the years Michael attended was open to conflicting interpretations. Catholic social teachings were from the beginning antipathetic to the assumptions of a capitalist world. Disciples of Thomas Aquinas knew from their master's teaching that "it is impossible for happiness, which is the last end of man, to consist in wealth." Aquinas knew nothing, of course, of the social ills associated with industrial capitalism, but seven centuries after his death some of his admirers would apply the standard of the organic community found in his writings to contemporary American society and find it wanting.[108]

Michael was a member of the St. Louis University High School chapter of the Sodality, a student group organized to promote lay piety and discuss spiritual writings. Prominent among the texts assigned to Sodality members was Leo XIII's 1891 papal encyclical *Rerum Novarum,* which condemned unchecked capitalism as a system in which "the teeming masses of the laboring poor [bear] a yoke little better than that of slavery itself."[109] In 1919, drawing upon *Rerum Novarum,* the American Catholic bishops issued a "Program of Social Reconstruction" that, while condemning socialism, called for federal old age pensions and unemployment insurance, public housing, progressive taxation, and the enforcement of labor's right to organize—anticipating virtually every important reform brought about by the New Deal (and some that weren't, such as worker participation in management).

Catholic theologian John A. Ryan played a major role in drafting the American bishops' 1919 statement on social justice. In 1920 he was appointed director of the social action department of the National Catholic Welfare Council, which gave him a prominent pulpit for his advocacy of the rights of workers. Drawing upon the papal encyclical, Ryan argued that "natural law" demanded that workers be paid a living wage, that workers had the right to form unions, and that the state had the right and duty to intervene in the economy and society to ensure the establishment of social justice.

In 1931 Pope Pius XI issued the encyclical *Quadragesimo Anno* to mark the fortieth anniversary of *Rerum Novarum; Quadragesimo Anno* again made the quest for "social justice" a priority for the church and also made clear the pope's antipathy toward capitalism: "It is obvious," his encyclical noted, "that not only is wealth concentrated in our times, but an immense power and despotic economic dictatorship is consolidated in the hands of a few."[110] The ideas put forth by *Rerum Novarum* and *Quadragesimo Anno* were widely discussed if not universally accepted within the Catholic community. In 1943–1944, for example, Michael's Sodality chapter discussed such topics as "the question of labor and capital," "a living wage," and the "right to strike."[111]

Of course, what the pope said and what ordinary Catholics chose to believe was church teaching were not necessarily the same thing at all. When the charge was made against Al Smith that if he was elected president he would radically reorder American society to fit the teachings of the encyclicals, Smith responded both with anger and some genuine confusion: "Will someone please tell me what the hell a papal encyclical is?"[112] Many American Catholics probably shared his puzzlement. In the 1930s and 1940s, Catholic liberals and conservatives alike claimed to be applying the teachings of the church to the political order. Using the same texts, prominent Catholics of opposing political persuasions hailed and denounced the New Deal. Rank-and-file Catholics tended to split the difference by loyally voting for Franklin Roosevelt and then tuning in Father Coughlin's anti-Roosevelt diatribes on Sundays on the radio.[113]

Students at St. Louis University High School, like their elders, absorbed their lessons selectively. Some would become passionate supporters of "social justice"; for others the term remained, at best, a vaguely remembered platitude. Michael's classmates became Democrats and Republicans, liberals and conservatives. With one prominent exception, few became socialists.

Catholic education thus did not provide Michael with any clearly defined political ideology or program. Instead, he gained a sense of moral gravity, which would stand him in good stead as he emerged as a social critic and a political dissenter.[114] In adulthood Michael would become an atheist. He thus might seem a prime illustration of Carl Jung's contention, in his 1938 study *Psychology and Religion,* that the lapsed Catholic was likely to swing to the opposite extreme. The "absolutism of Catholicism," Jung argued, "seems to demand an equally absolute negation."[115] Atheism (and in Michael's case, Marxism) thus amounts to a substitute religion for the former Catholic. But Jung's categories don't seem to do justice to Michael's evolution. Although at various points in his life he explored the outer edges of religious and political absolutisms, his personal affability, bohemian inclinations, and a measure of ingrained skepticism preserved him from the temptation of succumbing for long to any variety of self-righteous fanaticism.

Unlike the True Believer, Michael could tolerate error. The sins he had trouble tolerating, in himself or in others, were those of intellectual sloth and spiritual self-indulgence—particularly the kinds of sloth and self-indulgence that would deny the claims of community. "I grew up in [the Catholic Church]," Michael recalled later in life, "and from the time I was a little kid the Church said your life is not something you are supposed to fritter away; your life is in trust to something more important than yourself."[116] He would argue in his book on religion, *The Politics at God's Funeral,* that truly committed "believers and unbelievers have the same enemy: the humdrum nihilism of everyday life in much of Western society."[117] As Michael took off into a wider world in 1944, he began consciously to cultivate his distance from the humdrum.

CHAPTER TWO

Leaving Home, 1944–1947

Edward M. Harrington Jr. is not an easy man to place in the test tube of analysis.

Holy Cross student magazine
March 1947[1]

As Michael had contemplated his future in his last year at St. Louis University High School, his parents told him he could go on to any college in the country—so long as it was Catholic. Being a dutiful son, he raised no objection, but it is worth noting that the Catholic institution he chose—the only one he applied to in fact—was so far from home.[2]

As Michael prepared to leave for Holy Cross, Catholic higher education in the United States was enjoying the last years of its golden era. Male undergraduate enrollment in Catholic colleges increased fivefold in the years between the start of the First World War and the start of the Second World War.[3] The Jesuits alone maintained a system of twenty-eight colleges and universities across the nation, including such well-known institutions as Georgetown University, Fordham University, Boston College, and Holy Cross.

The students accepted by Holy Cross in those years had a sense of being a part of their generation's Catholic elite. Michael's high school classmate Bill Loftus enrolled in St. Louis University as a freshman in 1944. Tired of living at home, he decided in 1945 to transfer to another Jesuit school and went to talk to the dean of the College of Arts and Sciences: "I said, 'Father, I want to go to Georgetown.' And in typical Jesuit fashion he said, 'No you don't Bill, you want to go to Holy Cross. It's the best school we have.'"[4]

Despite the regard in which it was held in Catholic educational circles, Holy Cross was a regional institution in the 1940s that drew its students from Massachusetts and surrounding states. To come to the college from as far away as the Midwest, one of Michael's classmates recalled, was "like coming from Tibet."[5]

Founded in Worcester in 1843, the College of the Holy Cross was long regarded by local and state authorities as a nest of jesuitical subversion. For two decades, the Massachusetts legislature refused to grant the college a charter. It took the Civil War, a conflict in which thousands of Catholics from Massachusetts gave their lives for the Union, to discredit the anti-Catholic cause sufficiently for Holy Cross to win the right to award degrees in its own name.[6]

Hard feelings lingered. The tepid sentimentality of growing up Irish in St. Louis had not prepared Michael for the sharper ethnic and religious sensibilities prevailing at Holy Cross; there he encountered the "militantly paranoid" products of "the very real [Irish] ghettoes of the Northeast." His classmates sometimes described Protestants disparagingly as "APAers," in reference to a nineteenth-century anti-Catholic group, the American Protective Association.[7] Holy Cross was proud that it was one of its graduates who, at an alumni reunion dinner, had delivered the famed quatrain skewering the snobbish descendants of the Puritans: "And this is good old Boston,/The home of the bean and the cod./Where the Cabots speak only to the Lowells/And the Lowells speak only to God."[8]

Not that conversations with God were frowned upon at "the Cross." The Jesuits did their best to keep the college's religious mission uppermost in the minds of their students, who were assured by their professors that their integrated philosophy was the envy of their less fortunate Protestant counterparts at places like Harvard and Yale.[9] In "those pre-John XXIII philosophy and religion classes," Michael recalled, "when you were asked to prove the existence of God the professor was not soliciting your opinion on the subject."[10] Like all students at Catholic seminaries and universities, students at Holy Cross were expected to immerse themselves in the works of the great Catholic philosopher and theologian of the High Middle Ages, St. Thomas Aquinas, the "Angelic Doctor."

Catholic philosophers were convinced that the thirteenth century represented the period of the greatest intellectual breakthrough in the Christian tradition. Feeling besieged by the challenge of European rationalist philosophers, the church turned back to Aquinas in an attempt to put religious faith on a secure and demonstrable basis.[11] Neo-Thomism, as it had come to be called by the time Michael was in college, could draw on the masterful scholarship of twentieth-century philosophers like Jacques Maritain and Etienne Gilson. But in the hands of less inspired scholars and instructors, Neo-Thomism was reduced to a kind of basic training course for the religious enlisted ranks. Warren Coffey, a contemporary of Michael's at another Jesuit college, remembered of his own training in theology that they "all somehow became courses in apologetics, as though we were being equipped to pass our lives debating with Tom Paine or Bob Ingersoll."[12]

The campus, perched atop a high hill known as Mount St. James, had a sense of physical removal from the gritty industrial city that lay below. The students lived in dormitories where they were tightly supervised. They needed parental permission to go away for the weekend. Even a post-dinner stroll downtown was forbidden, except on Saturdays, and then it required a special pass. Seating was assigned at meals and in classes. Class attendance was mandatory. The Jesuits enforced a rigorous course of religious devotion. Students were required to attend morning mass six days a week (Sundays were the exception, on the assumption that good Catholic boys did not need coercion to observe so elementary a religious obligation). Attendance was taken, and if a student missed two masses in a week, he was not allowed to leave school on the weekend. When Bill Loftus arrived at Holy Cross after his year at St. Louis University, where he had experienced the relative freedoms of a non-residential program, he felt as if he had been sentenced as a "prisoner on the hill." There was also a dress code, although as Loftus recalled, Michael typically paid it the minimum necessary attention: "We were required to wear a jacket and tie to class, mass, and meals. His jacket might have lived on the floor, his tie was something he pulled blindly out of the closet and threw over his neck."[13]

Michael didn't find the restrictions at "the Cross" onerous. At sixteen he accepted the substitution of college authority for that of his parents as legitimate and natural. Going off to college was adventure enough for the moment. He arrived at the college determined to be accepted as a grown-up, a decision symbolized by his success in finally abandoning his childhood nickname "Ned." (Now he was known, like his father, as "Ed.") He welcomed the academic challenge, garnering A's and B's in English, history, and philosophy. Michael's favorite teacher at Holy Cross was Father William Brennan, chairman of the English department. Brennan taught Shakespeare, and it was under his influence that Michael chose "Hal, Prince and King" as the topic for his senior thesis.[14]

Shortly after Pearl Harbor, Holy Cross had adopted an accelerated program of studies that curtailed holidays and added summer sessions, allowing students to complete the normal four-year complement of courses in just three years. Even more than in high school, Michael was surrounded by and forced to compete with significantly older students. The Navy's V-12 training program brought hundreds of sailors to Holy Cross to work toward commissions as naval officers. They bunked separately from the other students, wore their uniforms, and marched to class. And, starting in 1944, the student body began to include a significant number of returning veterans.

War was on everyone's mind. Michael and his classmates wore class rings that bore the image of a mounted Christian knight, and the school's athletic teams were known as the Crusaders. In an essay in the college literary magazine, Michael celebrated the heroism and sacrifice of the church's warriors, missionaries, and martyrs: "Charles Martel, marching, with a song on his lips, against the Saracen . . . dauntless Xavier, dying on a steaming shore within the sight of a China that was denied him . . . Campion climbing bravely up a blood-stained Tyburn Hill." Michael was simultaneously stirred by the image of the contemporary crusader, "mourning the death of so many comrades" on "the red-stained coral strand of a Pacific island."[15] (He may have had in mind the four former Marines, veterans of "grueling months of the nerve-wracking island-hopping warfare" in the Pacific, who he profiled as a freshman writer for the Holy Cross student newspaper, the *Tomahawk*.[16]) Along with the other non-veterans enrolled at Holy Cross during the war years, Michael could not help being constantly reminded that he was missing out on the great crusade of his own era. "When life and death are cheap," he wrote in the school yearbook,

> the academic routine seemed trivial, too small in a world which knew so much of apparent greatness. . . . The few returned veterans immediately became the center of attention for all. The remarks went fast in the caf. 'D'ja know he got the Silver Star? Boy he saw some action.' They were older, a little more purposive, yet a little more restless.[17]

Tensions developed between the veterans and those who, because of age or disability or some other deferment, had stayed at home. Jack Drummey, who arrived at Holy Cross in the fall of 1945 after completing his military service, recalled the "envy and suspicion" that divided the two groups. Clothes defined status: "We had the 'glamour' of uniforms hanging in dorm closets." Some of the younger students took to wearing battle jackets bought in downtown Worcester.[18]

In the class history he wrote for his senior yearbook, Michael explored—or perhaps confessed—the psychological defenses the non-veterans used to offset their sense of having missed out on a great and vital and ennobling experience: "You could hear them in the caf. 'Me go? You're crazy, mac, crazy. I want to live.' Yet underneath the hard shell of their defense complex, they shared in the restlessness, they felt the incredible urgency of war, and life, and death."[19]

There is no way to know whether Michael's description of the inner conflict of the scoffers in "the caf" can be taken as a self-portrait. But his school transcript does reveal that, for at least a moment, he contemplated abandoning the contemplative life for a more direct involvement with that urgent world of war, life, and death. In the fall of 1945, with his eighteenth birthday finally approaching, he had his high school grades sent to the U.S. Naval Academy at Annapolis. Whether he went through with the application and was turned down for admission or whether he thought better of the plan with the end of the war is unclear.[20]

Notwithstanding his youth and the social and, perhaps, emotional liability of having missed military service, Michael again found ways to stand out among his classmates. His classmate Charles E. Fitzgibbon (no relation to the St. Louis FitzGibbons) remembered him as "brilliant, versatile, [and] fun-loving," a "guy with smiling eyes and an infectious grin."[21] As in high school, Michael played a large role in the school's publications, serving as sports editor of the *Tomahawk* his freshman year and then swiftly assuming editorship of its editorial page (Harrington, the 1946 yearbook noted, "has been doing one grand job as Sports Editor, a position which formerly was a senior prize").[22] He was elected managing editor of the *Purple,* the Holy Cross literary magazine, and "profile editor" of the yearbook, the *Purple Patcher.* He was elected president of the Holy Cross Debating Society and was part of the team that brought the college the trophy in the 1947 city tournament (besting Clark and Worcester Tech) and defeated Columbia on a trip to New York City. (The topic assigned to the debate team during Michael's senior year at Holy Cross was: "Resolved: That labor should be given a direct share in the management of industry." Whether he argued the affirmative or the negative case is unknown, but he did later comment that "in my own day as an intercollegiate debater we regarded it as a telling point, requiring no further clarification, that our opponent's position would 'lead to' socialism.")[23] Michael's gift for debate led to his selection as salutatorian of the class of 1947. He was also a member of the Sanctuary Society, whose members rose at dawn every morning of the academic term and donned cassock and surplice to assist the college priests in the celebration of the mass.[24]

A *Purple* profile of Michael in the spring of his senior year described his "most distinguishing characteristic" as "balance": "The field simply doesn't exist, except perhaps for the social life of the newt, in which he doesn't have definite and generally poignant views." And then, in more sincere tribute: "Within that close-shaven head is a firmly ingrained sense of humor, an eternally searching, incisive mind, a deep and sincere approach to his fellow man, and purposeful planning."[25]

Michael found ways to fit in and to excel. His classmates respected his abilities. For all that, he did not make any particularly close or lasting friends among them, apart from Bill Loftus, whom he had known from St. Louis days. A few other classmates wrote to him from time to time over the years or came to hear him after he became famous. But Michael chose not to sustain an intimate and ongoing relationship with any of them.[26] He was beginning to live a life defined in discreet episodes: When he finished with a place and an era, he tended also to be finished with the people associated with them. Even in college, many of his classmates had a sense that they weren't seeing much more of the real Michael than the glimpses or images he chose to reveal. "Edward M. Harrington Jr. is not an easy man to place in the test tube of analysis," the *Purple* declared in a thoroughly mixed metaphor: "[H]e presents to the casual observer the same dilemma which addled the minds of some of the most brilliant Shakespearian character scholars, . . . the dilemma which invariably arises from inherent contradictions of exterior appearances."[27]

Michael used his years at Holy Cross to experiment with and refine those shifting "exterior appearances." He struck poses and tried them out on classmates. A favorite was The Writer, somewhat distracted, attractively battered, jaded but still in quest of an elusive Truth. The photo that accompanied the profile in the *Purple* showed him at his "neat orderly desk" (buried deep in a disordered pile of books and papers), resting one arm on his typewriter while staring pensively away into the mid-distance. Michael's pose of premature world weariness was saved from absurdity only by a sly hint in his expression that, if challenged, he would be the first to acknowledge its obvious artifice.

Michael posed, but he also worked hard. He churned out poetry, fiction, and essays throughout his undergraduate years. The pieces he wrote for the *Purple* included: a one-act play in which Hegel, Kant, Descartes, and Nietzsche are confounded and mocked in their efforts to undermine the beliefs of a Catholic philosophy student ("KANT: Son, even though you are not there, . . . that is, you might be there, . . . but I just think you are there. . . . I am going to convince you."); a meditation on literary careers entitled "Posterity vs. Prosperity," in which Michael recommended that young writers reject both "commercial degradation" and "starving artistic perfection" ("Write, but always with the best that is in you. Sell, but never lower yourself to sell."); and an ambitious but callow essay on "Greatness" that bemoaned the passing of Roosevelt, Churchill, and even Hitler ("an evil man—but a great man") from the world stage, leaving only "economic panaceas, governmental directives, and the odd doings of Left Bank intellectuals [standing] where great men once walked."[28]

Despite the popularity of right-wing, populist Father Coughlin, in the 1930s Catholics had by and large voted their pocketbooks by supporting the New Deal and Democratic candidates. With the end of the depression and the coming of the war, new concerns pushed Catholic voters to the right, where their votes were welcomed by Republicans eager to bring an end to "twenty years of treason" in Washington. The Red Army's advance into eastern Europe and the threat of Soviet subversion and conquest were viewed with considerable alarm throughout the Catholic community, including its colleges. Anticommunism was linked in important ways with Catholic concerns about the immorality of the cultural elites—products of the Ivy League, like Alger Hiss, and fashioners of mass popular culture, like the Hollywood Ten.

Political concerns crept increasingly into Michael's writing. In his first conscious act of political rebellion—an "Oedipal reaction," as he would later call it—he began to describe himself as a Republican, an avowed admirer of "Mr. Republican," Robert Taft, the conservative Ohio Senator and presidential aspirant.[29] Although conservatism per se would not have troubled his parents, Republicanism of any stripe certainly represented a challenge to the loyalties he had been taught to respect as a child. In some ways, Michael's brief flirtation with the Republicans anticipated the political earthquake that would eventually destroy the New Deal coalition—the disaffection of urban, ethnic (and largely Catholic) voters with a liberalism out of touch with their social concerns. A foretaste of Democratic disasters in the making came during Michael's senior year at Holy Cross, when Catholic defections from the Democrats helped hand control of both houses of Congress to the Republicans for the first time since the 1920s.

Student political activism was rare at Holy Cross in the 1940s, but what there was of it was generated by the right rather than the left. During Michael's freshman year, student groups at the college adopted resolutions in praise of the House Un-American Activities Committee.[30] The next spring, Rev. J.F.X. Murphy, S.J., addressed a large audience of students on "Spanish democracy" and compared Generalissimo Francisco Franco to Presidents Washington and Lincoln. Father Murphy, the *Tomahawk* reported enthusiastically, had "cleared up" many of the "misunderstandings which the American people have about Spain."[31]

The unsigned editorials that filled the pages of the *Tomahawk* in the years when Michael oversaw the editing of its editorial page were not uniformly conservative; on issues less heated than the Communist threat, or where church doctrine was not involved, they sometimes edged toward liberalism. But on issues touching on Catholic social teachings—such as birth control (that "abominable . . . infamous . . . loathsome" and "hideous practice," as it was characterized in one editorial)—the invective flowed strictly from the right.[32]

It is impossible to establish with any certainty which editorials Michael wrote for the *Tomahawk*. But both the theme and the style of an editorial in the spring of 1946 suggest his authorship. "It was the master of the paradox, G. K. Chesterton," the editorial entitled "For the Radicals" began, "who remarked on the paradox of being orthodox and conservative in a world of radicals."[33]

British essayist and novelist Chesterton was a favorite of the Jesuits. Back in high school, Michael's favorite English teacher, Father Divine, had assigned Chesterton's essays to his class. A convert to Catholicism, Chesterton endeared himself to several generations of Catholic intellectuals and general readers before his death in 1936. He was their H. L. Mencken—bright and combative, not only a participant in the church's continuing celebration of

Aquinas and the High Middle Ages but also accessible and contemporary. The characteristic demand of Christianity, Chesterton once commented, was for "a new world." Seeking a third way between the extremes of capitalism and socialism, his theory of "distributism" promoted small property ownership as the basis of a pastoral, decentralized, and antistatist utopia. Dorothy Day, among others, was influenced by Chesterton's dreams of reviving peasant and artisan handicrafts as an alternative to industrial capitalism.[34]

Although Chesterton's influence had waned among general readers by the time Michael arrived at Holy Cross,[35] the college's literary-minded students still worshipped at his shrine. They could take or leave his social theories, but they admired the skillful wordsmith who, with pious wit, had fought famous literary battles in defense of the Christian faith against its rationalist detractors. A photograph in the 1946 yearbook showed Michael and his fellow *Purple* editors poring over manuscripts, and bore the caption "How did Chesterton say it?"[36]

This early immersion in Chesterton proved a lasting influence on Michael's writing, providing him with his characteristic opening literary gambit of the apparent paradox. As the *Tomahawk* editorial "For the Radicals" suggested, Chesterton's love of paradox was the defining mark of his essays, a means to get past the appearances of things, startling the reader into grasping ordinarily hidden truths by contradicting common ideas and reversing normal language (thus he would contend, in one of his most famous turns of phrase, that "there is nothing that fails like success").[37] More than an exercise in rhetorical self-display (although it was that as well), Chestertonian paradox represented a mode of thought consistent with both Chesterton's and Harrington's Catholicism—and with Michael's later turn to Marxism. (Christianity's animating myth is the story of the prophet who is executed as a man and rises from the grave as God. Marxism rested on the equally paradoxical premise that the capitalist bourgeoisie would act as its own gravedigger in creating the system that produced a revolutionary proletariat.)

As a good Chestertonian, the author of "For the Radicals" sought to shake the mental complacency of his readers by means of the unorthodox linking of Catholicism with radicalism, a political category that students of Michael's generation were accustomed to associate with the enemies of the church. Michael (if it was, indeed, Michael) argued that Catholic teachings represented "a radicalism which is derived from the continuity of two thousand years." A defense of traditional values in a society in which "the unusual has become usual" meant that conservatives were actually the true radicals of the age:

> For he is a radical who argues against divorce, he is a dissenter who argues against birth control; and the man who has the effrontery to claim that he

> 'believes' but he does not see is a rarity in this world of materialis. . . . Staid, unchanging, a rock in a swirling ocean of conflicting ideas, the Catholic Church stands out as the last stronghold of the radical. . . . A system which is two thousand years old, is the only radical in a world of conformists.[38]

At once earnest, provocative, dryly ironic, and playful, "For the Radicals" was an accomplished piece of writing for an undergraduate. It anticipated the style and strategy of the writer who would, a quarter-century or so later, begin his autobiography with the words "I am a pious apostate."[39] And it signaled its author's disdain for "a world of conformists," even if that meant embracing the normally despised identity of "radical."

Michael's period of conservative dandyism reflected more about his uncertainties regarding his old beliefs than it did about his new convictions. Michael's parents had sent him to Holy Cross confident that in doing so they were protecting him from the kind of harmful influences he might have encountered in a more secular environment. And to the extent that his Catholicism remained unshaken through his undergraduate years, they were not disappointed.

But Michael's ideas and interests were changing in other ways of long-term consequence. He had grown up in a city where segregation of the races remained the rule. Although the black population of St. Louis nearly tripled between the two world wars, white and black citizens seldom crossed paths. Blacks were not permitted to go to school with whites, or to eat in the same restaurants, or to sit beside them in movie houses and theaters. The widespread use of private restrictive covenants enforced residential segregation, penning the black community into the overcrowded wards of the eastern half of the central corridor and into the fringes of the downtown. Though, unlike the Deep South, there was no legal segregation on the street cars, St. Louis custom dictated that blacks move to the back of the car in any case. Michael's friends from those years do not remember him ever questioning those arrangements.[40]

There was little in the popular culture that would have pushed a young middle-class white boy, even one in a more northern-identified city than St. Louis, to wonder about racial inequality. When Michael was eleven, *Gone with the Wind* was released with great fanfare. Later, at the height of the civil rights movement, Michael would tell an interviewer that he had grown up with a "romantic identification with the Confederacy, which had much the best uniforms and much the best myth, the Ashley Wilkes' kind of stuff. . . . I used to think that the slaves really liked it under slavery."[41]

The neighborhoods he lived in and the Catholic schools he attended were lily white. Even the Harrington family maid was white. The only time

Michael saw black people in any significant numbers was when he rode the street cars that passed through the belt of black neighborhoods that surrounded downtown St. Louis—and that was considered a dangerous adventure. It was part of the lore of St. Louis University High School students during the war years that it was wise to avoid waiting on a traffic island for the streetcar on "pushing Tuesdays" and "shoving Thursdays," the days when blacks were supposedly carrying out a campaign to jostle whites off the sidewalk into the path of oncoming traffic.[42]

When Michael arrived at Holy Cross, he found himself again in a virtually all-white environment. Although a black student had been valedictorian of the college's first graduating class in 1849, few attended the school in subsequent years, and only one was enrolled in the years that Michael was an undergraduate.[43] Worcester's factories had always been able to depend upon a ready source of cheap European immigrant labor, funneled through Boston Harbor, and had attracted few blacks to the city. If Michael did interact with blacks in integrated settings during his college years, it would have been only on the occasional trip to Boston or New York City, or on the train ride back to St. Louis. Michael's very first short story for the Holy Cross literary magazine, published in the fall of 1944, depicted the rivalry of two black soldiers for the post of company bugler, and it was filled with comic racial clichés and stereotypical "Darktown" dialect: "Well, Jackson," Michael had one of his characters remark to the other as he challenged him to a game of dice, "Ah sure hopes that you is not disencouraged as not to enter the big city and perhaps shake those jumping African dominoes in a little game of skill and chance."[44]

But within a few months of arriving at Holy Cross, Michael abandoned the racial assumptions and stereotypes with which he had been brought up. His transformation may have been influenced in part by the 1944 decision of the St. Louis diocese to desegregate its own educational institutions. A few months before Michael left for Massachusetts, Father Claude Heithaus, the director of public relations at St. Louis University, electrified a student assembly when he proposed the admission of black students to the school. "Lord Jesus," he prayed aloud before the assembly, "we are sorry and ashamed for all the wrongs that white men have done to Your colored children. We are firmly resolved never again to have any part in them, and to do everything in our power to prevent them."[45] In response to Father Heithaus's challenge, St. Louis University admitted its first black students that very summer. The repercussions were felt throughout the St. Louis Catholic community. The conservative leader of St. Louis's Catholic hierarchy, Archbishop John J. Glennon, had given ground on the issue only grudgingly. But following Glennon's death in 1946, his liberal successor, Joseph E. Ritter, threatened to excommunicate opponents of the integration of Catholic schools. Michael's parents had never distinguished themselves as racial liberals, but neither were they dyed-in-the-wool racists. If the church said blacks and whites were equal, then as good Catholics that would become their creed as well.[46]

Even given the church's change of heart and policy in his hometown, it is striking that at Holy Cross Michael chose to speak out as often and as strongly as he did. It almost seems as if he decided he had a mission to do so. As one of the few Holy Cross students with direct experience of the Jim Crow system of segregation, he could lay claim to a certain expertise. He noted in the essay on "Greatness" in the *Purple* in 1946, "We stand so proudly in the glare of our technological development; yet the light switch is off on the development of ideas. . . . We can split the atom—but do we have a leader who can settle a racial question that threatens to plague society for generations to come?"[47]

Michael dealt with the "racial question" at greatest length in two earnestly didactic short stories he wrote for the *Purple,* stories that are also notable as his first known writings on the subject of poverty. In "The Little People," published in February 1945, he set his story in New York City ten years in the future. A new Great Depression has settled on the land: "A wind, brooding and chill, surged forth from the massing clouds above and swept down the dark, deserted streets of a large American city." Just a few years earlier, "victory bonfires" from the great war had burned everywhere. Now the men who had fought the war were unemployed and bitter, and "race hatred rose to an intolerable peak."

The story's protagonist, a jobless white veteran named John Spencer, has eyes that are "cold and cynical . . . burning with hatred." Feverishly searching for the work that would enable him to buy food for his hungry child, he happens onto a street battle between crowds of unemployed whites and blacks. When a squad of police arrives to break up the fight, Spencer wrests the gun away from one of them and uses it to shoot down "a young negro . . . his only offense his color." Spencer stumbles from the fight into a nearby Catholic church, where the priest is in the middle of delivering a sermon calling for the creation of a society governed by the principles of "Christian justice and Christian charity." Michael's protagonist is unmoved: "Ever since he had been a kid, this Holy Joe stuff had been too much for him." He leaves the church and, in a bungled attempt to shoplift a can of soup from a grocery store, is mortally wounded by the storekeeper. The storekeeper is gently reproachful as he kneels beside the dying man: "Gosh, buddy, why did you make me shoot? I would've given you the stuff, if only you'd have asked me. I got a wife and two kids myself, I know what things are like. You didn't have to steal." Filled with his own remorse, Spencer whispers his last words to the grocer:

> "I guess we're all in the same boat. All little guys, needing one another, and needing . . . needing Him, too . . . "
>
> His hand tightened on that of the grocer.
>
> "Say a prayer for me, buddy,—for me and all . . . the rest . . . of the little guys."[48]

In the second story, published in March 1946, Michael shifted the protagonist's perspective to that of a victim of racist violence. A black family from the Deep South is fleeing up the Mississippi River to start a new life. The family is motherless: She was killed by a mob of drunken whites two weeks earlier "because she's a nigger." The young daughter, Rose Marlowe, tearfully asks her father for reassurance: "Will it be different up there, Daddy?" Her father, Sam Marlowe, replies encouragingly: "They say up here they let you ride in the street-cars anywhere and go to the shows. The people up here, they got nothing against us. . . . Maybe, if we can get some money, we can send you to college some day."

When they get to their new home in an unnamed city (clearly intended to be St. Louis) the hardworking father opens a coal yard. Marlowe and his family scrape together a meager living amidst grim scenes of deprivation. Every day a "black trickle" of customers comes to the coal yard, "walking with the slow, uncertain gait of people who have no spirit. . . . Only the children, dirty and unkempt, frisked as they neared the yard, glad to have a place to play. And stretching out behind the dirty gray and black of the coal yard, were the littered pig pens of the slum dwellings." Marlowe's enterprise finds no reward in an unjust society, as a greedy white competitor incites a racist mob to attack his coal yard. Rose is raped in the assault, and Marlowe's hopes for the future are destroyed. In the end, as he reflects on his fate, he decides God must have

> made us something a white man could whip when he's mad. And made our women to be sneered at and followed. We're just a race in chains. A mistake. The only reason we're a mistake is because we're black. Black! Black! Black and fire, black and whip, black and desire! Blacks are made to die. No! That's not fair! How did they treat Him! He was like us.[49]

Although of slender literary merit, derivative in equal measure of pietistic conversion tracts and hard-boiled detective tales, Michael's short stories are still of interest for what they reveal of his emerging social concerns. His white and black protagonists, the "little guys," are brothers under the skin. Both are fathers victimized by a society that denies them the dignity of supporting and protecting their families. Christian teachings go unheeded, either because the way they are presented makes them seem of little relevance to the squalid conflicts of the streets, or worse, because they are discredited by the actions of pious hypocrites. John Spencer's bitter question after he leaves the church en route to his rendezvous with death, "Can bowing down before an altar put food in my kid's mouth?" goes unanswered in "The Little People." And in "The Sermon," the instigator of the lynch mob goes to church afterwards with an untroubled conscience and congratulates the minister for preaching a "fine sermon on tolerance." And yet, in the extremity of their despair, both Spencer and Marlowe still turn instinctively to the reassurance of Christ's message. Poverty and spiritual emptiness are linked in Michael's stories by the "dirty gray" and black hues that surround his characters. The monochromatic monotony is relieved only once in the two stories, in the scene in the church in "The Little People," where "flickering candles cut a crisscross pattern on the crimson draperies" and the afternoon sunlight "cut through the stained windows and formed rainbows along the marble altar rail."[50]

Michael was not yet ready to mount the barricades for civil rights or any other cause. Although he linked race hatred with economic competition and social distress, he was not smuggling an anticapitalist analysis into the pages of the *Purple*. Michael's sense of what constituted the good society was shaped more in terms of familial responsibilities, and a combined sense of spiritual and aesthetic fulfillment, than from any hint of a notion of class solidarity. The Catholic priest in "The Little People" is unable to sway John Spencer from his self-destructive path, but Harrington gives the priest enough space to suggest that in his sermon he spoke for the author as well:

> We forgot God. Why should He do anything for us? America too often has clasped hands with paganism. What has become of our reverence for woman and the family? We had our poisonous movies and our shows. We fed our youth with unbelief. . . . We had no norm. We lost the foundation of Christian truth.[51]

Michael was moving toward the view that the proof of Christ's promise of redemption could be measured best through the practical social consequences of Christian teachings. As he declared in his salutatory address at graduation in 1947, every man was created in "the image of God":

> The very foundation of democracy demands that we see our fellow man with the eyes of faith. The wealth or poverty of his fellow citizen, his color or his creed—these cannot be the determining norm of the true democrat. He is committed to the truth that every man has a moral worth and dignity . . . which comes from the fact that every man belongs to God.[52]

If Michael's political views were as yet only half-formed, his cultural stance at Holy Cross was taking on what would prove a permanent cast. Unlike the great majority of his classmates, he cultivated the stance of outsider and rebel. He didn't have to stray very far in those days to step outside the mainstream—polled in 1947, the graduating seniors chose Norman Rockwell as their favorite artist, *The Robe* as their favorite novel, Bing Crosby as their favorite singer, and Dinah Shore as their favorite "songstress."[53]

The circle of writers around the newspaper, the literary magazine, and the yearbook provided the closest that Holy Cross came to in the mid-1940s to a counterculture. Like aspiring writers at most American colleges since the 1920s, Holy Cross's literary elite was drawn to a somewhat contradictory mix of cultural ideals: the starving artist in the garret in Montmartre, or the wildly decadent, gloriously talented, and doomed flaming youth of an F. Scott Fitzgerald novel. Unlike their counterparts at more secular institutions, they added a third ideal type to the mix: the Catholic aristocracy of the British university system.

Bill Loftus was a prominent figure among Holy Cross's men of letters in those years. Back when Michael and he were classmates at St. Louis University High, Loftus had been described in the school newspaper as "the student most likely to succeed Virgil and make Homer blush with shame." Darkly handsome, and an honors student in high school, he had been editor in chief of both the yearbook and the newspaper his senior year. Bill and Michael shared an interest in writing and literature (and also in playing bridge, in which they both excelled) and remained close friends for a decade. This was in spite of Michael's mother's disapproval; she decided in Michael's high school years that Loftus was a bad influence on her son.

At Holy Cross Bill and Michael's friendship was deepened by their shared literary interests, their common outsider status as midwesterners, and the long train trips they made together back to St. Louis at Christmas.[54] Loftus became news editor of the *Tomahawk,* and his poetry was frequently published in the *Purple.* One classmate, who didn't care much for either of them, recalled that they "stuck closely together." They were both "brilliant boys . . . accomplished in letters, politics, poetry, and current events." But their classmate suspected the two midwesterners felt themselves superior to the "'bawstin' boys."[55]

In any case, both boys, long before they got to Holy Cross, would have sneered at the idea that a pietistic potboiler like *The Robe* had anything to recommend it as literature. "We were reading *very serious* things, like Tolstoi," Loftus recalled of their high school years. "For light reading we'd switch to Dostoevski." They also assumed that any books condemned by the church were probably worthy of at least a cursory inspection to make sure. In college they found sympathetic Jesuits who were willing to smuggle out books for them from "Gehenna," the section of the school library reserved for officially proscribed literature and strictly off-limits to students. By such means, Michael and Bill were able to read through the collected works of Freud by the time they had graduated from college, even though the church frowned on psychoanalytic theory and Freud was never assigned in any of their courses.[56]

Another book in which they shared an interest was Evelyn Waugh's novel *Brideshead Revisited,* published in its American edition shortly after Michael's arrival at Holy Cross. Waugh was a Catholic convert, which should have made him acceptable fare for Holy Cross undergraduates. But the Jesuits tried to steer their students away from him. His Catholicism was a little too raw and too fervent (too much the unreliable enthusiasm of a recent convert) for their taste. Waugh's casually tolerant treatment of homosexuality in *Brideshead Revisited,* particularly that of the spiritually troubled but appealing character Sebastian Flyte, was probably intended to provoke the ire of those puritanically minded English Protestants who had long regarded the Anglo-Catholic and Roman Catholic religious intellectual subcultures as foppish and effeminate. "Beware of the Anglo-Catholics," Waugh's character Charles Ryder was warned upon his arrival at Oxford, "they're all sodomites with unpleasant accents."[57] Loftus recalled that he and Michael read the novel "the minute we could secretly get a copy." Waugh's portrayal of the aristocratic, cultured, and hard-drinking student wastrels in *Brideshead Revisited* greatly appealed to Bill and Michael, offering the boys a vicarious taste of the freedoms they hoped to enjoy once they left Holy Cross. The book's dubious reputation among the Jesuits enhanced its literary appeal. "The act of rebellion of reading *Brideshead* was part of the charm," according to Loftus.[58]

Michael's parents were worried about the company he kept at Holy Cross. They were even more disturbed by a friend he made on another college campus. In his senior year at Holy Cross he began to date a Protestant undergraduate from Wellesley College. Michael had dated girls in high school and college but had never before had a serious romantic relationship. His sexual inexperience when he arrived at Holy Cross was so obvious that it became a joke among his older classmates, particularly the worldly wise military veterans; some of them checked into motels for sexual assignations under his name, because he was "the only known virgin on campus."[59]

When Michael's fellow seniors listed their "favorite women's college" in the 1947 yearbook, it was the nearby Catholic school, Regis College. Michael looked farther afield for female companionship—to the decidedly non-Catholic Wellesley College. There he was attracted to a bright and attractive, pony-tailed brunette named Joan Sayward. If Robert Taft was "Mr. Republican" to his admirers, Joan might have been dubbed "Miss Yankee Protestant," the child of rock-ribbed Republicans from Point Elizabeth, Maine. Michael and Joan met in the fall of 1946 on a blind date. Although the two were the same age, Joan was a freshman, so Michael enjoyed the glamour, in her eyes, of being a senior. (When Michael graduated in 1947, he was only 19 years old.) All that fall and spring they spent every available moment together. Joan later described herself as "green as grass" when she met Michael. Bill Loftus, who sometimes double-dated with the couple, remembered her as "a bit prim, like a character out of Nathaniel Hawthorne."[60] But the two fell passionately (if chastely) in love. Joan visited Michael once at Holy Cross for a football weekend; more often, he would hitchhike out on Saturdays to visit her for the day at Wellesley. To Joan, Michael was "very special, very imaginative, somewhat tormented." Michael wrote her poems (none of which have survived). They wandered hand in hand through the gardens, around the ponds, and beneath the stately trees of the Wellesley campus.[61] A letter Michael wrote to a friend a few years later captures some of the quality of their romance, although he viewed it by then from the pose of a self-mocking, mid-20s worldly cynicism:

> hitched in golden october to wellesley . . . almost like in movie; walked wistfully across meadowpath . . . looked at various spots . . . saw foot of stairs where i met joan sayward; looked at steps where we had sat; hitchhiked to n.y., got drunk; was unpardonably nostalgical. . . . think i am going through menopause (maybe infected ear).[62]

Michael and Joan did not discuss marriage, but they were courting in an era when any serious romantic relationship among young people of their social background presupposed marriage as the likely outcome. In the years Joan attended Wellesley College, her yearbook ran long lists of graduating seniors who were engaged or who had already earned their "Mrs. degrees." If Michael and Joan intended to win the approval of their respective families for a future match, they must have suspected that the prospects were poor. The Harringtons came east for Michael's graduation, and afterwards they all went for a vacation on the Massachusetts shore. Joan was invited to join them for dinner. The senior Harringtons were polite to their son's guest—Joan remembered Catherine as "flamboyant" and Edward as "subdued," which suggests that they were both playing their customary social roles, but her overall impression was that Michael's parents "probably weren't thrilled" by the relationship. Later that summer Michael came to visit her at her parents' house. The Saywards proved as polite, and as unenthusiastic, about their daughter's choice in young men.[63]

In the spring of 1947 Michael was still trying to be a dutiful son. He had excelled academically at Holy Cross and given his parents the great pleasure of hearing their son deliver the salutatorian speech at his graduation. Although he displayed the same shortcomings in the hard sciences that he had had in high school, his grades in other courses made up for the deficiency; he was ranked near the top of his graduating class at Holy Cross, thirty-ninth out of two hundred and forty-seven seniors.[64] He was accomplished, ambitious, and self-confident (so much the latter, in fact, that he predicted to classmate Bill Loftus on commencement day, "Someday I'm going to come back here and I'm going to speak at the commencement, and they're going to give me an honorary degree.").[65] He remained reliably devout as a Catholic. But Michael's parents had reason to feel some anxiety about his future plans. The relationship with Joan Sayward did not bode well and showed no signs of coming to an end. And there seems to have been a deeper disquiet troubling parents and child. Holy Cross had not worked out quite the way the Harringtons had expected. They didn't know everything Michael had been up to in college, but they sensed that something was amiss—they referred to it as his involvement in a "bohemian atmosphere." Catherine and Edward wanted Michael to become a lawyer like his father, and they were willing to pay for a law school education. To please them he applied to Yale Law School and was accepted.[66] But he still wasn't sure whether he would go. He told them he wanted to be a poet, not a lawyer. Finally they negotiated a compromise: Michael would go to Yale for a year and give the law a fair try before he decided on the alternative, less lucrative, and otherwise suspect career he had in mind.[67]

When Michael moved to New Haven in the fall of 1947 to start his first year of law school, the Harringtons must have been relieved. Their son was once again on track to the kind of respectable career and life they had always hoped he would pursue. It turned out to be the last time they would have that assurance.

CHAPTER THREE

"An Awful Lot of Soul-Searching," 1947–1950

"I think that New York is more amenable to my hope than St. Louis."

Michael Harrington
December 20, 1950[1]

There were very few memorable episodes in Michael's life that he didn't write about on one occasion or another later on, and usually at some length. So it is striking that in his memoir *Fragments of the Century,* he chose to devote all of four sentences to his experience at Yale. In *The Long Distance Runner,* the second volume of his memoirs, the only mention of Yale was a passing reference to his living quarters there. For Michael, law school was a detour from his sense of mission, however vaguely defined that remained for him at age nineteen. But the nine months he spent in New Haven would have important intellectual and ultimately political consequences for him.[2]

When Michael arrived at Yale, he moved into Room 2520 in the Sterling Law Building. His suitemate, Richard Fitzsimmons, was four years older and a military veteran. Arriving late at night and going straight to bed, Fitzsimmons didn't meet his suitemate until the following morning when "this guy came into my room, smoking a cigarette, and introduced himself as Ed Harrington. I sat up and said, 'How old are you?'" Fitzsimmons thought Michael "looked like a little boy."[3]

Notwithstanding the difference in their ages and life experience, the two suitemates did have some things in common. Both considered themselves loyal Republicans. And, like Michael, Richard came from a Catholic background. But unlike his suitemate, he had been educated in non-Catholic schools and found Michael's brand of Catholicism "very doctrinaire."[4]

Michael arrived at Yale in an uncharacteristically belligerent mood. Over the past few years he had acquired some of the defensiveness of his classmates at Holy Cross. He expected to be snubbed for his religious background and was determined, as he recalled later, to "show all of those Wasps from Yale—and from Harvard, Princeton, Amherst, and the like—that by God, we're as good as they are!"[5] This was the first time in his life that he had competed in an institution where he was surrounded by people of dissimilar beliefs.

Not only was he entering a secular institution, but it was a place that in 1947 stood as one of the nation's preeminent symbols of old-line New England Protestant cultural hegemony. Named for Yankee merchant prince Elihu Yale and founded by Puritan ministers, Yale was the third oldest university established in the English colonies of North America. For almost a quarter millennium, it had served as a bastion of the values and beliefs of the Northeast's Protestant elite.[6] As Michael was certainly aware, for most of those years Yale did not exactly seek out Irish-Catholics for admission. When the first Irish settlers arrived in New Haven in the mid-eighteenth century, they did not come in any scholarly capacity: A locally printed advertisement from 1764 announced the arrival of "A Parcel of Irish Servants, both Men and Women, just imported from Dublin in the brig Derby, and to be sold cheap." In the century that followed, New Haven had grown into a center of hardware, clock, and firearm manufacturing and had attracted a substantial Irish, Italian, and Jewish population.

The city was loyally Democratic in voting allegiance (the dissenters tended to cast their votes even further to the left—in the fall of 1947 the Socialist Party candidate for mayor in New Haven won over 11,000 votes, and nearby Norwalk and Bridgeport actually elected socialist mayors).[7] But as an institution, Yale did its best to pretend that neither the industrial revolution nor the New Deal had ever taken place. The landscaping alone spoke eloquently to this point. Adjacent to the campus lay a sixteen-acre green, bounded by three stately Protestant churches, an island of idealized New England village scenery. In 1951, marking the occasion of the university's 250th anniversary with a cover story, *Time* magazine declared that in "the best and truest sense of the word, Yale has stood from its earliest beginnings for conservatism triumphant."[8]

The law school, around which Michael's life in New Haven centered, shared the aesthetics, if not necessarily the politics, of the rest of the institution. The law school was founded independently in 1800 and affiliated with the university in 1843. The Sterling Law Building, though completed only in the 1930s, was designed to convey a sense of tradition, stability, and power. Housing both classrooms and residential suites, Sterling's quadrangle was decorated with elaborate stone carvings of bewigged jurists bearing scrolls and with Puritans leading Indians in prayer. The building's windows were leaded stained glass. Michael's suite came complete with a wood-burning fireplace and maid service.[9] Yale Law School functioned as the American equivalent of the *École Normale Supérieure*. It was the training place for leaders of American society; its graduates routinely went on to become partners in prestigious Wall Street firms, the deans of other law schools, and federal judges.[10]

When Michael entered law school, the Columbia sociologist C. Wright Mills was preparing to publish a study of white-collar professionalism. Mills described the law in the 1940s as a profession chiefly devoted to shaping "the legal framework for the new economy of the big corporation," which it was coming to resemble in organization and values. "More than a consultant and counselor to large business," Mills declared, "the lawyer is its servant, its champion, its ready apologist, and is full of its sensitivity."[11]

Surprisingly, Yale Law School proved an exception to Mills's generalization. To the horror of some of its older alumni, it had developed a reputation—even a notoriety—for unabashed liberalism. In the 1930s and 1940s the Yale law faculty were on the whole ardent supporters of Franklin Roosevelt and were committed to an ideal of public service that led many of them to take on assignments with New Deal agencies. Professor William O. Douglas served as chairman of the Securities and Exchange Commission (SEC), where he became part of Roosevelt's inner circle of advisers and poker buddies; Roosevelt appointed Douglas to the Supreme Court in 1939. Professors Abe Fortas, Wesley Sturges, and Thurman Arnold all worked for the Agricultural Adjustment Administration (AAA), and Arnold went on to play a major role in the antitrust division of the Justice Department.[12] These were men who believed in the beneficence of a powerful federal government, who mistrusted unbridled corporate power, and who assumed that an important part of the mission of intellectuals and academics was to act as the advisers to elected officials.

Michael never took courses with the more famous veterans of New Deal service, most of whom had moved on by the time he arrived. But he did take a torts class with Fowler V. Harper, who had worked in Washington in a variety of official capacities during the Second World War, before arriving as a faculty member at Yale Law School the same fall that Michael arrived as a student. Fowler also had connections farther left, as a leading member of the National Lawyers Guild in the 1940s. Asked once by a newspaper reporter why he always seemed to "follow the communist line," Fowler retorted that "sometimes it appears that the communists follow my line. They're always welcome to agree with me, but I don't see how I can be blamed when they do." Years later, Fowler would be involved in the early days of the "Griswold" case, in which the Supreme Court overturned Connecticut's ban on birth control counseling and established a controversial constitutional "right to privacy."[13]

Michael also took a course with a younger professor, Eugene Rostow, who would go on to considerable fame in the early 1960s as part of the "best and brightest" in the Kennedy and Johnson administrations. Rostow was born into a socialist family; named for Eugene Debs, he cast his first vote in a presidential election for Norman Thomas. By the time he joined the law school faculty he had decided that Karl Marx was "talking nonsense" about economics. He became, as was made abundantly clear in his later career, a fierce anticommunist. But as far as domestic economic policy was concerned, Professor Rostow was no conservative. He did his own stint of government service during the Second World War, when he served in the State Department as an administrator for the lend-lease program. Returning to Yale at the end of the war, he initiated a course entitled "Public Control of Business," which Michael took in the spring of 1948; here Michael gained his first acquaintance with the writings of John Maynard Keynes. The course, as Rostow later described it, "preached the gospel that the state had tremendous responsibilities. You couldn't rely on laissez-faire."[14]

In his encounter with Keynesianism, Michael was perhaps relearning old lessons. His grandfather Patrick could have and probably had taught him the same lessons about the virtues of deficit spending and public works in times of economic downturn, albeit with less elaborate theoretical grounding. But the emphasis Michael encountered at Yale on "legal realism" did present him with a perspective he had never considered before. Legal realists challenged the formalism of traditional legal thought, with its insistence that abstract principles were the genuine and proper basis for judicial decisionmaking. On the contrary, as a curriculum committee of the Yale Law School declared in a report in the mid-1940s, "law must be studied as part of the social process."[15] As one of legal realism's intellectual forebears, Oliver Wendell Holmes, had argued in the 1880s, the development of law was the product of "the felt necessities of the time, the prevalent moral and political theories, intuitions of public policy, avowed or unconscious, even the prejudices which judges share with their fellow men."[16]

Later on, as a Supreme Court justice during the Progressive Era, Holmes issued a celebrated dissent in the case of *Lochner v. New York*. The majority of the Court had rejected a New York law that would have restricted the number of hours bakery workers could work to ten a day; this was, in the opinion of the majority, unwarranted interference with the freedom of contract. Holmes, to the contrary, argued that "general propositions do not decide concrete cases." The constitution had not been established "to embody a particular economic policy." Neither Holmes nor most of the legal realists who followed in his footsteps were socialists. But they did take for granted a far greater degree of indeterminacy in the law's meaning than the systemizing theorists who preceded them would ever have tolerated.[17]

All of Michael's previous intellectual training had been shaped by the assumption that timeless and sacred principles determined right conduct and belief. Now, as Yale classmate Bill Hegarty put it, Michael was enrolled in an institution "designed to disabuse you of the idea that the law came from Olympus and was immutable." It was bound to be, in Hegarty's words, "an awakening to someone of Catholic background, used to hearing 'this is the way it is.'" Legal realism, as presented at Yale Law School in the mid-1940s, was at once pragmatic and iconoclastic, skeptical and optimistic. Hegarty remembered that Rostow's course in particular "would shake your sense of infallibility, papal or otherwise." Rostow taught his students that, for better or worse, "human beings had shaped the system."[18]

Michael's intellectual and political assumptions were being shaken not only in the classroom but in debates and conversations with his closest friends in New Haven. At Yale Law School, unlike Holy Cross, nobody was holding any sympathy meetings for Franco's Spain. According to Michael's fellow student Jerry Davidoff, the class of '50 at the law school was united politically by "a feeling that the world could be remade." The crusading spirit and liberal idealism of the New Deal and the war years were still very much in evidence among them. The United States government had ended the depression, had mobilized the nation's industrial might and manpower for a global war, and had emerged victorious over the forces of reaction, prejudice, and aggression. There was also a great deal of interest in and sympathy for the British Labour government that had come to power in 1945.[19]

The deterioration of Soviet–American relations, the Republican triumph in the 1946 congressional elections, and the Truman administration's attempts to purge the government of "disloyal" employees were disturbing trends, but few of Michael's classmates expected that the United States was on the eve of a decade of conservative reaction. Two hundred students turned out at a forum sponsored by the law school student association to hear Arthur Garfield Hayes, director of the American Civil Liberties Union (ACLU), denounce Truman's newly instituted federal employee loyalty review board as a "gestapo-like operation." The students attending the meeting adopted a resolution calling for the abolition of the House Un-American Activities Committee (HUAC).[20] Many students in Michael's class hoped that former Vice President Henry Wallace would galvanize a liberal counterattack and turn the usurper Harry Truman out of the White House the following year. When Wallace spoke at the New Haven Arena in September, over 6,000 enthusiastic supporters paid admission to hear his call for "a program of progressive capitalism which will end for all time the threat of depression."[21]

Among Yale undergraduates in the late 1940s, the law school became a byword for leftism—sometimes sinister, sometimes comic. In 1951, William F. Buckley Jr., a sophomore at Yale when Michael arrived, would make his reputation as conservative *enfant terrible* with the publication of *God and Man at Yale,* his scathing survey of Yale's "socialistic" curriculum. In the preface to the book he noted that "for practical reasons" he was restricting his survey to the undergraduate departments of the university, "even though some of the graduate departments, the Yale Law School in particular, would provide far more flamboyant copy."[22]

That Michael's political views in September 1947 were far closer to those of William F. Buckley than, say, Henry Wallace made him an oddball at the law school. At Holy Cross, the inherited and usually unquestioned loyalties of his classmates to the Democratic Party had provided little challenge to Michael's newly proclaimed Republicanism. In late night bull sessions at Yale, he faced a more informed opposition from men who were older and spoke with the authority of elite college educations and military service.[23] The champion debater of Saint Louis University High School found himself increasingly unsure of the views he defended against the arguments and gibes of his new liberal and radical friends. He took out a subscription to the *Nation,* in part to prove his open-mindedness, and to his own surprise found himself persuaded by much of what he read in it. Within a few months, his conservatism was crumbling. He lost his enthusiasm first for Robert Taft, then for the Republican Party, and finally for the capitalist system. He would later credit his Yale classmates with converting him to socialism, though none of his classmates remember him announcing such a conversion, and there is no evidence that he involved himself with any of the radical organizations available to him on the Yale campus.[24]

Michael's sense of religious certainty was also under assault. His classmates particularly delighted in baiting him on questions of sexual morality. Monroe Singer, who lived in the neighboring suite and was a frequent participant in those late night debates, remembered Michael denouncing the conclusions of the Kinsey Report, whose value-neutral report on "Sexual Behavior in the Human Male" was published in the spring of 1948. And yet, at the same time, Michael was experiencing an increasingly obvious conflict, as Singer recalled, over "certain elements of Catholic dogma that went against his grain intellectually." Richard Fitzsimmons remembered that in the early months at Yale, Michael would drag in Thomas Aquinas as "his answer to every problem," be it theological, political, legal, or moral. But by the end of the school year, the citations of Aquinas had all but disappeared from Michael's debating arsenal.[25]

Whatever anxieties Michael felt at Yale about his ability to hold his own academically were soon put to rest. Michael organized and led the exam study sessions at the end of that semester; to Richard Fitzsimmons it seemed almost as if Michael were a teacher leading a graduate seminar.[26] Of the six courses Michael took that semester, he received a grade of 80 or higher in three of them ("Criminal Law and Administration," "Judicial Process," and "Torts"); a grade 80 or above was rated as "Excellent" on his law school transcript. Only a grade of 67 (deemed "Satisfactory" on the transcript) in "Contracts" dragged his overall average for the semester below 80.[27] Michael's grades won him the distinction of becoming an editor of the Yale Law Journal.

Receiving his grades was both the high point and the beginning of the end of Michael's law school education. "The day I knew I was going to quit," he later reminisced, "was the day I got my grades. . . . I didn't want to leave as a failure. I wanted to show that I could do it if I wanted to, could be in the top ten percent of an elite law school."[28] The second semester at Yale he almost completely stopped studying for his classes, although his grades barely suffered. An hour or so a day of reading allowed him to coast by. He abandoned the law library, preferring the comfortable easy chairs and the collection of poetry available in the undergraduate library. Contracts and torts could not compete in his affections with the poems of Rainer Maria Rilke. One day, Richard Fitzsimmons decided to test him on Rilke, memorizing a few of the poems. "I asked him what was Rilke really trying to get across in the final stanza of such and such a poem?" Without missing a beat, Michael recited the lines in question and then offered a lucid mini-lecture on Rilke's mystical lyricism.[29]

When he wasn't reading law or poetry, Michael enjoyed the freedoms that he had dreamed about while "a prisoner on the hill" at Holy Cross. He was still dating Joan Sayward, and even debated with himself whether he would marry "outside the faith," but by mid-year the question became moot as the two drifted apart. He saw other girls, although none seriously.[30] The law school suites were a sociable community; there were frequent parties and card games and a lot of social drinking; Michael's torts professor, Fleming James, occasionally wound up sleeping on their couch after a late night of revelry. Michael whiled away many hours in nearby student hangouts, nursing a cup of coffee at George and Harry's coffee shop or drinking beer at the Old Heidelberg bar. The Schubert Theater, a few blocks away, brought in Broadway-bound try outs and revivals; he saw Henry Fonda star in *Mr. Roberts* in January. He also began going to the ballet, a newly discovered pleasure that became a passion. His taste ran to Balanchine, rather than to what he dismissed as the "prettified banality" of the nineteenth-century classics.[31]

From New Haven to New York City, it was only about an hour's journey by train or car, and Michael began to explore the city that year. Previously he had seen little more of it than the immediate vicinity of Penn Station, where he changed trains on his way to or from St. Louis. Now his guide was a fellow law student named John Dickinson, who lived across the hall in Sterling, and who was co-owner of a bookstore on the corner of Waverly and MacDougall Streets in the Village. Dickinson fascinated many of the law students with his outspoken radical politics (unlike most, he proved an unwavering Wallace supporter), as well as with his flamboyant lifestyle.

Dickinson's girlfriend, a Sarah Lawrence undergraduate, spent many nights with him at Yale, a virtually unheard of practice in the Sterling Law Building in those years. With Dickinson and a few others, Michael began haunting the bookstores and bars in Greenwich Village. If it got too late to return to New Haven, they would sometimes sleep over in the back room of Dickinson's bookstore.[32]

It was a pleasant enough life, and not very demanding. With a reputation already established as one of the best students in his class, Michael could easily have drifted through another two years of law school and then had his pick of secure and well-paying jobs. But for the first time in his life, and much to his parents' consternation, Michael did the unexpected. The law, he decided, was not for him. He was going to be a writer. Before the spring semester was finished he had applied to and was accepted by the graduate program in English at the University of Chicago.[33]

Michael tried his best to soften the blow to his parents. He sent them a three-page letter in April, explaining his decision. "Dear Mom and Dad," he wrote:

> In keeping with our rule of not keeping anything back, I want to tell you what I've decided in the last few weeks. I'm quite sure now that I don't want to come back here next fall—that I don't want to go on with the law.

He had, he reminded them, agreed only to try law school for a year, to give him the opportunity "to mature" and "get away from the bohemian atmosphere" he had immersed himself in at Holy Cross. He had enjoyed his first semester at Yale, when he had been able to immerse himself in "broad, humanizing ideas, the philosophy of law, the main concepts and problems of the judicial system." But now the focus of his courses had changed to drier and more technical subjects. The law, Michael argued, "just doesn't fit my way of thinking." He had even reached the point where he was hoping he would be drafted into the army, "so that I could have time to think and write and get away from law." The year at Yale had served only to remind him how much he had always wanted to make writing his career, "in some shape or form—and that I want to work at it full-time and not as an extracurricular activity." He hoped to take a "crack at English," and hoped his parents would "do the same as you did for the law"—which was to say, provide him both their moral and financial support. He concluded with a long apology for having thrown "cold water" on their hopes. Michael said he was "truly sorry and not at all ungrateful because I do realize that the reason you have those hopes is because you have always been so very interested in me and given me so much." He assured his parents, with the usual uncertain punctuation of his correspondence, that "if theres a single word in this letter thats in the least bit ungrateful then thats not the meaning that I wanted the word to have."[34]

Michael's parents could not have been pleased by his defiance, mildly and apologetically phrased as it was, but they went along. The fact that Michael was moving back to the Midwest and would be closer to home may have helped them to reconcile themselves to the idea. And there was always the chance that after a year of sowing his literary oats, Michael would get over his antipathy to the law and return to Yale. So in September, Michael moved to Chicago to take his "crack at English."

In contrast to the silence with which he passed over his year at Yale, Michael devoted pages of affectionate prose in his memoirs to his year at the University of Chicago, that "Left Bank of the mind where ideas, like the poems and paintings of Bohemia, were their own excuse for being."[35]

It proved a very good year for Michael, the best of his entire college experience. He loved the social freedoms he now enjoyed (unlike Holy Cross), as well as what he was studying (unlike Yale). He loved the excitement and variety of the intellectual community around the university. And in personal terms, the year in Chicago provided the twenty-year-old with his first chance to lay claim to a new independence and identity. His parents were still paying the bills, but this was the first time he had gone to a school that they had not chosen or approved for him. It was also the first place he had gone where his circle of friends and acquaintances was completely new (at Holy Cross Bill Loftus had been a reminder of life in St. Louis; at Yale, he had still seen a lot of Joan Sayward). Now there were no ties to the past, except those he chose to bring up himself. As if to symbolize the transition, in the fall of 1948 Edward Michael Harrington Jr., formerly and variously known as "Neddie," "Ned," and "Ed," began introducing himself to people by the name he would use for the rest of his life—"Mike Harrington."[36]

Michael would remember the year at Chicago as a kind of "explosion of the intellect." He "read like a madman" to catch up on the debates in his classes and in student hangouts like Reader's Drugstore and the University Tavern. The Aristotelians and the anti-Aristotelians "fought pitched battles" over such questions as "Is 'Murder in the Cathedral' a play? Is 'Death of a Salesman' a tragedy?" He was writing poetry, and everyone he knew seemed to be writing a play or a novel. He had a brief love affair with a woman he would identify as "Lindy" in his memoirs. Lindy was writing a novel that dealt candidly with the sex lives of people at the University of Chicago "and sometimes used real names, a fact that enlivened meetings of the Creative Writing Club where manuscripts were read." When she and Michael broke up, he recalled, "she threatened to write a novel about me."[37]

Michael would recall walking home one night a few months after his arrival in Chicago, thinking about an exam he was supposed to prepare for the next day. Instead he stopped at a bookstore and bought a copy of Joseph Conrad's *Victory,* a "poignant account of how man can't hide himself from life and love." Intending to read only a few pages, instead he stayed up most of the night to finish the book:

> That epitomized the spirit of Chicago in those days: there were even some students who waited for months to go to the registrar's to find out their grades on the grounds that a professor's opinion of their work was an irrelevance. And there was a rage to talk, to discuss, to articulate, that surged through bars and drugstores and love affairs.[38]

Not that his grades seem to have suffered as a result of his nonacademic enthusiasms. He took nine courses that year, ranging from "Methods of Literary Study" to "Donne and the Metaphysical Poets," and received more A's than B's and nothing below that.[39]

Among the topics that Michael had a rage to discuss that year were his ever-growing religious doubts. He sought out fellow Catholics on the largely non-Catholic campus. Jim Finn, a fellow graduate student in English, was sitting in the Modern Language Reading Room at the university when he glanced up to see "a young blond guy standing at the side of my cubicle." He introduced himself as Mike Harrington:

> "Interesting magazine, isn't it?" he asked. I looked down at my desk to see what he was referring to. The only visible magazine was the latest issue of *Commonweal,* which I had been reading. "Yes," I agreed rather dimly, not knowing quite where to go from there. But Mike did. He had used the *Commonweal* to find out whether I was a Catholic. That fact established, our conversation was launched. It led us, over a short time, to talk about religion, our backgrounds, our favorite authors, our uncertain plans for the future—and all the great questions of life.[40]

Michael finally decided that he could not accept "the concept of a God who would send somebody to hell for all eternity." And having broken with Catholic orthodoxy on a single question, Michael discovered, as he would say later, that the "Jesuit house of cards that [he] had been installed in at Holy Cross and at St. Louis" had collapsed around him. He decided sometime that year in Chicago that he was no longer a Catholic—although he chose not to share that dramatic news with his parents just yet. His split with the Church was still conditional; he later described it as an "indecisive apostasy."[41]

Michael would describe 1948 as "the last year of the thirties," with Harry

Truman waging a populist-flavored "give 'em hell" campaign against the Republicans. Whether that was true for the country as a whole, there was certainly a 1930s flavor to political debate on the University of Chicago campus—nowhere else, except perhaps in the city colleges of New York, was the partisan war among student Communists, Socialists, and Trotskyists still being waged with such intensity. The Young Progressives brought Henry Wallace to campus; the Socialists brought Norman Thomas. Wallace's supporters cheered as he denounced "fake liberals" who were rushing to enlist in the anticommunist crusade; Thomas's supporters cheered as he denounced "the Communist Wallaceites."[42]

If Michael attended any of these events, he made no mention of them subsequently. Certainly the idea of joining an organization, handing out leaflets, or marching on a picket line had little appeal to him. Michael's radicalism circa 1948–1949 was more about aesthetics than class struggle: "Capitalism was not so much cruel and exploitative as crass and vulgar."[43]

Perhaps the most formative political experience for Michael at Chicago was his coming to know, or at least know about, university president Robert M. Hutchins. A product of Oberlin College and Yale Law School, Hutchins enjoyed a meteoric academic career, becoming dean of the Yale Law School (where he gave the institution its "legal realist" leaning) and then moving on to become the "boy president" of the University of Chicago in 1929. He reorganized Chicago's undergraduate curriculum around the study of "Great Books" and abolished fraternities and the football team. Very much a "public intellectual" before the term had been invented, Hutchins reached out to the broader non-university public through speeches, writing, and a weekly radio program.[44] As one of his biographers noted, his goal was to create a "cohesive moral community" at the University of Chicago, drawing upon his experience of attending Oberlin.[45] Hutchins's emphasis on the moral responsibilities of the intellectual's quest for truth was not unlike the ideals of Catholic education that had sustained Michael in earlier years. Michael described the spirit at the University of Chicago fostered by President Robert M. Hutchins as "Aristotelian-Thomist Bohemian," which he defined as "an iconoclastic respect for standards" combined with "a contempt for middle-class utilitarianism."[46]

Hutchins's reforms were not universally popular. The University of Chicago had long been targeted by the Hearst press and by conservatives in the Illinois state legislature as a stronghold of subversion and immorality. Hutchins's bold defense of academic freedom made him a hero to students and faculty alike in the 1930s.[47] But in the late 1940s, attacks escalated. In the spring of 1949, Hutchins was summoned to testify before the Illinois legislature to respond to charges that the university was harboring Communist sympathizers on its faculty. There he was badgered by no less a celebrity than the chief investigator for the House Un-American Activities Committee, J. B. Matthews. Why, Matthews demanded to know, did the university persist in making its research facilities available to an emeritus professor at the medical school who had been accused of Communist affiliations? Hutchins would not concede that the professor in question was a Communist, but in any case her associations on campus were now limited exclusively to tending to her laboratory mice. Matthews retorted heatedly: "May I ask if in your educational theory there is not such a thing as indoctrination by example?" To which Hutchins replied mildly, "Of mice?"[48]

Hutchins defined an ideal of intellectual grace and political independence that Michael admired greatly, and for the rest of his life he would acknowledge his indebtedness to Hutchins's example.[49] There was a strongly ethical—even religious—component to Hutchins's vision of the responsibilities of intellectuals (he was himself the son of a professor of theology at Oberlin). In the spring of 1946, Michael had praised the devout Catholic as "the only radical in a world of conformists." Three years later, at the graduation ceremony at the University of Chicago, Michael sat in the audience and listened as Hutchins described "the educated man" in very similar terms. In a time of "unanimous tribal self-adoration" such as Americans were going through in the late 1940s, the educated man "must keep his head, and use it. He must never push other people around, nor acquiesce when he sees it done. He must struggle to retain the perspective and the sense of proportion that his studies have given him and decline to be carried away by waves of hysteria. He must be prepared to pay the penalty of unpopularity."[50]

However inspiring Michael found Hutchins's words and example, he still had no clear idea of how he was going to exercise his own responsibilities as an educated man. He had no intention of going back to law school, and, M.A. in hand, he was no closer to the goal of being "a writer" than he had been before his year in Chicago. He returned home to St. Louis that summer at loose ends. Notwithstanding his decision the previous winter to leave the church, Michael took on the project of writing a pamphlet for a Jesuit publishing house. Entitled *Cana Catechism*, Michael's first published writing outside of school newspapers described how parishes should go about staging religious retreats for Catholic married couples. It was full of practical tips for organizers, such as: "Experience shows that Cokes and coffee are the most practical thing to serve, and should appear at long conferences between meetings and after the gabfest at short conferences." The fact that he published the pamphlet under the name "Ed Harrington" suggests that he wanted to establish some distance between this project and the new identity he had forged as "Mike" in Chicago.[51]

Michael took on another job that year after returning to St. Louis that turned out to be of vastly greater importance in his life and legend. Years later he would present it as the turning point in his life:

> Without any idealistic thought on my part, and through the influence of a cousin and ward leader, I was given a job in the Pupil Welfare Department of the St. Louis Public Schools. I was assigned to the Madison School, located in an Arkansas sharecropper district down near the river, not far from a "Hooverville," one of those colonies of driftwood and tincan shacks that had survived from the Depression. One rainy day I went into an old, decaying building. The cooking smells and the stench from the broken, stopped-up toilets and the murmurous cranky sound of the people were a revelation. It was my moment on the road to Damascus. Suddenly the abstract and statistical and aesthetic outrages I had reacted to at Yale and Chicago became real and personal and insistent. A few hours later, riding the Grand Avenue streetcar, I realized that somehow I must spend the rest of my life trying to obliterate that kind of house and to work with the people who lived there.[52]

Michael may have undergone the change of heart he describes in the manner in which he remembered it (although none of his surviving friends and family can recall any announcement on his part of a dramatic social awakening). The records of the Division of Pupil Welfare of the St. Louis Board of Education show that Edward Michael Harrington Jr. was employed for a total of three days in September and October 1949, making $10 a day, and with the designation "substitute home teacher." The records may be inexact about his actual assignment; indeed, he could have been working as a truant officer and not a teacher. But he did not last a week in either capacity. In the fall of 1950, back in St. Louis again, he worked an additional four days for the board of education. "I started work this week," he wrote to a friend in New York that fall, "but not as a case investigator. I am a teacher—of history this week—at Roosevelt high school, a 'substitute' for someone who is sick." He did that job for two days. At the end of the letter he appended a note, "I am back as a welfare worker." All told then, Michael's "social work" career consisted of somewhere between two and—at most—five days of actual employment. He did not exactly lie about his experience of being a social worker in subsequent accounts, but he was certainly deliberately vague about its duration.[53]

In any case, Michael was unhappy wasting his time in St. Louis. Here he was, five years after setting off for Holy Cross, living in his boyhood bedroom in his parents' house. He looked up old friends and sampled the distractions offered by St. Louis high society: "I thought it only mildly embarrassing to go to a large debutante party at a country club in St. Louis and sit in front of a swimming pool filled with flowers and drink some rich father's whiskey while trying to convince a friend that capitalism was a rotten system."[54] He found a bar near the levee on the Mississippi called "Little Bohemia," where he could talk longingly with "the painters and other regulars" about "art and psychoanalysis and the motherland of Greenwich Village."[55]

By December he was fed up. He announced to his parents that he was moving to Greenwich Village to be a writer. All of Michael's well-honed diplomatic skills in handling his parents did not avail him this time. He had a fierce argument with his mother, who wanted him to stay in St. Louis, or at least go back to Chicago to complete a Ph.D. in English. Michael could not be swayed from his plan, nor his mother from her disapproval. When he left St. Louis this time, he left without even Catherine's grudging approval. She did not say good-bye and refused for several weeks to write to him.[56]

When Michael arrived in New York, he found temporary accommodations in a friend's dorm room at City College. He later would take pleasure, and some measure of literary license, in exaggerating his provincialism. "I wanted to get to the Village," he would relate of his first day in New York, "but not appear as a Midwestern Square, so I asked someone at the 137th Street subway station how to get to the Village Barn, a tourist mecca on 8th Street. The straw fell gently out of my hair onto the platform."[57] He had, of course, already been to the Village on numerous occasions during his year at Yale Law School, and with a knowledgeable guide. But it was certainly true that he still had a lot to learn about the lay of the land. On that first night in New York he found his way first to Louis's bar on Sheridan Square and then moved on to the Cafe Bohemia on Barrow Street. "It was then in a lesbian phase," Michael would recall, "and, like all straight young men from the Middle West, I found that fascinating. I got into conversation with an attractive young woman, but then her girl friend appeared, angry with my heterosexual poaching."[58]

Greenwich Village consisted of two square miles in lower Manhattan, stretching from Spring Street to 14th Street and from the Hudson River to 2nd Avenue, centered on Washington Square Park, with a population in 1949 of about 80,000, occupying a wildly miscellaneous collection of stately federal and Greek revival mansions, well-preserved brownstones, aging six-story walk-up tenements, converted factory lofts, and newer high rise apartments. Its meandering streets had defied the best attempts of nineteenth-century city planners to impose upon it the gridiron pattern that came to characterize New York north of 14th Street, and it would in a few years become one of the centers of resistance to the mid-twentieth-century cult of "urban renewal," when residents successfully fought off plans to run a "downtown expressway" through the heart of Washington Square.[59]

Greenwich Village occupied mythic as well as geographical space. Since the beginning of the nineteenth century, a number of celebrated misfits had called it home: Tom Paine lived on Grove Street in the West Village at the time of his death in 1809; Edgar Allen Poe lived on West 3rd Street in 1845 when he published "The Raven." The heyday of the Village came with the turn of the century, when a critical mass of talented and discontented artistic and political rebels arrived on the scene and launched such enterprises as the *Masses* magazine, founded in 1911, and the Provincetown Players, founded in 1916. A place of refuge had become a community. *Masses* artist John Sloan climbed with several friends to the top of Washington Square Arch in 1916; firing cap pistols and setting aloft red balloons, they declared Greenwich Village "a Free Republic, Independent of Uptown."[60]

So Greenwich Village came to represent a new promised land, where the sons and daughters of the American hinterland and middle class could shed the proprieties, inhibitions, and prejudices of their upbringings, in pursuit of (alone or in combination) real life, art, revolution, love, sexual fulfillment, and notoriety. The "doctrine" of the Village, as codified by the left-wing literary critic Malcolm Cowley in his memoir *Exile's Return,* included such ideas as "salvation by the child" ("each of us at birth has special potentialities which are slowly crushed and destroyed by a standardized society"), "self-expression" ("each man's, each woman's purpose in life is to express himself . . . through creative work and beautiful living"), "paganism" ("the body is a temple in which there is nothing unclean"), and "living for the moment" ("seize the moment as it comes . . . dwell in it intensely"). Michael, with varying emphases at different moments in his years in Greenwich Village, would subscribe to every item on Cowley's list.[61]

Another enduring part of the Greenwich Village myth, beloved by successive waves of old-timers and burdening successive waves of newcomers, held that the best days of the Village were already long past.[62] Cowley, who arrived in Greenwich Village in the 1920s, in exile from his native Pittsburgh, was pained by the realization that in the "prewar" Village, which he had just missed, "Bohemians read Marx, and all the radicals had a touch of the bohemian. . . . Villagers might get their heads broken in Union Square by the police before appearing at the Liberal Club to recite Swinburne in bloody bandages." But then Cowley had shared Paris in the 1920s with the "Lost Generation" writers, so it cost him little to concede the decline of the Village.[63] By the time Michael arrived, another war had come and gone, and cultural obituary writers were waxing nostalgic over the vibrant and now definitely dead-and-buried Village they had been privileged to know in the 1920s and 1930s. (But, they "were all wrong," Michael would remark dryly several decades after his arrival. "The Village did not die until after I got there.")[64]

A new generation was gathering in the Village in the years following the

Second World War, and if Swinburne was no longer in vogue, the imagery of poets on the cultural—if not necessarily political—barricades had lost none of its appeal. Michael's old high school and college classmate Bill Loftus had arrived in Greenwich Village before Michael. "For all of us," he recalled, "the ideal was Montmartre in the 1890s. That's what we were trying to recreate in the Village." Arthur Moore, a writer and editor who came to the Village in the late 1940s and met Mike shortly after his arrival in the city, bumped that ideal up to "Paris in the 1920s." David McReynolds, a radical political activist who arrived in the Village a few years after Michael, wrote home to a friend in Los Angeles on the occasion of his first visit in 1953: "I wish you could see Greenwich Village. I am sure you would like it. Shops are on every side of you, with all kinds of ceramics, paintings, books, odd musical instruments—a fantastic hodgepodge of people and objects and stores that are gentle and funny and a combination of Cocteau and Capote."[65]

Part of the appeal of the Village was the anomalous position it maintained at the cutting edge of avant-garde, while at the same time harkening back to earlier premodern forms of community. Thinking back twenty years after his arrival on the appeal of Greenwich Village, Michael described it as "small, organized on a human scale." By the time he had been there a few years he would "know half of the people in Washington Square Park on sight." It was a place "large enough to have a sense of community . . . and small enough for everyone to remain an individual."[66] It also required a kind of specialized knowledge to live in the Village, not readily apparent to the uninitiated, such as why, when one walked westwards from Washington Square Park on 4th Street, one came in due course to West 13th Street, or how one was supposed to find the way to Chumley's on Bedford Street, a restaurant and bar famed both for its appeal to Village writers and for its lack of any sign outside indicating its presence.

Michael celebrated his first Christmas in New York in his new apartment on West 15th Street between 6th and 7th Avenue, in a building tucked in between Mother Zita's Home for Friendless Women and Dykes Lumber Company. He split the rent with Bill Loftus, who was then a graduate student at Columbia. The two of them shared a bath with the occupants of three other apartments. The sanitary conditions left something to be desired: Within a few weeks, both of them were infested with pubic lice.[67]

Perhaps it was discomfort from crabs, perhaps it was post-Christmas letdown, perhaps it was the bleakness of late December weather in New York, or perhaps it was the understandable loneliness of a still very young man who still very much wanted to please his parents that led Michael to write a long letter to "Mom and Dad" shortly after Christmas Day.

He began in chatty fashion. "Christmas was very enjoyable—as much as the first Christmas away from home could be." With three friends, University of Chicago classmate Bill Smith, Mark Hazeltine, and Tommy Jackson, he had prepared Christmas dinner on a two burner stove: "steak, french fries, string beans, pear salad, burgandy, coffee ice-cream, coffee and the like."[68] Later in the evening other new acquaintances, including Arthur Moore, Jack Patterson, and Ed Donais, arrived and "we had a wonderful little session of beer drinking." Christmas dinner was quite a contrast from his usual fare since arriving in New York, "a concotion called Broadcast corned beef hash which serves two (with catsup) for thirty five cents. Amazing what you can do when you cook for yourself."

Done with the pleasantries, he moved on to his real purpose for writing:

> And now for some news. I know that you all have every right to be angry with me, but I ask you to remember that the whole thing is better to have happened this way. I have decided (after an awful lot of soul-searching) that I really want to take the doctorate—and at Chicago! I now feel a certainty about things. I came up here to write, yet I have realized that many things make it the wrong place to come, and make Chicago the right place to go. I suppose it was obvious to you, but I had to learn that an eight hour day in a publishing house, or in almost any kind of work that does not directly concern itself with teaching, is a drain on creative energy. I have not read as much since I have arrived in New York—I have only written as much (as Chicago) by the dint of a lot of concentration and will power.

Michael's confession continued onto a second page:

> And then there is Greenwich Village and the 'Artist's Life.' The only thing it does is ruin artists. It no longer means artistic freedom, it now means sexual freedom. In this short time, I have grown afraid of these people who sit around in bars and talk literature all the time, talk of creating all the time, and never get to anything more than sitting around in bars. It seems to me that their whole concept of an 'artists life' is a fairly thinly disguise for imorality and not too much more.

Michael had shed the belief that he had argued for so "vigorously" the previous summer, namely, that "the academic life is not for the artist." Now, he could "think of nothing that would help my writing more than . . . holing up in a room in Chicago and reading for eight hours a day. It would certainly be better than anything offered around here."

Miserable and contrite as he sounded—and probably felt—Michael wasn't prepared to return home just yet. He proposed that he remain in New York for two more months and return to Chicago in early March in time for the spring term, confessing that the additional two months would amount to "a glorified vacation . . . and . . . I have had quite a vacation already." He concluded with a final apology: "I know this letter comes as a shock—especially considering my attitude when I was home a few weeks ago. But blame my pride and nothing else." He signed the letter "Ned."[69]

There is no record of Catherine and Edward's reactions to this act of confession by their wayward son. Possibly they were gratified that he had finally seen the light. Perhaps they had grown a little wary over the preceding year and a half and were reserving judgment until they saw what Michael would actually wind up doing that spring. Michael's plea for an additional two months "vacation" in a community he professed to despise was not entirely encouraging. In any event, whatever Michael's intentions were in late December 1949, two months later he was not packing his bags for Chicago.

Michael's prospects and attitude had brightened considerably in that interval. After ridding themselves of their case of crabs, he and Bill Loftus moved to a larger apartment at 708 East 5th Street, between Avenues C and D in the East Village, which they shared with a third roommate, Bill's Columbia classmate Curtis Brown.[70] Also, and for the first time in his life, Michael began to support himself. At first he wrote articles for the *Columbia Encyclopedia,* where University of Chicago acquaintance Bill Smith worked as an editor and farmed out articles to his friends. Then he got a job in March as a writer-trainee with *Life* magazine, making $90 a week, a magnificent sum in those days for a young single man without responsibilities.[71]

Michael had also begun to enjoy a certain celebrity among the drinking circles of the Village. Having eventually found his way to the San Remo bar on his first night in town, he soon became a regular. The San Remo, located on the corner of MacDougall and Bleecker Streets, still enjoyed a considerable reputation as a writer's bar when Michael arrived, although it was soon to go in eclipse; when David McReynolds came to New York for the first time in 1953, Bayard Rustin warned him that the San Remo was a place for "people who discuss books they haven't read, art they haven't painted, theater they haven't seen."[72] But in the late 1940s it still counted James Agee, John Cage, Merce Cunningham, Allen Ginsberg, Paul Goodman, Jack Kerouac, and Judith Malina among its regulars. Maxwell Bodenheim, who was living the miserable life of an aging alcoholic, but enjoying the romantic aura of the "doomed poet," would come in and trade freshly scribbled poems for drinks at the bar.[73] Mary McCarthy, touring the Village on behalf of the *New York Post* in 1950, pronounced the San Remo the "American Café de Flore." Michael himself would describe the bar as "the united front of the Village," since its clients included, in addition to the writers, Communists, Socialists, Trotskyists, and potheads.[74]

Amidst this raffish crew, the twenty-two-year-old newcomer from the Midwest soon made his mark. Jim Finn, his University of Chicago classmate who had also moved to New York, thought of Michael as someone who not only was "very social and gregarious" but carried himself with a triumphal aura: "We thought of him as a golden boy. He was blond and very young and he had this uninterrupted success academically. He communicated this feeling that he was going to be very successful in whatever he did."[75] A young woman named Barbara Bank met him in 1950 in the San Remo. She remembered him as "charming in a boyish way, literary, serious about society, struggling with religious belief." Barbara invited Michael to a party over at Norman Mailer's loft on First Avenue, where, "goggle-eyed," Michael met the Village's cultural aristocracy—writers, painters, gallery owners—and even saw Marlon Brando across a crowded room. Mailer was only five years older than Michael and had only two years earlier become an overnight sensation with the publication of *The Naked and the Dead.* Politically radical, he was flirting at the time with a kind of neo-Trotskyism. Michael was awed in his presence, and flattered that he had "a marvelous memory for names of nobodies from St. Louis."[76]

No one among his circle thought Michael would remain a nobody from St. Louis for very long. But Michael's new friends did have a sense that they were dealing with someone who was still in some fundamental ways unformed. With Barbara Bank, Michael visited mutual friends one summer in the early 1950s at a rented beach house on Oyster Bay. They all wrote limericks about each other. The one about Michael went: "Mike waited each year for the spring,/And the changes in doctrine 'twould bring,/One year God's repression,/The next, sex expression,/Now changing the world's quite the thing."[77]

The other thing that happened to Michael that spring is that he fell in love. It didn't take him long, although he made a brief detour in search of a fantasy lover, a "lesbian ballerina," who he could convert to a lifetime of heterosexual bliss. He used to drag Bill Loftus along as he would troll the lesbian bars in the Village, until they were chased out by some "hulking female" who resented the presence of male interlopers.[78]

That phase of Michael's love life came to an abrupt end when he met Margaret "Peggy" Brennan. Peggy Brennan was a 1949 graduate of Manhattanville College (where her classmates included Jean Kennedy and Ethel Skakel, who would later marry Robert F. Kennedy). She had grown up on Long Island, one of six children of a prosperous cement contractor. Her background was as solidly Irish-Catholic as her name; one of her older sisters became a nun. When Michael met Peggy she was twenty-two years old, the same age he was, and living in Long Island City, where her roommate was Bill Loftus's fiancée.

Peggy was struck by his intensity, seeing him as "someone with a mission," but also as someone who "didn't quite know what to do" with himself. He was "very very pale, with a crew cut, and very slim." She was swept off her feet.

Unlike his fantasy lesbian ballerina, or even his Protestant girlfriend from Wellesley, Peggy was a girl he could bring home to mother, and soon did—she came to visit the Harringtons that fall. Catherine was enchanted by the new girl friend ("smitten" is the word Michael used to describe his mother's reaction).[79] Irish-Catholic Peggy was her dream daughter-in-law—and the means by which Michael could be re-tethered to his faith and middle-class respectability. When they were in St. Louis together that fall, Catherine insisted that Michael take Peggy out dancing, even though Michael hated to dance; finally giving in, Michael put on a suit and tie, drove Peggy to a local nightspot, and spent the evening talking without once stepping on the dance floor. For months after she returned from the visit to St. Louis, Peggy was bombarded by letters from Catherine, who wasn't going to let this one get away.[80]

If not much of a dancer, Michael could be quite romantic in other less conventional ways. They would go to the ballet or stay home and listen to Peggy's record collection. Michael would read poetry to her (his own, sometimes). One evening Michael and Peggy went with Bill and his fiancée to Louie's on Sheridan Square, where Michael delivered an impromptu calypso rendition of the evening's adventures. Mostly, Peggy remembered Michael "talking, talking, talking. About what he was reading. Where he was going or where he was trying to go. What he was reading. Where his soul was."[81]

Michael was writing to as well as talking to Peggy Brennan. His letters to her that year represent the largest surviving cache of his personal correspondence. And they coincide with the final tumultuous struggle he would wage, with himself and with his parents, before committing himself to a life devoted to "changing the world."

In May, Michael left New York. First he made a brief trip home to St. Louis and then moved down to Washington, on assignment as a *Life* writer-trainee. He had already decided that he was going to resign his job at the first opportunity, thus fulfilling the prediction of the personnel director at *Life,* who had opposed hiring him in the first place because, as he told Michael at the time, "you are not our kind of person."[82]

"Dear Peg," Michael wrote from Washington at the end of May, on "Time Incorporated" stationery. "The die has been cast":

> When I went home, I talked to mother, and told her that I was going to quit my job and go into welfare work. She balked—but, wonderful woman that she is, not half as much as I thought. Finally, we agreed that I would go and speak to Father Wade, the chairman of the Philosophy department at St. Louis University. I told him that I was out of the Church, and told him that

> I wanted to go into welfare work. His comments were magnificent—he understood. But he told me to tell my mother that I was out of the Church. He said that I had a positive duty to go the way my conscience told me, regardless of what any person, no matter how near, might think. But he said that I should at least tell her that important factor in my decision. I did, and she came through beautifully, desiring only to do what was right for me. And she took it upon herself to tell my father of my decision (not of the church) because she knew that the greatest anguish would come from him.

Michael had already applied for a job with the American Friends Service Committee (AFSC), the Quaker social action organization—that is what he meant by "welfare work." He had not yet heard back from them, but he was determined to resign from *Life* as soon as possible:

> I will probably have about a hundred and fifty dollars when I hit the streets, and that is enough for a month—or more if I play it close. And although I could stay on until I have a job for sure in welfare work there are other things that you have to think about. All of those trite statements about "selling your soul" and the enervating effect of work for *Life* are true. I still count my poetry important—if you take the word as not only the writing, but all that is symbolizes, the consciousness, the awareness of every moment, the reading, and seeing, and thinking and frustration and all the things—that is important, and I will have a few precious weeks to do nothing but that.[83]

One month later, however, he was still in Washington, still selling his soul to *Life* magazine. "Dear Peg," he wrote on June 29, "I can hardly wait to get out of this prison—or to open the door in the back of my mind, where waits myself independent of trivia and facing issues. It can't last much more than two weeks though."

Now, not only was he facing a quandary over his career choice (the AFSC had since turned him down due to a lack of funds),[84] but he had returned to the state of religious anguish that he had seemingly disposed of on his last trip to St. Louis when he announced to Father Wade and finally to his mother that he had left the church for good:

> I am actually physically sick over the breakdown in my spiritual life. I can't write much of a letter since nothing has happened to me since I last saw you—except for me to realize that the point of crucial importance is to establish some basis for virtue, some rule, within the confines of my other beliefs. I need God as I need food and sleep, but tracing his face with my fingers seems a long way off—a terribly long way.

Swiftly recovering from the depths of spiritual anguish, in the next paragraph he asked Peggy to do him a favor:

> Could you get up early and go down and get me some [ballet] tickets. At least four nights. I am enclosing fifteen dollars—if all that is left is good seats, go ahead and buy them. This is a cry from the wilderness and I hope you will help me.[85]

This cycle could clearly have continued for some time: guilt over prostituting himself to Luce publications, anguish over neglecting his poetry, spiritual uncertainty increasingly flavored by a heavy dollop of existential philosophy ("I have been reading Nicolas Berdyaev," Michael wrote to Peggy in May. The Russian Orthodox philosopher, who as an exile in France had associated himself with the left-wing French Catholic journal *Esprit,* was to Michael "mystic, wonderful and terrifying—the last because of the tremendous demands he makes on you if you believe him, something of the horror of freedom that I understand exists in Kierkegard and Satre.").[86] The impact of all of this was only somewhat softened by the good seats he could now afford to buy at the ballet.

But at this point Michael's personal biography intersected with world history, and his life's dilemmas were given a decisive shove toward a final resolution. In the predawn hours of June 25, soldiers of the North Korean People's Army had crossed the 38th parallel dividing North and South Korea and driven straight for the South Korean capital of Seoul. South Korean resistance had collapsed. Late in the evening of June 29, the same day Michael wrote to Peggy in search of spiritual solace and ballet tickets, General Douglass MacArthur, commander of the United States Far Eastern Command, cabled the White House, requesting the immediate dispatch of two U.S. Army combat divisions to South Korea (American warplanes were already in action over the Korean peninsula). The first elements of the U.S. Expeditionary Force arrived on July 1 and were in combat on July 5. On July 7, the United Nations Security Council voted to approve an American resolution establishing a UN command to coordinate military efforts in defense of South Korea. On August 2, following a month-long retreat down the Korean peninsula by UN forces, U.S. Army engineers blew up the last bridge over the Naktong River, which marked the western border of the remaining fifty- by one-hundred-mile enclave still held by UN forces along the southernmost coast of Korea, an area known as the Pusan Perimeter. President Truman regarded the hostilities in Korea as the start of the Third World War.

Two days after the siege of the Pusan Perimeter began, Michael resigned from *Life* magazine. He returned to New York briefly, but did not have the luxury of tending to his poetry. He and Bill Loftus both received draft notices that summer. Bill quickly joined the Navy; Michael, unsure of his course, returned to St. Louis.[87]

There he wrestled with his options. He decided he couldn't bear arms in Korea. Just when and how he decided that he was a pacifist remains unclear. He gave no previous indication to his friends of pacifist beliefs, nor did he display any qualms in peacetime about registering for the draft. The war itself seems to have been the catalyst for his new conviction that the taking of human life was a sin he could not commit. But his position was complicated by the state of spiritual disarray in which he found himself that spring. Only religiously motivated pacifists could lay claim to conscientious objector status; those who objected to war but did not believe in a Supreme Being were out of luck.[88] Michael considered the possibility of going to prison as a draft resister. At that stage in his life, with few attachments and little sense of direction, political martyrdom in the antiwar cause was not without a certain appeal. But he was deterred by the thought of how such a decision on his part would affect his parents. After all he had put them through in the past few years, he did not feel that he had any right to inflict further pain and humiliation upon them.[89]

On September 16, 1950, Michael telegraphed Peggy to announce his decision:

> ENLISTED SWORN IN ARMY MEDICAL CORPS GIVE FINN TICKET WILL WRITE LOVE MIKE.[90]

"Dear Peg," Michael wrote from St. Louis on September 27:

> I don't want to recount that day and a half before the resolution. It was hectic and charged, frantic. Then came the decision, the enlistment. Am I happy about it? I don't know. I feel that I satisfied the demands of my conscience, then. But since then a new principle has come into my mind, and I don't know how to evaluate it. Was it my duty to announce my belief, to witness it before the government? I don't know. The remorse that I didn't has one of two sources: a petty desire to be a romantic figure, a poet, to novelize myself, [and] a strong desire to accept fully and unhesitatingly the consequences of belief, and even to seek them out.

Now that he had made his decision, he hoped for an early call-up to active service: "The action of saving life, of attempting to help a fellow man, I am sure has value and it is good. May it come soon and questions of analysis be forgotten in the movement of hands."[91] Expecting to be in uniform no later than Thanksgiving, he begged Peggy to come to St. Louis for a visit before that. Meanwhile, there was little to do. He put in a few more days as a social worker and teacher for the board of education. Mostly he read. Immersed in Kierkegaard, Harrington wrestled with the questions of authenticity and meaning; was the purpose of his life to be found in the contemplative or the actual? Michael looked to his own experience for answers. He had begun substitute teaching at Roosevelt High School in St. Louis and discovered (after two days) that the experience had served to "crystallize the great methodical problem" of existence for him. As he wrote to Peggy:

> I spend the day being outward. Talking to a group of young people, giving them "facts." I come home, and I seek inwardness. Perhaps there is the pattern of what one must be. A constant tension of the inward and the outward, without a final answer, and only a dissatisfaction with whatever emphasis has the upper hand at the moment. And hope is for that which cannot be willed, but which can only happen, a moment which is of its nature mystical for the two are resolved, and the outward, the structure of the act, is filled with the inward. It is strange. The whole meditation leads on to the feeling of "I am I."[92]

Human consciousness, freedom and nothingness were, of course, the leitmotifs of existentialist philosophy, then enjoying a considerable vogue on both sides of the Atlantic. Existentialists rejected absolute values and philosophical system-building. Individuals truly existed only by living intensely conscious lives, vividly aware of and defining themselves through the choices, the anguish, and the burdens of human living.[93] Despite the talk of "nothingness" and the "absurd," existentialism did not necessarily lead to nihilism, relativism, or an embrace of the sensual. Ethical values could be created through action. "I am conscious of the terror of freedom," Michael wrote to Peggy:

> Of consciousness. I ride alone in the car, and I realize how much it hurts to be aware. Do I suffer? Yes—and no. Yes, there is the actual feeling there, experienced. No, I would not wish that feeling would not be there, for it is so much a part of me, that to wish it away is to wish myself away.[94]

As if Berdyaev and Kierkegaard weren't enough, he was also on a self-described "Dostoevsky kick":

> I have finally reached the brothers K (after the Possessed, the Idiot, Crime and Punishment, the six short novels). And yet Fydor seems limitless. Crime and Punishment, I found on rereading, will bear an absolute existential analysis. Its no secret that Doestoevsky is a white haired boy in that school, but I was amazed at how detailed the correspondence was. And now the Brothers is much more clear than when I read it before.[95]

Late November brought another "Dear Peg" letter. "It is bleak Thanksgiving, and though I love bleakness when I in myself do not have it, and am outside of it, the coincidence makes things difficult." And then still another report on his reading:

> I am just starting Karl Jaspers "Perennial Scope of Philosophy" and I found this magnificent statement: "A truth by which I live stands only if I become identical with it; it is historical in form; as an objective statement it is not universally valid, but it is absolute. A truth which I can prove stands without me; it is universally valid, unhistorical, timeless, but not absolute; rather it depends on finite premises and methods of attaining knowledge of the finite." Glory be [to] Kierkegard, Marcel—and Jaspers.[96]

Michael kept reading, and waiting for the notice that his unit was being called up for duty. Thanksgiving came and went; American forces in North Korea neared the Yalu River before being driven back in disorder by hundreds of thousands of Red Chinese "volunteers," but still no notice came to the Harrington house from the military authorities. It finally occurred to Michael that if he was going to "hurry up and wait" for the army to settle his fate, he could do it in New York just as easily as in St. Louis. That, of course, entailed yet another battle with his mother. But by this time Michael seemed to have finally taken Catherine's measure. "Dear Peg," he wrote on December 20:

> Mother has begged me to stay. She is in bad physical condition (generally run-down, more than anything) and the next two weeks will be rather bad. I have refused to stay. I feel that her physical condition is party mental—that it will develop every time I announce a departure. I believe that the thing must be done with, and done now. I think that New York is more amenable to my hope than St. Louis—even if it is only for two months (which I think it will be). But most of all, I think that my relationship with my parents must be defined, now and for good. This process could be endless, and though the direct shock is hard on them (but my father is resigned!), it is better than a long drawn out process. Strangely enough, the war is a reason to go, not to stay. The old ideas of security, of foreknowledge and predictability, are finished for our generation. We must accept a day to day life and make our reconciliation on the basis of ultimates.[97]

On January 3, 1951, Michael arrived back in New York City. He was no longer adrift. He was there to stay.

CHAPTER FOUR

The Life of a Saint, 1951–1952

There was a standard Catholic Worker statement in my time. People would ask, "What are you here for?" And we would sometimes say, "Well, I want to be a saint." That was considered a perfectly rational and legitimate thing to say.

Michael Harrington,
July 7, 1988[1]

The April 1951 edition of the *Catholic Worker* newspaper featured a wood print by the artist Fritz Eichenberg, a regular contributor to its pages. Entitled *The Lord's Supper 1951*, it depicted eleven men in ragged contemporary garb gathered round a table for a meal. Christ sat in the foreground. And, peeking shyly through a half-opened door was a young man in a long coat, with a magazine tucked in his pocket. The twelfth apostle was about to arrive on the scene. Eichenberg's wood print ran in the newspaper about a month after Michael arrived as a volunteer at St. Joseph's House, the Catholic Worker soup kitchen and residence on the Lower East Side. Though Eichenberg never said so, it is a common belief among Michael's fellow Catholic Workers that he was the model the artist had in mind for the tardy twelfth apostle.[2]

Michael had returned to New York City from St. Louis on board the "Southwestern Limited" on Wednesday, January 3, 1951. If he had picked up a copy of the *New York Times* on his arrival, he would have found the news almost universally grim. "Chinese Red Troops Closing on Seoul After Smashing Through UN Lines," read the headline over the newspaper's lead story that day. "Foe Swarms South." In Washington, D.C., the 81st Congress had adjourned the previous day, having failed to deliver many of Harry Truman's "Fair Deal" social welfare proposals but voting at the last minute for an additional $20 billion in emergency funding for the U.S. military for fiscal year 1951. In New York City on Tuesday, 247 men had lined up outside the Army-Air Force recruiting headquarters on Whitehall Street to enlist, while 500 or so besieged the Navy recruiting office on lower Broadway. Recruiting officers were delighted but also realistic in their appraisal of the motives of the new recruits. Most of them faced imminent draft calls and having "seen the handwriting on the wall" were signing up for branches of the service, or training specialties, that would allow them to avoid the meat-grinder of infantry combat in Korea. Those who remained behind were also being urged to serve. The New York City Office of Civil Defense had launched a recruiting drive on Tuesday for 500,000 civil defense volunteers. According to civil defense director Grover A. Whalen, applicants would be "carefully screened," would be required to sign loyalty oaths swearing allegiance to the Constitution, and would be asked to reveal any past or current associations with organizations on the subversive list of the attorney general of the United States. Among other useful skills, civil defense volunteers were to be instructed in first aid treatment of flash burns, radiation sickness, and temporary blindness, as well as in the use of pocket dosimeters, film badges, and Geiger counters.[3]

Michael's friend and former roommate Bill Loftus had meanwhile completed his own training as a naval officer. On January 27, Michael made a brief trip to Wilkes-Barre, Pennsylvania, to act as best man at Bill's wedding. He proved somewhat of a trial to the groom. The first crisis was easily resolved: Michael showed up without the cufflinks he needed for his dress shirt, so Bill lent him a pair. Then, just before the service began, when they were standing in the sacristy, Michael said to the priest, "Oh Father, I don't know if this makes any difference, but I'm not a practicing Catholic at the moment." It made quite a difference to the priest who, in Loftus's recollection, "went to smithereens." Bill's own father was pressed into emergency service in place of Michael.[4]

But within the next few weeks, Michael was back in the church. He credited his return to Catholicism to a "French Jansenist" and a "Danish Protestant"—Blaise Pascal and Søren Kierkegaard—both of whom had earned a place on the church's *Index Librorum Prohibitorum.* Pascal, the seventeenth-century Jansenist (an extreme conservative current within the Catholic Church emphasizing divine providence), argued that the certainties of faith could not be grasped through reason but only through the heart; Kierkegaard, a nineteenth-century Lutheran, insisted that Christianity was a mode of living that consisted in appropriating and assimilating the message of Christ into one's own existence. As far as the Vatican was concerned, both propositions undermined the teaching authority of the church. But Michael found his faith rekindled by these supposedly heretical ideas. "One night while reading [Pascal's] *Pensées* after a long immersion in Kierkegaard," he recalled:

> I decided in a most unjesuitical fashion to return to Catholicism. I no longer felt that I could prove my faith, but now I was willing to make a

> wager, a doubting and even desperate wager, on it: *Credo quia absurdam.* I believe because it is absurd. . . . Early the next morning I went over to Our Lady of Pompeii, an Italo-American church in the South Village, and went to confession to a priest who hardly understood English. That was well enough since it had been an exciting two years away from the prohibitions of Rome. That afternoon I searched out the Catholic Worker.[5]

"Mike was not a great one for discussing things," his friend Arthur Moore would recall. He had given his circle of friends in New York few hints that he was wrestling with questions of faith and commitment:

> I remember he just sort of said, "Well, I'm going to the Catholic Worker," and then he went. Some of these decisions later seemed as great turning points in his life, but at that time they didn't seem all that earth shaking because there wasn't a great deal of agonizing and discussion.[6]

Michael, however, was always better communicating with women—especially young and attractive women—than with men. After the letters she had received from him the previous fall, Peggy Brennan was not surprised by his decision. And Barbara Bank always remembered the dramatic gesture that he made one "snowy wintry eve" shortly before he joined the Catholic Worker. After telling her of his plans, he reached into his pocket and gave her all the money he had with him.[7]

"All I knew of the Catholic Worker when I walked into its House of Hospitality," Michael would write in his memoirs, "was that it was as far Left as you could go within the Church."[8] The Catholic Worker movement was founded in 1933 by Dorothy Day and Peter Maurin. Day, born in Brooklyn in 1897, could have joined (although she never did) both the Daughters of the American Revolution and the United Daughters of the Confederacy. Her father's family was Scotch-Irish with southern roots, her mother's family English and New York Episcopalian. She had a rootless childhood, due to her father's peripatetic career as a sports writer. Throughout her childhood, and as a young woman, she was strongly if episodically attracted to Christianity, in varying denominational hues. She also read widely in the literature of protest and revolution, including books by the anarchist Peter Kropotkin and by socialist novelists Jack London and Upton Sinclair. She joined the Socialist Party in Urbana, where she had enrolled as a student at the University of Illinois, and when she came to New York in 1916 she found a job as a journalist with the *Call,* a daily socialist newspaper.

Day arrived in New York at a time of revolutionary exhilaration; she was thrilled to listen to speeches by IWW firebrands like Elizabeth Gurley Flynn, and she met such imposing figures as the anarchist Alexander Berkman and the exiled Russian revolutionary Leon Trotsky. Later, in 1917, she joined the staff of the *Masses,* where she became friends with editors Max Eastman and Floyd Dell and with the writer Mike Gold. When the *Masses* succumbed to wartime repression, Day moved on to other radical publications, including the *Liberator* and later the *New Masses.* She remained close to Gold and others who would become Communists, although she herself never joined the party. With Gold and her close friend from University of Illinois days, Rayna Simons Prohme (a friend destined to take part in the Chinese Revolution, before dying of illness in Moscow), Dorothy sat "on the ends of piers singing revolutionary songs into the starlit night, dallied on park benches, never wanting to go home to sleep but only to continue to savor our youth and its struggles and joys."[9]

During and immediately after the First World War, Day drifted through several love affairs and a brief and unhappy marriage; she had an abortion, for which she would atone the rest of her life, and attempted suicide. Eugene O'Neill read poetry to her in Greenwich Village dives, and her circle of friends included writers John Dos Passos, Malcolm Cowley, Allen Tate, and Hart Crane. She traveled in Europe and Mexico, lived in Chicago, New Orleans, and Los Angeles, wrote a novel, and tried her hand at Hollywood script-writing. Spiritually as well as geographically and vocationally adrift, she often sought comfort in neighboring Catholic churches, without formally committing herself to the faith. For several of her happier years in the mid-1920s, she settled on Staten Island in a common-law marriage with Forster Batterham. Batterham was an anarchist with no use for either the institution of marriage or organized religion. When Dorothy not only became pregnant but decided, upon the birth of her daughter Tamar Therese, to have the baby baptized and to join the Catholic Church herself, he abandoned Dorothy and the child.

As a Catholic, Day still remained a committed radical, although now she now wrote more for the liberal Catholic weekly *Commonweal* than for the Communist *New Masses.* One of the main appeals of Catholicism for her was that it was the church of the urban poor. In December 1932, in the depths of the depression, she traveled to Washington to cover a Communist-organized "hunger march" for *Commonweal.* Where, she wondered, was her beloved church in the midst of this enormous social crisis? Why were the Communists the only ones who seemed prepared to take action? She prayed at a shrine in Washington for guidance. And on her return to New York she found it, in the somewhat unlikely form of Peter Maurin.

Maurin was fifty-five years old in 1932. A short, weather-beaten man of peasant stock, born in southern France, Maurin had been a member of the Christian Brothers order and then of various small Catholic anarchist and pacifist circles in France. In 1909 he emigrated to Canada, and in 1911 to the

United States. He drifted from one low-paying job and city to another, until he found himself in New York in the early 1930s. Dismissed by most of those who encountered him as a crackpot (even Dorothy Day would later concede that "Peter was hard to listen to"),[10] he liked nothing better than to get into shouting matches with the more secular radicals of Union Square, trying to persuade them that Catholicism not Marxism offered the true guide to remaking society. He began writing a series of "Easy Essays," short phrased lines outlining his social philosophy. In December 1932, at the suggestion of the editor of *Commonweal,* Maurin showed up on Dorothy Day's doorstep. After she overcame her initial skepticism, he persuaded her that together they should start a lay Catholic movement, loyal to but independent of the church, devoted to improving the lives of the poor along the lines of Catholic social teaching. Though Maurin was an eccentric character (he gave up bathing in the early 1940s as a distraction from spiritual values), Day idolized him: "He was my master and I his disciple," she would say of Maurin in *The Long Loneliness.*[11]

The first issue of the *Catholic Worker* newspaper was published on May Day 1933 and sold for a penny in New York City streets. From an initial press run of 2,500 copies, its circulation rose dramatically in the years that followed, peaking at a 185,000 on the eve of the Second World War. The newspaper attracted volunteers who staffed the soup lines in the thirty-two Houses of Hospitality, spread across twenty-seven cities, that had been opened by 1941, plus about a dozen Catholic Worker farms. In 1938 the soup line at the Mott Street House of Hospitality alone was feeding over 1,000 people daily. And, in what turned out to be its most lasting importance, the movement that Day and Maurin had begun trained a generation of dedicated and talented young Catholic activists and intellectuals who would go on to play significant roles within the church, the labor movement, and various social reform movements. There were any number of individual radical Catholics who had preceded Dorothy Day; but Catholic radicalism in the United States was largely her invention.[12]

The Catholic Worker fell on hard times in the 1940s. By the early 1950s, the circulation of its newspaper was only a third of what it had been in the late 1930s, and the number of Houses of Hospitality it maintained fell to fifteen. But, intellectually, it was a vibrant time to come to the Worker. The younger generation of Catholic Workers in particular felt themselves to be part of a broad, international current of experiment, challenge, and change within the church. As Michael would note, the talk at the dinner table in St. Joseph's House was often "of Jean Danielou, Henry De Lubac, Yves Congar, Jacques Maritain, Gabriel Marcel, Romano Guardini, and the other, mainly European, thinkers who were, without knowing it, preparing the way for Vatican II."[13] Nor was this discussion only of relevance to Catholics. The "personalism" associated with such French Catholic thinkers as Jacques Maritain would, through direct and indirect channels, have a significant impact on the broader politics and culture of the 1960s. Personalists rejected the materialism and absolutism of much of nineteenth-century philosophy, feeling that it reduced humans to mere phenomenal beings who easily lost their identities in the collectivities of the family, the community, class, and the state. Instead, personalists insisted on the uniqueness and autonomy of the human self and on the responsibility of individuals to involve themselves in the great social and moral issues of their times. There was an obvious kinship between these personalist ideas and those of the existentialists. With its emphasis on the imperative of providing an immediate and individual response to injustice and crying human needs, personalism represented an alternative both to mass collectivist movements, like communism and fascism, and to the managerialism of social democratic and liberal welfare states. In postwar France, the personalists associated with Emmanuel Mounier's journal *Esprit* challenged Christian Democracy and Gaullism from an independent position on the Left.[14] It was perhaps Peter Maurin's greatest contribution to the future of Catholic radicalism in the United States that he was the first one to draw Dorothy Day's attention to the intellectual resources offered by the French personalists.[15]

Peter Maurin was four years dead when Michael arrived at Chrystie Street. Dorothy Day was still the dominant figure of the movement (as she would remain until her own death in 1980). "Whenever we made a decision," Michael would later say of the Catholic Worker, "we all had a completely democratic, anarchist discussion, and then Dorothy made up her mind."[16] Or, as another Catholic Worker once said, "Dorothy wanted to be an anarchist, but only if she got to be the anarch."[17]

In 1951 Dorothy Day was fifty-three years old. That was just a year and a half older than Michael's mother—which may be part of the explanation for the appeal of the Catholic Worker to him. In Day, Michael found another devout and maternal figure to obey—except that this one, unlike Catherine, gave him the permission he sought to live in New York and proclaim himself a radical. Day had, as Michael remembered her, a "severe, almost Slavic, and yet very serene face. With her hair braided around her head and the babushka she sometimes wore, she might have been a peasant or, had the Dostoevsky she read so avidly written of women as he did of monks, a mystic in one of his great novels."[18]

Michael and Dorothy Day shared more than their love of Doestoevsky. Both had come to New York to find their destinies as writers (although Dorothy Day was born in Brooklyn, she spent most of her childhood and adolescence elsewhere). Both were drawn to the life of "the other"—to the bohemian life of Greenwich Village, to the poor, and in the case of Dorothy

Day, to Catholicism. When Michael arrived at the Catholic Worker, Day was in the midst of writing her autobiography, *The Long Loneliness.* She began the book with a chapter called "Confession," writing of her own political involvements before joining the Catholic Church: "I do not know how sincere I was in my love of the poor and my desire to serve them." Mixed in with and corrupting her altruism was the desire "to write, to influence others and so make my mark on the world." She chastised herself for her "ambition" and "self-seeking" in those early years.[19] In the prologue to the first volume of his own memoirs, published two decades later, Michael, in contrast, declared that he was not interested in writing a "confession." His story of gaining self-knowledge involved leaving the church, not joining it as Day had done; this was his "pious apostasy." Still, there was more than a hint of Day's influence visible in Michael's subsequent writings about himself. He too would worry about the conflict between loving humankind in the abstract and his own often ambivalent feelings toward the real, living human beings whom he encountered in his life. The title of the second volume of his memoirs, *The Long Distance Runner* (another figure famed in contemporary literature for loneliness), recalled, either by accident or intention, that of Day's autobiography.[20]

Michael had been living on MacDougall Street with his friend James Finn since returning from St. Louis. It was a ten minute walk east to the St. Joseph House of Hospitality at 233 Chrystie Street, a block off the Bowery, the heart of New York's skid row. St. Joseph's had been headquarters of the Catholic Worker movement and newspaper for less than a year when Michael made his way there; the movement had lost the lease on its longtime home on Mott Street in Little Italy the previous year. The new St. Joseph House was a five-story, redbrick building, once handsome, and still retaining an elaborate New Orleans-style iron grillwork in the front, but run down and grimy. The two bottom floors provided rooms for business and editorial offices, a meeting room, a dining room that could accommodate fifty, and a kitchen. The top three floors provided bedrooms that were shared by a half dozen or so middle-class Catholic Workers (those for whom poverty was "voluntary") and forty or more itinerant boarders whose poverty was not a matter of choice, and often related to alcoholism. A statue of Saint Joseph, patron saint of work, stood on the front steps of the building; Day would sometimes turn its face to the wall as an act of ritual shaming when donations were not coming into the movement in sufficient quantity.

Many middle-class volunteers, wearing their hearts and anguish on their sleeves, made their way to the Worker; few stuck it out for very long. As Garry Wills would note, the Catholic Worker movement often provided a "way station for troubled young men."[21] Betty Bartelme, a young woman who had already spent several years as a volunteer with the Catholic Worker, remembered Michael's first appearance: "He was wearing a tweed coat with some of the buttons missing. Someone asked me, 'Do you think that boy is poor or is he sloppy?' I said, 'I think he's sloppy.'" Tom Sullivan, whose own connection to the movement extended back to the mid-1930s, gave Michael a quick glance that day and assumed he was just "another hand to help mail out the papers."[22]

Michael was immediately put to work folding copies of the next issue of the *Catholic Worker.* The *Catholic Worker* was an eight-page tabloid, published monthly, and featuring a mixture of the homely and the exalted in its columns. There were accounts of life on Maryfarm (one of the Catholic Worker's surviving rural outposts), devotional and political essays, reprints of Peter Maurin's thoughts, book reviews, and an occasional piece of original journalism on topics un- or underreported in mainstream newspapers, such as prison conditions and labor struggles. The circulation of the newspaper had plummeted from its high point in the 1930s, but even with only 58,000 copies of each issue printed in the early 1950s, its circulation was roughly that of the combined circulations of the *Nation* and the *New Republic,* the two preeminent liberal weeklies.[23] Dorothy Day was no longer involved with the day-to-day editing and production of the newspaper, as she had been in the 1930s. Still, there was no question that it was her paper; when something was proposed that she didn't like, such as an editorial endorsing Adlai Stevenson for president in 1952, she simply put her foot down and refused to allow it be published. She also didn't hesitate to rewrite her authors, inserting her own words under their byline.[24]

It soon became clear that Michael had more to contribute to the *Catholic Worker* than his ability to fold paper. By the time the next issue came out he was listed on the masthead as one of three editors. Over the next several years he used the newspaper to explore and develop the concerns that he had first expressed in his tortured letters to Peggy Brennan. If he suffered under Dorothy's editorial heavy-handedness, he kept it to himself.

One of Michael's first published pieces made him a legend at the Catholic Worker. House manager Tom Sullivan gave him a translation of Jacques Maritain's *Man and the State,* recently published by University of Chicago Press, to review. A leading figure in the revival of Thomist philosophy, as well as the intellectual leader of liberal French Catholicism, Maritain was not the most accessible of writers.[25] Sullivan recounted the story:

> He took the book and in forty-five minutes read it and reviewed it. What was he trying to pull off? I hadn't read the book, so I couldn't tell whether he had really dealt with that book or not. So I turned the review over to somebody else who *had* read it, and she says, "Yes. It's a very good review." . . . That was the first thing we printed of Mike Harrington's.[26]

In his review, Michael praised Maritain's willingness to adapt St. Thomas Aquinas's teachings on natural law to modern conditions. "Natural law," Michael argued, "is not merely a static, ideal order existing independently of man, to be consulted like a geometric theorem." (Clearly Michael's brush with "legal realism" at Yale had done its work.) "It is within history. It is an inclination toward good, and a progressive understanding of the terms of that inclination, primarily through intuition, not through reason."

In practical terms this meant that the Catholic Church should seek to "proclaim the good" but not to impose its views through legal coercion on either its own followers or a broader public. The church's "proclamation must be consonant with freedom and must be practical." Attempts to enforce morality through censorship of books and movies, or through the legal prohibition of birth control, should thus be abandoned: "Maritain holds that the state should allow different ways of worship, modes of behavior, and ethical conceptions, in order to 'avoid greater evils' (that is, the ruin of the society's peace and either the disintegration or petrification of conscience.)"[27]

Such limits of the church's authority represented a pressing question for those on the Catholic Left in the 1950s. Paul Blanshard, an ordained Congregationalist minister and former Socialist, had published a series of best-selling books attacking the Catholic Church on civil libertarian grounds, criticizing its support for censorship, its opposition to birth control, and its attempts to secure public funding for parochial education. Blanshard denied any religious bigotry, but in his critique of the church's authoritarian structure he certainly harkened back to earlier nativist themes. Catholics were appalled by Blanshard's comparisons between communism and Catholicism; in his 1951 tract *Communism, Democracy, and Catholic Power* Blanshard declared that "the Kremlin and the Vatican are far more conspicuous in their similarities than their differences."[28]

Michael was surely aware of Blanshard's attacks, and like other Catholic radicals he found himself on the defensive. Not so Dorothy Day, who had no problem at all with acknowledging the church's authority, even as she did her best to subvert the authority of the secular state. As she once proclaimed famously, "If the Chancery [the administrative offices of the New York diocese] ordered me to stop publishing the *Catholic Worker* tomorrow, I would."[29] Michael would later call Day "a real Pius XII Catholic," and he complained that her habit of referring to arch-conservative Cardinal Spellman as "our dear, sweet cardinal" drove him crazy.[30] Day's meekness in the face of the church hierarchy was a matter of principle with her, but it also served as a stratagem for getting her own way.

In March 1951 Day was summoned by the New York Chancery office and ordered by Monsignor Edward Gaffney either to cease publication of her newspaper or drop the word "Catholic" from its title. The paper's outspoken pacifism and its casual use of the word "anarchism" had drawn complaints from influential conservative Catholics. Day consulted with the staff of the paper. She recorded in her journal that Michael, who had been at the Worker for only a month at that point, "urges me to fortitude and the fighting against obscurantism in the Church." Day finally smoothed over the controversy with a letter to the Chancery promising to do better in observing proprieties. Both Michael and fellow editor Bob Ludlow, to whom she showed the letter before mailing it, disapproved of her approach. They were humiliated by her submissive tone. But since the paper did not change its tone or politics noticeably in the months and years to come and continued to use the word "Catholic" in its title, Day's tactical retreat proved the wisest course.[31]

Michael learned the lesson and soon attempted a similar strategy in defending existentialism against official church disapproval. Pope Pius XII had condemned the teachings of the existentialists in 1950, which should have settled the question once and for all for devout Catholics. But having just read himself back into the church via existentialism, it's not surprising that Michael found the pope's pronouncement less than persuasive. He was faced with a contradiction between his renewed commitment to the doctrine of papal infallibility and his continuing affection for the ideas of some of his favorite writers. Could the two be reconciled? Michael was determined to try. His next book review for the *Catholic Worker,* a consideration of *Being and Having* by the French Christian existentialist Gabriel Marcel, appeared in August 1951, exactly one year after the papal encyclical condemning existentialism. Michael trod a careful line, throwing certain unnamed existentialists to the wolves, while exempting Marcel from the general condemnation of existentialism clearly suggested by *Humani generis:*

> Papal authority creates respect which is founded on faith in Christ, and is superior to rational conviction. But from this position, I think Catholics have little to fear from M. Marcel—and much to gain. On the whole, I do not think he maintains those existentialist propositions condemned by the Pope.[32]

Michael was determined to be a good Catholic. At the same time, he was determined to test the limits of dogma, not so much through a direct challenge to authority, but rather through a strategy of filling in the empty spaces in papal pronouncements with his own ideas and values. The church condemned birth control, and Michael accepted its teachings (contributing, in fact, his own column to the *Catholic Worker* denouncing the practice)—but the Church should avoid the error of seeking to reinforce morality through means of legal coercion. The pope says existentialism is bad; so be it. But surely the Holy Father did not mean to include the good Monsieur Marcel among those whose ideas were unacceptable to the faithful. Michael was, in effect, bargaining with the church: he would be a good Catholic, so long as he had the space to investigate, play with, and make up his own mind about new ideas and doctrines.

In the months that followed, Michael contributed a steady stream of reviews to the *Catholic Worker,* sometimes several in a single issue. These included reviews of many works of Catholic philosophy, such as Emmanuel Mounier's *Be Not Afraid,* but also non-Catholic works such as Martin Buber's *Paths in Utopia,* Hannah Arendt's *The Origins of Totalitarianism,* and Ralph Ellison's *Invisible Man.*[33] He also developed several regular "journalistic" beats, including political repression in Franco's Spain (a touchy subject for American Catholics, given their near-universal support for the Nationalists during the Spanish Civil War) and, closer to home, labor struggles on the New York waterfront.[34]

One of Michael's articles from this period stands out in retrospect, although it attracted little attention at the time. The June 1952 issue of the *Catholic Worker* featured a piece by him entitled "Poverty—U.S.A." Michael set out to challenge the current economic consensus that "things are pretty good." Citing the 1950 U.S. census, Michael noted that 50 percent of American families had incomes of less than $3,100, at a time when the minimal decent income for an urban family of four was estimated at $3,295. A quarter of American children lived in families with incomes of less than $2,000 a year; over half of the non-white population had incomes of less than $1,500 a year. "It goes without saying," Michael concluded, "that the incomes structure just described must be changed."

Michael added an interesting caveat to his article, intended to demonstrate the moral superiority of the Catholic Worker's religious radicalism to the blend of economic determinism and ends-justify-the-means cynicism that he believed characterized the outlook of more secular radicals, particularly Marxist revolutionaries. In doing so, he introduced a dichotomy between the head and heart, and between the pressing social needs of the present and the vision of a transformed social order in the distant future, that became a recurring theme in his political writings. If the problems of the poor were understood as and reduced to "the means toward the well-being of some future generation, as merely an incitement to class consciousness on the part of those involved," he warned,

> then we have changed people into objects, means. The problem must be faced as one of the future—and of the present. Immediate relief through any means which are not clearly immoral must be studied. To think otherwise, to view this poverty as a force in a historic [dialectic], is not only the

> dehumanization of the poor; it is the dehumanization of him who thinks it. The reaction to this poverty should be partly one of calculation, of how can it be erradicated, but it must also be of the Beatitudes, of hunger and thirst for Justice, of love and grief for what goes on before our eyes.[35]

"Hunger and thirst for Justice," Michael would later decide, required conceding a good deal more to the head ("calculation") than he believed to be the case in 1951, though he would never abandon the values that inspired "love and grief" for the plight of the poor.

Like many similar experiments in utopian living, the vices of the old world proved easier to critique than to cast aside. When a high school student named John McDermott, later to become a distinguished philosopher, came to volunteer at St. Joseph's House in 1951, he heard Michael referred to "as the guy with the typewriter."[36] Privileges were few at St. Joseph's House, which made them all the more noticeable when they existed; Roger O'Neil remembered that a few of the Catholic Worker volunteers felt "intellectual envy" of Michael and resented the time he spent reading books and writing long and complicated essays for the newspaper.[37] "There were tensions about me" at the Catholic Worker, Michael would later tell an interviewer.[38] For the first time in his life he found himself placed on the defensive for having intellectual interests, an unwelcome novelty that strained even Michael's famous affability. Ed Egan recalled a night at the Worker when someone at the dinner table was upbraiding Michael for being a snobbish intellectual. "Mike exploded and said, 'Look, there are three hundred books upstairs in my room. You are free to borrow any one of them, read them, and then talk to me. Otherwise, shut up.'"[39]

Michael soon became a favorite of Dorothy's. Day appreciated the intellectual luster that Michael was bringing to the pages of the newspaper. She also appreciated the social graces his mother had instilled in him. Michael found Day surprisingly "old-fashioned" in some ways and recalled that she "loved the fact that I held the door open for her and pulled her chair out."[40] If there was one role that came naturally to Michael, it was that of the good son. Of course, Michael's close relationship with Day did nothing to allay the envy of those who already resented his presence at the Worker.

In the 1930s, Catholic Worker houses provided services to poor people whose misfortunes were usually the clear result of circumstances beyond their control: men and women who, until the onset of the Great Depression, had worked hard and steadily, cherishing their homes and communities, only to find themselves dispossessed by the failures of the capitalist system. These poor were easy to sympathize with and even idealize—they were the poor of Steinbeck novels and Dorothea Lange documentary photographs. But the poor who sought out the hospitality of St. Joseph's in the early 1950s were not the sturdy unemployed of depression memory; they were the pitiful unemployable—aging, alcoholic, crippled, and often mentally disturbed. "Our ideal," Michael would recall of his days at the Catholic Worker, "was 'to see Christ in every man,' including the pathetic, shambling, shivering creature who would wander in off the streets with his pants caked with urine and his face scabbed with blood."[41]

But those who took shelter at St. Joseph's did not always give the volunteers who tended to them the satisfaction of idealizing them. Michael long remembered a conversation he had with an aging alcoholic, a man by the name of John Derry, who had been staying at St. Joseph's for some time. When Michael explained to Derry that his alcoholism was an evil to be borne rather than an evil he had committed, the older man curtly set him straight: "You're wrong, Michael. I'm a sinner and I'm going to go to hell for it."[42]

The Catholic Worker was a two-tier society: There were mercy-givers and there were scholars, and Michael clearly fell within the latter category.[43] He did not often serve food on the bread line, and when he did, it was not with any great sense of fulfillment. As his fellow Catholic Worker and good friend Eileen Fantino remembered: "He was not a very hands-on person."[44] His happiest time at the Worker was the six months he spent as night watchman, which gave him the chance to stay up all night and read or write poetry.[45] Betty Bartelme remembered that Michael "was not the favorite of the people who came in off the street. They were not taken with Mike. I think that's because he didn't really understand them. He was sympathetic towards them, but he couldn't really communicate with them."[46]

If Michael's attempts to apply the Sermon on the Mount in daily life sometimes seemed a little forced, no one doubted the sincerity of his spiritual commitment. Following Day's example, Michael became a daily communicant. In addition to attending mass, he would recite the hours privately, "so it would be typical for me to be in church, not once, but two or even three times during the course of the day."[47] In early January 1952 Michael wrote an elated letter to Jim Finn, reporting on his spiritual condition:

> this catholicism is sensational. have become insufferably religious. use short breviary—which is psalms according to the various hours—and have found it wonderful. am trying to be, with varying success, a daily communicant. proposition: living a catholic life impossible without living a sacramental life, i.e. regular mass and communion. . . . all of these things which are asked of us r.c.'s are intellectual game unless attempt is made to live the thing; and if the attempt is made, the trying becomes easier. . . . will never again try to lead a r.c. life without living one. the consolation is amazing—which is some thing which a bourgeois intellectual (ugh) like myself learns

> with great surprise. and living the liturgical year gives a significance to time and events—all during advent, found myself in something of a turmoil of happiness, not that nonsensical, sickly piety, but something real fine. actually was glad christmass because it was the day of Incarnation.[48]

Only a year earlier, Michael had despaired of ever "tracing God's face" again; now he had re-embraced the familiar religious beliefs of his childhood with the fervor of the newly converted. Of course, being *very* Catholic was also a way for him to distinguish his own beliefs from those of run-of-the-mill philistine Catholics. "Our complaint," Michael would remember, "was not that Cardinal Spellman was too Catholic but that he was not Catholic enough."[49] Garry Wills noted that Catholic liberals in the 1950s went on retreats to picturesque Trappist monasteries; the Catholic liberal "made ceremony less vulgar by making it even more exotic. It was not Rome he disliked in his churches; it was Peoria"—or, in Michael's case, St. Louis.[50] At the same time, Michael and his fellow Catholic Workers were so intimate with the church's traditions that they felt free to mock them. To mark the occasion in 1952 when the Vatican declared the assumption of Mary into heaven as official church doctrine, Michael's fellow Catholic Worker Ed Egan composed a little ditty that included the line, "Now that there is one more of us, you can adore the four of us."[51]

As Michael would remember of his days at the Worker, it was considered a "perfectly rational and legitimate thing" to say that one's ambition in life was to become a saint.[52] Among the favorite saints in the movement were two St. Theresa's, known familiarly among the initiate as "big T" and "little T."[53] "Big T," or Theresa of Avila, was a sixteenth-century Spanish nun and foundress of a reformed Carmelite order of nuns. The order placed a great emphasis on poverty, hardship, and solitude, signified by the coarse brown wool habit and leather sandals worn by its followers. "Little T" was Theresa of Lisieux, a French Carmelite nun in the late nineteenth century who died at the age of twenty-four without having accomplished much, but who left behind a short spiritual biography that found a wide readership. The emphasis on simplicity and service was, of course, what made both of them of interest to Day, who was writing a biography of "little T" when Michael was at the Worker (eventually published in 1961) and who had named her only daughter Tamar Therese after "big T."[54]

There were jokes about saints, as there were about other sacred symbols. Even Day, who tended toward humorlessness in such matters, told Dwight Macdonald in 1952, "We Catholics talk about the saints and the martyrs, but I've heard it said that the Catholic Workers are made up of the saints, and the martyrs are those who are willing to live with the saints."[55]

Day expected her followers to embrace a life of voluntary poverty. The problem was in deciding where such a life shaded off, on the one side, into a mortification of the flesh and, on the other, into bohemianism. Day's own lifestyle may have seemed eccentric to outsiders, but hers was a chastened eccentricity that insisted on at least some of the bourgeois proprieties. She took her clothing from the old clothes bin at St. Joseph's House, just like everyone else, but she saw no virtue in a lack of personal hygiene. "There is a Bohemianism of the religious life among young people as well as Bohemianism in the labor movement," she complained in *The Long Loneliness* in 1952,

> and it too smacks of sentimentality. The gesture of being dirty because the outcast is dirty, of drinking because he drinks, of staying up all night and talking, because that is what one's guests from the streets want to do, in participating in his sin from a prideful humility, this is self-deception indeed.[56]

In Michael's case, an embrace of dishevelment was not so much affectation as having finally arrived in a setting where his natural inclinations fit in with the norm. When Peggy Brennan brought him home to meet her parents in the summer of 1950, when he was still respectably employed by the Luce publishing empire, Peggy's mother took her aside and whispered in amazement, "That young man has two different color socks on."[57] At the Worker his dearest possession, apart from his books, was an old seersucker jacket that had been donated to the movement by Day's old friend, the poet Alan Tate. Even though the jacket was several sizes too small for Michael, he "was proud to wear the raiment of an established poet."[58]

Michael would later speak disparagingly of the fanatics at the Catholic Worker "who always wanted to go whole-hog and share toothbrushes and all that kind of stuff."[59] He would recall the "rotten food" at the Catholic Worker with particular horror: "We bought the cheapest cuts of meat or begged for the meat the butchers were about to throw out. We usually made our own bread. Sometimes bakers would give us stale bread. And I said to myself, 'This is not good.'"[60]

But memory, and the subsequent elevation of his tastes, may have tricked him. Friends from the period don't remember his ever expressing any distaste for the fare at Chrystie Street. In December 1951 Michael went to have Christmas dinner with his friend Molly Finn. As she recalled the evening: "I fixed a very elaborate dinner with suckling pig. I'll never forget Mike sitting there shoveling in all this food saying, 'We had a great meal at the Worker yesterday. We had some hot dogs and greens.'" She was convinced "he really couldn't tell the difference."[61]

Michael's voluntary poverty bore only superficial resemblance to the real thing, as he himself would readily concede. He had given his spare change away to Barbara Bank on the eve of his departure for the Worker, but when he came to the Worker he still had several hundred dollars saved up from his months at Time-Life—and with no rent to pay, meals to buy, or clothing to purchase, that went a long way. He also received an occasional check from home. And he carefully preserved one good suit for those occasions when his parents sent him a train ticket to St. Louis. If Michael found himself temporarily penniless, like other Catholic Workers he could go to Tom Sullivan who would dole out a dollar or two for a haircut or some other personal necessity.[62]

Notwithstanding the resentment that Michael aroused among some of the older generation at St. Joseph's House, he quickly became the center of a lively social circle among younger Workers. "Everyone was enchanted by Mike's good looks, his charm, his brilliance, his erudition," recalled Roger O'Neill. "Mike was always dazzling."[63] Betty Bartelme held out longer than most. "I wasn't very taken with him at first," she recalled. "Michael had a lot of charm, and he exerted it when he wanted to. He couldn't bear not to have people like him." Bartelme finally succumbed to the Harrington charm the day he called her up and said, "How would you like to go for a walk? It's a beautiful day." "I was pleased and said, 'OK, that would be nice.' So he came over and we went for a walk and ended up walking back and forth in front of the RCA Building, on a picket line for the radio and television writers union. That was Michael's idea of a walk."[64]

There were those at St. Joseph's House who spent their days and nights as if they had taken vows of temperance and chastity as well as poverty. In *The Long Loneliness* Dorothy Day described a typical day in the life of Bob Ludlow, "one of the most disciplined members of the Catholic Worker." Up at six, mass at seven, a bowl of cereal for breakfast, nine to five at his desk. "In the evening he reads from six to ten-thirty, goes out for coffee and a short walk, and is in bed at eleven. You can set your clock by him."[65]

For most of the younger volunteers, however, their idea of an evening out was by no means restricted to coffee and a short walk. The quest for sainthood, Catholic Worker-style circa 1951–1952, involved sacrifices and hardships, to be sure. But it was not a cloistered existence, nor did it lack its small redeeming pleasures—mostly innocent, but not always of the sort that Day approved. "It was a great fun time," Betty Bartelme remembered, "and that's something that nobody who has written about the Worker has captured."[66] Geography trumped ideology; on New York's Lower East Side the homeless poor had placed themselves in inconvenient propinquity to the fleshpots surrounding Washington Square and stretching into the West Village. These were the same places, or the same kinds of places, where Day, in her not easily forgotten because well chronicled ill-spent youth, had also passed many pleasant hours. As Malcolm Cowley remarked famously in *Exile's Return*: "The gangsters admired Dorothy Day because she could drink them under the table."[67] At the Worker there was a cult of Day as contemporary saint—

but there was also a cult of Dorothy as former sinner. There was endless speculation among the staffers about Day's pre-Catholic past, which she tried without much success to discourage and censor. People wondered how many of, and who among, her many literary and political acquaintances had actually been her lovers. Mike's contemporary Ed Egan recalled "everybody revered Dorothy and told terrible stories about her."[68]

Nearly twenty years of close involvement with the alcoholic excesses and wreckage of the Lower East Side had, understandably, turned Dorothy Day into a confirmed teetotaler. Michael tried, at first, to conform to her standards. But that effort lasted only a few months. As he confessed in a letter to Jim Finn in August 1951: "fell off the wagon last night. behaved disgracefully, i.e. drank until four in the san remo, the first time in months and months. am therefore poohed."[69] Michael was soon back to his regular drinking habits, although in a new setting. Fashionable opinion among Greenwich Village's cultural and political elite was turning against the San Remo—the victim of its own success, it was now scorned as a watering hole for tourists and poseurs.

The bar Michael would make his own for the next decade was the White Horse Tavern on the corner of Hudson and West 11th Streets in the West Village, a hangout for a variety of grizzled longshoremen, accomplished writers, aspiring folksingers, would-be revolutionaries, gay intellectuals, and assorted other bohemians. Poet Delmore Schwartz drank there; so did novelist James Baldwin and cartoonist Jules Feiffer; so did a young and ambitious Democratic Party political operative named Daniel Patrick Moynihan. So, later in the decade, did Tom, Paddy, and Liam Clancy, and Tom Makem, who as the Irish balladeers known as the Clancy Brothers would help spark the folk song revival of the 1960s and popularize the wearing of white Aran sweaters. It is surprising that no one ever wrote a folk song about the White Horse; it seemed such a perfect embodiment of a cultural moment and stance. Dan Wakefield, born and raised in conservative Indiana, discovered the White Horse in the mid-1950s. He recalled that in its back room, after many pints of ale,

> the Irish rebellion and the Spanish civil war seemed to blend together in one grand battle of noble underdogs against tyrant oppressors, waged from the dawn of history, and any rousing song of freedom stood just as well for the brave lads of Spain or Ireland, either one—or for any of us who had left home to come to the Village.[70]

On Sunday afternoons Norman Mailer held court for a circle of writers including Vance Bourjaily, Calder Willingham, John Clellon Holmes, and William Styron. The poet Dylan Thomas once mentioned to a college audience that he was a regular at the White Horse, an indiscretion that, to Michael's dismay, brought "every English major in the Northeast corridor" to the White Horse for a beer and a reverent look around. Michael would later claim he deserved a measure of literary fame for having stood next to Thomas at the urinal in the men's room at White Horse minutes before the alcoholic poet collapsed of a cerebral seizure and was carried off to St. Vincent's hospital to die, too sodden with drink by then to do much raging against the dying of the light. "I was in the Horse every night for more than ten years," Michael wrote in his memoirs with only slight exaggeration (he did occasionally pass nights in other cities). "As the people of Königsberg were said to set their clocks by Immanuel Kant's walks, you would see me, punctually dissolute, appear on week nights at midnight and on weekends at one o'clock."[71]

Day seemed genuinely bewildered by the ability of her young disciples to combine their spiritual commitments with such worldly goings-on. According to Eileen Fantino: "If Dorothy thought we were staying out late, and she was wondering what was going on, she would suggest that we go on a retreat." The young volunteers responded to that kind of advice as might be expected. As Betty Bartelme recalled: "We used to kid her, and call her 'Mother Superior' behind her back."[72]

Day was even more prudish about sex. She felt a maternal responsibility for protecting the young people in her charge from impure acts and thoughts. One evening at the Worker, at the dinner table, Michael was reading a psychiatric study of autoerotism. Dorothy got terribly upset. "Michael!" she announced sternly. "We do not even *talk* about such things!"[73] Of course, the very conditions of life associated with the Catholic Worker—voluntary poverty and communal living—made it difficult for the volunteers to follow the church's prescription for appropriate sexual behavior, that is, within marriage and for the purpose of procreation. Michael's relationship with Peggy Brennan did not survive his first year at the Worker. He proposed marriage to her in January 1952, but her father refused to hear of it. Just how, he wanted to know, did Michael expect to support children, let alone a wife, while committed to a life of voluntary poverty? Michael and Peggy had a tearful parting in Penn Station one wintry night (he was off again to see his parents in St. Louis), and they never saw each other again.[74]

Most of the resident volunteers at St. Joseph's House were men. But young women like Eileen Fantino, Betty Bartelme, and Mary Ann McCoy came by on a regular basis to help out with the bread line and the newspaper, and they stayed to socialize on the weekends with Michael and other young male volunteers. There were occasional romances; Michael and Betty Bartelme were briefly involved in the summer of 1952. Still, Day's worries about sexual misbehavior were needless. Much of the socializing between the sexes took place in crowds, not among couples, and in public spaces like Washington Square or the White Horse. Michael reported to Jim Finn in January 1952 on his sex life, or rather on its absence, a state of things he did not seem to regret: "do not wish to brag, but with the aid of grace have been able to avoid even commiting a serious act (other conditions aside) for many months."[75] Even on those occasional nights when the young volunteers failed to return home to St. Joseph's House it didn't mean they had any serious moral transgressions to report to their confessor. Bogdan Denitch, a young socialist who became intimate with Michael and his friends at the Worker in 1951, recalled how sometimes, instead of heading off to the White Horse, a whole gang of young Catholic Workers would descend on his apartment on Greenwich Street with a case of beer:

> There were a number of extremely attractive women around the Catholic Worker who drank with us and were a part of our circle, but who did not sleep with any of the guys. They would spend Saturday night with us drinking, and wind up sleeping on my couch. Then they would have to wake up early to go to mass. Nobody messed with them. They'd hug and kiss, but that was that.[76]

On the whole, notwithstanding Dorothy Day's personal lack of interest in feminist ideas, the Catholic Worker movement in the early 1950s seems to have achieved a kind of rough equality among men and women, something that at the time was as rare in radical circles as in mainstream society. According to Roger O'Neil, "What was unique about the Worker, even if there was no conscious sense of feminism, was that you could meet a whole range of women that you could have these platonic relationships with. Most people don't get this opportunity."[77]

The Catholic Worker ideal, in Dorothy Day's phrase, was to be "fools for Christ." Catholic Workers had to be prepared to accept a position on the margins of society and to endure whatever contempt, hostility, or ridicule that entailed. "When I was at the Worker in '51 and '52," Michael would tell an interviewer some years later, "we appeared at that point as a small band of nuts. . . . Totally marginal radicals."[78] But, paradoxically, it was while he was at the Worker that Michael took his initial steps toward influencing a broader audience. His first-ever experience speaking as a visiting speaker at a college came under the auspices of the Catholic Worker in November 1952: "The University of Vermont in Burlington asked Dorothy Day to speak," Michael would recall, "and in her grand style Dorothy assumed that the invitation was for the Catholic Worker movement rather than for her, and sent me to substitute."[79] The event, scheduled for November 19, was not simply a speaking engagement but a debate with William F. Buckley. The question on which they were set to clash was "Is our Educational System leading us down the road to Socialism?" Michael had reviewed *God and Man at Yale* the previous year in the *Catholic Worker*, ironically praising Buckley's consistency as a conservative:

> Conservatives usually excoriate "unbridled" capitalism in theory, though they are hard put to name any case of its existence. Mr. Buckley saves us that tiresome argument. He is in favor of laissez-faire capitalism in a very literal, Manchester sense which has been condemned in so many papal documents that it would verge on the heretical to agree with him.[80]

Meeting Buckley for the first time in Vermont, Michael found him "gracious, personable, friendly," as he noted in a letter to his parents shortly afterwards. It was the beginning of a life-long and respectful relationship between the two political adversaries, who would spar on numerous occasion in public forums, including repeated appearances on Buckley's television show *Firing Line.* (Buckley had a gift for constructing such relationships with men of the Left—over the years he would develop similar ties with Dwight Macdonald, Allard Lowenstein, and Murray Kempton.)

Michael seems to have had the better of that particular evening, at least insofar as one can judge from the coverage of the student newspaper. Mr. Buckley, a student reporter noted,

> although adept with statements such as "If you want socialism in this country just sit back and relax," and "The educators are giving it to you in greater and greater measure," was never able to substantiate his motives. Mr. Harrington was, however, able to use the example of our present system—that teaching in our schools is pledged to capitalism or maintaining the present property relations.[81]

Ned O'Gorman, then an undergraduate at St. Michael's College and later a notable poet, attended the debate. He was impressed by both Buckley and Michael, although as a reader of the *Catholic Worker* he was inclined to support Michael in any case. He remembered Michael's side of the debate being "like throwing fat on the skillet. He was absolutely, totally, intellectually vibrant. You knew that when he spoke, he spoke what must have been the truth."[82]

"The debate itself went wonderfully," Michael reported to his parents, offering a professional assessment of his opponent:

> To Buckley's credit, it is rather difficult to attack academic freedom in front of a university audience. He was at the disadvantage. However, his

presentation, from a purely rhetorical point of view, was not at the high level that I had been told it would be. This was especially true in his constructive speech—his rebuttal was pretty good. At any rate, the audience—in terms of applause, questions, etc.—was on my side, but again, I think they were before the debate even began.

Michael was happy to be able to report to his parents that he had enjoyed the support of the local Catholic clergy that evening:

> Four priests were present. Three of them I later learned were from St. Michael's College [in nearby Colchester, Vermont]—the President, Dean of Studies, and a Prof. The other priest I didn't know. When I saw them, I thought they might launch into me for my views and side with Buckley. But two of them spoke during the question period—one the St. Mike's Dean of Studies—and both attacked Buckley! The St. Mike's guy went so far as to accuse B of "educational relativism"! The other priest made a point that I had made in both my speech and rebuttal—that Buckley did not accept the Encyclicals of the Pope and would not, in fact, allow them to be taught in his kind of a Yale University. It leant support to my claim that I was within the bounds of the Church to have these "official" representatives speak up.[83]

Buckley's memory of the debate remained vivid many years later. He too had a high professional regard for his opponent's debating skills:

> When he went to the Catholic Worker, most of the Catholic Church was very conservative, as it would be up until Vatican II. He was arguing a position that was not popular in what one might call the communion breakfast set. He was so much in command of his own arguments and pitch that he was effective. He was a very, very good polemical slugger. . . . In the first place, he was very quick. Secondly, he was very fluent, extremely keen in seizing the weaknesses of his opponent, whether those were analytical philosophical weaknesses, or whether or not they were exploitable vulnerabilities in terms of the sentiment of the audience.[84]

In a particularly shrewd insight into his opponent's style and appeal, Buckley would conclude that Michael "had the evangelist's pitch of voice. . . . There is a sense in which he was preaching to a parish of sinners who desire to repent. He would show them how to do it."[85]

Even after Michael left the church, the two men felt a kinship in their Catholic backgrounds, and their debates displayed a kind of religious intensity. On another occasion some years later, at Pepperdine University, the two engaged in an epic conflict of ideas, debating for two hours in the morning and two hours in the afternoon. According to Buckley: "It was really a situation in which we found ourselves fighting for each other's soul."[86] Michael grew fond of, if never personally very close to, Buckley. He would describe him as a "charming rogue," and he did his best to separate his attitude toward the man from his opposition to Buckley's political views and activities.[87]

There were other relationships that Michael forged during his time at the Worker that would prove to have lasting effects on his career. Among these was the friendship he made with a former Catholic Worker named John Cogley, whom he met in 1951. Cogley proved not only a good friend but a very helpful patron, for he was already an influential figure in liberal Catholic circles. Cogley was a dozen years older than Michael, and like Michael he was a transplanted midwesterner, though he came from a considerably more hardscrabble background. He joined the Catholic Worker movement in Chicago in 1937, published a Chicago edition of the *Catholic Worker,* and was in charge of Chicago House of Hospitality. But at the onset of the Second World War, he broke with Dorothy Day when she tried to enforce an absolute pacifist position on the movement. After service in the Army Air Force, he studied theology at the University of Fribourg in Switzerland, and upon his return to the United States in 1949 he joined the staff of *Commonweal* magazine, soon becoming its executive editor. Cogley and his coeditors made the magazine a hard-hitting liberal intellectual weekly, sympathetic to the nascent movement for change within the American and international Catholic community while addressing political and cultural issues of interest to a broader audience.[88]

Commonweal had broken step with the Catholic hierarchy in the 1930s when it espoused neutrality in the Spanish Civil War. In the early 1950s, it won equal notoriety for its criticisms of Senator Joe McCarthy. Anti-McCarthyism had its costs; in some circles, to be referred to as a "Commonweal Catholic" was equivalent to calling someone a Communist. The magazine was banned in some Catholic libraries; in others, it was kept beneath the counter and handed out only on request. On the other hand, *Commonweal* was one of the few Catholic publications that regularly attracted a sizable non-Catholic readership. Its circulation in the mid-1950s was about 20,000, on a par with that of the *Nation* and the *New Republic.*[89]

Cogley asked Michael to contribute to the magazine. His first assignment was, appropriately enough, to review a collection of essays on the lives of saints, edited by Clare Booth Luce, the conservative wife of his former employer Henry Luce. Michael had high praise for the essay by Trappist monk and pacifist Thomas Merton on John of the Cross (whose saying "When there is no love, put in love and you will take out love" was among the favorite quotations of the Catholic Worker), as well as for Karl Stern's essay on

Therese of Liseux. But he took issue with Mrs. Luce's portrait of Joan of Arc as "a symbol of legitimacy and law-and-order, a saint for the cold war."[90]

Over the next half decade Michael became a regular contributor to *Commonweal*'s pages, writing nearly four dozen reviews, essays, and articles on topics ranging from Russian history to existential theology to contemporary ballet. Like the *Partisan Review* writers of the 1930s and 1940s, Michael strove to attain a kind of universal competence in politics, culture, and the interrelations between the two. More than any other writing he was to do in the 1950s, his contributions to *Commonweal* introduced him to, and taught him how to write for, a large audience that did not necessarily share all his political presuppositions. (Among those who learned of Michael from his writing in *Commonweal* in the early 1950s and saw him as a role model was a young Catholic seminarian named Michael Novak, who became a liberal and antiwar activist in the 1960s and, later, an influential figure in the neo-conservative movement.)[91]

Perhaps the single most important contact Michael made while at the Worker was Dwight Macdonald, who had come down to Chrystie Street in February 1952 to prepare a profile of Dorothy Day for the *New Yorker.* Macdonald had been a key figure among the older generation of political intellectuals who had made their names in the partisan warfare between Stalinists and Trotskyists in New York in the 1930s and 1940s. During the Second World War, Macdonald had moved from Trotskyism to an idiosyncratic blend of pacifism and anarchism, abandoning his editorship of *Partisan Review* to publish his own influential journal, *Politics,* from 1944 to 1948. He had only recently joined the staff of the *New Yorker.*

Perhaps the most gifted satirist in American letters since H. L. Mencken, Macdonald regularly and elegantly eviscerated such unworthies as fuzzy-minded fellow travelers, self-absorbed Trotskyist ideologues, and academic purveyors of "middlebrow" culture. Unlike Mencken, he was neither misanthropic nor cynical. When he found someone worthy of celebrating, he lavished them with affectionate prose bouquets. "Like so many people," Michael recalled, "Dwight fell in love with Dorothy." Thus the opening sentence of the resulting two-part profile of Dorothy that Macdonald published in the *New Yorker* the following October announced, "Many people think Dorothy Day is a saint and that she will someday be canonized."

Michael was amused that Macdonald, without telling his editors, went so far as to allow Dorothy the chance to censor the article before it appeared; she used the opportunity to strike out the Malcolm Cowley quote about how she could drink the gangsters under the table.[92] Michael was mentioned only in passing in the article (and gently tweaked by Macdonald for confusing "seamen" with "longshoremen" in an article he had written for the *Catholic Worker*), but Day's young disciple apparently made a lasting impression on Macdonald—which would serve Michael in good stead a decade later when Macdonald decided to review *The Other America* for the *New Yorker.*[93]

Through Macdonald, Michael caught a glimpse of the "twilight of the *Partisan Review* world." He was invited to a party at Macdonald's apartment in 1952, where the feature of the evening was a living room performance of Purcell's *Dido and Aenas* by Noah Greenburg's opera company. Greenburg, a leader of the Trotskyist fraction within the seaman's union in the 1930s, would later go on to become founder of the Pro Musica, a group that specialized in and helped popularize Renaissance music. For Michael the evening proved a congenial synthesis "in which the lions and lambs of Marxism and high culture lay down together."[94]

Nineteen fifty-two was also notable for Michael as the year in which he finally attained his childhood ambition of becoming a genuine published poet. Five of his poems were accepted by and printed in the Chicago-based *Poetry* magazine. Sex and death and evil preoccupied the poems: The epigraph for one of them was a line from Augustine's *Confessions:* "A pear tree there was near our vineyard, laden with fruit, tempting neither for color nor taste . . . it was foul and I loved it." And in another poem he paid homage to James Joyce (whose influence was evident throughout his poetry):

That last second
Of his exile,
Were the knives
Laid out like
Bright pandybats?
Did his mind
Wander like Jews
And finally find
Some pun from
The Scandinavian
That told exactly
How ether smelled?
Or as the mask
Covered his face,
Did he sink back
Like Molly Bloom
And say, yes
Oh yes yes[95]

These first literary offerings would also turn out to be Michael's last published poems, although he kept working at his poetry for another two or three years. By that time he had realized that if he had some talent as a poet, he certainly lacked genius. If he couldn't be a lamb of high culture, he would have to be satisfied with being a well-read lion of Marxism.[96]

Overshadowing everything else in these years for Catholic Workers was the war in Korea. And that, too, contributed to their sense of isolation from the mainstream. After the Communist Chinese intervention was contained in the spring of 1951 and the war settled into stalemate, many Americans tried to put the ongoing conflict out of their minds. The continued bloodletting was unpopular and always hovered in the background of public consciousness and national politics; Dwight Eisenhower's election year pledge to "go to Korea" to end the war certainly contributed to his victory in November 1952.[97] But American society in 1951 had little of the committed "home-front" quality that had defined life between 1941 and 1945. The economy was booming as it had not for a generation past; consumer goods were in ample supply; and the popular culture industry was reaping record profits as it concentrated on escapist themes. In the movies, pulp paperbacks, comic books, and on television, anxieties about the state of the world were masked in tales of alien invasion, unleashed monsters, and hard-boiled detectives.[98] Communist espionage and subversion remained the most explosive issues in American politics. The rhetoric of religious war was popular, especially among the Catholic hierarchy; when Cardinal Spellman visited American troops in Korea in 1951 at Christmas, he composed a poem that ended: "The burst of bombs in Korea/And the Star above in Judea/Symbol alike Christ the King."[99] But for many Americans, the Cold War (including its hottest manifestation, the war in Korea) was a part-time preoccupation, a set of issues and worries that were neatly compartmentalized apart from day-to-day concerns.

Catholic Workers wanted to shake the complacency of the majority. "It is heartbreaking once again to see casualty lists in *The New York Times*," Dorothy Day wrote in the first issue of the *Catholic Worker* to appear after the start of the Korean War.[100] But Catholic Workers were uncertain how to make their views on the war known, apart from publishing their dissent in the *Catholic Worker*. Most of the extremely limited open "peace" activism of the period was conducted by the Communist Party and various front groups, with whom the Catholic Worker wanted no dealings.[101] Catholic Workers emphasized individual resistance to the war through conscientious objection or draft resistance; in this period, Michael himself contributed two articles to the *Catholic Worker* analyzing and taking issue with the church's traditional "just war" doctrine. Thomas Aquinas and other Catholic theologians who had contributed to the development of this doctrine had insisted that, among other requirements, in a just war the benefits of fighting a war must outweigh its evils. But Michael and other Catholic Workers believed that this principle of "proportionality" no longer applied under the conditions of modern warfare, given the immense destructive powers now employed by belligerents and the commensurate suffering of noncombatants. "We know that truth is cautious," Michael wrote in October 1951, "the Church slow; we pray for a deeper understanding of pacifism on her part; but we are not dependent on the future—we condemn this war as Catholics, today."[102]

In making his arguments for absolute pacifism, Michael was, of course, wrestling with a personal dilemma. He was, at that very moment, still a member of the United States Armed Forces, on reserve to be sure, but engaged in training for active duty and subject to call-up at any moment for dispatch to the battlefields of Korea or anywhere else military authorities should see fit to send him. In January 1951, a month before moving into Chrystie Street, he had transferred to an army reserve hospital group based in Brooklyn, to which he had to report every week for an evening of training. But the compromise that kept him from shaming his parents now shamed him in the eyes of his fellow Catholic Workers. "On drill nights," he would write in his memoirs, "I felt myself an outcast. I waited until everyone was at dinner and then sneaked out of the house in my uniform, the livery of my compromise. There was constant discussion of how I could be so unprincipled."[103]

It was bad enough when his bargain with the devil involved only one evening a week. But in the summer of 1951 he was ordered to Camp Drum for a full two weeks of training. He persuaded himself—if not his fellow Catholic Workers—that there was no hypocrisy or violation of pacifist principles involved in his going, since he would only be training for noncombatant service as a medic.[104] But when he arrived at Camp Drum, he discovered that the army was not concerned with his moral scruples. Having been ordered to take infantry training, he went to his company commander to complain. "It was a ludicrous scene," he would later write:

> I was terrified at my own audacity in challenging a gigantic system of authority. I also did not know how to salute, whether to keep my cap on indoors, or anything about military etiquette. I stood there, trembling and filled with the Holy Spirit, while the captain yelled at me that if I were a C.O., why in the goddamned hell had I volunteered for the army? In exasperation he finally said that I didn't have to take a rifle but that I must march with the troops to the first exercise. "What is that," I asked. "Calisthenics," he said.[105]

"Calisthenics" turned out to be practicing throwing hand grenades. In a letter to James Finn, written at the end of August, Michael explained what happened next:

> just returned from the army. almost went to the stockade. the bastards sent me to the 307th infantry btn for training. i demurred on the issue of a rifle,

> after much shouting by a full colonel, was told not to take one; i demurred on listening to a lecture on hand grenades, after a little thought by captain francis x driscoll, was excused; it demurred on marching with the troops, typing for the infantry, was finally (two and a half hectic days) sent back to the 344th general hospital. i now have demurred on the army. am no longer a 1-a-o. told them i was resigning. that fixed their wagon. they are checking on whether i can or no. so am i.[106]

Michael went to a Benedictine abbey for a three-day private retreat to consider his next move. On returning to New York, he turned in his army uniform and refused to go to any further drills. The army swiftly turned down his request for a discharge. Michael gave Jim Finn a progress report in January 1952, saying that he lived in constant expectation of seeing "an m.p. jeep pull up outside." He had met with a "mean-faced" captain in the adjutant general's office in New York whose "sole qaulification for the job seems to be a small, narrow mind. he says, no, no, no." Nonetheless, the fact that he had not yet been arrested led him to suspect that the authorities considered him more trouble than he was worth: thus far the army's policy "is that they want me to drop dead."[107]

In July 1952 Michael attempted to change his draft status by filing a conscientious objection form with his draft board in Saint Louis. "I believe in the teachings of the Catholic Church," he wrote, "and base my claim on the church's traditional theology of war. This involves superior obligations to those arising in human situations."[108] In August he was classified 1-A. He appealed, and this time the draft board granted him conscientious objector status. He still had to take a physical to determine his qualification for alternative service.[109] During the physical, the army's X-ray technicians made what he regarded as "an outrageous misreading" of his chest X-rays. They reported that he had tuberculosis, rendering him incapable of military service. He was promptly classified 4-F. "I was sure," Michael would later write, that "there was some coded note on my file to reject this crackpot one way or another."[110]

But the army medical staff may have made an honest mistake. However spiritually bracing Michael had found life at the Worker, it did not improve his health or appearance. The food at Chrystie Street was a nutritional disaster, with fresh vegetables showing up only for two months in the summer, when they were supplied from Maryfarm. Michael's sleep patterns were irregular because he chose to serve as a night watchman, because he spent a lot of evenings in the White Horse, and because of the noise level that could be expected in a crowded boarding house in a poor urban neighborhood. According to fellow Catholic Worker John Stanley: "There were rumors that [Michael] had developed TB, he looked so unwell. Grey pallor, very thin, of course, we smoked our lungs out. . . . Lots of coughing going on."[111]

Michael was dismayed that he was being let out of military service on medical rather than conscientious grounds. After his army physical he went to a doctor at the City Health Clinic for a second opinion. On learning that he was from St. Louis, the doctor told Michael that he was suffering from histoplasmosis, a relatively innocuous fungal disease common in the Mississippi valley. Symptoms include fever, coughing, and loss of weight and are similar to those of tuberculosis. Even when symptomless, the disease can leave spots on the lung, as it had in Michael's case.[112] Michael wrote to the draft board to tell them they had made a mistake, but he never heard back from them. Bill Loftus, Eileen Fantino, and Mary Ann McCoy were at the San Remo one day when Michael came in just after having received his new 4-F classification; Fantino remembered that it was one of the rare occasions when she saw him very upset.[113] In September 1953, when his 1950 enlistment expired, he was automatically awarded an honorable discharge from the United States Armed Forces. Despite himself, Michael was a veteran.[114]

Shortly before reporting to Camp Drum for military training, Michael took part in one of the few—and certainly the most celebrated—public demonstrations held against the Korean War. The demonstration was scheduled for June 25, 1951, the first anniversary of the start of the war. Michael was one of a half dozen or so Catholic Workers who joined another dozen or so brave souls to mark the occasion by marching through Times Square; it was, Michael noted in his memoirs, "a motley little band." Notwithstanding the lack of attendance, the demonstration was notable for including a number of people who would become influential public figures in the 1960s, including David Dellinger of the War Resisters League and Bayard Rustin of the Fellowship of Reconciliation. The march concluded at the corner of Seventh Avenue and 40th Street, where Michael mounted a soap box and spoke on behalf of the Catholic Worker. Michael was followed by a speaker from the War Resisters League and then by Dave Dellinger. Dellinger did not get very far in his speech before he was rushed by a man brandishing a stick he had ripped from one of the demonstrator's picket signs. Confusing the words "Catholic Worker" on one of the signs for "Daily Worker," the Communist Party newspaper, the man yelled that the demonstrators were "a bunch of Commies." Bayard Rustin intercepted him, handing him a second picket sign, which bewildered him sufficiently to make him drop both sticks. But he continued to yell that the demonstrators were traitors. What happened next is a famous moment in the history of mid-twentieth-century American pacifism. As Michael would describe it:

> Dellinger replied that we were pacifists, not Communists. Then, said the man, come down here so I can hit you and see if you really will turn the other cheek. Dellinger left the stand and walked over to reason with our

> disturbed critic. The latter planted himself carefully and punched Dellinger in the jaw, knocking him to the ground.[115]

After Dellinger was beaten to the ground, Bayard Rustin intervened, and in a textbook display of Gandhian tactics told the assailant to hit him instead. Now utterly confounded, the man calmed down, apologized, and departed. The whole event confirmed the belief of radical pacifists that principled nonviolence could overcome hatred and unreason.

Michael admired Bayard Rustin as the most physically fearless man he had ever met, but he was not as convinced as Rustin that the June 25 demonstration "proved the enormous power of nonviolence." His most lasting impression of the day's events was a sense of futility and ridiculousness: "I saw myself shuffling along in that pathetic little parade and I thought I looked like one of those cartoon figures with a placard announcing the end of the world."[116]

By now Michael was one of the Catholic Worker's most articulate spokesmen, and he was often pressed into service to answer the movement's critics. But he grew increasingly dissatisfied with his own arguments in favor of Catholic Worker-style politics. He never bought into certain fundamental beliefs of the movement, such as its agrarian antimodernism—what Peter Maurin, who was no mean hand as a phrase-maker, labeled the "green revolution."[117] Michael told Dorothy Day that if she really "wanted to go back to organic farming to grow the food for the world, you'd better have some plan for the several billion people who are going to starve to death."[118] One of the few privileges of life at the Catholic Worker was the chance to visit one or another of its farms, in Newburgh or on Staten Island, for spiritual reflection, or just as a form of rest and relaxation from the rigors of life on the Bowery. Such was not the case for Michael. Long before he became a Marxist, Michael already shared Karl Marx's contempt for the "idiocy of rural life." He found the Lower East Side of New York infinitely preferable.

In itself, Michael's lack of interest in becoming a peasant did not disqualify him from being a good Catholic Worker. More troublesome were his growing doubts about the political efficacy of being a saint. The question he had to decide was whether striving for sainthood was the necessary precondition for—or antithetical to—any hope for actually changing the world.

In April 1952, a little more than a year after Michael arrived at Chrystie Street, a former Catholic Worker named John Cort reviewed Dorothy Day's memoir *The Long Loneliness* for *Commonweal* magazine. Cort had joined the Catholic Worker as a young Harvard graduate in 1936. He was, in some ways, the Michael Harrington of his era at the Worker—bright, dedicated, pious, and an effective organizer. While living at the Mott Street House of Hospitality, he developed a broad definition of what it meant to perform "acts of mercy," pushing his fellow Catholic Workers to get off the bread line and on to the picket line, in particular by providing strike support for the newly organized and militant unions of the Congress of Industrial Organizations (CIO). Toward this end, he helped found a group in 1937 called the Association of Catholic Trade Unionists (ACTU). The ACTU went on to play a significant role in rallying Catholic support for trade unionism in the late 1930s and in battling the Communists for control of such key CIO unions as the United Auto Workers, the Transport Workers, and the United Electrical Workers in the 1940s and 1950s.[119]

But the ACTU's success did not impress Peter Maurin or Dorothy Day. They found the group's emphasis on gaining position within the labor movement at odds with the Catholic Worker's more transcendent vision of social change. "We published many heavy articles on capital and labor, on strikes and labor conditions, on the assembly line and all the other evils on industrialism," Dorothy Day wrote in *The Long Loneliness.* "But it was a whole picture we were presenting of man and his destiny and so we emphasized less, as the years went by, the organized-labor aspect of the paper."[120] As a result, Cort and other ACTU stalwarts broke with the movement in 1938.

Cort outlined his differences with the Catholic Worker in his 1952 *Commonweal* review:

> The big contribution of Peter Maurin was that he got Dorothy Day started. He had great gifts and a charming simplicity. But after the start, it seems to me, his influence led Dorothy deeper and deeper into the waters of contradiction and confusion.

Cort defended the ACTU against Day's charges in *The Long Loneliness* that it was a group preoccupied with "maneuvering" for power. To the contrary, those who sought to work within the established labor movement were performing, in Cort's view, "another form of the works of mercy, which, Dorothy never forgets to point out, include the business of instructing the ignorant and counseling the doubtful." Despite what he described as the "magnificent lessons" taught by the Catholic Worker about poverty and love, Cort denounced the "theoretical confusions of the movement, the sloppy thinking, the silly posturing as more-radical-than-thou, etc."[121]

Although Michael must have read Cort's critique, he offered no direct response. But in a letter to another critic of the Catholic Worker a few months later, Michael considered the dilemma of how a movement so ambitious in its ultimate aims, and yet so isolated in its immediate influence, could justify its existence. The "CW" he admitted,

> does not have a mass base—either among workers or the middle-class. Perhaps as a Personalist movement it is stopped from being a mass move-

> ment. It writes of an uncompromising, relatively absolute Christianity. It is extremely critical of the society in which we live. These things are necessary, *if there ever is to be a mass movement.* Such a movement, such a society, must have some vision of an ideal. . . . Let us plead guilty for having sometimes been arrogant toward the immediate needs of the worker. Let us plead guilty for having lost an orientation toward the working class. Let us plead guilty for having been uncompromising in a hostile fashion that alienated many. And I am quite serious. We are guilty of these.
>
> But on the other hand, we must conceive ourselves in terms of our function. No one can be the Knights of Columbus and ACTU and the CW simoultaneously. I hope we can conceive ourselves in the way in which Father Danielou speaks of prophets and the vocation of prophecy. Short-sighted perhaps (I hope we can change to a certain extent) where the immediate problem is concerned, but visionary in the best sense of the word where the transcendental values of Christ are concerned. It is a hard role to play. . . . Yet it is necessary that we have our pilgrims of the absolute along with the day to day, empirical routine of parish work. For the greater danger is that, in attempting to comprimise, to soft-peddle pacifism, to mittigate our criticism, that we will lose sight of our ideal.[122]

As a defense of the Catholic Worker, Michael's effort was sincere but highly qualified. Given the magnitude of his concessions—that the Catholic Worker had lost contact with the real needs of working people, that it was arrogant and self-isolating in its intense moralism—one might well question whether Michael felt that the movement's all too abundant flaws were indeed outweighed by its redeeming quality as a prophetic minority. And in his attempt to think strategically—to posit a connection, however vaguely defined, between the actions of a saving remnant of true believers and some future *mass movement* (his emphasis)—Michael was straying far from the Catholic Worker's accustomed rhetoric and conceptual terrain ("mass movement" was not a phrase appearing in either the gospels or in Peter Maurin's "Easy Essays").

In his letter to Jim Finn in January 1952, Michael returned to the issues raised in John Cort's *Commonweal* critique of the Worker. Couched in a rather obscure consideration of means and ends (Michael was generally a very clear writer; as a general rule, the harder his argument was to follow, the less sure of it he was himself), he was in fact conceding the heart of Cort's argument:

> at the heart of christianity is an uncomfortable, radical proposition—do good and avoid evil. this proposition does not make any reference to pragmatism. however, in general, morality is usually pragmatic . . . do not believe that one should become univocal too often, cf. [Bob] ludlow's

> extremism on the state. proper attitude is: the means are the end in the process of becoming. therefore, a social phenomenon is evil, i.e. should be absolutely shunned, when the means are such that they clearly and inevitably lead to an evil end. thus war. however, the state, the union, etc., though containing evil elements, are not inevitably tending toward evil. in a sense, the means have not taken on a solid form, and the question of becoming is still equivocal. in this situation it is possible to cooperate with the means in the hope of forming them toward the good.[123]

That is to say—although Michael was not yet willing to say it quite so baldly—that the Catholic Worker, with its emphasis on individual spiritual perfection, had cut itself off from any real possibility of influencing the institutional mechanisms ("the state, the union") through which effective social change had been achieved historically. Michael's intricate reasoning put him at odds with the flat certainties professed by most of his fellow Catholic Workers, who felt there was nothing "equivocal" about the state and who harbored profound doubts about any collective body larger than the family or the neighborhood parish—including labor unions. "Anarchists believe that the *whole* people composing a community should take of what governing is to be done," Dorothy Day wrote in *The Long Loneliness* in 1952, "rather than have a distant and centralized State do it." This had been a consistent position with Day, even back in the days of New Deal reformism, which she regarded with considerable suspicion (and Peter Maurin regarded with complete hostility).[124] Taken to its logical conclusion, that Catholic Worker stance precluded voting or sympathizing with any political party, however radical its pedigree. As Bob Ludlow wrote in the *Catholic Worker*'s November 1952 issue: "If a Socialist heads the State, if a Democrat heads the State, if a Republican heads the State, it is still a war State. If a pacifist runs for president when he becomes president he must shed his pacifism. He could not operate otherwise."[125]

Michael revealed something else of interest in his January 1952 letter to Jim Finn. As recently as the previous summer, when he gave a talk at Maryfarm on the virtues of utopian thinking, he had categorically rejected socialist teachings:

> We cannot, like Marx (and, tragically, like Lenin and Stalin), call for political revolution, a mere change in government or law. If revolution is to be successful, it must occur within society before a sudden moment of political upheaval gives it legal recognition.[126]

But it seems to have occurred to him soon after delivering this judgment that he had, in fact, never systematically read Marx or his twentieth-century disciples. So he began to work his way through the relevant texts. "Have been reading all kinds of stuff," he informed Jim Finn in January:

> karl marx: das kapital. very good, in parts. his analysis of the "division of labor" (how the factory system inevitably tends to specialization and concentration) is magnificent. am surprised at the eschatological element. the belief in the leap from necessity into freedom is sheer theology, and since it is conceived materialistically, fairly sentimental and unreal. also—a comment that others have made—his giving the proletariat a mystical function—making them a chosen race—is a little too religious for my maw, bad religion that is. do not think he understood the emergence of the white-collar class (this is more true in U.S., which much of marx doesn't fit anyway; incidentally, trotsky's marxism in u.s. is best short summary of k.m. i have seen); this white collar group is bound to the republican party and reaction by some sort of veblenesque category of conspicuously consuming their votes and identifying with the so-called upper class . . . also been reading trotsky; the revolution betrayed. contains a chapter, "Stalins Thermidor" which could be printed in a pcifist paper without comment. shows how a revolution by violence assures the rise of reaction by killing off the best revolutionary cadres, etc. applies it to october '17 and french uprisings in 1790, '48 and '71. Also read Lenin on imperialism. found it very informative.[127]

That Michael was not yet ready to proclaim himself a Marxist is evident in his attempt to co-opt Leon Trotsky, founder of the Red Army, into the pacifist camp. But the political antennae of so experienced a radical as Dorothy Day did not miss the accumulating signals of Michael's coming apostasy. She began to have long arguments with him about socialism. Already beleaguered at the Worker because of his unapologetic commitment to intellectual pursuits, he now found himself the target of renewed attack for his political convictions. And among his antagonists, no one proved more relentless—and infuriating—than Ammon Hennacy.

Hennacy had himself been a socialist years before Michael was born. But, imprisoned in Atlanta penitentiary for draft resistance during the First World War, he underwent a conversion experience that led him to renounce his former political beliefs, if not his dedication to revolution. He decided that Christ's Sermon on the Mount was the most revolutionary statement ever made, and henceforth he had no use for those who looked to statist solutions to social problems.[128] Over the next three decades Hennacy developed a reputation as an indefatigable activist engaged in what he called his "One Man Revolution" on behalf of anarchist and pacifist causes. He gained fame within pacifist circles for his flair for the dramatic, his fasting, and his advocacy of tax resistance as a strategy for opposing war. In 1952 he converted to Catholicism, although his conversion seemed to hinge more on an unreciprocated passion for Dorothy Day than any acceptance of papal authority. In August of that year he moved in to St. Joseph's House—where his roommate was Michael Harrington.[129]

Hennacy's companionship over the next few months was, perhaps, the worst privation Michael suffered in the nearly two years he spent at St. Joseph's, and it may well have hastened his departure from the movement (even so committed a Catholic Worker as Bob Ludlow eventually fled from St. Joseph's House rather than put up with Hennacy's company any longer).[130] Michael came to dread the coming of morning, knowing that Hennacy was lying in ambush for him across the room:

> When I'd first wake up, I wouldn't open my eyes. I'd first listen to see if he was around because I knew he'd be waiting, just waiting. He would say, "I knew a socialist in Ohio in 1911 who became a white slaver. I knew a socialist who used to beat blacks." I mean, he knew every horror story about socialists.[131]

Hennacy offered a somewhat different account of his relations with Michael in his privately published memoir *The Book of Ammon,* written in the 1960s: "I found myself going easy on Mike Harrington," he reported of their time as roommates at St. Joseph's, because "he got so much razzing from everyone else." (He also bragged that the bed-bugs that infested their sleeping quarters didn't bother him nearly as much as they did Michael.)[132]

In time, Hennacy became a symbol for Michael of everything he most disliked about the Catholic Worker's style of expressive politics. He regarded Hennacy's self-dramatizing direct action tactics, particularly his annual fasts, as a kind of spiritual showboating:

> I remember he would fast and picket on every anniversary of Hiroshima. . . . Every year, he would fast longer. I was there the year he fasted more than forty days. And there was, I think, a little pride that he had now out-fasted Jesus. That Jesus had only done forty days and Ammon had done forty-three or something like that. Take that, God![133]

Michael and Ammon Hennacy did have one thing in common: like John Cort in the 1930s, they were more interested in the picket line than the bread line. As Michael's fellow Catholic Worker Roger O'Neill recalled, Michael "was a leader. . . . He was in front of things and he made things happen."[134] One of the things Michael made happen was the Catholic Worker's participation in a support group for imprisoned labor activists in Spain, called the

Committee to Defend Franco's Labor Victims. And it was on a picket line sponsored by the committee in front of the Spanish consulate on Madison Avenue in March 1952 that Michael had a fateful encounter with Bogdan Denitch.[135]

Bogdan was unlike anyone Michael had ever befriended before. His father had been a Yugoslav diplomat before the war. Forced into exile first by the Nazis and then by Tito's Communist government after the war, the elder Denitch brought his family to the United States in 1946. Bogdan enrolled in City College soon afterwards, where, as Michael would later note, "he majored in student politics."[136] In 1948, at the age of eighteen, he joined the Young People's Socialist League (YPSL). The darkly handsome young refugee, who spoke with a thick Serbo-Croatian accent, cut a wide swath in anti-Stalinist student circles and seemed perfectly typecast as the romantic revolutionary intriguer. He was a tireless organizer with a bluff, enthusiastic style that tended to provoke strong if varying sentiments.

Among Bogdan's political skills was an aptitude for talent-spotting. On the picket line that day in March 1952 he "immediately noticed this smart guy who didn't look as flaky as the rest of the Catholic Workers, or as nutty as the anarchists." Bogdan, in his own words, attached himself "like a limpet mine" to Michael, hoping to recruit him in to his YPSL faction. Michael, already primed by his self-taught course in the Marxist classics, proved receptive. Bogdan bombarded him with books, magazines, and the works of anti-Stalinist novelists like Victor Serge—a shrewd maneuver, given Michael's literary inclinations. Within a few weeks he had signed up with YPSL. And the next time he was accused of talking like a socialist at the Catholic Worker, he pulled out his party card and displayed it with a satisfied flourish. Everyone was shocked, and Dorothy Day avoided him completely for the next few days.[137]

Michael and Bogdan wrestled over the questions of ends and means. Was personalist sainthood a selfish indulgence in an imperfect world? Together they read and considered the implications of Bertolt Brecht's play about the Chinese Revolution, *The Measures Taken,* in which the "young comrade" is instructed by his party elders in his error of putting "his feelings above his understanding." In the play's most famous passage, the Brechtian equivalent of the Greek chorus proclaims the essence of revolutionary morality:

With whom would the right-minded man not sit
To help the right?
What medicine would taste too bad
To a dying man?
What baseness would you not commit
To root out baseness?

If, finally, you could change the world
What task would you be too good for?[138]

For Brecht, the Stalinist apologist, Michael had no use. There were many forms of "baseness" Michael was not prepared to accept or perform. But Brecht the revolutionary philosopher interested him greatly. Bogdan remembered their long discussion about the play that

> had been used by Whittaker Chambers in testimony before HUAC to illustrate what monsters the Bolsheviks were. Mike and I agreed that, to the contrary, that Brecht offered a reasonable, intellectually subtle and sophisticated argument on behalf of the party which has a thousand eyes and sees in a thousand places. The central point is "change the world, it needs it." . . . The transition for Mike from the Catholic Worker to Marxism was one from sympathizing with the poor, performing good works, and mortifying the flesh, to asking the question, how can you end a system which produces the poor? In order to do that, you have to think in terms of power.[139]

Michael still considered himself a Catholic in good standing as he began his exploration of revolutionary Marxist literature. It bothered him when his mother told him that he could not be both a socialist and a good Catholic. Michael, of course, knew of the example of the French personalists who, although they described themselves as being neither of the Left nor the Right, in fact supported the socialist movement. But he needed sanction from an authority closer to home to appease his mother, and so he sought out the Jesuit scholar John Courtney Murray. Murray was the preeminent liberal Catholic theologian in the United States and would go on to play a central role in the deliberations of the Vatican II council, where he was an outspoken advocate for religious liberty. Murray reassured him that he could indeed be both a socialist and a Catholic, so long as he didn't embrace the materialist aspects of Marxist philosophy. But as late as mid-November 1952 Michael was still trying to reconcile his new political beliefs with his past religious devotion.[140]

Within a few weeks, however, he resolved the dilemma of the relationship between Catholicism and socialism by deciding to leave the church, this time for good. As the thrill of his (re)conversion to Catholicism had worn off over the past year, Michael's old doubts resurfaced. "My own Pascalian wager ended on a bus in December 1952," Michael wrote in his memoirs,

> when I was going to speak at a communion breakfast in Pennsylvania. By the time I arrived at the church I had decided that I could not go to com-

munion since I no longer believed in the faith, not even by way of an existential leap. I gave a little talk on civil rights and, to my embarrassment on the first day of my definitive apostasy, a woman came up to me and said that I had helped her become a better Christian.[141]

Having already rejected the idea of hell, he now rejected the idea of heaven as well:

> I said to myself, "But if there is no hell, and everybody's destined for heaven anyway, why was this earth created so miserably?" In a sense, there's a logic in the heaven-hell dichotomy because it says we were put on earth to freely choose which way to go. If I had decided I couldn't tolerate or believe in one of the options, then I had to reject the other one, too.[142]

Michael still retained a shaky belief in God (although that too would be gone in another year or two), but he felt he could no longer accept the teachings of any Christian church.[143]

Shortly after his fateful bus ride, Michael arranged to meet Dorothy Day for lunch at a restaurant on 2nd Avenue. He dreaded her reaction to the news of his decision to leave not only the Catholic Worker but the church. But she took it in stride, asking only one question: "Was it a woman?" "No Dorothy," Michael replied. "It's theology." And Day, who could be quite puritanical about sins of the flesh but quite tolerant of intellectual disagreement, supposedly replied, "Oh, I'm so happy to hear that."[144]

In moving from the Catholic Left to the Marxist Left, Michael had given up on sainthood. But the path he chose to return to the real world of political engagement and (he hoped) accomplishment was a curious one, since it involved enlisting in one of the most notoriously unworldly sects to be found on the American Left. It must have seemed to some of his more genuinely worldly friends in 1952 that he was trading one "small band of nuts" for another.

CHAPTER FIVE

Resolute Waiting, 1952–1956

*The failure of the socialist movement in the United States is rooted in its inability to resolve a basic dilemma of ethics and politics. The socialist movement, by its very statement of goal and in its rejection of the capitalist order as a whole, could not relate itself to the specific problems of social action in the here-and-now, give-and-take political world. It was trapped by the unhappy problem of living "*in *but not* of *the world," so it could only act, and then inadequately, as the moral, but not political, man in immoral society. . . . A religious movement can split its allegiances and live* in *but not* of *the world . . . ; a political movement can not.*

Daniel Bell
1952[1]

Michael Harrington chose to join the socialist movement the same year that sociologist Daniel Bell half mournfully, half mockingly sounded its death knell. In 1952, Princeton University Press published Bell's magisterial essay "The Background and Development of Marxian Socialism in the United States" as part of a two-volume survey of American socialist history, theory, and philosophy. Bell, who would become known in the course of the next decade as one of the preeminent "New York Intellectuals," had joined the Young People's Socialist League (YPSL) twenty years earlier at the age of thirteen. But he had since abandoned the ideological enthusiasms of his youth for a pragmatic liberalism and an increasingly influential career as writer, editor, and scholar. Bell had long been doubtful of the prospects for any radical reconstruction of American capitalism, but the final blow to his residual socialist sympathies came in 1948 with Norman Thomas's dismal showing in the presidential race. Shortly thereafter Bell began writing the essay that interred American socialism.[2]

Michael read Bell's essay soon after its publication. He was unpersuaded, feeling that Bell too confidently substituted an abstract if eloquent metaphor for a more complicated series of historical events and factors. After all, as a number of Bell's critics have argued subsequently, his essay failed to take in to account the fact that socialist movements in other parts of the world have not been crippled by the supposed dilemma of being located "in but not of the world," and even American socialism, at certain times and in certain places, had known a measure of practical success.

Michael was nonetheless intrigued by the political challenge Bell posed. How could one balance principle and pragmatism in an imperfect world? He was by no means certain of the answer. The Catholic Worker's synthesis of good works and visionary utopianism no longer seemed to him to be a sufficient response to the world's evils. He wanted to go beyond merely feeding and sheltering the least of Christ's brethren, to doing something to abolish the conditions that denied the poor adequate food and housing in the first place. That meant building a movement capable of acquiring and wielding political power—in Bell's terms, "being in and of the world." But could becoming a socialist in America in the 1950s actually help accomplish that end? Considering the marginal existence of socialism in the early 1950s, was Michael's new political allegiance simply another gesture toward the salvation of his own soul—only this time without the material discomforts associated with life in St. Joseph's House?

Michael's first and most pressing problem when he moved out of Chrystie Street at the end of 1952 was the practical one of how to pay the rent on new quarters. He solved that by taking a job as executive secretary of a left-wing legal advocacy organization known as the Workers Defense League (WDL). Founded in 1936, the WDL had a long and honorable record of defending union organizers from official and extra-legal repression. By the early 1950s, reflecting the changing political climate, the WDL's emphasis had shifted to civil liberties cases. Unlike the legal defense groups associated with the Communist Party and its supporters, such as the Emergency Civil Liberties Committee, the WDL was both anti-McCarthyite and anticommunist. Much of its financial backing came from unions with a long tradition of battling the Communists within the labor movement [active board members included James Carey, the president of the International Union of Electrical Workers (IUE), and Charles Zimmerman of the International Ladies Garment Workers Union (ILGWU)].

Norman Thomas, one of the WDL's founders, also remained actively involved in the group's affairs. Staff positions with the WDL were among the few patronage plums that the Socialist Party had at its disposal in the early 1950s, and with his legal training, Michael was certainly a logical candidate. For the next year and a half, he handled the WDL's correspondence, put out a newsletter, took the minutes at board meetings, and the like, and he had plenty of time left over for political work.[3]

Any illusions Michael may have cherished as to the immediate prospects of the socialist movement were soon discarded. In a self-dismissive note written in the spring of 1953, he described his recent political conversion to his University of Chicago friend Jim Finn: "have been working for last year within socialistparty u.s. not so much that it is effective (it isn't), but that one likes company in misery."[4]

Michael's departure from the Catholic Worker had left the outward contours of his life mostly unchanged. He moved from Chrystie Street to an apartment on West 10th Street, but he was still a frequent visitor at the Catholic Worker, especially for the Friday night meetings. He no longer acquired his clothes off the old clothes pile, but his dress remained casual. So did his housekeeping. A writer who visited his apartment later in the decade (when he had moved to another tiny set of rooms on Greenwich Street) left this description of home life chez Harrington:

> The most striking thing about the place was the juxtaposition of the two aspects of its owner—the involved and the detached, or, more precisely, the active and the contemplative. To one side of the room were the meticulously ordered bookshelves—one of those libraries that remind you you never really read Durkheim or Max Weber, much less St. Augustine—while everything else bespoke that antic disorder which is a sign of ideological involvement: beer bottles, half-empty peanut butter jars, notices on pink, pale blue and pale green paper, communications to temporary tenants advising about various exigencies of the committed life—plumbing conditions, garbage disposal arrangements, forwarding addresses—cast in the heroic phraseology of the Left: ("Comrades, the chain works with patience.")[5]

On most days he slept until late in the morning. In the afternoons and into the evening he wrote and tended to the other business that went along with his political vocation. Late at night he repaired to the White Horse Tavern for several hours of drinking, conversation, and folksinging. In the wee hours of the morning, his would usually be the lustiest voice heard in choruses of "Shoot me like an Irish soldier, do not hang me as a dog" and "It's Sister Jenny's turn to throw the bomb."[6]

Whenever possible, Michael would head home from the White Horse with an attractive female companion. His departure from the church ended any remaining ambivalence he had felt about the carnal sin of fornication. As he wrote to Jim Finn in the spring of 1953:

> have plumbed some of the depths, not of my evil, but of my stupidity, i.e. have continued to be irresponsible toward living persons. metaphor: abortion. guy and girl casually meet at party, drunkenly have sex. girl becomes pregnant. three choices; (1) marriage; (2) child to be born, soon to be

> abroad and unknown to you; (3) abortion. all three abhorrent. point: the seeming unproportion of procreative act to child created is symbolic of the whole rather whimsical system of causation in this rather whimsical world.[7]

In the fall of that year he wrote again to Finn, with more confessions, though this time it was hard to tell where soul-searching left off and boasting began:

> state of soul: lousy (could be related to state of body). tired of tom-catting. want to settle down. enter into Responsible Relationship or something like that. haven't yet. succession of women: one a nymphomaniac, one a virgin. both didn't work out for different reasons.[8]

Michael sometimes joked that under socialism all competition would cease—all except for the competition for women.[9] He was not always kind to the women whose favors he sought in the 1950s; even in an era when the sexually predatory nature of the male of the species was taken for granted, some of Michael's female comrades came to regard him as a particularly irresponsible womanizer.[10] But, as usual, Michael was good at disarming potential critics. "I am looking for the BSF of L" he would joke,—his personal shorthand for the "Bitter Sweet Face of Love."[11]

The White Horse was the place he most often sought out the BSF of L. The tavern was a playground for Michael, a place to meet his friends and make sexual assignations—but at the same time it was the place where he perfected the public presence that was to prove an essential part of his political craft. Michael drew people together around him who might not otherwise have been found sitting at the same table in the back room of the White Horse—Catholic Workers, *Commonweal* editors, socialists, anarchists, and the occasional liberal Democrat, like Daniel Patrick Moynihan. They were a good audience on which to test his ideas and arguments. He did a lot of thinking out loud in those long evenings in the back room of the tavern, and if a turn of phrase or a new perspective on some political or literary question won a favorable response from his listeners, it was apt to show up later in one of his speeches or articles. "A transcript of a barroom chat with Michael Harrington," an admiring journalist later noted, "would read like the first draft of a slightly discursive *New Republic* essay."[12]

His ideas took on force from his persona. When David McReynolds, a young Los Angeles socialist, visited New York in the autumn of 1953, he encountered Michael holding forth in the back room of the White Horse. By that time, McReynolds and Michael were at factional odds within the YPSL, but McReynolds still found it hard not to fall under Michael's spell.

"Spent the evening listening to Mike Harrington tell of his experiences in the Catholic Worker," McReynolds wrote to a friend back in California, "and realize how terribly superficial my whole life is."[13] Judith Malina, cofounder of the Living Theater, encountered Harrington the following year, 1954, in the White Horse. Though briefly smitten romantically by Harrington (she was too committed an anarchist to be won to his socialist politics), she described him in a journal entry with shrewd detachment and an actress's appreciation of a good performance:

> At the White Horse, Mike Harrington and his friends talk; most of it is chatter, but it's never the solemn defeatism of the [San] Remo. . . . Mike is heroic. . . . That is, he takes in the environment and its people and includes them in a generalization of which he is the center. Thus the hero is in control without needing to be in command. Mike is handsome and doesn't rave in extravagant adjectives about what he likes, but smiles acceptingly, and his approbation is highly valued.[14]

In his mid-twenties, Michael was no longer the dazzling newcomer from the Midwest. If he remained boyish in appearance, he now also conveyed the sophisticated assurance of a born-again New Yorker, with an intimate knowledge of the more bohemian quarters of the city. His circle of acquaintances and admirers grew ever wider, although the number of people with whom he was genuinely intimate remained distinctly limited. He was on his way to becoming an institution in the Village—not surprisingly, he was asked to contribute a piece to the first issue of the *Village Voice* when it began publishing in 1955.[15] He had established for himself what was already becoming a legendary past, but he continued to give the impression of someone whose best days were still to come.

What is hard to reconcile about these years in Michael's life is the gulf that had opened between his personal qualities—of which so many people thought so highly—and the character of his politics, which did not inspire the same universal admiration. For Michael didn't simply join the socialist movement in 1952; he also joined an ongoing faction fight within the movement—the kind of maddeningly petty squabbling that over the years has caused countless potential recruits to swear off any future involvement with the organized Left. But that was not Michael's reaction. Rather than remaining aloof or shrinking in dismay from sectarian bloodshed, he waded in happily. Daniel Bell, writing about an earlier generation of left-wing sectarians, could just as easily have been describing Michael and his young socialist comrades in the early and mid-1950s: They enjoyed "the illusions of settling the fate of history, the mimetic combat on the plains of destiny, and the vicarious sense of power in demolishing opponents."[16] It all seemed very unlike

Michael, who until now had been known for his combination of keen intelligence, modest charm, and self-deprecating wit. And yet Michael's fling with sectarian politics would prove a crucial episode in shaping the political vision that was to guide him in coming decades.

In 1953, the Socialist Party barely managed to pay the rent for an office and pay the salaries for a few staffers necessary to maintain a semblance of a national headquarters in New York City. It had reached that advanced stage of organizational decay where its most reliable source of income was from bequests left to it by its rapidly dying-off cadre of elderly members. The most valuable political asset remaining to the SP was Norman Thomas, its six-time presidential candidate. But notwithstanding his still considerable energy, Thomas was getting on in years; he was already in his late sixties by the time Michael joined the movement. And since 1950, when Thomas had tried unsuccessfully to persuade his fellow socialists to abandon their futile quadrennial exercises in presidential politics, he largely withdrew into his own letterhead operations, devoting himself to performing such good works for peace or civil liberties as he could without bothering himself with the organizational minutiae of keeping the SP alive. Were Thomas to have suddenly dropped dead in 1952, he would have left behind no credible successor. Without new blood and new leadership, it was an absolute certainty that the SP would soon lumber off to that elephant's graveyard of the American Left inhabited by the carcasses of the Socialist Labor Party, the Industrial Workers of the World, and the like. Indeed, Daniel Bell had already consigned the party to its dusty fate, writing in the conclusion to his 1952 essay that "American socialism as a political and social fact had become simply a notation in the archives of history."[17]

Thus when even a single young and politically talented recruit (and one with a good Irish-Catholic name, no less) came along and signed up with the Young People's Socialist League, older socialists took it as an occasion for celebration. Michael would soon give them reason to change their minds. For at the very moment when he was emerging as a YPSL leader, he was also attracted to a new adult mentor, Max Shachtman. And Shachtman's name, for reasons that require a brief historical detour, was anathema within the Socialist Party.

The Young People's Socialist League had been a blessing and a curse to the adult socialist movement for decades. Originating as a local youth circle launched by Chicago socialists in 1907, YPSL was established as the national youth affiliate of the Socialist Party in 1913. Those were heady years for American socialists. The SP grew to about 100,000, and in 1912 the party's presidential candidate, Eugene Debs, received nearly a million votes. The health of the adult movement was reflected in the lusty growth of its offspring. By the time the United States entered the First World War there were over a hundred YPSL branches in cities across the country, with a membership approaching 10,000.

The First World War brought the hardships of official repression and internal division to the YPSL, as it did to its parent organization. The Socialist Party splintered in 1919, with many of its former supporters departing for one or another of the two rival Communist groups that had sprung up in emulation of the recent Bolshevik Revolution in Russia. Establishing a pattern in which young socialists could be relied upon to choose the most extreme left wing of the alternatives put before them during any factional debate, the yipsels voted virtually en masse to affiliate with the Communists.[18]

After a decade in the doldrums, both the Socialist Party and its youth movement revived in the early 1930s. The onset of the depression and then Norman Thomas's vibrant presidential campaign in 1932 attracted thousands of young supporters to the movement. By the end of 1932, SP membership climbed to perhaps as many as 25,000, and YPSL membership to about 2,500. The party's influence and that of YPSL seemed to be spreading rapidly. In straw polls held that autumn at colleges and universities from Columbia to Colorado, Norman Thomas ran a close second to Franklin Delano Roosevelt in popularity, and in some instances even bested him. In 1932, YPSL's future seemed as bright as that of American capitalism seemed dismal.

In Debs's time, the YPSL, like the SP, had been primarily a working-class movement. Many of the young people attracted to the socialist cause in the 1930s were also from working-class backgrounds, but with an important difference. As a result of the assimilation of the previous immigrant generation, as well as of the expansion of higher education, the new recruits were bound for middle-class status and professional careers (even if in the midst of the Great Depression that seemed an unlikely outcome to them). Most of the new generation of yipsels came from college campuses—City College of New York, Brooklyn College, and the University of Chicago among them—and, accordingly, most of YPSL's activism in the 1930s (when it wasn't consumed by internal debates) took the form of vying for influence within various "mass" student organizations, like the student branch of the League for Industrial Democracy (LID) and the American Student Union (ASU).[19]

But even as Norman Thomas was attracting large and enthusiastic crowds in the 1932 election campaign, inside the Socialist Party rancor and discord were spreading. The division was in part generational and in part political. In the SP's internal battles, the yipsels initially lined up with Thomas and the left-leaning "Militant" faction against the more conservative SP "Old Guard." The Old Guard, who cut their political teeth in the Debsian era, were concentrated in New York City. They were, for the most part, Jewish, many of them foreign-born, with long-standing ties to the labor movement, especially the needle trades unions. They also controlled such important party institutions as the Rand School, publications like the *Jewish Daily Forward* and the *New Leader,* and radio station WEVD. The Militants, in contrast, in addition to being younger by several decades, were more likely to be native born and included in their ranks Protestants as well as Jews, and midwesterners as well as New Yorkers. And they were, like young radicals of most generations, impatient. As one of their number, Irving Howe, would recall: "The youth had entered the movement in the hope of creating a new world, a new life, and now the old-timers came along, grumbling about defeats, mistakes, betrayals."[20]

Though more "American" in background and style than their factional opponents, the Militants flirted at the same time with a kind of homegrown Leninism. They were eager for action and innovation; although critical of the Communists for their subservience to Soviet directives, the Militants also felt a sneaking admiration for the brash certainty with which Communists comported themselves. They were, for a period in the mid-'30s, willing to lend a sympathetic ear to Communist calls for a "united front." The SP's Old Guard, in contrast, had long before made up their minds about the utter incompatibility of their own politics with those espoused by sympathizers with the Soviet experiment; they also felt increasingly drawn toward the practical benefits offered the union movement in alliance with President Roosevelt and the New Deal. To the Militants and most of the yipsels (with a few exceptions among the latter, like Daniel Bell), any inclination to back a "bourgeois politician" like Roosevelt was a betrayal of the party's historical tasks at the very moment of the old order's final crisis. Left-leaning Socialists—persuaded by the seemingly irrefutable economic evidence of capitalism's imminent demise, competing with young Communists for influence and legitimacy on the campuses, and intoxicated by a romantic reading of the Marxist classics—debated long into the night over resolutions bristling with references to armed insurrection and the like.[21]

Thomas, the Militants, and the yipsels emerged victorious when the Old Guard (along with its substantial financial and institutional resources) pulled out of the SP in 1936 to form a new and more moderate group known as the Social Democratic Federation (SDF). The departing Old Guard also helped form the American Labor Party (ALP) in order to provide a place on the New York State ballot where former socialists could cast their ballots for President Roosevelt and other New Deal candidates without having to take the repugnant step of actually voting the Democratic line. (Ironically, within a few years the ALP would fall into the hands of the Communists; some of the Old Guard were then instrumental in forming New York's Liberal Party.)

Minus the Old Guard, the Socialist Party was now, in theory, free to realize its revolutionary ambitions. But the bright hopes of 1932 were not to be realized. Part of the problem was President Roosevelt. As Norman Thomas once quipped unhappily, the New Deal succeeded in carrying out the Socialist Party platform—"on a stretcher."[22] Thomas, who had received nearly 900,000 votes nationwide in the 1932 presidential election, received less than 200,000 in 1936, the year of Roosevelt's resounding landslide re-election victory.[23]

The SP's woes were only beginning. The battle between the Militants and the Old Guard had not yet subsided when a new factional war was sparked by American followers of the exiled Bolshevik leader Leon Trotsky. Trotskyists believed that a world proletarian revolution would come within their lifetime, but only after they had succeeded in discrediting the Stalinist betrayers of the international revolutionary cause.

Following their expulsion from the Communist movement in the late 1920s, Trotskyists around the world had been trying to find an appropriate organizational home for themselves. As Joseph Stalin consolidated his power in the Soviet Union in the early 1930s, Trotsky decided it was time for his followers to form their own rival vanguard parties, as constituent parts of a new revolutionary "Fourth International."

In 1936, however, Trotsky changed his mind. Craving the access to potential recruits offered by the socialist parties in Europe and America; he instructed his followers to disband their own parties and sign up as socialists. This maneuver (known as the "French turn," for the country in which it was first attempted) represented a dramatic shift for the Trotskyists, who had previously derided Socialists as reformist sell-outs, second in villainy only to Stalinists as misleaders of the working class. Trotsky himself had once famously jeered that Norman Thomas was a socialist only "as the result of a misunderstanding."[24] But Thomas's SP now appeared as an extremely important prize for the Trotskyist movement, despite its weakness compared to its European counterparts. American Trotskyists numbered no more than a few hundred throughout most of the 1930s—but that made them, nonetheless, the largest single such grouping in the world. If the "French turn" had a chance of working anywhere in the world, it was in the United States.

Although Thomas was committed to making the SP an "all inclusive party" of the Left, he was dubious about the proposed alliance with the Trotskyists. Unfortunately for the future of the SP, he allowed himself to be persuaded by his younger associates. The Militants were convinced they could control the Trotskyists, using them as additional organizational muscle in the struggle against the Old Guard. But, as Thomas had feared, the Trotskyists' loyalty to their new allies was, to say the least, conditional. They were determined to replace the ersatz Leninism of the Militants with the real thing, and they quickly organized an opposition faction within the SP. American

Trotskyists demonstrated in the late 1930s that a small band of highly disciplined revolutionaries could prevail against a larger opposing force—at least when that force consisted of fellow radicals rather than of the power of the capitalist state.

Within the American socialist movement, the Trotskyists concentrated on winning the allegiance of the yipsels, and young socialists responded eagerly to their overtures. The Trotskyists offered them something no one else on the Left could—the chance to cast themselves as heroic partisans of the Bolshevik Revolution without sharing the burden of apologizing for every current twist and turn of Soviet foreign policy.

In 1937, when the Trotskyists were finally expelled from the SP and went on to form the Socialist Workers Party (SWP), they took most of the yipsels with them. What they left behind were the wreckage of Norman Thomas's party and a lot of bitter memories. By the end of 1937, SP membership had dwindled to about 7,000, less than a third of what it had been five years earlier. Of course, the battle with the Old Guard and the appeal of Franklin Roosevelt were contributing factors in the SP's decline. But, tellingly, the Trotskyists actually *wanted* to take credit for the disaster. As SWP leader James Cannon would later boast, in a classic and unintended revelation of how the sectarian mind worked:

> Partly as a result of our experience in the Socialist Party and our fight in there, the Socialist Party was put on the side lines. This was a great achievement, because it was an obstacle in the path of building a revolutionary party. The problem is not merely one of building a revolutionary party, but of clearing obstacles from its path. Every other party is a rival. Every other party is an obstacle.[25]

Exquisitely skilled in the techniques of internal party warfare, the Trotskyists failed to beat their factional swords into plowshares once they had withdrawn into their own camp. No sooner had they enjoyed their "great achievement" within the SP than they turned those same lethal weapons on their own ranks.

This new round of strife was precipitated by the onset of the Second World War. Like most groups on the Left, the Trotskyists had been predicting war all through the 1930s and greeted its arrival in 1939 both as confirmation of their own political acuity and as prelude to renewed revolutionary upheaval. The world war of 1914–1918 had ended with the establishment of soviets (of greater or lesser endurance) in St. Petersburg, Berlin, Budapest, and even in Seattle. Lenin and Trotsky had advocated turning imperialist war into civil war, and as a result they had been lifted from obscurity to the commanding heights of revolutionary power three years into the last imperialist war; surely their formula would again work its wonders in the new imperialist war.

But the Trotskyists ran into problems applying this otherwise comforting analogy in 1939–1940, because this time a self-proclaimed socialist homeland was also involved. Despite the signing of the Nazi–Soviet pact in 1939, it was clearly not going to be long before the Soviet Union was pulled into the broader war, even if it was not yet certain on which side. What policy, then, should Trotskyists adopt on "the Russian Question"?

Throughout the 1930s, some Trotskyists had wondered how they could condemn everything Stalin did and stood for and yet still regard the country he led as the socialist homeland—a "degenerated workers state," as Trotsky described it. When war broke out, Trotsky insisted from his exile command post in Mexico that his followers around the world continue to make the "unconditional defense of the Soviet Union" a political priority. For Trotsky it was axiomatic that when two capitalist nations fought one another, revolutionary socialists should refuse to back either side. But in a war between capitalist and socialist powers, revolutionaries did not enjoy the luxury of adopting a "plague on both your houses" stance. True revolutionaries had to rally to the Soviet Union in its hour of danger. James Cannon agreed, and he attempted to hold his followers to that principle. But Max Shachtman, who along with Cannon had been one of the cofounders of the Trotskyist movement in the United States, broke with Trotsky and Cannon on the issue.[26]

Of all the mentors that Michael Harrington would adopt during his political career, including such notable figures as Day and Thomas, Shachtman was destined to exercise the most lasting influence upon him. Born in Warsaw in 1904, Shachtman was brought by his parents to New York City as an infant. He was a precocious student and entered City College at age sixteen, but a bout of ill health, along with more pressing political interests, soon led him to drop out. It was within the Communist and Trotskyist movements that Shachtman gained his true education and found the arena in which he could display his considerable intellectual gifts.

Cannon and Shachtman divided responsibilities and constituencies in the Trotskyist movement. Cannon was the Trotskyists' public figure; an effective if bombastic public speaker out of the Debsian and IWW tradition, he was immensely popular with the movement's small but capable circle of trade union activists. Shachtman, a foreign-born Jew with a New York accent and a calculating demeanor, was better suited to tending to internal party tasks and debate. He edited the Trotskyists' newspaper, the *Militant,* and its theoretical journal, the *New International.* He also served as Trotsky's secretary, personal emissary, and traveling companion. In his most significant achievement in the 1930s, Shachtman helped marshal evidence to discredit the Moscow trials that were then decimating the ranks of the Old Bolsheviks in the

Soviet Union. Shachtman became a kind of walking encyclopedia of international Communist lore; one of his favorite rhetorical devices was to list the names of Stalin's victims from within the Communist movement, country by country. To his admirers, and particularly to the young, college-educated recruits who came to the movement from the YPSL, Shachtman seemed a living link with the best traditions of the Russian and international revolutionary tradition.

Shachtman was also renowned for bravado performances in debate. Phyllis Jacobson, a young Trotskyist recruit, recalled that Shachtman's speeches "were always full of irony; they had very mordant wit. He knew words; he knew how to fire your imagination; he was a great mimic." Shachtman inspired his young followers with the sense of being part of the elect. Irving Howe, who had become known as one of "Max's boys" while still a high school student in the Bronx, commented in his memoirs: "If Shachtman, during one of his marathon speeches, made a joke about Karl Radek or threw out a fleeting mention of 'the August bloc,' those of us in the know felt as gleeful as a philosophy graduate student pouncing on a subtle point in a Wittgenstein blue book."[27]

Committed as he was to proletarian revolution, Shachtman was no Eugene Debs or even James Cannon. He could never have led a strike or administered a union. But he came along at the moment in the history of American radicalism when such capacities were beginning to diminish in importance in comparison to the ability to appeal to a different constituency—young people, particularly those with college backgrounds. Much more than Cannon, Shachtman had the ability to inspire youthful radicals. Julius Jacobson, like Howe a product of the Bronx socialist movement, remembered Shachtman as "a young man's person. It was part of his personality. He was a kibbitzer; he was fun to be with; you could make jokes with him; he was bawdy; he'd hug you; he'd pinch your cheek." From the 1930s through the 1960s, Shachtman's greatest political asset was his ability to attract talented disciples. The best and the brightest of them, from Irving Howe to Irving Kristol, eventually rejected the substance of Shachtman's teachings, but few regretted the rigorous political training with which he had endowed them.[28]

Although Shachtman's milieu may have been grubby radical halls, he was never simply a party hack. In the best Marxist tradition, Shachtman took ideas seriously as a way of understanding and changing the world. When those ideas began to seem inadequate to him, he moved on. His political formulas were often defined narrowly, and he was not above defending them with a witty demagoguery, but he was not dogmatically wedded to any set of inherited ideas. In the fall of 1939, finding his beliefs about the "Russian Question" at odds with those of his own long-time political hero Trotsky, he did not hesitate to follow through on the logic of his own position. In collaboration with New York University philosopher James Burnham, and drawing upon ideas previously circulating in the Trotskyist movement, Shachtman came to the conclusion that the Soviet Union was no longer a "workers state" at all, "degenerated" or otherwise. The Stalinist bureaucracy represented a new kind of ruling class that collectively controlled the means of production through its control of the state apparatus. The Soviet Union was thus an entirely new kind of society, neither capitalist nor socialist. It was instead a bastard hybrid that Shachtman labeled "bureaucratic collectivist." State ownership of the means of production in itself was not socialism; indeed, it could be the basis for fastening upon the working class a subordinate status more absolute and degrading than that prevailing under capitalism.

Shachtman's critique resembled, and to an extent drew upon, theories of "totalitarianism" that were growing ever more popular among radical intellectuals. In the aftermath of the Moscow trials, and particularly with the signing of the Stalin–Hitler Pact, many intellectuals came to regard Nazism and communism as simply two sides of the same coin. This analysis often went hand-in-hand with a sense of the futility of political action, a disenchantment with any kind of grand theory of society, and a fear of any mass mobilization of popular sentiment.[29]

But Shachtman's version of the totalitarian thesis was intended to have a very different effect on wavering radicals. The good news, as delivered by Shachtman, was that Stalinism, like capitalism, was a system that carried within itself the seeds of its own destruction. One need not choose between the two fundamentally flawed systems. There was another choice, a "third camp," the camp of genuine socialism, which stood equally committed to the overthrow of capitalism and bureaucratic collectivism. Regrettably this third camp had no country (and in most places did not even have a party) to call its own. But in the revolutionary upheaval that would surely be unleashed by the Second World War, both capitalism and Stalinism would be fatally weakened, and the workers of the world could resume their march down the path Lenin and Trotsky had blazed in 1917. There was no need to apologize for any aspect of Stalinism, because the system that had developed in the Soviet Union since Lenin's death and Trotsky's fall from power was in no way representative of genuine socialism.

In 1940 Shachtman and Burnham led their followers out of the Socialist Workers Party and formed a new group, the Workers Party. Having decided that Marxism, Leninism, and Stalinism were indeed one and the same phenomenon, Burnham soon parted company with Shachtman and embarked on a rightward ideological odyssey that led him to William F. Buckley's *National Review* in the 1950s. Shachtman was probably happy to see Burnham go; he did not comfortably share the limelight in the organizations he created. Members of the Workers Party subsequently became known in left-wing nomenclature as "the Shachtmanites."

In their habit of draping themselves in the mantle of the Bolshevik Revolution, in their selective reliance on historical analogy, and in their willful misreading of the temper of the American working class, the Shachtmanites seemed no different from the myriad of tiny radical sects that preceded or followed them into oblivion. But the Workers Party was not simply another collection of revolutionary flagellants confidently awaiting the millennium in blissful discomfort. From the beginning there was something that distinguished it from its competitors on the ultra-Left. The political language favored by the Shachtmanites was one of stern confidence: "history," "the masses," "the tasks of the moment," and so forth. But there was a continuing and growing tension between the conceptual limits imposed by this language and the dynamics of the political culture that characterized the group. This was a party founded on doubt rather than on certainty. In a 1944 article reviewing the origins of the Workers Party, Shachtman remembered:

> I had developed some doubts . . . on the correctness of our traditional position, without being able to say to myself, and therefore to others, that this position was fundamentally false and that an alternative position had to replace it. . . . Doubts are bridges you cannot stand on for long. Either you go back to the old views or move on to new ones.[30]

The Shachtmanites were usually at their politically most creative when they were beginning to doubt something they had previously taken for a certainty.

The Shachtmanites were never numerous; their organizational strength peaked in the mid-1940s at about 500 members. With industrial jobs suddenly easy to come by due to the war, Workers Party "colonizers" fanned out across the country to places like Buffalo and Akron. Some became deeply involved in rank-and-file labor insurgency during the era when the official union movement was committed to maintaining the "no strike pledge," and a few subsequently gained elected or staff positions within the industrial unions. The Workers Party newspaper, *Labor Action,* saw its circulation rise to 40,000 readers during the war. But few genuine workers actually joined the party organized in their name. Ernest Erber, organizer of the WP's Philadelphia branch and a former YPSL leader, concluded in 1943 that the party was never going to grow as long as it looked for its inspiration to the model of the Leninist vanguard:

> We live a life apart from our surroundings. We develop our own sense of values, our own moral concepts, our own habits, and even our own jargon. . . . Our training is in the tradition of the Jesuits. Money, position in

life, family, personal inclinations as to kind of work, place of work, place of residence, must all yield when necessary to the requirements of the party.[31]

Shachtman had no sympathy for Erber's doubts during the war, but afterward (and following Erber's departure from the party), the WP reconstituted itself with the somewhat more modest self-description of the Independent Socialist League (ISL).

The Shachtmanites were, of course, disappointed in their expectations that world revolution would follow on the heels of the Second World War. As Shachtman's former comrade Dwight Macdonald would note in his journal *Politics* in 1946, "Trotsky's deadline is here and the revolution is not."[32] But, unlike Macdonald, Shachtman and his remaining followers were intrigued by and found political consolation in both the British Labour Party's parliamentary electoral triumph in Britain in 1945 and the sweeping social reforms enacted by the Labour government over the next half decade. For the first time, Shachtman seriously considered models for the creation of socialism that did not require some final catastrophic political convulsion. Throughout the late 1940s and early 1950s, Shachtman and his followers continued to describe themselves as Leninists and still piously observed the Bolshevik holidays. But, in the final analysis, they no longer expected to participate in a repetition of the Bolshevik Revolution in America. With the formation of the ISL, Shachtmanites were envisaging a new role for themselves, what British socialists called a "ginger group," the left-wing conscience within a broader movement for social change.

The problem was that there was no such movement in the early 1950s, and the ISL remained as politically marginal as the WP had been in the previous decade. The group dwindled to a few dozen activists and a few hundred increasingly inactive dues-payers. Even Shachtman was rarely seen around the ISL office from week to week. After years of penurious existence as a full-time revolutionary, he moved out to Floral Park, Long Island, and began running a small mail order business marketing hi-fi components, while raising orchids as a hobby. If this descent into the lifestyle of the petit bourgeoisie was in any way troubling to the former aide-de-camp to Leon Trotsky, Shachtman kept his discontents to himself. Only occasionally would he rouse himself from self-imposed internal exile among his orchids for a gala public occasion such as his 1951 debate with Earl Browder (who by Soviet directive had been deposed as leader of the American Communists in 1945). Shachtman brought down the house on that occasion, when, after intoning the list of leaders of foreign Communist parties murdered on Stalin's orders, he pointed suddenly to an ashen-faced Browder and declared, "There but for an accident of geography sits a corpse."[33]

Aside from such symbolic triumphs, the only thing the remaining

Shachtmanites had going for them was their youth group, the Socialist Youth League (SYL). And there wasn't much there either at the start of the 1950s: several dozen members clustered around a few campus outposts. But, unlike their elders, the young Shachtmanites still had plenty of energy, and they had inherited an idea—the "third camp"—that made them attractive to other energetic young people like Bogdan Denitch and Michael Harrington, who were looking for a way out of radicalism's impasse.

The year Michael joined the Young People's Socialist League, he was in a select company: YPSL recruited all of sixty-two new members that year, making for a grand total of one hundred and thirty-four members nationwide.[34] In the inhospitable political climate of the McCarthy era, it is surprising that even that many new recruits could be found who were willing to put careers and reputations at risk; virtually everyday there were newspaper headlines recording the fate of individuals branded "security risks," hauled before congressional investigating committees, fired from jobs, denied passports, deported as undesirable aliens, and on and on, because of past political sympathies and affiliations. The Communists bore the brunt of this assault, but radicals of all stripes, including Norman Thomas socialists, could list their own martyrs to the Red Scare. With new blood in scarce supply, ambitious radical organizers looked for ways to recycle the existing supply. Accordingly, young anti-Stalinists in the 1950s spent an inordinate amount of time thinking up ways to raid one another's organizations. And no one devoted more time and passion to this enterprise than Bogdan Denitch.

Bogdan and Michael, as noted, had met on a picket line in 1952 and were soon fast friends as well as comrades. Bogdan had an even more pronounced tendency than Michael for romantic self-dramatization. A photograph taken of him in the summer of 1951—which he spent working in a Reading, Pennsylvania, factory along with a group of fellow yipsels—showed him sitting on a chair, bare-chested, holding a newspaper in one hand and a .45 automatic pistol in the other, while puffing contemplatively on his pipe—the intellectual as man of action. He particularly liked to enthrall attractive young women with imaginary tales of wartime resistance activities in Yugoslavia.

Bogdan was destined to be the most intimate male friend of Michael's adult life. Although two years younger than Michael, he would, at first, play the role of older brother—protector, benefactor, and instructor. Like many strong bonds, this was an attraction of opposites. Bogdan could be loud, crude, reckless. He took risks. Whereas Michael's defiance of bourgeois authority was limited to occasionally sneaking into a ballet at intermission, Bogdan would spend several years in the mid-1950s dealing with the consequences of having impulsively pocketed a pile of blank draft cards while reporting to his local draft board. But Bogdan also offered his friends a kind of practical generosity that Michael was incapable of, as he was the first to acknowledge. "The difference between Bogdan and me," Michael once remarked self-mockingly to Peter Novick (who had been recruited into the movement by Denitch in the 1950s), "is that I'm a warm, caring, sensitive person, and Bogdan is cold and unfeeling":

> Let me give you an example. Suppose you were sick. I'd be so upset, I'd go over to the White Horse and drink myself insensible with grief. If anyone came by, I'd say "Have you heard? Peter is sick. Isn't it awful? Let's drink to his getting better." But Bogdan! Would he fret, would he suffer, would he anguish? Not at all: he'd be too busy doing your cooking, recruiting girls to come up and rub your back, taking out your laundry. That's the difference between Bogdan and me—I'm a warm, caring person, and he's cold and unfeeling.[35]

According to a joke circulating in student radical circles in the 1950s: "If you sent Bogdan onto campus for 12 hours he will end up with a party group. If you sent him onto campus for 24 hours he will end up with a party group and two pregnancies. If you leave him on campus for 36 hours you will have three pregnancies and three factions."[36] Michael shared Bogdan's taste for women—in fact, sometimes for the same women, who they would become involved with serially. What was more surprising was how quickly he came to share Denitch's other passion.

Good-hearted, amiable Michael, defying expectations, proved a natural at faction fighting. Not the least of his gifts was the fact that he didn't look like a factional conspirator. Within the movement, as Bogdan later acknowledged, he and Michael functioned as a kind of "bad cop/good cop" team. In public settings, hard-nosed Bogdan Denitch would give the polarizing speeches and open-faced Michael Harrington would make the conciliatory appeals. In reality, behind closed doors and under Bogdan's tutelage, Michael displayed a hitherto unrealized skill and delight in sectarian strategy that matched Denitch's own. As Denitch recalled, "Mike was very much of a party-building type, which is something that people who write about Saint Michael will not tell you."[37]

Michael's decision to turn on his political elders in the Socialist Party in 1952–1953 was not simply a question of generational psychodynamics, although that undoubtedly figured in the conflict. There were genuine, troubling, and not easily resolvable issues involved. When the Korean War broke out, younger socialists by and large opposed American involvement. This was no more an abstract issue for young socialists in the 1950s than the Vietnam War would be for New Leftists in the 1960s. Some of Michael's comrades were drafted into the military; others were jailed as draft refusers, including YPSL's national chairman, Vern Davidson. Michael, of course, went through his own period of uncertainty over whether to serve in the military or resist the draft. Despite the SP's long tradition of antiwar militancy, the party's leaders decided they had no choice but to endorse the American war effort in Korea. The threat posed by communism had come to outweigh any other consideration in their minds. "The outstanding conflict today," Thomas and other prominent socialists declared in a manifesto distributed internationally during the war by the Voice of America, "is between democracy, with all its human and capitalist imperfections, and totalitarian despotism."[38]

Left-wing critics gibed that the SP had become "State Department socialists," and Thomas's support for the U.S. military role in Korea provided the Shachtmanites, ever-alert for organizational advantage, with an opening for yet another raid on YPSL. Young Shachtmanites in the SYL began to make overtures to the yipsels, encouraging them to join in common "third-camp" antiwar activities. Among other initiatives, Schactman's young disciples launched a new quarterly antiwar journal known as *Anvil.* Supposedly independent, *Anvil's* editorial board was heavily weighted with SYL members. Denitch was among the third-camp sympathizers recruited to its editorial board, and he, in turn, recruited Michael as an editor.[39]

For adult Socialists all of this stirred unpleasant memories. They were willing to put up with a certain amount of political impertinence from their youth organization (otherwise they weren't going to have a youth organization), but they had no intention of sitting by idly while Shachtman pulled off yet another successful pillaging operation within YPSL. The Socialist Party had maintained a long-standing ban against any collaboration between its members and "totalitarian" organizations, a ban that extended from Communists to Trotskyists and Shachtmanites—the latter two groups were included in the ban because of their attachment to the principles of the Bolshevik Revolution, if not the practices of the current Soviet regime. Accordingly, YPSL members were forbidden by the SP to sell, sponsor, or in any way promote *Anvil.* The yipsels chafed at adult interference and what they regarded as a denial of internal democracy. At YPSL's December 1951 convention, the antiwar faction (which at that point included both Denitch's "third campers" and a grouping of more traditional pacifists) gained control of the organization. In what amounted to tossing the gauntlet in the dust at their elders' feet, they passed a resolution warmly endorsing *Anvil.*[40]

Relations between the adult and youth group worsened steadily in 1952, the year that Michael joined YPSL. Denitch's faction edged out the pacifists as the leading voice in the group's left wing; Bogdan's then wife, Carol Denitch, took over as YPSL national secretary following Vern Davidson's indictment for draft resistance.[41]

Writing in the *Young Socialist Review,* YPSL's internal discussion bulletin, pacifist David McReynolds complained of the young Shachtmanites' pretensions of being "the vanguard" and of their tendency to turn everything into a theoretical debate: "I like a little theory now and then as much as the next man, perhaps a little better. But in the S.Y.L. you don't comment on the weather or women, but on the latest theory of the Master, i.e. Max."[42]

McReynolds, a UCLA student who had joined the Socialist Party in the fall of 1951, hoped to win the SP back to an antiwar position. He did not intend to needlessly antagonize its leaders, nor to split off a chunk of YPSL to augment the Shachtmanites. But in New York, that was exactly the direction in which Bogdan, now supported by Michael, was heading. They pushed ahead with plans for further and closer collaboration with the SYLers, including joint statements, forums, summer schools, and the like.[43]

Matters came to a head just as the Korean War—the initial cause of YPSL disaffection with the adult party—finally ground to its inconclusive halt in the summer of 1953. At YPSL's national convention, held in Reading in April, the delegates resolved to call a "Young Socialist Unity Conference" for the following fall—with invitations extended to the SYL and other groups—to realize the goal of creating a "unified National socialist youth organization."[44] The Denitch faction swept the elections for the YPSL's ruling National Executive Committee (NEC); Michael was among those elected to the NEC. Carol Denitch continued as YPSL national secretary until May, when Bogdan succeeded her in the post.

In the meantime, Norman Thomas's patience had run out. In May he proposed to the SP's national executive committee that YPSL be rebuked for inviting Shachtman as a convention speaker. Shachtman "is an able man," Thomas conceded. Nonetheless, YPSL's invitation had been "grossly improper," since Shachtman was someone:

> whose position is definitely opposed to democratic socialism as we understand it. . . . He is a modified Trotskyist and our trouble with the Trotskyist, Shachtman among them, is a matter of history. I think it is a rather serious matter when our youth section shows such decided Trotskyist sympathy.[45]

Charges and countercharges flew back and forth between the older and younger camps, some of them reflecting political differences, others clearly a product of a generation gap. (Norman Thomas was also upset that YPSL's 1952 May Day leaflet, designed by Michael and Bogdan, included a poem from e.e. cummings with the line, "there is some shit i will not eat.")[46] The SP finally cut off its financial subsidy to its youth group. Bogdan, Michael, and several other yipsels were called before a subcommittee of the New York Local of the Socialist Party and ordered to cease all collaboration with the

SYL immediately. When they refused, the Socialist Party suspended YPSL's New York district. Bogdan and Michael were unfazed; ignoring the SP's edict, they polled YPSL's dues-paying members in good standing—the sixty-three who still remained—on whether or not to disaffiliate with the adult movement. In August 1953, by a slim majority (thirty-five in favor—and of those, twenty of them from the suspended New York district), YPSL officially declared its independence from the SP. A month later, in a pride-saving gesture akin to shutting the barn door after the cows have fled, the Socialist Party formally expelled Bogdan, Michael, and other supporters of the split.[47]

Michael and Bogdan were still relative amateurs in such factional endeavors. Behind them stood the éminence grise, Max Shachtman. Shachtman had met privately and frequently with the rebel yipsels during the last months of the battle with the SP, helping them plot strategy. When the split occurred, he was doubtless pleased with himself for picking up some new and talented disciples. He probably also enjoyed the sheer sport of stirring up a faction fight in a rival organization. But the YPSL split was, in retrospect, an ill-considered move, revealing how much Shachtman—for all the rethinking he was doing on large political issues—was still the prisoner of old sectarian habits. For those socialists with long memories—which is to say virtually the entire Socialist Party in the early 1950s—Shachtman had confirmed his reputation as a malicious spoiler. And now Bogdan and, by association, Michael were similarly branded.[48]

With the YPSL tie to the SP severed, nothing stood in the way of the merger of the SYLers and the yipsels. Accordingly, at a three-day convention held in the ISL's loft on West 14th Street in February 1954, the merged organization, dubbed the Young Socialist League (YSL), was officially brought into existence. Max Dombrow, a veteran of the SYL, was elected the first chairman of the new group. For their part, the former yipsels were awarded with the top slots of the YSL's new publication. Bogdan and Michael shared the editorship of the "Young Socialist Challenge," a four-page sheet that appeared as a weekly insert in the ISL's newspaper *Labor Action.*

A year and a half later, when the YSL held its second national convention in Chicago over Labor Day weekend, Michael challenged Dombrow for the post of national chairman. Some delegates expressed doubts about Michael's commitment to the movement, but with his growing reputation as a writer and speaker, and given his midwestern Irish-Catholic (which is to say, non-New York, non-Jewish) background, his election was never really in doubt.[49] Debbie Meier, who was an "old-timer" in the movement, having joined the SYL at the University of Chicago in 1951, voted for Michael to succeed Dombrow, but she viewed him with some suspicion. "You'll probably be here today, and gone tomorrow," she would later remember telling him.[50]

Michael's increased prominence in the movement brought with it another, unwanted distinction—the surveillance of the Federal Bureau of Investigation. He first showed up in FBI files in 1952, when he signed a statement with other Catholic Workers calling for the commutation of the death sentences of Julius and Ethel Rosenberg, who had been convicted the previous year of atomic espionage on behalf of the Soviet Union. The Communist newspaper in New York, the *Daily Worker,* reported on the Catholic Worker statement—while failing to mention that in the same statement Michael and his associates had criticized the Soviet Union for executing political dissidents.[51] Thereafter, the FBI maintained at least an intermittent surveillance of Michael. In January 1953 an FBI informant "of known reliability" reported to his superiors that Michael, representing the Catholic Worker, had spoken at a meeting sponsored by the "Yonkers Committee for Peace," and that in calling for an end to the Korean War, he had "followed the regular Communist line as closely as an overt Catholic could do."[52] For all of its vaunted efficiency, the FBI continued, until August 1954, to confuse Michael with another Michael Harrington, a New York City longshoreman born in 1906 who had emigrated to the United States from Ireland the year after Michael's birth and who had died shortly after Michael had first moved to New York City.[53]

But with Michael's prominent role in the founding of the YSL, the FBI finally sorted out the various "Michael Harringtons" in its files and kept the live one under close and continuing surveillance thereafter. The Bureau soon compiled a complete list of his political associations, past and present employment, and residences, as well as many other items of greater or lesser consequence (including one tidbit that, if accurate, reveals an interesting fact about Michael's mother, Catherine: "[blacked-out] who may be identical with the subject's mother telephonically furnished information to the St. Louis [FBI] Office on January 23, 1947, concerning an individual who she recalled favored Russia in 1937").[54] In 1955, the FBI officially placed Michael on its "Security Index," designating him as one of 12,000 or so dangerous characters destined for a detention camp in the event of national emergency.[55]

Given his experience with the Workers Defense League, Michael was assigned the task of advising potential recruits of the legal headaches they might incur as a result of joining the YSL.[56] Though the YSLers differed in few particulars from the political outlook of the adult ISL, the fiction of the youth group's organizational independence was maintained carefully, at its founding convention and thereafter—not least because the ISL had been placed on the U.S. attorney general's list of subversive organizations in 1948, a status of legal pariahdom that carried with it a number of potential administrative penalties. Max Shachtman had to fight a nearly ten-year battle to regain his passport after the State Department decided that any travels he took abroad would be inimical to the best interests of the United States. A number of YSLers were dishonorably discharged from the military for subversive associations.[57]

Whatever formal disavowals they chose to offer regarding fraternal status with the ISL, delegates to the YSL founding convention were nonetheless proud to pick up the banner—and fulsomely employ the rhetoric—of the ISL's revolutionary third-campism. They adopted a resolution declaring that resisting the threat of "imperialist war" was to be the new organization's first priority:

> If a third imperialist war breaks out we will continue participating in the class struggle, always retaining our identity as a Third Camp; struggling for the victory of the working class and colonial peoples over our ruling class and over the representatives at home of the ruling class across the sea [i.e., American Communists].[58]

Neither the American ruling class nor the YSL's Stalinist rivals had much reason to take this challenge seriously. Bogdan, writing in *Labor Action* later that month, rather grandly proclaimed the YSL "without a doubt, the largest single socialist youth organization in the U.S." A few weeks later, speaking before a student audience, he conceded that the group had something "under 30,000" members. That was certainly true—the YSL had *considerably* under that number—perhaps seventy-five or eighty all told.[59]

The YSL's style was unabashedly hard-line and old-style Marxist. That did not make recruiting any easier. When Michael's friend Jim Finn returned to New York from Chicago in the mid-1950s to join the staff of *Commonweal,* Michael brought him to a meeting where Shachtman was speaking, hoping he would see the light. "I was sympathetic," Finn recalled, "but never got deeply involved. I knew I couldn't belong when I heard people call each other 'Comrade Harrington' and 'Comrade This' and 'Comrade That.'"[60]

What YSLers lacked in numbers, they made up for in energy and ambition. Soon after the YSL's founding convention, Bogdan and Scott Arden, a former SYLer, launched a recruiting tour that took them to a dozen cities and college campuses in the northeast and Midwest.[61] Oberlin College, with its abolitionist and social gospel tradition, proved the high point of the tour; there the two YSLers challenged two liberal professors who had served in the Truman administration to a public debate on American foreign policy. Several hundred students turned out, a large crowd for a radical meeting at the time; and at least in some accounts, the young Shachtmanites emerged victorious in the debate. About a dozen Oberlin students subsequently formed a "Eugene V. Debs club" on campus that was sympathetic to the YSL's politics.[62]

Tim Wohlforth, an Oberlin undergraduate, was among the few new members the YSL picked up in its first year. Like other youthful recruits from the provinces, impressed by reports of successful YSL activities in other locales published in the *Young Socialist Challenge,* he assumed that the movement he was joining was far more powerful than it turned out to be in reality. Moving to New York in 1955, he eagerly sought out the loft three blocks east of Union Square where the YSL was headquartered. Headquarters did not live up to his inflated expectations:

> The third floor at 114 West 14th Street in lower Manhattan was the nerve center of Max Shachtman's political empire. . . . The building was not easy to find. I walked past it twice before I spied it sandwiched between a pawnshop and a cut-rate variety store just west of 6th Avenue. . . . I walked up dark, dusty stairs past the second-story loft devoted to some obscure and not very prosperous aspect of the garment trade. . . . I found myself in a small hall that could seat sixty or so people, and that clearly had not been painted since the Shachtman group moved into the place after its birth in 1940. As you moved toward the back you went past a room stuffed with old volumes of . . . *Labor Action* and an antiquated hand-operated Addressograph machine. Next came a couple of cubbyhole offices for the "national staff" of the ISL and the YSL. . . . The street below teemed with people—shopping, going to work, going home. That life, however, did not make it up the two flights to the headquarters.[63]

What life there was in the cramped political corner inhabited by the YSL in the early 1950s centered largely about the writing, production, and distribution of *Labor Action* and the *Young Socialist Challenge.* As in the case of many small sectarian groups, it was not entirely clear whether the newspaper existed to promote the movement or the movement existed to promote the newspaper. When in 1954 Hal Draper, editor of *Labor Action,* chided ex-Shachtmanite Irving Howe for having abandoned "the struggle," Howe retorted, "What struggles does Draper have except the very real one to fill the pages of *Labor Action* every week?"[64]

In the *Young Socialist Challenge,* the mundane details of internal YSL life—"educationals," "socials," and "summer camps"—were covered in extensive if not always absorbing detail. Thus in September, readers who for one reason or another had not been able to attend the annual YSL summer camp over Labor Day weekend were treated to a blow-by-blow description of what each and every speaker had to say to the fifty- or sixty-odd enthusiasts who had turned out.[65] Let a YSLer somehow thrust himself into a broader political sphere (by, say, getting expelled from a rival organization) and *Challenge* editors deemed it an occasion worthy of headlines of a dimension not seen in most American newspapers since V-J day—not least because the editors were usually the ones being kicked out.[66]

The Shachtmanites were not, of course, the only ones on the Left spinning their wheels in the early 1950s. The Communists, and the more orthodox Trotskyists of the Socialist Workers Party, fared no better, nor did the radical pacifists who functioned in groups like the War Resister's League and the Congress of Racial Equality (CORE). In such difficult times, a certain degree of dogmatic self-absorption helped marginal political sects remain afloat. Andre Schiffrin—an activist in the 1950s in the Student League for Industrial Democracy (SLID), a group that suffered the distinction of being one of the Shachtmanites' perennial targets for infiltration—was no particular admirer of the ISL or the YSL. But he read the Shachtmanite paper regularly and would later pay ironic tribute to its editors: "You know, when you think back on it," Schiffrin mused, "*Labor Action* was an extraordinary thing, a well-edited and intelligent weekly newspaper that gave the illusion of there being an organization behind it."[67] The problem with *Labor Action* and the *Young Socialist Challenge* was not, like some kindred sectarian efforts, that they were filled with mindless ranting and raving. Rather, what made reading them so predictably and deadly dull was the distinctly limited set of ideas and concerns deemed worthy of intelligent comment by the editors. Someone whose sole knowledge of American politics in the 1950s derived from the pages of *Labor Action* and the *Young Socialist Challenge* might well have believed that the nation as a whole was absorbed with judging the relative merits of third-camp socialism versus bureaucratic collectivism. One disgruntled reader wrote a letter to the editor of *Labor Action* in 1953 declaring that "the preoccupation of the ISL with Stalinism borders on the pathological." As evidence, he pointed to a recent issue of the newspaper in which he had counted "the word *Stalin* and its derivatives and synonyms" a total of 114 times.[68]

For such a small organization, the YSL seemed to possess an enormous pool of writers whose talents could be drawn upon for its newspaper. The front page of the January 30, 1956, issue of *Challenge,* for example, was devoted to reports on international student protests. The story on India carried the byline of Michael Harrington; the story on Spain was written by one Edward Hill; and the story on Argentina was written by one Eli Fishman.[69] Unlike Michael, who could be found most afternoons in the 14th Street loft pounding out his articles on an old typewriter, Hill and Fishman were more elusive figures—although their writing styles bore an uncanny resemblance to Michael's own.

"Party names" were part of the Bolshevik tradition, and in some instances their use was justified as a means of preventing FBI harassment or loss of employment. But in Harrington's case, since he was a movement full-timer who did not hesitate to make his radical affiliations a matter of public record, the use of various pseudonyms in the *Young Socialist Challenge* served mostly as a means to disguise the large proportion of the newspaper that he wrote every week. ("Fishman" also functioned as a movement in-joke, parodying the tendency of Michael's Jewish comrades to adopt common Anglo-Saxon names as pseudonyms. Casual readers of the paper may well have assumed that Fishman was the real writer and that the blandly Irish "Michael Harrington" was more likely the product of someone's assimilationist longings and imagination.)

On their occasional forays outside the 14th Street loft in the mid-1950s, YSLers engaged in what they called "arena work." Various political movements and issues were identified as priorities: trade unions, pacifist groups, campus groups, civil liberties, and civil rights were the leading "arenas." Of these, at one time or another in the 1950s, Michael put his energies into all but the first.[70]

Coming to the YSL out of the Catholic Worker, Michael was a natural candidate to play a leading role in antiwar arena work. With the end of the Korean War, radical pacifist groups began to concentrate their protests against preparations for nuclear war, including nuclear testing and civil defense drills. Although the pacifists were no less isolated than the Shachtmanites in the mid-1950s, their creative use of Gandhian tactics of nonviolent civil disobedience anticipated and helped prepare the ground for the political insurgencies of the 1960s.[71]

From its founding, the YSL had sought to cultivate ties with radical pacifists. A. J. Muste, leader of the pacifist Fellowship of Reconciliation (and, in a brief quasi-Trotskyist phase in the 1930s, a former party comrade of Shachtman), was invited to speak at the YSL's first convention; David Dellinger, Michael's old acquaintance from the Times Square picket line, addressed the YSL's first summer camp. Michael, who was elected to the executive committee of the War Resisters League (WRL)—at the time the leading radical pacifist group—addressed frequent appeals in the pages of the *Young Socialist Challenge* for common action by pacifists and third-camp socialists. When Dellinger launched a new radical pacifist magazine, *Liberation,* in the spring of 1956, Michael had an article in the first issue and was listed on its title page as associate editor.[72]

But Michael never seemed all that committed to, or perhaps never felt very comfortable within, the pacifist arena. He soon stopped attending meetings of the WRL executive committee.[73] And, although he kept in touch with friends from the Catholic Worker, he did not join them when they decided to engage in acts of civil disobedience to protest New York City's annual civil defense drill.

For several years, Ammon Hennacy, Michael's political nemesis at the Worker, had been picketing government offices during civil defense drills.

Since he seemed an isolated nut, no one paid much attention to him. But in June 1955, a small group of radical pacifists, including Hennacy and Dorothy Day, gained considerable notoriety when they gathered in the park outside of city hall shortly before the annual city-wide civil defense drill was scheduled to take place. Twenty-eight protesters were arrested for refusal to take shelter. It was the first "mass" act of antiwar civil disobedience. Those who took part were prepared to go to jail for their beliefs; New York State law made refusal to take shelter during a civil defense drill a misdemeanor punishable by up to a year's imprisonment.

Among those arrested that day were a number of Michael's friends from the Catholic Worker, including Eileen Fantino and Mary Ann McCoy. Michael was in the White Horse when he heard of their arrests, and, with another former Catholic Worker, John Stanley, he walked to the night court at 100 Centre Street, where the protesters were to be arraigned. The actress Judith Malina was also among the defendants; she noticed Michael's "pale face" among the crowd of spectators. Judge Louis Kaplan, after delivering an impassioned lecture to Dorothy Day on how her actions might, if widely emulated, lead to the deaths of millions of New Yorkers, ordered the protesters held on $1,500 bail each, pending trial (eventually convicted, they would be sentenced to five-day jail terms).

Before that evening's session of night court came to an end, however, it would provide a foretaste of the kind of courtroom theatrics that would by the end of the next decade become commonplace. None of the defendants had been fed since their arrest at midday; some of them, including Judith Malina, were feeling a little light-headed by this time. When Malina heard a bailiff mispronounce Ammon Hennacy's name, she laughed giddily. Judge Kaplan asked her if she had ever been confined in a mental institution, to which Malina retorted, "No, have you?"

Outraged at what he perceived as an assault on the dignity of the court, Judge Kaplan ordered Malina's immediate commitment to Bellevue Hospital for psychiatric observation. She then leaped on top of a table, briefly eluding the two policemen who stepped forward to remove her from the courtroom. As she was dragged screaming from the room, her husband, Julian Beck, stood up in the spectators' section and yelled agitatedly, "She's a wonderful woman!" Others among the defendants and spectators joined this spontaneous chorus of protest, which did not end until the riot squad was summoned to restore order. In the confusion, Julian Beck slipped out without suffering arrest. No one remembers whether Michael lent his voice to the protest that night. But earlier in the evening, as he had walked to Centre Street with John Stanley, he remarked, "Every time I enter a courtroom, I become an anarchist."[74]

The next day Michael put up bail for Eileen Fantino and Mary Ann Mc-

Coy. Afterwards, he and Bogdan went out for coffee with the two young women, who were feeling exhausted but exhilarated from their experience. Michael "looked upset," Fantino recalled forty years later. "I think he may have felt that he should have been with us."[75]

But civil disobedience was not the Shachtmanites' style of politics; when it came to direct action, they preferred legal and orderly picket lines. Here Michael played an invaluable role. His Irish name and friendly manner made him an ideal picket captain, according to YSLer Jack Stuart's memory: "He was, of course, the person who always spoke to the cops when we had a demonstration because that insured we were not going to get savaged by them."[76]

Such outdoor forays were, in any case, rarely attempted. The young Shachtmanites envisioned political struggle as more of an indoors, twilight, internecine affair: a matter of debating-points scored, resolutions passed, and staff positions gained. Perhaps the most damaging example of where these inclinations led the YSL was displayed in their campaign to capture Students for Democratic Action (SDA), the campus affiliate of Americans for Democratic Action (ADA).

The ADA had been founded after the Second World War as a kind of "New Deal in exile," its most important leaders having served their political apprenticeships in Washington during Franklin Roosevelt's presidency.[77] But by the early 1950s, most American liberals understood perfectly well that, barring the return of a new Great Depression, a nostalgic attachment to the New Deal would only carry them so far; the future of liberalism was going to require new political ideas and constituencies. With its own membership draw mostly from the ranks of college-educated (and mostly Jewish) professionals, ADA naturally looked to the nation's campuses as a prime source of new liberal recruits.[78]

Founded in 1948, SDA's membership peaked soon afterwards at about 3,500. Its brand of anticommunist liberalism flourished as long as politically minded students were looking for an alternative to Communist-dominated campus front groups like the Young Progressives of America. It attracted some talented and ambitious figures; Allard Lowenstein was a member at the University of North Carolina in the late 1940s; Michael Dukakis was chairman of the Swarthmore College chapter in the early 1950s. But as McCarthyism decimated the campus Left, SDA was reduced to a few hundred members, whose delegates passed resolutions at annual conventions that were of little interest to any one at all outside their own organization—except to the Shachtmanites.[79]

The YSLer's attitude toward groups like SDA was decidedly mixed. On the one hand, like several generations of Marxists who had preceded them, they enjoyed mocking what they saw as the vacillations and delusions of middle-class liberals. Michael was no exception. Writing in the *Young Socialist Challenge* soon after the YSL's founding convention, he haughtily dismissed liberalism for its "essentially moralistic analysis of social change." Politics was more than simply a question of mobilizing "people with good will." "The socialist," Michael declared, "sees the labor movement as the growing edge of freedom not because of some abstract idealism but because of the objective conditions in which the worker finds himself. Will and sincerity are still important, but they must be related to actual social forces." And in a subsequent article, written under his "Edward Hill" pseudonym, Michael put forth an even more exacting standard of political purity:

> Anyone in the 20th century who wants to fight for democracy must understand the revolutionary crisis of our times, the struggle of workers and Asian peasants against capitalism and imperialism, their constant betrayal by the reactionary anticapitalism of Stalinism. This, we say, is a situation which requires some kind of coherent ("dogmatic") consciousness. It is also a situation which requires the taking of sides—for the workers and peasants—against imperialism whether it be Stalinist or capitalist.[80]

But if liberals were to be scorned because they weren't prepared to swallow the YSL's entire radical agenda, they were also to be courted, because where else would new Shachtmanite recruits come from? Accordingly, in 1955, with Michael as chief strategist, YSLers took over the New York regional organization of SDA. They did so through the tried and true sectarian tactics of attending every meeting, staying late, and voting as a disciplined bloc.[81]

In his memoirs, Michael would put a benign spin on the YSLers' role within SDA: "We had gained something of a hearing in SDA, primarily because of our principled defense of the rights of Communists."[82] In this instance, however, principle and political pragmatism meshed easily; the YSLers' defense of civil liberties for Communists was a useful device for splitting the opposition within SDA. Protecting the civil liberties for actual Communists (and not just those liberals unjustly accused as such) was a highly charged issue within SDA. ADA itself had been victimized by red-baiting; many Democratic Party leaders wished the organization would go away, since it proved a lightning rod for Republican partisan attacks (in the 1954 midterm election campaign, Vice President Richard Nixon accused the "red ADA" of "selling socialism under the guise of liberalism").[83]

Nixon to the contrary, the ADA was hardly "red" in sympathies; it was on the record supporting much of the anticommunist legislation of the era, including laws that allowed firing Communists from teaching positions. One of ADA's leading lights, Senator Hubert Humphrey of Minnesota, had sponsored the Communist Control Act of 1954, which made membership in the Communist Party a federal crime, punishable by imprisonment and fines.[84] YSLers sought to exploit the contradiction between SDAers' own liberal sentiments and the guilty consciences some felt because of the political compromises of their ADA elders. In this endeavor they were successful, bringing several dozen new members into the YSL, some of whom played important roles in the organization.

But if the YSLers intended their involvement in SDA to represent anything more than a raiding party, their success proved short-lived, as both ADA and the national leadership of SDA mobilized to repel them. SDA passed a resolution barring adherents of "totalitarian" organizations from membership and sought to expel the YSLers. Now, instead of arguing about the larger principle at stake—whether or not Communists should be thrown in jail for their beliefs—the debate among SDAers centered on the considerably narrower issue of whether or not YSLers had a right to belong to their organization.

Short of actually capturing SDA, nothing could have made the YSLers happier than coming under this kind of attack. Sectarians live for such moments. SDA's attempt to expel the YSLers gave them the morally bracing feeling of being persecuted for their beliefs (without, of course, facing any serious consequences, should they lose the battle). It meant that the world was taking them seriously. Michael devoted column after column of newsprint in the *Young Socialist Challenge* to a minute analysis of SDA's internal failings, alternately chiding, mocking, and denouncing the group's "right wing leaders" for cowardice and duplicity.[85]

Andre Schiffrin, an interested observer of the SDA imbroglio, was baffled at the time as to why the Shachtmanites thought they had any legitimate business in SDA at all, "other than acting out of an infatuation of getting in to organizations larger than themselves."[86] The YSL's operating premises—revolutionary socialist and "labor party"-oriented—were utterly at odds with those of the liberal Democratic SDA. And since even SDA's "right-wingers" were part of that small minority of students in the 1950s who actively favored civil rights and organized labor, they might well have been justified in wondering why they, of all people, deserved being singled out for harassment by their Shachtmanite critics.

In any event, what had been a small, ineffective, yet at least mildly virtuous organization in 1954 was, thanks to the Shachtmanites, reduced to an even smaller, even less effective, and totally demoralized organization by the summer of 1956. The debate over whether YSLers could belong to SDA went on so long, and the issue proved so intractable, that ADA eventually resolved the question by shutting down its student affiliate. The main consequence of the YSL's efforts to capture SDA was that the "silent generation" on American campuses grew even more silent.[87]

What was someone like Michael, with a reputation for intelligence and personal decency, doing mixed up in this kind of business? He wasn't the first, and he certainly wouldn't be the last, young radical to mistake the immensely satisfying logical consistency of a closed system of thought for objective reality. "Never before," Irving Howe would write of his own experience as a young Trotskyist in the late 1930s, "and surely never since, have I lived at so high, so intense a pitch, or been so absorbed in ideas beyond the smallness of self. It began to seem as if the very shape of reality could be molded by our will, as if those really attuned to the inner rhythms of History might bend it to submission."[88]

Howe had the excuse of entertaining his own delusions of revolutionary apocalypse in the midst of the worst economic depression ever to beset American capitalism. Michael's era of political grand illusions came in the early years of what turned out to be the greatest period of sustained prosperity in the history of the United States, a quarter century of steady employment and rising real wages for most American workers. While the Shachtmanites huddled in their dingy loft on 14th Street, the landscape of both the nation's countryside and its social relations was being transformed by the rise in home ownership, the spread of suburbs, and the abandonment of the old urban residential districts by the sons and daughters of the traditional ethnic working class. How could the young Shachtmanites, and Michael in particular, have been so blind in the face of what seemed so evident to everyone else?

As Dwight Macdonald once said of his opposition to the Second World War, a position he later recanted, there are mistakes, and then there are "creative mistakes." Macdonald's deeply cherished belief in 1941 that socialist revolution was the only way to stop Hitler was clearly an illusion. Still, it proved a "creative mistake" in that it permitted him to become an astute critic of the mass regimentation of opinion and the techniques of sanitized mass slaughter that, to one degree or another, characterized the conduct of the war by both sides in the conflict.[89]

The YSLers' doomsaying about the American economy a decade later was similarly mistaken. And yet, by refusing to participate in the "American celebration" of the mid-1950s, they proved alert to a few truths that escaped far more prominent and influential social commentators of the time. If the old Lower East Side or "Back of the Yards" style of working-class life was drawing to a close, America was still not becoming an egalitarian "middle-class society." A factory was not as pleasant a workplace as a boardroom; a working-class suburb was not as pleasant a place to live as an upper-class suburb; the working-class share of national income, augmented as it was by easy credit, still did not guarantee as secure a future as that enjoyed by those who owned or managed America's mighty industrial establishment. Thanks to their own "creative mistake," YSLers had no trouble understanding what former Shachtmanite Harvey Swados meant when he attacked "the myth of the happy worker" in an article in the *Nation* in 1955; it would take mainstream American journalists and sociologists another generation to catch on to the existence of "blue-collar blues."[90]

If in the mid-1950s, the young Shachtmanites had a tendency to bask in the rosy afterglow of '30s-style industrial strife and class conscious labor politics, it was not, after all, such a far distant past that they were idealizing. It had been less than a decade since the enormous postwar strike wave had brought out 4 million American workers to march on the picket lines; labor militancy in 1952 approached that level, with over 5,000 strikes breaking out that year. It had been only a half dozen years since Walter Reuther, leader of the million-plus members of the UAW, had threatened to abandon the Democratic Party for an independent, labor-organized political party. Surveying the attitudes of CIO officials in the later 1940s, sociologist C. Wright Mills discovered that 52 percent of them looked forward to the formation of a new labor party within ten years time. Unionized workers still voted along class lines, even if they cast their ballots for the Democrats and not the hypothetical labor party that the Shachtmanites would have preferred. Union members had been the mainstay of Harry Truman's surprise victory in 1948, and in 1952, despite Dwight Eisenhower's enormous personal popularity, 55 percent of all union members, and a whopping 75 percent of UAW members, had cast their ballots for Democratic presidential candidate Adlai Stevenson.[91]

YSLers listened eagerly when Shachtman and other ISLers with personal memories of the labor battles of the 1930s and 1940s instructed them in movement lore and strategy: "I learned my labor history from veterans," Michael would recall, "some of whom were still shop stewards or local union officers." (Among the ISL cadre still active in UAW affairs at that time were figures like Carl Shier, a leader in the UAW's Local 6 in Chicago, and Don Slaiman and Sam Fishman, veterans of the Buffalo UAW who would go on to bigger things, Slaiman as a staffer for the AFL-CIO's civil rights department in Washington, and Fishman as president of the Michigan AFL-CIO.)[92]

Young Shachtmanites were convinced that they, too, were going to play an important role in the labor movement's future and, accordingly, in the politics of the nation. Capitalist crises would recur. And with the return of economic hard times, YSLers reasoned, would come a resurgence of left-leaning rank-and-file caucuses in the big industrial unions, as well as independent labor parties in states like Michigan and New York. Just as their elders had been swept up in the industrial organizing campaigns of the 1930s and the wildcat strikes of the Second World War, so the new generation of Shachtmanites looked forward to the moment when their talents as organizers and agitators would be tapped by a revived, militant labor movement. This scenario proved seriously flawed, but stripped of rhetorical excess it was not completely implausible.

Michael wrote scores of articles and delivered at least as many speeches that faithfully outlined the YSL's optimistic prospectus for socialism's future. Alongside the sermons preaching the good news, he also advanced another vision of the socialist mission, at once more astringent and more romantic—and also very revealing of his own most deeply rooted motives for identifying himself with this seemingly hopeless cause.

In YSL circles, to say that someone's politics were "hard" was a compliment. To be "hard" was to be clear-thinking, unsentimental, dedicated (and, of course, for males, it carried other positive if unspoken connotations). There were people whose politics were hard and with whom the Shachtmanites didn't agree—even some they hated, such as the Communists. Still, in a curious way, the Shachtmanites respected the Stalinist enemy, for they recognized Stalinists as people who were serious about their politics, however wrongheaded. Liberals, on the other hand, got no respect at all, for they were "soft"—hesitant, compromising, moralistic (or feminine, in other words).[93]

But for all of his diatribes against liberals who preferred soft and mushy ethics to hard and concrete social forces, Michael didn't fool the *real* YSL hards. He was regarded, particularly by those closest to Max Shachtman, as pretty soft himself—fatally compromised by his middle-class origins, his elite education, his religious and pacifist past, and his continued preference for the company and conversation of all sorts of dissolute dilettantes in the back room of the White Horse. And, from their perspective, his YSL detractors had a point.

Differences between Michael and harder-line YSLers had already emerged within a few months of the group's formation. One quarrel concerned a theoretical question of seemingly monumental irrelevance: If a genuinely socialist government (i.e., not the bureaucratic collectivists of the Soviet Union) were to acquire atomic weapons, would it ever be justified in using them to defend itself against imperialist aggression? Michael said no; the hard-liners said yes. As Bogdan, who sided with Michael, later explained:

> Among the Leninist sects, one of the no-no's was to say that something was unimaginable, that you'd never do it, like "socialists never engage in

> torture." "You mean, if thousands of lives are at stake, and this White Guardist knows where the bombs are placed in the orphanage . . . " and so forth. Everything is supposed to be relative, depending on circumstance.[94]

When it came to atomic weapons, Michael argued that moral judgment had to be absolute not relative; under no conceivable circumstance could the use of such weapons be justified, regardless of whether they were good socialist or bad capitalist bombs. If he had to step outside the boundaries of conventional Leninist concepts and terminology to justify his position, Michael was willing to do so. He had left the church, but he had by no means abandoned all of its teachings or habits of thought. The Catholic Church's doctrine of "just war" considered a variety of factors relevant to judging the character of a conflict—not only for what end the war was being fought but also whether the means used to wage it were commensurate with any desirable ends that might be obtained. For Michael, nuclear weapons, by definition, stood outside the boundaries of the commensurate (American Catholic bishops would get around to adopting a similar position thirty years later). As Michael argued in an article in *Young Socialist Challenge,* the indiscriminate slaughter that would result from the use of atomic weapons had to be regarded as antithetical to socialist values, if socialism were to have any legitimacy as an alternative to the existing order. Marx, Lenin, and Trotsky had lived and died before Hiroshima; their would-be successors were "faced [with] an objectively qualitative break in the history of war demanding a rethinking of all old positions."[95]

Since in the spring of 1954 the YSL was even less well-supplied with nuclear weapons than it was with dues-paying members, it is tempting to dismiss this whole debate as merely another a grandiose and ludicrous exercise in ideological fantasy. Still, within the circles that Michael traveled in the mid-1950s the suggestion that classical Marxism was not an all-encompassing system for understanding the world was a decidedly heretical concept. As far as Michael was concerned, a capacity for simple moral revulsion—however old-fashioned or bourgeois its source—was, at least in some instances, a better source of political wisdom in the post-Hiroshima world than any amount of sophisticated dialectical reasoning. If Michael's qualms (and his YSL opponents' lack of the same) about the use of atomic weapons had little practical relevance in terms of policy, this debate certainly revealed a lot about their respective sensibilities. Michael aspired to be as *hard* in his politics as his comrades; but there were some lines he would not cross, even in the name of revolutionary necessity.

In his 1954 review of French existentialist Albert Camus's recently translated book *The Rebel,* Michael praised Camus for introducing "the language of morality into the practice of politics." Revolutions were made by individuals, and their outcomes had to be measured by the impact they had on individual lives, as well as by whatever greater historical purposes they proposed to serve. Michael emphatically endorsed the sentiments expressed in the book's most famous passage, where Camus says that a rebel is someone who vows to side always with the executed and never to be an executioner. That, Michael concluded, "is a great deal to say of anyone in the twentieth century."[96]

Michael was no longer interested in being a saint, an ambition that now seemed to him to consist of a self-absorbed quest to live apart from the concerns that governed the lives of ordinary people. At the same time, he continued to admire the personal commitment of some of the people he knew in the Catholic Worker and the pacifist movement, like Eileen Fantino and Mary Ann McCoy. If he no longer aspired to sainthood, he still cherished the hope of finding a way of living his beliefs, or at least of keeping the gap between the real and the ideal as narrow as possible. As Dwight Macdonald had written of the conscientious objector to the Second World War, "His day-to-day life and his long-range convictions, if they do not wholly coincide, are at least on speaking terms with each other."[97] As a socialist, Michael wanted to keep his life and convictions on similar "speaking terms." That's why he found Daniel Bell's essay on the failure of American socialism so troubling and provocative.

In an article in the *Young Socialist Challenge* in the spring of 1954, Michael credited Bell with raising "an interesting and pertinent question" for socialists. How was one to live "in and of the world" while also providing a radical challenge to the "here-and-now, give-and-take political world"? What did socialists have to offer to potential followers beyond "a large, over-all theoretical analysis" that proved difficult to apply in a meaningful way in daily life?

> Here I think one must turn to a concept which has been primarily worked out in the pacifist movement—that of the "witness." Such a position is one which is willing to recognize that a certain attitude may have no immediate relevance, but that it may well have a long-term meaning. Precisely because they had kept to their principles, those German socialists who were opposed to World War I were able to have a tremendous eventual effect, one which could not have been foreseen in the late summer of 1914 when "practicality"—socialism proceeding on German bayonets—ruled the day.

Michael conceded that the tension between political effectiveness and sticking to one's principles was not resolved easily. Still, although socialists should not revel in marginality as if it confirmed their purity of vision, they had to recognize that there were times when standing fast, even in isolation, was the only ethical—and ultimately, "practical"—thing to be done:

> When the socialist is "not of the world," i.e., sees no practical alternative . . . this does not mean that the non-socialist position is worth supporting. If the choice for the modern world is between socialism and barbarism (and I think it is), the answer is not to support barbarism because it is on the ascendant, but to continue to struggle for socialism.[98]

Although never an orthodox Trotskyist, Michael admired the exiled Bolshevik leader as one of those historic figures who had managed to combine original thought with great deeds. After Trotsky's assassination, his widow Natalya said of her martyred husband: "He knew himself the last fighter of an annihilated legion. . . . His duty was to maintain, clearly, accurately, a doctrine, a historic truth, a resolute waiting."[99] Michael was moved by this image of Trotsky as the "last fighter," an image that resonated with the literature of revolutionary defeat he was reading at the time.

The mid-1950s were not always Michael Harrington's finest hours; too much of what he said and did represented a sterile homage to the ideological preoccupations and tactical habits of his mentor Max Shachtman. On occasion, however, he stretched the limits of inherited doctrine in ways that suggested, if did not yet realize, a fresh approach to radical activism. Perhaps the best that can be said for Michael's politics in these years is that his version of "resolute waiting" did not preclude such an approach once new political opportunities began to open up in the later 1950s.

CHAPTER SIX

A Premature Sixties Radical, 1956–1960

A major political change is beginning in the United States, and if it continues to develop it will reshape American politics. It will result in a New Left.

Michael Harrington
1959[1]

Small radical sects exist to recruit. The numbers of new faces at a meeting, new subscribers to the newspaper, and new dues checks deposited in the bank are usually the only tangible measures of progress available to such groups. For the YSL in the early 1950s, those numbers were not encouraging. The young Shachtmanites were not oblivious to the obvious political disadvantages under which they labored. George Rawick, a graduate student in history at the University of Wisconsin, joined the YSL at its founding. In the summer of 1954, *Dissent* published his sober assessment of the political mood on college campuses:

> The present group of young undergraduates did not share, even indirectly, in any of the experiences of the nineteen-thirties, the war, or the immediate post-war period. . . . Most of them have known only hectic prosperity, suburbia, schools which consciously placed their emphasis on conformity . . . , television sets, the Korean war, the acceptance of the military as the norm rather than the unusual. Most accept America without dissenting, feeling that *on its own terms,* which they have internalized, it has for the most part succeeded.[2]

As veterans of campus organizing can testify, generalizations about student attitudes have a very short shelf-life. The style, content, and memory of the left-wing politics of the 1930s and 1940s had little meaning for college students in the early 1950s. But, beginning in 1956 or so, intimations of a new radical style and content began to be felt here and there around the country.

And although the Shachtmanites themselves had little to do with initiating that new politics, some young and eager faces did begin to appear at YSL meetings. A few of them, like Tom Kahn and Rochelle Horowitz, teenage undergraduates at Brooklyn College when they joined the YSL, would go on to become key behind-the-scenes figures in the early civil rights movement.

Older YSLers began to develop the heady feeling that they were on to something. In 1956, Debbie Meier was already a veteran of a half decade in the movement, having joined the SYL at the University of Chicago in 1951. She vividly remembered the difference it made in the mood of the YSL when this new wavelet of recruits appeared:

> We were euphorically happy to have young, lively, intelligent people coming in. . . . They were ambitious. They were competent. We had had the feeling about ourselves that we could only attract *nudniks*: who would join an organization that isn't going anywhere? If you were attracting people with ambitions, they must see in you that you have a future.[3]

But if by the mid-1950s YSLers were beginning to feel a measure of political optimism, some people—Michael chief among them—realized that they weren't going to get very far without making fundamental changes in the nature of the organization. When Michael joined the socialist movement in the early 1950s, he expected it to prove a losing proposition. Because he was steeped in the European literature of the century's revolutionary defeats, the prospect of a politics of heroic endurance did not much disturb him—and indeed, it held a strong romantic appeal. If believing in the necessity of revolutionary change doomed him to marginality, at least it was a margin he shared with men he regarded as models of integrity, intellect, and action—Trotsky, Serge, Koestler, Malraux, Camus—figures made all the more appealing to Michael because they had recorded their own doomed quest for freedom and equality in such felicitous literary style.

But now it began to dawn on Michael that more immediate and tangible rewards were within reach, both for the movement to which he belonged and for him individually. Michael responded to new opportunities with a political creativity and a sense of optimism that stood in dramatic contrast to the futile sectarianism of his early years as a socialist.

Ruth Jordan was one of the newcomers attracted into YSL circles in this period. As chairman of the Brooklyn College chapter of Students for Democratic Action, she had been opposed to the heavy-handed way in which the ADA pushed for the expulsion of YSLers from SDA. She became romantically involved with one of the YSL's leaders, who she later married. All of this should made her a prime candidate for recruitment by the YSL. Years later, explaining why in the end she refused to join, she recalled a meeting at the group's 14th Street loft. Her boyfriend was the main speaker that evening and was taken to pieces by his comrades in the discussion that followed. "I don't remember what the issue was. What I remember is the cruelty, the savagery, of the way they went at each other. They cut their intellectual teeth on each other. I remember walking away feeling absolutely staggered. I took it very personally."

Michael, who had been sitting in a different part of the hall during the debate, noticed her expression and came over to her afterwards:

> He said, "You're not happy with this." I said, "I will never join this organization. You people don't know anything about the way people learn about the world." And Mike replied, "Well, we're not quite an American organization yet." He understood that the YSL bore the marks of a group that was still very sectarian, and that they had a long way to go.

In what would become a familiar theme in Michael's political career, people were already beginning to draw clear distinctions between him and the organizations with which he was associated. Jordan went away, determined not to join the YSL, but also impressed by Michael. "He stood out in the group. He joked about sectarian issues, but he seemed to know more about America. He was an American. Everything about Mike said that."[4]

Michael had a gift of transcending his surroundings. People came to hear him speak in seedy little halls, where the dust lay deep on unsold copies of yellowing newspapers, and somehow came away thinking about the future potential of the Left, not its current straitened circumstances. Michael had not yet freed himself of the sectarian habits of mind that had shaped his politics in the early 1950s. But the gap between his personal appeal and what had been until then the generally unappealing character of his politics at least had begun to shrink.

What brought new members into a tiny sect like the YSL? Being a responsible member of the YSL involved a lot of meetings and a lot of evenings. Once a week a bundle of *Labor Action*s would show up in the mail and would have to be sold or, more often, passed out for free to those deemed potential recruits. There were assigned readings to complete, subscriptions to be sold, dues to be collected, reports to be filed.

But there were compensations. For the politically committed and the politically isolated (and, when applied to the American Left of the 1950s, those terms were virtually synonymous), there was, of course, the gratification of comradeship and a sense of being involved in a movement of national and even international scope. For the intellectually precocious or the intellectually unfulfilled, there was the opportunity to engage in learned controversy (through position papers, debates, and the close readings of sacred texts) within a community of fellow scholastics.

And for those who were unhappy in their personal lives, there was a sense of warm personal association with like-minded comrades in a transcendent cause. Speaking of her own emotionally deprived childhood, Rochelle Horowitz recalled, "We had this belief that our personal happiness would come from making the world better."[5] Movement romances were common, and homosexuals like Tom Kahn, as well as heterosexuals, could make liaisons without fear of harassment or ridicule.[6] And in Max Shachtman, young recruits had a paternal authority who was at once inspiring and doting: Debbie Meier would describe the YSL as "a whole bunch of siblings gathered around their father."[7]

For YSLers who lived in the hinterlands beyond the Hudson, the most important means through which the sense of connection with the larger movement was sustained was the periodic appearance of one or another of the "big names" from New York. When Shachtman's health permitted, which was less and less frequently, he would undertake a tour to visit ISL and YSL chapters across the country. And every YSL chapter could expect a visit from one of the national YSL leaders at least once a year. The value of the visit obviously varied with the identity of the leader. When Michael was elected YSL chairman in 1955, its worth suddenly appreciated considerably.

Michael went on his first national tour in the fall of 1955, a trip that, thanks to the careful attention the FBI paid to such matters, can be reconstructed in detail. Arriving at Antioch College in Ohio on November 16, Michael gave a talk on "Co-existence," in which he concluded (according to the likely oversimplified summary provided by an FBI informer) "that the only 'coexistence' that could exist between the United States and Russia is for the United States to become Socialist and the only way the United States would become Socialist is for the transfer of power from the controlling class to the workers." From Antioch he went on to Oberlin College, where on November 20 he "spoke against America's form of government and finished by saying that he really thinks a Labor Party is the real solution." Two days later he was in Chicago speaking on "Coexistence or Peace" at a meeting of the Chicago branch of the YSL ("HARRINGTON stated that although he was a conscientious objector for moral reasons, wars will not be stopped by individuals refusing to fight, but that whole social classes, especially the working class, refusing to fight would be more effective."). While in the city, he also spoke before a group of fifty students at the University of Chicago, "complaining about the restrictions that the government puts on people who join any radical organization." Then it was on to his final stop, Madison, Wisconsin, where the FBI's attention finally seemed to flag; all that was recorded about that occasion was that he spoke on an unnamed topic under the auspices of the Wisconsin Liberals Club.[8]

Typically, when Michael arrived on a campus, he would stay for two days and give two talks—one on a political topic, one on a question of cultural interest. The theme of his political talk would be determined both by current events and the YSL's current organizing strategy—sometimes he stressed the issue of peace, other times civil liberties, other times civil rights. In his cultural talks, Michael offered a "Marxist" approach to art and literature, but with a freewheeling approach that drew in many listeners otherwise disinclined to share his political views. After one talk at the University of Chicago, where he had gone on at great length defending the autonomy of artistic expression against any "vulgar Marxist reductionism," Debbie Meier came up to him and said, "Mike, you've got to admit that economics has *something* to do with art."[9]

Michael's periodic visits gave local chapters the opportunity for a public display of strength (which is to say, they might attract as many as forty or fifty people to a meeting instead of the usual half dozen stalwarts). The visits also gave local members a claim on Michael's attention for at least a day or two, during which he would mediate conflicts, dispense political advice and good cheer, and perhaps kindle a new or rekindle an old romance.[10]

Given the state of the YSL's bank account, Michael's national tours could be grueling expeditions. He would travel by Greyhound bus or hitchhike, grabbing meals at greasy spoons or campus cafeterias. In the absence of a local romantic attachment, he would bed down at night on some comrade's living room sofa. At each stop he had to be constantly "on," making speeches, courting potential recruits, and, above all, "being himself," which is to say generating warmth, openness, and optimism. He had to repeat himself constantly—not just in his set speeches but in the seemingly intimate and spontaneous conversations that followed—and make it all sound fresh and exciting each time. Debbie Meier would see him work this magic repeatedly in the 1950s when he came to Chicago for speaking engagements and stayed with her. Michael seemed to Meier then like someone whose "life was entirely out in the public, where there were a lot of people around. We didn't think of him as someone who belonged anywhere but in the public sphere, drinking and chatting and laughing." Only much later did it occur to her that there might be a considerable amount of strain involved in such performances. To all outward appearances, Michael seemed to thrive on this regimen.[11]

After so many years of being the youngest at whatever endeavor he pursued, Michael now enjoyed playing the role of movement veteran and older brother to younger radicals. By the end of the 1950s he began referring to himself as the nation's "oldest young socialist." As he approached his thirties, he had grown to his full adult height of six feet, and he cut a trim figure even in the baggy peacoats and other ill-fitting clothes he customarily wore. He was a man now, no longer a golden boy. His father had died in December 1955 of a sudden heart attack; Michael mourned his passing and remained dutifully attentive to his mother's needs. But although now a widow, Catherine Harrington was enjoying what were in some ways her most fulfilling years in St. Louis as a politically well-connected civic activist, lessening her need to live vicariously through her son.[12]

Michael still had the habit of looking to older people for guidance, Max Shachtman most prominently. But he was now increasingly looked up to as an authority in his own right. Michael had a gift for making young people feel that their political choices had a meaning and a future. According to Jack Stuart, who joined the YSL at Brooklyn College in 1956:

> I was young, and when I think back on it, I'm sure that there was a private Mike who may have felt differently at times. But he never seemed to get discouraged. Every now and then he would say to me, "You look like you need some pepping up, let's talk." I remember him using that phrase—"pepping up."[13]

"He was enormously likable," Columbia University YSLer Peter Novick remembered, "in that much-abused word, charismatic. People, including myself, wanted to ingratiate ourselves, feel close with him."[14] Michael basked in such approval and then added to his own charm by mocking this very tendency in himself. "Is there any chance of getting a meeting at Brandeis," he wrote to a student contact in 1957, "at which (a) I could speak to the cheering and entrhalled mass of the student body, and (b) I could bother the hell out of you and a few others on the general and specific subject of socialism?"[15]

Reporting on the results of his first national tour in 1955, Michael cautioned that the "student awakening has not yet taken place."[16] YSL membership that year probably remained less than a hundred, not much more than it had been at its founding. Two years, and as many national tours later, Michael could report that the YSL was up to about 250 members nationwide. It had active chapters in New York, New Haven, Pittsburgh, Chicago, Seattle, the Bay Area, and Los Angeles, as well as members at large in a number of other locations. Jim Robertson, the chairman of the Bay Area YSL, wrote to the national office in May 1957 to report that the chapter had recently recruited two new members, for a total of eighteen. Given the pool of available recruits at the time, the numbers were not insignificant. "We are in the extremely pleasant situation," Robertson wrote, "that the CP used to monopalize of picking up practically every young person who wants to be really active in radical politics and despite our internal factional struggles which must seem pretty peculiar to some of the new people coming around."[17]

The YSL was also developing peripheral circles of allies and sympathizers. YSLers were active in "Debs clubs" at Columbia University, Brooklyn College, and Bronx Science High School, in the Politics Club at the University of Chicago, the New Left Club in Philadelphia, the Dissent Club in Los Angeles, and the Social Renaissance Club at Berkeley.[18]

Michael established useful contacts on a number of other campuses where the YSL itself had yet to establish an organizational beachhead. One such contact was T. Robert ("Lefty") Yamada, a former University of Michigan student and a mover and shaker in Ann Arbor radical circles. (Among other distinctions, in 1958 Yamada would steer a Michigan undergraduate named Al Haber to join the Student League for Industrial Democracy [SLID] chapter on campus—which proved a crucial step in the emergence of the New Left, since Haber would oversee the transformation of the nearly moribund SLID into Students for a Democratic Society [SDS] a few years later.) In 1957, Yamada began picking up tremors of a coming generational revolt. He wrote to YPSL national secretary Dick Gilpin that fall, saying that he had a feeling that the "campus is opening up quite a bit. . . . I think tactically speaking this is the time to flood the campus with all sorts of speakers." One of the first speakers he had in mind, Yamada told Gilpin, was Michael Harrington. Yamada's comments to Gilpin provide a good measure of Harrington's growing reputation in non-YSL circles in the later 1950s. Yamada planned to

> throw an informal party for [Harrington] and invite all sorts of people to come to hear him. I haven't seen him for a long time and it'll be good to renew our acquaintances. I'll throw him to the academic wolves that are around who would want to talk to him not as a socialist but mainly for their own academic interests.[19]

Michael's growing reputation outside the YSL (and the back room of the White Horse) rested on a number of sources. His writings for *Commonweal* and *Partisan Review* helped establish his credentials among Yamada's "academic wolves" as an up-and-coming freelance thinker to whom it was worth paying attention. In an era when intellectuals opted increasingly for the security of a university affiliation and honed their academic reputations by writing for ever-narrower circles of specialist colleagues, the breadth of Harrington's interests, as well as his radical activism, set him apart. For many academics, otherwise comfortably ensconced on one or another well-manicured campus, Harrington was coming to represent a kind of lost ideal—the independent, urban political intellectual.[20]

Michael's association with Irving Howe's journal *Dissent* also served to spread his reputation in both political and academic circles. Howe had been one of Shachtman's bright young disciples in the 1930s and 1940s. But by the start of the 1950s he had grown tired of the tone and spirit of "sectarian agitation" that characterized Shachtman's ISL. In 1951, in a final attempt to refashion the group into something to which they could comfortably continue to pay their dues, Howe and his political ally Stanley Plastrik proposed that the ISL begin to let "our ideas speak for themselves, with dignity and restraint and sufficient subtlety to show people that we are not merely replaying the old records."[21] Shachtman's indifference to their plea prompted their departure soon afterwards.

Early in 1954, about the same time that Michael was helping found the YSL, Howe and Plastrik, along with Lewis Coser and several other refugees from the sectarian Left, brought out the first issue of their new quarterly journal entitled *Dissent,* a socialist publication based "on an awareness that in America today there is no significant socialist movement and that, in all likelihood, no such movement will appear in the immediate future."[22] *Dissent*'s appearance enraged ISL stalwarts; Shachtman went so far as to secure the passage of a resolution by the ISL forbidding members to write for the journal. But to Shachtman's dismay, and Howe's satisfaction, the YSL refused to follow their elders' example. Michael and Bogdan published a note in the *Young Socialist Challenge* welcoming the advent of *Dissent* and encouraging YSLers to read this "new forum for socialist views."[23]

Though only ten years Michael's senior, Howe's history of radical activism in the 1930s and 1940s marked him off as part of a preceding generation. Still, the two would soon grow close personally, or at least as close as two men not inclined to share confidences could become. In the mid-1950s they still found much on which they disagreed politically: Howe had little patience for what he regarded as the YSL's futile repetition of the sectarian mistakes of his youth, and Michael responded in kind. After one public meeting sponsored by *Dissent* on the future of socialism, Michael accused the journal's editors of seeking to "convert college sophomores into exhausted old men."[24] Howe, having heard it all before many times, took such polemics in stride; he soon invited Michael to become a contributor to *Dissent*'s pages, and in 1957 he added Michael to the editorial board.

Michael's first appearance in the pages of *Dissent* came in the spring of 1955. His target, the American Congress for Cultural Freedom (ACCF), was founded in 1951 as the American affiliate of a similarly named international group of anticommunist intellectuals. The congress represented a kind of upside-down version of the Popular Front coalitions of the 1930s, drawing together anticommunist socialists, liberals, and conservatives in common cause. The International Congress, which held its initial gathering in the tensely divided city of Berlin in 1950, had been endorsed by prominent political, literary, and cultural figures from twenty-one countries. Its political stance was anti-third camp as well as anticommunist. As Sidney Hook, a prominent participant, observed, at certain critical junctures in history "instead of saying 'Neither-Nor' and looking for other viable alternatives, we must recognize an 'Either-Or' and take one stand or another."[25] The American affiliate of the congress, founded the following year, initially attracted the support of a wide range of American intellectuals, including many prominent liberals and even such freewheeling radicals as Dwight Macdonald.

Michael argued in *Dissent* that although the European affiliates of the congress had held to the original purpose of defending cultural freedom against threats from any quarter, the ACCF had lowered itself to become a kind of intellectual front group for the U.S. State Department, "less an organization devoted to the defense of cultural freedom than an agency propagandizing the American party line." Michael's polemical thrust was closer to the truth than he could have known at the time; it would be another decade before it would be revealed that the congress had been funded by the U.S. Central Intelligence Agency (CIA) as a means of countering pro-Soviet and neutralist sentiments among European intellectuals.[26]

The ACCF's version of anti-Stalinism, Michael warned, was becoming "crude, promiscuous and often without positive content." In the name of anticommunist unity, the organization had "steadily drifted to the right" since its inception. The most principled liberals on its executive committee—he mentioned Arthur Schlesinger Jr. and David Riesman in particular—had either criticized various ACCF positions or resigned. (ACCF member Norman Thomas, Michael noted pointedly, had not chosen to follow their example.)

Michael was particularly disturbed by the presence of, and the influence wielded by, such "McCarthyite supporters" on the ACCF executive committee as James Burnham (who had actually resigned by the time the article appeared) and the former Communist agent turned informer, Whittaker Chambers. Irving Kristol, ACCF executive secretary, was another target of Michael's ire. A City College classmate and Trotskyist comrade of Irving Howe's, and briefly a Shachtmanite, Kristol would vehemently deny that he was a supporter of that "vulgar demagogue" Joe McCarthy. Nonetheless, he had offered the senator at least backhanded support when he remarked in a notorious article in *Commentary* (later circulated under the ACCF imprimatur): "There is one thing the American people know about Senator McCarthy: he is unequivocally anti-Communist. About the spokesmen for American liberalism, they feel they know no such thing. And with some justification."[27] The trouble with many of the ACCF's members, Michael believed, was that they were infected by the "'ex-Communist' syndrome": Bearing the scars of years of ideological infighting on the Left, they had come to believe that "only they can know the cunning and power of the enemy." This was not, Michael concluded, a state of mind "likely to make for either a supple politics or a firm defense of cultural freedom."[28]

Years later, when the truth about the CIA's involvement in such enterprises leaked out, younger radicals and some historians dismissed the entire anti-Stalinist Left of the 1950s as simply so many dupes and agents of the American national security apparatus—"servants [of the] secret police," in historian Christopher Lasch's astringent judgment in 1968. Michael was stung by such charges and, in response, cited his *Dissent* essay as "documented proof" to the contrary. He later reprinted it in a collection of essays, arguing in a prefatory note that in the 1950s there "were anti-Stalinist radicals like me who were outraged by the liberals who did indeed turn their backs on civil liberties in the name of anti-Communism."[29]

Michael's personal credentials in the defense of cultural freedom and civil liberties in the 1950s went well beyond the occasional essay. In defending the political freedoms of people with whom he had profound disagreements, he had his own brush with that all too prominent fixture of American political life in the 1950s, the House Un-American Activities Committee.

After leaving the employ of the Workers Defense League in 1954, Michael went through some lean months financially (he even took a temporary job as a soda jerk in a drug store to help make ends meet). But one day in early October, while he was visiting with friends at the Catholic Worker (and cadging a free meal, as he frequently did in those days), a long-distance call came in for him from John Cogley in Los Angeles. Cogley was on the West Coast scouting out contacts for a study he was undertaking on behalf of the Fund for the Republic on anticommunist blacklisting in the entertainment industries. He wanted to know if Michael was interested in working as his assistant. Michael was indeed, and he was soon bound for Los Angeles, his first trip to California and his first long-distance airplane flight. And for once he dressed appropriately, wearing a brand new suit that Cogley's fellow editor at *Commonweal,* Bill Clancy, had bought him for the trip.[30]

The Fund for the Republic was established by the Ford Foundation in 1951 to sponsor research and educational programs "directed toward the elimination of restrictions on freedom of thought, inquiry and expression in the United States."[31] The Fund was provided a generous endowment of $15 million, a guarantee of institutional independence from the Ford Foundation, and an energetic and controversial president in Robert M. Hutchins. Michael had already encountered Hutchins at the University of Chicago, where as president and chancellor of the university he had been an eloquent defender of academic freedom during the early years of the postwar Red Scare. As president of the Fund for the Republic, Hutchins's goal was to use the considerable resources at his disposal to establish a "university without walls," sparking the kind of informed debate that would increase public knowledge of both the value and fragility of traditional American guarantees of free speech, free association, and equal protection before the laws.[32] Not surprisingly, from its earliest days the Fund itself was a target for hostile scrutiny by right-wing commentators and politicians. Hutchins was unintimidated, even when Senator Joe McCarthy and Vice President Richard Nixon made hostile inquiries as to the Fund's political motives.[33]

In September 1954, the Fund's directors approved a new project, a study of blacklisting in Hollywood. This turned out to be the most controversial of all of its efforts in the 1950s. In looking for a director for the project, Hutchins had to weigh both the administrative and political qualifications of potential candidates. He needed someone who would be difficult to smear as a Communist supporter or dupe. He found his man in John Cogley. Cogley had impeccable credentials as an opponent of McCarthyism (he had recently written a widely noticed speech attacking McCarthy that was delivered by Chicago's auxiliary bishop, Bernard J. Sheil). And as a prominent Catholic layman, without any past connection with the Communist Party or its front organizations, he could deflect at least some of the antagonism that the study was bound to arouse from conservative critics.[34]

By the time Cogley had been hired to begin his research, the blacklisting system had been in place for almost seven years. The House Un-American Activities Committee, driven by its members' insatiable appetite for generating headlines, had conducted two rounds of hearings on alleged Communist infiltration of the film industry, in 1947 and 1951. HUAC claimed its most prominent victims in the "Hollywood Ten," a group of screenwriters cited for contempt of Congress and sent to prison when they refused on First Amendment grounds to answer questions about their affiliations with the Communist Party. After an initial show of resistance, the heads of the major Hollywood studios capitulated to the combined pressure brought to bear by HUAC and conservative political groups who threatened to boycott any films that involved writers, directors, or actors suspected of Communist sympathies. Henceforth those who had had the misfortune of signing the wrong petition, attending the wrong political rally, or, as was the case in many if not all instances, actually having been a member of the Communist Party faced formidable hurdles to employment in the film industry—unless they were willing to publicly recant and "name names" of those who had committed similar transgressions. The blacklist soon spread through the entertainment world, into television and radio.[35]

Having accepted directorship of the blacklisting study, Cogley moved quickly to hire a staff that grew to include ten researchers and writers who worked out of an office on Lexington Avenue in New York City. Michael, who Cogley later said "knew the ins and outs of the Communist Party better than any non-communist of my acquaintance," was one of the first hired, and he was the person Cogley relied upon most. At the end of October, Michael wrote to W. H. Ferry, Hutchins's chief assistant:

> The research which we have done so far indicates that blacklisting is a pervasive and extremely complex problem in the entertainment industry. Many conflicting groups within the industry—the Eastern financial executives for the movies, producers on the Coast, the networks, advertising agencies, the blacklistees, etc.—are involved. Because of this the task of documentation will be a difficult one.[36]

In the course of the year that followed, Michael and other researchers would interview hundreds of people in the entertainment industry on both coasts. Cogley did most of the writing of the final report.

Although Michael may have known the ins and outs of communism, Hollywood was terra incognita. The only contact he and Cogley had in the beginning was a troubled script editor with liberal sympathies who met with them covertly and reported that, whatever official denials they might hear from the industry, the blacklist was a omnipresent reality. The script editor put them in contact with Martin Gang, a liberal Hollywood lawyer who had made a career in the early 1950s of getting blacklisted actors back to work by "naming names" before the House Un-American Activities Committee.[37]

Cogley soon returned to New York, leaving Michael the tasks of pursuing further leads and hiring the rest of the West Coast research team. Michael wrote to Cogley on October 6 to report that he had persuaded Paul Jacobs to join the staff.[38] Michael had met Jacobs, an ex-Trotskyist and union organizer, before in connection with his work for the Workers Defense League. They soon became good friends. Michael would later describe Jacobs as "congenitally irreverent, serious, and puckish," and they worked well together (among other distinctions, Jacobs would be one of the few people with whom Michael, a notoriously irresponsible letter-answerer, would maintain a more or less regular correspondence over the years).[39]

Michael shuttled back and forth from New York to California, in a style to which he was not accustomed (and, in between his duties to the Fund, got to conduct YSL business along the way). He was not immune to Hollywood's glamour, although he made light of it ("Have made no progress with Marilyn Monroe," he noted in signing off one letter to Cogley).[40] He did find it bothersome that many of the people he interviewed were lying to his face and that by the rules imposed on him as a researcher he was unable to challenge their assertions. Such people included studio executives who persisted in handing out the official line that there was no such thing as a blacklist, and active Communists who pretended that they were "mere liberals" who had never paid a dime in dues to the party. However, some of the Communists he met in Los Angeles turned out to be more forthright, or at least presented a human face to that abstraction, the "Stalinist," that Michael had previously never seen. "In doing some library research," he commented in his memoirs,

> I had discovered that Dalton Trumbo, the blacklisted screenwriter, had boasted under his own byline in the *Daily Worker* that the party had kept anti-Communist content out of the movies. In my interview with him I rephrased his own statement and asked him if it was true. He denied it, and I let the matter drop. (Our policy was never to dispute an interviewee's statement, only to record it.) Half an hour later he suddenly looked at me, laughed, and said, "You son of a bitch, you read the article!" He then explained that it still wasn't true, that it was a rationalization for the Hollywood party's inactivity designed to mollify party critics in New York.[41]

Before his involvement with the blacklisting study, Michael had never actually sat down and talked with a Communist at any length. He had seen them mostly from a distance, usually in an antagonistic situation and through a haze of theories about "bureaucratic collectivism" and "totalitarianism." But when he went to Los Angeles, he was being paid to meet them face to face and to listen to their stories. Intimate contact with so many "Stalinists" softened some of Michael's previous political certainties. He recognized that a number of the Communists he met possessed admirable personal qualities, and that, notwithstanding continuing political disagreements, at bottom he and they shared many of the same values.[42] Thinking back a few years later on the blacklisted Communists he had met in Hollywood, Michael would write:

> There was a certain dignity to some of the Communists, and it was undeniable. They were victims and, however bad their politics, that fact gave them some peace of mind, some integrity. Many of them, I felt, were remaining in the Party primarily due to the diligent work of the FBI and House [Un-American Activities] Committee [in] the mistaken feeling that the only alternative to continued membership was informing.[43]

Michael's official responsibilities with the blacklisting project were completed by the end of 1955, when Cogley set out to write up his report. (Michael would remain employed by the Fund for the Republic as a researcher, writer, and consultant on a number of other projects in the years to come. The job not only provided him a few thousand dollars of income every year, but also included the equally welcome perquisite of "several transcontinental airline tickets a year which allowed me to agitate my way across the country in relative comfort."[44])

The Fund for the Republic's blacklisting study was released with considerable fanfare and comment, both critical and supportive, on June 24, 1956. Its two densely documented volumes, one devoted exclusively to the movie industry and the other to the television and radio industries, left little doubt that there did indeed exist a highly elaborate system in all of those industries for denying employment to people suspected of Communist sympathies—until and unless they gave evidence of sincere repentance, as measured by a willingness to provide information about others to the House Un-American Activities Committee or the Federal Bureau of Investigation.[45]

The penalty in the 1950s for those bold enough to question HUAC's methods often proved to be the chance to experience them first-hand. Four days after the Fund's report was released, Representative Francis E. Walters, the chairman of HUAC, issued a subpoena to Cogley to appear before the committee in Washington. Chairman Walters announced to reporters that the Fund for the Republic's report "levels very grave charges against organizations and persons in the entertainment industry whose efforts have been directed toward eliminating the menace of the Communist conspiracy in the United States."[46]

Cogley's appearance before HUAC was scheduled for July 10. Michael and Paul Jacobs accompanied him to Washington, to be available if necessary to testify on his and the Fund's behalf. Hutchins telephoned on the morning of the 10th to assure all three of them that the Fund would back them unconditionally, whatever the outcome.[47] Hutchins's wisdom in choosing Cogley as director of the project two years earlier was confirmed that day when he was escorted into the hearing room by his good friend Eugene McCarthy, then a young congressman. The Minnesota representative had his arm conspicuously draped around Cogley's shoulders as the two entered the room, a symbolic act of friendly protectiveness that could not have been lost on McCarthy's colleagues on the committee.[48]

By the standards of the era, Cogley was handled gently by his interrogators. Richard Arens, HUAC counsel (and a former aide to Senator Joe McCarthy), did not attack Cogley directly. Instead, he concentrated on Cogley's associates, including Paul Jacobs, who as an ex-member of the Young Communist League made an easy target. But Michael was Arens's main target. "Did you know," he demanded of Cogley, "at the time that you engaged Michael Harrington that he had been a member of the Young Socialist League?":

> COGLEY: I did not know what organizations Mr. Harrington belonged to at the time.

ARENS: Did you ascertain from him whether or not he was a Socialist?

COGLEY: You mean did I ask him, "Are you a Socialist?"

ARENS: Yes, did you ascertain from any source whether or not your assistant, Michael Harrington, was a Socialist?

COGLEY: I knew that he was a Socialist. I did not know what organizations he belonged to.

ARENS: Did you know he had authored a number of articles in the Labor Action publication of the Young Socialist's Challenge?

"No sir," Cogley replied, with more discretion than candor. Arens then questioned Cogley about Michael's affiliation with the War Resister's League and about the fact that he had once signed a petition seeking clemency for the Rosenbergs. Cogley attempted to defend Michael's credentials as a democratic socialist who was opposed to communism and mentioned his many "anti-Communist articles in the Catholic Press." But Arens would not be deflected:

ARENS: You of course are aware of the fact that Lenin, the key philosopher of communism, has said socialism is only one transition toward communism.

COGLEY: Yes, sir.

ARENS: And socialists are only people who are conducting the transition from democracy to communism.

When Chairman Walters asked Cogley at the end of his testimony if he wished to make a final statement, Cogley said simply, "I would like to know why I was called here." Walters replied, briskly, "We called you for the purpose of ascertaining what your sources were in order to determine whether or not your conclusions were the conclusions we would have reached had we embarked on this sort of project."[49]

For the rest of the week, HUAC heard from witnesses more to its liking. Among them was Frederick Woltman, a staff reporter for the *New York World Telegram and Sun* who had won a Pulitzer Prize for his journalistic attacks on the Communist Party. Woltman, like most of the other witnesses, managed to deny that there was any such thing as a blacklist in the entertainment industry, while implying that it wouldn't be such a bad thing if it did exist. As for the report's authors, he was willing to concede that neither Cogley nor Harrington were "Communists or sympathizers." Rather, he thought, "like Mr. [Robert] Hutchins, they are very mixed up." At the end of the week's hearings, to no one's particular surprise, Chairman Walters declared that the Fund's report "isn't worth the paper it is printed on. I do not think there is a blacklist. I cannot find evidence of it."[50]

In some quarters, HUAC's version prevailed: The *New York Daily News* headlined its account of Cogley's testimony "Bares Pinko Tint in Fund," though for some unknown reason its reporter described Michael as a "former socialist."[51] Elsewhere, however, there were doubts, criticisms, and denunciations. The *New York Times,* weighing in editorially on the side of the Fund for the Republic, declared:

> If the House Committee on Un-American Activities were really interested in examining all un-American activities it might long ago have used its great powers as an investigative arm of Congress to look into the thoroughly un-American art of blacklisting in the entertainment industry.[52]

The *Washington Post & Times-Herald* blasted the "highly offensive questioning" of Cogley by HUAC, particularly Arens's attempt to blur the differences between socialism and communism:

> Much of the most effective work against communism is done by persons and groups of Socialist persuasion—by Norman Thomas and the *New Leader* in the United States; by the Social Democratic parties in Europe which are mortal foes of communism. . . . The inquiry may not have disclosed much about blacklisting, but it disclosed a good deal about the thinking process of some of the investigators.[53]

The controversy over the Fund's report added to Michael's political reputation, although in a way he might have preferred to have been spared. In a feature article in the *World Telegram* in December 1956, Frederick Woltman described Michael "as a staff executive of the Fund for the Republic who is currently active in a revolutionary Marxist movement cited as subversive by the Attorney General."[54]

The day after Woltman's article appeared, someone from HUAC (possibly Arens, although the name is blacked out in the available documents) contacted C. D. DeLoach at the FBI to advise him that the committee would subpoena Harrington and several others associated with the blacklisting report to testify in January. DeLoach noted in a memo on the conversation that the HUAC official "thought there might be some questions we might want the Committee to ask these individuals which in turn could possibly be of interest to us in our investigations." DeLoach thought this a good idea and proposed that the FBI provide HUAC with "lines of questioning" on "a confidential and informal basis."[55] But, in the end, possibly mindful of the bad publicity that had dogged its first attempt to crack down on the Fund for the Republic, HUAC let the issue of the blacklisting report drop without further hearings or comment.[56]

The *Report on Blacklisting* did not end Hollywood's political inquisition. The blacklist's demise came in gradual stages, starting in 1960 when the influential producer Otto Preminger thumbed his nose at HUAC by giving Dalton Trumbo screen credit for the script for *Spartacus.* That same year, students in San Francisco staged the first mass protest outside of a HUAC hearing, an event that, as much as anything, signaled the arrival of a "New Left" in America. But the publication of the blacklisting study, and Cogley's successful defiance of HUAC in 1956, helped delegitimize and defuse the power of the witch-hunters. As Michael noted in *Commonweal* in the spring of 1958, "We have, in the past few years, been the fortunate beneficiaries of creeping civil liberties."[57]

For a decade, conservative Republicans had kept liberals on the defensive, lambasting them over issues such as Communist infiltration into government agencies during the New Deal era. Liberals learned to speak a language of chastened realism, fearful of the political enthusiasms of mass movements. William Butler Yeats's lines about the "rough beast . . . slouching towards Bethlehem" became a staple epigraph for liberal writers lending a touch of literary elegance to dour meditations on human nature. In his 1949 political manifesto *The Vital Center,* the liberal historian Arthur Schlesinger Jr. cited both science and religion, Sigmund Freud and Reinhold Niebuhr, to illustrate "the awful reality of the human impulses toward aggrandizement and destruction."[58]

But with the emergence of the civil rights movement in the late 1950s and early 1960s, a new generation of liberals found heroes, images, and legends of courage and righteousness that inspired them to bolder visions of social justice and equality. The civil rights movement was just the kind of mass popular insurgency that older liberals had feared as the harbinger of intolerance, irrationalism, and totalitarianism. Yet, as the struggle for civil rights unfolded, it was easy to tell the good guys (Martin Luther King, Bob Moses, Fannie Lou Hamer) from the bad guys (Bull Connor, George Wallace, Sheriff Rainey). The civil rights movement, dedicated to eradicating America's deepest and most enduring social shame, was at the same time an unmistakably American movement, combining revolutionary fervor and radical insight with values and language drawn from the nation's most cherished biblical and republican traditions. It gave people of liberal sympathies something concrete and meaningful to do to affirm their political values. Liberals no longer had to content themselves with subscribing to the *Nation* or *Commonweal* and shaking their heads in dismay over the latest excesses of McCarthyism. Instead, they could donate money, attend a benefit concert, collect signatures on a petition, write their congressmen, march, picket, and in some cases even risk their lives in the South on behalf of the civil rights cause. As Martin Luther King's biographer, Taylor Branch, has noted, a "civil rights subculture" grew up in the north in these years.[59] And, as often as not, the people who staffed the infrastructure of that subculture, who sent out the fundraising letters, organized the concerts, drafted the petitions, and attended to the myriad of other necessary organizational details came out of one or another of the small radical groups that had somehow managed to survive the depredations of the McCarthy era.

The socialist movement had known a long and ambiguous relationship with the struggle for black equality. In the Debsian era, socialists had been prominent among the founders of the National Association for the Advancement of Colored People (NAACP). On the other hand, they had often downplayed the importance of the struggle against racism, or, like Eugene Debs, they had acknowledged its importance while subordinating it to the struggle for revolutionary socialism. In the 1930s, it had been the Communists, not the socialists, who had made the cause of black equality a political priority and reaped the benefits in recruits and influence in the black community. (During "my years as a civil rights activist," Michael would later note, "I assumed that a really trained black militant of a certain generation had probably been in, or around, the Communist party.")[60] Norman Thomas and other socialists worked valiantly in the 1930s to unite black and white southern sharecroppers in common cause. But the results were meager.[61]

The early years of the Cold War had been lean times for advocates of civil rights. Like "peace," "equality" had become a suspect word, linked to communism in the eyes of many. Even the study of racial discrimination—never mind attempts to do anything to challenge such discrimination—invited hostile inquiries from professional witch-hunters; Swedish social democrat Gunnar Myrdal's 1944 classic *An American Dilemma* came under the hostile scrutiny of the FBI and various congressional investigating committees in the early 1950s.[62]

Michael's own involvement with the issue of civil rights began on a small scale in 1954, the same year as the Supreme Court decision that overturned "separate but equal" justification for segregating public facilities, when he joined the Manhattan branch of the NAACP. He was tutored in civil rights issues by Herbert Hill, a former socialist who had become labor secretary for the NAACP. Although Hill was himself white, he was deeply involved with and knowledgeable about black culture and politics; among other lessons, he taught Michael to abandon his snobbish political disdain for the NAACP as a "middle-class" organization. In the South, Hill pointed out, it was only the black middle class that enjoyed sufficient economic independence to risk joining a civil rights group, whereas in the north, particularly in places like Detroit, a large proportion of NAACP membership was in fact drawn from the ranks of the black working class. Hill accompanied Michael to his first

NAACP meeting and warned him to keep quiet, as he was probably going to be suspected of being a Communist infiltrator until people got to know him better.[63]

Michael's most important link to the civil rights movement, however, came not through Hill or the NAACP, but through black activist Bayard Rustin. Bayard was sixteen years older than Michael and possessed a political résumé that few on the Left could equal. Born in Pennsylvania and raised as a Quaker, he had joined the Young Communist League for a brief period in the late 1930s, before moving on to more politically congenial ties with the socialist and pacifist movements. Bayard had worked with A. Philip Randolph—the socialist leader of the sole black-led union in the AFL, the Brotherhood of Sleeping Car Porters—in organizing the all-black pro-civil rights March on Washington movement to pressure President Roosevelt to end racial discrimination in defense industry hiring practices. He had been a draft resister during the war, for which he served more than two years in a federal penitentiary. He had been a founder of the Congress of Racial Equality (CORE) and had participated in a pioneering "freedom ride" to challenge segregation on interstate buses in the South in 1947 (which earned him a thirty-day sentence on a North Carolina chain gang). Bayard had teamed up again with Randolph in 1948 in another successful campaign to end racial discrimination, this time in the armed forces. He also had been a close associate of A. J. Muste in the pacifist Fellowship of Reconciliation (FOR) from the early 1940s until his arrest in 1953 on a morals charge for homosexuality. This event led Muste to ask for Bayard's resignation from the FOR staff. Since then he had worked for the War Resisters League, but he kept a close eye on civil rights activities, watching for any opportunity to make a contribution.[64]

Bayard cut an imposing figure with his athletic build, angular face, and carefully cultivated and thoroughly incongruous British accent. He was a man of many talents: a gourmet cook (he supported himself in part by catering to a wealthy clientele on Park Avenue) and a talented musician (he toured as a back-up player for Josh White and Leadbelly), he was also a savvy political tactician. His commitment to social justice was the great passion of his life, and, as Michael had already had occasion to observe, he was a man of great physical courage. It would be his unkind fate to be one of the unsung heroes of the civil rights movement.

In December 1955 Rosa Parks was arrested in Montgomery, Alabama, for refusing to surrender her seat on a city bus to a white passenger. Spurred on by a local activist in the Brotherhood of Sleeping Car Porters, E. D. Nixon, as well as by others in the community, black ministers in Montgomery swiftly mobilized a boycott of the city's buses to protest Mrs. Parks's arrest and the indignities of segregated public transportation. A twenty-six-year-old, newly ordained Baptist minister, Reverend Martin Luther King Jr., was chosen to head up the Montgomery Improvement Association (MIA), which directed the boycott effort.[65]

By complete coincidence, the same week that the Montgomery Bus Boycott began in December 1955, the YSL issued its own call for a March on Washington to demand passage of a federal antilynching bill "to Stop the Racist Terror in the South."[66] This was a completely meaningless gesture, taken independently of any civil rights organization, and without practical effect since no such march was ever held; it was simply a way for the *Young Socialist Challenge* to trumpet the YSL's antiracist bona fides. But in the year that followed, the YSL's involvement with civil rights would take a leap from sectarian gesture to deep and practical involvement, largely because of the ties the organization had with Bayard Rustin.

Rustin recognized in the events unfolding in Montgomery a long awaited opportunity to try out Gandhian tactics of nonviolent resistance on a mass scale. In February 1956, with the blessings of Randolph and Muste, Rustin traveled to Montgomery. King welcomed him, and Rustin soon became a trusted adviser on questions of day-to-day tactics and on issues of nonviolent philosophy. It was Rustin, as much as any single individual, who helped broaden King's perspective to see that Montgomery could be the beginning of a massive and ongoing civil rights movement throughout the South.

Rustin remained in Montgomery only a few weeks; his northern sponsors began to worry that were his presence noticed by white authorities in Montgomery, they would use his history of Communist involvement, draft resistance, and homosexuality to discredit the movement. Returning reluctantly to New York in early March, he devoted his efforts over the next nine months to building northern support for the Montgomery struggle. With Ella Baker, a veteran civil rights activist, and Stanley Levison, a former Communist, Rustin formed a group called "In Friendship," which undertook fundraising on behalf of the Montgomery movement. The office on East 57th Street was staffed mostly by two recent YSL recruits, Tom Kahn and Rochelle Horowitz. As Horowitz told Rustin's biographer:

> Mike Harrington had known Bayard from earlier days, and after one of Mike's speeches to the Young Socialist League at Brooklyn College, he told Tom Kahn and me that we could do a very good thing by going up to an office in the East Fifties, where Bayard was building support for the Montgomery Bus Boycott. We went up and volunteered. We stuffed envelopes, worked on leaflets, and helped coordinate big fund-raising events Rustin and In Friendship were organizing. It was our first experience in the civil rights movement.[67]

It would not be their last. Rustin, Kahn, and Horowitz worked together on most of the important national civil rights events of the late 1950s, and again, after a hiatus of several years, on the March on Washington. Michael referred to them as the "Bayard Rustin Marching and Chowder Society."[68] Michael too would be enlisted from time to time in Bayard's operation.

Bayard's pacifism, and particularly his emphasis on using Gandhian tactics in the promotion of what he called "social dislocation," was far removed from the YSL's preferred style of political action. His willingness to reach out to ex-Communists like Levison, and to turn a blind eye to some of the not so ex-Communists who volunteered to help out, was also not customary practice within the YSL. But Bayard and the young Shachtmanites forged a mutually beneficial and durable relationship. Bayard gave the YSLers meaningful work to do and access—or at least the appearance of access—to the inner circle of the southern civil rights movement. The YSL in return provided him with selfless, competent, and disciplined political assistants. That Rustin and Tom Kahn soon became lovers helped cement the political alliance between them.[69]

In the aftermath of the Montgomery Bus Boycott, King and other civil rights leaders called on their supporters to join a "Prayer Pilgrimage" to Washington, D.C., to mark the third anniversary of the Supreme Court's desegregation decision. The YSL threw itself into the effort to bring students to the event.[70] Kahn and Horowitz again headed off to work with Bayard Rustin. At other places around the country, years of dutiful attendance at the small meetings of civil rights groups finally paid off. A Chicago YSLer wrote to Michael to report on the local YSL's efforts mobilizing support for the Prayer Pilgrimage:

> We are in a good position here to work thru the NAACP as you probably know. Saul [Mendelson] and Scott [Arden] are active in the Hyde Park unit, which is extremely enthusiastic about the Pilgrimage. . . . On campus, the YSLers are now considered quite old timers in NAA and are among the few most active people. So we will focus all our activity there.[71]

Thirty thousand people turned out at the Lincoln Memorial on May 17 for the Prayer Pilgrimage, with A. Philip Randolph presiding. It was the largest mass gathering in the history of the civil rights movement and the first major public protest to take place in Washington since Roosevelt had been in the White House. The crowd heard Martin Luther King deliver his first national address, with his much-noted refrain "Give us the ballot." It was the first time Michael had ever heard King speak, and he was impressed. With King's last "Give us the ballot" still echoing from the loudspeaker, Michael noticed that "grown and grizzled men standing on the steps of the Memorial had tears streaming down their faces."[72]

The "Bayard Rustin Marching and Chowder Society" helped stage two more marches on Washington before the end of the decade, organizing them out of the Brotherhood of Sleeping Car Porters office on 125th Street in Harlem. The first, the Youth March for Integrated Schools, held on October 25, 1958, proved somewhat of a flop. Martin Luther King, who had been scheduled to speak at the event, was instead convalescing from a wound inflicted by a mentally deranged black woman a few weeks earlier, and that held attendance down. Still, about 10,000 marchers, including contingents from a number of northeastern colleges, followed Jackie Robinson, Harry Belafonte, and Coretta Scott King on a route down Constitution Avenue to a rally at the Lincoln Memorial. (The *New York Times* relegated its account of the march to page 76, a fair measure of the amount of attention most of the nation was paying to civil rights at the time.)[73]

Randolph, Rustin, and their assistants decided to try again. New recruits helped out at the Youth March headquarters in Harlem and elsewhere around the country; these recruits included Bob Moses, then a New York City high school teacher, and Eleanor Holmes (later and better known as Eleanor Holmes Norton), then a student at Antioch College.

On April 18, 1959, buses from all over the northeast, from as far west as Chicago, and from a number of southern black colleges rolled into Washington for the Second Youth March for Integrated Schools. The mood of the marchers was upbeat, even exultant. The New York City buses carried a fairly large contingent of the offspring of the last generation of radicals, from a variety of usually antagonistic traditions. Michael recalled that on the trip down to Washington the old sectarian traditions were temporarily shelved: "Whatever our attitudes towards the Soviet Union or China, we all knew the same songs, so the buses would reverberate to 'This Land is Your Land,' the national anthem of the Left, and the ballads of the Spanish Civil War."

Twenty-six thousand people came by bus, train, and automobile that day to join the march. That was still a small number, compared to the gigantic crowds that would return again and again to Washington in the 1960s in support of civil rights and in opposition to the war in Vietnam. But to Michael, who winced at the memory of that awful afternoon in 1951 that he spent parading around Times Square with a dozen fellow malcontents, it seemed like a new era:

> Snugly secure in the little world of the New York Left and rolling toward Washington in support of a truly just cause, we looked out of the windows, particularly in the Negro sections of the cities through which we passed, and dreamed that this truly was our land.[74]

The "little world of the New York Left" went through other dramatic changes in the later 1950s—the most dramatic of all being the virtual collapse of American communism. By 1956, the Communist Party in the United States was a battered remnant of what it had been only a decade earlier. Its top leaders were either under indictment, in prison, or on parole; its political energies had been drained by the unceasing demands of its legal battles and by the party's decision to maintain an elaborate underground structure; its influence within the liberal community and in the union movement had long since been obliterated. Still, 20,000 or so die-hard members hung on, which to Michael in 1956 was "more people than we [in the anti-Stalinist Left] had ever seen."[75]

In February of that year, Soviet premier Nikita Khrushchev startled the delegates to the Soviet Communist Party's Twentieth Congress by denouncing his predecessor, Joseph Stalin, as a bloody, paranoid tyrant. Khrushchev's speech was at first kept secret, but experienced Kremlin-watchers knew something was up when the Soviet press began issuing condemnations of a vaguely described historical evil known as the "cult of personality."

American Communists were thrown into confusion by these developments; some, like *Daily Worker* editor John Gates and like-minded staffers on the newspaper, took it as a sign that their own party needed to come to a reckoning with its long history of uncritical apologetics on behalf of the Soviet Union. When the "secret speech" was finally published in Western newspapers in June 1956, the once "monolithic" American Communist Party came apart at the seams. Hard-liners, grouped around party chairman William Z. Foster, battled a dissident reform faction led by John Gates, who opened the pages of the *Daily Worker* to free debate. Many rank-and-file Communists responded in a spirit of guilt and anguish: "I do not want to belong to an organization whose members feel socialism should be imposed on the ends of bayonets," wrote one veteran of nearly twenty years in the party. "This is not the socialism I worked for and dreamed of."[76]

The Shachtmanites regarded these developments as both political vindication—after all, Shachtman himself had played a major role in exposing the Moscow trials back in the 1930s—and political opportunity. Their first response, characteristically, was to set out on a raiding expedition, hoping to pick up recruits from among the disillusioned ranks of the CP's youth group, the Labor Youth League (LYL). The *Young Socialist Challenge* put out a special issue with a banner headline specifically targeted for this audience, "To the Stalinist Youth in the LYL: Did a Lunatic Despot Build Your System?"[77] Steve Max, son of one of the dissident editors of the *Daily Worker*, would recall his sense of astonishment one April evening when, turning a sidewalk corner on his way to an LYL meeting, Michael suddenly leapt out of a doorway to thrust a copy of the *Young Socialist Challenge* into his hands. It was in spite of, not because of, such incidents that Max soon found himself working with young Shachtmanites in organizing the civil rights youth marches.[78]

Thousands of people left the American Communist Party in the spring and summer of 1956; thousands more would follow their lead the next winter, after Khrushchev sent the Red Army to crush the Hungarian Revolution. Within two years the CPUSA was reduced to a corporal's guard of about 3,000 members, heavily infiltrated by the FBI. The LYL, the Communists' youth group, was so demoralized by the de-Stalinization crisis that it voted itself out of existence in 1957.

In an article in *Commonweal* in February 1957, Michael analyzed the Communist Party's current woes. He wrote respectfully of the political soul-searching of *Daily Worker* editor John Gates, his coeditor Joseph Clark, and other Communist dissidents. The group most affected by the de-Stalinization crisis, Harrington wrote, consisted of

> a whole stratum of Party leaders who came into the movement through the Young Communist League in the thirties. . . . The things that makes the Gates faction different, qualitatively different, from the [hard-liners] is that it seems to contain people who are reacting honestly, if hesitatingly after so many years in the intellectual prison of Stalinist ideology, to the events that have been shaking the Communist world.

For Michael this was "evidence of something which I once wrongly thought was impossible: that even those who have participated in the Stalinist movement for years . . . can begin to make independent criticisms." The anti-Stalinist Left was going to have to reconsider its attitude toward men like Gates and Clark:

> It is now clear that there are people within the Communist Party who have made one extraordinarily significant break: they no longer simply accept the Moscow line. . . . We can no longer rule out a dialogue with these people, at least as long as they maintain their newly-won independence of thought.[79]

In the months that followed, Michael established his own dialogue with both Gates and Clark, debating them before large audiences on New York campuses.[80] Michael's decision to reach out to the dissident Communists reflected both his personal and organizational priorities. By the late 1950s, he was becoming a good deal less certain of his own absolute righteousness and more tolerant of the errors of others. Michael was developing a capacity for sympathetic political imagination not widely shared in Shachtmanite circles. He was able to set aside past rivalries and current disputes and to see the world through the eyes of others, at least for a moment. Today's political opponent, he had come to realize, might become tomorrow's ally; *Daily Worker* editor Joseph Clark, for one, would resign from the CP in 1957 and later became a personal friend and one of Michael's fellow editors at *Dissent*.[81]

Michael's new openness to contacts with Communists also represented part of an organizational strategy and a dramatic change in perspective on the part of the Shachtmanites. As the de-Stalinization crisis dragged on from month to month, and the Communist Party fell into ever deeper disarray, some new and interesting questions began to occur to Shachtman and his associates, including, Where would all those ex-Communists go? What group, if any, would now step in and take the Communist Party's place as the largest and most influential force on the Left? The problem the Shachtmanites faced in any potential "regroupment" of the Left was that their own organization, fatally tainted by its reputation for sectarian ruthlessness, simply did not represent a credible alternative to ex-Communists or independent radicals of any stripe. It was Michael's old nemesis within the YPSL, Dave McReynolds, who finally came up with the solution to the Shachtmanites' problem.

McReynolds was one of the few people active in the Socialist Party in the mid-1950s who was more concerned with the party's future than its past. At the close of 1955 the SP could count all of 691 members in good standing nationwide, most of whom lived in four states—146 in New York, 113 in Pennsylvania, 105 in Wisconsin, and 61 in California. ("We are 9 members, and many years in the Party," Morris Stempas, organizer for the Camden, New Jersey, SP Local wrote to McReynolds in 1956. "We used to be a large Branch but the most members have a bad habit, to die! natural I mean and the young ones are not interested."[82]) McReynolds undertook a survey of the remaining SP locals and sent out a bleak report to his political allies in the party:

> I am now convinced . . . that the Party cannot be rebuilt on the basis of its present membership. In Reading, for example [a Party stronghold in the Debs era, with over a thousand local members], I was told the Party is literally dying and there is no prospect of any new recruits. Those who remain in the Party are either people who stopped thinking years ago or people who, while active in various community groups, are not able to take leadership in organizing for the party.

McReynolds concluded that, "The people who ten years ago came into the Party are either not going anywhere or are going into either the ISL, the YSL, the SWP or the ADA, etc."[83] That was not surprising, given that the SP was virtually inactive, save for the increasingly pointless quadrennial exercise of running a candidate for president (in 1956, Reading lawyer Darlington Hoopes once again picked up the socialist standard in the presidential race—and was rewarded with a grand total of 2,119 recorded votes, about a tenth of the number he had received in 1952, and about one five-hundredth of what Eugene Debs and Norman Thomas had received in their best showings).[84]

In 1955, the SP opened unity negotiations with the Social Democratic Federation (SDF), the group that had split off from the party back in 1936 over differences in electoral strategy.[85] McReynolds initially opposed the merger, feeling that re-enlisting the SDF's elderly members would only hasten the SP's inexorable transformation into an old people's home. But then he had an inspiration. He dropped his opposition to the SDF merger (which took place in January 1957; for the next decade and a half the combined group would be formally known as the SP-SDF, though most members still referred to it as the SP). Instead, McReynolds used the merger as an argument for bringing in other groups who would strengthen the party's tiny activist wing. As he wrote in May 1956 in *Hammer and Tongs,* the SP's internal bulletin:

> There are . . . very few groups with which we could seriously consider merger. Perhaps the SDF, perhaps the Jewish Labor Bund, perhaps the ISL. . . . The real objective would be to create a new climate in which the Socialist party would again be the dominant, moving force on the scene—to create the kind of environment and atmosphere in which it would be natural for radicals to come into the Party individually.[86]

Like Shachtman, McReynolds was intrigued by the implications of the collapse of the Communist Party. McReynolds needed allies for his left-wing caucus, people with an activist orientation who knew how to get things done organizationally. And the Shachtmanites needed a new organizational home that would allow them to ditch the political baggage they had accumulated in twenty-odd years of sectarian existence. So an unlikely alliance was born among people who had themselves only recently been bitter political antagonists. McReynolds would work within the SP to bring in the ISL and the YSL, while the Shachtmanites would promote the idea that the SP was the natural center for a revived American Left. "Now is the time for socialism to rebuild," ISLer Herman Benson argued in the fall of 1956. The place for ex-Communists was with their fellow socialists in a broad, democratic socialist movement: "What we are describing is nothing less than the Socialist Party of Eugene Debs."[87]

The reference to Debs was carefully chosen; he was the one left-wing hero shared by both Communists and Socialists. And the SP itself, in its current decrepit condition, had little else to offer beyond a heroic historical legacy. "Weak, impotent, incompetently led as the Party is," McReynolds wrote to civil rights activist Carl Braden in 1957, "it remains a symbol which is worth capturing."[88]

McReynolds had brought a proposal to the SP's national convention in 1956 to explore the possibility of uniting with the ISL, but Norman Thomas responded skeptically: "I know this group," Thomas declared in the subsequent debate, "and the Shachtmanites would take this bunch over in a year." The motion was defeated by a better than three-to-one margin.[89]

But McReynolds was nothing if not tenacious, and after a two-year battle he eventually prevailed. He won because he managed to persuade enough SPers that they simply had no alternative. The YSL's 200-plus youthful members made it an attractive prize. And so did the fact that the YSL had Michael Harrington (although there were some SP leaders, like Samuel Friedman, who cited Michael's role in the 1953 YPSL split as precisely the reason they opposed the merger).[90]

The YSL meanwhile was undergoing its own internal battle over Shachtman's regroupment strategy. For many years Shachtmanites had been attacking the leaders of the Socialist Party as right-wing sellouts and apologists for American imperialism; they derided the SP itself as "the swamp." Now, it was precisely because the SP possessed a respectable centrist image and leader in Norman Thomas that the Shachtmanites sought affiliation.

In the ensuing factional struggle within the YSL, Michael proved that he had learned a thing or two about playing organizational hardball. In an ironic echo of the 1953 YPSL factional imbroglio, Michael brought charges of consorting with Trotskyists against the leader of the YSL's left-wing caucus, Tim Wohlforth (who had, indeed, been flirting with James Cannon's Socialist Workers Party), and had him expelled from the YSL. Wohlforth, in turn, accompanied by several score of YSL defectors, helped to form a new radical youth group, the Young Socialist Alliance (YSA), which affiliated with the SWP. (Wohlforth and some others soon departed the SWP's orbit for a succession of ever smaller and more purist Trotskyist sects of their own devising.)[91]

Norman Thomas, wavering in his opposition to the merger, wrote to Shachtman in the fall of 1957 asking for Shachtman to pledge "explicitly and honestly" that ISLers would "abandon existence as an organized caucus" if they were allowed to join the SP. Shachtman responded solemnly, "We are prepared to lean over backward to prove in deed that any concept of a 'raid' on the Party or the 'capture' of the Party is utterly alien to our views and intent."[92]

Thomas was eventually persuaded by Shachtman's assurances, and at the June 1958 SP national convention he voted along with a majority of the delegates to support the merger. But to placate merger opponents, the convention agreed to leave the final decision up to a party referendum. Thomas sent out a letter to party members later that month saying that he was now convinced that ISLers "will not act as a continuing caucus."[93]

When the votes in the referendum were counted on August 9, the merger was approved, though only by a margin of a few dozen votes.[94] The ISL promptly adopted a resolution providing for its own dissolution, declaring that its goal was now to join in building a movement

> broad in its composition, its outlook, its concepts; that avoids iron and sterilizing dogmas which it seeks to impose upon all others, including dissenters in its own ranks; that avoids the demand for conformity on all questions and problems that are of interest to it; that rejects all concepts of a "monolithic" party and barrack-room discipline.[95]

Over the next several months, ISL members across the country were allowed to join the SP on a prearranged state-by-state basis. YSLers, meanwhile, held a formal unity convention with YPSL in New York over Labor Day weekend to cement their alliance.[96] McReynolds and most of the yipsels felt that Michael should become chairman of the unified group. But the Shachtmanites demurred; they preferred to remain in the background, and so Eldon Clingon from YPSL (a future New York City councilman) was elected instead. Everyone, including Clingon, understood that it was Michael who was the real leader.[97] This was consistent with Shachtmanite strategy within the SP. They intended to keep "real SPers" in prominent leadership positions, so that it would not appear that any kind of political coup had taken place. As Michael recalled, there was something that their strategy had not reckoned on:

> When we went into the SP Max was very concerned that we not take it over. And the problem was that the SP was such a total shell that if you could breathe you would take it over. It was almost impossible not to take it over. The fruit kept falling off the tree, and Max kept putting it back up on the tree.[98]

The Shachtmanites' caution dismayed David McReynolds, who had engineered the merger precisely to undermine the power of the SP's moribund old guard.

In the months following the merger, YPSL's numbers were still pitifully small: It counted two hundred and thirty members in thirteen chapters nationwide: fifty-five in New York, twenty-five in Chicago, twenty each in Los Angeles and Berkeley.[99] But promising reports of YPSL's potential for growth had begun to filter back to SP headquarters from across the country. From Los Angeles, Charles Curtiss wrote to SP national secretary Irwin Suall in early October 1958:

> The good news is that at the local meeting yesterday—nine, count them—nine people applied for membership. These were mainly, although not only people who were waiting to hear of the ISL-SP unity. . . . Still to come are the ISLers proper. You can imagine our jubilation. In the scale of history nine is not very much—but in relation to our recent past and our needs, nine new members is a giant step forward.[100]

Immediately after the YSL-YPSL unity convention, Michael set off on a campus tour that lasted from September through December 1958. It was, he would later recall, the "truly climactic and most emotional" of all the touring he did in the 1950s, a "voyage [that] was a personal and political epiphany." Everywhere he went that autumn he found signs that "the sixties were beginning to stir within the fifties and our tiny socialist movement was emerging from its sectarian isolation." The tour took him to the former centers of YSL strength—Chicago, Antioch, and Oberlin (at the latter, 250 students, a third of the student body, turned out to hear him). But he also traveled to previously unexplored political territory. From Chicago he flew to Denver and borrowed a car to drive to the University of Colorado at Boulder. Then he flew on to Albuquerque to speak at the University of New Mexico, and from there he went to Los Angeles and then north. At Berkeley he spoke before an audience of about a hundred students, the first time in decades that a socialist speaker had been allowed on campus.[101] There he also met with members of SLATE, a left-wing campus political party founded in 1957 that was busily laying the groundwork for the free speech movement that would emerge at Berkeley a few years hence. From the Bay Area he went on to Portland and Seattle (where, in another foreshadowing of the sixties, his hosts casually offered him marijuana after dinner, from a sugar bowl placed on the center of the kitchen table). From Seattle he drove through the Cascade mountains to give speeches in Walla Walla and Chesney, Washington. He finished up with a speech at the University of British Columbia before returning to New York.[102]

In February 1959, Michael reported to the YPSL national executive committee on his tour, a report issued as a pamphlet entitled "The New Left: The Relevance of Democratic Socialism in America." (The term "New Left" was just coming into use in several countries that Michael looked to as political models—a loose grouping of independent radicals in France were being called the "Nouvelle Gauche," while in Britain the influential journal *New Left Review* had begun publishing in 1959, and "New Left clubs" sprang up around the country. The European New Leftists occupied a political space, in the words of Stuart Hall, a West Indian student at Oxford and one of the key figures in the early New Left, "where Stalinism ends and Social Democratic reformism begins.")[103] Everywhere he traveled in the United States that fall, Michael reported, he found "a mood of change." He found evidence of an American New Left being born in the civil rights movement, in the labor movement, in the "growth of liberal opposition within the Democratic Party," and in "a renewal of concern with our disastrous foreign policy." Taken together these movements and concerns suggested the possibility for an imminent "political realignment," the harbinger "not of a 'third' party of protest, but of a real, second party of the people."

Michael had spent much of his tour on campuses, and it was there, he argued, that "the prospects for a New Left in the United States are . . . most immediate." Students were rejecting the "compromise politics of American liberalism." Michael believed that in the place of the tepid reformism of the Stevenson campaigns in 1952 and 1956, the nation's colleges and university communities harbored

> the possibility . . . within the next year of developing a mass (tens of thousands) Civil Rights movement. If this does take place, its effect on all other areas of student life—general political discussion, the socialist discussion movement, the revitalization of the National Student Association, and so on—will be tremendous.[104]

In yet another measure of his expanding political horizons, Michael got to make his first trip to Europe in the summer of 1959. One of the crueler aspects of the McCarthy era for internationally minded American radicals was that it curbed their freedom to travel abroad. Michael had never before even applied for a passport; given the Independent Socialist League's presence on the U.S. attorney general's list of subversive organizations, it is doubtful he would have been given one if he had tried. But after the ISL was dropped from the subversive list in the summer of 1958, Michael was at last free to travel where he liked.[105]

He had long looked forward to the opportunity to meet with western European socialists. The Socialist International, the federation of world's socialist parties, had collapsed during the Second World War but was revived in a meeting in Frankfurt, Germany, in 1951. In the postwar years, European socialist leaders were influential figures in their own countries, in and out of government, and they were usually able to count on the backing of trade unions. Michael put great stock in such international affiliations, both out of ideological conviction, and doubtless also because it boosted his own and his comrades' self-esteem to think of themselves as allied with powerful and, in some instances, ruling parties abroad.[106] For years he had handled the YSL's correspondence with the International Union of Socialist Youth (IUSY), the youth affiliate of the Socialist International. He continued in this role with YPSL, which was afffiliated with the IUSY in 1958.

Ironically, Michael's first trip to meet with his foreign comrades was almost funded by the American Central Intelligence Agency. Two international Communist front groups, the International Union of Students and the World Federation of Democratic Youth, were sponsoring a world youth festival in Vienna from late July through early August 1959, intended as a showcase for Soviet propaganda. All six previous world youth festivals had been held in Soviet bloc cities, the most recent, in 1957, in Moscow. By shifting the festival to Vienna, organizers hoped to draw in a wider section of impressionable young people from non-Communist countries. But the Vienna festival would also prove a magnet for groups who wanted to challenge Soviet influence, including the International Union of Socialist Youth—and the CIA. To recruit young anticommunist Americans to travel to Vienna, CIA operatives secretly established and funded a supposedly private educational foundation known as the Independent Service for Information on the Vienna Youth Festival, with its headquarters in Cambridge, Massachusetts. They hired a young graduate of Smith College named Gloria Steinem to run the office.[107]

Michael wanted to be in Vienna for the festival, seeing it as an ideal opportunity to forge closer relations with young European socialists. Unaware of the CIA's role in the operation, he contacted the Independent Service office in the spring of 1959, asking for financial aid in purchasing a plane ticket to Europe.[108] At Steinem's suggestion, Michael sent a detailed political résumé to C. D. Jackson at *Time* magazine, who was in charge of vetting applicants for Independent Service aid. Jackson had a long association with *Time,* but before that he had served as an aide to General Eisenhower, planning psychological warfare strategies in Europe. After the war he helped set up Radio Free Europe (secretly financed by the CIA) and then spent a year working for Eisenhower in the White House as an adviser on Cold War planning. Even after returning to work for the Luce publications, he remained well-connected in the intelligence community, hence his work vetting recruits for Steinem's group.[109]

At the beginning of June, Steinem herself wrote to Jackson, putting forward the names of four candidates for whom she hoped to secure free transportation to Vienna—among them Zbigniew Brzezinski, then a young instructor at the Harvard Russian Research Center. Of Michael, she wrote that he was

> one of the most prominent young Socialist leaders in this country. He is not associated with the [Independent] Service, but his background as a leader in several organizations and as an associate editor to the magazine *Dissent* means that he is far too identifiable to participate in the Festival officially. He is an excellent public speaker and has on many occasions been able to turn the tide in public meetings. . . . Mike can pay for his own expenses in Vienna,

> and will be working with international Socialist groups as well as the Independent Service. He does, however, need free transportation by plane or by boat. I believe he has already sent you his resume.[110]

But within a few days an obviously disappointed Steinem had to report to Jackson that Michael had withdrawn his application.[111] Beginning to suspect that the Independent Service was considerably less independent than it pretended, Michael had brought the question of accepting funding to a meeting of YPSL's leaders. There was a long debate, in which, Michael recalled, "inevitably, someone pointed out that Lenin had accepted railroad transportation from the Kaiser when he went from Switzerland to Russia in 1917." The money was tempting, but Michael's comrades deemed it too politically risky to accept. He looked elsewhere and eventually came up with the price of the ticket on his own, departing for London on June 19.[112]

Although one American intelligence agency had been prepared to fund Michael's travels, another viewed the prospect of such a well-known threat to the national security loose in Europe with considerable alarm. Learning of Michael's travel plans through an informer, the FBI immediately went into action, notifying U.S. State Department legal attachés in London, Paris, Bonn, and Rome, as well as U.S. Army G-2 intelligence in Europe and the U.S. Air Force Office of Special Investigations, of his imminent arrival on the continent. Everywhere Michael went over the next two months, he was never far from the watchful gaze of one or another employee of the American government.[113]

Michael traveled first to London, where he met some of the leading members of the British New Left (and greatly envied their ties with both a new and vital peace movement, the Campaign for Nuclear Disarmament, and with the British Labour Party). After London, he traveled to Paris, a city he had long idolized as the birthplace of bohemia, and he was not disappointed; he described the pleasure of seeing the city "during a sunny summer when the bright awnings along the Seine were like Impressionist brush strokes."[114] In between sight-seeing, he also made contact with "Nouvelle Gauche" contacts. Michael was particularly interested in the French Left's debates over the Algerian revolution, identifying with those who resisted the war to restore French colonial control.[115]

From Paris, he continued on to Berlin, where the IUSY was holding a convention, prior to tackling the Communists in Vienna. In Berlin he enjoyed the perquisites that came with being an official delegate to a socialist conference in a city ruled by an up-and-coming socialist politician named Willy Brandt. These perks included the exhilarating experience of marching down the street with other young socialists from around the world, as a band from the city's sanitation department played "The Internationale."[116] The

Berlin Wall had not yet been constructed, so he had the opportunity to spend a day roaming through East Berlin. It was Michael's first contact with a Communist country, and he found ample validation of his anti-Stalinist views, feeling "repelled by a drab city with 1984 banners everywhere proclaiming, 'Work for Us is a Joy, for We Work to Build Socialism.'"[117]

Michael arrived in Vienna in late July for the start of the World Youth Festival. He was attending as an observer, not as a delegate, which meant that he wasn't allowed on festival grounds. About half of the 400 official American delegates consisted of people recruited through the Communist Party and its front groups; the other half had come on their own, or through the means provided by Gloria Steinem's operation. Michael kept his distance from the anticommunist Americans, suggesting in a report on the festival he wrote for *Commonweal* that "the unseen hand of the American government" was somehow involved in their activities. Michael roamed the borders of the festival, buttonholing as many of the foreign delegates as he could, especially those from Soviet bloc countries. He found the Poles most sympathetic, as he reported in *Commonweal*: "When confronted with the suppression of *Po Prostu* [an opposition journal briefly published during the unrest of 1956 in Poland], more than one Polish delegate was willing to admit that it had been a serious blow to change in the country." East Germans also offered guarded criticisms of the regime. Not so the Russians: "Those whom one could encounter outside of the official meetings were usually trained propagandists. 'I am an average Soviet citizen,' one of them told me in flawless English, "I work in the Soviet press project on the United Nations.'" Michael did manage to get into the fairground stadium for one of the official rallies, where, as he would later describe the occasion, "the crowd chanted rhythmically, hypnotically, *Mir y Drubja, Paix Et Amitié,* Peace and Friendship. It was my first totalitarian rally, and reminded me of the newsreels I had seen of Hitler at Nuremburg."[118]

Michael left Vienna on August 5, intent on being a tourist for the remainder of his trip. The FBI continued on his trail, following him to Rome. The FBI's female informant, whose identity remains a secret but who was evidently close enough to Michael to travel around the city with him and a few other friends, reported to the agency that she was "impressed with Harrington's extensive knowledge of religious significance of various religious points of interest." Michael and his companions had an audience with Pope John XXIII, "which quite impressed Harrington." Interestingly, the informer went on in her report, "In discussions, Harrington was a staunch defender of the Catholic tradition and [blacked out] was most surprised when Harrington stated that he was not now a practicing member of the Catholic Faith."[119] The FBI's final verdict on Michael's travels proved anticlimactic:

> It was indicated that the three above named individuals while in Rome spent their time *sightseeing* and *shopping*. They are not known to have received any visitors at the pensione nor to have made any telephone calls. Their activities in general gave rise to no suspicions.[120]

Michael returned to the United States later that month, full of enthusiasm for the prospects of the European Left and determined to return to Europe, to travel, and to write a book.[121]

But meanwhile there was much to do in the United States. As the 1950s came to an end, Michael was no longer thinking of himself, in Natalya Trotsky's phrase, as the doomed supporter of "an annihilated legion." Everywhere he looked, he saw confirmation of great changes in the making. Unrest in the Soviet bloc and the de-Stalinization crisis in the American Communist Party swept away the notion, popularized in the writings of George Orwell and Hannah Arendt in the 1940s and early 1950s, that totalitarianism was the wave of the future. Michael argued that it was time for American intellectuals to discard the equally mistaken notion that the spread of "mass culture" had destroyed the possibility of democratic radicalism in the United States.[122] A decade earlier, at Holy Cross, Michael had argued that religious conservatives were the true radicals, standing up for their beliefs in an era of rampant materialism. Now, drawing on his experiences as an itinerant socialist agitator, Michael concluded that an "other America" (this was the first time he had used that phrase in print), that is, an alternative America—a nation of generous democratic values and artistic and social creativity, a nation not "dominated by gadgets and mass media"—lay preserved beneath the surface of a homogenized, profit-driven mass culture.[123] In Seattle, for instance, where he had recently visited,

> the people live in the presence of Mount Rainier. . . . Driving in the city, one never knows when the turning of a corner will reveal the aspect of beauty. On a clear day, each hour, each period, is given a special definition by the mountain. And this geography enters into a culture. It is, of course, intermingled with the history of the region: logging, the IWW, the Seattle General Strike of 1919 . . . the weatherbeaten and brawling tradition of a port. Thus the coffee cups in many restaurants in Washington are bigger than they are in the East. Their shape developed out of an outdoor, working world and they are part of the texture of life in the area. At the trucker's stop in the Cascade mountains where breakfast is ten strips of bacon, four eggs, and a pile of home fries, these coffee cups are one of the forms defining a history and a way of living. They are related to the towering fact of the mountain.[124]

As an apprentice revolutionary in the 1950s, Michael had come to pride himself on his rigorous scientific socialism. But no stretch of dialectical materialism could get him from Mount Rainier to oversized coffee cups to the Wobblies. There was instead a kind of unabashed lyricism in the passage, reflective of Michael's earliest career aspirations as a poet. Long after abandoning his laureate aspirations, he retained the habit of viewing his possibilities and surroundings through a literary lens, a sometimes romantic projection of what a world in which he might play a role commensurate to his talents could be and should be like. His weather-beaten Seattle longshoremen were the literary brothers to the "husky boilermaker from Frisco" who, in John Dos Passos's *The Big Money,* hopped a freight car to join the protest against the execution of Sacco and Vanzetti (an event that led Dos Passos to declare, "all right we are two nations.")[125]

Although he would later be a critic of the more extravagant claims made on behalf of the revolutionary potential of the "youth culture" of the 1960s, Harrington's own radicalism at the turn of the decade contained within it a distinct countercultural strain. Not that he expected (or wanted) the masses to drop out and move to Greenwich Village. But he saw no contradiction between the personal impulses that had led him to the bohemian quarters of lower Manhattan and the larger social transformation to which he was committed.

As in traditional Marxism, there was a teleological element to Michael's socialism, but it was no longer (if it had ever really been) based on his acceptance of some iron law about the falling rate of profit or the like. It was instead closely related to the outsider's stance that he had chosen for his own cultural orientation. His youthful bohemianism was not shaped primarily by a desire to shock or deride his elders or mainstream culture. Rather, he assumed that what most people wanted, and lacked even in "the affluent society" of the 1950s and early 1960s, was some version of what he had already achieved in his personal life—that is the power of self-definition. Socialism would come—not in Michael's lifetime perhaps, but someday and inevitably—as people awakened to the claims of "moral solidarity" and to the joyous potential of "community and meaningful work."[126] Michael's radicalism had become hopeful, generous, and expansive. Although steeped in European intellectual theory (both Catholic and Marxist), his cultural impulses reflected a distinctly indigenous tradition of radical individualism. On the eve of the 1960s, he had come to believe that if the "other Americas"—the *alternative* America of intellectuals and students and artists and his Greenwich Village neighbors, and the *excluded* America of the poverty-stricken and the dispossessed—could unite in coalition with a democratic labor movement, they would represent a powerful redemptive force for social justice.

CHAPTER SEVEN

The Man Who Discovered Poverty, 1960–1964

The War on Poverty arose as much as anything from the socialist tradition of men like Michael Harrington.

Daniel Patrick Moynihan
August 1968[1]

In the spring of 1962, the *Village Voice* hailed its long-time contributor Michael Harrington, with a certain proprietorial pride, as "a vital voice of conscience for our times." The occasion was the recent publication of his book on poverty, *The Other America.* In December 1963, Norman Thomas wrote to Michael, who was then in Paris, telling him of his eagerness to see him on his return to the United States. "I cannot think of anyone to whom I look with more confidence to carry on the struggle for the acceptance of an enlightened democratic socialism in our country." And in November 1964 James Wechsler, the influential editor of the then liberal *New York Post,* described Michael in an editorial as "a quiet thunderer" and predicted he would emerge as the unifying figure of the "scattered legions among the liberal intellectual community, the civil rights activists and the more enlightened sectors of organized labor."[2]

In the early 1960s Michael did indeed seem—for the first time in his adult life—a man at one with his setting and his times. After ten years of involvement with small sectarian organizations of the Left, most of it spent in apparently wasted effort, he became celebrated as the man who discovered poverty—and he did so at precisely the moment when the United States seemed to be prepared to pay attention to and act upon such a discovery.

The writing of *The Other America* began with an invitation to lunch. Anatole Shub, an editor at *Commentary* magazine (and himself a man with an offbeat political background, as the child of an exiled Russian Menshevik leader), treated Michael to a meal one day in December 1958. Shub suggested that Michael consider writing an article for *Commentary* on poverty.[3]

Shub's editorial instinct proved inspired. But the logic of the assignment was not as self-evident at the time as it might seem in retrospect. Michael's claim to expertise on the subject of poverty was limited. He had caught a glimpse of St. Louis's poor, memorable but extremely brief, during his stint with the public school system. He had acquired a longer and more intimate exposure to poverty while serving the Catholic Worker movement, but for the most part he came in contact with only a small and exceptional subgroup of New York City's poor—aging, white, male, alcoholic derelicts. And, in the half dozen years since he had left the Worker, he devoted little attention to poverty in his writing, apart from the kind of ritual references one might expect from a devoted critic of capitalism. Those who read his articles in *Commonweal* knew him primarily as an authority on communism and secondarily as an aspiring literary critic; those who read his articles in *Dissent* knew him primarily as a writer concerned with civil liberties issues. Of the dozens of articles and reviews he contributed to the two journals in the 1950s, only a single one, an article for *Commonweal* in 1954 about public housing, even so much as touched on poverty as an issue of contemporary concern.[4]

Michael, of course, was hardly alone in his neglect of the topic. Liberal publications in the 1950s, not to mention the mainstream press, seemed to assume that American poverty was something worth writing about only in historical retrospect. There were, at the very start of the decade, a few exceptions to this generalization. In January 1950, the *New Republic* put out a special issue assessing "The State of the Nation" at mid-century. The editors noted that 10 million families, accounting for a third of the nation's population, had incomes of under $2,000 a year. This "persistent poverty in the bottom layer of our economy," they warned, would not disappear even with "continuing full employment." The editors recommended new federal programs for job training of the unskilled, along with unspecified measures on behalf of "older workers, minority groups, widows or the heads of broken homes, and others handicapped by disability or special circumstances."[5] A few months later, *Harper's Magazine* carried any article by economist Robert Heilbroner entitled "Who Are the American Poor?" In it, Heilbroner made use of what a decade and a half later became a cliché for characterizing American poverty, the paradox of "poverty amidst plenty." America's "unresolved hard core of poverty," Heilbroner declared, "limited one-quarter of our citizens to a standard of living far short of that which we required for our national health."[6]

After that, and for nearly a decade, attention to poverty in liberal publications languished. Writing in *Dissent* in 1955, Irving Howe chided contemporary social commentators for their preoccupation with the problems of the middle class (as in such recently published works as David Riesman's *The Lonely Crowd,* or William H. Whyte's *The Organization Man*). Why, Howe wanted to know, wasn't anyone interested in such problems as "the gradual decay of the New England textile towns or the social disruption of New York City under the pressure of Puerto Rican migration"? Why had no one considered "writing a sequel" to James Agee's quarter-century-old study of southern sharecroppers, *Let Us Now Praise Famous Men*?[7] Just as the words "peace" and "equality" suffered from association with Communist rhetoric and protest movements, so "poverty" was perceived as a politically dangerous topic; even the editors of *Harper's* felt it necessary to preface Heilbroner's article with the disclaimer, "In calling attention to one of the imperfections of our economy, [Heilbroner] assumes a basic condition of health which can stand examination."[8]

But the dearth of discussion of poverty was not simply a matter of political caution. Liberals in the 1950s were generally persuaded that the United States no longer had any serious structural economic problems requiring concerted government action of the sort they had applauded in the 1930s. Economic growth in and of itself was the key to the mopping up of any residual poverty left over from the days of the Great Depression. Roosevelt biographer and ADA activist Arthur Schlesinger Jr., writing in 1956, argued that liberals had to face up to "the challenge of abundance." The "quantitative liberalism" of the 1930s had focused on "immediate problems of subsistence and survival" that no longer were of relevance in the United States. "The issues of 1956," he suggested, "are no longer the issues of 1933." It was time to move on to a "qualitative liberalism" that would be dedicated, in ways that Schlesinger left somewhat vague, "to bettering the quality of people's lives and opportunities."[9]

Two years later, Schlesinger's colleague at Harvard and fellow ADAer John Kenneth Galbraith published a study of the postwar American economy entitled *The Affluent Society*. The book rose to the top of the bestseller lists, and its title became a celebratory catchphrase for the genius and bounty of the free market—not entirely what Galbraith had intended. Galbraith argued that, thanks to the adoption of Keynesian fiscal policies, the United States had attained a more or less stable and permanent state of prosperity. But he sought to shift the argument from the quantity of goods produced by the economy to the quality of life that resulted, and he drew a contrast between private opulence and public squalor, particularly in such areas of government responsibility as education, the environment, and the urban infrastructure. Like many liberals, Galbraith had come to take economic growth for granted; unlike many of them, he questioned whether economic growth was in itself the highest social good with which government should concern itself. Galbraith also noted, toward the end of his book, that not all Americans could be called affluent in any sense of the word. In a chapter entitled "The New Position of Poverty," he demonstrated statistically that "poverty does survive" in contemporary America. But he also argued that it had "ceased to be a general case" and now afflicted only individuals suffering from particular disabilities, or, at most, certain "islands" of backwardness, like the Appalachian region.[10]

When Michael accepted *Commentary*'s commission, Shub's suggestion may well have seemed to him just another writing assignment. In his apprenticeship as a freelance writer, he had developed a knack for expounding confidently and lucidly on all kinds of topics, from bolshevism to Balanchine. Like many another intellectual jack-of-all-trades who came out of or paid tribute to the *Partisan Review* tradition, he was a gifted intellectual borrower. In familiarizing himself with a new subject, he could quickly sense the difference between a strong and a weak argument. He was always on the lookout for a compelling phrase or theory to quote. Michael had a lot of other projects to work on; he was bringing out his first book (a collection of essays on contemporary labor that he coedited with Paul Jacobs), and he was also beginning to think about a much more ambitious effort, a study of the idea of cultural decadence in the twentieth century.[11] All he probably intended to accomplish in the article for *Commentary* was to provide an overview and a synthesis of current thinking on the problem of poverty—certainly he did not intend to write the successor volume to Agee's classic work on poverty in the thirties that Irving Howe was calling for in the pages of *Dissent.*

Michael's investigation of poverty coincided with a minor spate of journalistic interest in the topic: Among the recently published items that caught his eye were a chapter on urban slum life in *The Exploding Metropolis,* a recent book by Daniel Seligman of *Fortune* magazine; an article in *Harper's* magazine by Albert Votaw that described the plight of southern Appalachian "hillbilly" migrants in Chicago; and reports in the *New York Times* and the *New York Post* on the failures of "slum clearance" projects.

Michael may also have read several pieces that dissented from Galbraith's conclusions about the affluent society. In the *New Republic,* in October 1958, economist Leon Keyserling noted that in the previous year more than a quarter of all American families reported annual incomes below $4,000. "These people may be living in affluence compared to people living in India," Keyserling declared. "*But they are certainly living in poverty by any standard that should have meaning for us today.*"[12] Keyserling, who had served as chairman of the Council of Economic Advisers in the Truman administration, argued that "eggheads" like Galbraith and Schlesinger underestimated the need for strong federal policies, akin to those initiated in the Roosevelt and Truman administrations, to promote full employment.

A few months later, *The New Leader* ran a piece entitled "How Affluent Is

"Neddie" Harrington, St. Louis, circa 1942

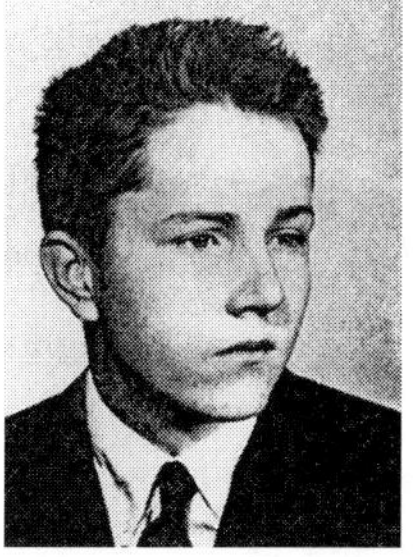

Edward M. Harrington, Jr.

CLASSICAL

Second Honors '41, '42; Sodality '41, '44; Dauphin '44, Associate Editor; U. Prep News '41-'44, Assoc. Editor '44; Speech Society '41, '42; Debating Team '42; Elocution Finalist '42; Latin Forum '43, '44; Literary Circle '44; Science Club '43, '44; Library Association '41; Radio Workshop '44.

"Ned" Harrington, St. Louis University High School Yearbook, 1944

"Ed" Harrington strikes a writer's pose, Holy Cross, 1947

Edward M. Harrington

BACHELOR OF ARTS

6186 McPherson Avenue, St. Louis, Mo.

. . . Ed, the oracle for the midwest . . . has worked for every publication on the Hill . . . and has done an excellent job with them all. Bane of his existence were Lambert and Markham . . . who used to wake him in the morning . . . with a bull whip in one hand . . . and a stack of assignments in the other . . . One of the best speakers in the B.J.F. . . . the wielder of a powerfully subtle pen . . . the owner of a personality which made all who knew him feel perfectly at home . . . Ed was a man for the Dean's List . . . a man for social recreation in a big way . . . and a man headed for Law school with a host of friends behind him . . . and a brilliant future ahead . . .

PATCHER Profile Editor 4; Purple 2, 3, 4, Managing Editor 4; Tomahawk 1, Sports Editor, Editorial Board 2, 3; B.J.F. 3, President 4; Sodality 1, 2, 3; Sanctuary Society 1, 2, 3, 4.

SENIOR THESIS

Hal, Prince and King

Edward Harrington, Holy Cross Yearbook, 1947

Dorothy Day, early 1950s

Michael as the tardy Twelfth Apostle, 1951

Bogdan Denitch, 1951

Norman Thomas, late 1950s

Michael Harrington at a Socialist Party conference, 1962

Michael in Paris, 1963

the village VOICE, *June 6, 1963*

Voice: Fred W. McDarrah

MARRIED IN PARIS on May 30 were **MICHAEL HARRINGTON** and **STEPHANIE GERVIS.** Miss Gervis, a free-lance writer, is the Voice correspondent in Paris, and Harrington, also a free-lance writer and one of the original contributors to The Voice, is author of the recently published, prize-winning "The Other America." He is an editor of New America and former assistant editor of the Catholic Worker. Miss Gervis had published articles in such magazines as Commonweal and the Nation. The Harringtons expect to return to the United States at the end of the year. They plan to live in the Village.

The Village Voice announces Michael's marriage, June 1963.

Max Schactman at a Socialist Party conference, 1962, Michael Harrington in the foreground

The Other America, 1962 hardcover, 1965 paperback

Lyndon Johnson, 1963

Sargent Shriver, circa 1964

Marching on Montgomery with Martin Luther King, Jr., 1965

Irving Howe, circa 1980

Michael, Stephanie, Alec, Teddy and Humphrey the dog, Larchmont, 1980

Stephanie, Alec and Teddy at the "Eurosocialism" conference, Washington, D.C., December 1980

Michael, Marjorie Phyfe, Gellerman, William Winpisinger, June, 1979

Our Society?" a reprint of a speech delivered by Senator Paul Douglas of Illinois. The occasion for Douglas's remarks had been an award ceremony at New York's Tamiment Institute, where *The Affluent Society* received the institute's annual prize for a book of "social significance." Douglas presented the award and, rather unusually for such occasions, took the trouble to think about and question some of the assumptions undergirding Galbraith's book. Douglas had the credentials to take on Galbraith; a former University of Chicago economist, he had been elected to the Senate in 1948; a stalwart ADAer, he was in the 1950s one of the few nationally prominent politicians who showed a consistent concern for the problems of the poor and the unemployed. Several of the proposals he brought (unsuccessfully) before the Senate in those years became hallmarks of John F. Kennedy's domestic policies—including government spending targeted to revitalize "depressed areas."[13]

In his comments that evening at the Tamiment, Douglas noted that "contrary to the title of Galbraith's book, not everybody is affluent in the United States." Being a "somewhat literal-minded fellow," Douglas had asked the Bureau of the Census for its most recently published data on family income. He discovered that roughly 25 percent of the country's families—all of whom, he argued, "can be regarded as being in a state of poverty"—had incomes under $3,000 a year. (Galbraith, in contrast, had used an annual income of $1,000 a year or less as his benchmark for determining the extent of poverty.) "It's not a third of a nation ill-housed, ill-fed and ill-clothed to which Franklin Roosevelt referred in his Second Inaugural," Douglas conceded, "but it is somewhere between one-quarter and one-fifth of the population."[14]

Michael never cited Keyserling's article or Douglas's remarks, but since he was reading around on the topic of poverty, it seems unlikely he could have missed them. It may be that the two pieces suggested to him an approach to the topic of poverty that he otherwise would not have taken—that is, counting the poor. Previous to this, Michael made infrequent and unsystematic use of statistical data of any kind in his writing. But his argument in his article for *Commentary,* appearing in July 1959, was driven by statistics, starting with its stark title, "Our Fifty Million Poor."

Using the same $3,000 annual income as Senator Douglas had as his benchmark for poverty (although arguing that it set far too low a standard for a minimally decent style of life), Michael concluded that somewhere between 40 and 60 million Americans were living in poverty in 1959, out of a population of just under 180 million. (His figures differed somewhat from Douglas's because he drew upon different sources: Douglas had used U.S. Census Department data, whereas Michael cited Federal Reserve Board and U.S. Commerce Department statistics.) Michael argued that his data disproved the "current myth" that the poor were a "small, rapidly declining group" likely to disappear entirely in the near future. To speak of the poor meant speaking, roughly, of one in every three Americans:

> As many as 50 million Americans continue to live below those standards which we have been taught to regard as the decent minimums for food, housing, clothing, and health. These millions are . . . a predominantly urban, white population; they have scarcely been affected by the reforms of the past quarter-century; and as a group they have profited least from the striking gains in productivity which have characterized the American economy since World War II.[15]

If all Michael had done was restate arguments already being made by Keyserling and Douglas about the continued existence of poor Americans, his *Commentary* article would likely have proven just another example of his episodic interest in the subject of poverty. But, in what proved a momentous act of intellectual borrowing, he added something else to the argument: the idea of the "culture of poverty."

The "culture of poverty" had been the guiding concept of *Five Families: Mexican Case Studies in the Culture of Poverty,* a recently published ethnographic study by the radically inclined anthropologist Oscar Lewis. Sociologists had long studied the "way of life of the poor," but until Lewis no one had argued that this way of life functioned as a distinct "subculture." Lewis contended that being poor was not simply a condition marked by the absence of wealth or material comfort; rather, poverty created "a subculture of its own," one that cut "across regional, rural-urban, and even national boundaries." In other words, however different their cultures of origin, poor people in Azteca, Mexico, might have more in common with their counterparts in San Juan—or, for that matter, New York—in terms of family structure, interpersonal relations, time orientation, value systems, and spending patterns than with other, better off people from their own countries.[16]

Echoing Lewis, Michael argued in *Commentary* that American poverty constituted "a separate culture, another nation, with its own way of life." Accordingly, a broad program of "remedial action"—part of a "comprehensive assault on poverty" on the part of the federal government—was needed if the problem was to be solved: "Housing, schools, medical care, labor standards, communal institutions must be combined in a broad planned program if any of these measures is to have real impact on poverty." The chances of that happening any time soon, Michael admitted, were slight. The liberal middle class had managed to "isolate themselves" from exposure to or knowledge of poverty. And the ruling conservative coalition in Congress had managed to block any real extension of the American welfare state since Roosevelt's second term in office. Until something changed, he concluded soberly, "it is likely that the poor will remain with us, through cycles of boom and bust and successive elections, and that their way of life will perpetuate itself, to their own hurt and the great damage of our own society."[17]

In his second article on poverty for *Commentary,* appearing in August 1960 and entitled "Slums, Old and New," Michael pronounced "postwar America's greatest single social scandal" to have been "its failure to provide adequate housing for its low-income groups." As in his first article, he made extensive use of the idea of a culture of poverty, contrasting the social disintegration characteristic of modern urban slums with a somewhat romanticized vision of the way things were in places like "Kerry Patch" and "Little Italy" at the start of the century. At the turn of the century, poor immigrant communities had been "a dynamic, creative part of American society," full of neighborliness, strong ethnic and religious institutions and bonds, and aspirations for a better life. The "changed slum" of contemporary America, in contrast, resembled its predecessors "only in dilapidation and overcrowding; for the new slum is conspicuously lacking in any central culture, and most often is based solely upon the integration of poverty with poverty, failure with failure." One of the most striking changes that had taken place in the past half century, Michael suggested, was in the character of family life among the poor. Whereas older slums had been characterized by "stable family life," the "rootless and transient" families found in the newer slums were frequently "female based," with children growing up without the presence of their natural fathers. Existing slum clearance and public housing programs, however well intended, only wound up "segregating the poor on the basis of class [and] caste," a condition that reinforced "slum psychology." In order to break the perpetuation of the culture of poverty in the new urban slums, Michael argued not only that existing public housing programs be expanded, but that such housing in the future should consist of "low-rise housing in relatively small units," interspersed among working- and middle-class neighborhoods.[18]

The timing of Michael's articles proved remarkably good. By the time his second article appeared, John Kennedy had spent several well-publicized weeks campaigning in West Virginia for the Democratic presidential nomination; the candidate and the press alike noted the decidedly unaffluent character of society in the mining towns of the state. Several months after Michael's second article appeared, CBS News broadcast a special hour-long documentary entitled "Harvest of Shame." Narrated by Edward R. Murrow, the documentary traced the plight of migrant farm laborers, many of them looking and sounding like they had just stepped out of the pages of *The Grapes of Wrath.* It received widespread attention, in part because it followed up on the earlier stories on the West Virginia primary, and in part because it was shown the day after Thanksgiving, when its message of "poverty amidst plenty" found a receptive audience.

Sensing that Michael had hit upon a hot topic, several publishers wrote to him asking if he would be interested in expanding the articles into a book. Heeding Max Shachtman's advice that the most valuable contribution he could make to the movement was to concentrate on his official duties within the Socialist Party, he threw the letters away without replying.[19] Nothing more might have come of the project, had it not been for the urging of Herman Roseman, a left-leaning economist of Michael's acquaintance who argued that Michael had a moral duty to "illuminate the reality that his profession ignored." Michael's old friend from Catholic Worker days, Betty Bartelme, who was working as an editor at Macmillan, put him in contact with Macmillan editor Emile Capouya, who offered him a book contract with an advance payment of $500. That "enormous sum," more money than he had ever been paid for any of his writing, clinched the deal.[20] Michael was soon on the road again, this time to gather material for the book, and publishing sections of his growing manuscript in *Dissent, Commonweal,* and other publications.[21]

But Michael had to squeeze his research in between many other political responsibilities. For much of 1960–1961, his involvement with the civil rights movement took priority over everything else.

There were really two civil rights movements in the 1960s. One, centered in New York with outposts in other northern cities, handled fundraising, publicity, and coalition-building for the movement and organized large, nationally focused events such as the March on Washington. The other and main movement, based in the South, grew out of the Montgomery Bus Boycott and the student sit-ins of the spring of 1960. It was oriented to local communities and favored tactics of direct action (including voter registration). The northern and southern movements were, of course, interrelated and symbiotic, and their differences in orientation reflected a kind of natural division of labor between the two regions. There were important figures, including Martin Luther King Jr., who shuttled back and forth between the two. Others, who got their start in one wing of the movement would shift their labors to the other: Bob Moses, who went from working with Rustin, Kahn, and Horowitz organizing the youth marches in the 1950s to leading the voter registration campaign in Mississippi in the early 1960s, is a case in point.

But the division of labor between the two civil rights movements also reflected, or perhaps engendered, a different political sensibility as well. For all of his long years of involvement in the movement, Michael's politics were formed independent of and outside of the civil rights movement. The "southern students," Michael wrote in an article for *The New Leader* in 1961, "come from a completely different background and are unrelated to the forces which have made for youth radicalism on the Northern campus. . . . [T]he Negro youths who take part in the sit-ins have not shared in the Northern experience of the decline of an existing student movement. They came fresh to their rebellion." Michael admired the spirit of the southerners but also felt it represented a potential weakness of the southern movement: "There have been few ideologically oriented, radical young people among them and they have not played a decisive role."[22]

Except for the occasional march or conference, Michael did not go south in the 1960s. He found it hard at first to appreciate the new style of politics being pioneered by the veterans of the sit-ins. The northern civil rights movement in which Michael figured as a respected political actor was older and more professional in its organizational structure and style of political work. Some of its most important leaders and organizers—A. Philip Randolph, Rustin, James Farmer of CORE—came out of or at least had close relations with the socialist movement. The southern movement, in contrast, was younger, less sophisticated ideologically, but more radical tactically. It favored an experimental and expressive political style that the northerners often found puzzling. After attending a student civil rights conference in the South in the fall of 1960, Michael came away extremely discouraged by the kind of "amiable, parliamentary chaos" that prevailed. It seemed to him that "the initial force" of the southern student movement "had been spent"; it was all so very different from the conventions he was used to, with their formal debates, resolutions, and caucuses. A year later he admitted publicly that he had been mistaken: "the Southern students have produced a full-time dedicated cadre," entirely on their own and without the guidance of more experienced leftists from the north, "and all the old theories about 'professional revolutionists' seem to have found a somewhat curious practical incarnation."[23]

It cannot be said of Michael, as it can be for so many other activists of the 1960s, that involvement in the civil rights movement changed his life. But his involvement in the movement would, nonetheless, have an important impact on him. It gave his politics a depth of human empathy and understanding lacking in the 1950s. He was forced to become aware of his own propensity, nurtured in brilliant and sterile debates in the YSL's loft, of thinking of blacks and other social groupings as abstract "social forces" who, favored with the proper political leadership, could be counted on to conduct themselves according to Marxist formulae. "Our sense of oneness with the masses," Michael would write in his memoirs, "was dangerously delusional. We had nominated ourselves as leaders on the grounds that our ideas were right. Later, when flesh and blood people, and not a Social Force, insisted on choosing their own spokesmen, we learned, sometimes painfully, that politics is not a folk song."[24]

On February 1, 1960, four black college students "sat-in" at a Greensboro, North Carolina, lunch counter to protest local segregation ordinances. Refused the cup of coffee they had ordered, they were back the next day—but this time with thirty compatriots. The next day there were over sixty, and the day after that several hundred. By then news of the protests had spread to black colleges across the south. Before the month was out, black students in Winston-Salem, Durham, Chattanooga, Nashville, and Montgomery, among other communities, had launched similar sit-ins. And by April it was estimated that more than 50,000 people had taken part in the movement. That same month, veterans of the sit-ins and sympathetic observers met in Raleigh, North Carolina, to form a new organization, the Student Non-Violent Coordinating Committee (SNCC).[25]

Michael followed these developments with great interest, if at a distance. He was in the midst of yet another national tour on behalf of YPSL when the sit-in movement broke out, and so he missed the April meeting in Raleigh. But he took part in another significant gathering that month in Ann Arbor, where, along with James Farmer, he was a featured speaker at a conference at the University of Michigan on "Human Rights in the North," organized by a new campus organization called Students for a Democratic Society (SDS). The meeting brought together for the first time the black veterans of the spring's sit-ins with white northern campus activists, the beginnings of what would prove to be a potent political alliance.[26]

Back in New York, Michael went to work on behalf of the current project of the "Bayard Rustin Marching and Chowder Society." The project was a letterhead organization known as the Committee to Defend Martin Luther King, which Bayard had established to handle publicity and fundraising chores after King was indicted on trumped-up tax evasion charges in Alabama. It was in the role of representative for Rustin's newest committee that Michael attended a National Student Association meeting on the sit-ins, held in Washington, D.C., that spring. "It was not then considered preposterous," as he would later note, "for a white radical to be a spokesman for a black leader."[27]

In the summer of 1960, the attention of the civil rights movement, like that of most of the nation, shifted to the presidential race. The Democratic national convention was scheduled to open in Los Angeles on Monday, July 11. Randolph and Rustin decided that they wanted to create a strong civil rights presence at the convention, reminding the presidential aspirants, as well as the delegates in charge of writing the party platforms, of the importance of the black vote. Michael was dispatched to Los Angeles to work with Clarence Jones, an influential black entertainment lawyer, to organize a mass march to the convention site on July 10, the Sunday before the official proceedings began. Michael arrived in Los Angeles in early June and immediately plunged into a series of meetings of black community leaders. He got along well with co-organizer Clarence Jones, who in a note to Bayard in late June commented: "Have greatest respect for Mike. Doing excellent job. Regards to Tom [Kahn]. Complete freedom of Negro people not far off when have dedicated *white* people of caliber of Mike and Tom."[28]

Not everyone in the black community welcomed Michael as warmly. While the city's highly factionalized civil rights leadership squabbled over issues of strategy and status, and the L.A. police department stalled on issuing the necessary parade permits, Michael found himself under attack from some black activists as an outside agitator. Others suspected him of being a Communist or, even less flatteringly, "a cop, a bill collector, or some other agent of hostile authority." Discouraged after several fruitless weeks of trying to unify the warring factions, Michael called Bayard in New York to confess failure. "My good friend," Bayard replied, "there is going to be a march. I know there is going to be at least one person on it. You."[29]

When July 10 arrived, it turned out that Michael would not have to march alone after all. Five thousand marchers, most of them from the local black community, followed Martin Luther King Jr., Roy Wilkins, and student sit-in leaders Bernard Lee and Marion Berry to the sports arena where the Democratic convention was to open the next day. The rally that followed was addressed by Senator Kennedy and other highly placed Democratic dignitaries. Kennedy assured his listeners that they could count on his support if he was in the White House, but he received a tepid and skeptical response from the crowd.[30]

Buoyed by the numbers who had turned out for the march, the organizers decided on the spur of the moment to set up a twenty-four-hour-a-day vigil outside the sports arena, to pressure the Democrats to adopt a strong civil rights plank for their 1960 party platform. Michael served as the vigil's picket captain, a role he thoroughly enjoyed. He was on his feet for hours every day, along with dozens and sometimes hundreds of supporters, waving picket signs, chanting, and singing. A contingent of Berkeley students came down to join the picket line, as did another group that came all the way from Cornell (and so did a University of Michigan undergraduate named Tom Hayden, who eight years later would be among the principal organizers of a very different sort of protest at a Democratic convention). CBS News filmed an interview with Michael the day that the Democrats adopted their civil rights plank, and millions of American television viewers that evening got to see a white man with an Irish surname, who wore a Los Angeles Dodgers cap to shade his fair skin, arguing that the Democrats' platform had not gone far enough in advancing the rights of the nation's black citizens.

Michael picked up Martin Luther King at the Los Angeles airport the day before the march on the convention and accompanied him when he testified before the convention platform committee. He also spent many hours keeping King company in his hotel room. This was the first time the two men met, and Michael was "astounded, and a little humbled, to realize that he was younger than I." In King's hotel room, he and Michael discussed political strategy and philosophy. King was being courted by representatives from the Kennedy camp asking him to endorse their candidate, and he asked Michael what he thought he should do. Michael told him not to endorse Kennedy, partly for the "stupid and sectarian" reason that he was unable "to advise anyone to back a 'bourgeois' candidate." There was also no guarantee that Kennedy would win in November, which meant that King would need to keep channels of communication open to Nixon. (Whether Michael's advice had much to do with his eventual decision is unlikely, but King refrained from formally endorsing Kennedy then, or in the general election.) The two also talked of their mutual interests in philosophy and politics. Michael came away from his discussions with King convinced that the civil rights leader was a democratic socialist in all but name. He found it heartening, he later wrote, that King had, "in the course of a much more profound political and intellectual journey than mine, come to a view of America and the world that I largely shared."[31]

Michael would meet King again a few months later, when both attended a SNCC-organized conference at Morehouse and Spelman Colleges in Atlanta. Michael was invited as a "resource person," once again representing the Committee to Defend Martin Luther King.[32] A number of Michael's SP comrades were also in attendance: Michael and Rochelle Horowitz helped lead a workshop on political action at the convention.[33] (Bayard Rustin, however, was conspicuous in his absence. George Meany, who was helping to fund the event from AFL-CIO coffers, intervened with SNCC to keep such a notorious radical away. That Rustin was a close associate of A. Philip Randolph, for whom Meany bore no love, did not help. SNCC leader Marion Berry wrote to Meany in September to assure him that "Mr. Bayard Rustin, Executive Secretary of the War Resisters League, who was listed as a participant is not now and will not be connected with our movement in the future.")[34] King invited Michael to his house in Atlanta for dinner and to continue the conversations they had begun in Los Angeles.

By the time of the Atlanta conference, SNCC was beginning to talk about shifting its focus from direct action protests against segregation to a voter registration campaign. As yet, the civil rights movement had encountered what, by later standards, would seem a very mild reaction from the defenders of white supremacy. No one was killed in the protests in 1960, although some were beaten and many arrested. Michael discussed the voter registration proposal with King and was impressed and sobered by King's response. "Some people would probably be hurt," King acknowledged. "There is a danger of death even. But we have no choice. We have to go there."[35]

Michael was also busy that fall with new duties as editor in chief of the Socialist Party's biweekly newspaper, *New America.* He brought out the paper's inaugural issue on Labor Day 1960. Michael was determined to make it a publication that would attract readers on its merits, rather than it being just another earnestly orthodox party organ on the order of the now defunct *Labor Action.*

With scanty resources, a neophyte staff, and no pretense of preserving the stance of journalistic objectivity prized in the mainstream press, *New America* was hardly in a position to compete for Pulitzer prizes.[36] But in its first few years the paper built a credible record for nonsectarian coverage of the issues and movements that would count in the decade to come. While the mainstream press was preoccupied with the horse race between Richard Nixon and John F. Kennedy in the fall of 1960, A. Philip Randolph's lead story for *New America*'s inaugural issue chastised both Democrats and Republicans for the failure of their parties to offer any kind of consistent and reliable support to the civil rights movement. Referring to the past summer's nominating conventions, Randolph declared, "Idealism and vision were to be found not within the convention halls but outside, among the thousands of civil rights supporters who marched on both conventions demanding Negro freedom now." Randolph predicted that the civil rights movement would soon launch "the kind of physical, and essentially nonviolent assault on reactionary institutions that the labor movement developed in its finest days."[37]

New America's insider's perspective on the civil rights movement would remain its most distinguished feature for the next few years, and its reporting conveyed the flavor and excitement of frontline correspondence from a war zone. In the spring of 1961, sixty-year-old Detroit socialist Walter Bergman and his wife Frances were among the first group of "Freedom Riders" who went south to challenge the segregation of the races on buses engaged in interstate travel. It proved to be a dramatic journey and a major step forward for the civil rights movement. Bergman sent in a first-hand account to *New America* of the attack in Anniston, Alabama, on the Freedom Riders' bus, whereby the bus he was riding in was assaulted by a racist mob and set on fire. (Bloodied in that attack, Bergman sustained permanent brain damage a few days later when the Freedom Riders were attacked again in the Greyhound bus terminal in Birmingham.)[38]

But not all of *New America's* pages were devoted to the blood, sweat, and tears of social struggle, and that, too, set it apart from the general run of left-wing newspapers. Michael modeled *New America* on the *Village Voice*: Among other borrowings, the newspaper ran Jules Feiffer's cartoons as a regular feature. *New America* also provided a professional apprenticeship for several journalists who would go on to careers writing for the *Voice,* including Jack Newfield (who Michael had recruited to YPSL in 1959) and Michael's sometime girlfriend Erika Munk.

Michael brought to *New America* a playful tone rarely encountered in American radical journalism, at least since the long-ago days when the Marxists, anarchists, feminists, and avant-garde artists of the Greenwich Village Left collaborated in putting out the *Masses.* In February 1961 New York City was paralyzed by a severe snowstorm. Surface transportation was immobilized, and businesses shut down. The average left-wing publication, had it even deigned to notice so trivial an event, would have used it as yet further proof of the inadequacy of public services such as snow removal under the rule of monopoly capital. Michael, instead, chose to celebrate the event in *New America* as a "blizzard utopia," a welcome occasion for subverting "the icy conventions of urban impersonality":

> Perhaps the strangest feeling in this was that one had the right to walk in the middle of the street. There were few cars, and the sidewalks were often impassable. As the people walked, there was a sense of the unusual, almost a mood of festivity, as if the city had been given back to its inhabitants.[39]

New America's appearance coincided with the start of the 1960 presidential campaign. This election year was to be the first time since 1900 that Socialists did not either run a candidate in their own name or endorse a third party candidate.[40] There had been some discussion within the party of running Norman Thomas and A. Philip Randolph on an independent ticket, but the opposition of liberal and labor groups who wanted nothing to drain votes from the Democratic candidate in a tight election put an end to that notion. Michael explained the new socialist strategy of working for "realignment" within the Democratic Party in an editorial in *New America*'s inaugural issue:

> American socialism must concentrate its efforts on the battle for political realignment, for the creation of a real second party that will unite labor, liberals, Negroes, and provide them with an instrument for principled debate and effective action. Such a party as the Democratic Party will be when the Southern racists and certain other corruptive elements have been forced out of it. Political realignment is a precondition for the resurgence of a meaningful Socialist politics in America; it is also a precondition for meaningful and progressive social welfare, labor, and civil rights legislation.[41]

The Socialists, or at least those who belonged to what became known within the SP as the "Realignment Caucus," conceived of their own role as a kind of ideological matchmaker in a grand majority coalition of progressive forces. "One of the most vital obligations of the SP-SDF," Michael would write in 1962,

> is to broaden the horizons of the thousands of good citizens who have been supporting one or the other of these progressive tendencies, to show their inter-relations, to help improve the sometimes not too good relations between civil rights advocates, municipal reformers, peace movement advocates and trade unionists, and to work with all of them and with the genuinely liberal politicians to forge a new dynamic coalition which will force a basic realignment in American politics.[42]

This was, to say the least, an ambitious strategy to be proposed by a group as marginal as the Socialist Party, considering that President Roosevelt had failed in his own attempt to purge the Democratic Party of its antiliberal elements in the late 1930s. But the proposal was not completely far-fetched, given the division of political forces at the start of the decade. The Democratic Party had survived the worst the Republicans could throw at it in the 1950s, including charges of treasonable behavior, without a significant erosion of support among its traditional constituencies. Republican control of the White House in the 1950s seemed to many Democrats a momentary aberration that could be explained as a product of the Cold War reversals of 1949–1952, as well as of the unassailable personal popularity of General Eisenhower. There was no liberal crisis of confidence at the end of the 1950s. Contenders for the Democratic presidential nomination still had to present themselves to their fellow Democrats as more or less ardent liberals in order to be taken seriously. And public opinion polls showed that in the nation as a whole just about as many Americans chose the designation "liberal" to describe themselves as those who were self-identified as "conservative" (with a large, uncommitted group in between).

If Marxist categories rarely fit exactly with American social realities, it still made a good deal of sense to think of politics in terms of class allegiances. The Democratic Party's popular base among white, urban, ethnic, working-class voters, as well as among urban blacks, seemed secure, notwithstanding growing conflicts in northern cities over issues of residential segregation. The labor movement was near the zenith of its postwar strength, representing a third of American workers and constituting a political force that, at least in some key electoral states, professional politicians ignored at their peril. In United Auto Worker president Walter Reuther, widely thought to be the heir apparent to AFL-CIO president George Meany, labor had a leader consciously committed to refashioning American politics along social democratic lines. "We feel that instead of trying to create a third party—a labor party," Reuther told one journalist in 1960, "we ought to bring about a realignment and get the liberal forces in one party and the conservatives in another."[43] Even more conservative labor leaders like George Meany viewed the new decade as the long-awaited opportunity to undo the legislative damage—such as the Taft-Hartley Act and various state "right-to-work" laws—inflicted on the movement during the years of Republican ascendancy.

To its proponents in the socialist movement, the realignment strategy had the advantage of seeming tough-minded and specific. It harkened back to the 1930s, the last great period of left-wing strength, but was flexible enough to accommodate the new movements arising at the start of the 1960s, especially the civil rights movement.

Within the Socialist Party, Max Shachtman was the acknowledged leader of the Realignment Caucus. As late as 1958, on the eve of the merger of the ISL with the SP, he had declared that he had "no illusions about the Democratic Party. . . . I cannot and will not support capitalist candidates and parties." But despite that seemingly ringing reaffirmation of the traditional Trotskyist electoral gospel, Shachtman had given up the illusion of seeing an independent labor party supplant the Democrats anytime in the foreseeable future.[44] That left him with the alternative of simply abandoning any hope of ever influencing electoral politics or of learning to live with the Democrats. By this point in his career, Shachtman had mastered the art of reversing himself without embarrassment; through conviction or guile he managed to convey the feeling (at least to his closest followers) that the new doctrine was merely the logical continuation of the old, even when the two were as antithetical as the choice between "labor party" and "realignment" politics. Shachtman now began to argue that the AFL-CIO's decision to use its influence within the Democratic Party, rather than pursuing an independent electoral strategy, in itself made the Democrats a "labor party," or would once the Southern reactionaries were thrown out.

Michael could not match Shachtman's chutzpah; when he changed directions, it was not without a few visible ideological stumbles. Formally committed as he was to realignment, Michael nonetheless predicted in the radical pacifist magazine *Liberation* that the victor in the 1960 presidential election "can now be predicted with scientific accuracy. It will be the Ruling Party in a walk."[45] And in November 1960, in what he would later regard as "one of the remarkably stupid actions of my political life," he wrote in Norman Thomas's name for president instead of pulling the lever for John F. Kennedy. The old inhibitions against voting for a "bourgeois" party and candidate were still too strong for him to do otherwise, whatever else his emerging notion of realpolitik might argue.[46]

Kennedy survived Michael's defection. But given his margin of victory in the race, it was a good thing for him that 10,000 or 20,000 other Democratic voters in New York, Illinois, or California did not similarly indulge themselves in the luxury of writing in Norman Thomas's name on their ballots. That was a lesson Michael would long remember.

With the Democrats back in the White House, the question for the Socialists became how best to pressure the new administration to embrace a genuinely liberal legislative agenda. Some veteran SPers, still gripped by nostalgia for the glory days of Norman Thomas's campaigns in the 1930s, argued that the party should resume running candidates under its own name. (In another lapse from his commitment to realignment strategy, Michael was persuaded to accept nomination as the Socialist Party candidate for the Manhattan city council president in the spring of 1961, though he never got around to actually campaigning for the post.)[47] Others favored a return to the labor party strategy, a viewpoint that was particularly prevalent within the YPSL. And there was also a group of onetime Shachtmanites like Debbie Meier and Saul Mendelson who, although resigned to the idea that there was no realistic alternative to supporting at least some Democratic Party candidates some of the time, favored putting most of the party's emphasis into supporting the peace and civil rights movements. The "Meier-Mendelsohn" tendency, as they were known, feared that Shachtman's new realignment strategy would lead the SP to seek to become "the left-wing of the Kennedy Administration."[48]

Michael had no intention of becoming an apologist for the new Democratic administration. In fact, he found little to praise in Kennedy's policies as they revealed themselves over the next two years, notwithstanding the carefully managed image of youthful "vigor" and idealism that led many Americans to regard their new president as a champion of social change. Michael's coolness toward Kennedy set him apart from some of his closest associates from the 1950s, such as John Cogley, who had joined the Kennedy campaign as a speechwriter (specializing in the delicate issue of religious freedom) in 1960.[49] Michael was also silent—it might seem almost resolutely silent—on the topic of Kennedy's Catholicism. He seemed unmoved by the fact that Kennedy had succeeded where Al Smith had failed in 1928 in demolishing the barrier that had kept Catholics out of the White House.

In 1960, Kennedy had run as a liberal. Theodore White would write in *The Making of the President, 1960* that "Kennedy's shock at the suffering he was seeing in West Virginia [where he campaigned hard to defeat Hubert Humphrey in the state's Democratic primary] was so fresh that it communicated itself with the emotion of original discovery."[50] In the fall, challenging Nixon's defense of the Eisenhower administration's economic record, Kennedy declared that the "war against poverty and degradation is not yet over," citing statistics showing millions of Americans living in substandard homes, and millions of elderly people living on inadequate assistance. (Although at least one historian has credited Michael's *Commentary* articles with influencing Kennedy's comments on poverty in 1960, there is no direct evidence that either Kennedy or his speechwriters actually had read them.)[51] Kennedy's promise that he would "get the nation moving again" was as vague about specifics as a good campaign slogan should be, but not so the party platform, adopted by the delegates at the Democratic national convention in 1960. Kennedy ran for office committed to a liberal wish list of bold initiatives; if elected, and true to these promises, he would raise the minimum wage, improve the conditions of farm workers, secure passage of national health insurance for the elderly, and launch a ten-year campaign to eliminate urban slums. The Democratic party platform also pledged vigorous enforcement of existing civil rights legislation and praised the student sit-in movement.[52]

But however sincere Kennedy may have sounded in campaigning on this platform in 1960, the final results of the election did little to reinforce his commitment to the pursuit of liberal reform once in the White House. His narrow margin of victory was hardly a resounding mandate for change. And, in contradiction to the usual pattern of American presidential elections, the Democrats in 1960 lost seats in both the House and Senate while taking back the White House. Thus Congress was even more firmly under the control of southern Democrats and conservative Republicans in Kennedy's first two years in office than it had been in the last two years of Eisenhower's administration. Kennedy was also eager to reassure a nervous business community that the return of the Democrats to power would not mean reckless spending or inflationary policies. He therefore decided even before he moved into the White House to defer potentially divisive reforms and spending measures until safely re-elected to his second term in office. In his inaugural address, as a result, the new president failed to mention domestic policy at all.

Within weeks of Kennedy's inauguration, Michael was writing in *New America* to criticize the president's "extremely cautious approach towards America's problems." The headlines over his articles that spring in *New America* manifested barely any enthusiasm for the administration's domestic proposals: "Labor, Rights Movements Restive on New Frontier" read one in March, followed by "Hostile Congress Fights Weak Anti-Recession Plan" in the next issue, and "Religious Issue Complicates Inadequate School Aid Bill" in the issue after that.[53]

Kennedy pushed some measures in the first years of his administration that had been kicking around liberal Democratic circles for the past half decade or so. In the spring of 1961, Congress passed the administration's Area Redevelopment Act, which provided loans to businesses willing to relocate to depressed regions like Appalachia, as well as grants for road and bridge improvement and a raise in the minimum wage over a two-year period from

$1.00 to $1.25. And in 1962, Congress passed the Manpower Development and Training Act, which created programs for the retraining of workers displaced by automation.

But Kennedy's few legislative achievements had little impact on the lives of Americans living in poverty. The Area Redevelopment Act, for example, produced a grand total of 350 jobs for all of West Virginia in the first year after its passage. In a resolution on "political action" that Michael drafted for the Socialist Party's national convention in June 1962, he credited the New Frontier with a "slight advance" in solving the nation's problems. But, he added, "measured against the hopes and aspirations of the millions who crave a broadening of civil liberties, an end to the shame of racial inequality, alternative roads to world peace and an end to economic injustice and unemployment, the record of solid accomplishments has been slim."[54] Many liberals, let alone socialists, found Kennedy's domestic record a distinct disappointment. John Roche, a Brandeis University political scientist who was elected chairman of Americans for Democratic Action in 1962, denounced Kennedy's "technocratic liberalism" and suggested that his administration could benefit from an infusion "of good old-fashion crusading zeal."[55]

With a more liberal Congress, of course, Kennedy might have attempted and achieved more. But he himself opposed some social welfare measures proposed by liberal Democrats in Congress, such as Pennsylvania senator Joseph S. Clark's call for a public works program to battle unemployment.[56] The lights certainly did not burn late in the White House while Kennedy fretted over the fate of his domestic programs. As he remarked to former Vice President Richard Nixon in the spring of 1961, "It really is true that foreign affairs is the only important issue for a President to handle, isn't it? I mean who gives a shit if the minimum wage is $1.15 or $1.25?"[57]

Kennedy's own economic advisers were unhappy with his course—not because they were particularly liberal or reform-minded in their concerns, but because they understood that the cautious "fiscal responsibility" of the Eisenhower era had led directly to what had proven—for the Republicans—the politically costly recessions of 1954, 1957, and 1960. Kennedy had inherited the latest of these economic downturns; in the early months of his presidency, unemployment was at its highest level in the United States since the onset of the Second World War. At first, Kennedy continued to mouth conventional sentiments about balancing the budget. A concerned Walter Heller, chairman of the Council of Economic Advisers, set out to tutor the president in the "New Economics." Over the next two years, Heller and others gradually convinced Kennedy that he had the power and the responsibility to shape the economy through the government's fiscal policies. A tax cut, even though it would end the budget surpluses of the later Eisenhower years, would stimulate economic growth. And the "rising tide" of economic growth would, as the New Economists were wont to say, "lift all boats." Wall Street would be happy, the middle class would be happy, and the poor (to the extent that anyone was thinking at all about their fate) would disappear.[58]

Nevertheless, there was little evidence to administration outsiders of the change in Kennedy's thinking: His occasional suggestions that the "stale phrases" and "myths" of traditional economics had to be rethought and revised were usually followed in short order by yet another pledge to balance the budget. And even if Michael had known about Kennedy's re-education in elementary Keynesianism at the hand of his advisers, it is unlikely it would have done much to improve his opinion of the president. Walter Heller's brand of economic activism was an example of what Michael, following John Kenneth Galbraith, would label "reactionary Keynesianism," that is, favoring tax cuts for the wealthy and middle class, rather than public spending, as the means of priming the pump of a sluggish economy. It was seen as a truism of American politics that "redistributionist" economic policies were the political kiss of death—except, it seems, when the redistribution of income was upwards.[59]

Michael was also concerned with Kennedy's record on civil rights. The president had backed off from his campaign pledge to end discrimination in public housing "with a stroke of the pen" by means of executive order; his brother and attorney general Robert Kennedy had responded to the Freedom Rides in the spring of 1961 with the suggestion that civil rights groups allow a "cooling off" period before pursuing their protest against segregation. In a political resolution Michael drafted for the SP in the summer of 1961, he denounced any suggestion that "social gains can be purchased with the rights of eighteen million Negroes. We find it incredible that it should be proposed to the Civil Rights movement that after almost one hundred miserable years of waiting since the Emancipation Proclamation, it should 'go slow.'"[60]

Michael was not a fan of the New Frontier—at home or abroad. From the first days of the new administration, Michael criticized Kennedy's obsession with overthrowing Fidel Castro. Unlike some sections of the American Left who were themselves enamored with the new Cuban regime, Michael and most of his fellow socialists regarded Castro as an unscrupulous dictator and, increasingly, a Soviet pawn. They felt, nonetheless, that the United States had an obligation to respect Cuban sovereignty and self-determination. In February 1961 Michael drafted a resolution, approved by the party leadership, warning the Kennedy administration to keep "Hands off the Cuban Revolution!"[61] When CIA-backed Cuban exiles made their botched landing at the Bay of Pigs in mid-April, Michael joined Murray Kempton and Norman Mailer as the headliners at a New York City protest meeting organized by YPSL. Michael was also one of several dozen liberal and leftist figures, ranging from Norman Thomas to Norman Podhoretz, to sign an open letter to President Kennedy opposing the invasion.[62]

After Kennedy's assassination, many former critics of the martyred president chose to gloss over their earlier anti-Kennedy sentiments. Michael proved no exception. He told an interviewer in 1966, "I had a premonition, I guess you'd call it. All the time I was writing [*The Other America*], I felt President Kennedy would read it."[63] But there is no evidence in the written record from 1961–1962 of any such "premonition" on Michael's part. He cast a justifiably skeptical eye at the time on Kennedy's limited legislative initiatives designed to improve the lives of the poor, and he had little reason to think that the president—or anyone else in Washington for that matter—would take the slightest interest in what he had to say on the topic of poverty.

The Other America was published in March 1962. It was a short book; at 186 pages, it was just over half the length of the original edition of Jacob Riis's *How the Other Half Lives*.[64] Brevity turned out to be one of its strengths. The nine chapters of *The Other America* could and often were read in a single sitting, which for some readers increased the sense of "the scales fell from my eyes." It was also a simple book with an easily grasped thesis. Although Michael had continued and broadened his readings in the sociology of the poor since writing his articles for *Commentary* and had picked up some new concepts, such as that of the "multi-problem family," his thesis remained essentially the one he had first sketched out for *Commentary*'s readers in 1959–1960.[65]

There were two essential points Michael wanted readers of *The Other America* to understand. The first was that, despite the apparent national consensus about the arrival of the "affluent society," widespread poverty continued to exist in the United States. There was "another America" of 40 to 50 million inhabitants living in the United States, "the unskilled workers, the migrant farm workers, the aged, the minorities, and all the others who live in the economic underworld of American life." This "invisible land" of the poor existed in rural isolation or in crowded urban slums where middle-class visitors seldom ventured. "That the poor are invisible is one of the most important things about them," Michael wrote in his introductory chapter. "They are not simply neglected and forgotten as in the old rhetoric of reform; what is much worse, they are not seen."[66]

Michael's second point, again familiar to readers of the *Commentary* articles, was that "poverty is a culture." Poor Americans were not simply distinguishable by their lack of adequate income. Rather, they are

> people who lack education and skill, who have bad health, poor housing, low levels of aspiration and high levels of mental distress. . . . Each disabil-

ity is the more intense because it exists within a web of disabilities. And if one problem is solved, and the others are left constant, there is little gain.

It was thus a delusion to believe, as many conservatives did, that poverty could be solved by exhortations to the poor to lift themselves up by their own bootstraps. And it was equally a delusion to believe, as many New Frontier liberals did, that the opportunities provided by a then rapidly expanding economy would automatically solve the problems of poor people. "Society," Michael concluded, "must help them before they can help themselves."[67]

In the introduction to *The Other America,* Michael wrote that the poor needed "an American Dickens" to make them visible to better-off citizens, by recording "the smell and texture and quality of their lives."[68] Michael quickly hastened to add that he was no Dickens. There was, nonetheless, a significant amount of literary craft involved in *The Other America,* notwithstanding the fact that Michael also strove to maintain an informal and almost conversational tone to his prose. In effect, Michael's creative achievement in *The Other America* included not only his description of the lives of the poor, but the creation of a public persona for himself. His tone throughout was modest, reasonable, and calm, and yet often and at the same time idealistic, impassioned, and inspiring. Unlike many radical pamphleteers, Michael had the ability to convey moral seriousness without lapsing into moralism. Although he talked in *The Other America* about the need for "outrage" over the conditions of the poor, there was no hint in his writing of the sanctimonious bullying of the middle class that pervaded so much of the radical style to come later in the 1960s. Michael's tone was intended to suggest that the reader was a reasonable person, just like the author, and reasonable people, once appraised of the plight of the "Other America," would agree on the need to find solutions. He eschewed polemics. The enemies Michael identified in the book tended to be such carefully distanced abstractions as "social blindness" or "the vocabulary of not caring," rather than identifiable individuals or social groupings. Though taking issue with government economist Robert Lampman's estimates that economic growth in and of itself would halve the poverty rate in the United States over the next two decades, Michael hastened to add that he did not wish to depict Lampman "as an enemy of the poor." The fact that he was interested in poverty at all was to his credit; he had "social eyes" and a "genuine concern for the poor."[69]

One of the ways in which Michael chose to reinforce the credibility of his authorial voice came at the cost of a troubled conscience. The only political affiliation that he revealed in *The Other America* was his past association with the Catholic Worker. The word "socialism" did not appear in the text. Michael agonized over the omission and later promised himself "that if I wrote a book without mentioning the word socialism, in the next book I wrote I would mention it all the time"—a promise fulfilled in his next dozen books, including several of their titles.[70] A sophisticated reader would, in any case, have no difficulty in discerning Michael's political credentials from various hints dropped in the text, such as his frequent praise for the labor movement and a familiarity (at the time uncommon outside the Left) with the lyrics of Woody Guthrie songs such as "Pastures of Plenty."

Michael often illustrated his points in *The Other America* with his favorite Chestertonian strategy of paradox. The "Other Americans" were "the victims of the very inventions and machines that have provided a higher living standard for the rest of society," because the mechanization of agriculture and the automation of industry had eliminated the kind of unskilled and entry level jobs that had previously sustained the poor.[71] The "welfare state benefits those least who need help most," because social security pensions and unemployment compensation payments were often unavailable to those with low incomes.[72] Poverty was "expensive to maintain," because poor communities required extensive public spending on fire, police, and health services.[73]

Michael frequently combined paradox with the theme of bringing hidden evils to light. Surface appearances were deceiving in the social landscape of the United States. "Beauty can be a mask for ugliness," which is why the affluent tourist passing through the Appalachian mountain range might miss the desperate quality of life of the rural poor in places like West Virginia.[74] "America has the best-dressed poverty the world has ever known," allowing the poorly housed, fed, and doctored to blend in with the more affluent fellow citizens when they ventured into public spaces.[75]

The way to peer through a deceptive surface, Michael suggested, was to enrich individual observation with social measurement. Following the pattern already established in his *Commentary* articles, Michael made extensive use of statistics in *The Other America,* but he almost always found a way to present them that would keep the nonspecialist reader's eyes from glazing over. "Sometimes in the course of an official Government report," he wrote, "a human being will suddenly emerge from the shadows of statistics and analyses."[76] Or, in another passage: "Sometimes the statistics of poverty can be read like a detective story."[77] The effect of the technique was to make author and reader allies in the struggle to come to grips with a vast—but understandable and thus solvable—social ill.

The Other America was a book about poor people, but it was not a book written for poor people. It was apparent throughout that the readers Michael was speaking to were citizens of the affluent society. Michael also made it clear that he did not imagine that the poor were finer, more authentic, or more generous human beings than their better-off brethren in the suburbs, as Jack Kerouac had recently done in *On the Road,* or as John Steinbeck had done in *The Grapes of Wrath* a generation earlier. The lives of the poor, as portrayed in *The Other America,* were generally nasty, brutish, and short, and they were that way precisely because they lacked such amenities of middle-class life as decent housing, education, nutrition, and medical care. Despite his sympathies, Michael felt no hesitation in presenting the seamier side of the lives of poor people—including alcoholism, domestic violence, sexual promiscuity, and even cruelty to the mentally retarded—without sentimentality. But, by making use of the notion of the culture of poverty, he could do so without simply reinforcing pre-existing prejudices against the poor. The culture into which the poor were born, the culture that was bred into them by their surroundings, was one of the many indignities that they suffered.

In the final chapter of *The Other America,* Michael asked his readers to make use of their "vision"—in two senses. First, he asked them to "see through the wall of affluence" and recognize the true dimensions of poverty in the United States and its cost in human dignity. Second, he declared that there must also be vision "in the sense of purpose, of aspiration." Michael summoned his readers to "war on poverty" not just for the sake of the poor but for their own sakes. Ending poverty was not a question of charity, although the charitable impulse was not to be scorned. Michael argued that Americans should be angry and ashamed to live in a society that, having the resources to provide everyone a decent standard of living, was instead divided into two nations. "The fate of the poor," Michael concluded, "hangs upon the decision of the better-off. If this anger and shame are not forthcoming, someone can write a book about the other America a generation from now and it will be the same or worse."[78]

The Other America enjoyed only modest sales in the months after its publication. Michael was not particularly surprised or disappointed. He told *New York Post* editor James Wechsler before the book came out that he would be happy if it sold 2,500 copies.[79] He nonetheless read his reviews carefully—a quarter century after *The Other America*'s publication he still had not forgotten an early and highly critical pre-publication review that appeared in the trade journal *Kirkus Reviews.*[80] But in general he had nothing to complain about. The reviews in the mainstream press were respectful and sympathetic. A. H. Raskin, the well-known labor correspondent for the *New York Times,* reviewed *The Other America* for the book review section in the Sunday *Times* and praised its "angry thesis." Simply to be reviewed in the *Times* served to legitimize Michael as a serious and respectable writer. But Raskin went further, making it clear that he felt radical criticism of American society was long overdue and welcome:

> Mr. Harrington does his best as stand-in for Dickens, with strong overtones of Jeremiah. He writes with sensitivity and perception as well as indignation. The Council of Economic Advisers might say, with justice, that

> he has overdrawn his case as to both size and intractability of the problem. That is no indictment. The chroniclers and celebrants of America's upward movement are plentiful; it is good to be reminded that we are still a long way away from the stars.[81]

The weekly journals of liberal opinion were, not surprisingly, equally enthusiastic. The *Nation*'s reviewer called *The Other America* "grimly impressive"; the *Reporter*'s reviewer described it as a "sobering, even shocking book." Writing in the *New Leader,* Robert Lampman praised *The Other America* (while offering a backhanded swipe at established liberals like Arthur Schlesinger Jr.) for "presenting a graphic rebuttal of the contention that the U.S. has solved the 'quantitative' economic problem, leaving only the 'qualitative' problem."[82]

In radical circles, *The Other America* was taken as the sign that Norman Thomas had finally found his heir apparent. Thomas himself, writing in *New America,* declared that Michael "has written a book which consciously or subconsciously, all of us Socialists have been waiting for."[83] In a front page feature article in the *Village Voice* that celebrated the publication of *The Other America,* J. R. Goddard hailed Michael as a virtual folk hero of the Left:

> Most know him as the masterful orator of the Socialist position. A few believe him to be the potential replacement for Norman Thomas as leader of the social-democratic left. Others (even right-wingers) admire his skills. . . . Still others know him as a kind and affable man in his mid-30's who tells funny stories in that garrulous Village forum, the back room of the White Horse Tavern.[84]

Notwithstanding the generally celebratory tone of the article, Goddard also wrote of his suspicion that Michael used his surface affability to "hide a moodier, more introverted person." Indeed, for someone who had just scored a significant literary success, Michael sounded a little cranky. He told Goddard he was getting tired of wandering from campus to campus as a kind of "Socialist jukebox." He planned to go to live in Paris sometime soon. And when he returned, he intended to leave New York, his home for the past dozen years, and move to San Francisco, "the Paris of America."[85]

There was nothing new about Michael's ambivalence about his political career. Ned O'Gorman, who had first encountered Michael debating Buckley at the University of Vermont in 1951, came to New York in the mid-1950s to attend graduate school and often shared a table with Michael at the White Horse. One evening he and Michael discovered that they both had fantasized about the pleasures of a British academic life, as enshrined and mythologized in the novels of C. P. Snow.

> We sat up one night talking about what a great life it would be if we could be in an oak paneled room at Oxford, and reading, and then you could get up in the morning and have tea and walk through these wonderful buildings and halls, and then sit and have really interesting discussions about what you had read.[86]

Michael's friend and comrade Peter Novick would catch occasional glimpses in the 1950s of "the old literary Mike." Michael would tell him about the great book on Western culture and decadence he intended to write someday: "He had the notion that at some point he would burst what he felt to be the confining bonds of politics, stop being a superannuated youth leader, and turn away from full-time political work toward things more literary and academic."[87]

Two years as editor of *New America* contributed to Michael's desire to get away and try something new. He had the feeling that he was wasting his talents, "doing many things; none of them well."[88] When Macmillan sold the paperback rights to *The Other America* to Penguin press later that spring (it was the first paperback book published by Penguin in the United States), Michael wound up with a check for $1,500, enough in the early 1960s for a plane ticket and a few months living expenses in Paris. He made plans to leave at the end of the year.[89]

But there was a complicating factor in Michael's life in the spring of 1962, and that was a new girlfriend. Michael's comrades were, of course, accustomed to seeing him in the company of good-looking women. Some of them were fellow leftists, but more often than not they were women he encountered elsewhere, with a style that set them distinctly apart from the movement norm. Fellow SPer Rob Tucker would recall that whenever he walked into "a grungy leftist office" and encountered "a malnourished young woman in exquisite clothes, looking like a refugee from *Vogue*, with a bored expression and a hatbox, I knew Mike Harrington was not far away." Michael's girlfriends, in Tucker's memory, "awed all of us."[90] But he didn't take them too seriously himself. In the years after he left the Catholic Worker, Michael had only one girlfriend he considered a serious marriage prospect. That was Sally Backer, a recent graduate of Sarah Lawrence College when Michael knew her, and the daughter of Dorothy Schiff, publisher of the *New York Post*. Michael seems to have made an equally strong impression on both daughter and mother: In the late 1950s, James Wechsler asked a friend of Michael's to tell him all about Michael because, he said, "I think he may be my next boss."[91]

After Michael and Sally broke up, he returned to playing the field. Michael was used to easy conquests, and he had fallen into the habit of treating the women in his life with a certain studied indifference. Rob Tucker remembered how the elegant young ladies Michael brought to the office would be abandoned by their escort, while he tended to the revolution: "We would sit down for an editorial conference and he would seem utterly at leisure as we all conversed; he would seem unaware that he was making a lady wait."[92]

Probably the last thing Michael intended to do in 1962, as he prepared to shuck off his official duties and responsibilities for a sabbatical year in Paris, was to get seriously involved with another woman. But then he met a leggy, red-headed, and quick-witted young woman named Stephanie Gervis.

Michael met Stephanie at the White Horse, where she had come one late winter evening with her then boyfriend, folksinger Tommy Makem. Stephanie was a few years out of Cornell, with a walk-up apartment on Carmine Street in the Village and a job as a reporter for a small newspaper in Westchester County, where she had grown up. Her first impression of Michael was not good. She didn't like his crewcut or his "very nasal voice."

Stephanie's initial indifference probably made Michael all the more interested. He asked her out for dinner at a Spanish restaurant on Greenwich Street, and when he came to pick her up at the White Horse he wore a jacket and tie—a sure sign to those who knew him that he was going to unusual lengths to win this woman's favor. As they left the tavern and crossed the street, he charmed Stephanie when he reached out and held her arm to keep her from coming to any harm from the passing traffic, a very un-White Horse-like gesture of chivalric tradition. But it was a subsequent date some weeks later that persuaded Stephanie that this was a man whose idiosyncrasies might be worth tolerating. Michael asked her to meet him at an antinuclear testing rally at the United Nations, where he was scheduled to speak. Stephanie was still trying to make up her mind if she and Michael had any future. The suit and tie were back in the closet. "There he was in his pea jacket and watch cap," she recalled of the rally. And then he went up to the microphone to deliver his speech to the crowd, and "suddenly there was this voice, so resonant and big. . . . I was just stunned."[93]

Theirs was a public and celebrated courtship, in part because Stephanie, like Michael, was in the habit of using her own life as the subject for her writing. When Jack Goddard left the *Village Voice* that spring for another job, he recommended Stephanie as his successor. Michael also put in a good word for her with *Village Voice* editor Dan Wolfe. So, starting that summer, the Stephanie Gervis byline began to appear regularly in the *Voice*, covering Village politics and culture.[94] In July, the *Voice* ran her tongue-in-cheek guide to sex for "Greenwich Village girls." Although the article ostensibly spoofed Helen Gurley Brown's recent bestseller, *Sex and the Single Girl*, those in the know could pick up more than a few barbed references to the *Voice*'s favorite radical leader. "What's available" in terms of male partners in Greenwich Village, Stephanie asked her readers, and then answered her own question:

"Just about anything. Poets, painters, sculptors, writers, folk singers, radicals, electricians, bartenders, etc. What are they good for? Sex. Also food and drink. . . . Radicals are good for nothing—they're always off making speeches." She went on to recommend the White Horse Tavern as the "Macy's" of Greenwich Village man-shopping, and she gave a few tips to women aspiring to attract the attention of the back room regulars:

> When in the White Horse, be an intelligent, controversial conversationalist. To do this you must be omniscient; there's nothing you don't know or haven't read. Always argue on the side of the man you're after. He will soon realize that two can pontificate better than one, and it will be a relief for him to be able to share the burden of constant pretense. Whatever you do, don't ask questions—people will think you're stupid. Of course, if you don't ask questions you may never learn anything new and really become stupid, but what you really are is not the point.[95]

Michael's friends, familiar with his incessant pursuit of the Bitter Sweet Face of Love, wondered how long he would continue to put up with this new, independent-minded partner. In a letter to Michael in mid-August, Paul Jacobs concluded with a cheery, "Best regards to you, and love to Stephanie—if you are still seeing her."[96] But somehow, despite some ups and downs, including a temporary breakup, they were still seeing each other in January when it came time for Michael to leave for Paris.

Stephanie accompanied Michael to Idlewild Airport on January 4 for a tearful farewell over martinis while waiting for Michael's Air France flight. Michael wrote long romantic letters from Paris; Stephanie, feeling abandoned, didn't reply. Then he wrote to declare that her silence must mean that she didn't love him after all. Stephanie called him in Paris to challenge his interpretation, and before the call ended it was agreed that she would come to Paris herself at the earliest possible moment. (An inveterate procrastinator, several months passed before Stephanie followed through on her decision, leading an annoyed Michael to start referring to her as *Gervis Immobilise.*)[97]

While Michael waited on Stephanie, he explored Paris. A high point of his first weeks in France came when he attended a poetry reading by the young Soviet poet Andrei Voznesensky, at the Vieux Colombier, an old avant-garde theater on the Left Bank. He spotted André Breton, the "lion-headed veteran of Paris surrealism" there, as well as the old Communist poet Louis Aragon.[98]

This was the Paris that Michael had read and dreamed about for years. He had long imagined himself, after a hard day of writing his book, sitting in cafes, arguing politics and literature with French intellectuals. But reality fell considerably short of fantasy. The French weren't friendly, and Michael's spoken French, although technically proficient (he had been tutored in French three times a week for five months before leaving New York), lacked confidence.[99] Michael soon became friends with an expatriate American painter named Don Fink, who had settled in Paris after the war. He found it frustrating that Fink made himself understood perfectly well using an idiosyncratic pidgin French, spoken with such "utter bravado" that it was treated respectfully by the French. Michael, in contrast, would go across the street every morning from his apartment to a little market and ask the shopkeeper, in technically perfect French, for two eggs, and every morning the same shopkeeper would feign total incomprehension. When Stephanie finally got to Paris, she had the opportunity to observe this routine: "It was like a little play. Every morning she would not understand a word he said." In general, Stephanie recalled, Michael would find himself "frustrated by France his whole life. It never lived up to his expectations."[100]

Stephanie arrived in mid-April. In anticipation, Michael had left his original lodging at the Rirabet Hotel for an apartment in the 13th arrondissement. Rue Arago was a little street full of Left Bankish charm, with a full complement of cheese shops, bakeries, and butcher shops, although the new apartment, lacking such amenities as refrigerator or private toilet, was more Michael's style than Stephanie's.[101] Michael wrote to Paul Jacobs soon afterwards to report that despite such hardships, and despite the fact that "April in Paris has been one long, unromantic drizzle," things were going well with the reunited lovers:

> Mlle. Gervis, to be Madame Harrington towards the end of May I think (I am seeing a lawyer today about the French bureaucracy and marriage) sends her best. . . . We saw "Mourir a Madrid" last night, a documentary on the Spanish Civil War. I am sure the Church will keep it out of the U.S. but it is one of the greatest, most moving films we've ever seen. Steph has been running around the apartment all day giving a clenched fist salute. She makes me feel old. I have had to teach her songs like The Four Insurgent Generals, the 15th Brigade, and Song of the United Front. I thought every little American child knew them, but apparently that doesn't cut for those born in the mid-Thirties.[102]

Michael called his mother from Paris to tell her of his plans and to invite her to the wedding. Catherine not only declined to attend but did not even want any wedding announcements to send to her friends. Stephanie, who was Jewish, got the distinct impression that Catherine, whom she had yet to meet, was not thrilled by the prospect of her son marrying quite so far out of the faith. So, minus his mother, Michael and Stephanie were married on

May 30, in the city hall of the 13th arrondissement, with Stephanie's parents and a few local friends in attendance.[103] *The Village Voice* and *New America* both took official notice of the wedding. So, too, did the FBI, which had kept careful tabs on every step Michael had taken since applying for his passport the previous November.[104]

Michael meanwhile was hard at work on his book on cultural decadence, for which he had received an advance from Macmillan that helped pay the bills in Paris ("a major, major effort," he reported in a letter to Paul Jacobs. "I think of it as much more ambitious and ranging than the last one").[105] And both he and Stephanie were doing as much freelancing as they could to pay the bills. Stephanie sent articles to the *Voice* on French culture and politics, written with her trademark acerbity. One of her articles, appearing in a September issue of the *Voice,* was entitled "The Last Time I Saw Paris I Fell into Deep Depression" and recounted the defects of their Rue Arago apartment, as well as the dismal shortcomings of Parisian cafe life. A "good weekday night at the Limelight or White Horse," Stephanie reported with a mixture of homesickness and Greenwich Village chauvinism, "can provide better booze, better conversation, and better stories to tell later."[106]

She also sent in an account of the march that she and Michael had joined in Paris in solidarity with the March on Washington in August. Several hundred Americans, including Don Fink, James Baldwin, novelist James Jones, and the musicians Hazel Scott and Memphis Slim, marched from the American church on the Quai d'Orsay to the American embassy at the Place de la Concorde to present a petition supporting civil rights.[107]

Michael traveled to Amsterdam in September, where he attended the Eighth Congress of the Socialist International as an official delegate of the American Socialist Party. He had earlier attended and spoken at a congress of the French Unified Socialist Party (PSU), but like most of his interactions with the French, it was a disappointment; after his speech, everyone ignored him. Not only were French socialists rude; they were also losers, unable to challenge Charles de Gaulle's popularity, even as they abandoned socialist principles in an attempt to outflank him politically. In one of her *Village Voice* dispatches, Stephanie acidly described an evening she and Michael had spent in a Left Bank cafe with an unnamed French Socialist intellectual "who exerted all his Gallic subtlety on the argument that if other countries have the bomb why shouldn't France."[108]

But the Socialist International meeting was different. It was a moment of high optimism for many European socialists. Willy Brandt, the mayor of West Berlin and a rising star in German politics, delivered one of the keynote addresses; his recent smashing re-election as mayor had put him in a strong position to challenge Konrad Adenauer's conservative government. British Labour Party leader Harold Wilson also spoke, amid signs of a

Labour electoral revival (realized the following year when Labour won a narrow parliamentary majority and Wilson became prime minister). The Socialist International delegates were also heartened by news from Rome of the Catholic Church's Vatican II Council, which suggested an "opening to the Left" on the part of the church.[109]

After the conference in Amsterdam, Michael and Stephanie went on to England, where they stayed with friends in London. Paul Jacobs joined them there; before he came, Stephanie wrote to beg him to bring along a three-month supply of birth control pills, which she could not obtain in Europe.[110] Michael soon afterwards added his own plea to Stephanie's in a letter to Jacobs: "I guess you got Stephanie's request for life-and-death pills. We are going to have a book before a baby."[111]

Somewhat to his chagrin, *The Other America* had made Michael a minor literary celebrity within the Soviet bloc, as Communist propagandists eagerly latched on to any evidence of economic or social problems within the capitalist world. The Soviet journal *International Affairs* published a review of the book in February 1963, calling it "a distress signal of social misery in the United States," though criticizing Michael (who it described somewhat fancifully as a "leader in the Catholic trade-union movement") for failing to analyze the "social laws" that created poverty under capitalism.[112] Without Michael's or Macmillan's permission, pirated editions of *The Other America* appeared in the Soviet Union and in Poland. The only way Michael could collect any royalties from the sale of his book in Eastern Europe was to travel there and spend his zlotys or rubles in-country. So from London, Michael and Stephanie flew to Warsaw in mid-November.

In Warsaw, they found evidence that American culture was influencing the young: In the main dining room of their hotel, couples were dancing the "twist."[113] But for the most part, Warsaw was as grim an illustration of the Stalinist legacy as Michael could have imagined. Everywhere they went they were shadowed by secret police agents. They visited the site of the Warsaw Ghetto, unmarked except for a small plaque, the whole area covered with blocks of dreary apartment buildings. Michael arranged a meeting in a Warsaw coffee shop with dissident Marxist philosopher Leszek Kolakowski; Kolakowski spent the whole time looking over his shoulder to see if anyone was eavesdropping. (Kolakowski was still officially a member of the Polish Communist Party at that time; when Michael asked another dissident intellectual in Warsaw why Polish Communist leader Gomulka had not had Kolakowski expelled, he received the wry explanation, "Because he does not want to drive the only Marxist in Poland out of the Party.")[114] In any case, it wasn't much fun spending zlotys in luxury starved Warsaw, so Michael and Stephanie left after a few days.[115]

From Warsaw they flew to Milan. The date was November 22. Italy would have been a great relief after Poland, had it not been for the news they received that evening. After unpacking in their hotel room, Michael and Stephanie went downstairs to have dinner. They were in the restaurant when a distressed-looking waiter came up to their table and said, in French, "It's so terrible, they have just killed Kennedy." Michael and Stephanie looked at each other, both thinking something had to be wrong with their French. So they asked him if he spoke English, and he repeated it in English. They left the hotel and went over to the Milan office of the Associated Press and read the wire copy from Dallas as it came in on the machine. When they returned to the hotel they encountered a couple of Texan tourists who, clearly undisturbed by the news of Kennedy's death, were debating what kind of rifle sight the assassin probably used. In contrast, walking past the headquarters of the Communist Party in Milan the next day, Michael was struck by the large poster mounted outside expressing deep grief over Kennedy's assassination.[116]

Michael had never been an ardent Kennedy fan, but after his death Michael credited the president with having "opened many windows" in American political culture: Kennedy's administration, Michael wrote in 1965, "if it did not provide profound answers, had the merit of raising profound questions."[117]

From Milan, Michael and Stephanie traveled first to Florence and then to Rome, where they arrived December 1. There they stayed with John Cogley, who was in Rome reporting for *Commonweal* on the sessions of the Vatican II Council, which had been initiated by Pope John XXIII the previous year.[118] (Michael was a strong admirer of the pope. Under his leadership of the church, the intense moralism and anticommunism of the 1950s was giving way to new concerns for social justice, religious liberty, and peace. His 1959 and 1961 encyclicals, *Ad Petri Cathedram* and *Mater and Magistra,* reiterated and expanded on the themes of social justice heard thirty years earlier in Piux XI's *Quadragesimo Anno.* Michael also admired John's 1963 encyclical *Pacem in Terris,* which condemned the nuclear arms race. He was saddened when John died soon afterwards, though hopeful that the reformist movement instituted during his brief papacy would continue to guide church doctrine and practice.[119])

After spending a week and a half in Rome, Michael and Stephanie went on to Naples. Three days later, on December 15, they boarded the passenger liner *Leonardo Da Vinci* for the return voyage to the United States and arrived in New York on December 23. The FBI agents who had kept close tabs on Michael throughout his year in Europe could now relax. "During the time they were in Italy," the FBI summary of Michael and Stephanie's European travels concluded, "they were not known to have engaged in any suspect activity."[120]

No sooner had Michael arrived back in New York than he discovered just how much of a celebrity he had become in his year abroad. The word was out that President Lyndon Johnson intended to announce a major new government initiative to combat poverty in his first State of the Union Address on January 8, and ABC radio network called to ask if Michael would serve as a commentator on Johnson's speech. Another call came from Georgetown University asking him to speak at a conference at the end of January on "Poverty in Plenty." Among his fellow speakers were Leon Keyserling, who had published his own study of poverty in the spring of 1962 under the auspices of the Washington-based and labor-backed Conference on Economic Policy, and Gunnar Myrdal, the Swedish social democrat and author of *The American Dilemma.*[121] United Autoworkers president Walter Reuther invited Michael to be the keynote speaker at the founding meeting of a new organization to be called the Citizens' Crusade Against Poverty.[122] Editors besieged him with commissions for articles on poverty; he soon would publish articles in such hitherto unknown literary territory as the *New York Times Magazine* and *Look Magazine.*[123] And there were requests for interviews: before the spring was over he had been the subject of articles in *Newsweek, Time,* and the *New York Times.* In a feature piece in the *New York Herald Tribune* that fall he would be dubbed "The Man Who Discovered Poverty." When Marilyn Magid of the *Herald Tribune* called his home to ask for an interview, Michael was out; Stephanie, according to the reporter's subsequent published account, "was noncommittal and courteous, if faintly ironic" when she answered the phone. "Let me know if you find him," she told Magid.[124]

Michael's comrades had awaited his return from Europe with much anticipation. Norman Thomas had even been talking him up as a possible presidential candidate for 1964.[125] But veterans of the movement also felt some trepidation about Michael's future plans. The Socialist Party had a long and, from its perspective, unfortunate tradition of serving as the training ground for bright young men who, as soon as they began to make their mark in society, stopped paying their dues to the party (Michael's favorite labor leader, Walter Reuther, was a case in point). Thus it was with a palpable sense of relief that the SP's national secretary, Irwin Suall, wrote to Norman Thomas in January 1964 to report that all was well on the Harrington front. Michael "certainly struck a gusher, didn't he?" Suall commented on the continuing attention attracted by *The Other America.* "We must continue to make good use of him—and he's more than willing. My impression is that his attitude toward the party and his political morale are even better than before he left."[126] But the Socialists knew they would have to share Michael with a broader world from now on. In February, the SP's national committee sent a cautionary note out to SP locals clamoring to have Michael come as a speaker: "Comrade Harrington is trying to finish his second book but finding it very difficult, due to requests to speak, both paid and unpaid."[127]

Michael had gained some inkling during the past year of his increasing fame at home. In December 1962, shortly before he left for Paris, he had spent an evening drinking and talking with Dwight Macdonald, who had been commissioned by the *New Yorker* to write a review of *The Other America.* When the review appeared, several weeks after Michael's departure from New York, it proved a sensation—at fifty pages it was the longest book review the magazine had ever printed, and probably the most influential. Despite some criticism of Michael's "impressionistic" use of statistics, Macdonald left little doubt that *The Other America* was a "most important" book. Macdonald concluded his review by calling for "direct intervention" on the part of the federal government to eliminate "the shame of the Other America."[128]

In late 1962 President Kennedy had asked Walter Heller to dig up some "facts and figures" on the nation's unfinished economic business, including "the poverty problem." There is little evidence to suggest that Kennedy at that moment had in mind any major antipoverty initiative, but he had retained a mild interest in the issue since the 1960 campaign. When Heller saw Macdonald's review in the *New Yorker* in February 1963 he passed it, or perhaps (memories vary) *The Other America* itself, along to the president.[129] Whether or not Kennedy actually read Michael's book, it was widely assumed in Washington that he had, and this assumption, plus *The Other America*'s own merits, made it required reading among those in charge of shaping and implementing the administration's domestic policies. A kind of informal task force, with a revolving membership drawn from the Council of Economic Advisers, the Labor Department, and other agencies and cabinet offices, met through the summer and fall of 1963 to discuss what, at least in some administration circles, was then being called a "Widening Participation in Prosperity" program.[130] According to James Sundquist, a political scientist who was involved in the early discussion and would go on to help draft the war on poverty legislation, *The Other America* brought an end to "piecemeal" thinking about domestic problems:

> The measures enacted [up through 1963], and those proposed, were dealing separately with such problems as slum housing, juvenile delinquency, unemployment, dependency, and illiteracy, but they were separately inadequate because they were striking only at some of the surface aspects of a bedrock problem, and that bedrock problem had to be identified and defined so that it could be attacked in a concerted, unified, and innovative way. Perhaps it was Harrington's book that identified the target for Kennedy and supplied the coordinating concept: the bedrock problem, in a word, was "poverty." Words and concepts determine programs; once the target was reduced to a single word, the timing became right for a unified program.[131]

On November 19, Heller met briefly with Kennedy in the White House. Kennedy told him he was still interested in seeing some sort of antipoverty program launched in 1964. Three days later, Kennedy was assassinated in Dallas. On the very next day, back in Washington, Heller met with the new president to brief him on, among other things, the still very vague plans for an antipoverty program. "That's my kind of program," Johnson told Heller. "Move full speed ahead." Johnson's emphasis on the need for haste reflected in part his desire to secure legitimacy in the eyes of the country by adopting as his own what was presented to him, not entirely accurately, as a legislative priority for John Kennedy. It also reflected an accurate political calculation that he had been presented with a remarkable, though undoubtedly short-lived, opportunity to push an ambitious package of social legislation through Congress. Just what that package should look like, he didn't know and didn't entirely care, so long as it was of suitably historic dimensions—which was to say, it should bear favorable comparison with Franklin Delano Roosevelt's New Deal. A scant six weeks later, in his State of the Union Address, Johnson declared that his administration, "today, here and now, declares unconditional war on poverty in America."[132]

Influential among policymaking insiders, at least to the extent that it defined poverty as a social and moral issue worth confronting, *The Other America* also found a much wider readership in 1963 and 1964 among the general public. Paul Jacobs wrote to Michael in Paris in May 1963 to let him know that: "Poverty and you have become inseparable and so I suppose the book must be doing very well. If it isn't, it isn't because people aren't talking about it."[133] By the time Michael returned to the United States, *The Other America* had indeed done well for a book on so somber a social issue, selling some 70,000 copies in hardcover and in the newly released Penguin paperback; it went through three additional printings in 1964, and two more in 1965. References to Michael's book became a virtually obligatory feature in the vast outpouring of journalistic commentary on poverty over the next several years; as *Business Week* noted in one such article in early February 1964, "*The Other America* is already regarded as a classic work on poverty."[134] *The Other America* was also paid the compliment of unattributed appropriation. Senator Hubert Humphrey published his own quickie book on poverty later that spring, which apart from frequent obsequious references to President Johnson, read like a gloss on Michael's book: "To most of us the poor inhabit a sector of society that we hardly recognize. They may come to do the laundry or fix the garden, but we barely see them as we speed by on the freeways or ride the commuter specials to and from the cities."[135]

There is no sure way to know just who was buying and reading *The Other America*, but it is probably safe to say that a significant number of them fit the description of the "amateur Democrat" that political scientist James Q.

Wilson had described in a 1962 book of the same name. These amateur Democrats, or Reform Democrats as they were more likely to call themselves, were for the most part urban, middle-class professionals, many of whom dated their political involvement to the Adlai Stevenson presidential campaigns of 1952 and 1956. Reform Democrats felt no loyalty to the old-style ethnic politics and political machines that had served the Democrats so well in the past, and in fact they often defined their politics first and foremost as "anti-boss." Wilson described them as people who see

> the political world more in terms of ideas and principles than in terms of persons. Politics is the determination of public policy, and public policy ought to be set deliberately rather than as the accidental by-product of a struggle for personal and party advantage.[136]

Among other characteristics, the amateur Democrats tended to be great readers. Not since the 1930s had so many books of social criticism found so wide a readership—and perhaps even more than in the 1930s, these were books that had significant political consequences. Jane Jacobs's *The Death and Life of Great American Cities,* published in 1961, punctured the myth of "urban renewal" and sparked a movement in defense of livable urban neighborhoods; Rachel Carson's *Silent Spring,* published in 1962, became the bible of a new environmental movement; Betty Friedan's *The Feminine Mystique,* published in 1963, contributed to the rebirth of American feminism; and Ralph Nader's *Unsafe at Any Speed,* an indictment of American car design published in 1965, led to movements for consumer safety and public interest lobbying.[137]

And although the "New Class" (as they were sometimes referred to) would be scored by conservatives for their alleged elitism, their favorite books, including *The Other America,* took as a basic premise the belief that one need not be a professional sociologist, biologist, engineer, or urban planner to understand what was wrong in American society and how to go about fixing it. As *Commentary* editor Norman Podhoretz (later one of the most caustic critics of the New Class) would write of his own reaction to reading about poverty in *The Other America* in the early 1960s: "In my judgment there was no question of the ability of the system to deal with such a problem; nor was there any question of how to do so. Like civil rights in the South, it represented a mopping-up operation, nothing more."[138]

On January 23, a month after his return to New York, Michael traveled to Washington to speak at the Georgetown University Conference on Poverty in Plenty. Like his fellow speakers Gunnar Myrdal and Leon Keyserling, Michael was critical of the limited scope of the president's proposed "war on poverty." At that time, estimates of the amount of funding Johnson intended to ask for from Congress for antipoverty programs ranged from a low of a quarter billion dollars to a high of one billion dollars. Michael suggested that even the higher of the two figures was no better than "the beginning of a beginning" of a real war on poverty.[139]

Following the Georgetown conference he returned to New York to work on his book. But scarcely had he settled back at his desk when he was called back to Washington. On February 1, President Johnson appointed Peace Corps director (and Kennedy brother-in-law) Sargent Shriver to oversee planning for the war on poverty. The appointment was intended both to convey the continuity between Kennedy's and Johnson's plans to eradicate poverty, and to bring into the antipoverty effort some of the reflected glow of the Peace Corps's popularity with the press and the public. Shriver, in turn, recruited Frank Mankiewicz, who had been directing Peace Corps operations in Peru, as a talent scout. Mankiewicz, who had met Michael in the 1950s and had read *The Other America,* mentioned his name to Shriver. "Who's that?" asked Shriver (*The Other America* had not, obviously, been read by everyone in Washington). And then, when Mankiewicz explained, Shriver told him, "Get him."[140] Mankiewicz called Paul Jacobs on February 2, and Jacobs called Michael.

The next day Michael and Jacobs were in Washington having lunch with Shriver and Mankiewicz and talking poverty programs. Michael warned Shriver that poverty would not be ended by spending "nickels and dimes." "Oh really, Mr. Harrington," Shriver replied. "I don't know about you, but this is the first time I've spent a billion dollars."[141]

Lunch turned into twelve straight days of continuous meetings and memo-writing as part of what came to be called the President's Task Force in the War Against Poverty, an involvement cut short only because Michael was committed to a series of speaking engagements in California in mid-February. At the first formal session of the task force, held on February 4 in Shriver's Peace Corps office on Connecticut Avenue, participants included Walter Heller, Secretary of Labor Willard Wirtz, Kennedy and Johnson speechwriter and political aide Richard Goodwin, Undersecretary for Health, Education, and Welfare Wilbur Cohen, and Adam Yarmolinsky, an aide to Robert McNamara in the Defense Department. It was, Michael would recall, "all very heady and exciting to be arguing with Cabinet officers and indirectly presenting memos to the President."[142] Paul Jacobs remembered their role in even more expansive terms. Since he and Michael did not have other official demands on their time, they were "the only two people in the group able to put in full time on the project." For a few days, Jacobs remembered, they even acted as administrative coordinators for the program, until government personnel were transferred from other agencies.[143]

But others remember their role differently. James Sundquist, who had been sent over from the Department of Agriculture to work as Shriver's assistant, described their contribution to the actual drafting of the antipoverty legislation as "negligible." The cabinet and other executive departments most concerned with the issue of poverty, including the Agriculture and Labor Departments, HEW, and the Budget Bureau made sure that their representatives went to every meeting and stayed as long as necessary to defend their own bureaucratic turf.[144]

Michael and Paul had no bureaucratic turf to defend, nor any political clout. So they wrote memos instead. They advocated creating what Michael called a "visionary division" or "a gadfly division" of the war on poverty, "which would be charged precisely with going beyond the present political and economic premises of the program," in thinking about ways to combat poverty in the coming years.[145] Frank Mankiewicz, who was friendly with both Michael and Paul, appreciated their contribution. They were definitely not "hard-headed Washington realists." But that wasn't their role. What they were best at was helping to "generate awareness" of the full dimensions of the problem of poverty. Michael urged the task force to keep in mind the levels of social alienation and rootlessness of the poor. "You know," he would say, for example, "most of these people never get any mail."[146]

Michael and Paul caused some consternation because of their habit of ending memos with the half-joking injunction, "Of course, there is no real solution to the problem of poverty until we abolish the capitalist system." According to one prominent figure in the planning sessions, who prefers anonymity, Michael and Paul were warned "by all means" to make sure "that none of their memos ever turned up on Capitol Hill."[147] Yarmolinsky, who became Shriver's deputy in the planning efforts, was the member of the task force least patient with Michael and Paul's perspective (perhaps because he came from a radical family background, which he had rejected): "They'd tell us over and over again what the problems were, but we said, 'what do you do about them? What kinds of legislation?' And it wasn't their bag."[148]

The two task force radicals did have at least one concrete policy suggestion to offer, and although it wasn't what Johnson wanted to hear, it wasn't all that radical either. Yarmolinsky assigned task force workers the job of writing a set of background papers on the solutions of poverty. A group that included Jacobs and Michael received the assignment of writing about jobs. On February 6 they sent a memo to Shriver arguing that "if there is any single dominant problem of poverty in the U.S., it is that of unemployment."[149] They went on to argue that the war on poverty should return to the tried and true model of the New Deal, creating massive public works projects to end unemployment and redistribute income to those most in need. That was also the approach favored by Secretary of Labor Wirtz and his assistant—and former White Horse regular—Daniel Patrick Moynihan (who coauthored the memo on jobs with Michael and Paul). Creating public works employment, however, was an expensive proposition; initial Labor Department proposals for jobs programs were in the $3 to $5 billion vicinity. And Johnson, with an eye to the upcoming presidential election, had committed himself not only to waging war on poverty but also to securing a tax cut and to reining in government spending. When Wirtz raised the question of a jobs program at a cabinet meeting with the president, Johnson didn't even bother to respond. He simply went on to the next item on the agenda.[150] The budget that the administration submitted and Congress passed for fiscal year 1965 represented a slight cut from that of the previous year.[151]

Johnson's own ideas about how to combat poverty were a contradictory mixture of warm memories of the New Deal (particularly the National Youth Administration, for which he had served as Texas state coordinator before entering Congress in 1937) and a conviction that simply giving money to the poor was both morally and politically undesirable. "You tell Shriver, no doles," was the message he gave to aide Bill Moyers to pass on to Shriver as planning for the war on poverty began. Public works, along with expanding existing welfare programs, was never considered as a serious option by Shriver's task force.[152]

Instead, the war on poverty chose to emphasize programs that would enable the poor to improve themselves—a "handup, not a hand out," as Shriver would put it. The poor would be provided with job training and other forms of educational benefits that would allow them to take advantage of the opportunities provided by an expanding national economy—hence, the title given to Shriver's package of legislative proposals was the Economic Opportunity Act.[153]

Michael found himself welcome but marginalized (or as Sundquist and Yarmolinsky would argue, self-marginalized) in the antipoverty task force. But there were some other radicals involved in the planning process who would have a much greater impact on the kinds of programmatic proposals that emerged from these deliberations. These were the "community action" advocates, a small cadre of unorthodox sociologists who had signed on to government service during the Kennedy administration to develop plans to combat urban juvenile delinquency. Their chief representative at the poverty planning sessions was Richard Boone, who argued that the frustrations associated with "blocked opportunity" were the cause of most of the social problems associated with poor communities, from low levels of aspiration to gang violence. As the discussion within Washington domestic policy circles shifted from the narrowly gauged effort to combat juvenile delinquency to the new emphasis on ending poverty, the community action advocates came into their own. They argued that poor neighborhoods should be "empowered" through federally initiated efforts in community organizing, a project undertaken with the "maximum feasible participation" of the poor.

Shriver was sympathetic to the notion of community action from the beginning. The Peace Corps had been running a form of community development for three years before Shriver got the call to head up the war on poverty; what's more, he had been friendly with radical organizer Saul Alinsky in the 1950s, when Alinsky was experimenting with community organizing through the Back of the Yards project in Chicago.[154] Michael himself was not unsympathetic to the concerns of those who argued for the community action approach. In *The Other America* he had contrasted the spirited, politically well-organized slum communities of the early twentieth century with the spiritless, disorganized slums of the 1960s. Michael recounted the history of the Montgomery Bus Boycott in *The Other America,* noting that it had had the entirely unexpected effect of lowering the crime rate in Montgomery's black community. "Thousands of people had been given a sense of purpose, of their own worth and dignity. On their own, and without any special urging, they began to change their personal lives; they became a different people. If the same elan could invade the other America, there would be similar results."[155]

Nevertheless, Michael remained skeptical about the idea that the government could step in to organize the poor in their own interest:

> Is it possible for governments to finance the self organization of the poor? Isn't it true that when you have a governmental program to organize the poor on their own behalf that, if it is successful, the first thing those people are going to do is hold a rent strike? The second thing they're going to do is send a committee to their local Congressman, and the third thing they're going to do is picket the Mayor. Can you expect, given the political structure of this country, governmental funds being used to overthrow governments?

Instead Michael would prefer to see "non-governmental agencies and individuals to involve themselves" in the organization of the poor, "because they need not have these restrictions."[156]

But if Michael had little to do with actually choosing the policies that would determine the ultimate success or failure of the war on poverty, he had a great deal of responsibility for how those policies would be justified to the public. When the Johnson administration marched off to wage its newly declared war on the domestic front, it was not so much against poverty as against "the culture of poverty." One of the reasons for the popularity of the notion of the culture of poverty was that as a descriptive label it seemed to carry great explanatory power, and in terms of policy it proved remarkably flexible. Over the next several decades the notion would, in fact, wind up being employed to support just about any solution to poverty that could be imagined across the political spectrum, from the most conservative to the most liberal, and even to the revolutionary.[157]

The irony is that the phrase with which Michael's name will always be identified most closely was one that he himself was not really committed to and may not have even fully understood when he used it in *The Other America.* Throughout the book, "culture of poverty" is used interchangeably with another term, "vicious circle," which had been a staple of reformist literature ever since the Progressive Era.[158] "Here is one of the most familiar forms of the vicious circle of poverty," Michael wrote in a typical passage from *The Other America*:

> The poor get sick more than anyone else in the society. That is because they live in slums, jammed together under unhygienic conditions; they have inadequate diets, and cannot get decent medical care. When they become sick, they are sick longer than any other group in society. Because they are sick more often and longer than anyone else, they lose wages and work, and find it difficult to hold a steady job. And because of this, they cannot pay for good housing, for a nutritious diet, for doctors. At any given point in the circle, particularly when there is a major illness, their prospect is to move to an even lower level and to begin the cycle, round and round, toward even more suffering.[159]

Michael wanted to impress his readers with the sense that poverty was not an easy condition of life to break away from. Everything conspired to keep those already in poverty mired in poverty. But nothing in the "vicious circle" of poverty, as described here, was culturally rooted in the sense that Oscar Lewis had meant when he talked about the culture of poverty as a kind of normative system at odds with the values of the larger society, an ingrained and unchanging way of life passed down from generation to generation. No part of Michael's vicious circle was related to the low level of aspiration that was supposed to characterize those living in the culture of poverty, nor to the tendency to indulge in immediate gratification, nor to the propensity for violence or sexual promiscuity. Poor nutrition, poor medical care, poor housing, and prolonged and frequent illnesses were conditions imposed upon the poor by a lack of income, not by cultural traits or behaviors that, presumably, could be exchanged for others. Everything Michael described in this particular example of the vicious circle could be improved through the simple expedient of additional family income.

Another of the chapters in *The Other America* was devoted to exploring the dilemma of poverty among the elderly. After reviewing government statistics showing that older Americans accounted for a disproportionate share of the population living below the poverty line, Michael asked rhetorically, "Who are these people? How did they come to the culture of poverty?" But in answering this question, he undermined its premise by making it clear that many of the elderly poor "had known days of good wages and working conditions" when they were younger.[160] In other words, these were people who became poor only upon retiring or being forced into permanent unemployment late in life. Was Michael asking his readers to believe that the elderly poor suddenly began displaying the characteristics of the "culture of poverty" after decades of enjoying steady work at good wages? Clearly, what Michael really meant to ask was, "How did these people come to be poor?"—that is, come to exist in an unfavorable economic condition—instead of, "How did they come to the culture of poverty?"—that is, display a set of behaviors and attitudes at odds with the dominant culture.

Oscar Lewis quickly noted the discrepancy between his own definition of the culture of poverty and Michael's economic interpretation, even if few other people did at the time. Lewis was annoyed by what he regarded as a misuse of his research. He had estimated that the culture of poverty characterized no more than a fifth of those living in poverty in the United States; Michael used the term far more loosely as a virtual synonym for being poor.[161] Were this simply a question of semantics, it would not have made much difference. But in misapplying the concept of the culture of poverty, and in proving so wildly and unexpectedly successful in popularizing that misapplication, Michael had handed a potent weapon to those who would, in subsequent decades, seek to undo the legislative legacy of the war on poverty. Within a very few years, the "culture of poverty" would be interpreted in ways antithetical to Michael's own understanding, values, and political aspirations, that is, as a way of depicting the poor as the authors of their own fate.

That possibility seemed remote in the spring and summer of 1964, as President Johnson masterfully manipulated the political levers needed to move the Economic Opportunity Act to approval by Congress. Michael argued in May that Johnson had chosen the terrain for his first big legislative effort shrewdly, since focusing on the poor lent him "a peculiar rhetorical advantage" in terms of American political culture:

> The poor are not a social and political class in the sense that organized workers are. If, for example, Johnson had approached democratic America in terms of the trade union vocabulary—full employment, minimum wage, shorter work week—that would have set off all kinds of class antagonisms, real and imagined, on the part of business. A well-fed executive can declaim against the surly, shiftless union members and their sinister leaders. But the American pattern of speech does not allow the same fury against

> the "poor," who are traditionally seen as victimized, unorganized and not menacing.[162]

There was some historical precedent for Michael's argument. During the Progressive Era, reformers had achieved their greatest legislative successes when they focused attention on groups such as poor women and children, who were viewed in some sense as dependent upon the generosity and good intentions of the larger society. Even while trade unions and male industrial workers in general remained objects of suspicion or fear on the part of middle-class voters, significant legislative gains were made in the battle to restrict child labor and regulate the conditions of work for women.[163]

The early reports on the war on poverty struck exactly the kind of "victimized [and] not menacing" note that Michael suggested Americans felt in regards to the poor. The face of poverty that turned up in the mass media in those days tended to be that of young white Appalachians. Lyndon Johnson did his part by making a well-orchestrated trip to eastern Kentucky in late April, where he visited with an unemployed coal miner named Tom Fletcher in his three-room, tarpaper-covered shack.[164] James Agee and Walker Evans's *Let Us Now Praise Famous Men* was back in print, after twenty years of being unavailable, and selling many more copies than it had the first time around. Harry Caudill's *Night Comes to the Cumberlands,* a portrait of life in southern Appalachia published in 1963, was also popular. "This is Daniel Boone country," Stewart Udall wrote of the Cumberland Plateau in his foreword to Caudill's book, a region where once "fiercely independent frontiersmen found in these isolated valleys the elements that sustained vigorous life."[165] As long as the poor continued to be thought of as the great, great grandchildren of Daniel Boone, the fortunes of the war on poverty would remain on the rise. What neither Michael nor Lyndon Johnson was considering in the spring of 1964 was what would happen if and when the iconic image of poverty shifted from a white Appalachian child to someone else—say a black welfare mother, or worse, a black street criminal. (Even in the spring of 1964, when the war on poverty was still generating reams of enthusiastic coverage in the nation's press, and when most Americans pronounced themselves in favor of Johnson's antipoverty efforts, public opinion polls nonetheless revealed that a plurality of Americans continued to believe that the poor were to blame for their own condition.)[166]

In August 1964, Congress passed the Economic Opportunity Act and appropriated $800 million to fund the Office of Economic Opportunity, the new agency that would oversee antipoverty efforts under the direction of Sargent Shriver. Michael praised the passage of Johnson's antipoverty program as a step "in the right direction." But in his frequent public speeches that year, such as one he delivered to delegates at the General Assembly of the Council of Jewish Federations and Welfare Funds held in St. Louis in November, he argued that to truly wage war on poverty, Americans would have to be prepared to spend a $100 billion over the next ten years. "Massive investments" in preschool education and public works programs were needed, as were increases in the level of social security payments, raises in the minimum wage, and the creation of a system of national health care.[167]

Although conservative critics of the war on poverty would continue to attack it as socialist inspired, Michael had long since worn out his welcome in official administration circles.[168] When Marilyn Magid asked Michael if he now felt "like part of the Establishment" he was not amused. It was, she noted, a question "he had apparently encountered once too often." Michael responded "slowly and distinctly" that "I have not—repeat not—been invited to dine at the White House."[169] Nor was he invited for the ceremony in the White House in August when President Johnson signed the new antipoverty act into law. Shriver, Yarmolinsky, and many others who had been part of the initial planning sessions for the legislation the previous February lined up to collect one of the seventy-two pens Johnson used in signing the act. Michael would not have gotten a pen if Daniel Patrick Moynihan had not thought to go through the line twice to pick up an extra one for him.[170]

Michael did not brood over LBJ's snubs. Indeed, he argued forcefully that fall that the Left should support Johnson's bid for election to the White House in his own right. "The defeat of Barry Goldwater," he wrote in the journal *New Politics* in the summer of 1964, "is a precondition for the future of democracy in the United States [and] a precondition for any development of the democratic left." Writing in *New America* in early September, when it had become apparent that Johnson was heading toward a landslide electoral victory on November 3, Michael looked forward to the election results as "a turn to, and a mandate for, the liberal Left."[171]

There was one dark cloud on the political horizon that fall that Michael had to acknowledge, and that was the war in Vietnam. In August, Johnson had ordered U.S. bombing raids against North Vietnam in response to alleged attacks on American destroyers by North Vietnamese PT boats in the Gulf of Tonkin. Johnson had used the events in the Gulf of Tonkin to secure passage of a congressional resolution supporting his actions in the region. Antiwar critics argued that the resolution amounted to a virtual declaration of war.

Although Michael criticized Johnson's continuing commitment to the "impossible war" in South Vietnam, he still chose to emphasize that Johnson was the lesser of two evils. Barry Goldwater had been calling for a sustained bombing campaign against North Vietnam and for the use of chemical defoliants to strip away the jungles and forests that gave cover to the Viet Cong. President Johnson, Michael wrote in *New America* in September, wasn't nearly as great a threat to peace as Goldwater, the "darling of the Big Bomber Boys" who would give military field commanders "the decision over atomic holocaust."[172] Norman Thomas, writing in the same issue of *New America*, was not as sanguine. Although declaring that it was "very important that the Goldwater-Miller ticket be overwhelmingly defeated," Thomas took a more critical stance on the administration's policy in South Vietnam. Quoting a letter he had recently sent to his old acquaintance Hubert Humphrey, Thomas declared, "I think a continuation of the Administration's present policy in South Vietnam . . . will lead to war almost as surely but by no means as rapidly as would Goldwater's. You are not protecting freedom in South Vietnam, but practicing power politics."[173]

In November the voters gave Johnson his expected landslide victory, handing him the electoral votes of every state except for Goldwater's home state of Arizona and five states in the deep South disenchanted with Democratic support for civil rights. Democrats gained two seats in the Senate, and thirty-seven in the House. Now, at long last, it seemed to be the liberals' turn to set the national agenda.

Few people on the American Left were better positioned to influence that agenda than Michael Harrington that fall. In November, he was installed with considerable pomp as chairman of the League for Industrial Democracy, the venerable educational wing of the socialist movement, founded in 1905 by Jack London, Upton Sinclair, and Clarence Darrow. Jack Newfield reported in the *Village Voice* that only three years earlier "Michael Harrington's reputation as a socialist preacher with the eloquence of Debs and a debater with the logic of a Talmudic scholar was confined to one faction of the Young People's Socialist League and the back room of the White Horse Tavern." Now, Newfield noted, Michael had been "knighted by Arthur Schlesinger Jr. as 'the only responsible radical in America.'" Norman Thomas, "beaming like a father," was among those present for the ceremony in the ballroom of the Fifth Avenue Hotel, along with such notables as Bayard Rustin, Daniel Bell, and James Wechsler. Bell joked to the assemblage that Michael was being promoted to the role of chairman of the "MASL—the Middle-Aged Socialist League."

In his acceptance speech, Michael outlined ambitious plans for LID's revival, including plans to hold a major conference the following spring to bring together American and European intellectuals, trade unionists, and civil rights activists to discuss the future of left-liberal politics. In addition, Michael noted, LID would continue to "subsidize [its] rapidly growing campus division, Students for a Democratic Society."[174]

In an editorial in the *New York Post* several days later, James Wechsler predicted that Michael was destined to play a "special role" in American politics: "Out of one man's commitment and conscience small miracles are sometimes wrought. In a time when 'consensus' politics too often clouds great questions, his clear voice may be heard in many provinces."[175]

All the years of patient waiting, building, and preparation on the part of Michael and his comrades seemed ready to come to fruition. The 1964 election was a triumph for those who dreamed of a "realigned" Democratic Party that would draw together the great forces of labor, liberalism, and the civil rights movement. Even the defection of the once solidly Democratic Deep South to the Republicans was a blessing in disguise, reducing the influence of the Dixiecrats within the councils of the Democratic Party. And who was better situated than Michael Harrington—the "man who discovered poverty," the man who had the ear of Martin Luther King, and Walter Reuther, and Sargent Shriver, the man with a following that reached from the liberal wing of the Catholic Church to Students for a Democratic Society—who better situated than Michael to bring together those "scattered legions" and unite them into a powerful redemptive force for equality and social justice?. In 1962 the *Village Voice* had described Michael as "a vital voice of conscience for our times"; in 1964 James Wechsler wrote that Michael was a "Man of his Time." What no one could have predicted was just how quickly his time was destined to pass.

CHAPTER EIGHT

Sibling and Other Rivalries, 1960–1965

Harrington was pivotal, for he was the one person who might have mediated across the generational divide.

Todd Gitlin,
former national president of Students for a Democratic Society (SDS)
1987[1]

Michael waited a long time for a new generation of young radicals to come along in America. Between 1952 and 1960 he had undergone a rigorous training in political theory and organizational know-how—which he was now eager to share with the newcomers. Of course, there were those among the older generation of radicals who argued that the best thing the veterans could offer the coming generation was a promise to leave them alone. The poet Kenneth Rexroth, whose own radical credentials reached back to the Communist-organized John Reed Clubs of the early 1930s, and who had in more recent years embraced a more anarchic politics, issued a warning in the *Nation* in the summer of 1960 to the students who had made headlines the previous spring by taking part in the civil rights sit-ins and anti-HUAC protests. News of the "New Revolt of Youth," he noted,

> reached the ears of all the retired and semi-retired and comfortably fixed pie-card artists of every lost and every long-since-won cause of the labor and radical movements. Everybody shouted, 'Myself when young!' and pitched in with application blanks. . . . As the kids go back to school this fall, this is going to be the greatest danger they will face—all these eager helpers from the other side of the age barrier, all these cooks, each with a time-tested recipe for the broth.[2]

But for Michael it was unthinkable simply to pass the torch on to the newcomers, wish them well, and stand aside. To begin with, he had not crossed to the other side of the "age barrier" nearly so long ago as someone of Rexroth's generation; in his own mind, at least, he was more older brother to the New Left than ancient patriarch. Even had he been as old as Rexroth, he would likely have felt the same obligation to pass on the lessons he had drawn from his own experience. Michael believed that genuine radicalism—the kind that was capable of holding on through tough times, the kind that could build and sustain a mass movement for social justice—was not simply a matter of generational identity or ideological conviction, much less a state of grace. It was instead a set of skills, attitudes, and principles that had to be learned—either from painful experience or from some other source.

Rexroth was, however, right about one thing: Michael did indeed see the New Left through an interpretative lens of "Myself when young!" He viewed his own past as a model for the new generation to follow, hopefully with fewer detours along the way. Just as he had moved from the other-worldly utopian pacifism of the Catholic Worker to a more worldly, sophisticated, and nuanced Marxism, so he hoped and believed that all the younger Michael Harringtons now appearing on campuses across the nation would do the same.

For the young to learn, the old had to be prepared to teach. But, echoing the young Karl Marx, Michael did not forget that it was "essential to educate the educator himself."[3] Writing in *Dissent* early in the 1960s, Michael warned "veterans of the radical movement" not to react too hastily when they heard New Leftists espousing apparently naive or apologetic views of third world Communism, especially in Cuba. Although such attitudes "must be faced and changed," the young were not going to be persuaded by means of adult edict:

> It cannot be done from a lecture platform, from a distance. Rather, the persuasion must come from someone who is actually involved in changing the status quo [and] someone who has a sympathy for the genuine and good emotions which are just behind the bad theories.[4]

Michael was determined to be that someone who combined the knowledge, credentials, and sympathies that could persuade the young to turn away from "bad theories" and embrace the democratic socialist alternative. In reaching out to New Leftists, he was not seeking a personal following. He did not want to make "Harringtonites" (a phrase he never used) out of young radicals; he wanted to make them socialists. The notion of an unorganized socialist struck him as an oxymoron. "The socialist movement," he would write, "is itself the embryo of socialism."[5]

What that meant in practical terms to Michael was that socialists had to be prepared to work with the organizational materials they had at hand—

which in the early 1960s consisted of, for all their admitted inadequacies, the Socialist Party/Social Democratic Federation, and the Young People's Socialist League. So when Michael reached out to the new generation of radicals, he did so both as an individual thinker and activist and—in what was for him a matter of a disciplined, principled choice—as a representative of the actually existing socialist movement. That Michael felt no conflict between those two roles did not mean, unfortunately for him, that there would be none—and in the end, his role as the latter would seriously undermine his appeal as the former.

In most histories of the 1960s, including those focusing on the history of the American Left, the Socialist Party to which Michael paid dues and owed allegiance receives but scant attention—and understandably so. At the start of the decade, the party's membership was at an abysmal low of about a thousand—less than a hundredth of its size a half century earlier. Of that thousand, perhaps no more than a few hundred could be counted upon as radical activists. The rest kept up their membership out of lifelong habit, or as a sentimental tribute to the tradition of Debs and Thomas. And yet, paradoxically, of all the left-wing groups in the country at the start of the 1960s, these very same Socialists were best positioned to take advantage of the improving prospects for radical politics.

Consider the situation in Berkeley, California, at the start of the 1960s. The New Left sprang from many sources and many locales. But surely no place in the country was more important in its genesis than Berkeley. "There on the edge of the Pacific," Michael would recall fondly, "a radical-Bohemian world existed that was very much like the one I had known at the University of Chicago in the late forties. At the Steppenwolf and the Blind Lemon [Berkeley coffeehouses] there was an ambiance of folk music, Marxism, and sexual freedom, the Left-wing trinity of that period."[6] In the late 1950s, Michael had made repeated trips to the campus of the University of California at Berkeley to drum up new recruits. And, as a result of his efforts and those of his comrades, on the eve of the 1960s, Berkeley was one of the strongholds of the SP and YPSL—and of Michael's own faction within those groups, the Shachtmanites. Richard Drinnon, a young historian at the University of California, reported in a letter to David McReynolds early in 1959 that a "strong contingent of former ISLers have moved into control" of Berkeley's SP chapter. It was to be expected, Drinnon wrote, that "comrades with such talent and discipline"—and here he mentioned by name Bogdan Denitch, Hal and Ann Draper, Stan Weir, and Barney Cohen—would exert "considerable power" within a local group that until recently had shown few signs of life. Drinnon was not entirely happy with this development, fearing that for all their talk of creating "an open, Debsian party," the familiar sectarian habits of the Shachtmanites would reassert themselves, scaring off newcomers.[7]

But such fears proved misplaced, at least in the short run. In Berkeley, and across the bay in San Francisco, a revitalized SP made its mark on the political map for the first time in decades. Berkeley YPSL, with just twenty members at the start of 1960, tripled its membership that spring. (Five dozen determined and energetic activists can make a big difference, even on a huge university campus like UC–Berkeley.) The yipsels were active in the local chapter of CORE and turned out in force to picket local Woolworth's stores in support of the southern civil rights sit-ins. They were also well represented at the May 13, 1960, demonstration at San Francisco city hall protesting hearings being held there by the House Un-American Activities Committee. That protest ended in a dramatic confrontation between the students and the police riot squad and was one of the formative events signaling the emergence of a new left.[8]

So in the first year or two of the 1960s, YPSL seemed to reinvent itself successfully as an activist organization. In the spring of 1961 five members of the Berkeley chapter were among the Freedom Riders arrested and jailed in Mississippi for challenging segregation on interstate buses.[9] That same year Dale Johnson, a young Bay Area radical not particularly sympathetic to the Socialists, reported in the New Left journal *Studies on the Left:*

> Since the May anti-HUAC "riots," new organizations and spontaneous protest movements have grown up: the socialist groups of the [Bay] area have reported a high degree of interest in their programs (the Young People's Socialist League and the Socialist Party-Social Democratic Federation of Berkeley, blessed with highly skilled leadership, have been particularly successful of late).[10]

In New York, Philadelphia, Chicago, and on a half dozen or so college and university campuses, the SP and, particularly, YPSL were beginning to develop a similar sense of local strength and élan in the early 1960s. Although SP membership failed to grow significantly (the number of new recruits continually offset by the number of veterans dying off), YPSL roughly doubled its membership every two years following its merger with the YSL, from 200 in 1958 to 400 in 1960 and over 800 in 1962. Low as these numbers were, they still put YPSL ahead of potential competitors on the Left; in 1962 YPSL counted several hundred more dues-payers in its ranks than the nascent Students for a Democratic Society (SDS). Being first on the scene awarded YPSL considerable advantage, evident not only in the quantity but also in the quality of those it was attracting to its meetings. An obscure young activist named Jerry Rubin was a card-carrying socialist in San Francisco in 1961; an equally obscure Stokeley Carmichael was among the Howard University undergraduates that Tom Kahn was able to interest in

YPSL that same year; while in New York City a Queens College undergraduate named Mario Savio liked to hang out in Washington Square Park and "listen to the socialist firebrands."[11]

At the start of the decade Socialists thus had at least as good a claim as any of the other existing radical groups to a future rendezvous with destiny. They were playing leading roles in the peace movement as part of such recently organized and fast growing groups as the Committee for a Sane Nuclear Policy (SANE) and the Student Peace Union (SPU). They had footholds of influence within the labor movement, at least within union staff, from the old needle trades to the New York teacher's union to the United Auto Workers. Most importantly, they had friends in high places in the civil rights movement, like Randolph and Rustin. I. F. Stone, a journalist more often associated in the past with the fellow-traveling circles around the Communist Party, celebrated the vitality and appeal of the Socialists in an article written for his *Weekly* shortly after the 1963 March on Washington. Stone had attended an SP-sponsored conference in Washington just after the march, where civil rights notables like Randolph and Rustin had addressed the crowd. In that ill-lighted hall, Stone declared,

> amid the assorted young students and venerables like Norman Thomas, socialism took on fresh meaning and revived urgency. It was not accidental that so many of those who ran the March turned out to be members and fellow travellers of the Socialist Party. One saw that for the lower third of our society, white as well as black, the search for answers must lead them back—though Americans still start nervously at the very word—toward socialism.[12]

And, of course, Socialists enjoyed the visibility and legitimacy that came from having someone like the vigorous Michael Harrington, as well as the venerable Norman Thomas, as their public face. Michael turned thirty-two in the spring of 1960. His membership in YPSL had lapsed the year before, so he could no longer accurately describe himself as "America's oldest young socialist." To the nineteen- and twenty-year-old aspiring radicals he was encountering on college campuses, he was now a distinguished elder. "I noticed the real change," Michael remarked to John Cogley in the mid-1960s, when students "began to call me 'Sir,' and refused to call me 'Mike.'"[13] But Michael wore his newly acquired adult authority lightly. He was an inspirational figure, admired for the quality of his ideas and his ability to give them eloquent expression, and also for the obvious sincerity with which he embodied them. Bob Ross, who as a freshman at the University of Michigan in 1960 was becoming involved in radical politics, encountered Michael giving a speech in Ann Arbor that year on the need for a "democratic social order." Ross remembered being "really charmed" by the fact that because Michael still retained a trace of his midwestern accent he pronounced it democratic social *ardor.* Tom Hayden, another product of the University of Michigan who met Michael for the first time that same year, would describe him as "easily the most charismatic of the political intellectuals" he encountered in the early 1960s. In 1961, in an article entitled "Who Are the Student Boat-Rockers?"—for, of all places, *Mademoiselle* magazine—Hayden listed Michael as one of three radical leaders over the age of thirty who had "won [the] respect" of New Leftists (the other two were C. Wright Mills and Norman Thomas).[14]

Michael's "charisma" was a product of personal poise, good looks, and intellectual sophistication. It also had something to do with his identity as a New Yorker. Michael Harrington, the St. Louis socialist, would probably not have enjoyed quite the same reputation as Michael the consummate New Yorker. Paul Cowan, a young New Leftist who joined the staff of the *Village Voice* in the mid-1960s, would later recall walking down West 4th Street to the *Voice*'s offices with fellow staffer Jack Newfield. Newfield told him that "he wouldn't change his job on the newspaper for any other in the world. A community that included Norman Mailer, Mike Harrington, Bob Dylan, and Tom Hayden seemed to him ideal."[15]

Michael was linked to the excitement of the contemporary Village, as well as to the great tradition of bohemian radicalism stretching back to Jack Reed and *The Masses,* and to Emma Goldman and *Mother Earth.* He was someone who wrote for and was celebrated in the pages of the *Village Voice,* who could be found on a Saturday afternoon listening to the folksingers in Washington Square Park, and who squired his attractive girlfriends, and later an attractive wife, to fashionable Village parties and watering holes. He may have graduated to the status of "sir" in the eyes of young radicals, but he definitely wasn't some tiresome old Leftist who looked and sounded like he was left over from the 1930s. He had a sense of personal style, even in his habitual dressed-down disarray. And style and self-presentation counted with this generation. It helped that Michael looked like a winner.

In the 1950s, those few young men and women who Michael recruited into the movement usually felt themselves culturally as well as politically dispossessed. Although some would develop into talented intellectuals or organizers, their beliefs set them off as eccentric social orphans. Not so the new generation that Michael was now encountering in campus lecture halls around the country. To be young and radical in the early 1960s was to be endowed with the expectation of coming into a large and well-deserved inheritance, for, as Bob Dylan would sing in 1962, "The times, they are a changin'." Whatever the newcomers were, they were not the last recruits of some doomed legion of the Left. Marilyn Magid, a New York reporter intimately familiar with the city's radical subculture, shrewdly surveyed the youthful audience who turned out to hear Michael speak on one occasion early in the 1960s:

> The audience seemed for the most part the same kids who have suddenly achieved visibility as they enact the sit-ins and demonstrations that are at the heart of [the civil rights] movement. Everyone knows by now what they look like—if not from those demonstrations, then from the lobby of the Bleecker Street Cinema or the audience at the Judson Memorial Church or the new places that have suddenly begun to burgeon east of Astor Place. The girls are prettier than the girls used to be at meetings of the Left—devoid altogether of the low-heeled Fabian look—faintly arty but with a minimum of hammered silver; they wear eye makeup but no lipstick. The boys are cooler, jauntier; they carry fewer library books (the paperback revolution having ensued in the meantime); they look less fiercely brainy and their complexions are better.

Michael's new following, Magid concluded, resembled nothing quite so much as "the entire incoming class at Swarthmore."[16] The incoming class at Swarthmore probably wouldn't have known what to make of a Max Shachtman; Michael Harrington, on the other hand, seemed at that moment as much culturally one of their own as Bob Dylan.

Michael's hopes for influencing the development of a New Left soon came to rest on his close relations with an emerging group of youthful organizers and intellectuals who called themselves Students for a Democratic Society (SDS). SDS grew out of the Student League for Industrial Democracy (SLID)—the same SLID that in the early 1950s had beaten off an attempted organizational coup by Bogdan Denitch's "Red Caucus." In 1958, Al Haber, a veteran of student politics at the University of Michigan, joined SLID at the urging of Michael's old Michigan friend "Lefty" Yamada; in 1960 Haber was elected president of the group, newly renamed as Students for a Democratic Society. Haber was determined to make SDS a multi-issue group, linking together activists on many campuses and in many causes who shared a radical democratic perspective, and breaking with sectarian traditions of other left-wing student groups. Haber invited Michael (along with Rustin, James Farmer, and other veteran radicals) to speak at the very first public event sponsored by SDS, a conference entitled "Human Rights in the North," held at Ann Arbor in the spring of 1960. The conference brought together some of the black students who had recently launched the sit-in movement in the South to meet with their northern campus sympathizers, and it was a significant success for the fledging SDS.[17] Michael was impressed, and resolved to stay in close contact with Haber and those he attracted to SDS. He found an official way to maintain contact when he was appointed the following year as a member of the student activities committee of the League for Industrial Democracy, the adult sponsor and bill-payer for SDS.

Haber's most important recruit in 1960 was an undergraduate from the University of Michigan named Tom Hayden. More than anyone else Michael would encounter in the early New Left, Hayden seemed cut out for the role of his political "younger brother." He was eleven years younger than Michael, an age difference only a few years greater than that separating Michael from Irving Howe. Like Michael he was raised in an intensely Catholic environment; the only child of a doting mother, Hayden early on displayed a knack for piety and intellectual achievement, winning plaudits for reading aloud from St. Thomas Aquinas to the nuns in his parish school when he was in second grade. Later on in college he would immerse himself in philosophy and political theory, influenced by many of the same authors Michael had discovered a decade earlier, including Albert Camus and Jacques Maritain.

But there were differences between the two men's backgrounds, as well. Hayden's childhood had been more abrasive than Michael's; his father was a heavy drinker, his parents divorced while he was a child, and money was scarce in the Hayden home. His disillusionment with Catholicism came earlier, too, than Michael's; he had no interest in going on with Catholic education after high school—thus his enrollment at Michigan in 1957. Like Michael, he gravitated to bohemianism, but of a more roughneck variety—a devoted Jack Kerouac reader, he enjoyed risking his neck on a motorcycle. All in all, there was a harder edge to his personality, and an angrier undercurrent to his politics. Irving Howe would conclude after a first tense meeting with Michael's new protégé that "in Hayden's clenched style . . . one could already see the beginnings of a commisar."[18]

But Michael saw in Hayden a kindred spirit—perhaps even an eventual successor. Although Hayden was, to Michael's eyes, "unprepossessing, a nondescript youth of no great presence," he detected burning in him "an intense Leftist commitment."[19] The two met for the first time at the SDS human rights conference in Ann Arbor in the spring of 1960, and then again that summer at the Democratic convention, where Hayden showed up hoping to interview Martin Luther King Jr. for the *Michigan Daily* and stayed to join Michael's picket line outside the convention hall. When Michael attempted to recruit him into the socialist movement, Hayden made it clear he was uninterested. "He'd say, 'I agree with you,'" Michael would recall:

> But where I disagree with you is that you use the word 'socialism,' which is a European word, which essentially cuts off your American audience. And

what he was essentially telling me was that he wanted to have a different language. He wanted to speak American.[20]

Though Hayden spurned Michael's political advances, the two nonetheless remained close. Hayden spent the next year finishing up at the University of Michigan, then "went south" in 1961 as SDS's representative to the civil rights movement. Michael came down to Austin, Texas, that fall on a speaking tour, and while there he attended Tom's wedding to fellow activist Casey Cason (the newlyweds read aloud passages from Camus as part of the service, a touch that Michael surely appreciated). In December 1961, when Hayden was released from jail in Albany, Georgia, after being arrested in a civil rights protest, he came back to New York to build support for SNCC's efforts in Albany; Michael introduced him to a cheering audience at a rally in a public school. And a few months later, when *The Other America* was published, Michael signed and sent Hayden one of the first copies of the book.[21]

Michael didn't give up hope that Hayden would eventually come around to some version of his own socialist politics, even if he wasn't interested in YPSL. "Some recent commentators have written eulogies to the non-ideological character of the youth movement," Michael noted in the *New Leader* in the spring of 1961 (possibly in delayed retort to Kenneth Rexroth):

> Usually, these writers are imposing their own disillusionment upon a movement which they see from a great distance. To be sure, the broad mass of involved students are not ideologically committed, but their impetus usually comes from conscious radicals: the sign-painters, the leaflet-writers, the activists.[22]

Over the next several years, he predicted, student activists with "a sophisticated political point of view" would continue to grow in importance within the movement, and as a result, the New Left "will lose its heavy emphasis upon the moral gesture."[23]

In fact, Michael was swimming against a heavier tide than he realized in his ingrained suspicion, left over from Catholic Worker days, of the politics of "moral gesture." Politically and culturally attuned as he was to the new generation of radicals, there was a kind of spiritual connection he could not or would not make to them. The new social movements of the 1960s shared transcendent faith in their mission, and that was true whether they looked to sacred or secular texts for inspiration. Paul Cowan, who was a peace and civil rights activist before joining the *Voice,* would remember of the era, "Whenever I attended one of [Pete] Seeger's concerts I felt a belief, nearly religious, that there was a generation of people like myself preparing to help America break free."[24] Civil rights activists in the South, and many of their northern supporters, had come to view "putting their bodies on the line" at the risk of arrest and beatings not only as an unavoidable occupational hazard but as a sign of grace won through redemptive suffering. In these years, unlike the early 1950s when Michael had passed through the Catholic Worker, the moral gesture proved to have a pragmatic side as well. As Martin Luther King and other civil rights strategists understood keenly, televised images of the violence visited upon nonviolent civil rights activists by their opponents—at Anniston, Montgomery, and Birmingham in 1961, Birmingham in 1963, and Selma in 1965—proved to be the movement's single most effective weapon in securing favorable policies and legislation from the federal government.

Although Michael admired the courage displayed by the Freedom Riders and other disciples of nonviolent civil disobedience, he had no desire to emulate them. Part of his dislike for the politics of direct action, as he readily acknowledged, was a healthy middle-class fear of violence. He had managed to avoid fistfights all his life, which, considering he spent so many of his evenings in taverns, took some doing. And in ten years of radical activism, including innumerable public demonstrations, he had never once found himself at the wrong end of a policeman's nightstick.[25]

Still, he was not completely immune to the spirit of the times, as became evident on a June evening in 1961. Michael had turned out on a picket line to support a group of New York City yipsels who were sitting-in in the West 66th Street offices of Leonard Goldenson, president of ABC/Paramount. The sit-in was in support of civil rights activists in Austin, Texas, who had for some months been picketing local Paramount-owned theaters to protest Jim Crow seating arrangements. Michael wasn't planning on staying long; he had even brought a date. But the evening took an unexpected turn when the sit-inners were picked up by some burly Pinkerton guards and New York City police and unceremoniously deposited outside on the street. Michael, along with several others, joined them in a spontaneous sit-in blocking the front doors to the building. The police moved in and arrested them all. Michael waved good-bye to his date, as he and his fellow arrestees were hauled away in the back of a paddy wagon, singing "We Shall Overcome." They spent a sleepless but not unpleasant evening in a holding cell in the 54th precinct police station before being bailed out in the morning; Michael helped the group pass the time by conducting an impromptu seminar on the political economy of poverty.[26]

That arrest proved an exception.[27] Mostly Michael kept doing what he did best—writing, touring, speaking, debating, and recruiting. Outside of the black movement, Michael had few competitors on the Left who could compare with his abilities as a speaker. The response recorded in a local newspaper after Harrington spoke on the campus of Savannah State College in the mid-1960s was typical:

> A tall man with blue eyes in a ruddy face, Michael Harrington has not lost the eagerness of his youthful college days. . . . His words tumble out. Emphasis follows emphasis. He is so imbued with his topic one feels he can hardly wait to give one knowledge. An audience of students, faculty, social workers, and others rose in tribute at the end of the lecture.[28]

As the venue suggests, Michael's speaking engagements not only kept increasing in sheer numbers of places he visited, but also took him places where as a socialist he would never before have been able to get a hearing. For the first time since his Catholic Worker days, for example, he was able to appear as a speaker at Catholic colleges: In 1961 alone, he spoke at Albertus Magnus College, Manhattan College, Notre Dame, and Fairfield University, as well as before a regional meeting of the National Federation of Catholic College Students.

Thanks to the spirit of questioning and reform that John Paul XXIII was encouraging within the church, Michael could not have asked for a better moment to re-enter the Catholic community, as a friend if not a believer. Michael "has been prominent in liberal circles," a feature writer for the Holy Cross student newspaper wrote in 1962, about the college's newly famous alumnus, "but his liberalism is of the kind espoused by Pope John; it is certainly in no sense communistic or socialistic."[29] The young liberal and (occasionally) radical activists Michael met in Catholic colleges still had a sense of isolation from their peers. But he found them impressively thoughtful and articulate (and clearly identified with them). As he wrote in *Dissent* in 1962:

> Precisely because they were living in a generally conservative milieu and come from a tradition historically hostile to the left, their views seem to have more intellectual substance that those of their non-Catholic similars. . . . They work through to their convictions and must be prepared to defend them.[30]

Michael gained many admirers among politically active students in the early 1960s for his debates with prominent right-wing anticommunists. Often the topic was civil liberties. Many public universities retained bans on politically controversial speakers or attempted to regulate student political activities. For student leftists, setting aside such bans and regulations was part of the unfinished political business of the 1950s, and also a precondition for more broadly focused political activity in the 1960s.

Michael tangled more than a dozen times with the ultra-conservative journalist Fulton Lewis III, who had helped the House Un-American Activities Committee (HUAC) produce the documentary film "Operation Abolition," which labeled the anti-HUAC demonstrators in San Francisco as a collection of Communist agents and their dupes. (Michael would refer mockingly to his opponent in these debates as "the imaginative and creative technical director of Operation Abolition.") Their climactic debate came before an audience of a thousand delegates at the annual congress of the National Student Association in 1961 in Madison, Wisconsin. In the debate that followed a showing of "Operation Abolition," Michael easily bested his opponent, and the NSA overwhelmingly voted through a resolution condemning HUAC.[31]

Michael was sharp and funny in these debates and seemingly never lacked for a telling anecdote or statistic to back up his arguments. Rob Tucker, a fellow SPer, remembered how Michael once countered the famous right-wing chestnut about the high suicide rate in social democratic Sweden when the point was raised by a conservative debater:

> Mike said, "I never thought I'd hear anyone ask about the Swedish suicide rate except as a joke! Look, the Swedes have *always* had a high suicide rate. It has something to do with Ingmar Bergman and long cold winters. Besides, how do you explain that the homicide rate in the United States is 408 per cent higher than in Sweden?"

Impressed with the ease with which Harrington rattled off the statistic, Tucker asked him afterwards where he had found it:

> He said, "I made it up."
>
> "You *what?*"
>
> "Well, there *is* a statistic that's approximately the one I gave. Who remembers things like that? In a debate, you make it up."[32]

Michael took greater care in debates with opponents for whom he had greater respect, like his familiar nemesis William F. Buckley Jr. The careers of the two men, however widely separated by ideology, had continued to parallel one another in interesting ways. Both made their careers as public intellectuals outside of academia. Both had become emblematic figures for their respective points of view. Both, after some years on the margins of American politics, were seeking to influence and transform one of the two major parties, Michael through the realignment strategy, and Buckley through support for a Barry Goldwater presidential candidacy. And both were bidding for the allegiance of the new generation on campus.

In September 1960, Buckley hosted the organizing convention of Young

Americans for Freedom (YAF) at his Sharon, Connecticut, estate. The new group grew out of the "Youth for Goldwater" movement that had promoted the presidential nomination of the conservative Arizona senator at the 1960 Republican convention. The delegates adopted a statement of conservative ideals, which came to be called the "Sharon Statement," celebrating individual liberty while calling for an escalation of the Cold War. Buckley hailed the meeting as a harbinger of future conservative triumph within the Republican Party and in the nation, commenting in the *National Review* that "what is so striking in the students who met at Sharon is their appetite for power."[33]

The YAF's first big show of strength came with a "World Liberation from Communism" rally in Madison Square Garden in the spring of 1962. Barry Goldwater was the keynote speaker. Eighteen thousand young conservatives turned out for the evening and waved placards reading "Better Dead than Red" and "Stamp Out the ADA." Michael mocked the professionally produced event as having "all the spontaneity of the Komsomols marching in Red Square," but the size and fervor of the audience persuaded other observers that students of the sixties were going to prove even more conservative than their predecessors in the 1950s. "I'm a conservative," an expensively dressed and elderly character declared in a Jules Feiffer cartoon in the *Village Voice,* while grimly spouting a litany of conservative slogans: "Keep Red China Out of the U.N., Overthrow Cuba, Up Barry Goldwater." And then, with a happy smile, he concluded in the final panel: "It's good to see I'm still in step with the college kids."[34]

Michael and others were determined that the YAF's claim to represent the viewpoint of the young would not go unchallenged. In an event that would be impossible to imagine just a few years later (and that has been overlooked in subsequent accounts of the early New Left), Americans for Democratic Action (ADA) and Students for a Democratic Society (SDS) cosponsored a picket line in front of Madison Square Garden the night of YAF's big rally. Fifteen hundred young protesters chanted slogans like "HUAC Must Go!" and "John Brown Yes! John Birch No!" Then they marched sixteen blocks through Manhattan's streets to their own "Stand Up for Democracy" rally in the St. Nicholas boxing arena, where a crowd of 3,000 liberal and radical partisans heard a roster of speakers denounce the Right.

James Wechsler chaired the event, which included speeches by Michael, Congressman William Ryan, New York State assemblyman Mark Lane, and ADA stalwart Hubert H. Humphrey. Senator Humphrey received a tepid response from his listeners, as he accused both "the extreme right and the extreme left" of sharing a "lack of faith in the democratic process." It was Michael who won the heart of the audience, with a rollicking, radical, hard-hitting speech. Given the evening's theme—opposition to the far Right in

American politics—he could have chosen to concentrate his fire on Goldwater and Buckley. Instead, he combined a call for liberal/radical unity around a common domestic agenda with an uncompromising indictment of the Kennedy administration's Cold War polices, as represented in its hostility to Cuba and its nuclear brinkmanship. At the end of his speech, according to the *Voice,* he received a "huge stomping ovation" from his young listeners.[35]

While Michael's personal reputation among New Leftists soared, the fortunes of the groups he represented failed to keep pace. By 1962 the Young People's Socialist League had begun to trod the now classic path toward sectarian oblivion. YPSL's strength peaked in mid-February of that year, when it helped organize a well-attended demonstration in Washington, D.C., against nuclear testing.[36] But the young socialists were already getting bogged down in yet another round of factional disputes—this time between old-line and new-line Shachtmanites (that is, between those favoring a "labor party" approach to American politics, and those who favored a "realignment" within the Democratic Party). The days when yipsels could be found freedom-riding, picketing, and sitting-in were coming to a close; instead they preferred to huddle in their caucuses, churning out an endless stream of densely argued, single-spaced, mimeographed polemics. In 1964 the "left wing" gained control of the organization—and then itself splintered immediately into four separate factions.[37] Dave McReynolds was moved to complain in a memorandum to other socialist leaders that he could not think of "a single major constructive thing" that YPSL had done on its own in recent years, "except issue discussion bulletins that have grown larger and larger as YPSL has grown smaller and smaller."[38] Norman Thomas, all too familiar with YPSL's predilections for ideological onanism, started telling potential young recruits that they should join SDS instead. In 1964, shortly before the SP gave up and dissolved YPSL, Thomas wrote to a political acquaintance and said that he was "terribly disappointed" in what had happened to the group: "I had hoped they would develop along the lines of the Students for a Democratic Society."[39]

Meanwhile, back in SDS, Tom Hayden was wrestling in the spring of 1962 with the dilemma of how the new generation of radicals could learn to "speak American." He did so with a deadline to meet. On June 12, SDSers from around the country were scheduled to gather in Port Huron, Michigan, at a lakeside camp lent to them by the United Auto Workers. There they planned to adopt an organizational manifesto for SDS. Throughout the spring, Hayden, immersing himself in the works of thinkers such as John Dewey, Albert Camus, C. Wright Mills, and Michael Harrington, sent out a series of memos on, and drafts of, the manifesto, both to SDSers and to the Student Activities Committee of the League for Industrial Democracy, on which Michael sat. In one of his memos, Hayden outlined the problems faced by a small group of politically marginal radical intellectuals such as SDS:

> Objectively we are "out" politically. We do not have access to the circles of men and institutions making final and decisive decisions. . . . Furthermore, we will be "out" if we are explicitly socialists, or if we espouse any minority political views honestly (we can be further "in" if we are willing to call socialism liberalism, or if we are willing to say "the free world" instead of the "capitalist bloc"; but these, again, amount to sacrificing intellectual independence.[40]

The existing "socialist parties," Hayden continued, were "in shambles" and had little to offer to New Leftists as organizational or intellectual models: "their vision is clouded by sectarianism or queer jargon; as for relevance, they have little, except as the[y] infiltrate non-socialist ranks." Hayden, thinking back on comparable moments in the history of the American Left, mused, "I have the impression that we have been our own leadership to a far greater degree than most 'student radicals' of the past." New Leftists were going to have to figure out on their own how to pursue "a politics of vision and relevance."

Notwithstanding his disdain for the organizations with which Michael was associated, Hayden clearly remained in dialogue with his socialist mentor in the months leading up to the Port Huron convention:

> A moral aspiration for social equality, unaccompanied by a political and economic view of society, is at best wistful (I think I mimic Harrington) and, at worst, politically irresponsible. But an economic and political analysis, without an active, open moral pulse, dwindles to uninspired and uninspiring myopia.[41]

As Michael read through Hayden's various political musings that spring, he may have been reminded occasionally of his younger self. Just ten years earlier, in the spring of 1952, he had attempted to come to grips with the same set of issues—although set forth in rather different terms—as he justified to himself and others the "uncompromising, relatively absolute Christianity" of the Catholic Worker movement. "It is a hard role to play," he wrote then:

> Yet it is necessary that we have our pilgrims of the absolute along with the day to day, empirical routine of parish work. For the greater danger is that, in attempting to comprimise, to soft-peddle pacifism, to mittigate our criticism, that we will lose sight of our ideal.[42]

In 1962, as ten years earlier, Michael was seeking to strike the proper balance between his "parish work" and the "pilgrimage of the absolute." Sometimes he leaned one way, sometimes the other. When he appeared in the company of Senator Humphrey at the SDS-ADA anti-Goldwater rally that spring, he chose to be a radical pilgrim rather than a moderate parishioner; despite the temptation to strike a note of seamless liberal–radical unity in the face of right-wing Republicanism, he had neither mitigated nor soft-peddled his opposition to the current Democratic administration's foreign policy. After a decade of experimenting with this equation, Michael trusted himself to make such judgments. At Port Huron it became apparent that he did not trust others, especially others younger than himself, to do the same.

Fifty-nine delegates, representing the eleven SDS chapters then in existence, as well as observers and speakers from the League for Industrial Democracy and other interested groups converged on June 12 at Port Huron. Michael arrived the first afternoon in the company of Donald Slaiman, a veteran Shachtmanite who was then on the staff of the AFL-CIO's civil rights department. They were scheduled to appear together that evening on a panel on the labor movement, an event that had been scheduled by the SDSers as a goodwill gesture toward the concerns of their LID elders. En route from the airport, there were already omens of discord; SDSer Richard Flacks, who had picked Michael and Slaiman up at the airport, was repelled by Slaiman's blustering "old-line Marxism," something that mixed oddly with his insider role in the AFL-CIO. To Flacks, Slaiman seemed "a caricature of a labor bureaucrat."[43]

Michael arrived in a combative mood. Earlier in the week he had discussed Hayden's most recent rough draft with Rochelle Horowitz and Tom Kahn, who were also coming to the convention. The three of them agreed that it was seriously flawed: It awarded students the leading role as agents of social change; it criticized the labor movement for suffering a "crisis of vision"; and it suggested that "older radicals" were too prone to treat any discussion of the nature of the Soviet Union as a "closed question."[44]

Had Michael and Tom Hayden sat around a table in the back room of the White Horse in June 1962 to hash out these issues, they might have found that they agreed more often than they disagreed. Michael certainly did not underestimate the political importance of the student movement, nor did he believe that the labor movement was above criticism.[45] As for the nature of the Soviet Union, Michael did take an uncompromising position—the USSR's "bureaucratic collectivist" character was indeed a "closed question"—but, as he had just finished arguing in the pages of *Dissent,* young radicals' "bad theories" (and here he specifically cited their attitude toward Communist countries such as Cuba) needed to be countered with due attention to the "genuine and good emotions" that lay behind them. And, even in the realm of theory, most SDSers did not differ all that greatly from Michael in their attitude toward the Communist world in 1962. SDSers felt that their vision of the good society—a "participatory democracy"—was at least as much at odds with communism as with capitalism. Where they differed with their LID elders was mostly in the quality of their emotional response to the Soviet threat. Instead of seeing the Soviet Union as a totalitarian empire on the march to world conquest, the SDSers regarded it as a conservative "status quo" power, more concerned with sealing off its borders than expanding them.

Michael and Tom as individuals, and even as representatives of LID and SDS, might have resolved such differences elsewhere. But the meeting hall at Port Huron was not the back room of the White Horse. The setting aroused instincts in Michael more akin to those he used to feel in the dusty YSL loft where he had sharpened his rhetorical skills in the 1950s. Michael appeared at Port Huron in his "hard" infighter role, not as the "soft" conciliator he played on other occasions. He wasn't in Port Huron to represent himself; he was there, in his own mind, as spokesman for the socialist movement and its most cherished loyalties, traditions, and beliefs. He had once again strapped on the armor of the doomed legion of the Left. As he would later write of his mood at Port Huron, he felt himself emotionally "in solidarity with the Russian oppositionists, the Left Socialists and anarchists in the Spanish Civil War, the Hungarians invaded by the Red Army in 1956, and the Poles in their endless struggle for freedom and decency in the shadow of Soviet power."[46] All of these were worthy and sympathetic constituencies, to be sure, but appearing in their stead did not bring out Michael's best qualities in the give-and-take of political discussion. Nor was he playing simply to an audience of young, inexperienced radicals at Port Huron, with their bad theories and good emotions, but also to some of his oldest and closest comrades, all of whom were, in Shachtmanite terms, "hards." That made a crucial difference in the tone and substance of what followed on the evening of June 12 and its aftermath.

At the panel that evening Michael and Slaiman denounced Hayden's draft in scathing tones. Hayden, stung by the attack, refused to give ground. The argument continued late into the night, adjourning to the dining room, where, as the quantity of beer consumed increased, the voices grew louder. Other SDSers listened in dismay.

There is no record of the actual discussion that evening; much of it revolved around the issues of anticommunism, and whether or not the wet-behind-the-ears SDSers had earned the right to criticize an old fighter for labor's cause like George Meany. But there was also a subtext, which

Michael would come to see as his "emotional overresponse" to what he perceived as "an Oedipal assault on the father-figure":

> I'd always been the youngest at every thing I'd ever done. I graduated from college at nineteen; I was the youngest editor of *The Catholic Worker.* My self-image was as a *young* person. . . . Up comes this younger generation. I think that they are ignoring my honest, sincere and absolutely profound advice. And this struck at my self-image.[47]

Michael left the convention the next morning for another speaking engagement. Horowitz, Kahn, and YPSL chairman Richard Roman remained and soon got into their own squabble with SDSers over another issue, the question of whether a seventeen-year-old visitor from the Communist Party's new youth group, the Progressive Youth Organizing Committee, should be allowed to attend the convention as an observer. To allow him to attend, Steve Max recalled, seemed "tantamount to diplomatic recognition" of Russia in the eyes of the yipsels, but their objection seemed bizarre to the SDSers. Ironically, by the time the dispute was resolved in favor of seating the Communist teenager, he had gone home.[48]

After such stormy opening sessions, the remaining two days of the conference proved remarkably productive, as delegates worked intently to revise Hayden's draft. The final version was clearly intended as a generational manifesto, reflecting the experiences and outlook of those who stood on the brink of adulthood at the start of the 1960s. "We are people of this generation," the statement began, "bred in at least modest comfort, housed now in universities, looking uncomfortably to the world we inherit." SDSers committed themselves to a struggle for "participatory democracy," which to them meant transforming American politics through the creation of new forms of decentralized democracy that would supplement existing representative institutions and, hopefully, draw citizens directly into political decisionmaking. In programmatic terms, there was little in the statement that could not have been agreed to by most liberals in 1962. SDSers endorsed civil rights, federal antipoverty initiatives, increased spending on education and mental health facilities, and the like. And even on foreign policy, a far touchier issue, SDS did not veer far from the liberal consensus. Although the statement retained a sentence criticizing "unreasoning anti-Communism," Richard Flacks added a passage that declared SDSers "in basic opposition to the communist system. The Soviet Union, as a system, rests on the total suppression of organized opposition. . . . The communist movement has failed, in every sense, to achieve its stated intention of leading a worldwide movement for human emancipation."[49]

At the conclusion of the Port Huron convention, most SDSers felt that they had just lived through a moment of political epiphany; that they had created a radical document that could "speak American" to their generation. But there were three delegates in attendance who did not share the general euphoria—the three yipsels, Tom Kahn, Rochelle Horowitz, and Richard Roman. Becky Adams, former student body president of Swarthmore College, was part of the group redrafting the portion of the statement dealing with the sensitive issue of communism and anticommunism, along with Flacks and Richard Roman. She was put off by what she regarded as Roman's single-minded ideological preoccupation: "It seemed to me that [his] only interest was in getting his language into the statement. It was obvious he was on a mission for [the Socialist] party. He was insensitive and stubborn. He repeated himself again and again."[50]

If the yipsels won no popularity contests among the SDSers, they did win at least a qualified victory at Port Huron for their positions. They had arrived determined to root out from SDS's manifesto any sloppy or insidious ideological concessions toward the Soviet Union or communism, and they had largely succeeded in that end. Furthermore, SDS criticisms of the labor movement were toned down, and the final version included a sentence, composed by Bob Ross, declaring, "Middle class students . . . have yet to overcome their ignorance, and even vague hostility, for what they see as 'middle class labor' bureaucrats."[51] Moreover, in the elections that concluded the convention, Tom Kahn was added to SDS's national executive committee, where Richard Roman already had a seat. Of course, the final draft of the Port Huron statement would not have passed muster at a YPSL convention—but then this wasn't a YPSL convention. Had they chosen to do so, Kahn, Horowitz, and Roman could have gone home to New York and declared victory.

Instead, when Michael called Horowitz a few days later to ask how things had gone, she told him that the SDSers had made no substantive concessions on the issues he had raised while at Port Huron.[52] Michael was furious, convincing himself he was being mocked and betrayed by the SDSers. Without waiting to review the final version of the Port Huron statement for himself, he summoned an emergency meeting of LID leaders to discuss their wayward youth affiliate. On June 28, twelve days after the conclusion of the convention, a subcommittee consisting of LID chairman Harry Fleischman and executive secretary Vera Rony met with Hayden (elected at Port Huron as SDS president), Al Haber, Bob Ross, and Steve Max to discuss the problems LID had with the SDS's manifesto. The debate was heated, but Hayden and the others were able to clear up at least some of the misconceptions about the actual content of the statement—such as Rony and Fleischman's mistaken belief that it contained an explicit condemnation of the LID.

But LID would not leave well enough alone. A week later Hayden and

Haber were summoned to appear before the entire LID board to defend their views. In the meantime, they were forbidden to put out any mailings or other communications under SDS's name.

Ten years earlier, this kind of set-piece generational battle within the Left would have had an easily predictable outcome. Michael had been through a similar imbroglio in 1953 when the SP had cracked down on his rambunctious faction of YPSL. This time Michael was the one playing the role of adult heavy, and it would be surprising if he did not look to the past for guidance in handling SDS. When Michael challenged Norman Thomas's authority in 1953, Thomas had thrown him out of YPSL. But in the end everything had come out right: Michael had in time seen the error of his ways; he and Thomas were now the closest of comrades and friends. Now that he was on the other side of the generational fence, confronting a new group of unruly youngsters, Michael likely decided that it was better to rein them in early on. Hayden and Haber and a few others might go away mad, but SDS could be placed under the caretaker leadership of some reliable yipsel, and in the end the deposed SDSers would likely return to the fold, a little bit chastened and a lot wiser from the experience.

At the LID board's meeting on July 6 with the SDS leaders, Michael zealously played the role of chief inquisitor. He unleashed a barrage of new objections to what had been said and done at Port Huron—objections that struck the SDSers as ranging from nonsensical to mean spirited. Calling SDS a "non-organization," Michael now denied that the Port Huron convention had had any legitimacy at all (something he had not thought to mention while he was attending it). The delegates to the convention, he charged, were unrepresentative of the organization. What was more, they had been rushed to conclude their deliberations on the SDS manifesto with unseemly haste: Four days was much too short a time for such a convention to meet. In order to have adequate time to consider the issues before them, SDSers should have stayed at Port Huron for at least ten days.[53]

Turning to the issue of the single young Communist who had shown up hoping to attend the convention as an observer, Michael treated his appearance as evidence of a deliberate provocation on the part of SDSers, and also as an attempt to create an ongoing alliance—a "united front"—with the Communists. "You knew this would send LID through the roof," Michael thundered at Hayden and Haber. "This issue was settled on the left ten or twenty years ago—and that you could countenance any united frontism now is inconceivable." When Hayden protested that if Michael would take the time to read the Port Huron statement, he would see that it clearly condemned communism, Michael was unbending: "Documents shmocuments. Slaiman and I said that this was antithetical to the LID and everything it's stood for." Michael then condemned SDSers for electing Steve Max to succeed Hayden as the organization's new field secretary. After all, Max had once belonged to the Communists' Labor Youth League, and his father had once been managing editor of the *Daily Worker.* It didn't seem to matter to Michael, who had befriended several prominent ex-Communists since 1956, that both the younger and elder Max had publicly broken with the Communist Party during the de-Stalinization crisis. In fact, probably more than anyone else in SDS's leadership, Steve Max (along with fellow ex-LYLer Richard Flacks) shared Michael's perspectives on domestic realignment and even on the Soviet Union.

After the meeting, the LID board took Hayden, Haber, and Max off salary, appointed YPSL chairman Richard Roman as interim secretary of SDS, and, most memorably, changed the locks on the SDS office. These measures had no practical effect (the SDSers picked the locks and retrieved the all-important mailing lists from the office) and served only to cement the conviction of the New Leftists that their LID elders were not only irritable and unreasonable, but also undemocratic in their outlook. As Tom Hayden told Jack Newfield a few years later: "It taught me that Social Democrats aren't radicals and can't be trusted in a radical movement. It taught me what Social Democrats really think about civil liberties and organizational integrity."[54]

Eventually, through the intervention of Norman Thomas and a few of the more conciliatory LID board members, a compromise was patched up. SDS leaders sent a written appeal to the LID board defending the Port Huron statement that was about half as long as the statement itself. Michael finally got around to reading the amended version of the document adopted at Port Huron and discovered, as he would later admit, that the SDSers had actually "responded quite generously to my criticisms."[55] At the end of the summer, he and Thomas made a pilgrimage of reconciliation, meeting with SDS leaders at the National Student Association's annual convention in Columbus, Ohio. Michael offered an apology for his actions, which went some way toward "patching up a working relationship," as Steve Max, who was present, recalled.[56] The LID agreed to resume paying Hayden's salary (though still refusing to pay Max's—SDS members taxed themselves to make up the difference).[57]

Michael's contrition at Columbus was genuine. As he would confess in 1988, long after he had been forgiven by those he wronged at Port Huron, he had been guilty of displaying

> a rude insensitivity to young people struggling to define a new identity [and had] treated fledgling radicals trying out their own ideas for the first time as if they were hardened faction fighters whose lives were perversely dedicated to principles I abhorred. I then compounded that stupidity by

making an alliance with the old guard of the League for Industrial Democracy . . . against my former protégés.[58]

The story of what happened at Port Huron and in its aftermath circulated by word of mouth through the student radical elite; Todd Gitlin, a peace activist at Harvard but not yet an SDSer, heard about it later that year and thought it sounded "like an Alice in Wonderland version of what I had read about the long-gone internecine left-wing strife of the Thirties." It was not, he recalled, "the sort of thing to make my heart beat fast for the 'democratic Left.'" But, as he would also note, "Port Huron hadn't been terribly public, and the LID's parental inquisition had been kept in the family."[59] It wasn't until 1966, with the publication of Jack Newfield's popular account of the origins of the New Left, *A Prophetic Minority,* that a critical account of Michael's role at Port Huron was widely circulated—and Newfield's report that Michael had since "publicly apologized to SDS" (as well as the fact that Michael contributed a preface to Newfield's volume), helped take some of the sting out of the revelation.[60]

Although Port Huron was a significant moment in SDS's history, its importance in Michael's life can be easily exaggerated.[61] When the dust had settled, Michael remained in demand as a speaker by SDS chapters and kept up friendly contacts with a number of Port Huron alumni. "Dear Mike," Bob Ross wrote to him from Ann Arbor in December 1962, "I understand you're becoming a rather prominent guy. So be it. Soon we can take a new tack: Harrington is a New Frontier member of The Establishment. Etc." If the SDSers had really regarded Michael as such, there wouldn't have been any point in kidding him about it—especially since the next thing Ross did was ask for a favor. The campus SDS chapter was going to sponsor a series of forums on contemporary political concerns that spring, and they hoped Michael could come out as keynote speaker to kick off the series.[62]

So it is a mistake to read back into the early 1960s—even the post-Port Huron early sixties—the kind of categorical rejection of Michael's views that characterized the New Left later in the decade. As it turned out, Michael wasn't able to go to Ann Arbor for the SDS forum—notwithstanding Ross's offer of "20–25 bucks" as honorarium—since he was already in Paris. But had he not left the country for his year's sabbatical from politics, he would have had more opportunity to smooth over the ill feelings left over from Port Huron.

By the end of 1963, when Michael returned to the United States, SDS's leaders had made the fight against poverty an organizational priority—a decision that should have brought them even closer to the author of *The Other America.* SDSers were influenced by predictions that the postwar economic boom was about to come to an end, as automation displaced increasing numbers of formerly well-paid industrial workers. This swelling army of the unemployed would add to the numbers, and potential political importance, of that bottom third of the American people already excluded from the rewards of the affluent society. The goal of young radicals, Tom Hayden argued, should now be the creation of "an interracial movement of the poor." Part of the appeal of this strategy was that it allowed SDSers to emulate the community organizing tactics pioneered by young civil rights activists in the South. "Can the methods of SNCC be applied in the North?" Hayden asked in an SDS newsletter in the spring of 1963.

One of the things making it possible for SDSers to answer Hayden's question in the affirmative was a grant of $5,000 from the United Auto Workers to set up an Economic Research and Action Project (ERAP). Over the next two years SDS-ERAP projects were set up in a dozen cities, from Newark to Chicago to Oakland. Several hundred SDSers were eventually drawn into the projects, including many of the group's founding generation (now increasingly referred to as the "old guard"). While ERAP made some political contributions, particularly to the emerging "welfare rights" movement, its strategic assumptions proved wrong. Far from the economy slumping and unemployment growing, the United States was about to begin a half decade of dizzying prosperity (in part because of factors the SDSers could not have known about, including the effects of government spending on the Vietnam War). In any event, the chief political consequence of the departure of Hayden and others to the northern slums was that the campus organization they had founded so recently, already deficient in its supply of thirty-to-sixty-year old mentors, would be lacking even the guidance of radicals in their mid-twenties.[63]

Tom Hayden wrote Michael a friendly letter soon after his return from Europe, describing plans for ERAP. Michael was skeptical about ERAP's prospects, suspecting that the impetus behind the SDSers turn to community organizing was a product mostly of their subjective desire to merge themselves with "the people." But for the time being, he avoided making any public criticisms. He refrained in part because he had no desire to stir up the embers of the Port Huron conflict. He also shared the ERAP analysis that automation was about to displace large numbers of workers.[64] And he could hardly overlook the symbolic importance of the UAW's contribution to ERAP—here, seemingly, was concrete evidence that SDSers were prepared to work with the mainstream of the labor movement in common cause. Finally, as Hayden himself suggested in his letter to Michael, ERAP could be seen as a complementary rather than a rival approach to Michael's preferred strategy of political realignment; if ERAPers helped encourage the northern poor to go to the polls, as civil rights activists were encouraging blacks in the South to do, their combined votes might help turn the Democratic Party leftwards.[65]

As long as poverty was regarded as the biggest issue confronting the nation, Michael's standing with the New Left was reasonably secure. For every New Leftist in 1964 who had read Marx, Lenin, Mao, or Marcuse, there were dozens who had read *The Other America.* That made Michael a very in-demand campus speaker that year. At Berkeley in February 1964, he spoke to an enthusiastic audience of a thousand students about the promise of the newly announced war on poverty. But its promise could not be realized, he emphasized, unless "an anti-poverty party" of liberals, labor, civil rights activists, and others took over the Democratic Party.[66]

Michael also took part in some of the early planning sessions for what became known as the Freedom Summer project. First proposed by liberal activist Allard Lowenstein, the idea of bringing hundreds of volunteers from northern colleges down to Mississippi to help out in a voter registration campaign in the summer of 1964 was taken up by SNCC and other civil rights groups. The organizers hoped that the presence of the young northerners—most of them whites, some of them well-connected politically—would force the federal government to step in to protect civil rights workers in the South, something it had not done very zealously in the past. In addition, movement strategists intended to organize black voters into a new organization, the Mississippi Freedom Democratic Party (MFDP), which would challenge the seating of the state party's delegation to that summer's Democratic national convention—since as things stood, blacks were excluded from choosing delegates. While on the West Coast in February, Michael helped sound out some prominent Democrats on the idea of supporting the MFDP's challenge to the Mississippi regulars, and in the end the California Democratic Council became the first important liberal grouping to offer its backing.[67]

Busy with his speaking tour and with finishing the book he had started in Paris, Michael did not make it to Mississippi that summer (he finally got there in September, speaking at a black church in Biloxi on behalf of the MFDP, and feeling very exposed traveling the back roads from Jackson to Biloxi just weeks after the bodies of three Freedom Summer volunteers had been found beneath an earthen dam nearby). But if Michael wasn't part of Freedom Summer, *The Other America* certainly was. It had been among the books that project volunteers had been assigned before arriving in Mississippi, and it found readers in freedom schools and jailhouses that summer. A student who was jailed for organizing a voter registration meeting in Drew, Mississippi, wrote home to his parents: "One of the guys had a battered copy of *The Other America* so we divided up chapters. I got the dismal one on the problems of the aged. . . . To be old and forgotten is certainly a worse sentence than mine (I wouldn't recommend the book for those planning to do time)."[68]

Just four years earlier, Michael had helped organize a march and picket line at the Democratic convention in Los Angeles in an attempt to get the party to adopt a strong civil rights plank in its platform. Most of the delegates at Los Angeles that year had been more concerned with the horse race among would-be presidential contenders than with what seemed the peripheral issue of civil rights. On the eve of the 1964 convention, the situation was reversed. No one had any doubts that Lyndon Johnson would be the party's presidential nominee in the fall. The only substantive issue facing the delegates in Atlantic City was how to handle the challenge of the Mississippi Freedom Democratic Party to the seating of the all-white delegation of party regulars. The Socialist Party's position on the eve of the convention in August was unequivocal. As *New America* declared editorially: "The fight over the seating of the Mississippi Freedom delegation will be a test of organized liberalism's commitment to put its principles into action."[69]

In the end, "organized liberalism" failed the test. President Johnson, hoping to hold down the defection of white southern voters to Barry Goldwater, instructed his convention managers to make only the most minimal gesture to civil rights supporters. Johnson put pressure on Hubert Humphrey—his not yet officially sanctioned running mate—and Humphrey in turn called in Bayard Rustin and others to help make the MFDP amenable to some compromise. In the end, two "at-large" seats were offered to MFDP delegates, as well as a promise that in the future the Democratic Party would insist on integrated delegations. The Mississippi regulars meanwhile could take their seats as planned.[70] Fannie Lou Hamer, who had electrified the country with her televised testimony before the convention credentials committee about the beatings of civil rights workers in Mississippi, spoke for the entire delegation when she responded contemptuously to the proposed compromise: "We didn't come all this way for no two seats!"[71]

Rustin had not been alone in supporting the compromise—Martin Luther King Jr. had also urged the MFDP delegates to accept it. But Rustin, who was increasingly regarded within the civil rights movement as a self-interested and conniving insider rather than as a selfless and outspoken agitator (which had once been his reputation), took most of the blame for it. "You're a traitor, Bayard, a traitor!" one SNCC organizer yelled at him during a tense meeting in Atlantic City.[72] Michael, out of personal loyalty and political conviction, sided publicly with Rustin—which he need not have, since he had played no role in forging the compromise. Shortly after the Democratic convention, Michael urged MFDP supporters to put aside their bitter feelings and look to the future. Although the MFDP did not receive "justice" at Atlantic City:

> What it did do, and the fact is momentous, was to force the President of the United States and undisputed leader of the Democratic Party to make

> a compromise. From the standpoint of ethical rights, the Freedom Democrats received much less than their due, which was everything they asked. From the standpoint of politics—the measure of a political convention—they succeeded tremendously. . . . [The] potential of that victory for 1968 is tremendous.[73]

A few months later, Michael, along with Al Lowenstein and Bayard Rustin, met with a delegation from SNCC to sort out the ill feelings left over from the convention. Rustin and Lowenstein argued that they had not "favored the compromise" but merely suggested to the MFDP delegates that they consider it. The SNCC leaders—Jim Forman, Ella Baker, and Ivanhoe Donaldson—were unimpressed with the distinction. "For them, even to have considered the possibility of something less than total and complete victory—to argue on grounds of political practicality—was treasonous," Michael later wrote. "As a result, a difference on tactics was turned into a bitter dispute over principles."[74]

Like SNCC, the white New Left regarded the compromise offered to the MFDP as a betrayal and as proof of the bankruptcy of liberalism. Before Atlantic City, Todd Gitlin would later write, "liberalism posed a dilemma" to the New Left. "Afterwards, it was an obstacle."[75] After the convention, Tom Hayden played a key role in reshaping the views of his fellow New Leftists, just as he had at Port Huron. In a private letter in January 1965, SDS president Paul Potter wrote of Hayden: "Tom seems to be moving closer and closer to a position that the liberal establishment (if not all liberals) constitutes the most dangerous enemy we confront."[76]

For a few months more, Michael remained immune to the ill will gathering to his left. The return of the Freedom Summer veterans to college campuses in the fall of 1964 brought with it a renewed wave of campus activism, this time drawing on the direct action tactics the volunteers had picked up in Mississippi. Nowhere were the results more dramatic than at the University of California at Berkeley, where Freedom Summer veteran Mario Savio challenged the UC administration's clumsy attempts to restrict political advocacy on the campus. Before the Free Speech Movement (FSM) ran its course at Berkeley, administration buildings were occupied, the police were called in, and hundreds of students were arrested. It proved the template for hundreds of campus rebellions over the next half dozen years. Michael was an outspoken supporter of the movement: The FSM, he wrote, made "an excellent case . . . for breaking the law"—which for him was high praise indeed.[77]

Although the Free Speech Movement would be remembered, among other things, for launching the slogan "Don't Trust Anyone Over Thirty," there were people over thirty the FSMers trusted. One of them was Michael. He spoke in Berkeley in October 1964 at the invitation of the campus SDS chapter, in a meeting chaired by Professor Lewis Feuer of the university's sociology department.[78] After Michael had finished urging the students to vote for Lyndon Johnson in November, Feuer raised a cheer from the audience when he remarked that he would rather vote for Michael Harrington as a socialist candidate for president than for the man nominated as that year's Democratic candidate.[79]

The spring of 1965 would prove a memorable one for Michael, for many reasons. Never before had he felt so much reason for political optimism. He took part in the most inspirational political event of his life in March, when he responded to Martin Luther King's call for northern supporters to join civil rights activists on the final day of a march from Selma to Montgomery, Alabama. Since January, King, the Southern Christian Leadership Conference (SCLC), and SNCC had been conducting an all-out campaign for voter registration in Selma and neighboring counties. The authorities had responded as violently and stupidly as civil rights strategists had hoped. The violence peaked on "Bloody Sunday," March 8, when a mounted posse, armed with clubs and whips, trampled peaceful demonstrators who had attempted to cross the Edmund Pettus Bridge on the first leg of a protest march to the Alabama state capital. Televised scenes of the resulting carnage sickened northern viewers and prompted President Lyndon Johnson to announce his intention to bring voting rights legislation to Congress that year. On March 21, as King and several thousand others crossed the bridge on a new march to Montgomery, public opinion polls showed that three-quarters of all Americans backed the proposed voting rights act.[80]

Michael flew to Montgomery on March 25, part of a "fly-in" sponsored by the Village Independent Democrats that brought over a hundred marchers to join the throngs coming from around the country. Michael's traveling companions included Rustin, A. Philip Randolph, and a rising liberal politician named Ed Koch. Koch, who had been a combat infantryman in Europe during the Second World War, called the experience of marching through the black sections of Montgomery like "marching through Paris again with the liberation army." Michael remembered how, as they marched through the slums, some of Montgomery's blacks "stared in disbelief," others wept, while still others fell into the line of march. The marchers headed downtown to the Alabama state house, from whose steps two years earlier newly elected Governor George Wallace had declared, "Segregation now! Segregation tomorrow! Segregation forever!" Montgomery had served briefly as the capital of the Confederacy during the Civil War. There were no American flags to be seen on the state buildings, only the Alabama state flag. Someone in the crowd began to sing the "Star Spangled Banner." As thousands of others took up the song, Michael would recall, it sounded to his ears "like a revolutionary anthem."[81]

Martin Luther King made one of his finest speeches to the crowd that day—many who heard it thought it was even better than the "I have a dream" speech of two years earlier. King's speech concluded with a line that Michael would make a standard part of his own speeches. King predicted that civil rights activists would lead the nation to redemption, and in the not so distant future. "How long?" he called out to the crowd—and then, answering his own question, declared: "Not long. Because the arm of the moral universe is long, but it bends towards justice."[82] Back in New York, Michael pointed to the Montgomery rally as a model of "a new Populism." The coalition of civil rights groups, religious groups, liberals, and labor unions who had joined together in singing the national anthem that day, he wrote, represented "the human potential for a new American majority."[83]

Lyndon Johnson's landslide victory in 1964 brought with it a vastly expanded Democratic majority in Congress. Fifty-one freshmen Democrats took their seats in the House in January 1965 and helped pass landmark liberal legislation establishing Medicare and Medicaid, federal aid to secondary schools, national endowments for the arts and humanities, new environmental standards, immigration reform, and a federally guaranteed right to vote. Liberals and labor leaders were understandably elated, seeing the opportunity to revive goals put on hold since the late 1930s: AFL-CIO president George Meany reported to the 1965 AFL-CIO convention in San Francisco that "the New Deal proclaimed in 1933 has come to a belated maturity under LBJ in 1965."[84] Echoing Meany, Michael called for a "Third New Deal" to carry out an expanded war on poverty, with government economic planning, "massive social investments," and the "creation of a new human care sector of the economy."[85] That fall he went to Washington to take part in a planning session for the White House Conference on Civil Rights, scheduled for the spring of 1966. Along with the other delegates he was invited to a Texas-style buffet dinner in the White House, and Lyndon Johnson shook his hand. Mississippi civil rights leader Aaron Henry came over to him and marveled, "Mike, we're eating barbecue in the White House."[86]

But at the very moment when Michael's political optimism was at its highest, his sense of personal well-being was collapsing. In early March he was out on the West Coast, giving speeches in Santa Barbara, Sacramento, and Los Angeles. It proved an exhausting schedule, all the more so for the socializing and drinking he was doing. On Saturday night, March 13, he attended a party in the fashionable Bel Air section of Los Angeles, where he admired his hosts' extensive collection of modern art and got to meet actor Edward G. Robinson. The next morning he got up early and drove to San Diego, where he was scheduled to deliver a speech on poverty, this time at a Unitarian church. Nothing could be more routine for this veteran speaker.

But, as he would later recount, when he reached the podium, he had a new and alarming reaction:

> I suddenly felt faint and had to grip the sides of the lectern in order to keep my balance. Then the sense of being on the very edge of losing consciousness became so intense that I had to sit down and explain to the audience that I was indisposed and could only go on if I were seated.

Somehow he managed to get through the rest of the speech and fled to his motel room, sweating profusely. He wondered if he was suffering heart troubles, and he flew home the next day and called his doctor. But there was nothing physically wrong with him. The problem lay elsewhere. "I had read my Freud," Michael recalled later. Most of his friends had been or were in the midst of psychoanalysis. He could analyze a poem or a movie for its hidden psychological symbolism. He was a thoroughly sophisticated student of the psyche: "Only I had never met my own id, at least not face to face. Now . . . my unconscious had seized me by the scruff of the neck in a surge of pent-up destructive fury."[87]

A month later, Michael began analysis with New York psychoanalyst Elizabeth Thorne, a process that lasted over the next four years. What they found to talk about remained their secret. In the chapter of *Fragments of the Century* in which he discussed his breakdown and eventual recovery, Michael acknowledged that "decisive childhood relationships with my mother and father would be critical in a study of my intimate self." He then changed the subject to the "public causes of my private woes."[88]

Michael entitled that chapter "Success" and argued that it was the arrival of fame and (modest) fortune that had done him in in the spring of 1965. Seventeen years earlier, he had turned away from the path of conventional achievement by leaving Yale Law School. Fourteen years earlier he had embraced a life of voluntary poverty with the Catholic Worker. For more than a decade since leaving the Catholic Worker, he had still managed to hold his average annual income to under $5,000, except for one exceptionally prosperous year when he worked for the Fund for the Republic. Upon returning to the United States in December 1963, however, success was "thrust upon" him. Suddenly everyone wanted to hear from the man who discovered poverty. His speaking opportunities multiplied, and his speaking fees jumped to as high as $1,500 a speech. Even with a third of that amount going to the booking agency, and even holding to his commitment to give two free speeches for every paid occasion, his income in 1964 jumped to $20,000. On one occasion in the spring of 1964, speaking before an audience at the Center for the Study of Democratic Institutions in Santa Barbara, Michael's old patron Robert Hutchins introduced him as "the only man ever to get rich off of poverty." In the audiotape of the event, Michael's response—a very weak chuckle—can be heard in the background.[89]

Michael would explain his emotional problems in 1965 as the product of this conflict between his previous image of himself as selfless and marginal and the new realities of his life, post-*The Other America.* And that is certainly a plausible explanation. But as he himself implied, it may not have been the entire story. Whatever deeper explanations he and his analyst probed in those years remain confidential—as perhaps they should. There is, however, a hint of another explanation for Michael's crisis that spring, from a public source, that is at least worth noting.

For his eightieth birthday celebration the previous November, Norman Thomas was given a sizable check by his admirers to distribute as he saw fit.[90] In the months that followed he wrote checks of varying sizes to deserving groups on the Left. The largest checks went to the Socialist Party, and *New America. Dissent,* SDS, and SNCC all got smaller checks. So did the League for Industrial Democracy; Thomas wrote a check for $150 to LID and sent it in early March.[91]

Michael returned home from San Diego in a state of acute discomfort and exhaustion on March 15. But sometime the next day he managed to look over the correspondence that had accumulated at the LID office while he was gone. Finding Thomas's check, he fired off a telegram in response:

> Just returned from speaking tour. Shocked and dismayed to discover your token contribution to LID. Personally—and this message is without consultation with any liders—it is as if you gave a tip to the only organization attempting to revive the concepts of democratic and political allocation of national resources. Upset you did not discuss your low evaluation of LID with me. Perhaps you think we should end the organization.[92]

Thomas, perhaps alerted to Michael's emotional fragility, did not respond in kind but instead waited a few days before writing Michael a conciliatory letter:

> I do not think you, or rather we, should end the LID. On the contrary, under you and Tom Kahn, I have new hopes for that organization and its capacity to raise money. I am especially hopeful for the work of the Students for a Democratic Society, if it can be kept in close and friendly touch with the parent LID organization.

Thomas noted that he had given $500 of his own money to LID in the past year and had pledged more.

> Once more, let me repeat that I think you and the new organization of the LID can get money easier than these other organizations. Perhaps I am wrong but I can only use my best judgement. You are experienced enough to know how many times over I could have spent that generous check in good causes in which I am myself more or less involved.[93]

The matter was smoothed over and soon forgotten. But why had Michael lashed out so wildly? His emotional distress, as he described it in his memoir, was something he turned inward, as depression and anxiety, not outward as the kind of anger and paranoia evident in his telegram. He doesn't seem to have acted out aggressively against anyone else in his circle. Indeed, some of his long-time friends were completely unaware of the breakdown, except to the extent that they may have noticed he was more withdrawn than usual.[94]

Norman Thomas was the latest and most prominent of a long string of adult mentors and models to whom Michael had played the role of good son. However, unlike his relationship with Dorothy Day and Max Shachtman, Michael's role vis-à-vis Thomas was not only that of good son but also that of likely and imminent successor, or so many people thought. Perhaps that was not a role Michael (who had so recently complained about feeling like a "socialist jukebox") looked forward to playing with entirely unmixed enthusiasm. Perhaps Thomas had the misfortune of standing in for all the others, starting with Michael's mother (the mother who had so recently refused to attend his wedding), for whom he had long labored to fulfill ever higher expectations. Perhaps . . . but the point need not be belabored with further speculation. The only thing that can be said with certainty is that an accumulation of tensions in Michael's life, some of recent origin, others presumably of longer duration, reached critical mass in the spring of 1965 and left him with "a fearful case of social vertigo."[95]

In the months that followed, Michael gradually refashioned a confident public presence. He found he could short-circuit impending anxiety attacks if he could first visit the room or hall where he was scheduled to appear; he would stand behind the rostrum for a minute or two looking out over the empty seats to get the feel of the place. And although he recognized that alcohol had contributed to the onset of his initial breakdown, he found that it helped to have a drink before speaking. That was not a problem in the evenings, but he now felt odd when he had morning speaking engagements, for which he prepared with a breakfast of "tea, toast, and a dry martini."[96] With a new attentiveness to his personal health, he also gave up smoking cigarettes.

It seemed to help. Three months after the terrible day in San Diego, he was giving a speech before an audience of 400 civil rights activists in Atlanta, without apparent difficulty. Still it would not be until 1970 that he felt capable of casually accepting an invitation to deliver a speech and "mak[ing] it without careful prior calculations and a drink."[97]

Michael's breakdown preceded by only a few months the publication of his new book, *The Accidental Century,* the "major, major effort" that he had described in a letter to Paul Jacobs while writing it in Paris, a book he thought of as being "much more ambitious and ranging than the last one."[98] Its reception by critics and the public could not have done much to improve his mood in the later months of 1965.

The Accidental Century was a mélange of literary criticism, social analysis, and revolutionary theory—in Michael's own phrase, an attempt "to marry engineering and philosophy." The book represented a grand synthesis of virtually every writer Michael had admired since high school, from Aristotle to Yeats. The book's thesis was that "political and social imagination" had not kept up with the revolutionary impact of new technologies—as a result the past hundred years had proven an "accidental century." But now, at least in the industrial West, humanity stood on the verge of the end of scarcity and could begin the process of consciously creating new freedoms:

> To talk of capitalism as an economic system is the first step away from fatalism. If it is the machines alone which have created all these changes, then the best that one can do is pray to the computers and production lines that they will become more benign. Such an approach leads to a modern animism that invests technology with the spirits that once inhabited trees and storms. But if it is man's use of machines—the economic system—that is responsible for what is happening, then the direction of events can be altered.

This position allowed Michael to claim, with his familiar love of paradox, to be writing "a hopeful book about decadence."[99] The authors he most admired were, virtually without exception, profoundly pessimistic about the human condition. But Michael managed to tease out, at least to his own satisfaction, an underlying optimistic message within their works.[100]

The Accidental Century was an ambitious attempt to justify Michael's belief in mankind's collective capacity for creating a better world, marked not only by affluence but by genuine liberation of the human spirit. But read as contemporary social analysis, it bewildered many of its readers and most of its reviewers. Even those well disposed to Michael on the basis of *The Other America* seemed a bit mystified. A favorable review in the *San Francisco Chronicle* summarized Michael's thesis briefly, noting that it was "more theory than social investigation" and suggesting that it was "unlikely" that the book would "prove to be as influential as his previous one."[101] To some reviewers, Michael had committed the offense of being obviously better read than they were: *Life* magazine's reviewer called *The Accidental Century* a "confused, contradictory and often incoherent book," in which the author "wanders off into barely relevant discussions of Nietzsche, Joyce, Proust and Mann."[102] Michael's socialist convictions, which had gone unmentioned in *The Other America,* now worked against him. "Isn't human freedom most endangered," the book reviewer in *Newsweek* wanted to know, "by the corruptibility of any all powerful government?"[103]

One of the shrewdest reviews of *The Accidental Century* appeared in William F. Buckley's *National Review.* M. Stanton Evans took a respectful if bemused tone toward the book and its author, describing Michael as "an intelligent young man of collectivist tendency who, having been educated at Holy Cross and Yale, decided he was a Socialist and was plain-spoken enough to designate himself as such." Noting that Michael discussed no significant American authors in his survey of modern literature, Stanton observed: "Mr. Harrington is, in truth, a kind of European in our midst" whose view of American capitalism is

> roughly comparable to what might be expected from some of the literary figures he examines—distant, truncated, sometimes illuminating for its very strangeness, but thoroughly alien in both idiom and aspiration to the whole point and purpose of the American experiment.[104]

Like Tom Hayden, Evans evidently felt that Michael just did not know how to "speak American."

Of course, Michael was perfectly capable of writing in an American idiom, and had he chosen to write *The Accidental Century* in the voice he had previously employed in *The Other America* it might have found a broader and more sympathetic readership. He must have been bitterly disappointed with its reception; in any event, it would be another three years before he again ventured into print with a new book. And in the future his books would not aspire as much to high political and cultural theory as they would to a kind of higher journalism.

It is unlikely that *The Accidental Century* found much of a readership on the New Left. Michael and his politics were fading into the much disdained catalogue of the irrelevant, when they were not regarded as completely pernicious. In the spring of 1965 Michael was sitting out active involvement in ongoing political debates as a result of his emotional difficulties. Still, he could not avoid the spillover of rancor from the increasingly frequent clashes of the New Left with the social democratic Left. The most famous of these occasions, as celebrated at the time as the Shachtman–Browder debate had been for an earlier generation of leftists, was the clash in a New York City hall in early May between Irving Howe and Tom Hayden. Their topic was "New

Styles in Leftism." Hayden, wearing a worn sweatshirt and speaking in what Jack Newfield called "a tense staccato voice," denounced mainstream liberal, church, and civil rights organizations as bureaucratic shells, "more responsive to pressure from the government than they are to their own rank and file." Howe, in turn, baited Hayden on his attitude toward the Soviet bloc, which Hayden stubbornly refused to label totalitarian. In the end Hayden stormed out of the hall, blinking back furious tears.[105]

In an article in the *Nation* the same week, Newfield (who had sympathies for both sides in the conflict) bemoaned the growing estrangement of New Leftists from "the handful of radicals who fought so bravely through the 1950s":

> Immediate predecessors like Socialists Bayard Rustin and Michael Harrington are repudiated on the absurd ground that they have "sold out to the Establishment"—Rustin because he supported the 1964 moratorium on street demonstrations and the compromise offered the Mississippi Freedom Democratic Party at the 1964 Democratic convention, and Harrington because he is a consultant to Sargent Shriver and Walter Reuther. The new radicals also reject the Rustin-Harrington theory that social change is achieved by an institutionalized coalition of church, labor, Negro and liberal groups reforming the Democratic Party.[106]

Not only were the clashes between generations on the Left coming more frequently, they were also drawing the attention of the mainstream press. *Newsweek* reported in May 1965, with some wonder, "Suddenly, it seems, America has a left wing again." The article was illustrated with a cartoon solar system depicting the groups "In orbit on the Left." There were "Stalinist fragments" floating around in the far reaches of the solar system, with SDS and SNCC represented somewhere closer in, and the Socialist Party just outside the warm radiance of "The Center" of American politics. Patronizing to the New Left (its proponents invariably described with some descriptive phrase such as "chubby-cheeked" or "bearded") *Newsweek*'s article was more respectful of the "tough-minded" and "steadfastly anti-Communist" spokesmen for the Socialists, including Howe, Rustin, and Harrington. *Newsweek* reported that the socialist elders held "ambivalent attitudes" about the New Left:

> On the one hand, they cherish any vague stirrings on the left. On the other, they feel that the new radicals are dangerously innocent about the danger of authoritarian domination of the movement. . . . Their hope—and it is the hope of most realistic liberals—is that time and the miraculous potential of America will blunt the harsh alien edge of the New Left

> and make its radicals genuinely effective operatives within the traditional American consensus.[107]

But neither time nor miracles were on the side of the "traditional American consensus" in the spring of 1965. A new issue had arisen, destined to wreck not only the relation of social democrats to New Leftists, but also the very stability of the American political universe: the Vietnam War.

CHAPTER NINE

Socialists at War, 1965–1972

One reason the kids don't listen to us or listen only with contempt is precisely because in our concern to be politically effective we have spoken lies and left truth to the poets.

David McReynolds
November 30, 1967[1]

In the late winter of 1965 President Lyndon Johnson dramatically increased the scope of American commitment to the war in Southeast Asia, first by ordering American warplanes to undertake a sustained bombing campaign against North Vietnam, and then by sending the first openly designated U.S. ground combat forces to South Vietnam. By the end of 1965, there would be nearly 200,000 Americans in Vietnam, with hundreds of thousands more on the way.

Contrary to the legends that would later spread on the Left, Michael opposed the war, and from its beginning.[2] That the Socialist Party would do so as well seemed a foregone conclusion. Socialists, after all, had a long history of antiwar opposition, most proudly represented by memories of Eugene Debs's thundering condemnation of the First World War. That tradition had fallen on hard times by the 1950s, but it had never completely died out. In the early 1960s it seemed to be reviving. Socialists had endorsed and joined the first small public protests against the war in Vietnam in 1963. The following year, the SP's election platform declared that "under no circumstances should men and money be invested further in war in Southeast Asia."[3]

Within weeks of Johnson's initial escalation of the war, a mass antiwar movement sprang up around the country. In March there were teach-ins against the war at the University of Michigan and at dozens of other campuses across the country. In April SDS staged the first major anti-Vietnam War demonstration in Washington, D.C. Local antiwar organizing committees sprang up in big cities and college towns across the country and made the first tentative efforts to forge a national coalition.

Michael accurately described the antiwar movement in these early months as "inchoate and without structure, but drawing upon deep sentiments of moral idealism."[4] Revolutionaries and reformists, Communists and Trotskyists, radical and religious pacifists, New Leftists and others may have been convinced that they and they alone were in possession of the proper formula for opposing the war. But with all the jockeying for position and influence that went on in those early days of the antiwar movement, none gained a dominant position. The movement against the war proved so ideologically diverse, and so geographically dispersed, that no single political group could possibly have determined its character and outlook. "Coalition" may have become a dirty word among certain sections of the Left, where it was used to describe a politics dependent on retaining the goodwill of a Lyndon Johnson or a George Meany. But the antiwar movement itself proved one of the most genuine and successful coalition efforts ever launched by American radicals.

Michael spoke out against the escalation of the war in early April 1965, predicting in a column for the *New York Herald Tribune* that the "fate of Appalachia may well be determined in the jungles of Viet Nam." He feared that the war would "once again put the American social conscience in a deep freeze." Although the United States may have been "rich enough" to have both guns and butter, Michael believed that "the politics and psychology of military mobilization" amounted to "a declaration of war on the war on poverty."[5]

By the time Michael's column appeared, controversy was brewing over SDS plans for an antiwar protest in Washington. SDS's decision to sponsor the march and rally had initially been welcomed by elders of the socialist and pacifist movements, who were glad to see young people taking the initiative in opposition to the war. Norman Thomas wrote to A. J. Muste in March, saying that he hoped to be able to attend and suggesting that it would be a good idea if SDS and the increasingly moribund Student Peace Union were merged into a single organization.[6]

Others, however, including Bayard Rustin, worried that by failing to make clear that opposing a war against a Communist enemy was not the same as being in favor of the victory of that enemy SDS would not stage the right kind of antiwar protest. Michael spoke to the march's organizers about these concerns; he and others were not reassured when a piece of doggerel appeared in an SDS publication a month or so before the march, declaiming, "And before I'll be fenced in/I'll vote for Ho Chi Minh/and go home to the North and be free."[7] As at Port Huron, the question of Communist participation also proved troubling. SDS had opened the march to any individual or group opposed to the war—and this policy of "non-exclusionism," as it was termed, was taken as another worrisome sign in Michael's corner of the Left.

Fearing a political fiasco that would tarnish the entire peace movement, Rustin and others wrote and circulated a statement critical of the march, which they released to the press on the eve of the SDS march. Thomas and Muste and others initially sympathetic to SDS's project were convinced to sign on. The statement expressed "interest and sympathy" for the motives leading students to protest the war, but went on to criticize SDS for allowing certain unnamed "elements" to participate. Legitimate antiwar protest, the signers declared, should be restricted to "groups and individuals who, like ourselves, believe in the need for an independent peace movement, not committed to any form of totalitarianism nor drawing inspiration or direction from the foreign policy of any government." The liberal *New York Post* followed up the release of the statement with an editorial accusing SDS of planning a "frenzied, one-sided anti-American show" in Washington.[8]

Within a few years, much of the New Left would indeed come to identify emphatically and uncritically with "one side"—the Communist side—in the Vietnamese conflict, as images of heroic guerrillas brandishing AK-47s became a staple feature of SDS's *New Left Notes.* Whether that outcome was a foregone conclusion in 1965 is less certain. SDS's official call for the march was indeed radical by the standards of the time, but it was neither frenzied, pro-Communist, nor anti-American, unless one assumed that unsparing criticism of American foreign policy automatically fell into those categories.[9]

On April 21, some 25,000 demonstrators turned out in response to SDS's call, the largest antiwar demonstration in American history at that point. The march and rally was spirited but also moderate in its tactics and slogans. There was no civil disobedience, let alone violence. There were as yet no Viet Cong flags to be seen and no chants of "Ho-Ho-Ho Chi Minh/the NLF is gonna win" to be heard. SDS president Paul Potter gave the closing speech that day, declaring that it was time to "name the system" that "justifies the United States or any country seizing the destinies of the Vietnamese people and using them callously for its own purpose." He did not, however, actually give the system a name, though some voices from the crowd shouted out suggestions such as "capitalism" or "imperialism."[10]

Conceding afterwards that the event was far from the pro-Communist outing they had been led to expect, Norman Thomas and A. J. Muste both came to regret their criticisms of the march. Thomas publicly apologized for having signed the statement. And Muste decided that SDS had been right to insist on the principle of non-exclusionism; he applied it in the antiwar coalitions over which he presided until his death in 1967.[11]

Meanwhile, the Committee for a Sane Nuclear Policy (SANE), a liberal antiwar group, also turned its attention to the war, sponsoring a rally in Madison Square Garden in June with 18,000 in attendance, as well as its own march on Washington in November, which brought out another 25,000 participants. The SANE events attracted a generally older and more respectable crowd than the SDS march, but young and old, liberals and radicals, were present at both. Despite the dispute over the SDS march, political and generational lines in the antiwar movement were not yet firmly drawn. The SP's newspaper ran a favorable report on the SDS march, and SDS endorsed the SANE rallies in New York and Washington.[12] Norman Thomas remained a much-sought-after speaker for campus antiwar rallies; in May 1965 he took part in the massive Berkeley teach-in. Meanwhile SANE, eager to tap the energies of younger antiwar protesters, invited SDS president Carl Oglesby to give the concluding address at its November rally; his speech got the most enthusiastic response of any that afternoon.

The escalation of the war coincided with the onset of Michael's nervous breakdown. He was not a signatory of the Rustin-Thomas-Muste statement, although he agreed with its sentiments. He was trying to limit public speaking engagements, which he found stressful. He did not appear on the podium at either of the two SANE rallies that year, though he joined the crowd in November, where he "listened with pride and affection as Norman Thomas told the throng at the Washington Monument that he did not want to burn the flag but rather to cleanse it of the stains of Vietnam."[13] Michael's few public comments about the antiwar movement through mid-October suggested at least general approval. In one of the weekly columns he was now contributing to the *New York Herald Tribune,* Michael argued that youthful antiwar protesters were "rendering a profound service to this country and the world" by provoking debate over the Vietnam War.[14]

Before the month was out, however, he shifted directions. In a statement coauthored with Rustin, Howe, and several other luminaries of the anti-Stalinist Left, Michael threw down the political gauntlet to those in the antiwar movement who offered "explicit or covert political support to the Viet Cong." The statement criticized unnamed groups of antiwar protesters who hoped to "transform the protest into an apocalypse, a 'final conflict' in which extreme gestures of opposition will bring forth punitive retaliation from the authorities."[15]

This proved to be one statement too many in terms of Michael's reputation among youthful antiwar protesters. He had once again forgotten the rules he himself had laid down in *Dissent* in 1962 on how to correct the excesses of the young:

> It cannot be done from a lecture platform, from a distance. Rather, the persuasion must come from someone who is actually involved in changing the status quo [and] someone who has a sympathy for the genuine and good emotions which are just behind the bad theories.[16]

It wasn't that the criticisms in this latest pronouncement weren't cogent, and even prophetic. As of the fall of 1965, the most apocalyptic action taken by antiwar demonstrators anywhere in the country was an attempt in August by Berkeley students to block troop trains passing through Oakland, California. It would not be long, however, until the moral imperative to end the war would move others to violent street confrontations, and, in a few instances, to acts of terrorism.

In fact, that fall there were people in SDS who shared worries similar to Michael's. Lee Webb, part of the SDS "old guard," warned in a working paper presented at the December 1965 SDS national conference that the group was now influencing its members "to become more militant rather than more radical." The "rich internal life" of early SDS was a thing of the past, replaced by "the calls to fight the draft, stop a troop train, burn a draft card, avoid all forms of liberalism. . . . Thus commitment, confrontation, martyrdom, anger become the substitute for intellectual analysis and understanding."[17]

The problem with this latest broadside from Michael and his comrades lay not so much in content as in form. It established the reputation of the "anti-Stalinist Left" as a group that had little to offer to the cause of peace in Vietnam—little, that is, except for criticisms of those who were actually trying to stop the war. It didn't help that the average age of the anti-Stalinists was a decade or two older than the average antiwar protester; nor did it help that Irving Howe had a hard time controlling his anger or curbing his sarcasm in exchanges with younger political opponents.[18]

But it wasn't simply a generation gap that kept the anti-Stalinist Left from getting across their message. A useful contrast is provided by journalist I. F. Stone, who was closing in on sixty years of age when Johnson escalated the war, and whose weekly newsletter was widely read by antiwar activists. In articles for the *Weekly* in the fall of 1964, Stone had helped discredit the government's account of the Gulf on Tonkin incident. In December of that year he had spoken at the SDS National Council meeting, arguing the case for a U.S. pullout from Vietnam; his speech was one of the factors leading SDS to call for its march on Washington. Thus, Stone was a natural choice for SDS to invite to speak at the rally in April. His turn at the podium came immediately after folksinger Phil Ochs had sung a musical parody, mocking liberals as sellouts and hypocrites. Stone was annoyed and blasted Ochs: He was a liberal himself, he told the crowd, and he had seen "snot-nosed Marxist Leninists" come and go, and he wasn't impressed by their pretensions. In the years that followed, Stone repeatedly criticized "stunt-mongers and suicide tactics" in the antiwar movement—but because his commitment to ending the war was so clearly established, he also continued to get a respectful hearing in the antiwar movement and the New Left.[19] By comparison, Michael, Howe, and Rustin lacked the credentials in the eyes of young antiwar protesters that would have made their unsolicited advice seem cogent, useful, and well intended.

The anti-Stalinist Left also assumed that its anti-McCarthyite credentials needed no burnishing and would serve to bolster its authority in the dispute over the role of Communists in the peace movement. But that was ancient history to young antiwar activists, who had not been around to read Michael's critique of Sidney Hook in 1956, and who were infuriated to find themselves being red-baited by the media, politicians, and government officials. Just a few weeks before the anti-Stalinists denounced Communist influence in the peace movement, Attorney General Nicholas Katzenbach had responded to a nationally organized day of antiwar protest by declaring that "there are some communists involved in it. We may very well have to prosecute."[20] It was perhaps unfair, but certainly not surprising, that young protesters would not always distinguish between malevolent and well-intentioned finger pointing at the Reds in their midst.

In mid-November, Michael returned to the fray with an article in the *Village Voice* entitled "Does the Peace Movement Need the Communists?" Once again he argued that "the only effective peace movement" would be one that disassociated itself from "any hint of being an apologist for the Viet Cong." He criticized the few protesters who had begun showing up at antiwar rallies carrying Viet Cong flags. And he argued that the demands of the antiwar movement should be for negotiations between the contending parties in Vietnam, leading to a cease fire and free elections. Should the Vietnamese then choose a Communist government, that was their business. But "under no circumstances" would he personally "celebrate a Viet Cong victory."

Michael challenged the mood of "anti-anti-Communism" that was growing within the antiwar movement. Tom Hayden and Staughton Lynd had declared earlier that year in an article in the journal *Studies on the Left* that they "refuse[d] to be anti-Communist." While describing the Hayden-Lynd position as "the historical product of honest experience," Michael chided their political inconsistency: "I do not think that one can be in favor of defending the outcasts and victims of Mississippi and Harlem but be indifferent about those in Hanoi and Peking." He insisted that radicals should not be afraid of the label "anti-Communist." "[If] they ask the peace movement, 'Are you Communist?' it should answer, 'No,'" not in capitulation to reactionaries but "because it is for one man, one vote everywhere in the world."[21]

"Does the Peace Movement Need the Communists?" displayed some of the familiar virtues of Michael's best political writing. While staking out his own position very clearly, he was respectful of the motives of those he criticized and phrased his criticisms in a language ("one man/one vote") that should have resonated with its intended audience. Instead, for antiwar protesters it seemed to miss the point. As one of Michael's critics wrote in a mocking reply to the editor of the *Voice:* "Why can't Mr. Harrington be a little less pragmatic and/or principled, and a little more sensible?"[22] Much more than the incident at Port Huron in 1962, Michael's stance on the war in the fall of 1965 proved a dividing line in his political relations with the New Left, and with many others involved in the protests against the Vietnam War. Carl Oglesby, elected president of SDS in 1965, had—in his own words—"loved and admired" both Michael and Irving Howe in the early 1960s. Although he had never met either man, he felt as though he knew them: He had been a *Dissent* subscriber, had read *The Other America,* and as a former graduate student in English had been much taken with Howe's study of *Politics and the Novel.* But by the fall of 1965 he had changed his mind: "Here were these guys I admired so much denouncing me as a Red because I wouldn't criticize both sides [in the war] equally—which seemed bullshit because both sides weren't invading each other equally, weren't napalming each other equally."[23]

Michael misread the temper of the antiwar movement, and as a result he was slow in thinking about the challenge that the Vietnam War presented to the anti-Stalinist Left. If the protests against the war were developing in ways that worried Michael, it was hardly because of the presence of members of the Communist Party in either the leadership or ranks of the movement. In fact, Communists consistently proved among the more conservative voices within the movement, in terms of the tactics and slogans they advocated. They did not believe in civil disobedience, let alone violence; they did not wave Viet Cong flags, or burn American flags. And—like the Socialists—they believed that the peace movement should call for "negotiations" to end the war, instead of the more radical demand for immediate withdrawal of all U.S. forces from Vietnam.[24] Implying that it was Communists who were somehow responsible for the sins and errors of the peace movement, as Michael did in his *Voice* article, made no sense to young protesters. Whatever mistakes they may have been making, they knew that they had arrived at them on their own.

As Oglesby's comments suggest, Michael's call for negotiations as the solution to the Vietnam conflict also failed to convince antiwar activists. The third-camp socialist position, as it had been developed in the 1940s and 1950s, insisted on an equal condemnation of both war camps in the Soviet-American confrontation. In the early 1960s, socialists active in the peace movement had applied the formula to the issue of the nuclear arms race, insisting that both sides in the Cold War were equally culpable for putting the world at risk of atomic annihilation. The call for "No Tests, East or West" made sense to young antiwar activists drawn to groups like the Student Peace Union: The fallout from Communist bombs was self-evidently just as deadly as that produced by capitalist bombs. In 1965 the call for negotiations in Vietnam—rather than for an immediate U.S. withdrawal, which would have amounted to a Communist victory—seemed consistent with this tradition to Michael and his comrades.[25]

But with the Vietnam War, the terms of the debate had shifted in ways that made this formula seem irrelevant. Even antiwar protesters who had no particular sympathies for the Viet Cong—and they were always a majority of those who turned out for the big antiwar protests—did not feel obliged to "even-handedly" criticize both sides in this war. In the eyes of Michael's critics, the issue at stake in Vietnam simply did not turn on the question of whether or not Ho Chi Minh was a Stalinist, but on whether the United States had the right to unleash its vast technology of destruction on a poor and distant country like Vietnam, in defiance of the very principles of national self-determination that Americans supposedly cherished. The "really objectionable section of Harrington's article," Charles Hook declared in a letter to the editor of the *Village Voice,* came not with his analysis of the role of Communists in the peace movement

> but in his statement on what peace in Vietnam really means. Harrington calls for negotiations with the Viet Cong (NLF). Negotiations for what? Negotiations to determine how big a slice of Vietnamese territory the United States shall get for its military invasion? . . . Did Mr. Harrington call for negotiations between the Russians and the Hungarians to determine how much of Hungary the Soviet Union would control after it invaded Hungary in 1956?[26]

That Charles Hook was not an SDSer but rather president of the Student Peace Union added to the force of his criticism. Even in those corners of the antiwar movement where their influence had been strongest, socialists were now beginning to be regarded with distrust. They fell into disfavor with others on the Left not so much because they were viewed as being hard on Communists as because they were viewed as being soft on the warmakers in Washington.

Taken together, the anti-Stalinist Left's various pronouncements about the shortcomings of the antiwar movement in 1965 gave the impression that they had already, in their own minds, lost the battle to influence the movement. There was a kind of self-fulfilling prophecy involved in this process, because if anti-Stalinists weren't prepared to work on behalf of the antiwar movement—while fighting within it for their own political perspective—then other views were by necessity going to come to the fore. It was as if Michael and his comrades were in a rush to claim the role of a defeated and excluded opposition—something that, of course, had been the fate of anti-Stalinists in the 1920s, 1930s, and 1940s. But this time their assumption of this role came at a moment when they still had a good chance to emerge, if not victorious, at least in a position of influence comparable to that of their rivals on the Left.

The anti-Stalinists were not the monolithic bloc they may have appeared to be to outsiders. Irving Howe wasn't entirely sure how he felt about the war in 1965; he still seemed to think that some kind of democratic third force might yet emerge in South Vietnam to stand up to both the American-backed military regime and the Communists.[27] He was also, by training and inclination, a polemical slugger who seemed driven in the mid-1960s to take on the New Left on every available occasion, regardless of personal or political consequences. And it wasn't just New Leftists infatuated with third world revolutions who annoyed him; he harbored an equally strong dislike for "moral absolutists" of any kind, including pacifists.[28]

Bayard Rustin took part in the early protests against the war more out of force of habit than conviction; by mid-1965 he was in the midst of abandoning his pacifist convictions and affiliations and would soon resign from the War Resisters League and the editorial board of David Dellinger's *Liberation* magazine. In the political circles in which he was beginning to move, the more he was reviled by pacifists or New Leftists as an apostate, the higher his political stock rose.[29]

Michael's case was different. He may have shed his own pacifist convictions in the early 1950s, but he never lost his pacifist sensibilities. He hated war in general and the Vietnam War in particular. And he had genuine sympathy for antiwar protesters, even when they engaged in actions he thought were politically futile, counterproductive, and self-destructive. Unlike Howe, and certainly unlike Rustin, Michael acknowledged on a number of occasions over the next several years that his own formulas for correct political behavior did not seem sufficient to cope with the moral challenge posed by the war.

The first of these occasions came in early November 1965, when a twenty-one-year-old Catholic Worker volunteer named Roger LaPorte set fire to himself in front of the United Nations building to protest the war (one week earlier, the Quaker Norman Morrison had committed suicide on the steps of the Pentagon). LaPorte lingered near death for over twenty-four hours before succumbing to his injuries, telling those who struggled to save his life: "I am a Catholic Worker. I'm against war, all wars. I did this as a religious action."[30] Michael was both shocked and moved by LaPorte's actions and defended him against suggestions that his had been the act of a madman. Recalling his own experience as a Catholic Worker in the early 1950s, Michael wrote that "it was the society as a whole that seemed mad, and it was the passionate voice of conscience which seemed the only real sanity."[31]

But Michael did not often permit himself to indulge the "passionate voice of conscience" in these years. It wasn't that he was unaware of its claims on his attention; but as he suggested in a review of Christopher Lasch's *The New Radicalism in America* for *Commonweal* in September 1965, there were other voices that had to be heeded as well. Lasch's influential book offered a series of biographical portraits of intellectuals, starting in the Progressive Era and continuing to the early 1960s, who had been trapped between the "polarities" of "accommodation to power" and "principled ineffectiveness." Lasch was most critical of his intellectual forebears who had chosen to support American entry into the First World War under the illusion that by doing so they could shape wartime mobilization to serve the cause of social reform. This compromise of intellectual and moral independence, in Lasch's account, had proven a delusion; only passionate (and politically doomed) naysayers such as Randolph Bourne came off looking well in *The New Radicalism.*

Michael was more sympathetic than Lasch to the dilemmas faced by the Progressives. Intellectuals, he wrote, inevitably faced an "uncomfortable tension" between "integrity and impotence, flexibility and betrayal." There was no single formula for principled political behavior. In different historical eras, different balances would have to be struck, according to circumstance and opportunity. In the early 1950s, Michael contended, when there was no movement for fundamental change afoot or even on the horizon, the radical intellectual "was obliged to seek his own alienation." In the 1960s, with a widening of the possibilities for securing real social gains, "the radical must brave semi-commitments." *The New Radicalism in America,* Michael argued, "misses the ambiguity of the radical who must exist in mid-air between sectarian irrelevance and successful betrayal."[32]

Foremost among Michael's own commitments in these years was his support for the Socialist Party, for the party's "realignment" faction, and for his faction's undisputed leader, Max Shachtman. He clung to these allegiances even as many of his closest friends and comrades from the 1950s, like Bogdan Denitch and Debbie Meier, drew back from Shachtman in disagreement and dismay. "People in the New Left used to say to me, 'Mike sold out,'" Meier would recall. "I thought to myself that, in an odd way, his loyalty to Shachtman was the opposite of selling out. He could have been a very popular figure in American political life. He cut himself off with his strange attachment to the Shachtmanites."[33]

Since the ISL's merger with the SP a half dozen years earlier, Shachtman—who turned sixty-one years old in 1965—had kept a low profile within the merged organization, in part to avoid raising concerns that he was plotting to capture it, in part because of the burdens of ill health and aging. He still consulted regularly with a small circle of political comrades, Michael among them, but they had to travel to his house in Floral Park to meet him.

By most measures Shachtman's life had been a failure, marked by the wasting away of the series of marginal groups he had founded and led and by the defections of once close and trusted associates. The revolutionary socialist dreams of his youth had long since disappeared, followed in turn by the collapse of his hopes for a labor party. The publication of his collected essays in 1962, *The Bureaucratic Revolution,* garnered a polite review in *Dissent* but was otherwise all but universally ignored.[34]

But ailing and isolated as he was, Shachtman remained as politically ambitious as ever. Since he was incapable of creating powerful institutions *on* the Left, he began instead to think of already existing powerful institutions *as* the Left.[35] And chief among the pillars of his imagined Left was the AFL-CIO. The sheer size and wealth of the trade unions, compared to any other potential constituency of the Left, seemed to dazzle Shachtman and rendered irrelevant any questions about what they actually stood for politically. In the 1950s, the Shachtmanites had celebrated Walter Reuther of the UAW as the embodiment of their hopes for a revitalized class-conscious labor movement. By the mid-1960s, their iconography of working-class heroes had moved upwards and rightwards: Now it was George Meany, president of the AFL-CIO, who seemed to them to embody all that was good and decent (and powerful) in the union movement. In time the Shachtmanites constructed a veritable Meany cult of personality, singing his praises on every possible occasion. An affectionately drawn cartoon portrait of Meany, with his trademark cigar clenched between his teeth, became as regular a feature in *New America* as Che Guevera's bereted visage did in the underground press.[36]

Where once Shachtman dreamed of leading the dispossessed, he now settled for influencing the well connected. The great victories celebrated in the Shachtman camp came when one or another of his lieutenants managed to secure a staff position within the trade union hierarchy. Don Slaiman led the way with a position at the AFL-CIO's civil rights department, where he gained the ear of George Meany's assistant Lane Kirkland. Bayard Rustin, increasingly a Shachtman acolyte, was hired as director of the newly established A. Philip Randolph Institute in 1965. Meany no longer regarded Rustin, as he had as recently as 1961, as a dangerous radical. Heavily subsidized by the AFL-CIO, the Randolph Institute performed various good works in the labor movement, such as running apprenticeship programs to prepare minority workers for membership in the building trades unions. But the institute also served as the vehicle through which Rustin could act as the labor movement's quasi-official deputy to the civil rights movement. In addition, it provided staff positions and salaries to various other Shachtmanites, including Rochelle Horowitz, who was hired on as the institute's administrative secretary.[37]

Closer to home, Shachtman's wife, Yetta Barsh, became secretary to Al Shanker, president of the powerful United Federation of Teachers (UFT) in New York City, and YSL veteran Sandra Feldman became one of his troubleshooting aides. Shanker, an effective and ambitious union organizer, was a rising contender for leadership of the UFT's parent union, the American Federation of Teachers (AFT). The AFT was becoming strategically important within the national labor movement; along with other unions of public employees, it would expand its membership dramatically in the 1960s and 1970s, in marked contrast to the declining fortunes of the major industrial unions. An alliance with Shanker was thus valuable currency in intra-union affairs.[38]

Shachtman's strategy for exercising stealthy influence within the councils of the powerful was both abetted and threatened by his affiliation to the Socialist Party. On one hand, the SP, and particularly its youth affiliate, gave him access to new recruits. YPSL, dissolved in 1964 when it had passed into the hands of its left-wing faction, was reconstituted in 1966, this time firmly under the control of its right wing, and would be the source of such talented up-and-coming young Shachtmanites as Josh Muravchik. Shachtman's socialist affiliations also provided him access to those labor leaders like Shanker who retained fond memories of their own youthful left-wing indiscretions—in Shanker's case, as a member of the Columbia University SLID chapter in the early 1950s. As an independent operator, without his link to the SP, Shachtman could not have traded nearly as effectively on the claim to be the guardian of the Debs-Thomas tradition.

On the other hand, Shachtman knew that the SP was useful to him only so long as it remained inoffensive to George Meany. And that meant, among other things, that Shachtman could not permit the Socialists to take a strong stand in opposition to the Vietnam War, which Meany ardently supported. Since 1960, the AFL-CIO had served as a conduit for millions of dollars of American aid from the State Department to anticommunist unions in South Vietnam. At the December 1965 national convention of the AFL-CIO, the delegates voted with near unanimity for a resolution proclaiming that "the nation's working men and women . . . support the Johnson Administration in Viet Nam." When UAW secretary-treasurer Emil Mazey dared suggest that antiwar protesters had a right to be heard, he was publicly rebuked by Meany. At a later convention, Meany declared that he "would rather fight the Communists in South Vietnam than fight them . . . in the Chesapeake Bay."[39]

Ten years earlier, Shachtman would have labeled Meany's position "Stalinophobic"—shaped as it was by the AFL-CIO's bitterly anti-Soviet international affairs director Jay Lovestone. But Shachtman had come to believe that Lovestone—an old rival of his from the days when they were both young and up-and-coming Communists in the 1920s—was right. It no longer seemed impermissible to Shachtman for socialists to take sides with a capitalist government in a war with a Communist government; indeed, committed as they were to the existence of free and independent labor movements, they had no choice but to do so. Shachtman's change of heart on his third-camp philosophy first became known publicly in April 1961 when he gave a speech in San Francisco and offered a qualified endorsement to the

Cuban exile landings at the Bay of Pigs (there were, he pointed out, some trade unionists, "good, stout, working-class fighters," in the ranks of the invasion force). In the summer of 1965, Shachtman announced that he opposed American withdrawal from South Vietnam. It was not, he assured his listeners at a *Dissent* forum in New York, that he favored the existing South Vietnamese regime; again, as at the Bay of Pigs, he was merely siding with good trade unionists and other democrats whose cause would be lost if the Communists came to power in South Vietnam.[40]

Shachtman's increasingly conservative outlook led to a new wave of defections among his followers. Some, like Hal Draper and Julius Jacobson, broke publicly and bitterly; others, like Bogdan Denitch and Debbie Meier withdrew with less fanfare.[41] As his circle of long-time political intimates shrank, Shachtman grew ever more attached to the few who remained loyal. He spoke of Tom Kahn and Rochelle Horowitz as his "children," and they would serve him for the remainder of his life with filial devotion. His ties to his most famous disciple, Michael Harrington, proved more troublesome.[42]

Michael had not agreed with Shachtman on the Bay of Pigs, nor was he swayed by Shachtman's views on Vietnam. But he agreed that tactically the SP had to handle the issue of Vietnam gingerly, if it hoped to realize its domestic agenda. At planning sessions in the fall of 1965 for the upcoming White House Conference on Civil Rights, Michael listened as A. Philip Randolph called on the delegates to endorse a vastly expanded war on poverty, one that would be prepared to spend tens of billions of dollars in place of current appropriations of little over a billion a year. Although the White House remained unresponsive, and the conference delegates never got a chance to vote on the proposal, Michael, Rustin, and others decided to make Randolph's proposal the centerpiece of their domestic strategy. They drafted a model "A. Philip Randolph Freedom Budget," calling for the expenditure of more than 180 billion dollars by the federal government in a ten-year campaign to eliminate poverty in the United States. John Kenneth Galbraith endorsed the proposal, as did a number of prominent labor and civil rights leaders.[43]

But the Freedom Budget was a hopeless cause from the moment it was first proposed. Although President Johnson pledged in his 1966 State of the Union Address that the United States was "strong enough to pursue our goals in the rest of the world while still building a Great Society at home," he had in fact largely lost interest in his own domestic programs by then—and in any case, had never envisioned social welfare spending on the scale called for by Randolph and his supporters.[44] The midterm elections in 1966, in which the Democrats lost forty-seven seats in the House of Representatives and three in the Senate—most of them liberals, some of them of the stature of Illinois senator Paul Douglas—signaled the beginning of the end even for Johnson's limited war on poverty. The term itself soon vanished from White House rhetoric.[45]

Michael, however, despite his own dire prediction in the spring of 1965 that the fate of Appalachia would be decided in the jungles of Vietnam, clung to the belief that President Johnson's interest in domestic reform could be revived. The United States, he insisted on numerous occasions in the mid-1960s, could indeed afford both "guns and butter"—even if personally he wasn't happy about the guns. "Whatever your opinion on the War in Vietnam," Michael told the audience at an antipoverty conference in 1966, "there is no reason that the poor should pay for it. There's enough money floating around in the form of excess profits and high incomes to finance both [guns and butter], if we decided we wanted to."[46]

Michael wasn't the only political leader on the democratic Left who was torn between revulsion for the war and a desire to keep open lines of communication with the White House. Martin Luther King Jr., at the urging of Bayard Rustin, at first attempted a similar strategy. King spoke out against American involvement in Vietnam, but he avoided taking part in or endorsing demonstrations against the war. King attended the White House Conference on Civil Rights in 1966, unlike the youthful militants of SNCC who boycotted the event to protest the war. But in the year that followed, King decided that for conscience's sake he had to join in active opposition to the war, regardless of political costs. Rustin, who by now had completely severed his links to the peace movement urged him not to do so. But others, including Norman Thomas, supported his decision. On April 4, 1967, at a meeting in New York City's Riverside Church, King issued what he called his "declaration of independence" from the war in Vietnam. In a speech far more radical than any given back in 1965 at the SDS march, King described the American government as "the greatest purveyor of violence in the world today." As a dedicated pacifist, he was first and foremost opposed to the war because of his moral objections to the use of violence. He also issued a ringing challenge to Lyndon Johnson's belief (still shared by Michael) that Americans could enjoy both guns and butter. "A few years ago," King declared, "there was a shining moment" when it seemed "as if there was a real promise of hope for the poor":

> Then came the build-up in Vietnam, and I watched the program broken and eviscerated as if it were some idle political plaything of a society gone mad on war. . . . So I was increasingly compelled to see the war as an enemy of the poor and to attack it as such.

King concluded by calling the war a "symptom of a far deeper malady within the American spirit," and he called on the nation to atone for its sins with a "radical revolution of values."[47] King had come to believe that no issue confronting the country was more important than the war; whatever political influence he might sacrifice in the short term was of incidental consequence compared to the necessity of bringing the conflict to an end.

Michael agreed—at least in retrospect. In his autobiography, published a half dozen years after King's "declaration of independence," Michael contrasted King's behavior in 1967 with that of Rustin. Describing him as "the bravest man I've ever known, and certainly one of the most dedicated and committed militants," Michael averred that Rustin nonetheless "made the wrong decision" when he decided

> to subordinate his antiwar convictions to what he became convinced were the imperatives of domestic coalition politics. He was wrong because this position presumed that social conditions could succeed while the war raged, and because it ignored one agony in order to deal with another. It was wrong, and it was understandable. It was his love of justice in America that led Bayard to ignore monstrous injustice in Indochina. Martin King made the other, the right decision. With the knowledge that he was imperiling, if not destroying, his access to the White House, King became an outspoken critic of the war. But to say that Bayard was wrong in his choice is hardly to condemn him. T. S. Eliot once said that the greatest treason "was to do the right thing for the wrong reason." How, then, does one judge a man like Bayard, who did the wrong thing for the right reason?[48]

A fair and compassionate question, but one that could be applied to its author as well. It is difficult to avoid the conclusion that in contrasting King's position with Rustin's, Michael was displacing some guilty feelings about his own role vis-à-vis Vietnam.

Personally appalled by the war, Michael did not allow himself to issue the kind of passionate and uncompromising moral condemnation of it so evident in King's speech. Time and again throughout the 1960s he would refer to the war as a "tragedy"—as if it were an earthquake, a hurricane, or a plague. He could never bring himself to say that the evils of the war were the product of human agency. It was as if the war had been set in motion by an act of God, rather than on the orders of the president of the United States. It wasn't that Michael felt any special attachment to Lyndon Johnson. But by not blaming Johnson for the war, he also could avoid blaming those among his closest and longest-standing political comrades who were supporting the slaughter LBJ had unleashed. He could continue to view them as good socialists with whom he differed on peripheral issues such as how best to end the war, while remaining allied with them on the crucial domestic issue of realigning the Democratic Party.

In 1966 Michael attended a private meeting at Bayard Rustin's apartment to discuss Vietnam. Shachtman considered the meeting important enough to make one of his rare trips into the city from Floral Park. Irving Howe was there too, along with a contingent of *Dissent* editors. Howe by this point had given up his earlier illusions that some kind of "third force" was likely to emerge in South Vietnam to save the situation. Michael agreed with Howe; as he wrote in the *Village Voice* that year, misguided French and American policies in Vietnam over the past twenty years had driven "the courageous youth of the ex-colonial world" to embrace the anticolonial insurgency led by Ho Chi Minh. The result was that eventual Communist victory was all but inevitable, and in any event a lesser evil to an endless or expanded war.[49] Shachtman disagreed, and with the rhetorical overkill he often employed when he wanted to intimidate opponents, he proceeded to attack the *Dissent* group "as a bunch of totally committed Gandhian pacifists who were against the use of violence under all circumstances."[50] Michael and Howe and the others from *Dissent* were taken aback as they listened to Shachtman justify supporting the U.S. war indefinitely. As terrible as the war was, as reprehensible as the Saigon regime had proven itself, anything was preferable to "Communist victory." The American war effort must continue until the Communists were beaten. Offers of negotiations were permissible, but only if hedged with enough conditions to make it impossible for the Communists to accept.[51]

Michael heard what Shachtman was saying about the war, yet he failed to draw what seems in retrospect the obvious conclusion: that if Shachtman and his supporters took part in organizing an "antiwar" group, they were dissembling. As he would later put it, he could not bring himself to believe that "the comrades of my youth, who had fought against the Korean War, who had spit in the eye of the FBI," had changed their opinions and allegiances so completely.[52] That Shachtman was hard-nosed and unsentimental about issues of war and peace, Michael was prepared to admit; that he was actually pro-war was inconceivable.

And so, the following spring, Michael helped Shachtman and others organize a new group called Negotiations Now, which promoted itself as a responsible, moderate alternative to the irresponsible, radical groups calling for the immediate withdrawal of U.S. forces from Vietnam. Although it listed some influential sponsors on its letterhead, including John Kenneth Galbraith, Arthur Schlesinger Jr., and Martin Luther King, Negotiations Now was organizationally little more than a front group for the Shachtmanite faction of the Socialist Party. The group helped nudge a few former supporters of the war, like Schlesinger, into taking their first public stance critical of the Johnson administration's policies. But Negotiations Now's chief function was to serve as the SP's placeholder in the antiwar movement—something they could point to when challenged to show that they too were working to bring the war to an end. Negotiations Now also served as a convenient podium from which the Shachtmanites could criticize the rest of the antiwar movement as being, in contrast, extremist, misguided, and objectively pro-Communist.[53] It was a sham operation. "In the immortal words of V. I. Lenin," as Michael acknowledged in retrospect, the Shachtmanites "supported Negotiations Now the way a rope supports a hanging man."[54]

While *New America* devoted endless columns to praising the (mostly imagined) achievements of the SP's antiwar front group, it denounced most of the major antiwar demonstrations organized by others from 1965 through 1972. The usual charge was that protesters were insufficiently evenhanded in their opposition to the war: The 1967 Spring Mobilization demonstration in New York City, which turned out 300,000 antiwar protesters to march from Central Park to the United Nations building, was condemned in the paper because it "makes no demands on the Communists, as well as the United States, to de-escalate and end the war."[55] Official condemnations of this sort did not always stop individual Socialists from joining the demonstrations. Norman Thomas, at Martin Luther King's personal request, introduced King for his speech at the rally, and Michael marched anonymously with the crowd.

Even in the case of the few antiwar events judged politically acceptable, Socialist spokesmen launched shrill attacks on those whose opposition to the war drew on different assumptions than their own. In a report on a December 1966 antiwar rally sponsored by SANE and endorsed by the SP, Paul Feldman, the Shachtmanite editor of *New America,* devoted several paragraphs to denouncing folksinger Pete Seeger, who, having "dutifully set to music every twist and turn in the Communist line from the time of the Hitler-Stalin Pact, . . . has no more business at a peace rally than Robert McNamara since he also is an uncritical supporter of one side in the war." Dr. Benjamin Spock, I. F. Stone, and others came under similar attack.[56]

Not all party members were oblivious to the political costs involved in the SP's self-righteous abstention from antiwar activism. Donald Henderson, a member of the SP's national committee, wrote to Norman Thomas in 1967 to complain about the coverage of the antiwar movement by *New America:*

> The paper does not appeal to the American left, its subscription is dropping under the current Editorship while the Left grows. . . . Large sections of the Party find it more of a hindrance than a help. . . . Comrade Feldman either has applied extremely bad political judgement in the paper or he is wielding a very well honed sectarian sword.[57]

Although Michael never denounced individual antiwar opponents the way his Shachtmanite comrades did, he could not help being associated with their divisive tactics. David McReynolds was among those who ran afoul of the Shachtmanites, as he played an important role assisting A. J. Muste in organizing the antiwar coalition that staged the Spring Mobilization in April 1967. In an exchange that year in the *Village Voice,* McReynolds noted that he, like many others in the antiwar movement, had "been accused, and by personal friends of Mike Harrington, of being soft on communism, of supporting Hanoi, etc."[58]

McReynolds resigned from the SP's national committee in 1965 to protest the party's indifferent response to the war; while putting most of his political energies into the activities of the War Resisters League in the years that followed, he also helped organize an antiwar faction in the party that called itself the "Debs Caucus." Michael shared the general Shachtmanite view of McReynolds as a hopelessly muddled dilettante who did not share their hard-headed commitment to the labor movement or to the realignment of the Democratic Party. McReynolds, in turn, regarded Michael as untrustworthy; and, as he would be honest enough to acknowledge, he was jealous of Michael's preeminence in the SP and of the affection Michael received from Norman Thomas.[59]

Notwithstanding their mutual antagonisms, McReynolds sensed Michael's unease over the war, recognized his value as a movement leader, and tried repeatedly to shake him free from his Shachtmanite allies. In November 1967 he wrote an essay for the *Village Voice* entitled "Letter to the Men of My Generation," by which he meant his fellow anti-Stalinist radicals of the 1950s, in general, and Michael in particular. "Some of you," he wrote,

> good friends and old associates—suggest we will lose our effectiveness if we speak the full truth about the war. . . . We organize a 'Negotiations Now!' movement because we think 'Withdrawal Now!' would fail to win support. And yet what have we to negotiate except the roads our troops will follow as they withdraw? Do we have any right to negotiate the kind of government we shall leave behind us?[60]

Michael responded in the next issue of the *Voice,* repeating his criticisms of both Vietnamese Communism and the slogans and tactics of the antiwar movement: "I can't participate in demonstrations that will alienate people from the antiwar cause. . . . I can't endorse middle-class elitism or regard middle-class psycho-drama as a substitute for serious politics." But, in another of those moments when he allowed his own doubts to surface, he confessed to "being emotionally dissatisfied with my own position. This war is so ugly and horrible that I want to do something more personal, more involved than simply being rational and political."[61]

McReynolds challenged Michael's distinction between the "personal" and the "rational and political" in the next issue of the *Voice:*

> What is politically sound is generally morally defensible, and what is morally imperative generally proves politically sound in the long run. . . . Mike should not be too worried by public reaction to peace demonstrations, nor too eager to keep them respectable. The history of social change shows that any action which brought a controversial issue to the attention of the public aroused tremendous negative reactions. . . . Think of the struggle against slavery, the struggle for women's rights, the struggle of labor, and the Negro struggle.[62]

But, if McReynolds was still eager to engage Michael in debate, many others on the Left had by now decided that he was past all hope of salvation. As one *Voice* reader wrote in response to the Harrington-McReynolds exchange, Michael had become to the Vietnam War

> what Albert Camus was to the Algerian [conflict]. Camus . . . disappointed history by his equivocal role during the Algerian Revolution. . . . Camus' tragedy, like Harrington's, was his inability to comprehend the phenomenally cruel and undemocratic nature of his nation's behavior. . . . I know that I will always think of Harrington as the man who woke up a sleepy 1950's student generation and who reminded a nation of the problem of its poor. But . . . I will disconnect those actions from his pitiful inaction against the war.[63]

Michael regarded his position on Vietnam as an example of the triumph of the head over the heart, of prose over poetry. But Vietnam was not the kind of issue that lent itself to staking out the "responsible" middle ground. When Americans grew disenchanted with the war, it was not the supposedly measured response of "negotiations now" but the passionate avowal of "immediate withdrawal" that engaged them. Certainly that was true of the liberal Democratic constituency that the Socialists most hoped to influence. By 1970 both SANE and Americans for Democratic Action (ADA) had switched from supporting negotiations to calling for unilateral U.S. withdrawal. By the following year, public opinion polls showed that 60 percent of Americans favored a pullout from Vietnam, "even if the government of South Vietnam collapsed." And that spring, for the first time, a majority of Americans declared that the war was "morally wrong." Fearful of being too radical, the Socialists in fact tailed far behind shifting public opinion on the war. To many antiwar activists, the Socialist Party's position on the war thus seemed esoteric at best, or, at worst, an intentional backhanded endorsement of American involvement.[64]

Michael had managed to work himself into a position where both opponents and allies regarded him with contempt. The left wing of the SP despised his position on the war; the right wing of the SP despised his position on domestic politics.

In terms of political strategy, Michael and Shachtman were theoretically aligned as advocates of the realignment of the Democratic Party. But just who was worthy of being "realigned" in the progressive Democratic majority of the future was increasingly a divisive issue within the SP's Realignment Caucus. This debate within a tiny isolated corner of the Left would both reflect and, to a surprising extent, influence a fundamental reordering of American politics over the next decade.

For Michael, as for Shachtman, it was gospel that the union movement was an essential component of any effort to remake American politics and society: "Even if labor does not score a breakthrough in new areas of organization," Michael wrote in 1968, "it will still represent the largest organized body of Americans committed to economic reform."[65] However, Michael did not share Shachtman's increasing tendency to link the cause of social justice solely with the well-being of trade unionism, and the well-being of trade unionism solely with whatever George Meany's views on current issues might entail. For one thing, Michael recognized that the old industrial order that had provided the setting in which both Karl Marx and George Meany had worked out their fundamental worldview was in the midst of a dramatic period of change and transformation. The industrial working class represented a declining proportion of the working population in the United States, whereas non-blue-collar occupations were among the fastest growing segment of unionized workers. "The theory of the working-class' historical mission has been undermined by the technological revolution," Michael wrote in early 1966. "No single class, but a coalition of progressive social forces, is now necessary to achieve a radical democratic transformation of society."[66]

Organized labor could not prosper without new allies drawn from the ranks of middle-class social movements. By 1967 Michael had come to describe these allies as the "conscience constituency"—a new phrase in his political vocabulary The phrase harkened back to A. Philip Randolph's description of the groups supporting the 1963 March on Washington as a "coalition of conscience," and also to the antebellum division between "conscience Whigs" and "cotton Whigs" in the north. Drawing on works that included John Kenneth Galbraith's *The New Industrial State* and David Bazelon's *Power in America: The Politics of the New Class,* as well as on discussions within the New Left on the growing importance of a "new working class" of scientists and technicians, Michael came to identify the educated middle class as a key component in his strategy for remaking the Democratic Party and American society.[67] He wrote in the *Village Voice* in 1967:

> From Marx to [C. Wright] Mills, the Left has regarded the middle class as a stratum of hypocritical, vaccilating rearguarders. . . . But now, it is pos-

> sible . . . that a new class is coming into being. . . . By education and by work experience this new class is predisposed toward planning and economic rationality. . . . It is now possible . . . that the American economy is creating a social structure which vastly enlarges the conscience constituency.[68]

The notion of the conscience constituency appealed to Michael on two grounds. First it could be squared with his ingrained Marxist belief that the decisive political issues were decided by the clash of rising and falling classes. "In the next decade" Michael wrote in his 1968 book *Towards a Democratic Left* (a work that was, in part, Michael's attempt to create a sort of Port Huron statement for the conscience constituency), "professional and technical jobs will grow faster than any other, and their increase will be concentrated in education, space, urban problems and medical services." This new class could be "an ally of the poor and organized workers"—or, if its potential was overlooked by the Left, "their sophisticated enemy."[69]

Another reason that Michael liked the idea of the conscience constituency was that it validated his old idea about the "other America"—that is, the existence of an alternative America of generous democratic impulses deeply rooted in the national culture. In the idea of a conscience constituency, he saw the possibility of a mass social base that might realize a truly visionary politics:

> The famous American knowhow can be directed to unmet social needs like housing, public transportation, and the dilapidated public sector. The country can decide to find a less terrifying way to subsidize research and development than through the arms industry. Considerations of beauty and social consequence can be politically programmed into economic calculations, the boundaries between work and leisure can be redrawn to suit human needs, the university can be turned into something better than a technological trade school.[70]

The Shachtmanites did not share Michael's enthusiasm for the "conscience constituency." They liked neither the theory nor the social grouping it celebrated. They preferred to refer to liberal professionals as the "new class"—a term that in Shachtmanite usage invited comparison with the new class of Communist bureaucrats in eastern Europe described by Milovan Djilas.[71] There is a curious parallel between the political direction that the Shachtmanites took in the mid-1960s and that taken by their hated rivals on the New Left: Both came to use the word "liberal" as a political epithet. Thus YPSL, at its founding (or rather re-founding) convention over Labor Day weekend 1966, adopted a resolution committing the organization to "defend the Labor Movement against all reactionary attacks and middle class liberal cynicism."[72]

Although Michael, too, defended the labor movement against its critics on the right and the left, his emphasis was always on the need for the liberal middle class to join with other groups, including unions, in a mutually beneficial political alliance. In February 1967 he spoke at Harvard University at the invitation of the school's newly formed YPSL chapter. He told his audience in this bastion of both class privilege and New Left activism:

> I think it conceivable that students could form the basis, on the one hand, for a snob politics, for an anti-popular politics, for a reactionary politics, for a middle class, smug, self-satisfied politics. On the other hand—and this is the trend which appears to me much more dominant recently in the United States—the vast increase in the number of educated people in this country could provide the basis for a conscience politics: for people who are driven to change the society not out of a material need alone, but out of a spiritual and intellectual need as well.[73]

That 700 students had turned out to hear Michael speak on this occasion was a hopeful sign. That he was speaking at Harvard at the invitation of the Young People's Socialist League, and not at the invitation of Students for a Democratic Society, was less promising. The Harvard-Radcliffe YPSL chapter, one of the largest and most active in the organization, proudly claimed "over twenty" members in the spring semester of 1967, at a time when the SDS chapter had at least five times that number. SDS chapters could be found in many less prestigious and more working-class universities, from San Francisco State to Kent State, where yipsels were a completely unknown breed. In the summer of 1968, *New America* hailed the fact that YPSL had "close to 500" members—that year SDS's national membership was approaching 100,000.[74]

So Michael was preaching in the wrong church. Of course by 1967, he was unlikely to find many converts within the New Left, regardless of who invited him to speak. Michael Kazin, one of the SDSers who heard Michael speak at Harvard that spring, found him eloquent and inspiring, but irrelevant, because he so clearly "wasn't a revolutionary."[75] Disillusionment with the "liberal establishment," anger over the war, and a desire to keep ideological pace with an ever more militantly inclined black power movement, reinforced all the tendencies within SDS to embrace the politics of "the moral gesture" that Michael had early on and presciently warned against.[76] The best he could hope to do was to be in a position to re-establish contacts with student radicals, if and when they abandoned their current ultra-revolutionary convictions. At a conference of socialist leaders in May 1967, Michael cautioned against strident denunciations of the New Left: "They will make mistakes, but they are the people—when things get better—that I'll have to work with."[77]

New Leftists had come to reject the very idea of reform as a pernicious snare designed by "corporate liberals" to entrap the politically unaware. Tom Hayden declared in 1967 that there was

> little evidence to justify the view that the social reforms of the past thirty years actually improved the quality of American life in any lasting way, and there is much evidence which suggests that many of the reforms gained were illusory or token, serving chiefly to sharpen the capacity of the system for manipulation and oppression.[78]

New Leftists regarded the war on poverty as a particularly cruel deception. SDSer Richard Rothstein, like Hayden a veteran of the ERAP project, declared in 1968 that he and his comrades were

> now enemies of welfare state capitalism, with little faith or desire that the liberal-labor forces within this system be strengthened vis-à-vis their corporatist and reactionary allies. We view those forces—and the social "reforms" they espouse—as being incompatible with a non-interventionist world policy and as no more than a manipulative fraud perpetrated upon the dignity and humanity of the American people.[79]

Michael readily admitted that the existing American welfare state, "ill-financed and bureaucratic" as it was, often created "humiliating dependence and fear" among its intended beneficiaries. But he insisted that it be seen as a genuine social gain, won through "a major upheaval of the workers, from the bottom up" in response to the hardships of the Great Depression. As for the war on poverty, it was "certainly inadequate," but "it is not a fraud."[80]

Michael understood why New Leftists were drawn to extreme gestures of alienation, and he expected them to outgrow them, since he had been through that stage himself. But he seemed less certain as to how he should respond to the rise of black militancy and black nationalism in the later 1960s, for the rage of black militants was not something that he could subsume into the category of "myself when young." When Malcolm X was assassinated in Harlem in February 1965, Michael did not join the chorus of those who noted smugly that Malcolm's chickens had come home to roost, that violent speech begets violent acts, or that those who live by the sword should be prepared to die by it. "America does not understand men with black skins and men who are poor," Michael wrote in the *New York Herald Tribune:*

> People tend to think of Negroes as middle class whites in disguise and of the poor as solid citizens who temporarily don't have money. . . . And then they look at someone like Malcolm and judge him as if the alternatives were a comfortable, happy career or a willful choice of violence. Malcolm was born into the underworld. . . . And at the end, he may well have been trying to do something that few people ever achieve: to rise completely above the premises and assumptions of his childhood and youth.[81]

Michael took on the difficult role of explaining the position of the militants to moderates, and that of the moderates to the militants. When rioting broke out in the Watts neighborhood of Los Angeles in August 1965, resulting in six days and nights of violence that left thirty-four dead in its wake, Michael was staying nearby in Santa Barbara. Shortly afterward he met with Rustin, who had come out to Watts with Martin Luther King to help restore calm. On the devastated streets of Watts, Michael reported in the *New York Herald Tribune,* Rustin heard over and over again a "significant and curious term":

> The people, Rustin told me, referred to the arson and looting and bloodshed as their "manifesto." . . . If the United States as a whole suffered an unemployment rate like that in Watts, I suggest that there would be riots in every city and they would be made by white men as well as black.[82]

Michael tried to explain the furies sweeping through the black communities of the urban north. At the same time, he lent his support to those who offered a moderate political alternative, including Martin Luther King and Bayard Rustin. Rustin had fallen into disrepute among black militants, not only for his role at Atlantic City but for his insistence, spelled out in a famous article in *Commentary,* that it was time the civil rights movement shifted "from protest to politics." Rustin, Michael wrote on one occasion, "has been wrongly accused of going over to the Establishment because he doggedly and courageously insists on working to assemble an antipoverty majority under the most difficult of circumstance. His tactic does not 'sound' radical—but in fact it goes to the roots."[83]

Michael also defended another old acquaintance, Daniel Patrick Moynihan, against attacks from the Left. Moynihan was not a political comrade like Rustin, but he was someone whose judgments Michael respected. He and Moynihan had argued on the same side in the Shriver task force for a war on poverty that emphasized jobs creation, although to no avail. The following year Moynihan gained national notoriety as the author of a U.S. Labor Department study entitled *The Negro Family: The Case for National*

Action, better known as "the Moynihan Report." Moynihan described what he called a "tangle of pathology" that had undermined the urban black family in recent years. Moynihan's intention in analyzing black family structure fully conformed with the reformist goals of the war on poverty and drew heavily on studies of ghetto life by black social scientists like E. Franklin Frazier and Kenneth Clark. Although there was nothing startlingly new about Moynihan's observations, the word "pathology" leapt off the page of his report, infuriating black readers who took it as an insult, and persuading many white readers that the problems of the black community were so intractable as to be impervious to government social welfare programs. Michael read the Moynihan Report more sympathetically than its critics. He had yet to make up his mind about the implications of its critique of the black family, but he certainly agreed with the policy conclusions Moynihan himself drew at the time: "As the Moynihan Report itself makes plain, unemployment and under-employment are fundamental to the problems of the Negro family." The solution to the social ills of the ghetto was not (as Moynihan himself would later come to argue) a "benign neglect" but rather a large-scale federal effort to put black men back to work.[84]

Michael's sympathies remained with the black movement for equality. But he no longer enjoyed the sense of belonging to a "beloved community" that he had known in the early days of the 1960s. He still traveled frequently to Harlem for meetings with A. Philip Randolph at the Brotherhood of Sleeping Car Porters headquarters. But where he had formerly felt "so righteous and innocent and safe in the ghetto," now every time he ventured into black urban neighborhoods, he was "apprehensive and fearful."[85]

Michael's most important continuing connection with the civil rights cause was in his role as a member of Martin Luther King's "research committee," an informally organized New York- and Chicago-based group of advisers, who, starting in 1964, met three or four times a year with the SCLC leader to help him devise movement strategy. It was in this capacity that he took part in the early discussions for King's proposed "Poor People's Campaign" in the winter and spring of 1968. In an attempt to pressure the federal government to expand its antipoverty programs, SCLC planned to bring thousands of poor people of all races to Washington for a sustained campaign of marches, lobbying, and sit-ins. At a meeting of the research committee on January 29, King asked Michael to draft a manifesto for the campaign, laughingly telling him, "You know, we didn't even know we were poor until we read your book."[86]

Michael agreed to take on King's assignment, but he and Rustin remained skeptical of the strategy that SCLC was now following. The movement, they felt, could not content itself with "one more moral victory and an actual defeat," as had been the case two years earlier in Chicago when King led an ill-starred drive for "open housing." As Michael wrote in the summer of 1968, describing his and Rustin's involvement with the Poor People's Campaign:

> Rustin urged King to state his broad, far-reaching program for the abolition of poverty *and* a series of demands which might be won immediately. King agreed with the logic of Rustin's position, yet at the same time he clearly sympathized with the emotions of others at the meeting who talked of pushing nonviolent resistance to the point of civil dislocation. These two positions called for quite different tactics; King, it seemed to me, found it difficult to choose between them.[87]

A little over three months later, Martin Luther King was struck down by an assassin in Memphis, Tennessee, where he had gone to support a strike by the city's sanitation workers. Michael flew to the city two days later to join a memorial march. There he saw representatives of the same coalition of forces who, three years earlier, had defiantly sung the "Star Spangled Banner" in the streets of Montgomery—blacks, unionists, liberals and radicals, religious leaders. This time there were no songs, and no cheering crowds. In the deserted streets of downtown Memphis, the only sound to be heard, Michael would report, was "the eerie tread of feet."[88]

The Poor People's Campaign went on without King. Several thousand self-selected representatives of the Other America took up residence in a collection of shacks and tents along the Capitol Mall, a ramshackle encampment grandly and inaccurately dubbed "Resurrection City." Despite his misgivings, Michael couldn't stay away from such a gathering. On June 19 he traveled to Washington to take part in a "Solidarity Day" march that Rustin had helped organize, a large, peaceful, and integrated event that was supported by liberal trade unions as well as civil rights groups. Momentarily encouraged, he went over to Resurrection City the next day as an invited speaker. He made, he recalled, "a brief but pointed attack" on the hypocrisy of well-off Americans who piously told the poor "to stop asking for handouts. . . . I said if this society would only treat slum dwellers as well as home builders, and hungry children as well as corporate farmers, it would take a step towards justice, not charity."

Given the setting, his message, and his reputation, Michael was expecting a friendly reception. Here he was, the man who discovered poverty, speaking on behalf of the poor to Resurrection City's "Poor People's University." Instead, as he finished speaking, an "angry—almost psychotic" black man in the audience lashed out at him, calling him "Whitey":

> [He] told me that he would not fight my war, did not support my social system, and would not leave the mall where he had built a home for him-

self. . . . At one point he asked me directly whether I thought he lacked money. His point was that he, and his brothers, were rich in spirit, while the affluent—liberal, radical, or conservative—were poor in spirit and that dollars were therefore not decisive. I said that I thought a hungry person could use money. He replied: "I can always get a brick and go to Safeway."[89]

Michael listened quietly to the man's long and incoherent harangue, fearing if he didn't he might come under physical as well as verbal assault. "Finally his passion was spent and the meeting was over," Michael would write in his memoirs. "I almost ran out of the camp and along the walk past the Lincoln Memorial, fleeing what seemed to me the shambles of the beloved community."[90]

There was still time in that crowded year for Michael to be drawn into one more disaster for race relations, and that was the Ocean Hill–Brownsville controversy. In September 1968 the United Federation of Teachers went on strike when the board of education for the Ocean Hill–Brownsville district of the New York school system refused to reinstate a group of white teachers it had transferred out of the district. The Ocean Hill–Brownsville Board of Education, like the Brooklyn neighborhood it represented, was overwhelmingly black, whereas the teachers in the district's public schools, as was true throughout New York, were mostly white, and often Jewish. What began as a labor dispute quickly took on racial overtones. The Shachtmanites, with their close ties to the UFT, were inevitably drawn into the fight—in fact, the UFT's official field representative to Ocean Hill–Brownsville was veteran Shachtmanite Sandra Feldman. (Ironically, two years earlier, Al Shanker had approached Michael and asked him to write an article on the UFT's support for the principle of decentralizing the powers of the New York City school system, in the name of the same ideal of "community control" now being championed in Ocean Hill–Brownsville. Furthermore, the LID had sponsored a series of off-the-record meetings between the UFT, the black community, and city hall on ways to implement community control. But issues of who controlled curriculum, and hiring and firing, had proven intractable, especially when charges of racism and anti-Semitism muddied the more abstract policy issues.)

When the strike broke out, Michael was privately disturbed by what he saw as the UFT's racially polarizing tactics. Nevertheless, he and Tom Kahn served as cochairmen of a pro-UFT "Ad Hoc Committee to Defend the Right to Teach," whose advertisement with twenty-five signatories appeared in the *New York Times* on September 20. In response, community control advocates turned their fire from Shanker to Michael. He was attacked in the pages of the *Village Voice* by Nat Hentoff, and in the *New York Review of Books* by Dwight Macdonald, who had initially been one of the signatories of the pro-UFT advertisement but then switched sides in the controversy. Even by the contentious standards of New York intellectuals, this was a bruising affair in which personal friendships of many decades were severed. It was also organizationally costly: Several prominent members of both the SP and the LID left in protest because of the pro-UFT position taken by those organizations. Worst of all, Ocean Hill–Brownsville was a disaster for Michael's coalitionist strategy, prefiguring, as he would later write, "the split in the liberal-labor-black movement, which was the precondition of Republican presidential power for the next two decades."[91]

Michael had begun the 1968 presidential campaign with high hopes that the long-predicted realignment of the Democratic Party into a unified and genuinely liberal political party was in the offing. While radical organizers were taking the issue of the war to the streets, a new generation of young, issue-oriented liberals were making inroads into the Democratic Party. Allard Lowenstein wanted to give them an antiwar candidate to support in the 1968 election. He and Jack Newfield had met with Robert Kennedy in September 1967, but after three hours of eloquent argument they failed to persuade the ultra-pragmatic Kennedy that he had a real chance to win. So Lowenstein looked elsewhere and eventually recruited Senator Eugene McCarthy to challenge Johnson in the Democratic presidential primaries.

While old-line political insiders scoffed, the McCarthy campaign in New Hampshire attracted an army of youthful volunteers and tapped an undercurrent of deep anxiety among voters about the course of the war. Although he did not think much of McCarthy's chances, Michael declared his support for the senator's campaign in speeches and in an article in *Commentary*.[92] The Shachtmanites, however, despised McCarthy as an elitist, dilettante spoiler. When some Harvard yipsels had the temerity to join McCarthy's campaign in New Hampshire, they had to face the wrath of the YPSL National Executive Committee. McCarthy's campaign was illegitimate, YPSL's leaders declared, because "the mass social forces of the American left—the labor and major Negro organizations" had already endorsed Lyndon Johnson for re-election.[93]

But if YPSL and the AFL-CIO considered the 1968 Democratic presidential nomination a closed question, the voters of New Hampshire did not. President Johnson did not campaign in New Hampshire, but his surrogate spokesmen made it clear what the president thought the stakes in the primary were; the Democratic governor of New Hampshire labeled McCarthy "a champion of appeasement and surrender." The Democratic senator from New Hampshire declared that a McCarthy victory would be good news for "draft-dodgers and deserters." Pro-Johnson newspaper advertisements declared that a vote for McCarthy was a vote for Ho Chi Minh.[94]

Notwithstanding this barrage of abuse, McCarthy's cause prevailed. On

March 12, New Hampshire voters handed him a stunning moral victory with 42 percent of the vote against the incumbent. Robert Kennedy, ruing his caution of the previous fall, entered the race for the Democratic nomination four days later. And on March 31, a beleaguered Lyndon Johnson announced that he would not be a candidate for president in the upcoming election. The nation was stunned; liberal Democrats and antiwar protesters were elated.

The euphoria proved short-lived. Martin Luther King's assassination a few days later, and the wave of rioting that followed in over a hundred cities around the country, was a grim reminder that the social optimism of the early 1960s was not going to be easily restored. The liberals themselves could not agree on a common candidate or strategy for the upcoming election. Many McCarthy supporters resented Kennedy as a Johnny-come-lately trying to horn in on a political opportunity that he had lacked the courage to create for himself.

Michael disagreed. He embraced Kennedy, feeling that he had "the better possibility of uniting the white working class and the black poor and of thus bringing middle class liberals and radicals into a genuine majority coalition."[95] Michael traveled to Indiana just as the primary campaign opened up there to give a previously scheduled speech at Butler University. In a press conference before the speech, he announced his support for Kennedy. Later that evening in a restaurant, he ran into Richard Goodwin, who he knew from the days of Shriver's antipoverty task force. Goodwin was sitting with Robert Kennedy and introduced the two men, who had not met previously:

> "Mike gave you a good endorsement today, Senator," Goodwin said by way of introduction. Kennedy thanked me and then Goodwin added, "He said he couldn't back Rockefeller [a candidate in the Republican primary] because he won't spend $150 billion on the cities." "My God," Kennedy replied with a smile, "you didn't say that I would, did you?"[96]

Kennedy bested McCarthy in Indiana, and the two contenders headed for the West Coast for further primary battles. McCarthy handed Kennedy a surprise defeat in Oregon, a state where Michael's conscience constituency had long been a force in Democratic party politics. In an effort to help shore up Kennedy's liberal credentials, Michael headed out to California in late May to campaign on his behalf, speaking on campuses in the company of such Kennedy supporters as the former SNCC leader John Lewis and the farmworker leader Cesar Chavez. For Michael, the presence of the three of them on a platform together—a white radical intellectual, a black civil rights activist, and a Chicano labor leader—symbolized the possibility that a

Kennedy campaign and presidency could be the making of a new majority coalition in American politics.[97]

Once again that spring, an assassin's bullet laid low the hopes of liberal reformers. Kennedy was slain on June 4 at the moment of his triumph in the California primary. Two days later, Michael viewed Kennedy's body lying in state in St. Patrick's Cathedral. SDS founder Tom Hayden was there too, weeping; it was the first time in years that he and Michael had turned out for the same event. Michael rode on the funeral train that carried Kennedy's body from New York City to Washington, D.C., where the newest Kennedy martyr was to be buried next to his brother in Arlington National Cemetery. Michael sat for a while with Daniel Patrick Moynihan, who in a mood of Irish fatalism declared, "By God, the only thing we do well is to bury our dead." Michael watched the crowds that had gathered along the tracks to witness the passing of the funeral train, sometimes singing, more often silent, many of them, he guessed, from the "other America," since "the affluent never live in sight of the tracks but the poor do." They stood along the tracks "mourning their own aspirations along with the man who had spoken for them."[98]

After Kennedy's death, Michael resumed his support for Eugene McCarthy. He campaigned for McCarthy in the New York primary, during which he took to quoting Charles Dickens's opening lines from *A Tale of Two Cities:* "It was the best of times, it was the worst of times."[99] Just before the Democratic convention, Michael took part in a McCarthy benefit at the hip New York night club Cheetah, organized by writers William Styron and George Plimpton. Among the authors reading from their works that evening were poets Allen Ginsberg and Richard Wilbur and playwright Arthur Miller. Despite the quality of literary talent represented in the room, Joe Flaherty reported in the *Village Voice* that "the most moving reading" consisted of Michael reciting from *The Other America:*

> It wasn't the words but Harrington himself that touched the crowd. While most of his generation is corrupted by the longing for power, or maddened by despair (a despair that certainly should be shattering to Harrington since he championed the two Kennedys), he remains constant to one goal—to change the lot of the poor in America. When he ended his plea, as usual, the audience was struck by the decency of the man.[100]

In Chicago, in August, the party regulars pushed through the nomination of Hubert Humphrey. Only eight years earlier, in what now seemed like ancient history, Michael and Tom Hayden had walked together on a peaceful picket line for civil rights outside the Democratic convention in Los Angeles—and both of them would have welcomed the nomination of the staunchly liberal Humphrey over the centrist John F. Kennedy. Now Hayden was leading antiwar protesters, some of them bearing Viet Cong flags, in bloody clashes with Mayor Daley's police. Michael, perhaps sensing disaster, stayed away.

Appalled by Humphrey's nomination, his temporizing on the issue of the war, and the blood shed in the streets of Chicago, many liberal Democratic voters decided to sit out that year's elections. Michael was not among them; now that Humphrey was selected as the Democratic candidate, he argued, liberals and radicals had to hold their noses and vote for him. It was, he wrote in *Dissent,* a matter of "straight lesser-evilism." It was true that Humphrey had been both an "enthusiastic booster of the horror in Southeast Asia" and "had shamelessly kind words for Mayor Daley after the police lawlessness in Chicago." Nonetheless, Michael chided those "middle class puritans" who planned to stay home on election day. The alternative was to "condemn the American people—and particularly the black, the poor, and the young—to four years of Richard Nixon."[101]

As Michael prepared to vote for Humphrey in November, he also sought to shore up the forces in the Democratic Party that had opposed Humphrey's nomination in the first place. In October, he helped found the New Democratic Coalition, an alliance of Kennedy and McCarthy backers who sought to wrest control of the party away from the regulars before the next presidential election.[102] Michael felt that Humphrey's victory at the Democratic convention and Nixon's victory in November were historical accidents that should not obscure the astonishing political progress of the liberal cause in the past year. Writing in *Dissent* just before the November election, he argued that whatever the final outcome would prove to be, the triumphs of the McCarthy–Kennedy forces in the spring of 1968 were no "transitory" phenomenon. Rather, they reflected "the growth of a college-educated constituency in which quantitative expansion may well have turned into something qualitatively new: a mass base for 'conscience politics.'"[103]

Michael took part in one other political campaign in 1968. It was a campaign far less consequential in the nation's history, but one of great importance in his own life. It was a struggle for control of the Socialist Party. Although the Shachtmanites controlled the party press, the LID, and the YPSL, they had yet to succeed in taking over the SP itself. That would change in July at the party' national convention, when after many months of careful preparation, the Shachtmanites secured a majority on the ruling national committee. They elected Michael as party chairman. With Norman Thomas hospitalized and clearly living his last days, Michael's election signaled his new status within the movement. When Thomas died in December, at the age of eighty-four, Michael contributed an obituary for him in the *Village Voice:* "Midwestern, with a heritage of Protestant conscience and a touch of Lincoln in his tall commanding presence," he wrote, Thomas was, "like Gene Debs, a man for whom socialism was personal and ethical." And now that he was gone, there was no one but Michael who could plausibly inherit the mantle of "Mr. Socialism," which Thomas had inherited from Debs.[104]

Ironically, however, Michael's real power in the Socialist Party was weaker after 1968 than before and would dwindle steadily over the remaining four years he stayed a member. Having used Michael's prestige for their own purposes, the Shachtmanites no longer needed him. He could go off and give his speeches; he could write his articles and books; he could preside at conventions and banquets. But he would soon learn that being Mr. Socialism in the public eye did not give him an equivalent, or indeed any, authority within the Socialist Party. In war, God tends to favor the side with the biggest battalions; in left-wing factionalism, He favors those who have paid staff positions at their disposal. There were no "Harringtonites" in administrative positions in the LID or the SP who could do his bidding—only Shachtmanites whose loyalties lay elsewhere, and who increasingly made no secret of their contempt for Michael. "I was standing out in front singing pretty songs, and they were in the backroom running the operation"—that's how Michael later characterized his role in the last years of the Socialist Party.[105]

Just how little influence he wielded became embarrassingly evident in the spring of 1969 at the LID's annual award luncheon. In 1968 the LID's "man of the year" award had gone to Ralph Nader, a choice that reflected Michael's desires to build bridges to issue-oriented liberal activists. In 1969, without consulting Michael, Tom Kahn offered the award to Hubert Humphrey. Irving Howe, a member of the LID board, wrote to Tom Kahn to protest his fait accompli:

> Let me begin with something that may seem strange to you. I think I should say: we are really against the war. Mike, I, the *Dissent* people. It's not just a matter, with us, of covering our left flank, or responding to campus sentiments, or cursing the war because it interferes with domestic needs, and breaks up potential domestic alliances. We think it is a reactionary war. Exactly what you and some of your close friends think on this isn't after all these years, clear to me. Are you really for the war but think it expedient not to say so? Are you against the war but think it inexpedient to say so? And to say that you have worked to bring the war to an end isn't a sufficient answer. Prowar people can have decided that is necessary. . . . I mention this, to repeat, because you must understand that we're not acting out of pique, but out of what we regard as a) principle and at least as important b) the intense difficulties that the LID action have created for Mike and myself in our little worlds.[106]

But of course, that was precisely the point of the award. The Shachtmanites wanted to create difficulties for Michael with liberals and others on the Left who despised Hubert Humphrey. In the end, Michael boycotted the luncheon, although he attended some of the panel discussions.[107]

Even in the face of provocation, Michael would not break with the Shachtmanites. He was, however, becoming bolder in his own criticisms of the war. In the fall of 1969, for the first time, he actually gave a speech at an antiwar rally, during the October moratorium against the war.[108] By the following January, he decided that the antiwar movement had been right to emphasize the demand for a U.S. withdrawal from Vietnam, rather than simply negotiations. "I believed that a negotiated settlement was the only way out of Vietnam," he confessed in an article in *Dissent* that month. Now, however, with the Saigon regime committed to "subverting even the possibility of a settlement," and with 40 percent of the American public favoring U.S. withdrawal, Michael decided that "only an American commitment to withdraw can make a negotiated settlement possible."[109]

The fact that the war in Vietnam was now being conducted by Republican Richard Nixon rather than Democrat Lyndon Johnson, made it easier for Michael to rethink old assumptions. He was also encouraged by the growing antiwar sentiments within the labor movement itself. A new antiwar group called Labor Leadership Assembly for Peace was first organized in Chicago in the fall of 1967 and began to chip away at the impression that Meany spoke for the entire labor movement in his support for the war. The decision by the UAW to withdraw from the AFL-CIO (for reasons other than the war) also undercut Meany's authority. And Walter Reuther finally came out against the war in 1969, joining his brother Victor Reuther and UAW secretary-treasurer Emil Mazey, who had been enthusiastic backers of the Labor Leadership Assembly for Peace. In New York City, Victor Gotbaum, president of the American Federation of State, County, and Municipal Employees (AFSCME) District 37, had long been outspoken in opposition to the war, and in May 1970 he helped organize a student-labor coalition that brought out 50,000 demonstrators to protest Nixon's invasion of Cambodia.[110] Michael had previously taken the AFL-CIO's conservatism in foreign policy as a given. But with antiwar sentiment breaking out within the labor movement, he began to reconceive the battle for "realignment." Perhaps in the process of realigning the Democratic Party, it might also be possible to do some realigning of the labor movement, with Socialists allying themselves with progressive unionists against the AFL-CIO old guard.

Michael was also heartened by political changes taking place within the Socialist International. Western European social democrats were growing restless with Cold War assumptions and policies. In West Germany, Willy Brandt led the German Social Democrats to adopt a policy of *Ostpolitik,* seeking openings to Eastern Europe and the Soviet Union, hoping that détente with the Communist bloc would in time open up the possibility for the reunification of Germany. Like most Western European socialist leaders, Brandt carefully refrained from any public criticism of the American war in Vietnam, though he felt it was a disastrous policy.[111]

The Swedish Social Democrats, in contrast, made no secret of their opposition to the war. Since the mid-1960s they had been providing asylum to American military deserters, and in the fall of 1969 Swedish prime minister Olof Palme compared the U.S. intervention in Vietnam to the Soviet invasion of Hungary in 1956 and of Czechoslovakia in 1968.[112] Michael had met Palme the previous summer at the Socialist International Congress held in England and had been very impressed. Palme was then forty-three, just a year older than Michael. Here he was, leader of the longest-ruling socialist party in the world, the one that provided its citizens with the most generous welfare state, and yet he was not afraid to speak his mind on an issue of conscience like the Vietnam War.

In the spring of 1970 Michael and Stephanie, at Palme's invitation, traveled to Stockholm. They arrived there on May 12, just a little over a week after four students had been killed during antiwar protests at Kent State University. Given the turmoil and violence in the United States, they were astonished with the casual circumstances that marked their meeting with Palme and his predecessor in office, Tage Erlander. They met in the entrance way of an office building in downtown Stockholm, where the two Swedish leaders were "unescorted, unguarded, apparently unremarked by passers-by, walking in the front door without any fanfare. No police were necessary." As the four of them rode up the self-service elevator together to the offices of the Social Democratic Party, Michael kept thinking, "Is this what being civilized really comes down to?" Upstairs, over coffee and pastry, they talked of the fall elections in Sweden and the war in Vietnam, marveling at Nixon's "politically disastrous" invasion of Cambodia.

Later, Michael attended a meeting at the University of Lund where Palme was scheduled to speak. Three thousand students crammed into a hall built to accommodate one-third that number. Palme entered, again alone and unguarded. For the next two hours he answered questions put to him by the students, many of them coming from a vocal and hostile Maoist contingent. When faced with the "inevitable accusation that he had sold out socialism," Palme replied that revolutionary parties around the world, "after making their violent revolutions," would send delegates to Sweden "to find out what to do." Michael was tremendously impressed. If the leader of the Swedish government could take time off to debate radical students and win them over to his own politics, how could he do any less back in the United States?[113]

But the euphoria of the Swedish visit did not last long after his return to the United States. American Socialists were preparing for their biannual convention in June, and Michael once again chose to ally with the Shachtmanites. Along with Penn Kemble, he drafted a resolution on the Vietnam War designed to paper over the chasm between the SP's pro- and antiwar wings. Its call for a "cease-fire and speedy disengagement from Vietnam" was so hedged with qualifications as to be meaningless. If the Saigon regime showed a willingness to consider democratic reforms, for example, then the pace of withdrawal should be slowed. At the same time, the resolution declared, the peace movement should demand that all North Vietnamese troops be withdrawn so that "it cannot be accused of encouraging or aiding a communist military victory in South Vietnam."[114] An alternative resolution, calling for unilateral U.S. withdrawal from Vietnam, was voted down by a three-to-one margin.

A despairing David McReynolds finally resigned from the SP. The "SP I knew," he wrote in his letter of resignation, had died long before:

> [It] would have been more decent had it been allowed to die a natural death. Instead, the shell, the title, have been taken over by those who do not share its traditions, and who have made of the SP an effective front for the establishment. Our hopes, back in 1958, for a new, broader party, bringing together the thousands of democratic radicals who had no home, proved foolish.[115]

When a sympathetic account of McReynolds's resignation appeared in the *Village Voice,* Michael wrote in to take issue. "In McReynolds' fantasy, the Shachtmanites are pro-war right-wingers and agents of Hubert Humphrey." Although he personally favored a "speedy, unilateral withdrawal" of all U.S. forces from Vietnam if the Saigon regime refused to reform, Michael defended the SP's compromise on the issue and even claimed that it set a standard for civilized debate: "Unless the entire Left learns to act in this spirit, then intransigent moralism will guarantee the victory of the Right."[116]

McReynolds responded the following week, addressing one last weary personal appeal to Michael:

> One of the reasons I privately urged Harrington not to accept the post of Party chairman at the June convention was that I knew he would inevitably be forced into a position of defending positions that are not even his own . . . and would no longer be a spokesman for a broad range of democratic socialists. . . . While Mike speaks well and writes well, he has very little clout within the Party of which he is chairman. . . . Irwin Suall,

Tom Kahn, Penn Kemble—they have clout and much more to do with shaping Party policy than Mike.[117]

And yet, even as Michael was helping the Shachtmanites retain control of the SP, he was finally coming to realize that he had less in common with them than with their factional opponents. After years of camouflaging their real views, the Shachtmanites came out in the open with a pro-war "Statement on Vietnam" that they circulated among the delegates at the June convention. Although they described their position as one of "critical support" of the war, it was hard to see where, if at all, they were critical of Nixon administration policies. The South Vietnamese, they declared, were fighting for "self-determination"; the issue in Vietnam was one of democracy versus totalitarian communism; a "real peace" required the defeat of the Communists; the South Vietnamese government should be provided with the level of aid that would allow "the maximum possible number of American forces [to] be withdrawn."[118]

This proved too much for Michael to let pass unanswered. In August he responded with a nine-page, single-spaced mimeographed rejoinder. The "Statement on Vietnam," he declared,

> is based on an abstract, ahistorical application of universal principles to an extremely complex reality. It would commit the Party to a principled support of American foreign policy in any conflict with Communism; it endorses the unconscionable and self-defeating tactic of supporting reactionary anti-Communism as a lesser evil to Communism; it offers no hope in Vietnam for either changing the regime or for peace.

In what sounded like an echo of the kinds of criticisms his position on Vietnam had received in the pages of the *Village Voice* over the past half decade, Michael took issue with the Shachtmanites for conjuring up an "abstract either/or world," in which the United States was imagined to be "defending 'self-determination' in South Vietnam":

> In the complicated reality, this country sent 500,000 foreigners to Vietnam and used its awesome air power to kill Vietnamese, i.e. the members of the very nation whose right to self-determination we are theoretically defending, and to attack a North Vietnam which is both Communist and the outcome of an armed struggle for national self-determination. This took place because, as a result of French colonialist, Diemist and Thieu-Ky policy, aided and abetted by the United States at every turn, a not inconsiderable segment of the indigenous nationalist sentiment became Communist or accepted Communist leadership.

If the United States remained committed to the policies embraced by both the Nixon administration and the signers of the "Statement on Vietnam," then, Michael predicted, "the killing in that impossible, unwinnable war which we never should have joined will go on." Comparing those consequences with the "possible risks" involved in an immediate U.S. withdrawal from Vietnam, Michael then declared, "I am ready, morally and politically, to accept the latter as an obvious lesser evil."[119]

Shachtman was furious, and from his perspective justifiably so. As he wrote to Rochelle Horowitz in September, Michael's criticisms were

> directed at the comrades whom he helped make the leadership of the Party at its recent convention when he already had their Statement [on Vietnam] in hand, and from whom he accepted the chairmanship of the Party; at the comrades who constitute the leadership of the caucus for which he was the spokesman at and before the convention; at still the same comrades with whom he found it desirable and possible to compose a common 'compromise' resolution on Vietnam, which he championed at the convention in opposition to the convention minority whose resolution was substantially identical with his own position, a fact which he does not find the space to acknowledge.[120]

From that moment on, Shachtman never again spoke to Michael.

Michael was now a pariah within Shachtman's newly renamed "Majority Tendency" caucus. Other socialists, particularly younger ones who shared his antiwar views, prodded him to break with the Shachtmanites. In the spring of 1971, the leaders of the Harvard and Tufts YPSL chapters sent him a pointed appeal: "We have been at a loss to understand how you can so consistently ally yourself with people who support a criminal war against the peoples of southeast Asia . . . a war which (to us this much seems desperately obvious) no socialist could support."

Describing Shachtman as "a man who has made a lifetime occupation of ravaging the left in search of followers prepared to embrace his momentary whims," they called on Michael to break with him and to take a stand within the SP "in support of your own publicly announced views on the war":

> The SP and YPSL have tried to pretend for the past six years that the war would quietly pick up and go away if only they ignored it. . . . The war remains the vital issue for the nation, for the left, for the party. We hope that the considerations of internal party politics which guided your past actions will be set aside in the interests of the overwhelming priority of the war.[121]

Whether it was this appeal—which, unlike most of the letters he received, he retained in his personal files—or the accumulated weight of insults he had been handed by his former allies, Michael was finally moved to action. At the end of June he sent a letter to a few long-time party comrades, including Carl Shier in Chicago and Julius Bernstein in Boston. The Shachtmanites, he wrote, were "feeling their oats":

> Whether they want to take over the Party completely and drive those of us who disagree out of the organization, or into inactivity, I am not sure. Thus far they have met very little resistance from us and they may simply be pushing as far as they can go and be prepared to retreat when challenged. . . . I don't want to conduct a factional war to the knife against them but to challenge them clearly and openly with the assumption that they can be won, or made, to accept real coalition politics.

Michael's own analysis of the dynamics of the Shachtmanite faction did not, however, offer much encouragement for the belief that they could ever be won to his vision of "real coalition politics":

> They constitute a world of their own in New York based on the Party and related institutions and the UFT. There is constant political and organizational contact during the day and social contact at night. They increasingly view political questions from an organizational perspective. . . . They have moved back from coalition politics to the concept of a labor party, i.e. of the trade unions as the only factor worth really taking into account and with the 'new politics'—the liberal and radical middle class—dismissed or attacked.[122]

In September, the SP's national committee considered a proposal to have the party merge with a small group of elderly Jewish social democrats known as the Democratic Socialist Federation (DSF). This was a group that had originally split with the "old guard" in 1936 and then refused to rejoin the SP when the Social Democratic Federation did so in 1957, because they remained suspicious of Norman Thomas's pacifism. Thomas's death removed that obstacle. It was clear to all concerned that if the DSF members joined the SP, they would shift the center of gravity in the organization even further to the right.[123] Michael suggested postponing the merger until after the next SP national convention, scheduled for 1972, due to "serious disagreements within the Party on the issues of Vietnam, electoral action and with regard to the very nature of the Party itself."[124] But he was voted down, as Tom Kahn and others counterattacked, accusing him of attempting to "disrupt and factionalize the Party."[125]

If Michael had taken his stand against the Shachtmanites in 1968 he would have found plenty of allies within the SP. But by 1971 most of his potential supporters had already voted with their feet. The first thing he had to do was to try to draw disaffected socialists back into the party so they could lend support to his new "Coalition Caucus." He wrote to old comrades to see if he could get them to rejoin. Debbie Meier and Bogdan Denitch, among others, signed up. Irving Howe, who had never formally joined the SP, proved a tougher sell. Michael reported to him in the fall of 1971 on his plans:

> At the last meeting of the SP National Committee we dissolved the Majority Tendency and began what will certainly develop as a faction fight in the period leading up to the 1972 Convention. I got involved in this with the greatest reluctance given both my personal predelictions toward writing and speaking rather than organization and a sense of weariness that, after all these years, one more internal hassle is necessary. And yet I think it has to be done. The coalition perspective is, I am more and more convinced, the only viable program for Left politics in America. . . . The problem is not that Tom, Penn and company have established such good working relations with the Meanyites but that they pursue that one strand of coalition policy with such a single minded fervor that they will drive everyone else away. In jargon, they are retrogressing to the old labor party perspective. And in foreign policy terms they are approaching the positions of the *New Leader* during the Joe McCarthy period.[126]

Howe responded sympathetically:

> I have the sense that in the last year they have gone rather berserk, in a kind of lemming fanaticism, no qualifications, no modulations. . . . What finally depresses me is their vulgarity of mind, and this I take to be a function of Max's desperation: his tacit conclusion that nothing is left in the world to stop the triumph of Stalinism except the U.S., and that only Meany-Lovestone see the need, etc. You are right, of course, in saying that they are resurrecting Cold War Socialism.

But Howe was not persuaded that any good could come from a faction fight within the SP: "Suppose you achieve your objective, and there is a balance of the two factions: will that be any good?"[127]

"Perhaps it is my eternal optimism," Michael wrote back,

> but I am still convinced of the essential rightness of the coalition perspective, that it is possible to beat Nixon and that, if that is done, there might be surprising possibilities. . . . And finally I guess there is an element of

sentimentality in my feelings: that I owe it to [Norman] Thomas and the whole tradition of the SP not to passively allow the Party to be turned over to those kinds of politics.[128]

In October Michael traveled to California to woo members of the "Debs Caucus" to back his cause. They were not, however, quick to forgive or forget Michael's role at previous SP conventions. As Harry Siitonen, a Debs Caucus member, wrote to him early in 1972, his call for resistance to the Shachtmanites "comes as a matter of too little and too late":

> It does little good to say, 'we told you so,' but all this might have been prevented as late as the 1970 Convention, if the antiwar wing of the Realignment Caucus had taken its stand then and had not agreed to caucus discipline on the key issue of Vietnam. . . . You yourself were the leading spokesman on the convention floor for the so-called "compromise" on Vietnam, which allowed the ultra-rights to seal their grip of control on the Party.

Despite his "considerable disagreements" with Michael, Siitonen still regarded him as the nation's "leading Socialist thinker, writer and lecturer. You are one of the few who has made an original creative contribution to Socialist thought in many years and you're recognized for it." But, in Siitonen's opinion, Michael's talents would be "utterly wasted" in any attempt to "salvage anything out of the insane viper's nest the SP has become." Instead, he urged him to create a "new Democratic Socialist organization in which you would . . . play a leading part."[129]

While Michael searched for allies, the Shachtmanites were not idle. In March 1972 they pushed through the merger of the Socialist Party and the Democratic Socialist Federation. One of the great advantages of the merger from the Shachtmanites' perspective was that it provided the occasion to demote their former factional ally. No longer SP chairman, Michael was now merely one of three cochairman of the SP-DSF, along with Bayard Rustin and Charles (Sasha) Zimmerman, a DSF member and vice-president of the ILGWU. "A New Day for American Socialism," proclaimed a banner headline in *New America* after the merger. "Prospects for growth," declared Irwin Suall, who chaired the unity convention, "are better today than at anytime since the 1936 split in the Socialist movement."[130]

One of the things the Socialists had going for them in 1936 had been a leader who, to the public at large, symbolized the socialist cause. By creating a ruling triumvirate for the new SP-DSF, the Shachtmanites may have imagined they were tripling their visibility. But Rustin was not widely known as a socialist, and outside of the readership of the *Jewish Daily Forward,*

Zimmerman was not known as anything. Only Michael had a real claim to the role of America's leading socialist. A few weeks after the merger, John Lester Lewine, a veteran of forty years in the party, wrote to the newsletter of the Boston SP Local to express his dismay at recent developments in the party:

> Whatever reservations some comrades may have concerning some of Com[rade] Harrington's actions and views, his importance to the S.P. is incommensurable. No one in the U.S.A. approaches him in importance. He is 'Mr. Socialism U.S.A.' in the seventies, just as Eugene V. Debs was in 1917, Morris Hillquit in 1920 and Norman Thomas from 1932–1965. That doesn't mean that any of those comrades was flawless, nor immune to criticism. Loyal and informed socialists differed with all of them—and frequently were right! But they were all absolutely essential to the party's image and growth. To discard Com. Harrington—or to place him in such a position that he could not function properly—would be an act of unforgivable folly.[131]

While the contending forces within the SP prepared for a final showdown, a much larger political drama was being played out nationally. Senator George McGovern of South Dakota had picked up the antiwar banner that Eugene McCarthy carried in the 1968 primary and this time was carrying it to victory over party regulars like Hubert Humphrey. Michael had originally supported Maine senator Edmund Muskie's bid for the nomination, feeling he would be the strongest candidate the Democrats could put up against Nixon. But when Muskie dropped out in March, Michael switched to the McGovern camp.

The Shachtmanites, for their part, had pinned their hopes initially on Senator Henry (Scoop) Jackson of Washington, a hard-line anticommunist known as the "Senator from Boeing" for his support of defense spending. A number of yipsels enlisted in Jackson's campaign and Tom Kahn signed on as a speechwriter. Then when Jackson dropped out of the race later that spring, the Shachtmanites switched their support to their former favorite, Hubert Humphrey.[132]

In May, Michael informed the SP's national secretary, Joan Suall, of his intention to endorse McGovern's candidacy for the Democratic nomination. Suall wrote back urging him to delay the announcement, since, "There are serious political implications for the Party and the YPSL involving an officer's endorsement at this time when only 2 candidates are battling it out—Hubert Humphrey and George McGovern," particularly in terms of potential impact on "our allies . . . in the labor movement." Since Bayard Rustin had already announced that he intended to give his personal endorsement to Humphrey, Michael made it clear to Suall that he felt under no obligation to keep his own preferences secret.[133]

In June, McGovern defeated Humphrey in the California primary and secured his nomination. McGovern's triumph was the product of a transformed liberalism. Liberals no longer shied away from the idea of crusades and mass movements, as they had in the late 1940s and through the 1950s. Nor was there any shortage of new movements with which they could ally themselves: Growing organizations promoting civil rights, civil liberties, environmentalism, and feminism, among a host of other worthy causes, competed for their attention. The new party rules adopted after the 1968 convention, plus a widespread resentment among rank-and-file Democratic activists against the old party regulars, worked to McGovern's advantage. The number of women and minority delegates selected for the nominating convention tripled from 1968 to 1972; the number of delegates under the age of thirty increased tenfold. The delegates to the 1972 convention were also inordinately well educated; nearly 40 percent of them held postgraduate degrees. The conscience constituency was coming into its own.

Michael's concern was not simply in helping McGovern win—like every other astute observer of American politics in 1972, he realized early on how unlikely that outcome would prove come November. Rather, he hoped to establish a working relationship with those who secured McGovern's nomination, as the SP had failed to do with McCarthy and Kennedy supporters in the aftermath of the 1968 campaign. "McGovern's useful activists," Michael wrote in July in *New America,* "will be shaping America's politics for years to come and they are likely to remain left of center."[134] In a letter to Coalition Caucus supporters about the same time, he was even more enthusiastic:

> Some of us—myself most emphatically included—enormously underestimated the potential of the new strata as the McGovern campaign so clearly shows. In retrospect it is clear that we should have been in that McGovern campaign from the start. In saying this I do not want to suggest that the future is rosy: they still might steal the nomination from McGovern; and if he gets it Nixon could beat him, and even beat him big (though I tend to discount the Goldwater analogy). It is also true that he might win. In either case . . . we can see a huge constituency open to our ideas.[135]

Michael's other concern was to help the McGovern forces heal the breach with traditional Democratic constituencies, especially the unions. On its face, that should not have been a difficult task to accomplish, since McGovern was probably the most pro-union nominee the Democrats had ever chosen to run for president. Trained as a historian before entering politics,

McGovern had written his doctoral dissertation about the "Ludlow massacre" of 1914, an important occasion in labor's chronology of martyrdom; when it was revised and published as a book in 1972 it carried the dedication "To the American Coal Miner."[136] Once in Congress, McGovern rarely deviated from labor's legislative agenda, earning a 93 percent legislative rating from the AFL-CIO's Committee on Political Education (COPE). And the platform his supporters adopted at the Democratic convention in Miami included a host of progressive proposals long supported by the labor movement, including national health insurance.[137] But McGovern's antiwar stance, and the fact that he owed labor nothing for his nomination, made him anathema to George Meany. For the first time in its history the AFL-CIO declined to endorse the Democratic presidential candidate, proclaiming official neutrality in the race between Nixon and McGovern—notwithstanding the fact that just four years earlier Meany had declared that Nixon's election as president "would be a disaster for the ordinary people of this country."[138]

The twenty-seven-to-three vote for neutrality in the AFL-CIO's executive council was testimony to Meany's personal power within the labor movement; but the fact that unions representing nearly half of the AFL-CIO membership subsequently endorsed McGovern on their own was equally powerful testimony to the growing split within the movement. Among the "McGovern unions" in the AFL-CIO were such powerful political players as the Machinists, the Communications Workers, and the American Federation of State, County, and Municipal Employees. The United Auto Workers, which had split with the AFL-CIO in 1968, also strongly backed McGovern's candidacy.[139]

For a dozen years the Shachtmanites had fought within the SP for the position that radicals should help realign the Democratic Party leftwards. Now that the Democratic Party had taken a decisive leftward shift, supported by the unions that had the strongest ties to progressive and even socialist traditions, they did everything they could to contribute to the defeat of the party's presidential candidate. Tom Kahn, who had signed on as a speechwriter for George Meany after his stint with Senator Jackson, wrote the anti-McGovern speech that Meany delivered to a convention of Steelworkers unions in September. One of the lines became legendary in socialist circles because of Kahn's resort to gay bashing. "We listened for three days to the speakers who were approved to speak by the powers-that-be at that convention," Meany said to the Steelworkers, following Kahn's script:

> We listened to the gay-lib people—you know, the people who want to legalize marriage between boys and boys and between girls and girls. . . . We heard from the people who look like Jacks, acted like Jills, and had the odor of johns about them.[140]

On a slightly more elevated level, *New America* missed no opportunity to denigrate McGovern's candidacy: Typical headlines included "McGovern Underestimates the Communists" and "Jewish Voters Disaffected from Democratic Ticket" In the fall, the newspaper carried "An Open Letter to George McGovern" from one-time Marxist philosopher Sidney Hook, arguing that "Nixon is the Lesser Evil" in the presidential race.[141]

At its September meeting the SP's national committee voted to "endorse" McGovern. But their statement of endorsement was reminiscent of the Shachtmanites' Negotiations Now strategy within the antiwar movement, which is to say that it was intended to undermine the cause it ostensibly served. Supporting McGovern like the proverbial rope supported the hanged man, the SP national committee decried his "neo-isolationist and conservative" foreign policy and denounced the "authoritarian leftist" and "elitist and anti-labor" groups allegedly supporting his candidacy. David Selden, an SP member and president of the American Federation of Teachers (soon to be ousted from that post by Al Shanker) wrote to SP leaders to protest:

> George McGovern is the closest thing to a Socialist to run for President since Norman Thomas. Instead of trying to ape the inane official AFL-CIO policy, *New America* should fulfill its Socialist function by calling for a restructuring of the labor movement to make it more representative of the principles of progressive unionism.[142]

In his own letter to Coalition Caucus supporters, Michael described the SP's position on the presidential race as a "shamefaced, negative statement of an unfortunate preference for McGovern." The Shachtmanites were "not simply objectively taking a pro-Nixon line; they are subjectively, consciously and enthusiastically for McGovern's defeat."[143]

Two weeks later, on October 14, Michael sent a "Dear Bayard and Sasha" letter to his fellow chairmen of the SP-DSF, announcing his intention to resign publicly from his chairmanship the following week:

> At the recent meeting of the Party's National Committee I discovered that the Majority was split between those who are straightforwardly for McGovern's defeat—and therefore for Nixon's victory—and those who privately share that attitude but, for tactical reasons, are unwilling to state it publicly.[144]

On October 22, Michael publicly announced his resignation, decrying the fact that "the historic party of Eugene Victor Debs and Norman Thomas is today doing the work of Richard Nixon."[145]

On November 7, Nixon won his expected landslide, taking better than 60 percent of the popular vote and the electoral votes of every state except Massachusetts. Nixon's supporters included a majority of Catholics, a majority of blue-collar workers, a majority of members of union families, and more than a third of registered Democrats. Of the traditional Democratic constituencies, only blacks and Jews remained loyal to McGovern. The "Goldwater analogy," rejected by Michael that spring as he considered McGovern's prospects, in the end proved appropriate.

The Shachtmanites rejoiced. The 1972 campaign could not have gone better from their perspective, given the entrée it wound up providing them to the highest levels of the union movement and to the conservative wing of the Democratic Party. Their talents were now recognized and put to use. Tom Kahn became George Meany's executive assistant and from there would move on to become director of the AFL-CIO's foreign affairs department. Penn Kemble became executive director of the Coalition for a Democratic Majority, a newly organized advocacy group for the anti-McGovern wing of the Democratic Party that was closely tied to the AFL-CIO hierarchy. Al Shanker, who had served as an early and important patron for the Shachtmanites, later paid tribute to their "tough political education": "They know they will never attain power electorally. So they learn other things—how to caucus, organize factions, draw up policy papers, handle ideas. It's a good training ground for politics."[146]

The only thing tempering the joy of the Shachtmanites as 1972 drew to a close was the fact that Max Shachtman himself was not there to witness the victory. Shachtman died of a heart attack on November 4. Tom Kahn mourned his passing in the pages of *New America.* How ironic, Kahn mused, that Shachtman should die just at the moment when the "full fruits of his achievements" in the "reunification and reorientation of the democratic socialist movement" were being realized.[147]

In a feature article in the *Wall Street Journal* early in December, reporter James Ring Adams described Michael's resignation as chairman of the Socialist Party as "a turning point in the recent history of the moderate American left." It was "the successful first skirmish of a mounting attack against the New Politics . . . on such traditional liberal fronts as the intellectual community, the labor movement and the Democratic Party itself." Ring's article drew extensively on his interview with Kahn, who sneered at Michael not only for his political misdeeds but for the company he kept: "Mike is part of the Jimmy's crowd. [Jimmy's was a bar on Sheridan Square.] That's where the *Village Voice* crowd, the [Bella] Abzugites, the New Classniks hang out."[148]

Later that month the Shachtmanites held yet another party convention. They cemented their victory over the SP's left wing by renaming the group Social Democrats, USA (SDUSA). Michael was among the minority voting in opposition. SDUSA spokesmen claimed 18,000 members; in reality, total membership was perhaps 1,600. From 1960 to 1972 Socialist membership had increased by 600—and that figure included a number of members who were just waiting for Michael Harrington to make up his mind about what he would do next before they sent in their resignations.[149]

"What conclusion does one draw from this sad little history?" Michael asked in his 1973 memoir, *Fragments of the Century,* after recounting his losing battle with the Shachtmanites:

> Many radicals would, I am sure, say that it all goes to prove that when a socialist mixes in capitalist politics, he is selling out and has taken the first step down the slippery slope that leads to conservatism. Nonsense. The vocation of a radical in the last portion of the twentieth century is to walk a perilous tightrope. He must be true to the socialist vision of a new society and constantly develop and extend its content; and he must bring that vision into contact with the actual movements fighting not to transform the system, but to gain some little increment of dignity or even just a piece of bread.[150]

Though saddened that some of his "good comrades fell from that tightrope," Michael did not see any reason to re-evaluate his own commitment to creating a "left wing of the possible" within the Democratic Party. But in the years that followed, he did rethink his own role in the 1960s, particularly in the antiwar movement, and found himself to have been in the wrong. Socialists, he wrote in one of his last reflections on the topic,

> had been quite wrong to demand small group standards of political correctness in what must inevitably be the ideological sloppiness of a huge mobilization. We should have acted . . . like everyone else: speaking our mind from the podium even though we differed, sometimes significantly, from those who talked before and after us.[151]

The political costs of that mistake were heavy ones—for Michael, for the cause of democratic socialism, and for the antiwar movement. In his response to the central issue of the 1960s, Michael let pass the chance of a lifetime to make a democratic socialist perspective relevant to the hundreds of thousands of Americans who supported the antiwar movement. On one occasion, speaking before a large audience of student radicals at Cornell University in 1971, Michael failed to make many converts to his own brand of pragmatic radicalism. Yet, as one of the unpersuaded New Leftists in the audience that day wrote later in the student newspaper, Michael is "a man whom you want to like and agree with."[152]

The Vietnam War destroyed the Socialist Party, and with it Michael's chance to reshape and reinvigorate the entire democratic left in America. That it could have been otherwise is suggested by the fact that in the later 1960s and early 1970s, the sharpest prodding and most telling criticisms that Michael faced came not from the New Left, or from those sections of the Old Left cherishing pro-Communist sympathies, but rather from those with whom he shared organizational affiliations and political assumptions. As a young Socialist Party member named Hendrick Hertzberg wrote in a letter to Harrington in 1972, "Vietnam is the kind of basic litmus test that Stalinism was twenty and thirty years ago. . . . If the SP is no longer in any way an important organization, that's only because it has misplaced its soul."[153]

CHAPTER TEN

Starting Over, 1973–1980

"Who knows? Maybe we can yet do something!"

Irving Howe to Michael Harrington
July 13, 1973[1]

In the spring of 1973, Daniel Bell wrote a letter to Irving Howe, chiding his fellow New York intellectual for having abandoned a "literary sense of 'complexity'" when it came to understanding contemporary social issues. In particular, Bell urged Howe—and his comrades at *Dissent*—to abandon the habit of treating controversies over federal welfare policy as a kind of morality play, with liberal champions of antipoverty programs cast as heroes and their conservative opponents as villains. The tone of too many pieces in Howe's quarterly, Bell argued, sought to imply that

> "we" ("we happy few") do know the answers. But the fact is that the liberal-left does not. Its strength is a moral attitude in which it stresses priorities for the disadvantaged and the exploited, but to assume that because one has a moral strength, a practical solution follows, is false. The fact is that what the '60s programs showed is that nobody had any answers, and that everybody was sliding from program to program with no knowledge of what would work. . . . Mike Harrington [was] on the Shriver antipoverty task force, but if Mike would come out of his closet he would have to admit that he had no program, and that his fallback was always, spend more money. And that is not the answer. Money does not change social habits, repair broken families, give better education, etc.[2]

Howe passed Bell's message on to Michael. Bell had long been a figure to be reckoned with in Michael's life, serving as a kind of skeptical political conscience for him. In the early 1950s, Michael had wrestled with Bell's famous judgment that the failure of American socialism derived from "its very statement of goal and in its rejection of the capitalist order as a whole," a stance that meant that it "could not relate itself to the specific problems of social action in the here-and-now, give-and-take political world." For the next decade Michael had sought the formula by which socialists, who were, in Bell's terminology, "*in* but not *of* the world," could somehow act effectively to change that world in the "here-and-now"—and do so without abandoning their vision of an eventual and profound transformation of economic and social relations. His search for the proper balance of pragmatism and principle led him to write *The Other America* in 1962, to join in the deliberations of the war on poverty task force in 1964, and to pursue the strategy of creating a coalition within the Democratic Party that could function as "the left wing of the possible." Surely all that should have proved that he was willing and able to take a stand *in* the world that he was committed to changing.

But now, some twenty years later, Bell was once again calling him otherworldly, moralistic, and impractical—not because Michael clung to a sectarian vision of an anticapitalist utopia, but because he had allied himself with the indisputably "of-this-world" Lyndon Johnson in developing and promoting a war on poverty in the 1960s.

Bell's accusation that Michael's strategy for ending poverty came down to the call to "spend more money" had a familiar ring to it. On the day after his re-election in November 1972, President Nixon told a reporter that the failure of the Great Society in the 1960s had been the result of "throwing money at problems."[3] Conservative Republicans had been grumbling about costly boondoggles on behalf of lazy and undeserving welfare recipients since the New Deal era. What was new in the 1970s was the support that such views were beginning to receive from other quarters. A group of liberal intellectuals that included Bell, Nathan Glazer, Irving Kristol, Norman Podhoretz, and Daniel Patrick Moynihan played a particularly important role in the political legitimation of the conservative critique of welfare; these intellectuals responded to the upheavals of the 1960s by turning against beliefs and policies they had once helped promote.

Michael first took note of the phenomenon in 1970, and not entirely unsympathetically. After all, he shared with the group—if perhaps in milder form—their discomfort with cultural radicalism, their opposition to the confrontational politics of the New Left, and their fear of the antiwhite and anti-Semitic tendencies within the black power movement. When asked that year by a *New York Times* reporter to comment on a recent *Commentary* article by Nathan Glazer, in which the Harvard sociologist said that he no longer felt comfortable with the term "liberal" and would rather be known as a "mild conservative," Michael responded lightly: "I would give him absolution and tell him some of his sins are not necessary to confess."[4] Glazer had long been a man of the Left, and his ties to democratic socialists reached back to his days as a City College undergraduate in the 1940s; he and Michael had worked together as recently as 1968 as supporters of Bobby

Kennedy's candidacy in the California Democratic primary. Michael was hopeful that Glazer and others of like mind would come around once again to being good liberals, once the campuses and inner cities settled down (and indeed, despite misgivings, Glazer would support McGovern's bid for the presidency in 1972, as would Daniel Bell).

Within another couple of years, however, the rightward-evolving viewpoint of the group that Michael would dub "the neo-conservatives" ceased being a joking matter for him.[5] The neo-conservative intellectuals, many of whom were cosmopolitan New York Jews, had been schooled in the rigors of left-wing debate, and were formidable and sophisticated foes. The traditional intellectual Right tended to consist of economists and philosophers—along with the occasional hard-to-classify gadfly like William F. Buckley—and had lacked social scientists, who, for most of the twentieth century, had gravitated to the liberal or left-wing side of the political spectrum. But the neo-conservatives of the 1970s were masters of the language of public policy and thus well prepared to fight liberal advocates of the social welfare state on their own terrain.[6]

In an ironic twist, the neo-conservatives took Michael's notion of the "culture of poverty" and, turning it on its head, used it as an argument *against* pursuing a federal war on poverty. In *The Other America* Michael had argued that structural barriers to social mobility helped create and perpetuate a set of *symptoms*—low aspirations, drug and alcohol abuse, petty criminality, and the like—that distinguished those living in the culture of poverty from mainstream middle-class Americans. Neo-conservatives, in contrast, came to see in such attitudes and forms of behavior the operative *cause* for poverty, to which any systemic explanation of the obstacles to social mobility took second place. "The lower-class individual lives in the slum and sees little or no reason to complain," Harvard political scientist Edward Banfield declared in his influential 1970 study *The Unheavenly City*.[7] The typical "other American" in Banfield's account, far from being a helpless victim (and thus an appropriate object for sympathy and outside help), was instead the author of his own fate:

> He does not care how dirty and dilapidated his housing is either inside or out, nor does he mind the inadequacy of such public facilities as schools, parks, and libraries: indeed, where such things exist he destroys them by acts of vandalism if he can. Features that make the slum repellent to others actually please him.[8]

Nathan Glazer, Banfield's colleague in the Harvard sociology department, took this argument a step further in an article in *Commentary* in 1971, significantly entitled "The Limits of Social Policy." Glazer believed that the increasing reliance of poor Americans on the support provided by various federal welfare programs had served only to encourage the weakening of "traditional structures" like family, neighborhood, and church that previously had helped alleviate the burdens of poverty. "What keeps society going," Glazer wrote, "is that most people still feel they should work—however well they might do without working—and most feel that they should take care of their families—however attractive it might on occasion appear to be to desert them."[9]

The trouble with the poor, as the neo-conservatives saw it, was that they had adjusted to a condition of permanent dependency—on AFDC, food stamps, Medicaid, and other benefits provided by liberal bureaucrats. Those who professed to be interested in aiding the poor by means of expanding the welfare state were, in effect, the poor's worst enemies, fastening the shackles of degradation and demoralization upon them more securely than if they had simply been left alone.

President Nixon, among other Republicans, read Glazer's article as confirmation of his own long-standing doubts about the wisdom of the welfare state. Within the Democratic Party as well, neo-conservatives began to find a sympathetic hearing, particularly within its moderate and conservative wings. Searching for a way back into the White House, prominent Democrats concluded that their party's public identification with the cause of the poor and minorities was proving to be a losing electoral proposition.[10]

Michael was personally acquainted with many of the leading apostles of neo-conservatism. A few of them, like Irving Kristol, were old adversaries and thus easy to dismiss. Until very recently, others had been political allies. Michael always tried to separate political disagreements from personal relations—in part because he was not a hater by temperament, and in part because he recognized that given the cycles of political fashion and debate this year's opponent could become next year's ally. So in responding to apostates like Glazer, Bell, and Moynihan, he went out of his way to concede their "decency and intelligence."[11]

But if he was prepared to be civil, he was not prepared to give ground on the substantive issues raised by the neo-conservatives. Beginning in 1973, and for the remainder of his life, he regarded his ongoing debate with the neo-conservatives over the lessons to be drawn from the history of the war on poverty as his most important political priority. It was a battle he fought with genuine zeal, not only because he was convinced of its intrinsic importance, but also because it was a battle he was free to fight with a clear conscience and a sure grasp of his position—the two things that had eluded him in the years when the Vietnam War had dominated the political terrain.

Michael may have had Bell's 1973 letter in mind when he wrote an article later that year for *Dissent* on "The Welfare State and Its Neoconservative Critics." "The experimentation of the Great Society programs in 1964 and 1965 does not prove, as many assume, that the Government failed because it tried so much," he contended. "Rather it illustrates the penny wisdom and pound foolishness of getting everyone excited about an imminent utopia and then investing funds that . . . are not enough for a modest reform."[12] The war on poverty was a failure not because the government had thrown money at problems but because (and here he delighted in quoting a comment by Daniel Patrick Moynihan from his book *The Politics of the Guaranteed Annual Income*) the "social reforms of mid-decade had been oversold, and . . . underfinanced to the degree that seeming failure could be ascribed almost to intent." The overwhelming bulk of increased federal spending on social welfare from the mid-1960s through the mid-1970s was for programs that benefited the middle class rather than, or as well as, the poor—chiefly Social Security and Medicare. The budgets for those two programs alone increased by just under $45 billion in the 1960s. In contrast, the Office of Economic Opportunity, the chief disburser of funds targeted for the war on poverty, limped along on an average annual budget of just over a billion dollars a year, between its formation by Johnson in 1965 and its dismemberment by Nixon in 1973.[13]

Michael also challenged the neo-conservative assumption that the consequences of government action were, "more often than not, unintended and usually negative." According to neo-conservatives, government programs fostered a dependent, hustler-like mentality among the poor, rather than stimulated them to efforts to improve their own lot in life. Thus neo-conservatives argued that means-tested programs like Medicaid (federally subsidized health insurance for poor people) had the collateral effect of discouraging the poor from seeking the jobs that would lift them out of poverty. Once they began earning their own independent income, they would have to pay for health coverage from private insurers—and the loss of Medicaid would be enough to discourage some welfare recipients from seeking out and accepting employment. That there was some truth in this argument, Michael readily conceded. Those among the poor capable of functioning as rational economic actors could only be expected to play the hand dealt them to their own greatest relative advantage. But this was not an example of the federal government attempting to do too much, as the neo-conservatives would have it. Rather, it served as a perfect illustration of the kinds of consequences to be expected from the self-defeating timidity of America's "pinch-penny" social welfare programs. If the United States provided national health insurance to all its citizens, like most other western democracies, there would be no disincentive for advancing from poverty to self-supporting employment. The negative economic consequences of Medicaid were thus "not the result of the immemorial frailties of the human condition, but of our own conscious, perverse, and reversible political decisions."[14]

Michael did not want to be boxed into a narrow defense of the Great Society by the neo-conservative counteroffensive. The vast expansion in AFDC rolls in the 1960s and early 1970s was not his idea of enlightened social policy—though in the absence of more ambitious federal efforts to promote full employment it remained a necessary evil. For both practical and political reasons, he much preferred government programs that worked to benefit all Americans, rather than those targeted for the poor—especially since for many Americans the categories of poor and non-white had come to seem one and the same. Programs that "deal with the special needs of blacks and other minorities" would work better, and enjoy greater support, Michael believed, if they were "designed so as to raise the living standards of others, the white working class in particular." Government programs to promote full employment, for example, bettered "the bargaining position of all workers," while improving "the relative position of the most vulnerable more than that of any other group."[15]

The limitations of existing welfare programs did not, however, justify the neo-conservatives' "preference for the unplanned, and even the irrational, as opposed to conscious government policy." In reality, Michael concluded, "the failures of the welfare state in recent years are the result of its conservatism, not its excessive liberalism or, more preposterously, of its radicalism."[16]

Michael's defense of the welfare state was both spirited and nuanced—but hardly popular. The very fact that he offered it in the pages of *Dissent* (circulation 5,000) rather than in any of the mass media outlets that had been available to him in the heyday of the Great Society was a good illustration of how much the political climate had changed in the past decade. Attacks on social programs by neo-conservative intellectuals and the politicians who promoted their views struck a responsive chord with an electorate increasingly prone to mistrust anything proposed by the federal government, from the war in Vietnam to the war on poverty. According to public opinion polls, the percentage of Americans who agreed with the statement that they could trust the government in Washington "to do what is right" declined from 76 percent in 1964 to 54 percent by 1970; by 1980 the figure would drop to 25 percent.[17] Voter cynicism and apathy were evident in declining turnouts for national elections. In 1972 the turnout fell five percentage points from the 1968 level, and it continued to drop steadily over the next decade. The decline was greatest among lower-income groups most likely to have a stake in social welfare programs. And the Democrats, as the party identified in the public mind with big government, saw their support erode among the reduced number of Americans who still bothered to go to the polls. In the mind of many voters, liberal Democrats had become the partisans of "special interests"—not just welfare recipients, but blacks, feminists, the elderly, and labor bureaucrats—whereas it was Republicans who spoke confidently in the name of unifying national interests and purpose.

Given the shifting tide of political sentiment, and given his own rough treatment at the hands of long-time comrades in the Socialist Party, this would seem to have been a logical moment in Michael's life for him to reevaluate his socialist commitments. In an era when it was becoming hard enough to defend liberal welfare programs on their own merits, why should he make the job even more difficult by doing so as a socialist? The man who discovered poverty, now widely acknowledged as one of the nation's leading public intellectuals, wasn't going to fall back into obscurity simply because he was no longer chairman of the Socialist Party or its equivalent.[18] Why then continue to put up with the organizational headaches, petty intrigues, and dreary squabbles of the ideological Left, and why provide his enemies with a convenient way of misrepresenting his beliefs, when he might accomplish as much—and likely more—acting as an independent social critic?

But there is no evidence that Michael ever gave serious thought to abandoning either his socialist vision or affiliation. He had no desire to strike out on his own as an "independent radical," a category of political actor he regarded with some disdain. Perhaps it was a measure of his religious background and training that still affected his outlook: As he liked to say of himself, "you can take the boy out of the church, but you can't take the church out of the boy."[19] Protestants can, if need be, worship and serve God on their own (and many prefer to do so); a Catholic needs infrastructure. Politics was not just a question of belief for Michael—it demanded a commitment to building institutions and to defending traditions. Giving people a radical analysis but failing to give them a cause to commit themselves to, an organization to join, some way of applying their analysis to solving short-term problems and imagining long-term alternatives, seemed to Michael inadequate if not irresponsible.

He acknowledged in a 1974 article for the *Nation* that most Americans continued to associate the word "socialism" with "totalitarianism, foreign ideology [and] atheism." Still, he argued, there were politically compelling reasons why liberals and socialists alike should cooperate in dispelling such illusions, for as long as socialism remained a taboo word in American political discourse, the possibilities for far-reaching and effective liberal reform would also be hampered:

> American anti-socialism . . . helps create self-fulfilling prophecies which are extremely useful to the conservative cause. If the public is persuaded that the private sector, with its managed desires, its built-in obsolescence, its enormous unpaid social costs, is the realm of freedom, then politicians

> will see to it that the public sector is as underfinanced and shoddy as possible. Which of course then proves the public sector is bad, the private sector good.[20]

Like many of Michael's pronouncements on American politics, this sounded better in the abstract than it did as a practical guide to, say, getting elected to office. Was it really worth accepting the immediate disadvantages that attached to the socialist label, for the hypothetical gains that he assured liberal readers would eventually ensue? If pressed, Michael would likely have conceded the difficulties involved in this course in the short run; but at the same time he would have maintained the value of sustaining a transcendent vision of political justice and equality in the long run.

In the introductory chapter of *The Politics at God's Funeral*, published in 1983, Michael discussed the implications of eighteenth-century philosopher Immanuel Kant's argument that God's existence cannot be proved:

> So God is not the basis of morality, for morality rests upon reason, and reason cannot demonstrate that God exists. He is, rather, a *postulate* of morality, a being who gives us cause to act upon the categorical imperatives of the conscience. One acts "as if" God were there.[21]

Socialism for Michael had become a kind of Kantian categorical imperative, as well as the core of his political and personal identity. To satisfy the demands of conscience, "one acts 'as if' God were there," one acts *as if* socialism were a real possibility. Socialism was also a compelling narrative, just like the biblical account of the teachings and actions of the Judeo-Christian God. It offered Michael a place at center stage in an enduring historical drama; it gave him a sense of connectedness with a heroic (if tragic) past and with an uncertain (but hopeful) future still unfolding. This was not a fanatic's faith, for it had no impending apocalyptic or millennial deadlines attached to it; Michael had no illusions of seeing socialism in his lifetime, nor did he believe that the movement represented the inevitable outcome of great historical forces. Socialism was a process, rather than a result, and there was never going to be a final moment of triumph when the red flag was raised over the prostrate capitalist foe.

But neither was the world static and unchanging. The accumulation of thousands of small and often hidden changes in politics, in economics, and in culture would some time or another add up to a transition—if not a revolutionary leap—to a qualitatively different world, where human existence was governed not by necessity but by freedom. He took this belief on faith, because no better proof was available, and he believed it wholeheartedly.

Michael's personal commitment to the socialist cause had, by the early

1970s, taken on what he described as a "Pascalian cast"—the same term he had used to describe his return to the church in 1951. Just as he had passed through a crisis of religious faith and found that he still wanted to be a Catholic in the early 1950s, now he passed through a political crisis and found that he still wanted to live his life as a socialist. Both decisions required him to make an "existential wager" with the universe. "Socialism is still beginning," he wrote in 1973, "a task to be accomplished, not a destiny to be awaited."[22]

So persuaded himself, there was nothing to do but start over and to try to build yet another organization to take the place of the now defunct Socialist Party. Accordingly, at his invitation, a hundred or so people met on a Saturday in early February 1973 at New York University for the start of a weekend-long conference on "The Future of the Democratic Left." By Sunday's sessions, which moved to a seedy welfare hotel on New York City's West Side, only a few score of stalwarts remained. But this "defeated remnant of a defeated remnant," as Michael would describe them, included some of his longest-standing and closest associates—Irving Howe, Debbie Meier, and Bogdan Denitch were among their number. As a cohort of veteran radicals, they were linked by common history and strong friendships and unfazed by the prospect of starting organizationally from scratch. Their only serious disagreement came over the question of what to call themselves. Feeling that they had lost the franchise on "Socialist Party," they finally agreed upon an alternative—the Democratic Socialist Organizing Committee (DSOC).[23]

The designation "organizing committee" conveyed a deliberately modest self-evaluation: It was meant to suggest a group that would be involved in an ongoing process of innovation and transition, rather than one that was setting up shop as a fully defined entity. At the same time, for radicals of a certain vintage, the name carried with it echoes of the heroic days of the Left in the 1930s, when, as the ground troops for new industrial unions like the CIO's Steel Workers Organizing Committee, young socialists of various ideological stripes set out to conquer the antilabor bastions of corporate America.[24]

Having settled the issue of what to call themselves, the group elected Michael as DSOC chairman and agreed to hold an official founding convention in the fall. Then, in a gesture Michael found both appropriate and a little embarrassing, the founders of this newest venture on the Left closed their meeting by singing the old socialist anthem "The Internationale." "That is how revolutions go forward sometimes," Michael wrote in his 1973 autobiography, "in such ridiculous settings, sometimes among just a few people."[25]

One thing was certain. This was a revolution that was going to have to be fought on a shoestring. Jack Clark, a former UMASS–Amherst student who had been part of YPSL's minority antiwar faction, became DSOC's entire paid staff. He worked at first out of a spare room in Debbie Meier's Upper

West Side New York apartment, and later from a tiny basement office just down the street (when the sewer connection for the building above them backed up, which it did frequently, work would have to be suspended). DSOC's monthly newsletter (a biweekly newspaper like that published by the SP throughout the 1960s was way beyond their means) made its first appearance the following month, with an appeal from the new chairman to his readers to help build "the left wing of realism."[26]

DSOC's first organizational priority was, by necessity, that of recruiting, so Michael set off that spring on a familiar mission, a speaking tour that took him to Chicago, Detroit, Grand Rapids, New Haven, Stony Brook, and Washington, D.C. He sold the new organization to potential recruits with a rhetoric of pragmatism, lightly tinged with prophecy. "We stand chastened by the past, but look hopefully to the future," he wrote in the spring in a brochure advertising DSOC's upcoming convention. "We identify with the tradition of Eugene Victor Debs and Norman Thomas—with a socialism which is democratic, humanist, and antiwar," he wrote in a draft resolution to be voted on by delegates at the convention. "We are not an anointed vanguard. . . . We are a modest but hopeful new beginning."[27]

Given the political climate, the modesty in Michael's formula may have seemed more appropriate than the hopefulness. President Nixon's decisive re-election the preceding fall had drawn "the sixties" to a conclusive end. Publicly, the president pledged to use his second term to dismantle the federal initiatives in social welfare that had emerged during the Great Society (and that, with his acquiescence, a Democratic Congress had further expanded during his first term in office). In the privacy of the Oval Office, he swore vengeance on opponents and critics among the nation's liberals and radicals. (Among the names already assembled on a secret "enemies list" by White House Counsel John Dean for the president's consideration was that of Michael Harrington—a status that Michael was proud of when he learned of it in the summer of 1973.)[28] Although in January the Watergate burglars had gone on trial in Judge John Sirica's courtroom in Washington, and in February the U.S. Senate had established a Select Committee on Presidential Campaign Activities to look into the previous year's campaign abuses, the president was more popular at the start of his second term than at any other moment in his years in the White House, with polls showing 68 percent public approval.[29]

Meanwhile, potential opposition forces on the liberal and radical Left were on the defensive and in disarray. While McGovernite liberals licked their wounds, other Democrats laid plans for a purge of "New Politics" perspectives and advocates from the party leadership. The Shachtmanite-staffed Coalition for a Democratic Majority (CDM), which became the chief voice of neo-conservatism within the Democratic Party, was the best-organized of the anti-McGovern forces; shortly after the 1972 election, the CDM, in alliance with the AFL-CIO and backers of Senator Henry Jackson, ousted McGovern ally Jean Westwood as chair of the Democratic National Committee.[30]

To the left of the Democratic Party, the political situation was even more dismaying. The bloom had long since departed the New Left. SDS collapsed in 1969 in a final paroxysm of revolutionary posturing, scattering its 100,000 or so adherents to the winds. A few dozen of the group's most notorious veterans carried on as the "Weather Underground," setting off an occasional bomb in public buildings—inevitably inviting comparison with the isolated Japanese soldiers who skulked in the underbrush of South Pacific islands in the years after the Second World War. The legions of campus activists who made the 1960s forever synonymous with words like "protest" and "confrontation" were dispersing to graduate schools and professional careers, marriages and mortgages. "Where are they now?" stories about former student revolutionaries reinventing themselves as BMW-driving stockbrokers would soon become a media staple.

Looking back later on the early 1970s, Michael would claim that all he had then seen looming on the horizon was "a long miserable stay in the trenches." But that overstates his pessimism. In reality, he faced the mid-1970s with an exhilarating sense of new possibilities opening up. Nixon's coattails had proven remarkably short in November 1972, and Democrats retained healthy and liberal-oriented majorities in both houses of Congress—in the House they had held their losses to twelve seats, and in the Senate they had even managed to pick up two seats. From Michael's perspective, the liberalism of the early 1970s was vastly preferable to that prevailing a decade earlier. Liberals had abandoned their Kennedy-era commitment to "bear any burden and pay any price" in the Cold War; they had provided legislative and political substance to their earlier tepid commitment to the cause of civil rights; and they no longer regarded economic growth in and of itself as the chief solution to social problems. At its 1969 national convention, Americans for Democratic Action adopted a resolution calling for a "massive redistribution of wealth and power in America." Michael, who had become an ADA board member in 1970, probably had the group's 60,000 members in mind when he declared in 1973 that there were "more closet socialists in the Democratic Party than in all the socialist groups in the United States combined. It's time they came out of the closet."[31]

Michael was also hopeful about prospects for re-establishing good relations with New Left alumni and alumnae. He had bided his time since the late 1960s, waiting for the moment when the ultra-left enthusiasms of the younger radicals would fade sufficiently to resume dialogue. If the now "twenty-something" radicals were no longer to be found at the barricades,

Michael did not believe that they had undergone a mass conversion to the status quo. It was too much to expect that a majority of New Leftists were going to remain "lifelong militants," he wrote in 1973, but he still expected them to remain "affected positively by their youthful militancy all their lives." SDS was dead and gone, and no plausible successor organization had appeared on the scene; but across the country thousands of its former adherents were involved in burgeoning groups of radicals in the professions, in alternative newspapers and community organizing projects, in environmentalist and feminist groups, and even in the labor movement. At the local level, radical activists probably had stronger institutional roots than at any time since the height of Debsian socialism. What they lacked—and what Michael proposed to provide—was a national organizational presence and a unifying political perspective.[32]

Finally, Michael and his comrades felt optimistic because they at long last had liberated themselves from the burden of apologizing for the ever rightward migration of their Shachtmanite associates. Veteran Chicago socialist Carl Shier wrote to a friend in May 1973 that it was a "great feeling not to have to explain away our fellow comrades pro war Viet Nam position."[33] Even Irving Howe, usually the gloomiest of political prognosticators, allowed himself a rare moment of mild enthusiasm in a letter to Michael that summer. "Who knows?" he scrawled at the bottom of a note about Michael's contribution to an upcoming issue of *Dissent.* "Maybe we can yet do something!"[34]

At forty-five, Michael was no longer the "oldest young socialist in America." His hair was graying and his face lined, though tennis and a enviable metabolism kept him reasonably trim. His eyesight weakened, and he began to wear glasses (these served him well as a prop in his speeches; when he wanted to lay special emphasis on a point, he would whip them off and gesture with them at the audience). As a journalist noted in a profile of Michael for the left-wing magazine *Mother Jones* in the mid-1970s, the cover photos of Michael's books had shifted in recent years from that of "moody young militant in a blue denim jacket" to "urban academic in black trenchcoat and paisley tie."[35]

In addition to a slight spiffing up in his wardrobe, there were three major changes that took place in Michael's life from the late 1960s through the late 1970s. One such change was that for the first time since leaving the employ of Time-Life in 1950, he found himself holding what the outside world would consider a real job.[36] Friends like Irving Howe, who had long worried about Michael's financial prospects, lobbied Joe Murphy, the newly installed president of Queens College, on his behalf.[37] Queens College, part of the City University system of New York, was in the midst of an enormous expansion in its student population, having grown from 5,000 students in the early 1960s to nearly 35,000 by the mid-1970s, making it the third largest college in New York State. The student body was mostly white and working class of Jewish, Irish, and Italian backgrounds, although it included an increasing number drawn from new immigrant groups like Koreans and Soviet émigrés. Whatever their ethnic origins, most Queens undergraduates were the first in their families to go to college. These were commuter students, many of them attending school part-time and working outside jobs to pay for their education.

Murphy, a tough-talking product of New York's Left (his mother Jewish, his father that rare character, an Irish working-class Stalinist), was happy to hire radicals to teach these students, figuring they had greater need to be exposed to politically unorthodox ideas than their more privileged peers at private institutions. And he didn't much care if his new hires had jumped through the conventional academic hoops. In recruiting Michael as a visiting professor in the political science department at Queens in 1972, Murphy overlooked the fact that Michael's highest academic degree was a master's in literature (in fact, he had never taken so much as a single course in political science in his years at Holy Cross or thereafter). A year later, Michael was appointed a regular member of the Queens political science department, and in 1975 he was tenured. "It never occurred to me that he could be persuaded to go permanently into academic life," John Kenneth Galbraith wrote in his letter of recommendation when Michael came up for tenure. "Queens College is to be credited with an imaginative stroke of the first magnitude."[38]

As Galbraith suggested, Michael was a distinguished appointment for Queens; in reflected prestige for the institution, he was well worth what he was paid. But by most accounts, including his own, he was no more than a dutiful professor. Apart from the days he was scheduled to teach, he was rarely seen on campus. His lecture courses, on topics such as "Power in America" and "Twentieth-Century Social Movements" were known among Queens students as "guts," with many recommended but few required texts, no exams, and few papers. Michael was well aware that he was providing his students with a credential not a worldview; the students who took political science lecture courses at Queens, he would write, were doing so "in order to get into law school, not to learn about the institutions of their country and the world."[39] Like most professors, he found teaching seminars a more gratifying experience, and although he scrupulously avoided recruiting from his classes, a number of his seminar students found their own way into DSOC. He felt that the best class he ever taught at Queens was an evening course in a labor studies program where most of the students were union activists. They pleased him with their willingness to "counter my theories with their experience."[40]

Michael's new career provided a welcome measure of financial security, including health benefits. It also allowed him to take his place within the ranks of the union movement as a member of the Queens College Local of the American Federation of Teachers (the only other time he had belonged to a union was a brief stint as a member of the American Newspaper Guild, while a writer-trainee at Time-Life). And, occasionally, his teaching and other interests coincided, as when a seminar he taught on religion and politics helped him sort out ideas for his 1983 book, *The Politics at God's Funeral.* But otherwise, the job at Queens was a sideline to his real life and interests. Colleagues at the DSOC office would kid him when students from his classes would call asking to speak to "Professor Harrington."[41]

A second major change in Michael's life was that he was now a father to two sons, Alexander, born in 1968, and Teddy, born in 1971. He was a loving parent but one who, having grown up an only child, hadn't quite bargained on the chaos that two small children could produce in the close quarters of a New York City apartment. Though he craved peace and quiet, he could not enforce it, for like his own father he had no inclination to be a disciplinarian: "He would sort of yell and scream and stamp his feet," according to his wife, "but he wouldn't follow up. He would say, 'Stephanie, do something.'"[42]

A young and growing family made life in New York City—heretofore among Michael's greatest joys—an increasing burden. The Harringtons moved three times in the decade after Alex's birth: first, in 1970, to an apartment on Perry Street and then again in 1976 to one on Mercer Street. Each time they wound up with less, not more, living space than in their previous residence. But the size of their apartment wasn't the only way in which life in the city was becoming problematic. Rents were skyrocketing; the schools were deteriorating; and life on the city streets was becoming more abrasive. Broken glass and dog droppings littered the streets; Alex and Teddy were harassed and sometimes mugged when they ventured outside alone; Michael himself was assaulted for no reason by an angry black man one day while on an outing with the boys. Nor could they escape reminders of the city's deteriorating state by staying indoors: Their apartment had metal shutters across the windows, and the insurance company would not agree to provide the Harringtons with renter's insurance until they installed a burglar alarm. This was not the benign New York whose late night streets Michael had roamed with impunity as a young man.[43]

In the summer of 1979, the Harringtons decided that they had had enough—a decision that led to the third major change in Michael's life. They packed up and moved to the suburbs—not to the fanciest suburb available to New York commuters (they deliberately avoided looking for houses in wealthy Scarsdale) but to the more modest, if still securely middle-class, community of Larchmont in Westchester County, where they purchased and moved into a two-story, three-bedroom frame house on a quiet street.

Michael's pending move to the suburbs soon became a matter of comment among both friends and enemies. One of Michael's strongest supporters in the New York City labor movement was Victor Gotbaum, who since 1965 had led AFSCME's District 37, which represented most of the city's public employees. Michael had been trying to patch up relations between Gotbaum and New York's recently elected Democratic mayor, Ed Koch, who was no longer the ardent liberal he had been when Michael first encountered him in Village Independent Democrats' loft on Sheridan Square in the early 1960s. When Gotbaum gave a dinner party in 1979 and invited both the Harringtons and Koch (and the mayor's frequent escort, former Miss America Bess Meyerson), Michael welcomed the occasion as an opportunity for some political fence-mending. Instead, the evening wound up in a loud and angry argument between Gotbaum and Stephanie over the morality of the Harringtons' flight from the city. Mayor Koch, Michael remembered, "seemed to enjoy the moment immensely."[44]

The *New York Post* ran a gleefully malicious story under the headline "Socialist Leader Flees to Larchmont." When Irving Kristol heard the news, he wisecracked that Michael's new political slogan should be, "Think Left! Live Right!" The story migrated to the editorial page of the *Wall Street Journal*, and elsewhere, each time with the same implied moral: America's leading socialist was just another hypocritical limousine liberal, full of sympathy for the poor but unwilling to spend any time in their proximity. Michael, rarely thin skinned in political controversies, couldn't seem to help sounding defensive whenever this topic came up—something it seemed to do at regular intervals for the rest of his life. "There are all kinds of people who think that, if you've written books on poverty, then you should be poor too," he complained to a reporter in 1987. "And that's garbage! Friedrich Engels was a businessman, for Christ's sake!" Even Karl Marx, after years of enduring urban poverty "eventually moved out . . . to the suburbs so that his daughters could find some eligible guys to marry."[45]

In the first months after the move, Michael pined for life in the city. Marty Peretz, publisher of *The New Republic,* suggested in 1980 that he write something about suburban living. Michael refused: "It is one of the more miserable experiences of my life," he responded to Peretz, "and I'm just not ready to commit an article." Among other complaints he had about his new residence was that "we have been utterly, completely and totally broke since we bought the damned house."[46] Within a few years, however, he began to appreciate the virtues of his semi-pastoral life, at least on a part-time basis. He enjoyed walking Humphrey, the family dog, in the quiet neighborhood streets and watching the leaves change in the fall. Michael could find dashing historical parallels in the most unlikely places: He once remarked to his son Alex that looking out his study window at the blue sky reminded him of how Trotsky would do the same from his fortified compound in exile in Coyoacan, Mexico.[47] Of course when this particular exile got tired of staring out the window, the city was only a pleasant half hour or so away by train. If anyone suffered from the move, as Michael himself acknowledged, it was Stephanie. She found herself in the not entirely congenial role of full-time suburban matron, without easy access to her own accustomed haunts and friends in the city. Michael, meanwhile, was out of town at least a hundred nights every year. When Pittsburgh DSOCers complained that Michael hadn't bothered to meet with them when he visited the city to give a talk at Carnegie-Mellon University, he responded with uncharacteristic testiness: "You should know that in this period I have been taking planes roughly three times a week and at almost every stop have met with DSOC members and locals. My family occasionally likes to see me and I do have some responsibilities to them."[48]

As his boys grew up, Michael drew closest to his eldest, Alex, who came to share his political and intellectual interests. Alex went off to Columbia University, where he studied Russian literature and acting and became a socialist activist himself. Michael was immensely proud when Alex was arrested in a campus protest. Teddy, on the other hand, was more involved in athletics than books and had little interest in his father's politics. Michael made an effort to spend time doing the things the boy liked, such as going to Yankees games (in high school and college Michael had been a sports columnist, and his interest in professional athletics was revived for the first time in years through Teddy's influence). Still, the youngest son grew up resenting his often-absent father. "In the suburbs," Teddy would recall, "everyone's dad was around going to their Little League games and football games. My dad was always out giving speeches, or teaching in Paris." It may have been Teddy, as well as Stephanie, that Michael had in mind when he confessed in *The Long Distance Runner* that his life-long love affair with "ideas and ideals" had come at a personal cost, since it meant there was "not too much energy left over for the intimacy and personal love that is supposed to be the essence of my imagined future."[49]

So it was as a gray-haired professor and father of two, and no longer as a young firebrand, that Michael presided over DSOC's founding convention in New York in October 1973. "Today we begin the work of building the seventies Left," Michael told the 400 delegates and observers in the ballroom of the McAlpin Hotel on West 34th Street at the opening session—the line was a sly if unacknowledged paraphrase of Lenin's famous greeting to Soviet delegates in revolutionary Petrograd in 1917, "We shall now proceed to construct the Socialist order!"[50]

Although the in-jokes in Michael's speech were derived from his sectarian years, his overall message embodied the militant moderation he had come to espouse in more recent years: "We must go where the people are, which is the liberal wing of the Democratic party," Michael told the assemblage. Radicals should get over their love affair with being principled losers: "Victory, even limited victory, is radicalizing. Defeat, even glorious defeat, convinces people you can't fight city hall. It is time to speak our own name in the Democratic party, to become a conscious visible presence." Most of all, he emphasized, it was time to put aside the quarrels of the 1960s and to unite all who could be brought together into the democratic socialist movement.[51]

If DSOC's 1973 convention did not exactly rival the 1917 Congress of Soviets of Workers' and Soldiers' Deputies in historical significance, Michael still had reason to be pleased by the gathering. The delegates included some highly prized luminaries from the union movement, including AFT president David Selden; Ralph Helstein, emeritus president of the Amalgamated Meat Cutters and Butcher Workmen; and Victor Reuther, the retired former international affairs director for the UAW. Helstein and Reuther were elected as vice-chairmen of DSOC, and Selden was elected to its national board. Despite efforts by DSOC's rivals in SDUSA to discourage attendance by members of foreign socialist parties, David Lewis, parliamentary leader of Canada's New Democratic Party, spoke to a convention-eve meeting, and the French Socialists, Swedish Social Democrats, and British Labour Party all sent fraternal greetings. Such gestures provided good harbingers for Michael's campaign, launched the preceding spring, to gain DSOC official recognition as a member-party of the Socialist International.[52]

In addition to the radical and labor veterans at the convention, there was a respectable turnout of young people. According to the *New York Times,* about half those in attendance appeared to be of college age, with contingents of students from Harvard, Yale, and Columbia.[53] Veterans of sixties radicalism were, for the most part, still keeping their distance from Harrington. But the New Left journal *Socialist Revolution* ran a favorable piece about the convention by historian Ron Radosh (himself a product of the Communist youth movement of the 1950s as well as of the New Left of the 1960s). Radosh called on New Leftists to "treat Michael Harrington and the rank-and-file of his DSOC as serious comrades who . . . are engaged in a task similar to ours."[54]

Grander political events worked to confirm Michael's political optimism. The revelations of the Senate Watergate hearings in the summer of 1973 fatally tarnished Nixon's reputation; the president's personal approval rating plummeted to 40 percent by July; and by the time of the DSOC convention, the nation was in the grip of the unprecedented constitutional crisis that doomed the administration. AFL-CIO president George Meany, who had made such a singular contribution to the president's re-election the previous year, now denounced Nixon's "dangerous emotional instability."[55] Democrats looked forward eagerly to the upcoming midterm elections in 1974, and the list of would-be Democratic presidential nominees for 1976 grew ever more crowded, including such liberal stalwarts as Sargent Shriver, Morris Udall, Birch Bayh, Fred Harris, and Frank Church.

Not only Nixon but "Nixonomics" were in trouble. Warning signs of economic difficulties had been mounting since the late 1960s: The United States lost a million manufacturing jobs between 1966 and 1971, the American economy posted an international trade deficit in 1971 for the first time in the twentieth century, and, unusually, both unemployment and inflation (the word "stagflation" yet to be coined) were on the rise in the early 1970s. Through a combination of wage and price controls and Keynesian stimulation (the Defense Department, for example, ordering a two-year supply of toilet paper in 1971), Nixon had temporarily managed to turn the economy around in time for the 1972 election year. But by 1973 such economic gimmickry was no longer sufficient to stave off mounting economic difficulties; unemployment and inflation reappeared, real wages and real family median income fell, as did productivity and growth rates. And to top it off, the Organization of Petroleum Exporting Countries (OPEC) launched an oil embargo in the fall of 1973 that led to dramatic increases in energy costs. The long postwar boom was at an end, and Americans knew it. By the end of 1973, 85 percent of those questioned in a Gallup poll expected economic hard times in the coming year.[56]

All of this seemed to bode well for Michael's strategy for building "a new majority for social change." Debate could now shift from issues that until recently divided Democrats—such as the Vietnam War—to the economic issues that had historically served as a unifying symbol for the party. As Michael argued in the *Newsletter of the Democratic Left,* organized labor and New Politics liberals alike should now "focus on what could unite them: full employment, including economic and social rights for the minorities; the Kennedy-Griffiths health insurance bill; a guaranteed annual income, etc."[57]

But Michael had not fully reckoned with the changes that the sixties had wrought in American political culture—changes from which even DSOC's founding convention would not prove immune. Although the public sessions that weekend ran smoothly, discord was building just below the surface. On the evening the convention adjourned, Michael and Stephanie went to a celebratory party at Debbie Meier's apartment. No sooner had he walked through the door than he found himself hustled into a back room by a group of disaffected women delegates and roundly chastised for gross insensitivity to feminist concerns. Although there were women like Debbie Meier and others involved in DSOC's nascent leadership, the proceedings of the previous two days had still been dominated by Michael's version of an old-boys network; the convention had not included a single female speaker on its program. Michael didn't emerge from the room until five hours later, to find the party over.[58]

The party was also over, in another sense, for the Marxist-inspired version of bread and butter radicalism with which Michael was most comfortable. Michael's rude introduction to the basic principles of feminism was a good measure of how his involvement in the Socialist Party had isolated him from some of the more significant political currents of the preceding decade; DSOC was now going through battles over women's issues that had been fought out in other quarters of the Left a half dozen years earlier. Whereas male leaders in the New Left had, rather famously, not always proved receptive to the new feminist consciousness, in the Socialist Party in the 1960s and early 1970s, even the women were usually indifferent, if not openly hostile, to the movement. In December 1970, for example, Socialist Party member Midge Decter debated feminist leader Gloria Steinem at a meeting sponsored by the New York SP Local. Decter declared flatly that the feminist movement "springs not from oppression. It arises from a desire to evade the responsibility that freedom entails. Women's lib allows some women to blame men for their own inadequacies." Michael didn't share Decter's overt contempt for the movement (which reflected her general hostility to anything associated with the "New Politics"); on the other hand, with women in the SP voicing such opinions, he wasn't exactly pushed to embrace the insights of feminism.[59]

In starting DSOC, Michael had assumed that his main rivals would be other Marxist-oriented groups (just a few months before DSOC's convention, a meeting in New York drew some 1,200 participants to a discussion of the need for a "new communist party"). In the 1970s, however, democratic socialists and Leninists alike faced a more profound challenge from radical groupings and tendencies that jettisoned the Marxist preoccupation with issues of class for a politics centered around questions of sexual, racial, or cultural identity.

The 1960s slogan "the personal is political" had served initially as one of the unifying themes of the New Left. Politics, as Tom Hayden and others had insisted from the very beginning of the movement, was more than a matter of elections and legislation; it was also a question of how individuals could live a satisfyingly "authentic" life. What the founders of the New Left had not foreseen was the way in which personal politics would bring questions of identity to the fore, eclipsing the universalist claims of previous radical traditions. By the mid-1960s, young black militants felt that they could no longer share organizational ties with their former white allies; by the late 1960s many radical women felt they had to separate themselves from the "male Left"; by the early 1970s the women's movement itself was riven with divisions along lines of race and sexual orientation.[60]

Michael was more than willing to list feminists, along with environmentalists, peace activists, and even gay rights supporters, among the supporters of his new progressive majority. But he worried that some of the issues these movements deemed most important, like abortion or gay rights, would prove divisive—and, in particular, scare off organized labor.[61] Nor, at the beginning of the 1970s, was he ready to concede that anything in the feminist indictment of male supremacy might conceivably apply to his own leadership within the movement.[62]

Over the next few years, DSOC took steps to increase the role and visibility of women in the organization, including adopting a provision in 1979 that 50 percent of all members of its national committee be women. By the 1980s Michael was capable of writing that "the most radical movement of our times has been the challenge to the most ancient form of oppression on the planet," the rule of men over women.[63] The fact that some sections of the labor movement were themselves becoming more sympathetic to the new social movements that grew out of the 1960s—as evidenced by the formation of the Coalition of Black Trade Unionists (CBTU) in 1972 (formed out of frustration with the AFL-CIO's "neutral" stance in that year's presidential election) and the Coalition of Labor Union Women (CLUW) in 1974—also made it easier for Michael to incorporate a broader conception of legitimate issues and concerns within his political vision.[64] Still, he remained an unreconstructed Marxist in many ways, for whom conflicts based upon class remained paramount. The trick, as he saw it, was to come up with issues vital to the interests of the labor movement that could also appeal to the Left's other constituencies.

DSOC's chairman was the first to acknowledge that the group was an inadequate tool for changing the world—all that he claimed for it was that it was better than the existing alternatives. Michael made a point of telling new, and especially young, recruits, that socialism was not coming anytime soon. What they could hope to accomplish in their lifetime was the re-creation of a viable and ongoing socialist movement and tradition in the United States. And, for a few years at least, they and he seemed to be succeeding in that goal. DSOC counted about 500 members at the time of its founding convention in 1973; by the end of the decade that number had increased eightfold. Finances improved sufficiently to allow DSOC to move into a larger office, located, per tradition, in New York City's Union Square. And enough young members had joined by 1975 to justify the creation of a DSOC Youth Section, which within five years would grow to a thousand members with organized chapters at thirty campuses.

DSOC was never simply a vehicle for Michael Harrington as, say, the Rainbow Coalition was for Jesse Jackson. Michael regularly found himself on the losing side on issues, small and large, in DSOC's internal debates. But that he was DSOC's primary attraction was clear to everyone involved. Skip Roberts, a Vietnam veteran, union organizer, and Democratic Party activist who joined DSOC in 1973, was proud to identify himself to fellow trade unionists, or anyone else, as a "Michael Harrington socialist": "I could take Harrington out and sell him. Nothing to be ashamed of, or try to hide. You can point out, 'that's right, I'm a socialist because of Michael Harrington.'"[65]

Joe Schwartz, a Harvard graduate student in political science who would join DSOC's national staff as a Youth Section organizer, described Michael as a "totemic" figure for the group:

> Here was the touchstone of the socialist movement. Here was the place you got the sense that you were part of something significant. People in the Youth Section used to bring their parents to hear Mike speak to validate their beliefs. You know, "I'm not a nut. Here is a person of real substance, who's on TV, who is taken seriously by the mainstream media. You see, we're not crazy."[66]

Mike did look good on television, and over the years he learned the art of the ten-second sound bite. In the 1980s, when he was invited to become a weekly commentator for National Public Radio's *Morning Edition,* he mastered the art of delivering a two-and-a-half-minute commentary on current events. But what really set him apart was his ability to deliver an old-fashioned hour-long speech; he was, as DSOC colleague Harold Meyerson recalled, "the last white boy in America who could give a speech."[67]

Peter Mandler, another DSOC youth activist in the late 1970s, developed a keen appreciation of the craftsmanship that went into a typical Harrington speech. As he took the podium, Michael would invariably announce that he would be making three points, whatever the topic or occasion, and then go on from there. "The three points were the basic structure," Mandler recalled:

> Into that structure could be plugged, modularly, virtually any sub-argument that he had at any point in recent memory packaged up for himself. He was very confident that the world cohered—"Marxism is a science," was one of his favorite ironical aphorisms—and each sub-argument, if appropriately selected, could just slot down into one of the three points. Sometimes the sub-arguments would string together into a long digression—and you could see him pause at the end of such a string, look down at the index card with the three points, take a little breath, and effortlessly shift back onto the main track. It was a talent which made anyone who ever organized a meeting for him fall instantly in love with him. It was so reassuring. You never had to worry about failure or a lapse, and, incidentally, it made you too feel that the

> world cohered, and that our moral position within the world both made that coherence obvious and indicated an immediate program of action.[68]

Michael's speeches mixed analysis and passion in equal measure. He ended many of them by slightly misquoting Martin Luther King at the rally on the steps of the Alabama state house in the spring of 1965: "The moral arc of the universe is long, but it bends towards justice."[69] The effectiveness of any given Harrington speech could be measured in applause—and in the number of potential recruits he left behind for DSOC organizers to sign up. One young woman who heard Michael speak on a college campus in 1980, apparently as part of a class assignment, recorded her reaction in a handwritten essay that her teacher later forwarded on to him. "I feel the most important thing I learned from Mr. Harrington's speech is that it is time for me and others like me to open our eyes and start participating in our countries government," she wrote with equal measures of political innocence and enthusiasm:

> I have never taken the time to sit down and study what is going on within our system. . . . Mr. Harrington's speech scared me into opening my eyes and my mind to what is going on around me. He showed me that through all the complicated reteric of government (which is what I hated and therefore turned my back on the full picture) that there is a basic underlying system that our country is functioning in. One that he feels is standing in place for the few elite and crushing the rest. . . . Mr. Harrington has done his "homework" and it is about time that I (and others) do ours. With Mr. Harrington and others out there like him, why haven't the people noticed them and give themselves a chance to learn the most important thing of their life: how our system works to govern.[70]

The possibility that this particular listener's reaction was colored by a desire to win the approval of a left-leaning professor can't be excluded (although ungraded, the essay bore the teacher's written comment "Very Good"). But if so, that too was simply a measure of new political opportunities opening up for Michael's message. Unlike the later 1960s, when his over-thirty status, his moderate views, and even his ability to deliver a well-thought-out and coherent speech made him an object of suspicion to campus New Leftists, the 1970s were a decade in which Michael could win a sympathetic hearing from both students and the new generation of junior faculty, many of them veterans of sixties activism now beginning the long climb up the academic ladder. Michael was always nostalgic for the bygone Debsian days when the Socialist Party carried electoral clout in cities like Reading and Butte. As a personal presence, however, he was ideally suited for an era in which the political base for radicalism, such as it was, had shifted to cities like Ann Arbor, Cambridge, Santa Monica, and Ithaca.

In between speaking tours, Michael wrote steadily. Between 1972 and 1989 he published twelve books, including two works of autobiography, two books on poverty, several works on socialist history and theory, and a study of the crisis of contemporary religious belief.[71] The books were widely reviewed, but their sales were disappointing, at least compared to the phenomenal success of *The Other America.* The best-selling book was *Socialism*, published in 1972, which sold over a hundred thousand copies in paperback, and influenced many readers with its argument that the "real Karl Marx" was a radical democrat, not a would-be dictator. But the rest of his books did not do nearly as well. The 15,000 hardcover sales for his 1976 work of political theory, *The Twilight of Capitalism,* was about average. Michael liked to joke that the elderly Mrs. Marx would chide her feckless son, "Karl, why do you keep writing about capital and never making any?"[72]

Perhaps a more telling indicator of the problem with his books was how quickly they went out of print. Many of them represented popularizations of the works of other Marxist theorists like Nicos Poulantzas, proving too dilute for the true *marxisantes* among his audience and too abstruse for everyone else. Michael's long-time publisher, Simon and Schuster, finally dropped him as an author in 1980. Even some of his closest associates felt that Michael was writing too much, too quickly. Irving Howe told him repeatedly that he should cut back on public speaking and devote more thought to his books, to no avail.[73]

But the books were important to Michael, evidence to himself that he wasn't simply a "socialist jukebox." He worked hard on them, rising at five in the morning to get in a few hours of uninterrupted reading and writing before the other demands of his days overwhelmed him. And the books brought him a certain amount of gratifying attention in the press and from the public; it was not uncommon after a speaking engagement for listeners to gather around and get his autograph on the latest Harrington publication.

And so, through the mid- and late 1970s, DSOC grew, slowly but steadily adding a campus chapter here, recruiting a union staffer there. That hardly made it a large or in any way representative organization; of its few thousand members, about a fifth were concentrated in New York City, and of those, more than half could be found residing in four contiguous assembly districts on Manhattan's west side.[74] Still, DSOC's growth seemed respectable to radicals whose formative political memories dated back to the 1950s. At Youth Section gatherings, Michael liked to tell the young delegates that it was "1958" all over again; after meeting with a group of radical activists at the

University of Michigan in 1979, he noted in an article for the *New Republic* that he felt "as if I had gone two decades into the past and was meeting again for the first time with Tom Hayden and Al Haber."[75]

For a year or so after DSOC's founding, Michael and his comrades searched for an issue and a strategy to make a name for the group; as DSOC staffer Jack Clark recalled, "We sort of kicked around trying different things."[76] They made their share of missteps. In response to the rapid rise in energy prices that followed the 1973 OPEC oil embargo, DSOC launched a campaign to impose government regulation on the oil industry on behalf of consumers, labor, and the environment. But if the oil companies would win few popularity contests with the American public in the mid-1970s, Michael's proposals found even fewer supporters. When he keynoted a "teach-in" at Columbia University on the energy crisis in the spring of 1974, the *New York Times* reported that only a few dozen of the already converted bothered to attend, while outside, on a warm sunny day, "hundreds of students frolicked, obviously more interested in solar energy than any crisis variety."[77]

In a more promising initiative later that year, Michael ran for a delegate seat from New York City's Seventeenth Congressional District (which included Lower Manhattan and Staten Island) to the first-ever midterm conference of the Democratic Party, scheduled for December 1974 in Kansas City. Much to his own surprise, he won—in part because of support from liberal Democrats in Greenwich Village, and in part because some of the conservative Irish Catholic voters on Staten Island took one look at his name on the ballot and concluded mistakenly that Michael must be one of their own.[78]

The midterm conference was a legacy of McGovern's triumph at the 1972 Democratic nominating convention. Liberal delegates had pushed through a resolution requiring the party to hold a national conference in two years time to discuss its position on the issues confronting the nation. The idea was to elevate discussion within the party to a more principled level than the usual political horse-trading. By doing so, the party's issue-oriented activists (the backbone of the McGovern candidacy) hoped to consolidate their influence vis-à-vis party officials, regulars, and machine politicians. Michael was delighted at the prospect the conference offered for nudging the Democrats a step or two along the way toward "something vaguely resembling a party," if not European-style ideological coherence.[79]

When Michael and fellow DSOCer Marjorie Phyfe Gellermann (appointed as an alternate delegate from Staten Island) headed off to Kansas City in December, they carried with them large bundles of a special issue of *The Newsletter of the Democratic Left* addressed to 2,000 fellow delegates.[80] Democrats were in an optimistic mood as they met in Kansas City, having witnessed the spectacle of Nixon's resignation the previous August, and having trounced Republicans in the congressional elections that followed in the fall (they gained fifty-two seats in the House and four in the Senate to add to their existing majority). A large field of contenders for the 1976 presidential election, many of them drawn from the party's liberal wing, attended the convention in hopes of securing supporters. But Michael warned the delegates to beware of overconfidence. One of the more troubling indicators visible in the 1974 elections was the extremely low voter turnout, with only 38 percent of eligible voters participating. Although this low turnout worked in the short term for the benefit of the Democrats, it was an "ominous trend" for the future. Something had to be done to re-involve ordinary people in determining the political direction of the country, and gloating over Nixon's downfall, however gratifying, was not going to do it. What the Democrats needed to do now, Michael argued, was to shift their fire to "Nixon's economic Watergate": the combination of rising inflation, declining real wages, rising unemployment, and declining economic productivity that had kicked in in the aftermath of the 1972 election. The United States, Michael declared, faced "the most severe economic and political crisis since the Great Depression." To lead the nation out of its economic doldrums, and at the same time to rebuild its own political fortunes, the Democratic Party was going to have to become "at least as imaginative and innovative as it was during the New Deal. Only now that the reform and accomplishments of the New Deal are part of the status quo, we must be prepared to go beyond them—far beyond them."

Among the specific measures he called on the Democrats in Kansas City to endorse were commitments to full employment, to shifting taxes off working people and the middle class and onto the corporate rich, to a crash program for the development of new energy sources, and to a cut in the defense budget, with the resulting savings "devoted to meeting social priorities."[81]

Kansas City proved a mixed success. The Shachtmanite-staffed Coalition for a Democratic Majority arrived at the convention bent on punishing the adherents of the New Politics. George Meany's political lieutenant, Al Barkan, sought to use the occasion to roll back the party reforms that had lessened the influence of labor officialdom in choosing the Democratic presidential nominee in 1972. They did not prevail, but then neither did Michael's side. There were, no doubt, many delegates in Kansas City sympathetic to Michael's call for a revival of the party's traditional support for social reform efforts. But whatever the merits of his proposals, he discovered that it wasn't enough to list them in a newsletter and expect supporters to come flocking. The regulars who ran the convention saw to it that few controversial issues made it to the floor, and those that did were deftly compromised.[82]

The DSOCers at Kansas City were there on their own. They had few ties or even acquaintances among the other liberal and radical forces represented at the convention. Michael and fellow DSOCer Gellermann felt distinctly lonely at a "socialist breakfast meeting" that they hosted for delegates one morning; practically no one showed up for an event that, as Michael later wrote, was the epitome of "our innocence and helplessness. . . . It was not enough, we realized, to be abstractly right. . . . It was also necessary to have something to do."[83] DSOC, in other words, was going to have to move from political advocacy to political organizing, if it had any hopes of influencing the "here and now" in the 1970s.

One year later, in December 1975, Michael, Marjorie Phyfe Gellermann, and Jack Clark sat down and laid plans for a campaign to influence the platform of the 1976 Democratic Party presidential campaign and, in doing so, to create an ongoing organized presence within the party for DSOC and its allies. As outlined in notes from their meeting, the new strategy would entail the following:

> Build a programmatic tendency of the democratic Left in the Democratic Party and related constituent organizations (women's movement, trade unions, etc.)
> Create a presence for that tendency at the Democratic convention
> platform cttee.[committee] fight
> floor fight like '68 peace issue fight
> getting some of the planks adopted
> having delegates, speechwriters, lobbyists, people testifying before platform cttee. identified with our program. . . .
> Getting DSOC members and locals actively involved in project[84]

Michael wanted to call this effort the "America Can" campaign—a rallying cry meant to suggest that, contrary to the neo-conservative gospel, the country's social and economic problems *could* be solved through resolute federal activism. Others objected to the boosterish ring to the slogan—and some thought it suggested nothing so much as the name of a container manufacturing corporation. In the end, DSOC adopted the strategy but renamed it "Democracy '76."

The Democracy '76 campaign (which went through another name change a year later to become "Democratic Agenda") allowed DSOC over the next several years to play a role far disproportionate to its numbers. As one commentator noted at the time, DSOC's 3,000 or so activists had managed to play a role in the Democratic Party roughly commensurate to that of the 300,000-strong American Conservative Union within the Republican Party. This was a measure both of DSOC's success and of American liberalism's disarray. Michael and his comrades were doing for liberalism what it could not seem to do for itself, which was to set forth a coherent response to the conservative attack on the welfare state.[85]

Crucial to Democratic Agenda's success were the ties that Michael had forged in recent years with the "McGovern unions"—the major industrial and public employee unions that had broken with Meany in 1972 to back the Democratic presidential candidate. The most important of these were the United Auto Workers, led by Doug Fraser; the American Federation of State, County, and Municipal Employees (AFSCME), led at the national level by Jerry Wurf and in New York City by Victor Gotbaum; and the International Association of Machinists (IAM), led by William Winpisinger. The fact that powerful unions were willing to work openly with a socialist group (and that Winpisinger actually joined DSOC, and became a vice chair of the organization) boosted DSOC's standing even with unions that had not backed McGovern. By the end of the 1970s the AFL-CIO's Building and Construction Trades Department was taking out ads in DSOC's newsletter saluting the organization, prompting *Business Week* to report that "Socialism" was "no longer a dirty word to labor."[86]

As an assistant to UAW president Doug Fraser, Don Stillman worked closely with Michael on projects like Democratic Agenda. He recalled that Fraser, and other top UAW leaders, had a "very positive, very supportive" attitude toward Michael that reflected their own and their union's history:

> They came of age in a period when the discussion over ideology had been a central part of trade union life and politics. They had a comfort level with the word "socialism" that came out of that history. And Mike was able to express his political philosophy in accessible terms that rank and file and secondary leadership people in the UAW could identify with. When you are doing trade union work as a daily matter, dealing with a hundred different crises, you don't have the luxury of thinking through economic planning and how it might serve working people. Mike had the time and ability to provide us with intellectual ammunition that we could appropriate in greater or lesser amounts. And, of course, his enemies were our enemies.[87]

AFSCME president Jerry Wurf had been a YPSL member while a teenager in Brooklyn in the 1930s, and he remained a lifelong admirer of Norman Thomas. Steve Silbiger, a DSOC activist in the 1970s and an AFSCME lobbyist, thought that Wurf supported Democratic Agenda because "Mike was somewhat of a nostalgia trip for him and marginally useful":

> Also, Wurf's big thing was tweaking the AFL-CIO. He hated the Shachtmanites; he hated Tom Kahn. He saw them as people who kept the labor

> movement behind, and as people who weren't as smart as he was—which was true. So this was a way of annoying them.[88]

Whatever motives led particular union leaders to provide the funding, Democratic Agenda quickly became a going concern, with an office, newsletter, and paid full-time staff, including Marjorie Phyfe Gellermann serving as its director. Five hundred people turned out for its kick-off meeting in February 1976 in Washington, D.C., to hear Winpisinger, Congressman John Conyers, and others call on the Democrats to be true to their traditional constituencies and programs. In his own speech to the gathering, Michael denounced two prominent "neo-liberals," Democratic governors Jerry Brown of California and Michael Dukakis of Massachusetts, as "deserters from the liberal Democrats . . . who compete with their old enemies in avowing their lack of faith in the capacity of this society to deal with the crises which are all but overwhelming it."[89]

At the start of 1976, the race for the Democratic presidential nomination was wide open. Michael gave his personal endorsement to Arizona congressman Morris Udall, but Udall and other liberals in the race soon faded, as dark horse candidate Jimmy Carter surprised party insiders with a series of early primary victories. Early on Carter had benefited from the support of the UAW and AFSCME—who saw him as the best way to derail George Wallace's popularity among southern Democratic voters. But for the most part he owed his triumph to a shrewd appreciation of the power of media, which anointed him "front-runner" after he made a stronger-than-expected showing in the Iowa caucuses.[90]

Michael was prepared to support virtually any candidate the Democrats nominated that year, except for Wallace. He put most of his political energy into the attempt, through Democratic Agenda, to shape the party's platform. And the issue to which he attached the most weight that year was full employment. In 1975, California congressman Gus Hawkins and Minnesota senator Hubert Humphrey had proposed a Full Employment and Balanced Growth Act, better known as the "Humphrey–Hawkins bill." The bill revived Franklin Roosevelt's 1944 pledge to guarantee a job to every American who wanted one. Bertram Gross, a DSOC member who had helped draft the original full employment bill of 1944 (adopted in diluted form in 1946) was one of the drafters of the new bill. And Hawkins, an influential figure in the Congressional Black Caucus, had been one of Michael's political allies in 1960 when he organized the march on the Democratic convention. The new bill was intended to add teeth to the 1946 measure, requiring the federal government to coordinate its economic policies to achieve "full employment," taken to mean an adult unemployment level of 3 percent or less. The bill went through several versions, each one less sweeping in its provisions than the last. But Michael became a strong advocate for Humphrey–Hawkins; whatever its shortcomings as policy, it made up for them in philosophy, particularly in its underlying assumption that employment was a "right" of workers, as precious as any other protected by the Constitution.[91]

Long before the Democrats met in New York in July for their convention, it was clear that, like it or not, Jimmy Carter was going to be their presidential nominee. Candidate Carter was not a fan of Humprey–Hawkins (though he eventually and grudgingly endorsed it). But Democrats were hungry for the victory they felt Carter could bring them in November, and liberals were hopeful that he could be nudged to the left once in the White House. George McGovern personally helped derail an incipient "anybody but Carter" movement among delegates at the convention—a generous political gesture considering the fact that Governor Carter had not supported his party's presidential candidate in 1972. And at the convention's rousing final session, Carter delivered an unabashedly liberal speech, describing himself as a died-in-the-wool Democrat in the tradition of Roosevelt, Truman, Kennedy, and Johnson. The evening closed with the delegates spontaneously joining in singing "We Shall Overcome," many of them with tears streaming down their faces.[92]

Carter made other gestures toward the party's Left, selecting Humphrey's fellow liberal from Minnesota, Walter Mondale, as his running mate. And he instructed his point man on the platform committee, Joe Duffy, to do what he could to satisfy the concerns of the Democratic Agenda caucus. As a result, the campaign platform the Democrats adopted in July was full of promises of support for full employment legislation and national health insurance, as well as of pledges to institute limits on defense spending and nuclear arms development—in Michael's judgment "probably the most liberal [platform] in the history of the Democratic party."[93]

Michael was a vocal supporter of the Carter–Mondale team in the fall campaign. He wanted to make sure that there would be no massive defection of Democratic voters on the Left, such as the one contributing to Humphrey's defeat in 1968. On the day before the election, he debated Socialist Workers Party presidential candidate Peter Camejo before a gathering of several hundred students at Queens College. The SWP clung to its traditional view that support for a Democrat—any Democrat—was a betrayal of socialist principles and could not be justified by the argument that Carter represented a "lesser evil." "The people that run this country can *always* find somebody else that's worse," Camejo told the audience. "They want you to stomach Carter, they put up Ford. If they want you to vote for Mussolini, they'll run Hitler." Michael, in rebuttal, dismissed the SWP's "revolutionary fantasies." Jimmy Carter was not the man he would have chosen as the Democrats' candidate, but Carter's program deserved support. The "actual working class" as opposed to the SWP's "imaginary working class" was going to vote Democratic in November, because it understood that "Carter is better for full employment, for national health, for tax reform, for all kinds of issues that affect our lives."[94]

Michael was right about the election's outcome, but he was on shakier ground in interpreting the source of Carter's victory. Carter, he wrote soon after the election, "owes his victory to a coalition of trade unionists, blue-collar workers, blacks and Hispanics (particularly the Chicanos in the Southwest), lower-income voters, liberals, city dwellers and the like."[95] Neither Carter nor most political analysts agreed with Michael's assessment. Whatever concessions he may have made on platform issues at the Democratic convention, Carter understood that his real appeal in this first post-Watergate election was his status as an "outsider," untainted with close association with Washington's traditional movers and shakers—including its liberals. The other credentials that were vital to his victory were those of being a white southerner and pious Baptist: Although a majority of white southerners voted for Ford, Carter offset Republican strength in the south with a strong showing among "born-again" Christians; that, plus a solid black vote, gave him the edge he need to carry ten of the eleven former Confederate states in the election.[96]

Once in office, Carter proved a throwback in Democratic politics to the pre-New Deal era: a moralist and technocrat, more concerned with efficiency than equality, he was a kind of latter-day version of an early twentieth-century Progressive. Eliminating government waste engaged his interests far more than any possible expansion of the welfare state bequeathed him by his predecessors. In the name of efficiency, he launched an antiregulatory drive midway through his administration, deregulating the transport and phone industries, whittling away at the hard-won environmental and occupational safety gains of the previous decade. And given the unpalatable choice in economic policy between reducing unemployment at the risk of increasing inflation (the instinct of his liberal advisers), or doing the reverse (the instinct of his conservative advisers), he much preferred the latter. By 1978, he was committed to a conservative, monetarist approach to solving the inflation problem through higher interest rates.[97]

In January 1977, as Carter took his oath of office in Washington and DSOC met in Chicago for its third convention, all that was in the future. DSOC's meeting was a festive occasion. There was no more "remnant of a remnant" rhetoric to be heard. Many of the delegates felt that they had turned a corner in the past year with the adoption of the Democratic Agenda strategy. The organization's membership was now over 2,000 and climbing. Journalist Henry Fairlie, who covered the meeting for the *New Re-*

public, wrote an article so fulsome in its praise that DSOC immediately reprinted it for distribution:

> They will bring to bear on Jimmy Carter the weight of his promises, for they believe in those promises, having in part been responsible for writing them into the Democratic party platform last year. That is all they are asking: that he should look to his own promises. I would not underestimate the political vitality of these people. I think they have an uncommon access to this administration; I think they are skilled at the electoral level, and skilled, then, in their impact on Congress and state legislatures; I think they are mobilizers, that their name is exact: *organizing* committee.[98]

Within a year, DSOC, along with the labor movement and much of the liberal community, had given up on the president they had supported in 1976. The trade unions were particularly disenchanted with the administration's lukewarm support for a labor law reform bill that would have streamlined National Labor Relation Board procedures. Facing waves of layoffs, plant-closings, and a sophisticated and well-financed union-busting campaign by major corporations, the unions were feeling besieged by the mid-1970s. Between 1974 and 1976 alone, unions lost nearly 350,000 members nationwide. Overall the percentage of the American workforce represented by unions declined from nearly 30 to just over 23 percent between 1970 and 1980; by 1978, the union movement began a long decline even in its absolute numbers, notwithstanding the entry of many millions of baby boomers into a steadily expanding workforce. [99]

The labor law reform bill was intended to help reverse that decline by making it easier for the unions to make use of the federal machinery set in place in the 1930s to guarantee workers' rights to collective bargaining. The bill passed the House of Representatives in 1977 but stalled and eventually died in the Senate, due to staunch corporate opposition and to the Carter administration's decision to delay a vote on the measure pending ratification of the controversial Panama Canal Treaty.[100] After the bill's defeat, UAW president Doug Fraser resigned from a committee of union and business leaders devoted to encouraging labor-management cooperation, declaring that American business leaders had evidently "chosen to wage a one-sided class war."[101]

If this was class war, Carter had no intention of enlisting on labor's side. Wedded to the "outsider" strategy that had served him so well in 1976, he felt that he had more to gain by distancing himself from the core constituencies of the Democratic party than by investing political capital in helping them achieve their legislative goals.[102] On the first anniversary of Carter's victory,

Democratic Agenda staged a candlelight march on Democratic National Committee (DNC) headquarters to demand that the president honor his campaign promises. Carter ignored them.

The Democrats had another midterm convention scheduled for December 1978, this time to be held in Memphis. To prevent any controversial debates in Memphis that might embarrass the Carter administration, the DNC instituted a new rule requiring that one quarter of all delegates had to sign a petition to get a resolution on the floor of the convention, and such petitions had to be presented to DNC headquarters three days *before* the convention opened. With 1,613 delegates coming to Memphis from across the country, that seemed a secure bastion against a runaway convention.

But the party establishment hadn't reckoned on Democratic Agenda, which ran a virtuoso campaign to get its issues heard in Memphis. Marjorie Phyfe Gellermann and Skip Roberts ran a boiler room operation from New York City, contacting delegates and asking their support. Three years of political networking paid off, as Democratic Agenda tapped a deep anti-Carter sentiment within the party. Pledges of support flooded the Democratic Agenda headquarters. Four hundred and three was the magic number of signatures required; on the day of the deadline, Democratic Agenda had gathered four hundred and nine signatures on four separate resolutions. Roberts flew down to Washington to deliver the required signatures to the DNC just before the deadline. "The White House was just in a panic," Roberts recalled. "It was amazing. The party was so alien to them. They were really outsiders."[103]

The press scented a good story but sought to personalize it into a battle between President Carter and Massachusetts Senator Edward Kennedy, who despite denials was thought to be considering a run against Carter in 1980 presidential primaries. Carter press secretary Jody Powell denied to reporters that the Memphis convention would be the scene for a confrontation between the two: "The dispute which appears to be on the horizon in Memphis is not between the President and Senator Kennedy," Powell declared, "but between the Administration and the Democratic Agenda."[104] The blandly non-ideological nature of American party politics was, for once, facing a serious challenge from the Left. "If this were France," House Speaker Tip O'Neill declared on the eve of the midterm convention, "the Democratic Party would be five parties."[105]

Democratic Agenda's supporters caucused in Memphis on the eve of the convention. They sought to win approval by the convention of four resolutions challenging Carter's domestic priorities, including a call for national health insurance and for the creation of a government-owned gas and oil corporation on the model of the Tennessee Valley Authority. The most important resolution, however, focused on economic policy and was an unambiguous condemnation of Carter's record thus far:

> The problems which confronted this nation in 1976 have not been solved, yet it appears that the fiscal year 1980 budget will cut many social programs below "current services" levels, while allowing the military budget to grow. The proposed reductions, together with current economic policies, may well result in a recession and a rising unemployment rate in 1980—in direct violation of the Humphrey-Hawkins Full Employment Act.[106]

The Carter camp put their best people on the floor in a determined effort to head off political disaster: Hillary Rodham, wife of the newly elected Democratic governor of Arkansas, Bill Clinton, was among the Carter floor whips.

Although many Democratic Agenda supporters sported blue-and-white Kennedy for President buttons, the Senator himself did not arrive until the second day of the convention and spent only six hours in Memphis. It was Michael, along with UAW president Doug Fraser, who were the acknowledged leaders of the anti-Carter insurgents. Michael told Democratic Agenda supporters that "the road to victory in 1980 lies in implementing the 1976 platform."[107] But in the end, contrary to Jody Powell's prediction, it was Kennedy who stole the show. Carter had received a tepid response from the delegates when he addressed them on Friday. The Carter forces slotted Kennedy's speech to Saturday afternoon, figuring it would be the moment when it would receive the least attention. But when Kennedy spoke, he received a standing ovation for what the *Nation* called a "rip-roaring, stem-winder of a speech calling for national health insurance *now*."[108]

All four Democratic Agenda resolutions were defeated, but the margin was too close to give the Carter forces much comfort. In a front page analysis of "The Message of Memphis" on the day following the convention, *New York Times* political writer Hedrick Smith declared that

> the fact that nearly forty percent of the party's activists were willing to go on record against Mr. Carter on what John C. White, the Party chairman, made a virtual vote of confidence in the President, was firm indication of the schism that has developed between the White House and the liberal wing of the party.[109]

"It was an electric moment," UAW staffer Don Stillman recalled: "A sitting Democratic president had come quite close to a humiliating rebuff at the hands of his own party."[110] According to DSOC staffer Jack Clark,

Memphis was for Michael "a political fantasy come true." Here he was, after nearly twenty years of pursuing a "realignment" strategy, allied with some of the nation's top labor leaders in devising and carrying out a joint strategy for pushing the Democratic party leftwards.[111]

Unfortunately for Michael and his colleagues, it proved a Pyrrhic victory. Carter did not back off from his increasingly conservative domestic policies. The economy did slide further into recession. Ted Kennedy, emboldened by the response he had received in Memphis, moved into open opposition to the administration, and opinion polls through most of 1979 showed him trouncing Carter in the 1980 presidential primaries. Michael early on declared himself a supporter of a Kennedy candidacy.[112] But Kennedy stumbled badly in the opening days of his candidacy, appearing confused about his own reasons for running, other than fulfilling the family legacy. And, in November 1979, the capture of the American embassy in Tehran by Iranian militants, and the subsequent furor over the American hostages in Iran, guaranteed Carter's renomination at the 1980 Democratic convention.

For their part, the Republicans nominated former California governor Ronald Reagan at their convention that summer. Michael, who had so strongly argued that Carter was a "lesser evil" to centrist Republican Gerald Ford in 1976, seemed almost indifferent to the possibility that an ultra-conservative "greater evil" might take office in January 1981. DSOC refused to endorse Carter's candidacy. Environmentalist Barry Commoner was running as a third party candidate in the election, and Michael, who usually denounced such efforts as divisive and futile, took a benevolently neutral stance on his candidacy. He urged disaffected Democrats to vote but did not formally endorse either Carter or Commoner.[113]

Michael's political judgments that fall seem to have been influenced by his moment of triumph in Memphis. It was almost as if he had come to believe that the Democratic Party's midterm conventions were of greater importance than the presidential election. "If Carter wins in November," he wrote in October 1980, "he will be a lame duck president in 1982, unable to dominate the midterm convention as he did in 1978 at Memphis; if Carter loses, the internal structure of the Democratic Party will be wide open. In any case, if the Party's Left will take the 1982 meeting seriously, it should be able to win there and write its own program."[114] In the November 1980 issue of *The Newsletter of the Democratic Left,* writing before the outcome of the election was known, Michael urged DSOCers active in the Democratic Party to view the events of 1980 as a temporary setback; regardless of whether Carter or Reagan sat in the Oval Office come January, left-wing Democrats should emulate their opponents on the Right, and be "as aggressive as the Goldwater-Reaganists in the long march through the Republican party."[115]

The 1970s were fated to be a decade that few Americans would later feel nostalgic about. It was a confusing, muddled period that seemed to lack character and definition—at best, a petty "Me Decade" of self-indulgence, drift, and disillusionment. But for DSOC, the seventies had been years of triumph. Michael's brand of moderate, pragmatic radicalism seemed in the "here and now" of the Carter years to be working. In little over a half decade of effort, democratic socialists had established themselves as a force to be taken seriously within the Democratic Party. Having done so much better than they expected in the 1970s, Michael and his comrades were unprepared for just how badly things would go for their political project in the 1980s.

CHAPTER ELEVEN

Coming to an End, 1981–1989

I am not a Labor Leader. I do not want you to follow me or anyone else; if you are looking for a Moses to lead you out of this capitalist wilderness, you will stay right where you are. I would not lead you into the promised land if I could because if I could lead you in, some one else would lead you out.

Eugene Debs
1910[1]

If Michael seemed relatively indifferent to the prospect of a Reagan victory in the fall of 1980, the first year of the new administration served as a powerful stimulus to concentrate his mind. The president's inaugural in January 1981 was so devoted to the values and display of conspicuous consumption (Nancy Reagan's wardrobe alone cost $25,000) that it distressed some stalwart members of his own party. "When you've got to pay $2,000 for a limousine for four days," complained the Republicans' former conservative standard-bearer Barry Goldwater, "at a time when most people in this country just can't hack it, that's ostentatious."[2]

In his Program for Economic Recovery, introduced to Congress in February 1981, Reagan declared that the goal of his administration would be to "nurture the strength and vitality of the American people by reducing the burdensome, intrusive role of the federal government." The economic rationale that would guide the administration's domestic policies was known as "supply-side economics." If the tax burden was reduced, supply siders argued, then savings and investment (supply) would increase. The increase in capital in the hands of corporations and private individuals would in turn accelerate economic growth, and thus (somewhat counterintuitively) wind up producing *more,* not less, tax revenue. If the theory was correct, permitting the American people to pay less taxes would for the first time in decades allow the federal government to balance its budget. It was, in effect, the promise of a free lunch. Candidate Reagan promised that if he was elected president, the federal government would enjoy a balanced budget by 1984. Although some critics questioned the logic of the supply-side theory (before he gave up his own hopes of becoming the Republican presidential nominee, George Bush had called it "voodoo economics") and others charged that supply-side economics was merely an updated version of the old "trickle down" theory with the already wealthy as its greatest beneficiaries, many voters found it attractive.[3]

The 1980 election handed the Republicans control of the Senate as well as the White House and cut sharply into the Democratic majority in the House. Some of the most prominent spokesmen of Democratic liberalism, including Senators George McGovern of South Dakota, Frank Church of Idaho, Birch Bayh of Indiana, and Gaylord Nelson of Wisconsin, had been sent packing, and the survivors in both houses of Congress showed little stomach for resisting the new president's program. Within the first six months of his inauguration, Reagan gained congressional approval for his tax cut, accompanied by spending cuts of more than $70 billion for federal social welfare programs. AFDC and the food stamp programs each lost 14 percent of their funding in the first Reagan budget; social service block grants to states were cut 20 percent; child nutrition programs were cut 28 percent; and a public works employment program, CETA, was completely eliminated. Under toughened eligibility guidelines nearly 200,000 disabled people were dropped from the rolls of Social Security Disability Insurance by 1982. For the "other Americans" already tough times got that much harder. The poverty rate climbed from under 12 percent of the American population in 1980 to over 15 percent by 1983. Children were particularly hard-hit; two years into the Reagan administration over 20 percent of American children were being raised in poverty.[4]

In a speech to a standing-room-only audience at the University of Maine on the second anniversary of Reagan's inaugural, Michael described the president as "a genuine radical," the only American leader in recent memory to enact his campaign promises into law. That was "refreshing," Michael declared, paused, and then delivered his punch line: "It's unfortunate that the program he ran on was insane and cruel."[5]

The 1980s proved to be the 1960s turned upside down. In 1961 a charismatic young president took the oath of office, celebrating public service and sacrifice for the common good as the highest civic virtues. Kennedy may not have had much personal interest in domestic social reform, but he helped create a political climate in which a book like *The Other America* could find a hearing. In 1981 a similarly personable though much older president took the oath of office, proclaiming that government was the source of the American people's troubles and celebrating the relentless pursuit of individual wealth and advancement as their antidote.

These very different presidencies put the spotlight on equally divergent works of advocacy. Michael had authored the best known source of policy inspiration in the Kennedy/Johnson years; right-wing authors George Gilder and Charles Murray provided the equivalents during the "Reagan Revolution." Gilder's 1980 best-seller, *Wealth and Poverty*, a Book-of-the-Month Club selection that carried an ecstatic blurb from Reagan's budget director David Stockman, made the case for another set of "other Americans"—the nation's long-suffering capitalists:

> One of the little-probed mysteries of social history is society's hostility to its greatest benefactors, the producers of wealth. . . . There is something, evidently, in the human mind, even when carefully honed at Oxford or the Sorbonne, that hesitates to believe in capitalism: in the enriching mysteries of inequality, the inexhaustible mines of the division of labor, the multiplying miracles of market economics, the compounding gains from trade and property.[6]

Michael was not persuaded: "Gilder is long on crackpot anthropology," he commented in his review of *Wealth and Poverty*, "because he's short on economics."[7] Gilder's weakness for purple prose and his faith in Victorian generalizations about the nature of the sexes ("Money is far more immediately decisive in the lives of men than women, and women often fail to understand what is at stake among men at work")[8] would eventually turn his book into a rarely cited curio, even in conservative circles.

Far more influential in the long run was Charles Murray's 1984 book, *Losing Ground: American Social Policy 1950–1980*, a work of earnest analysis and passionate advocacy that came buttressed with sixty-odd pages of tables, footnotes, and bibliographic references.[9] Among its other features, *Losing Ground* abounded in references to *The Other America*. The 1960s were a time, Murray wrote, when "books became banners for causes." Michael had been the "pamphleteer" of the poor, "*The Other America* their Common Sense." In Michael's view, as Murray summarized it, "*Poverty was not the fault of the individual but of the system.*" Murray agreed. But *the system*, in his version, had nothing to do with the inequities or irrationalities of capitalism; rather it consisted of the "entire federal welfare and income-support structure for working-age persons," which worked in perverse ways to persuade the poor that it was worth more to them to collect welfare than to seek individual self-improvement. The solution Murray offered was breathtakingly simple—the abolition of the federal welfare state. This act of social "triage" would "leave the working-aged person with no recourse whatsoever except the job market, family members, friends, and public or private locally funded services."[10]

The same year that Murray published *Losing Ground*, Michael brought out a new book of his own entitled *The New American Poverty*. For twenty years he had resisted proposals to write a successor volume to *The Other America.* But in the face of the Reagan administration's claims that the extent of poverty in the United States was greatly exaggerated, Michael felt he had to respond. Poverty was not disappearing; it was changing. The "new 'Other America'" was in some ways worse than the version prevailing at the start of the 1960s. It was "more systemic and structured," due to the combined impact of factors such as corporate globalization and domestic deindustrialization. As he summed up his argument, "One reason that young men in the winter of 1983 had to ask New York City for beds for the night was that there were steel mills in South Korea."[11]

Just as Michael figured into Murray's book, so Murray made an appearance in Michael's. Michael had not yet seen *Losing Ground,* but he criticized an earlier article by Murray advancing a similar argument that had appeared in the neo-conservative journal *Public Interest.* Murray, Michael averred, was the right-wing equivalent of a "vulgar Marxist," a social theorist who believed in a "one-to-one relationship between the economic and the political or the psychological." Murray's portrait of the poor was of a group of people poised to leap into new values and behaviors the instant federal welfare policies changed: "Increase the welfare benefits and, by lightning calculation and utterly rational action, the poor, the blacks, will drop out of the labor market."[12]

Later, when Michael had had the chance to read *Losing Ground,* he returned to the attack in the pages of the *New Republic.* Murray's "crunched numbers" falsely linked the introduction of Great Society programs with increases in long-range poverty. The statistics in *Losing Ground* purported to show, for example, that the rate of black male labor force participation dropped dramatically in the late 1960s and early 1970s, a change that he attributed to increased welfare benefits. What Murray either didn't notice or chose not to acknowledge was that the rate of black male labor force participation had begun its precipitous drop in the late 1950s—that is, before the war on poverty and the expansion of AFDC rolls could have had any effect—which suggested that other factors, such as deindustrialization, may have been the real explanation for the phenomenon.[13]

Though argued with his usual lucidity, Michael's book on the "new poverty" read like the work of a man who was growing somewhat weary of pointing out the obvious. In the preface, Michael reflected on the reception his first book on poverty had received in the 1960s, and on why, in contrast, it was unlikely his current effort would achieve similar attention:

> Crises, particularly at first, do not make people radical or compassionate. They are frightening, and most people concentrate on saving themselves. Thoughts of "brothers" or "sisters," who are moral kin but not one's blood relatives, are a luxury many cannot afford.[14]

It was one thing to reveal the existence of a previously hidden poverty at a time when most Americans were feeling optimistic about their individual and collective economic future, but quite another to draw attention to the structural causes of the already visible poverty of the 1980s at a time when the unemployment rate was in double digits, real wages were falling, and two-income, middle-class families were struggling to stay afloat in a sea of personal debt. And what was more, the visible face of poverty in the 1980s was no longer that of some young white child far off in an Appalachian mining town and glimpsed in a photograph in the pages of a newsmagazine. It was much more likely to be the face of some all-too-physically-present and intrusive adult male minority panhandler, camping out in the public spaces of major cities. When reporters and social scientists talked about poverty in the 1980s, they tended to use terms like "the underclass" rather than "the poor"—the latter a phrase retaining some residual claim on public sympathy, the former a classification suggesting that those to whom it applied had few if any redeeming qualities.[15]

Reagan's two terms in the White House not only represented a watershed in public attitudes toward the poor but also established a new pariah category in the United States—liberals. The term "liberal" itself was effectively turned into an epithet—the "L-word." Whereas in 1960 almost every potential nominee as the Democratic candidate for president—John Kennedy, Adlai Stevenson, Stuart Symington, Hubert Humphrey—welcomed being called liberals (Lyndon Johnson, ironically, being the sole exception to that rule), by the time the 1980s were over no serious Democratic presidential contender would or could admit to owning such self-damning beliefs.

In September 1981, Michael wrote with disgust of the "Democratic collapse" in the face of the new administration. With the exception of the Congressional Black Caucus,

> the Democratic party either stood idly by while reactionaries mounted their savage attack on social programs, particularly those aimed at helping the working poor, or worse joined in the destruction of gains they themselves had pioneered.[16]

But by that September the first signs were appearing that the honeymoon was coming to an end for the Reagan Revolution. For Democrats, painful memories of the previous November's debacle began to fade, and questions arose as to just how meaningful a mandate Reagan had gained for his radical new policies. Reagan ran in 1980 against a singularly unpopular and inept incumbent opponent who had been visibly floundering for some time in the face of economic downturn and foreign policy humiliations. Carter carried the burden of the nation's recent past, a burden made heavier by his moralistic calls for restraint and self-sacrifice; Reagan was packaged as the candidate of a brighter, beckoning future, promising unlimited growth and affluence. Exit polls suggested that many Reagan supporters in 1980 were "anybody but Carter" voters who would have cast their votes for third party candidate John Anderson (who on many issues stood to Carter's left) had Reagan not been in the race. The new president's broad appeal was marked by the fact that one half of the blue-collar Democratic voters who had supported Edward Kennedy in the spring 1980 Democratic primaries turned around and voted for Reagan in the fall general election. But this fact also suggested the need for the new administration to tread carefully, lest the so-called "Reagan Democrats" be driven back to traditional loyalties.[17]

And that is just what seemed to be happening from the fall of 1981 well into 1983, as Reagan's strategy for economic recovery exacted a high price on ordinary Americans. Despite the assurances of the administration that a "safety net" would remain in place to protect the deserving poor, it was difficult to avoid evidence of increasing social misery in the early 1980s. More ominously, from Reagan's perspective, it wasn't just the poor that were hurting. Four million American workers lost their jobs between the spring of 1981 and the fall of 1982, many of them previously well-paid industrial workers. Unemployment stood at just under 7 percent when Reagan took office in 1981; by November 1982 it was approaching the 11 percent mark, the highest since the end of the Great Depression.[18] Newspapers carried dozens of stories about displaced "rust-belt" workers who were reduced to sleeping in their cars or on the streets as they searched for employment in the South and West. "Homeless Crisscross U.S., Until Their Cars and Their Dreams Break Down" read a headline in the *New York Times* in December 1982, invoking memories of the Joad family in *The Grapes of Wrath*.[19] The one thing no Republican president wanted to do was invite comparisons with Herbert Hoover. But even such fervent supporters of the administration as the editors of the *Wall Street Journal* were forced to concede the parallel. In July 1982 the *Journal* noted editorially that the current economic recession "set postwar records in unemployment and hit some states like a depression." Maintaining a stiff upper lip, the editors argued that, properly considered, that economic record was to the credit of the Reagan administration. After all, recessions played "an important role in economic growth. They weed out inefficient, outmoded enterprises and free resources for new ones. The Reagan administration is the first in memory to . . . deal with a slump by doing nothing."[20]

That kind of logic played better in the editorial offices of the *Journal* than it did with unemployed steel and auto workers who were unlikely to think of their personal difficulties as a benign and necessary precondition for the return of economic growth.[21] In November 1981, the director of economic surveys for the Gallup Organization warned that "Reagan does not have a mandate to bring about recession." If the economy continued to slide, he warned, "attitudes will begin to shift against [Reagan] very fast."[22] The Democrats had a good year in 1982, winning back twenty-seven seats in the House of Representatives in the midterm elections—better than twice the number of seats the Republicans had gained in the 1978 election. By January 1983, Reagan's approval ratings in the polls had declined to 35 percent—less than Nixon's in the Watergate summer of 1973. All of this seemed to suggest that Reagan, like the hapless Democrat he replaced in the White House, was going to prove yet another one-term president.

The most visible opposition to the Reagan program in the early 1980s came not in Congress or in the Democratic Party but on the streets. The spirit of "the sixties" and the new forms of political protest that had been developed on the Left in that decade turned out to have greater vitality than many commentators had previously assumed. By the Carter years, direct action protests against nuclear power sites were becoming frequent and sizable. An accident at the Three Mile Island nuclear facility in Pennsylvania in the spring 1979 galvanized mass protests against the nuclear power industry. Over 100,000 marched in a "No Nukes" demonstration in Washington in May 1979. Michael was among the speakers at the event, although he was overshadowed by actress Jane Fonda, whose antinuclear thriller "The China Syndrome" had coincidentally opened that same spring.[23] The following spring Michael was back in Washington, this time as a featured speaker at an antidraft rally initiated by DSOC. Over 30,000 mostly student-age demonstrators protested the Carter administration's plans to require young men to register for the draft for the first time since the end of the Vietnam War. For Michael, who appeared on the podium alongside draft resistance leader David Harris and the Reverend William Sloan Coffin, this was a chance to make amends for his absence during the antiwar protests of the 1960s. "We are here," he told the crowd in his address that day, "in the words of Norman Thomas to cleanse the American flag and not to burn it. We are the real patriots."[24]

The protests of the later Carter years would be dwarfed by those of the early Reagan era. And, much to Michael's satisfaction, the first of these huge protests was organized by the labor movement. In August 1981 the Professional Air Traffic Controllers Organization (PATCO) went on strike. Their employer was the federal government, and because of their vital role in insuring the safety of the nation's air traffic, they were bound by a no-strike provision in their contract. President Reagan responded by firing the entire workforce and ordering that substitute controllers be hired in their place. To the AFL-CIO this proved too great a challenge to ignore, even under such a conservative and ineffective leader as Lane Kirkland, George Meany's protégé and successor. And so, at the AFL-CIO'S call, over a quarter million trade union members and supporters gathered in Washington, D.C., for a protest rally and march on September 19, dubbed "Solidarity Day."

For a decade, Michael had been talking about the need to assemble a coalition of the "Three Georges"—the union members led by George Meany, the New Politics activists led by George McGovern, and the populist-oriented followers of George Wallace (in the latter case, minus their racist elements).[25] Solidarity Day seemed to represent just such a gathering. Although sparked by the PATCO firings, the protest was not limited to narrow union issues. According to a report in the *New York Times,* "the issues that caused the most anger included Social Security cuts, high interest rates, cutbacks in school lunch programs and cuts in the college student loan program."[26] A fifty-year-old union carpenter from New Jersey told a reporter, "I thought protest marches were for kids who had too much time on their hands. The kids would come down here, have riots, smoke marijuana, and tear down the system." But now, he mused, he was the one marching on Washington, because the Reagan revolutionaries were "trying to put the working man down. They're trying to make this a different kind of country."[27]

The presence of feminist, peace, and civil rights groups in the line of march that day reinforced the "sixties" flavor of the event, as did Pete Seeger's performance of "Solidarity Forever" from the podium. At the invitation of William Winpisinger, Michael happily took his place among the rank and file of the Machinists' union contingent, along with about 700 other DSOCers. It was an exhilarating day for them. William Serrin, the *New York Times* labor reporter, talked to Michael after the event and quoted him as saying that the gathering in Washington "consisted of genuine American workers [and] not a bunch of 'pie carders.'" (As Serrin explained to those *Times* readers not well versed in American labor folklore, Michael had "used an old Industrial Workers of the World term for those employed by the union establishment, who the I.W.W. charged sold out for the comfortable notion of pie in the sky.")[28]

The following spring it was the peace movement's turn to challenge Reagan in the streets. Michael joined with 750,000 others in New York City to support the call for a "nuclear freeze"—an immediate halt to the arms race by the United States and the Soviet Union. It was the largest political demonstration in American history.[29] And in August 1983, on the twentieth anniversary of the civil rights movement's original March on Washington, another quarter million protesters, Michael among them, marched to the Lincoln Memorial to protest the Reagan administration's record on race relations.[30]

So Michael and his comrades spent a lot of time in other people's parades in the early 1980s. But what, specifically, could they contribute to the anti-

Reagan cause as democratic socialists? Michael had built DSOC's political strategy and identity in the 1970s around an attempt to shift the Democratic Party leftward. At Memphis in 1978 it seemed to work. But Memphis turned out to be the high-water mark for Democratic Agenda.

Michael had assumed that the failed presidency of a conservative Democratic president would naturally serve to strengthen the position of the party's left. After all, if Carter had listened to his Democratic Agenda critics, he would not have provided a prototype for the Reagan Revolution in his use of unemployment to combat inflation, in his zeal for deregulation, and in his support for increased military appropriations. Michael hammered this point home repeatedly in his writings and speeches in the early Reagan years. In the fall of 1982, he was the featured speaker at a conference of social workers in East Hartford, Connecticut, where a sympathetic audience cheered his sallies against Reaganism. "A rumpled figure with tousled grey hair and half glasses," a reporter from a local newspaper wrote of the event, "Harrington rasped, poked the air and gently joked with his audience." Though the audience laughed "on cue to his references to Nixon and Reagan," Michael warned them that Reagan's shortcomings as an economic policymaker were not going to win the next election for the Democrats: "Let's suppose the Democrats get back into power. What are they going to do? Take us back to Jimmy Carter? It was he who put Reagan in." It was "a virtue" to oppose Reagan, Michael added, "but it's not a program."[31]

But there was a flaw in Michael's reasoning. If Carter had gone down to defeat at the hands of a moderate Republican like Gerald Ford, the surviving Democratic incumbents might have agreed that it was in the party's best interest to adopt a more left-leaning program, in order to set it apart both from Carter's failed policies and from those being adopted by the new Republican administration. But the fact that victory had gone to an ultra-conservative Republican like Reagan taught the Democrats a very different lesson than the one Michael thought they should learn. The center of political debate had shifted so far to the right that Democrats decided they would have to adopt at least some of Reagan's policies and rhetoric as their own as protective coloration on hostile political terrain.

Democratic Agenda also proved the victim of its own Memphis success. The Democratic Party establishment was not oblivious to the lessons of that conference and would not be blindsided again. The entire DSOC/Democratic Agenda strategy was fatally wounded by a simple organizational measure when Democratic National Committee chairman Charles Manatt limited attendance at the 1982 Philadelphia midterm convention to party appointees and officials.[32] Democratic Agenda subsequently disappeared, without so much as a formal notice of disbandment.

Michael had other organizational matters that needed tending to that year. As DSOC grew in the 1970s, its membership rolls displayed a curious demographic feature. The bulk of the organization's members were either over forty or under twenty-five. The missing middle consisted of people in their late twenties through their thirties who had come of age politically in the 1960s. Old suspicions and divisions left over from the days of Port Huron and the Vietnam War survived among many former SDSers and other veterans of the New Left. "We were always paying for the Sixties," recalled Jo-Ann Mort a DSOC activist who joined while a student at Sarah Lawrence in the late 1970s. The title of a generally sympathetic article about Michael that appeared in *Mother Jones* in 1977 spoke volumes about the unfinished business of the previous decade: "An Irresistible Profile of Michael Harrington (You Must Be Kidding)."[33]

Michael was determined to wipe that slate clean. He did so with repeated public apologies for Port Huron (they appeared so often that one veteran of SDS's founding convention was finally moved to write a personal letter in the mid-1980s and told him he could stop already).[34] And in 1982 he presided over the merger between DSOC and a rival left-wing organization called the New American Movement (NAM) to form Democratic Socialists of America (DSA). With the founding of DSA, Michael would write, "I had finally expiated my stupidity in SDS."[35]

NAM's history stretched back to the start of the 1970s, when a group of activists and intellectuals influential on the New Left, including Michael Lerner, James Weinstein, and Staughton Lynd, decided to form a successor to SDS.[36] This would be a post-student organization, though one heavily influenced by the experiences of student radicals in the 1960s. From the early New Left and the civil rights movement, NAM took an emphasis on the importance of local community organization; from the later New Left it took a mixture of Marxism and feminism. At the same time, NAM discarded the confrontational politics and tempered (if never entirely eliminating) the third world romanticism of the late 1960s. And, unlike latter-day SDSers, NAM members no longer cherished an apocalyptic notion of revolution lying just around the corner. SDSers had favored T-shirts bearing a likeness of slain Cuban revolutionary Che Guevera as a fashion/political statement; NAM's T-shirts featured the likeness of imprisoned Italian Communist theorist Antonio Gramsci and his dug-in-for-the-long-haul slogan, "Pessimism of the Intellect, Optimism of the Will."

At NAM's founding convention in Davenport, Iowa, there was no talk of this new movement being only a "remnant of a remnant": NAM's founders believed that within a short time thousands, if not tens of thousands, of New Left veterans would join up. These expectations were disappointed. The frenzied crack-up of the organized New Left disposed most of its former adherents to deep suspicion of any attempt to create a new national organization, even one that, like NAM, took antisectarianism as a founding principle. And so, for the next decade, NAM struggled along, with a small and rapidly turning over membership. Its most prominent early leaders left for other ventures—James Weinstein to found the weekly socialist newspaper *In These Times,* Michael Lerner to found the radical Jewish monthly *Tikkun,* and Staughton Lynd to organize unemployed steelworkers in Youngstown, Ohio.

Roberta Lynch was one of the founding members who remained with NAM. Like most of her NAM comrades, she initially regarded DSOC as a group hopelessly compromised by its social democratic illusions and bureaucratic habits. In 1977, she was elected NAM's national secretary and was an invited guest at that year's DSOC convention. In a follow-up report for *In These Times,* she roundly criticized DSOC. The organization's approach to electoral politics "serves to obscure the class nature of the Democratic party," and its ties with established union leaders had led it to "ignore the necessity for rank-and-file activity and union democracy." Only as a kind of afterthought did she mention that it might be time for competing groups of democratic socialists to abandon "worn-out categories" and "self-righteous posturing."[37]

Irving Howe once described how some American Communists in the 1930s, almost despite themselves, began to adapt their political tactics and outlook to better fit the special circumstances of American life. The changes were often slight, and the thinking behind them muddled. But, he added (in words that some critics applied to his own transformation from sectarian revolutionary to democratic socialist), "most changes of thought occur hesitantly, and language always lags behind impulse and feeling."[38] Something very similar was happening with NAM's cadre of former New Leftists in the 1970s. In Roberta Lynch's case, the new "impulse and feeling" came as she was drawn in the late 1970s to a local reform group called the Progressive Chicago Action Network, which tried to bridge the racial chasm in Chicago politics and in doing so helped lay the groundwork for Harold Washington's successful mayoral campaign in 1983. NAM, she felt, was totally irrelevant to this endeavor; it was simply not capable of being "real world" enough.[39] DSOC's success with the Democratic Agenda strategy made NAM leaders like Lynch take a second and more thoughtful look at the organization. In Chicago, as in a number of other places around the country, NAM and DSOC began cooperating on common projects; some individuals paid dues to both groups; and from various sources, both within NAM and DSOC, proposals began to surface for a merger of the two groups.

It has always been easier to split radical groups than to bring them together, and it took several years of intense negotiations to pull off the merger of DSOC and NAM. But both sides eventually recognized that they potentially had much to gain in joining ranks. DSOC had greater national visibility than NAM, and a good network of contacts within the Democratic Party and the union movement. NAM had strong local chapters in a number of places, including on the West Coast, where DSOC had always been weak. In negotiations that took up a good deal of time and energy for both groups in 1980–1981, NAM wound up making most of the ideological concessions: The merged organization, it was agreed, would strongly back the state of Israel and would adopt DSOC's perspective on the Soviet Union and other Communist nations, which was (in homage to Max Shachtman's theory of bureaucratic collectivism) that they were not to be considered "socialist." DSOC, in turn, made organizational concessions to NAM, including opening up regional offices in Chicago and San Francisco under the direction of NAM veterans (NAM particularly wanted to avoid having the merger produce yet another New York-centric radical group).[40]

The merger was officially cemented at a unity convention in Detroit in March 1982, with the founding of Democratic Socialists of America. For a few years, DSA served as a conduit for one-time New Leftists to make the transition to mainstream electoral politics and union activism (Roberta Lynch herself became an AFSCME staffer in Chicago). DSA, as hoped, proved to be more than the sum of its two constituent parts. DSOC had about 4,000 members at the time of the merger, and NAM brought in about 800 more; by 1983 DSA counted a full 7,000 members. DSA was, as its brochures noted proudly, "the largest democratic socialist group in America since the 1930s."

But these (relatively) good times would not last long. DSA membership dropped to 6,000 by 1985 and to 5,000 by 1987. A long-developing financial crisis (unpaid printers' bills and the like) came to a head just after the merger, and as a result the recently opened regional offices in Chicago and San Francisco were shut down. Feminist writer and NAM veteran Barbara Ehrenreich, who became cochair of DSA in 1983, did not get along with Michael. Some former NAM leaders became members of a "Green Caucus" within DSA (favoring more emphasis on social movements like gay liberation, less on the labor movement); others withdrew from active involvement.[41] Part of the problem was demographic: Those thirty-something activists whom Michael so desperately wanted to attract to the new organization were finding themselves taking on other responsibilities in the 1980s. As *Socialist Forum,* an internal discussion bulletin of the organization, noted in 1986, "A DSA 'baby boom' of sorts is underway, and child care and parenting responsibilities are cutting still further into the discretionary time our members have available."[42]

The main problem DSA faced, however, was that it failed to invent a meaningful political role for local members to play *as socialists.* Individual DSAers were involved with issues that ranged from opposing American policies in Central America to defending reproductive rights. They were members or staffers of trade unions, environmental groups, peace, civil rights, and feminist organizations. Beyond wearing a DSA button to the meetings of these other groups, however, there was seldom any meaningful connection between their socialism and their other activism. DSA's rhetoric stressed the interconnectedness of issues and movements. But given inevitable conflicting demands over the allocation of time and money, involvement in DSA often proved one interconnection too many.

Michael never quite seemed to grasp the problem. After all, he didn't have any trouble integrating the role of socialist and political activist in his own life. That's what his entire life consisted of—he was "America's socialist." As DSA political director Jim Shoch recalled of DSA's organizational problems in the mid-1980s:

> We would organize these big meetings and Mike would blow into town and speak to a large crowd and he would go back home and think, "Boy, socialism is on the march." In private I would say to him, "Mike, this is not happening." And he would say, "Look, I just went out to Boise and there were 400 people there." What he didn't see was that the local in Idaho hadn't met in a year.[43]

It wasn't Michael's fault, but the fact remained that being America's socialist was a lot more meaningful than being Boise's socialist.

Increasingly in the 1970s and 1980s, Michael wasn't just America's socialist; he was also a socialist of international prominence. In his 1988 memoir, *The Long Distance Runner,* he predicted that when the history of the last quarter of the twentieth century came to be written "the Socialist International will take up less than a chapter and considerably more than a footnote."[44] Whether or not that turns out to be the case, the fact that Michael's account of his own involvement with the Socialist International (SI) took up fully three of the ten chapters in that book is suggestive of how much importance it had come to carry in his life.

In a profile of Michael that appeared on CBS's Sunday morning news show in 1982, correspondent Jerry Landy introduced the segment by noting Michael's participation the previous autumn in a meeting of Socialist International leaders at the Elysee Palace in Paris:

> Israel's opposition leader, Shimon Peres, was there. So was Willy Brandt, the former chancellor of West Germany. The host was the new Socialist president of France, François Mitterrand. They are men of power in their countries. The American Socialist in attendance was Michael Harrington. Back in his country, Michael Harrington is not a household word. Nonetheless, he has shaped American political thinking and he's trying to do so again.[45]

"The SI was Mike's baby," is how his colleague Jo-Ann Mort described DSOC's and DSA's international affiliations.[46] From the start, Michael handled relations with the SI with little consultation with others in the organization. He conducted the delicate negotiations that allowed DSOC to join the SI as a "consultative member" in 1976 and move up to full member status in 1978 (with rival SDUSA, already an SI affiliate, fighting to keep DSOC out every step of the way). Unlike many other leaders of the SI's constituent parties, he wasn't busy running a country, so he was increasingly entrusted with the job of drafting the resolutions, programs, and manifestos issued in their collective name.

DSOC was admitted to the Socialist International in the same year that West German socialist leader Willy Brandt became SI president. Michael had first encountered Brandt in 1959, when he had gone to West Berlin as a delegate to an international conference of young socialists. Brandt made his name both in German politics and internationally as the mayor of that beleaguered city; he had been in office when John Kennedy stood before the Berlin Wall in 1963 and declared, *"Ich bin ein Berliner."* Brandt and Kennedy were much alike—in their youth, their good looks, and in their views; some called Brandt the "German Kennedy." Since then, Brandt had gone on to both political triumph and disaster: He was foreign minister in West Germany's coalition government in the late 1960s and then became Germany's first postwar Social Democratic chancellor in 1969. While in office, Brandt promoted an *Ostpolitik* (eastern policy, opening to the east), hoping to normalize relations both with Communist East Germany and the Soviet Union. In 1974 he was forced from office as a result of a spy scandal in his government, but he remained the leader of the German socialists.[47]

As president of the SI, Brandt once again acted boldly, this time to break the organization out of what he referred to as its "European ghetto" (besides those to be found in places like Canada, Australia, and Japan, the SI counted few member parties outside of Europe in 1976). Brandt was determined to shift the focus of the SI's political concerns from the East–West confrontation to the relations between "North" and "South"—that is between the highly developed industrial nations of Europe and North America, and the developing nations of Central and South America, Africa, and Asia. From the 1950s through the mid-1970s, Michael would write of the SI, it was

> primarily an 'old boys' reunion of European Left politicians with an ideology shaped in the coldest days of the Cold War. Under Brandt, it has become a dynamic institution in which the non-European parties are in a majority and its politics, though based on consensus, have moved steadily toward the left on issues of peace, the Third World, the environment, and social movements.[48]

Bernt Carlsson, a Swedish socialist and general secretary of the SI from 1976 through 1983, was instrumental in realizing Brandt's vision. The SI encouraged the development of, and extended recognition to, new member parties throughout the Third World. Reclaiming some of its nineteenth-century revolutionary heritage, the SI made a particular effort to reach out to struggling insurgent movements in southern Africa and Central America. "Our main task in life is not to be anti-Communist," Carlsson declared in 1981, explaining the SI's role in the Third World: "Our task is to promote democratic socialism as an alternative to both Communism and capitalism."[49]

As an expression of this new orientation, Michael was appointed by Brandt as the American representative to the SI's Committee to Defend the Nicaraguan Revolution, which was chaired by Spanish Socialist leader Felipe Gonzalez. In June 1981, as the Reagan administration was gearing up its "secret war" on the Nicaraguan government, Michael and other committee members traveled to Managua and met with Sandinista leader Daniel Ortega. Michael had steeled himself against the temptation to become a "revolutionary tourist," swayed by the romance of Third World national liberation struggles into apologizing for dictatorship. But having bought a copy of the opposition newspaper *La Prensa* in Managua, he decided that whatever its sins, the Sandinista government could not be judged a totalitarian state.[50]

Michael came to know a good many other Socialist leaders. Some of these relationships, as with the regally inclined Mitterrand, remained formal. With others, like Olof Palme of Sweden, Shimon Peres of Israel, Neil Kinnock of Britain, Ed Broadbent of Canada, and Michael Manley of Jamaica, he developed the kind of friendly acquaintanceships where he could sit down with them over a beer and exchange stories. It was, for Michael, as if the back room of the White Horse Tavern circa 1955 had gone global. The good feelings were mutual. According to Pierre Schori, the Swedish Social Democratic Party's spokesman for foreign affairs, Palme regarded Michael as a kind of "soul brother." Palme was not alone among SI leaders in thinking that "if Mike had been a European politician, he would have been prime minister."[51]

Michael readily acknowledged that flying off to cities like Paris, Geneva, Madrid, and Vienna on a semi-regular basis was not exactly the most onerous task he faced as America's leading socialist. He confessed to a reporter in 1987 that he loved "all the formal protocol, the elegant dinners, all that."[52] He was scrupulous about raising the money for his SI-related trips from outside his own organization's coffers, frequently by selling articles about the latest turns in SI policy to interested magazines, like the *New Republic*.[53]

Still, some of his colleagues felt that he was laying undue emphasis on the importance of his contacts with the SI, seduced by the glamour of his powerful new associates. What difference did his ability to have lunch with Mitterrand in the Elysee Palace make in the United States? How many

Americans even knew that something called the Socialist International existed, let alone cared what causes and movements it chose to endorse in the various resolutions that Michael helped draft?

But Michael thought his involvement with the SI did make a difference, and in 1980, to prove the point, he tried to bring the SI home to America. With generous funding from the German Marshall Foundation, DSOC staged a "Eurosocialism conference" in Washington, D.C., on the first weekend in December 1980. Twenty-five hundred people attended the two day conference. Brandt, Mitterrand, Palme, Spain's Felipe Gonzalez, and Joop Den Uyl, prime minister of the Netherlands, were among those who participated. Seldom had Washington played host to such a distinguished assemblage of past, present, and future European leaders. And seldom was so little attention paid when they did. There was no television coverage at all, and of the major U.S. newspapers, only the *Washington Post* carried any articles. Michael was particularly disturbed by the *New York Times*'s decision to ignore the Eurosocialist gathering, an omission that he attributed to the ideological hostility of the *Times*'s managing editor, Abe Rosenthal. The AFL-CIO's international affairs office, under Tom Kahn's direction, had campaigned for months to sabotage the conference (which Kahn referred to snidely as "that Eurocommunism conference").[54] Kahn's efforts were not successful in discouraging European attendance, but they did work to scare off American liberal politicians who were conspicuous in their absence (DSOC member Ron Dellums of Oakland was the only congressman to address the conference; Michael introduced him to the audience as the "socialist caucus of the United States Congress").[55]

Seven years later Michael was still brooding about what had happened. He devoted a half dozen pages in *The Long Distance Runner* to revealing "the hidden history of the Eurosocialism conference," which, he wrote, "might seem more fascinating than the event itself."[56] It seems unlikely, however, that even lavish media coverage, or the attendance of the entire Democratic congressional delegation, would have lent the affair any more fascination or lasting significance for the American public. This was one of the few instances where Michael's romantic conception of himself and his role in the world led him into a stubborn and continuing unwillingness to face up to reality. And the reality was, for better or worse, that Americans simply did not look elsewhere in the world for inspiration in remaking their own society. Any movement founded on the belief they ever would was deluding itself.

Frustrated as he was by the failure of the Eurosocialist conference, it was probably just as well for Michael that it had not drawn greater attention. The more his name was linked in the public mind with foreign leaders and foreign doctrines (however democratic their credentials), the less, not the more, influential he would become. By the 1980s Michael had emerged as a kind of icon of authentic American radicalism. Nobody, or next to nobody, read his books or turned out for his speeches because they hoped to learn more about the Swedish socialists' "solidaristic wage policy" and other of Michael's enthusiasms. They listened to him because he had come to serve as the voice of collective conscience for those who were disturbed by the values of Reagan's America. He told the nation uncomfortable truths in a way that made people want to do something about them. "There is still a fresh breeze in the way Harrington talks about politics and policies," the *Boston Globe* reported after Michael gave a talk at Harvard University in 1983. "Harrington's mobile Irish face and twinkling eyes have graced a thousand lecture platforms, union halls, hearing rooms of Congress. And even under Reagan he does not despair." His eloquence helped, as did his obvious breadth of knowledge. But what really defined his public image was the sense he projected of being a practical idealist. "Harrington has assumed the mantle of the late Norman Thomas," the *Boston Globe* continued. "But unlike the cerebral Thomas, Harrington's socialist commitment is more grounded in the union hall and the workplace."[57]

Michael was never entirely comfortable with his own semi-deification. He remembered how it had annoyed Norman Thomas to be put in the position of "a socialist who threatened no one and nothing—who was a palpably decent man of conscience and commitment—who could be revered on ceremonial occasion and cited to prove that the country was genuinely tolerant and democratic." He was afraid when his life was over that all he would have accomplished was the construction of "a lesser Norman Thomas."[58] But there was not much he could do about it, except occasionally poke fun at himself. After speaking at the dedication of a new DSA office in Baltimore in 1982, he reported to readers of *Democratic Left* that it had been, in most respects, a "euphoric" event": "The only negative note: a sympathetic article in the Baltimore *Sun* calls me the 'grand old man' of American socialism. Actually, I am a closet youth."[59]

In 1984, noting that "voices from the left" seemed "strangely muted" in that year's presidential election, the Sunday *New York Times Magazine* devoted ten pages to the transcript of a conversation between Michael and Irving Howe, in which the two men reviewed the history of socialism from the days of Norman Thomas to the present, concluding that "by now, practically everyone of the Left agrees that the Democratic Party, with all its faults, must be our main political arena."[60]

Walter Mondale was the Democratic candidate for president in 1984, and he represented the kind of campaign coalition that Michael had been calling for the past two decades. Mondale's supporters included organized labor and the conscience constituency, the AFL-CIO and the National Organization for Women. "The Mondale campaign united all of the class and social forces we had deemed essential," Michael noted ruefully after the election, "and went down to ignominious defeat."[61]

That outcome was partly a matter of circumstance. Two years earlier, at the height of the Reagan recession and the depth of Reagan's public approval, Michael had warned Democrats not to bank too much on continued hard times to deliver them the White House in 1984. He recalled the example of the 1972 election, where Nixon managed to get the economy out of recession just long enough to secure his own re-election. "Is such a miraculous convergence of economic trends and presidential political advantage to be ruled out in 1984," Michael asked:

> Reduced rates of inflation, lower interest rates, discipline restored in the factories through fear of unemployment, lower real wages, obsolete plants shut down at the mere cost of lost jobs and communities, could all work to put America on the road to a corporate dominated recovery financed by the misery and lowered living standards of the great mass of Americans. That will not resolve the structural crisis of the American economy. It could secure a temporary remission of some of the worst symptoms of that crisis just in time to help re-elect Ronald Reagan.[62]

That turned out to be a pretty accurate prediction. The economy bottomed out a few months later and then, fueled by deficit spending and a defense build-up (a policy of "unconscious Keynesianism" as Michael called it), began to expand. By the fall of 1984 unemployment had dropped 3.5 percent from the height of the Reagan recession in 1982 (although at 7.3 percent it was at a rate that would have crippled the election chances of any incumbent in the 1950s and 1960s). The poverty level also declined nearly a full percentage point from 1983 to 1984 (although at 14.4 percent it was higher than it had been in any year since the launching of the war on poverty—with the exception of the first two years of the Reagan administration).[63]

Mondale pointed to the discrepancies in the Reagan record (particularly the fact that Reagan had promised in 1980 to balance the budget by 1984, instead of sending it into a record deficit). But the voters, famously characterized by short memories, did not seem to care. Reagan promised to fix the country's economy, and he had delivered, so what was Mondale complaining about? It was, as the Reagan campaign ads put it, "Morning in America." Mondale was just a gloomy holdover from the bad old days of Jimmy Carter, a nay-saying preacher of restraint and also (however inconsistently) a tax-and-spend liberal. There were plenty of special circumstances that could be cited to explain the Mondale defeat, just as there had been in determining the outcomes in 1968, 1972, and 1980. But Michael was now willing to acknowledge that American politics was changing in ways that he had not fully understood before.

Four days after Reagan's re-election, Michael drove to Princeton University to take part in the centennial observance of Princeton alumni Norman Thomas's birth. This was a gala event, part academic conference, part veterans' reunion for the socialist movement. Michael's speech came on the second evening of the three-day observances. He chose to speak of mortality—not the death of an individual but the death of a tradition.

Michael had read and been impressed by the recently published biography of Eugene Debs, by Cornell historian Nick Salvatore, another participant in the conference. He quoted this passage from Salvatore's book to the audience that night:

> The faith of Debs and his followers in the redemptive power of the ballot is, from a current perspective, simply staggering. They took the republican tradition seriously and stressed the individual dignity and power inherent in the concept of citizenship. While frequently vague over exactly how to transform their society, these men and women had no doubt but that, if the people united, the vitality of that tradition would point the way.[64]

That was Debs's world. But what about the political world of 1984? "The radical republican notion of 'citizenship' which both Debs and Thomas incarnated, is disappearing," Michael told his listeners:

> The grandchildren of men and women who once stayed late into the night at the Grange hall or the union hall, talking intensely with each other about what kind of society they wanted to build, now stay home watching TV. If they participate at all in shaping their collective future, it is most likely by opening a computer-generated envelope from some committee in New York or Washington.[65]

Michael said nothing that evening of his own role in the socialist movement. But it was hard to avoid the implication that both he and the movement he represented may well have outlived their time.

Something else happened that weekend to make Michael think of mortality—this time his own. While waiting at a traffic light on the drive down to Princeton, he happened to touch the left side of his neck. There he discovered a bump. He decided it was probably a swollen gland, but just to make sure, he scheduled an appointment with his doctor upon his return to New York. His doctor concurred with Michael's self-diagnosis; the bump was nothing to be concerned about.

Michael was just fifty-six years old in 1984 and had enjoyed a lifetime of good health. His role model, Norman Thomas, was still alive and vital into his eighties. Michael really did expect to grow up to be the "grand old man" of socialism. But all around him, death was beginning to claim family members, old friends, and political associates. In 1980 alone, his mother, Dorothy Day, and Al Lowenstein had died.[66] And in 1982 Michael lost a good friend and comrade to cancer, DSOC's organizational director Selma Lenihan. In the 1950s, some of his comrades in the Young Socialist League had imagined themselves to be "dead men on leave" because of their revolutionary aspirations. By the 1980s Michael had reached an age where he really was a dead man on leave—the only question being whether that leave would extend for a few more decades or only a few more years.

At the end of January 1985 Michael returned to the same doctor for his annual physical exam, who discovered the same bump on his neck and this time took it more seriously. Michael was dispatched to a specialist who, after tests and another few days wait, confirmed what Michael already feared. The bump was cancerous; in technical terms it was a "metastatic carcinoma," a secondary growth indicating the existence of a still more serious primary cancer lurking somewhere else in his body, probably in the head and neck. The day he learned the news he became fixated on the title of a classic polemical essay that Leon Trotsky had penned in 1939: "From a Scratch to the Danger of Gangrene." In his own case, Michael reflected with grim irony, it was "from a bump on the neck to metastatic carcinoma." In the weeks of depression that followed he would imagine his own memorial service, and weep.[67]

Another month would pass before he had a complete picture of the threat he faced. In March he entered St. Vincent's hospital in New York City for exploratory surgery, the first time in his life he had ever been a patient in a hospital. The primary cancer was found at the base of his tongue. Given its location, it was probably the product of years of heavy drinking and smoking (although he had given up the latter a full twenty years earlier). His doctors prescribed seven weeks of radiation therapy.

During these months of treatment, Michael noticed that the familiar religious phrases of his childhood were echoing in Latin in his imagination: "*Magnificat anima mea. . . .* My soul doth magnify the glory of the Lord." Given the circumstances, it would not have been strange for him to reconsider and reject his thirty-odd year commitment to atheism. A few days before he was scheduled to return to the hospital in July for surgery to remove the remaining cancerous growth on his neck and tongue, Michael had lunch in New York with his childhood companion and cousin Peggy FitzGibbon. Peggy had grown up to pursue a religious vocation, as a nun of the Cenacle order. Michael told Peggy that he still deeply loved the Catholic Church and found its rituals immensely beautiful and comforting. But he could not bring himself to believe in God. If he did die on the operating table and somehow found himself dispatched to heaven, he told Peggy, at the first opportunity he was going to accuse God face-to-face of mumbling to humankind.[68]

The accusation would have to wait. He awoke from surgery not in heaven but in the hospital, spent an uncomfortable week in an intensive care unit, and then returned to his life and politics. The operation was a success, cancer leaving behind only its detritus: a scarred neck, a stiff left arm, and a frequently parched mouth, since he had also lost some of his saliva glands.

For the next two and a half years he was as busy as ever, speaking and writing, organizing conferences, flying to meetings of the SI, trying to keep DSA afloat. His political optimism revived; he sensed that the Democrats had a good chance to return to power in 1988. He was also intrigued with Jesse Jackson's bid for the Democratic presidential nomination. Not that he thought that Jackson could win but that he was raising all the right kind of issues. Jackson was eager for Michael's support and asked him to do some speechwriting for him in 1987.[69]

In November 1987, finding it increasingly difficult to swallow, Michael went back for another checkup. The doctors found a new and this time inoperable tumor in his esophagus. They gave him six months to two years to live. He decided that day that he would write another book, one that would consider the past and future of socialism. He began a debilitating monthly schedule of chemotherapy sessions that left him weighing forty pounds less than in his prime and looking markedly older than his actual age. Too weak to do much speaking or traveling, he even had to skip that year's DSA national convention in December. Instead, he concentrated on writing, bringing his legal pads with him to the chemotherapy clinic to scribble in while awaiting treatment.

As news about his declining health spread in the year that followed, Michael began to hear from old friends and comrades, and from some old adversaries too. Among the many personal letters he received in those months, wishing him well or saying good-bye, one of the most eloquent came from William F. Buckley:

> I saw you briefly on tv yesterday (you were making a brief appearance in behalf of socialism), and I rejoiced both that your appearance was brief, and that you looked so well. . . . I have said a special prayer for your recovery. . . . Meanwhile, take care of yourself: You are a brave and admirable man, the daemons to one side.[70]

There were more formal tributes: in newspaper editorials, from international unions, from city councils, and even from a reunion of SDS veterans.

The most elaborate came at the end of June 1988 in the Roseland Dance Hall in New York. It was billed as a "Celebration of Michael Harrington," marking Michael's sixtieth birthday and the publication of his memoir *The Long Distance Runner.* "When word gets around that you're dying," he remarked to a reporter a few days before the gathering, "everyone calls you a nice guy." Gallows humor aside, he really did want to be there, asking his doctors that spring to keep him alive long enough to make the celebration.[71]

He was in good form at Roseland, where 600 paying guests assembled to honor him. He described Ronald Reagan to one reporter covering the gathering as "his therapist." The president had given him "a will to live. I want to be around for the post-Reagan period."[72] Speakers included Gloria Steinem, Cesar Chavez, William Winpisinger, and Ed Broadbent.[73] Senator Edward Kennedy spoke as well, and in his tribute declared:

> In our lifetime, it is Mike Harrington who has come the closest to fulfilling the vision of America that my brother Robert Kennedy had, when he said, "Some men see things as they are and say 'Why?' But I dream things that never were and say 'Why Not?'". . . . Some call it socialism; I call it the Sermon on the Mount.[74]

When it was Michael's turn to speak, he related a parable that he had used on many other occasions:

> In desert societies, water is so precious that it is money. People connive and fight and die over it; governments covet it; marriages are even made and broken because of it. If you were to talk to people who have known only that desert and tell them that in the city there are public water fountains and that children turn on the fire hydrants in the summer and frolic in the water, they would be sure you were crazy.
>
> They would assume that, at night, people must come out of their houses to fill buckets and hoard water. For they know, with an existential certitude, that it is human nature to fight over water. It is in our genes.
>
> Our problem is that humankind has lived now for several millennia in deserts of various kinds. Our minds and emotions are conditioned by that bitter experience. There are some who loathe to leave behind the consolation of familiar brutalities; there are others who in one way or another would like to impose the law of the desert upon the Promised Land.
>
> Yet there are signs that we are, without really having planned it that way, marching out of the desert. We are beginning to know that we can end the invidious competition and venality which we had come to think were inseparable from our humanity. You and I accept the fact of societies in which at least one doesn't die of thirst. Water is the one thing that has

been socialized. Hoarding it, fighting over it, marrying for it are *not* part of human nature after all—*because we have confidence that it will be shared.*

So why can't we go a little further and imagine societies in which each person also has food and shelter? In which everybody has an education and a chance to know their value? Why not?[75]

After the speeches, there was music. The crowd sang Woody Guthrie's "This Land Is Your Land," accompanied by Tommy Makem on banjo, and by Michael waving a long-stemmed red rose to the beat. And then, without accompaniment, the gathering ended with the singing of "The Internationale."[76]

He felt better in the fall and began traveling and speaking again. Throughout the winter and spring of 1989 he kept up a schedule that many a healthy sixty-one-year-old man would have found taxing. January took him to the University of Minnesota and MacAlester College in Minneapolis, and, most memorably, to Dublin, where he delivered the annual James Larkin Memorial Lecture on behalf of the Federated Workers' Union of Ireland. (Larkin, an Irish trade unionist and socialist, had spent nearly a decade in exile in the United States before Ireland gained its independence; among other distinctions, he had campaigned for Eugene Debs in the 1912 election.) This was Michael's first and only visit to his ancestral homeland.[77]

In February, Michael spoke at Brandeis, Temple, and the University of Pennsylvania, and at the annual winter conference of the DSA Youth Section, meeting at Columbia University. He told a hundred or so campus activists gathered for the occasion that he knew that not all of them would remain life-long supporters of the socialist cause:

Some of you, God bless you, will pay your dues, you'll be around for a while, and then you'll leave. You will be enriched somewhat and when you get older, you'll say, "Oh, I was a socialist when I was a youth . . . but I got older, I got smarter, I gave up that stuff." But you'll probably remain, at least, a good liberal. You'll go to a reproductive rights march, you'll campaign against aid to the contras. You'll do fine things and I just wish that there were more of you.

But it was to the others that he really wanted to direct his comments, those who would remain life-long socialists. They would see many "ups and downs" in their lifetime, "and in America," he added, "from my experience in forty years of the movement, I've got to tell you that the downs tend to predominate." Still, he hoped they would hang in there, understanding the interconnected nature of the many struggles they would find themselves involved in:

What we are dealing with is not simply an economic transition, or a political transition. What we are dealing with is the emergence of a new civilization. What we are dealing with are new ways of life for all the people of the Earth. By the end of the 21st century existence will nowhere, in any way, look like it looks like now. And if you know that and even though you know in your lifetime there will be no answer, but you understand that if there is the least possibility of freedom being the answer, it is worth a lifetime commitment. That's what holds you together. This movement should enrich you, this movement should allow you to lead a different kind of life. This is not a burden. At its best this is a movement of joy. . . . You will have an opportunity to make these ideas come alive.[78]

March brought him to Notre Dame and then to the annual Socialist Scholars conference in New York City. He had to skip the meeting of SI leaders in Vienna that month because of his health; but in a letter to Willy Brandt, Michael assured him that he would be coming to Stockholm for the next Congress of the Socialist International in June, "barring any utterly unforeseen medical events."[79] In April he traveled to Marquette University and delivered the Stanley Plastrik Memorial Lecture at the CUNY Graduate Center in New York.[80]

When he wasn't on the road, he worked with fierce concentration on his final book *Socialism: Past and Present.* It opened with a hundred-page tour de force survey of the history of socialism in the nineteenth and twentieth centuries, with the familiar Harrington emphases—on the democratic Marx, on the ambivalent nature of the socialist revolution that Lenin made in 1917 and its descent into a murderous bureaucratic collectivism by the 1930s, on the appeal of the Soviet model to various third world nations and, in turn, the appeal of authoritarian third world socialisms to young radicals in the West in the 1960s. In succeeding chapters he laid out the case for a politics of "visionary gradualism" devoted to the creation of a democratic, decentralized, market-oriented socialism for the twenty-first century. He remained a Marxist to the end, regarding capitalism as a self-contradictory system that drew people together in productive enterprise and yet drove them apart through the unequal distribution of resources. He called this "an unsocial socialization." He ended by posing a question about his preferred alternative, socialism:

More than a hundred years ago, it understood the basic tendency of capitalist society, that drive toward an unsocial socialization. And it counterposed a vision of democratic socialization, one that has in fact inspired almost every gain in human freedom in modern times. But when socialism tried to implement that concept of a new civilization that went beyond simple reform, it was sometimes disastrously wrong or else vague and

> merely rhetorical. The question is: Can socialism learn from the defeats and betrayals that resulted from its flawed understanding of its own profound truths?[81]

By the time the book came out, Michael would be back in the hospital. He wasn't able to fly to Stockholm for the SI's congress after all. Instead, DSOC and DSA veteran Skip Roberts traveled in his place and presented a copy of *Socialism: Past and Future* to Willy Brandt, to whom it was dedicated. The congress delegates elected Michael as honorary president of the Socialist International.[82]

Michael got to celebrate one final May Day, but few who saw him that month expected to be celebrating Labor Day with him. He gave his final talk in New York City to a luncheon meeting of the Metro Labor Press Council, a group of reporters and editors from New York-based union newspapers, held at NYU on May 5. He spoke of the need to rebuild labor's image as a progressive force in American society after a decade in which the movement had been stigmatized as greedy and outdated. Several times in the course of his speech he was forced to stop by coughing fits, but each time he composed himself, started again, and finished strongly.

Dinah Leventhal, a twenty-two-year-old DSA activist was among those in the audience. She had been working as an editorial assistant for the Amalgamated Clothing and Textile Workers Union (ACTWU) newspaper since her graduation from Harvard University the previous year, and in July she would begin a new job as DSA's national youth organizer. After the luncheon, she and Michael talked for a few minutes. He reminisced about his own days as a YPSL organizer, hitchhiking around the country in the late 1950s and gathering material that he would use in *The Other America:*

> He said he had felt an incredible degree of freedom and learned so much in those years. He said I should make the most of it, being an organizer and traveling around, getting to see the country and getting to know what the country was all about. He really loved this country and thought that you had to love the country to be a radical, to be a socialist, and to want to change it.[83]

Michael had eleven weeks remaining. After a final trip to Iowa City on May 6 to speak at a law school commencement, he grew too sick for any further public appearances. He spent most of June in the hospital. When it became clear that there was nothing that doctors could do for him, he was sent home to Larchmont, where he died on the last day of July 1989.

In a famous speech in 1910, American socialist leader Eugene Debs disavowed the role of revolutionary tribune of the people. Many years later

Michael cited the speech as containing his "favorite quotation on what it means to be a true democrat." "I would not lead you into the promised land if I could," Debs declared, "because if I could lead you in, some one else would lead you out."

Debs nonetheless remained a larger-than-life symbol of republican manhood and redemptive martyrdom to his many admirers, exercising what his contemporary Max Weber called "charismatic authority." In his biography of Debs, Nick Salvatore wrote that the old campaigner "crystallized for many the meaning of Socialism." So did his successor Norman Thomas. As Michael would write of Thomas, his very bearing seemed "to incarnate a peculiarly American and Protestant sense of social justice and personal authority." So in time, minus the Protestantism, would Michael.

In the years since Michael's death, no claimant has emerged to pick up the mantle of Debs and Thomas and Harrington. Michael seems to represent the end of the line. Like his predecessors, he believed that to awaken the conscience or change the consciousness of a nation, one had to be prepared to build an organization, start a publication, speak in a thousand halls to crowds of hundreds, or scores, or tens, if necessary, recruiting one's followers from those converted by the sound of one's voice and the strength of one's arguments. An honorable, even heroic, vision, it was also, as Michael reluctantly conceded in the last years of his life, one for which there remained precious little room in American political culture.

NOTES

Preface

1. Michael Harrington interviewed by Rosalie Riegle Troester, July 7, 1988, p. 24, transcript from the Catholic Worker Archives, Marquette University.
2. E.M. Forster, *Howard's End* (New York: Penguin, 1986), pp. 151–152.
3. See, for example, Irwin Unger, *The Best of Intentions: The Triumph and Failure of the Great Society Under Kennedy, Johnson and Nixon* (New York: Doubleday, 1996), p. 65.
4. "Required Reading," *Time*, June 8, 1998, p. 108.
5. Forster, *Howard's End*, p. 85.
6. Michael Harrington, *Fragments of the Century* (New York: Saturday Review Press, 1973); *The Long Distance Runner: An Autobiography* (New York: Henry Holt, 1988). Also see Robert A. Gorman, *Michael Harrington: Speaking American* (New York: Routledge, 1985).

Chapter One: *Community, Family, and Faith, 1928-1944*

1. Karl Marx and Frederick Engels, *Letters to Americans, 1848–1895* (New York: International Publishers, 1953), pp. 25–26.
2. Jean Fahey Eberle, *St. Roch's: The Story of a Parish* (St. Louis: St. Roch's Parish, n.d.). I am grateful to Msgr. Sal Polizzi of St. Roch's Church for making a copy of Michael Harrington's baptismal certificate available to me.
3. *St. Louis Post-Dispatch,* February 28, 1928.
4. Quoted in David Burner, *Herbert Hoover: A Public Life* (New York: Knopf, 1979), p. 201.
5. W. A. Swanberg, *Norman Thomas: The Last Idealist* (New York: Scribner's, 1976), p. 112; *St. Louis Globe Democrat*, October 19, 1928, p. 24.
6. For one historian's appreciation of St. Louis's virtues, see George Lipsitz, *The Sidewalks of St. Louis: Places, People, and Politics in an American City* (Columbia: University of Missouri Press, 1991), passim. The St. Louis World's Fair is described in James Neal Primm, *Lion of the Valley: St. Louis, Missouri* (Boulder, Colo.: Pruett Publishing Company, 1981), pp. 395–418.
7. Primm, *Lion of the Valley*, pp. 9–10, 16.
8. Alice Lida Cochran, *The Saga of an Irish Immigrant Family: The Descendants of John Mullanphy* (New York: Arno Press, 1976), passim. Adolphus Busch (of Anheuser-Busch fame) and the ragtime composer Scott Joplin were among other men who came to St. Louis and found fame and wealth. See Primm, *Lion of the Valley*, pp. 347–349, and Lipsitz, *The Sidewalks of St. Louis*, pp. 69–70.
9. The parochial records of Glanworth Parish in County Cork list Patrick's birthdate as May 4, 1861. I am grateful to William Fitzgibbon, the grandson of Patrick's brother David, for this and other information about Patrick's life in Ireland. Letter from William Fitzgibbon to the author, February 10, 1992.
10. Letter from Peggy M. FitzGibbon to the author, October 4, 1992. Peggy M. FitzGibbon, a great, great granddaughter of Patrick R. Fitzgibbon, is the unofficial family historian of the FitzGibbon clan; the family tree she assembled proved an invaluable resource for this biography. [Readers of these footnotes should not confuse her with the other Peggy FitzGibbon in these pages, who was Patrick's granddaughter and Michael's first cousin.] Additional details on family history came from Bishop Edmund Fitzgibbon, a distant Irish-born cousin of Michael's who is today the bishop of the Catholic Diocese of Warri in Nigeria. Letter from Bishop Edmund Fitzgibbon to the author, December 8, 1992.

11. *Guide to Cork* (London: Ward, Lock & Co., n.d.), p. 81. According to Bishop Edmund Fitzgibbon, "the last Prior in the Dominican Abbey near the village of Glanworth was a William Fitzgibbon. He and the monks were put to death by the Cromwellian soldiers who destroyed the Abbey. I do not vouch for a secure [family] connection [but] William is a recurring Fitzgibbon family name." Letter from Bishop Edmund Fitzgibbon to the author, December 8, 1992.
12. James S. Donnelly Jr., *The Land and the People of Nineteenth Century Cork: The Rural Economy and the Land Question* (London: Routledge and Kegan Paul, 1975), p. 86.
13. Ibid., pp. 88–91.
14. Ibid., pp. 120, 125.
15. On weather conditions in 1872, see Ibid., p. 148. In the four decades after the potato famine, nearly 425,000 people emigrated from County Cork, proportionately more than from any other section of Ireland, Ibid., p. 227. U.S. census records for 1900 confirm the 1872 date of immigration. See *Twelfth Census of the United States: 1900,* microfilm reel 896, vol. 95, e.d. 259, sheet 3, line 30. (The *Fourteenth Census of the United States: 1920,* microfilm reel 953, vol. 103, e.d. 581, sheet 13, line 99, lists 1878 as Patrick's date of immigration, which probably reflected Patrick's failing memory or a mistake by the enumerator.)
16. Author's interview with Peggy FitzGibbon, November 3, 1990. William Fitzgibbon, grandson of Patrick's brother David, recalled family stories that in Patrick's time "horses tied up outside the church were 'borrowed' and were returned after wild gallops to the same place sweating and panting to the puzzlement of their owners." Letter from William Fitzgibbon to Peggy M. FitzGibbon, February 22, 1991. When Michael made his first trip to Ireland, a few months before his death, he proudly told an interviewer from an Irish newspaper that his grandfather "fled to the US to escape the police." Peadar Kirby, "Perhaps the 90s Will Be Socialist," *Alpha* (Dublin), February 17, 1989, p. 15.
17. According to U.S. census records, Patrick's future wife, Nellie Dillon, immigrated to the United States two years before her mother Ellen followed. *Twelfth Census of the United States: 1900,* microfilm reel 896, vol. 95, e.d. 259, sheet 3, lines 31, 37. Patrick's brother John and his sisters Norah and Margaret all made the journey to the United States. David, the youngest brother in the family, also tried to leave, but his mother followed him, caught up with him in Queenstown (Cobh), and brought him home. Patrick's three remaining sisters, Bridget, Mary, and Kate, married local farmers. Letter from Bishop Edmund Fitzgibbon, December 8, 1992.
18. Letter from Peggy M. FitzGibbon to the author, October 4, 1992.
19. Letter from William Fitzgibbon to Peggy M. FitzGibbon, February 22, 1991; letter from Peggy FitzGibbon to Peggy M. FitzGibbon, February 19, 1991.
20. Etan Diamond, "Kerry Patch: Irish Immigrant Life in St. Louis," *Gateway Heritage* 10 (Fall 1989), p. 27.
21. On the proportion of immigrants among St. Louis's population, see Primm, *Lion of the Valley,* p. 332, and Lipsitz, *The Sidewalks of St. Louis,* p. 42. On nativist violence in the 1850s, see Primm, *Lion of the Valley,* pp. 177–179; 333.
22. Lipsitz, *The Sidewalks of St. Louis,* pp. 95–98; David Herreshoff, *American Disciples of Marx: From the Age of Jackson to the Progressive Era* (Detroit: Wayne State University, 1967), pp. 59–67.
23. Primm, *Lion of the Valley,* 327–331; David T. Burbank, "The First International in Saint Louis," *Bulletin of the Missouri Historical Society* (January 1962), pp. 163–172; David B. Roediger, "'Not Only the Ruling Classes to Overcome, But Also the So-Called Mob': Class, Skill, and Community in the St. Louis General Strike of 1877," *Journal of Social History* 19 (Winter 1985), pp. 213–227.
24. J. L. Spalding, *The Religious Mission of the Irish People and Catholic Colonization* (New York: The Catholic Publication Society, 1880), p. 127.
25. Steven P. Erie describes Irish-American working-class support for labor and socialist parties in the 1870s and 1880s in *Rainbow's End: Irish-Americans and the Dilemmas of Urban Machine Politics, 1840–1985* (Berkeley: University of California Press, 1988), pp. 49–50.

But such examples of radicalism remained localized and proved ephemeral. Also see L. A. O'Donnell, *Irish Voice and Organized Labor in America: A Biographical Study* (Westport, Conn.: Greenwood Press, 1997).

26. I am grateful to Martin Towey for recounting this incident to me. By the time Michael was growing up, in the mid–1930s, socialism in St. Louis counted proportionately more supporters among the faculty at Washington University than it did among the city's workers. Author's interview with Martin Towey, May 14, 1992.
27. Letter from William Fitzgibbon to Peggy M. FitzGibbon, February 22, 1991, in author's possession.
28. Bishop Edmund Fitzgibbon met Patrick on Patrick's visit to Glanworth in 1936: "He was introduced to us children as an important 'son of the soil.'" Letter from Bishop Fitzgibbon to the author, December 8, 1992. According to William Fitzgibbon, "versions of the successes and achievements of 'Uncle Johnny' and 'Uncle Patsy' in St. Louis have been current in my family for several generations, . . . beginning with poverty and menial tasks and ending with promotion to the highest public offices in St. Louis. The achievements of one generation became intermingled with those of another until it was difficult to establish what, if anything, they had actually done in that city."

    Letter from William Fitzgibbon to the author, December 14, 1992. Patrick did his best to preserve his memory in Ballylegan, sending the family an oil painting of himself as a child, which still hung in the cottage on the Fitzgibbon family farm in the 1980s when his niece Peggy visited. Author's interview with Peggy FitzGibbon, November 3, 1990.
29. Michael Harrington, *Fragments of the Century* (New York: Saturday Review Press, 1973), p. 7; author's interview with Peggy FitzGibbon, November 3, 1990. Patrick's obituary appeared in the *St. Louis Globe Democrat,* April 17, 1945. His naturalization date is listed in his entry in the 1920 census and in the naturalization records of the Missouri Circuit Court, 22nd Judicial Court, for the May term of 1884, p. 463. I am grateful to Melvina Conley, archivist for the Missouri Circuit Court, for making this information available to me.
30. Author's interview with Peggy FitzGibbon, November 3, 1990; letter from Peggy FitzGibbon to Peggy M. FitzGibbon, February 19, 1991. According to the *Twelfth Census of the United States: 1900*, microfilm reel 896, vol. 95, e.d. 259, sheet 3, line 31, Nellie Dillon was born in 1868 and immigrated in 1882.
31. Letter from Peggy M. FitzGibbon to the author, October 4, 1992; letter from Peggy FitzGibbon to Peggy M. FitzGibbon, February 2, 1991. On Irish fertility patterns, see Robert E. Kennedy Jr. *The Irish: Emigration, Marriage, and Fertility* (Berkeley: University of California Press, 1973), pp. 173–205.
32. Author's interview with Peggy Fitzgibbon, November 3, 1990.
33. Author's interview with Peggy Fitzgibbon, November 3, 1990. Richard, J. Emmet, and David W. FitzGibbon all became lawyers (the remaining son, Matthew P., who was somewhat of the family ne'er-do-well, took a job with the city water department, which he lost during the depression).
34. Frank Brennan, who grew up in Kerry Patch and who later lived on the same street as the Harringtons in St. Louis's West End, delighted in telling this story in later years. Author's interview with Bill Loftus, July 17, 1993.
35. Author's interview with Ed Brungard, December 14, 1990.
36. When she was in her fifties, Catherine received national recognition in an article in the *Saturday Evening Post* on St. Louis city politics, which described her as a "civic-minded housewife" and a "volunteer spark plug." Joe Alex Morris, "How to Rescue a City," *Saturday Evening Post*, August 18, 1956, p. 56. Also see Marjorie Louise Purvis, "Saint Louis Women of Achievement and Community," Ph.D. diss., St. Louis University, 1973, pp. 27, 28, 34, 37, 42, 45, 65–66; *St. Louis Globe Democrat*, July 10, 1955; December 30, 1956; January 22, 1957; *St. Louis Post-Dispatch*, July 10, 1955.
37. Author's interview with Father Frederick Zimmerman, December 13, 1990; interview with John Padberg, December 13, 1990.
38. Some of Catherine's insecurities stemmed from her family's long residence in Kerry

Patch. She may also have felt herself slighted in her father's attentions, since she was neither the first nor the favorite daughter in the household. Author's interview with Bill Loftus, September 27, 1991.

39. "The mother, like the nun, was retired and secluded, cloistered in her home. Like a saint, her sacrifices went unknown and unacknowledged." Colleen McDannell, "Catholic Domesticity, 1860–1960," in *American Catholic Women: A Historical Exploration,* ed. Karen Kennelly, C.S.J. (New York: Macmillan, 1989), p. 59.
40. Purvis, "Saint Louis Women of Achievement and Community," p. 27.
41. Author's interview with Ed Brungard, December 14, 1990.
42. Author's interview with Peggy FitzGibbon, November 3, 1990; interview with Bill Loftus, September 27, 1991.
43. Edward's one-paragraph obituary in the December 30, 1955, *St. Louis Globe Dispatch* notes a brother surviving in San Diego and three sisters living in St. Louis. (Catherine's obituary, in contrast, ran to two columns and included a photograph.) The *Fourteenth Census of the United States: 1920,* microfilm reel 961, vol. 120, e.d. 526, sheet 10, line 1, lists Edward's birthplace as Missouri, his father's birthplace as Ohio, and his mother's in Ireland. Edward first appears in *Gould's Saint Louis Directory* in 1905, and every year subsequently except for 1918. I have been unable to find any surviving descendants of the St. Louis Harringtons. Michael's childhood friend Ed Brungard recalled that "Eddie Harrington came from a large family. The Harrington family had six or seven brothers. But I never met any of them." Author's interview with Ed Brungard, December 14, 1990. Michael told Stephanie Harrington of his father's desire to be a cartoonist. Author's interview with Stephanie Harrington, November 12, 1992.
44. *Martindale Hubbell Law Directory,* vol. 1, 1931 (New York: 1931), p. 1347; Michael's father took out an advertisement for his services as "Attorney-at-law, Patents and Patent Causes" in the 1928 *Polk-Gould Directory.*
45. The 1920 U.S. census reported that Edward was living with his sisters Kathryn, age twenty-six, and Ellen, age twenty-four.
46. According to Virginia Brungard's son Ed (who became Michael's closest childhood friend) Catherine "met Eddie and decided Eddie was going to be her man." Author's interview with Ed Brungard, December 14, 1990.
47. Letter from Peggy M. FitzGibbon to the author, October 4, 1992.
48. The Kingsbury neighborhood is described in *St. Louis: Its Neighborhoods and Neighbors, Landmarks and Milestones,* ed. Robert E. Hannon (St. Louis: St. Louis Commerce and Growth Association, 1986), pp. 112–116.
49. Author's interview with Ed Brungard, December 14, 1990.
50. Author's interview with Ed Brungard, December 14, 1990; interview with Richard Dempsey, May 16, 1992.
51. Author's interview with Ed Brungard, December 14, 1990.
52. Martin Towey, "Hooverville: St. Louis Had the Largest," *Gateway Heritage* 1 (fall 1980), pp. 4–11; Primm, *Lion of the Valley*, pp. 468–469.
53. Harrington, *Fragments of the Century,* p. 1.
54. Author's interview with Stephanie Harrington, December 3, 1992.
55. In 1957, Catherine took a job as a counselor at Harris Teachers College, where she worked until her retirement in 1971. "Catherine Harrington Dies; Was Civic Leader," *St. Louis Globe-Democrat*, July 25, 1980. I appreciate the help in obtaining Catherine's academic transcript provided by Stephanie Stueber, C.S.J., director of college relations at Fontbonne. The observation about Catherine's study habits was from Ed Brungard. Author's interview with Ed Brungard, December 14, 1990.
56. "Once Known for Her Own Record, Now She Is Michael's Mother," *St. Louis Post-Dispatch,* January 20, 1971. Catherine later donated the collection of children's books she had assembled for Michael to a Catholic missionary, who took them back with him to Honduras.
57. Michael Harrington, *The Other America* (New York: Macmillan, 1962), front piece; *Fragments of the Century,* p. 1.

58. Marion Magid, "The Man Who Discovered Poverty," *New York Herald Tribune Magazine,* December 27, 1964, p. 9.
59. Letter from Michael Harrington to Peggy Brennan, May 29, 1950, in author's possession. Michael also describes his father as "gentle" in his autobiography, *Fragments of the Century*, p. 1, and in the acknowledgments to *The Other America.*
60. Edward M. Harrington, "Agamemnon," The Holy Cross *Purple,* vol. 57, April 1945, pp. 373–374. Also see the description of "Doctor Carl Mason," a man "who relied on a yearly American Legion Convention, or perhaps a game of bingo at the Elks' Club to fill adventure's needs for a year," in Michael's short story "Exit Smiling," *Purple*, vol. 57, January 1945, p. 225.
61. This was a story that Michael later told his wife. Author's interview with Stephanie Harrington, December 3, 1992.
62. Author's interview with Martin Towey, May 14, 1992; Primm, *Lion of the Valley*, p. 462.
63. "The law is flexible," Judge FitzGibbon once told a reporter. "If a man comes before me who's supposed to be a criminal, I'm the one who decides whether he is or not. I'm the one who says whether he's going to jail. And if I think he's not such a bad soul, I'm the one who can give him a break." Some of the men he sent to prison became his friends, and he would help them find jobs or make loans to them after their release. "David W. FitzGibbon Dies; Judge with 'Biggest Heart,'" *St. Louis Post-Dispatch*, April 6, 1982, p. 10.; "A Judge Who's Firm but Fair," *St. Louis Globe-Democrat*, April 9, 1966, p. 3.
64. Author's interview with Peggy FitzGibbon, November 3, 1990.
65. Michael Harrington, *The Long Distance Runner: An Autobiography* (New York: Henry Holt, 1988), p. 4.
66. Harrington, *Fragments of the Century,* p. 8.
67. Harrington, *Fragments of the Century,* p. 4. Also see Margaret Sullivan, "Fighting for Irish Freedom: St. Louis Irish-Americans, 1918–1922," in *The Irish: America's Political Class,* ed. James B. Walsh (New York: Arno Press, 1976), pp. 184–206.
68. Harrington, *Fragments of the Century,* pp. 5–6. Harrington's observations are supported by recent scholarship. See Martin Towey, "Kerry Patch Revisited: Irish-Americans in St. Louis in the Turn of the Century Era," in *From Paddy to Studs: Irish-American Communities in the Turn of the Century Era, 1880 to 1920,* ed. Timothy J. Meagher (Westport, Conn.: Greenwood Press, 1986), p. 157.
69. On FDR's courtship of Irish-Americans, see William V. Shannon, *The American Irish* (New York: Macmillan, 1973), pp. 328–329, 347–348, 352–353.
70. *Angels with Dirty Faces* and *Going My Way* are discussed in Les and Barbara Keyser, *Hollywood and the Catholic Church: The Image of Roman Catholicism in American Movies* (Chicago: Loyola University Press, 1984), pp. 62–67, 98–107. According to Bill Loftus, he and Michael went to see *Going My Way* in 1944. Author's interview with Bill Loftus, July 15, 1993.
71. Author's interview with Father Robert Henle, December 13, 1990.
72. *Chaminade College Elementary and High School Catalogue,* 1940, p. 12.
73. I am grateful to Alyce M. Hrdlicka, alumni/public relations director at Chaminade, for providing me with a copy of Michael's school transcript and a 1940 Chaminade catalog.
74. Author's interview with Ed Brungard, December 14, 1990.
75. Author's interview with Ed Brungard, December 14, 1990.
76. Author's interview with Peggy FitzGibbon, November 3, 1990. In 1987, Michael told reporter Bella Stumbo that had he revealed his desire to become a poet as a child, he would have been stigmatized as a homosexual. See "The Lonely Fight of Last Old Leftist," *Los Angeles Times*, April 4, 1987.
77. Author's interview with Ed Brungard, December 14, 1990.
78. Author's interview with Father John Padberg, December 13, 1990; Harrington, *Fragments of the Century,* p. 10. The origins of St. Louis University High School are described in Michael's yearbook, the *Dauphin* (St. Louis: 1944), and in William B. Faherty, S.J., *Better the Dream: Saint Louis: University and Community, 1818–1968* (Boulder, Colo..: Pruett

Publishing, 1990), pp. 8–12, 286. I am grateful to Eleanor McCarthy, assistant librarian at St. Louis University High School, for her help researching school publications.

79. St. Louis University High School *Dauphin* (St. Louis: 1941).
80. Paul Johnson, *A History of Christianity* (London: Weidenfield and Nicholson, 1976), pp. 304–305.
81. Michael noted Trotsky's views on the Jesuits in *Fragments of a Century,* p. 8. Another observer who made the Jesuit-Bolshevik comparison was Michael's future coeditor at *Dissent,* Lewis Coser, in "The Militant Collective: Jesuits and Leninists," *Social Research* 40 (spring 1973), pp. 110–128.
82. Peter McDonough, *Men Astutely Trained: A History of the Jesuits in the American Century* (New York: The Free Press, 1992), pp. 136–137, 149.
83. Author's interview with Father Robert Henle, December 13, 1990. Wade grew up as part of the only Catholic family in Whitesboro, Texas. His father reputedly strapped on two revolvers and single-handedly dispersed a mob bent on burning down a black neighborhood after a local white woman was raped. Wade was liberal in his own political sympathies and was interested in the appeal of Marxism to western intellectuals. As chairman of the philosophy department at St. Louis University he raised a lot of eyebrows by sponsoring a speaking engagement at the university by the French Marxist Roger Garaudy. He was also, in later years, fiercely critical of what he felt was the relativism and intellectual dishonesty of many liberals. Wade was known to advise students to consider whether they might be happier as atheists, agnostics, Methodists, or Lutherans, telling them that "it's better to be a good Lutheran than a bad Catholic." Rev. James F. Meara, S.J., *For the Sake of Argument: A Portrait of Father William Ligon Wade, S.J.* (St. Louis: Jesuit Community at Saint Louis University, Inc., 1976), pp. 32–33, 35–36, 46–47.
84. Author's interview with Father Robert Henle, December 13, 1990.
85. John W. Donohue, S.J., *Jesuit Education: An Essay on the Foundations of Its Idea* (New York: Fordham University Press, 1963), pp. 143–148.
86. St. Louis University High School *Dauphin,* 1942.
87. Author's interview with Father John Padberg, December 13, 1990.
88. Author's interview with Richard Dempsey, May 16, 1992.
89. St. Louis University High School *Prep News,* October 29, 1943, p. 4; April 21, 1944, p. 4.
90. Author's interview with Msgr. Jerome Wilkerson, May 13, 1992.
91. Author's interview with Father John Padberg, December 13, 1990; interview with Ed Brungard, December 14, 1990; interview with Bill Loftus, July 20, 1993.
92. Michael's high school classmates continue to refer to him as "Ned" Harrington to this day, but in the school newspaper he was alternately "Ned" and "Ed" (and only for comic effect, "Neddie"). See, for examples, *Prep News,* October 8, 1943, p. 4; October 29, 1943, p. 4; April 24, 1944, p. 4. Michael's adolescent wit was attested by Richard Dempsey and Father John Padberg, as well as by the 1941 yearbook. Author's interview with Richard Dempsey, May 16, 1992; interview with Father John Padberg, December 13, 1990; St. Louis University High School *Dauphin,* 1941.
93. Harrington, *Fragments of the Century,* pp. 10–11.
94. Author's interview with Bill Loftus, September 27, 1991.
95. Author's interview with Richard Dempsey, May 16, 1992; interview with Ed Brungard, December 14, 1990.
96. Author's interview with Father John Padberg, December 13, 1990.
97. Harrington, *Fragments of the Century,* p. 11. I am grateful to the Rev. Leo Dressel, president of St. Louis University High School, and his assistant Bob Lynch for making a copy of Michael's transcript available to me.
98. For a sample of Michael's high school prose, see St. Louis University High School *Prep News,* October 8, 1943, p. 4.
99. St. Louis University High School *Dauphin* (St. Louis: 1941); St. Louis University High School *Prep News,* May 5, 1944, p. 4. John Padberg recalled Michael as the "gentle scoffer" of the class. Richard Dempsey remembered him as "affable and friendly" al-

though "not really part of any particular clique at the high school." Jerome Wilkerson remembered him as "a cocky, colorful fellow. He wasn't a big athletic hero, or anything like that, but he was bright and he knew he was bright." Author's interview with Father John Padberg, December 13, 1990; interview with Richard Dempsey, May 16, 1992; interview with Msgr. Jerome Wilkerson, May 13, 1992.

100. Interview with Msgr. Jerome Wilkerson, May 13, 1992; interview with Bill Loftus, September 27, 1991. In 1942, when St. Louis University High School tied for city champs, the team of Richard Dempsey and Michael Harrington won three matches in the Clayton tournament, one in the Webster tournament, and lost one in the St. Charles tournament. St. Louis University *Dauphin,* 1942, pp. 60–62.
101. St. Louis University High School *Prep News*, March 31, 1944, p. 2.
102. Tom Dooley's St. Louis years are chronicled in James T. Fisher, *Dr. America: The Lives of Thomas A. Dooley, 1927–1961* (Amherst: University of Massachusetts Press, 1997), pp. 12–24.
103. Fisher, *Dr. America,* pp. 26–27. Michael would later tell his son Alex that he arrived at Holy Cross without any sexual experience. Author's interview with Alex Harrington, September 27, 1991.
104. Harrington, *Fragments of the Century,* p. 12.
105. Author's interview with Richard Dempsey, May 16, 1992; St. Louis University High School *Prep News,* pictorial section, spring 1944; *Prep News,* October 8, 1943, p. 4.
106. John Padberg recalled that in the last months of high school, the war "impinged" on Michael's relations with his classmates. "They were aware that he was two years younger than we were, and that he had the opportunity to go to college right away, while a fair number of people in our class knew that they were going to go right into the army." Authors interview with Father John Padberg, December 13, 1990.
107. Castro's comments are quoted in Tad Szulc, *Fidel: A Critical Portrait* (New York: William Morrow and Co., 1986), p. 117.
108. Quoted in David Shi, *The Simple Life: Plain Living and High Thinking in American Culture* (New York: Oxford University Press, 1985), p. 9. Also see Alan Brinkley, *Liberalism and Its Discontents* (Cambridge, Mass.: Harvard University Press, 1998), p. 289.
109. *Rerum Novarum* is quoted in David J. O'Brien, *American Catholics and Social Reform: The New Deal Years* (New York: Oxford University Press, 1968), p. 14.
110. Quoted in George Q. Flynn, *American Catholics and the Roosevelt Presidency* (Lexington: University of Kentucky Press, 1968), pp. 24–25.
111. St. Louis University High School *Dauphin,* 1944, p. 59. Also see Flynn, *American Catholics and the Roosevelt Presidency,* pp. 22–26.
112. Quoted in O'Brien, *American Catholics and Social Reform,* p. 45.
113. As David O'Brien noted, "American Catholic social thought in the 1930's was characterized by unanimous acceptance of official Church teachings and wide and often bitter disagreement as to their meaning and application." *American Catholics and Social Reform,* p. 100.
114. As one of Michael's most astute interviewers wrote, "[If] the Jesuits do not specialize in breeding Socialists, they do excel in developing rigorous dissenters, who retain the mode, if not the content, of Jesuit training." Marion Magid, "The Man Who Discovered Poverty," *New York Herald Tribune Magazine,* December 27, 1964, p. 9.
115. Carl Gustav Jung, *Psychology and Religion* (New Haven: Yale University Press, 1938), p. 23. More recently, historian Tony Judt noted the "symbiotic relationship" between Catholic and Communist beliefs in France in the postwar era: "both represented world outlooks that were pessimistic about humanity but optimistic with regard to history." *Past Imperfect: French Intellectuals, 1944–1956* (Berkeley: University of California Press, 1992), p. 88.
116. Microfiche transcript of CBS *Sunday Morning News,* October 10, 1982. The interviewer was Jerry Landy.
117. Harrington, *Fragments of the Century,* p. 3; *The Politics at God's Funeral: The Spiritual Crisis of Western ivilization* (New York: Holt, Rinehart and Winston, 1983), pp. 10–11.

Chapter Two: *Leaving Home, 1944–1947*

1. Holy Cross *Purple,* March 1947, pp. 485–486.
2. According to Michael's high school transcript, Holy Cross was the only school he asked to have his grades sent to. Also see Holy Cross *Crusader*, March 1, 1968, p. 2.
3. The figures on college enrollment are from William M. Halsey, *The Survival of American Innocence: Catholicism in an Era of Disillusionment* (Notre Dame: University of Notre Dame Press, 1980), p. 53.
4. Author's interview with Bill Loftus, September 27, 1991.
5. Letter from Jack Drummey to the author, February 15, 1992.
6. Until 1865 graduates of Holy Cross received their degrees through Georgetown. Seven Holy Cross graduates were among those who died in the Union's cause in the Civil War. The early history of Holy Cross is recounted in Walter J. Meagher, S.J., and William J. Grattan, *The Spires of Fenwick: A History of the College of the Holy Cross, 1843–1963* (New York: Vantage Press, 1966), pp. 17–107.
7. Michael Harrington, *Fragments of the Century* (New York: Saturday Review Press, 1973), p. 5.
8. Quoted in Meagher and Grattan, *The Spires of Fenwick,* p. 151.
9. Harrington, *Fragments of the Century,* p. 14.
10. Michael Harrington, "Change and Holy Cross," *Stars and Stripes*, June 16, 1971, p. 13.
11. William M. Halsey describes the "robust enthusiasm" with which American Catholics embraced neo-Thomism in *The Survival of American Innocence*, pp. 138–168. On the influence of neo-Thomism also see Margaret Mary Reher, *Catholic Intellectual Life in America: A Historical Study of Persons and Movements* (New York: Macmillan, 1989), pp. 114–118. Among Aquinas's teachings was the belief that the pursuit of wealth was an unworthy occupation for Christians and could not lead to happiness; only through achieving the "vision of the divine essence" could humans know true happiness in this life.
12. Warren Coffey, "Jesuit Education: Between Two Worlds," *Ramparts* 2 (March 1963), pp. 10–14.
13. Harrington, "Change and Holy Cross," p. 13; author's interview with Bill Loftus, September 27, 1991.
14. Author's interview with Bill Loftus, September 27, 1991. No copy of Michael's senior thesis has survived in either Michael's papers or the Holy Cross archives. Gerry Martel, Michael's roommate at Holy Cross until his departure for military service, was a classmate in one of Brennan's literature classes. He wrote to Mike in 1988, recalling, "I got an 'A' in 'Ma' Brennan's class because E.M.H. [Michael] wrote a Sonnet for me." Gerry Martel to Michael Harrington, August 12, 1988, Democratic Socialists of America office files.
15. Edward M. Harrington, "Crusader—A Reply," Holy Cross *Purple,* February 1946, pp. 256, 258.
16. Ed Harrington, "Four Marine Veterans, Chums, Fought Together," Holy Cross *Tomahawk*, September 20, 1944, p. 1.
17. Edward Harrington, "Senior Class History," Holy Cross *Purple Patcher,* 1947.
18. Letter from Jack Drummey to the author, February 15, 1992.
19. Harrington, "Senior Class History."
20. Edward Michael Harrington transcript, St. Louis University High School. According to Jane H. Price, archivist at the Naval Academy, the academy does not retain records of applicants who did not enroll at the academy, nor is there any way to determine whether Harrington was nominated for admission. I am grateful to Ms. Price for sending me a copy of the 1945 "Regulations Governing the Admission of Candidates into the Naval Academy as Midshipmen."
21. Letter from Charles E. Fitzgibbon to the author, October 8, 1991.
22. Holy Cross *Purple Patcher,* 1946.
23. Harrington, "Change and Holy Cross," p. 13.
24. Holy Cross *Purple Patcher,* 1947.
25. Holy Cross *Purple,* March 1947, pp. 485–486.
26. Michael's Holy Cross classmates, by and large, pursued conventional careers and held

conventional political views in later years. That may have been a factor in Michael's failure to keep in close contact with them in later years. Gerry Martel, Michael's freshman roommate, stayed in closer touch with Michael after graduation than most, seeing him "every five to ten years or so." "His lifestyle and mine were different," Martel recalled: "Money and the trappings of an affluent American are my modus operandi." Although he claimed that Michael chastised him for his "decadent" ways, Martel always felt that "my life is better for having known Edward Michael Harrington." Letter to the author, August 12, 1991.

27. Holy Cross *Purple*, March 1947, pp. 485–486.
28. Edward M. Harrington, "Philosopher's Stone," Holy Cross *Purple*, February 1947, pp. 386–392; "Posterity vs. Prosperity," Holy Cross *Purple,* November 1946, pp. 85–88; "Pause for Greatness," Holy Cross *Purple,* December 1946, pp. 226–229.
29. Harrington, "Change and Holy Cross," p. 13. Michael used the term "Oedipal reaction" when interviewed by Diana Trilling in March 1976. I am grateful to Diana Trilling for permission to quote from this interview.
30. "O'Brien Defies Communism," Holy Cross *Tomahawk*, January 10, 1945, p. 2.
31. Holy Cross *Tomahawk*, March 21, 1945, p. 1.
32. Holy Cross *Tomahawk*, April 30, 1947, p. 2.
33. Charles E. Fitzgibbon, Michael's classmate and the editor in chief of the *Tomahawk* in 1946, believes that "both the viewpoint and writing style" of "For the Radicals" were "consistent with my memories of Ed." Letter to the author, October 8, 1991.
34. On Chesterton's influence at the Catholic Worker, see Mel Piehl, *Breaking Bread: The Catholic Worker and the Origin of Catholic Radicalism in America* (Philadelphia: Temple University Press, 1982), pp. 71–72. On distributism, also see Christopher Hollis, *The Mind of Chesterton* (London: Hollis & Carter, 1970), p. 14.
35. Hugh Kenner, *Paradox in Chesterton* (New York: Sheed & Ward, 1947), p. xi.
36. Holy Cross *Purple Patcher,* 1946. According to Bill Loftus, Michael had been "constantly exposed" to Chesterton since his high school days. Author's interview with Bill Loftus, April 12, 1993.
37. Quoted in Garry Wills, *Chesterton: Man and Mask* (New York: Sheed & Ward, 1961), p. 38. "The special rhetorical purpose of Chesterton," Hugh Kenner noted, "is to overcome the mental inertia of human beings, which mental inertia is constantly landing them in the strange predicament of both seeing a thing and not seeing it. When people's perceptions are in this condition, they must, in the strictest sense of the words, be made to renew their acquaintance with things. They must be made to see them anew, as if for the first time." Kenner, *Paradox in Chesterton*, p. 43. Also see Wills, *Chesterton: Man and Mask*, p. 37.
38. Holy Cross *Tomahawk*, May 8, 1946, p. 2.
39. Harrington, *Fragments of the Century,* p. 3.
40. Katherine T. Corbett and Mary E. Seematter, "'No Crystal Stair': Black St. Louis, 1920–1940," *Gateway Heritage* 16 (fall 1995), pp. 82–88.
41. John Cogley interview with Michael Harrington, "Strictly Autobiographical—By Request," audiotape of a radio broadcast, sponsored by the Center for the Study of Democratic Institutions, Santa Barbara, California, spring 1965.
42. James Neal Primm discusses St. Louis's segregation ordinances in *Lion of the Valley: St. Louis, Missouri* (Boulder, Colo.: Pruett Publishing Company, 1981), pp. 435–439. The information about "pushing Tuesday" and "shoving Thursday" came from my interview with Bill Loftus, September 27, 1991.
43. According to Father Paul Nelligan, S.J., college archivist, the first significant numbers of blacks students were enrolled at Holy Cross in 1968. Telephone conversation with the author, March 30, 1993. I am grateful to Jo-Anne Carr, assistant archivist at Holy Cross, for checking the records of the classes of 1944–1947.
44. Edward M. Harrington Jr., "G. W. Jackson—Solid Sender," Holy Cross *Purple,* October 1944, p. 23.
45. Quoted in William B. Faherty, S.J., *Better the Dream: Saint Louis: University and Community, 1818–1968* (St. Louis University, 1968), p. 341.

46. Donald J. Kemper, "Catholic Integration in St. Louis, 1935–1947," *Missouri Historical Review* 73, no. 1 (1978), pp. 1–22. Michael would note Cardinal Ritter's role in the desegregation of Catholic schools in his autobiography, *Fragments of the Century,* p. 6.
47. Edward M. Harrington, "Pause for Greatness," Holy Cross *Purple,* December 1946, pp. 226–229.
48. Edward M. Harrington, "The Little People," Holy Cross *Purple,* February 1945, pp. 263–271.
49. Edward Harrington, "The Sermon," Holy Cross *Purple,* March 1946, pp. 326–333.
50. Harrington, "The Little People," p. 268.
51. Ibid.
52. Edward M. Harrington Jr., "Salutatory Address—Class of 1947," Holy Cross Archives.
53. "Senior Favorites," Holy Cross *Purple Patcher,* 1947.
54. Author's interview with Bill Loftus, September 27, 1991.
55. Letter from Jack Drummey to the author, February 15, 1992.
56. Author's interview with Bill Loftus, September 27, 1991, and April 12, 1993.
57. Evelyn Waugh, *Brideshead Revisited: The Sacred and Profane Memories of Captain Charles Ryder* (Boston: Little, Brown and Company, 1945), p. 26.
58. Author's interview with Bill Loftus, April 12, 1993. Michael's classmate Charles Fitzgibbon also recalled the popularity of *Brideshead Revisited* at Holy Cross. Letter to the author, May 25, 1993.
59. Author's interview with Alex Harrington, September 27, 1991.
60. Author's interview with Joan Sayward Franklin, March 18, 1992; interview with Bill Loftus, April 12, 1993. Sayward's picture appears in the 1950 Wellesley College yearbook; she looks proper and determined in the photograph and like all her classmates wears the then obligatory string of pearls around her neck. Wellesley *Legenda,* 1950, p. 116.
61. Author's interview with Joan Sayward Franklin, March 18, 1992.
62. Michael Harrington to Jim Finn, November 16, 1953, in author's possession.
63. Author's interview with Joan Sayward Franklin, March 18, 1992.
64. Edward Michael Harrington transcript, College of the Holy Cross, and College of the *Holy Cross Catalogue,* 1944–1945, 1945–1946, and 1946–1947. I am grateful to the Holy Cross registrar's office for making Michael's transcript available to me, and to Rev. Paul J. Nelligan, S.J., college archivist, for copies of the college catalogues.
65. Author's interview with Bill Loftus, September 27, 1991.
66. Michael also had his grades sent to Notre Dame University that spring; whether or not he was accepted, and what he intended to study there, is unknown. Edward Michael Harrington transcript, St. Louis University High School.
67. Letter from Michael Harrington to "Mom and Dad," April 18, 1948. Michael discussed his agreement with his parents to attend Yale for a year in his interview with Rosalie Riegle Troester in 1988. Michael Harrington interviewed by Rosalie Riegle Troester, July 7, 1988, p. 24, transcript from the Catholic Worker Archives, Marquette University.

Chapter Three: *"An Awful Lot of Soul-Seaching," 1947–1950*

1. Michael Harrington to Peggy Brennan, December 20, 1950, copy in author's possession.
2. For Michael's published references to Yale, see Michael Harrington, *Fragments of the Century* (New York: Saturday Review Press, 1973), p. 64, and *The Long Distance Runner: An Autobiography* (New York: Henry Holt, 1988), p. 123.
3. Author's interview with Richard Fitzsimmons, February 7, 1992.
4. Ibid.
5. Michael Harrington interviewed by Rosalie Riegle Troester, July 7, 1988, p. 24, transcript from the Catholic Worker Archives, Marquette University. An edited version of this interview appears in *Voices from the Catholic Worker,* ed. Rosalie Riegle Troester (Philadelphia: Temple University Press, 1993).
6. Yale's founding is described in Brooks Mather Kelley, *Yale: A History* (New Haven: Yale

University Press, 1974), pp. 3–28. A good description of New Haven a decade before Harrington's arrival can be found in the Federal Writer's Project publication, *Connecticut: A Guide to its Roads, Lore, and People* (Boston: Houghton Mifflin, 1938), pp. 222–253.

7. *New Haven Journal Courier,* October 7, 1947, p. 1; November 5, 1947, p. 1. Municipal socialism in southern Connecticut had, by this time, very little of the crusading spirit of the Debsian era left in it; there was a saying in the Socialist Party that a Bridgeport socialist "was a Republican who believed in mass transit." R. W. Tucker, "Rise and Decline Among the Reds," (privately published, 1991), p. 8. Virtually the entire Connecticut state membership left the Socialist Party in 1950 in a dispute over electoral tactics. Daniel Bell, "Marxian Socialism in the United States," in *Socialism and American Life*, vol. 1, ed. Donald Drew Egbert and Stow Persons (Princeton: Princeton University Press, 1952), p. 402.
8. "The Steady Hand" *Time,* June 11, 1951, p. 74.
9. Author's interview with Bill Hegarty, October 10, 1992; interview with Richard Fitzsimmons, February 7, 1992; Harrington, *The Long Distance Runner*, p. 123. The early history of the law school is recounted in Kelley, *Yale: A History*, pp. 200–208.
10. Author's interview with Richard Fitzsimmons, February 7, 1992 ; David Margolick, "Another Public Drama Puts Yale Alumni Out Front," *New York Times*, March 20, 1992, p. 16. Among Michael's classmates at Yale, Thomas Black became the chief judge of the eastern district of the United States District Court; John Power became the CEO of Aetna Insurance Company; Don Turner became a distinguished professor of law at Harvard University; and Norman Redlich became dean of the New York University Law School. Byron "Whizzer" White, who would be appointed to the U.S. Supreme Court by President John F. Kennedy, was starting his final year in the law school when Michael arrived in New Haven; White worked as a student waiter and served Michael his meals that year in the law school's baronial dining room. Among later graduates, Yale Law School could count Bill Clinton and Hillary Rodham Clinton.
11. C. Wright Mills, *White Collar: The American Middle Classes* (New York: Oxford University Press, 1951), p. 123.
12. On the role of Yale law professors in the New Deal, see Jerold S. Auerbach, *Unequal Justice: Lawyers and Social Change in Modern America* (New York: Oxford University Press, 1976), pp. 181–184; Laura Kalman, *Legal Realism at Yale, 1927–1960* (Chapel Hill: University of North Carolina Press, 1986), p. 130; and Alan Brinkley, "The Antimonopoly Ideal and the Liberal State: The Case of Thurman Arnold," *Journal of American History* 80 (September 1993), pp. 557–579.
13. David Garrow, *Liberty and Sexuality: The Right to Privacy and the Making of Roe v. Wade* (New York: Macmillan, 1994), pp. 148, 230.
14. Author's interview with Eugene Rostow, August 6, 1991.
15. Quoted in Laura Kalman, *Legal Realism at Yale,* p. 17.
16. Oliver Wendell Holmes, quoted in Peter Novick, *That Noble Dream: The "Objectivity Question" and the American Historical Profession* (Cambridge, U.K.: Cambridge University Press, 1988), p. 146.
17. Morton J. Horwitz, *The Transformation of American Law, 1870–1960: The Crisis of Legal Orthodoxy* (New York: Oxford University Press, 1992), p. 202; Malcolm Feeley, "Legal Realism," *The Guide to American Law*, vol. 7 (West Publishers, 1984), pp. 129–131.
18. Author's interview with Bill Hegarty, October 10, 1992.
19. Interview with Eugene Rostow, August 6, 1991. A visiting British Labour MP assured a meeting of the Yale Political Union that year that "my government believes that planning in the economic field can be combined with personal liberty." *Yale Daily News,* February 26, 1948, p. 1.
20. *Yale Daily News,* November 14, 1947, p. 1.
21. Author's interview with Jerry Davidoff, March 19, 1992; Diana Trilling's interview with Michael Harrington, March 1976, p. 9; *Yale Daily News*, September 24, 1947, p. 1; September 30, 1947, p. 1; October 9, 1947, p.1; April 12, 1948, p. 1; *New Haven Journal Courier,* October 9, 1947, p. 1. Most of the Yale student support for Wallace waned in 1948 as it became clear how closely tied his campaign was to the Communist Party.

22. William F. Buckley Jr., *God and Man at Yale: The Superstitions of "Academic Freedom"* (Chicago: Henry Regnery Company, 1951), p. xvii.
23. Diana Trilling's interview with Michael Harrington, March 1976, p. 8.
24. Writing to Yale classmate Jerry Davidoff in 1982, Michael noted the "bizarre fact that I became a socialist at Yale Law School, largely because of the arguments of members of the class of '50." Michael Harrington to Jerry Davidoff, July 5, 1982, in author's possession. I'm grateful to Jerry Davidoff for providing me with a copy of this letter. Also see Michael's contribution to "The Nation at 100," *Nation,* July 5, 1965, p. 18.
25. Author's interview with Monroe Singer, February 8, 1992; interview with Richard Fitzsimmons, February 7, 1992.
26. Author's interview with Richard Fitzsimmons, February 7, 1992.
27. Edward Michael Harrington Yale Law School transcript for 1947–1948, in author's possession.
28. Michael Harrington interviewed by Rosalie Riegle Troester, p. 24.
29. Author's interview with Richard Fitzsimmons, February 7, 1992.
30. Author's interview with Joan Sayward Franklin, March 19, 1992; interview with Richard Fitzsimmons, February 7, 1992.
31. Author's interview with Richard Fitzsimmons, February 7, 1992; interview with Jerry Davidoff, March 19, 1992. *Yale Daily News,* September 18, 1947, p. 23; October 18, 1947; p. 7, January 13, 1948, p. 6. Michael discussed his preferences in ballet in a column for the *New York Herald Tribune* in the 1960s. Michael Harrington, "Yes, But Is It Art?" *New York Herald Tribune,* May 16, 1965, p. 11.
32. Author's interview with Monroe Singer, February 8, 1992.
33. Michael seems to have considered another career alternative that spring. The Yale Law School registrar noted on his transcript, "Not returning 1948 fall term. Volunteered with Naval Reserve." Edward Michael Harrington transcript, Yale Law School, 1947–1948, in author's possession.
34. Letter from Michael Harrington to Catherine and Edward Harrington, April 18, 1948, in author's possession.
35. Harrington, *Fragments of the Century,* p. 36.
36. Author's interview with Jim Finn, September 27, 1991.
37. Marilyn Magid, "The Man Who Discovered Poverty," *New York Herald Tribune Magazine,* December 27, 1964, p. 10; Harrington, *Fragments*, p. 35.
38. Harrington, *Fragments of the Century,* p. 36.
39. Edward Michael Harrington transcript, University of Chicago, in author's possession.
40. Jim Finn, "A Radical Commitment," *Commonweal* 116 (September 8, 1989), p. 467; author's interview with Jim Finn, September 27, 1991.
41. Diana Trilling's interview with Michael Harrington, March 1976, p. 5; Harrington, *Fragments of the Century,* p. 17.
42. *Chicago Maroon,* October 8, 1943, p. 3; October 12, 1948, p. 1; October 22, 1948, p. 1; May 6, 1949, p. 1.
43. Harrington, *Fragments of the Century,* p. 65.
44. William H. McNeill, *Hutchins' University: A Memoir of the University of Chicago, 1929–1950* (Chicago: University of Chicago Press, 1991), p. 97.
45. Ibid, p. 164.
46. Harrington, *Fragments of the Century,* p. 36.
47. McNeill, *Hutchins' University,* pp. 62–65.
48. William V. Morgenstern, "Springfield Summary," *University of Chicago Magazine* 40, June 1949, p. 4; Mary Ann Dzuback, *Robert M. Hutchins: Portrait of an Educator* (Chicago: University of Chicago Press, 1991), pp. 201–202.
49. For Harrington's tribute to Hutchins, see his entry in the symposium on "Robert Hutchins' Platonic Grove," *Nation,* July 30, 1988, p. 124.
50. Press release dated June 21, 1949, Robert M. Hutchins Papers, box 28, folder 2, Department of Special Collections, University of Chicago.

51. Ed Harrington, *Cana Catechism* (St. Louis: The Queens Work, 1950), p. 15. The title of the pamphlet derived from a passage in the Gospel of John that describes Jesus performing the miracle of turning water into wine while attending a marriage ceremony in the village of Cana in Galilee. The pamphlet was written "from the notes of Edward Dowling, S.J.," a leading exponent of the conferences, so it's hard to tell where Dowling stops and Harrington begins. Only in a few passages does a distinct Harrington voice emerge, such as the following: "Cana is by no means a subversive movement (unless it is considered un-something-or-other to dedicate yourself to subverting de-Christianized marriage) but it can learn from the Russians. We have found that a Cana 'cell' in the home, a small meeting of friends informally gathered together, can produce concrete results" (p. 18).
52. Harrington, *Fragments of the Century,* p. 66. In *The Long Distance Runner,* Harrington again refers to "that rainy day in St. Louis in 1949 when I accidentally happened to be a social worker and blundered into an encounter with an outrageous, unnecessary misery" as the day that changed the course of his life. Harrington, *The Long Distance Runner,* p. 10.
53. Edward M. Harrington Jr., personnel file, St. Louis Board of Education, 1949–1950 (in author's possession). I am grateful to Donald D. Shipp, director of employee processing for the Saint Louis Public Schools, for making these records available to me. Michael refers to his substitute teaching in a letter to Peggy Brennan, October 13, 1950, copy in author's possession.
54. Harrington, *Fragments of the Century,* p. 65.
55. Ibid., p. 33.
56. Author's interview with Stephanie Harrington, July 24, 1991.
57. Michael Harrington, "'A San Remo Type': The Vanishing Village," *Village Voice,* January 7, 1971, p. 3.
58. Harrington, "We Few, We Happy Few, We Bohemians," *Esquire,* August 1971, p. 101.
59. For an overview of Greenwich Village history and some striking photographs of the district as it appeared in the late 1950s and early 1960s, see Fred W. McDarrah, *Greenwich Village* (New York: Corinth Books, 1963). On urban renewal and Greenwich Village, see Jane Jacobs, *The Death and Life of Great American Cities* (New York: Vintage, 1961), pp. 360–361.
60. Robert Rosenstone, *Romantic Revolutionary: A Biography of John Reed* (New York: Random House, 1975), pp. 104–105.
61. Malcolm Cowley, *Exile's Return: A Literary Odyssey of the 1920s* (New York: Viking Press, 1951), p. 60.
62. Russell Jacoby offers an enlightening tour of the numerous times the Village has "died," in his study *The Last Intellectuals: American Culture in the Age of Academe* (New York: Basic Books, 1987), pp. 31–34. Also see Sally Banes, *Greenwich Village 1963: Avant-Garde Performance and the Effervescent Body* (Durham, N.C.: Duke University Press, 1993), pp. 29–30.
63. Cowley, *Exile's Return,* p. 66.
64. Harrington, *Fragments of the Century,* p. 39.
65. Author's interview with Bill Loftus, September 27, 1991; interview with Arthur Moore, September 28, 1991; letter from David McReynolds to "Ben," October 9, 1953, David McReynolds Papers, Swarthmore College Peace Collection, series 2, box 1.
66. Harrington, "We Few, We Happy Few, We Bohemians," pp. 102–103; Harrington, *Fragments of the Century,* pp. 42, 44.
67. Author's interview with Bill Loftus, September 27, 1991.
68. Note Michael's misspelling of "burgundy." When I quote letters like this, I will copy them exactly as they were written and I will not insert the customary *sic.*
69. Letter from "Ned" Harrington to "Mom and Dad," n.d. [December 1949]. In author's possession.
70. Author's interview with Bill Loftus, September 27, 1991.
71. Author's interview with Bill Loftus, September 27, 1991; interview with Arthur Moore, September 28, 1991.

72. David McReynolds to "Ben," October 9, 1953, McReynolds Papers. Michael conceded that the customers of the San Remo were given to "cultured superficialities" in conversation, but he argued that "our phoniness had high standards. We postured about the first rate, about Proust and Joyce and Kafka, the later Beethoven quartets and Balanchine choreography, Marx and Lenin." *Fragments of the Century,* p. 46.
73. Barry Miles, "The Beat Generation in the Village," in *Greenwich Village: Culture and Counterculture,* ed. Rick Beard and Leslie Cohen Berlowitz (New Brunswick, N.J.: Rutgers University Press, 1993), p. 170; McDarrah, *Greenwich Village,* p. 64.
74. Harrington, *Fragments of the Century,* pp. 40, 45.
75. Author's interview with Jim and Molly Finn, September 27, 1991.
76. Harrington, *Fragments of the Century,* pp. 42–43.
77. Letter from Barbara Bank Fussiner to the author, August 1, 1991.
78. Author's interview with Bill Loftus, September 27, 1991.
79. Michael Harrington to Peggy Brennan, September 27, 1950, copy in author's possession.
80. Author's interview with Peggy Brennan Mitchell, October 22, 1992.
81. Author's interview with Peggy Brennan Mitchell, October 22, 1992; interview with Bill Loftus, September 27, 1991.
82. Harrington, *Fragments of the Century,* p. 66.
83. Michael Harrington to Peggy Brennan, May 29, 1950, copy in author's possession.
84. Michael later told an interviewer about his experience with the AFSC: "I've chided them about that, and they've sort of agreed that maybe they made a mistake." Troester interview with Harrington, pp. 1–2.
85. Michael Harrington to Peggy Brennan, June 29, 1950, copy in author's possession. Interestingly, Michael signed this letter to Peggy as "Ned." She found that surprising, because he had earlier told her he only wanted to be known as "Mike," which is how he signed his letter to her in May. To her, it suggested the depth of his confusion and uncertainty at the time. Author's interview with Peggy Brennan Mitchell, October 22, 1992.
86. Michael Harrington to Peggy Brennan, May 29, 1950, copy in author's possession.
87. Author's interview with Bill Loftus, September 27, 1991.
88. Remembering his own turmoil around the issue of conscientious objection in this period, Michael would later argue for the right to "selective" conscientious objection, open to atheists and agnostics, as well as religious pacifists. See Michael Harrington, "Politics, Morality, and Selective Dissent," in *A Conflict of Loyalties: The Case for Selective Conscientious Objection,* ed. James Finn (New York: Pegasus, 1968), pp. 219–239.
89. Michael told Peggy Brennan that he couldn't bear the idea that people in St. Louis would say that his parents had "a no-good son who wouldn't serve his country." Author's interview with Peggy Brennan Mitchell, October 22, 1992.
90. Michael Harrington telegram to Peggy Brennan, September 16, 1950, copy in author's possession.
91. Michael Harrington to Peggy Brennan, September 27, 1950, copy in author's possession.
92. Michael Harrington to Peggy Brennan, October 13, 1950, copy in author's possession.
93. Michael remained a Kierkegaard enthusiast, even after he had resolved his post-adolescent identity crisis. In a review of a study of Kierkegaard published in *Commonweal* three years later, Michael called him "one of the greatest of modern thinkers." For Harrington, Kierkegard's "real significance" was "more prophetic" than formally philosophical: "a violent affirmation of the crucial character of the relation of the individual to God in the face of systems and historicisms." Michael Harrington, "An Examination of Greatness," *Commonweal* 59 (December 18, 1953), pp. 289–290.
94. Michael Harrington to Peggy Brennan, October 13, 1950, copy in author's possession.
95. Ibid.
96. Michael Harrington to Peggy Brennan, November 25, 1950, copy in author's possession.
97. Michael Harrington to Peggy Brennan, December 20, 1950, copy in author's possession.

Chapter Four: *The Life of a Saint, 1951–1952*

1. Michael Harrington interviewed by Rosalie Riegle Troester, July 7, 1988, p. 7, transcript from the Catholic Worker Archives, Marquette University.
2. The drawing appeared in the *Catholic Worker,* April 1951, p. 1; on Michael, and others' conviction that he was the model for the Eichenberg drawing, see Troester interview with Harrington, p. 16.
3. *New York Times,* January 3, 1951, pp. 1, 12, 17.
4. Author's interview with Bill Loftus, September 27, 1991.
5. Michael Harrington, *Fragments of the Century* (New York: Saturday Review Press, 1973), p. 18.
6. Author's interview with Arthur Moore, September 28, 1991.
7. Letter to the author from Barbara Bank Fussiner, August 1, 1991.
8. Harrington, *Fragments of the Century,* p. 18. Michael may have exaggerated his ignorance. When he was growing up, there was an active branch of the Catholic Worker in St. Louis that maintained a soup line and a shelter for the unemployed. Moreover, Michael had been a reader of *Commonweal* magazine at least since his days at the University of Chicago, and Catholic Worker founder Dorothy Day was a frequent contributor to its pages. On the St. Louis Catholic Worker, see Janice Brandon-Falcone, "Experiments in Truth: An Oral History of the St. Louis Catholic Worker, 1935–1942," in *A Revolution of the Heart: Essays on the Catholic Worker,* ed. Patrick G. Coy (Philadelphia: Temple University Press, 1988), pp. 313–336. For Dorothy Day's contributions to *Commonweal* in this period, see, for example, "The Scandal of the Works of Mercy," *Commonweal* 51 (November 4, 1949), pp. 99–102, and "Traveling by Bus," *Commonweal* 51 (March 10, 1950), pp. 577–579.
9. Dorothy Day, *The Long Loneliness: The Autobiography of Dorothy Day* (New York: Harper and Row, 1952), p. 69.
10. Day, *The Long Loneliness,* p. 199.
11. Ibid., p. 166.
12. Mel Piehl, *Breaking Bread: The Catholic Worker and the Origin of Catholic Radicalism in America* (Philadelphia: Temple University Press, 1982), p. 25.
13. Harrington, *Fragments of the Century,* pp. 18–19.
14. On the role of Mounier and *Esprit,* see John Hellman, "The Opening to the Left in French Catholicism: The Role of the Personalists," *Journal of the History of Ideas* 34 (July 1973), pp. 381–390. James J. Farrell makes a persuasive case for the importance of "personalism" (which derived from a variety of other sources, as well as the French Catholic philosophers) in his book *The Spirit of the Sixties: The Making of Postwar Radicalism* (New York: Routledge, 1997).
15. Farrell, *The Spirit of the Sixties,* p. 12.
16. Troester interview with Harrington, p. 18.
17. Tom Cornell quoted in *Voices from the Catholic Worker,* ed. Rosalie Riegle Troester (Philadelphia: Temple University Press, 1993), p. 72.
18. Harrington, *Fragments of the Century,* p. 20.
19. Day, *The Long Loneliness,* pp. 9–12, 60.
20. Michael Harrington, *The Long Distance Runner: An Autobiography* (New York: Henry Holt, 1988), p. 9.
21. Garry Wills, *Bare Ruined Choirs: Doubt, Prophecy, and Radical Religion* (Garden City, N.Y.: Doubleday and Co., 1972), p. 59.
22. Author's interview with Betty Bartelme, March 17, 1995; Nancy Roberts, *Dorothy Day and the Catholic Worker* (Albany: SUNY Press, 1984), p. 146.
23. Dwight Macdonald made the comparison between the circulation of the *Catholic Worker* and the two preeminent liberal weeklies in his essay, "The Foolish Things of the World, II" *New Yorker* 18 (October 11, 1952), p. 46.
24. Day attained "some kind of height or depth of editorial *chutzpah,*" Catholic Worker Edward Egan would recall, "when she took out a paragraph of something Mike Harrington

had written and inserted a paragraph she thought was better under his name." Interview with Edmund J. Egan, October 1968, p. 15, Dorothy Day-Catholic Worker Collection, series W-9, box 1, Marquette University Archives.

25. In a letter to Jim Finn in 1952, Michael recommended he read Maritain's *Preface to Metaphysics,* a "great, great book." He suggested that Finn, no novice in the field, "read [the] first chapter four or five times over a three week period; then you will be able to read [the] rest of the book easily." Michael Harrington to Jim Finn, January 4, 1952, copy in author's possession.
26. Interview with Tom Sullivan, June 24, 1976, p. 7, Dorothy Day-Catholic Worker Collection, series W-9, box 2, Marquette University Archives.

    Sullivan's memory was faulty on one point. Michael's first article for the paper, which appeared on the front page of the March 1951 issue, recounted a recent incident in the Louisiana State Penitentiary, where thirty-seven convicts had slashed their own Achilles tendons in a protest against the brutality of the prison guards. Michael concluded: "The heel-slashing at the Louisiana prison is not a mere indictment of one warden or one governor, or one prison system. It is an indictment of the apathy of the people who leave it to the representatives to legislate humanitarianism." Michael Harrington, "Convicts Protest Prison Brutality by Slashing Heels," *Catholic Worker* 17 (March 1951), p. 1.
27. Michael Harrington, "'Man and the State,'" *Catholic Worker* 17 (May 1951), p. 4.
28. Quoted in Martin E. Marty, *Modern American Religion,* vol. 3, *Under God, Indivisible, 1941–1960* (Chicago: University of Chicago Press, 1996), p. 160.
29. Quoted in Dwight Macdonald, "The Foolish Things of the World," p. 39.
30. Troester, *Voices from the Catholic Worker,* pp. 75, 123.
31. William D. Miller, *Dorothy Day: A Biography* (San Francisco: Harper & Row, 1982), pp. 427–429.
32. Michael Harrington, "Existentialism," *Catholic Worker* 17 (June 1951), p. 5.
33. Michael Harrington, "Paths in Utopia," *Catholic Worker* 17 (July-August 1951), p. 3; "Hannah Arendt," *Catholic Worker* 18 (November 1951), p. 4; "Emmanuel Mounier," *Catholic Worker* 18 (March 1952), p. 4; "Invisible Man Is a Novel," *Catholic Worker* 18, (June 1952), p. 4.
34. For examples of Harrington's journalism, see "Spanish Workers Strike," *Catholic Worker* 17 (June 1951), p. 1; "The Seamen Strike," *Catholic Worker* 18 (November 1951), p. 1; and "Archbishop Criticizes Spanish Regime," *Catholic Worker* 18 (January 1952), p. 1.
35. Michael Harrington, "Poverty USA," *Catholic Worker* 18 (June 1952), p. 7.
36. Author's telephone interview with John McDermott, February 4, 1992.
37. Author's interview with Roger O'Neil, April 6, 1991.
38. Troester interview with Harrington, p. 17.
39. Author's interview with Ed Egan, October 30, 1992.
40. Troester, *Voices from the Catholic Worker,* p. 74.
41. Harrington, *Fragments of the Century,* p. 18.
42. Troester, *Voices from the Catholic Worker,* p. 132.
43. Piehl, *Breaking Bread,* p. 174.
44. Author's interview with Eileen Fantino-Diaz, March 16, 1995.
45. Troester, *Voices from the Catholic Worker,* p. 128.
46. Author's interview with Betty Bartelme, March 17, 1995.
47. Troester interview with Harrington, p. 3.
48. Michael Harrington to Jim Finn, January 4, 1952, copy in author's possession.
49. Harrington, *Fragments of the Century,* p. 22.
50. Wills, *Bare Ruined Choirs,* p. 39.
51. See Edmund J. Egan interview, Dorothy Day-Catholic Worker Collection. The song was heard outside the walls of St. Joseph's as well. Jim Finn remembers Michael singing it at the White Horse later in the 1950s. Author's interview with Jim Finn, September 27, 1991.
52. Troester interview with Harrington, p. 7.
53. Troester, *Voices from the Catholic Worker,* p. 125.
54. In her autobiography, Dorothy Day recounted one of her favorite stories about Theresa

of Avila: "Once when she was traveling from one part of Spain to another with some other nuns and a priest to start a convent, she was thrown from her donkey. The story goes that our Lord said to her, 'That is how I treat my friends.' And she replied, 'And that is why You have so few of them.'" Day, *The Long Loneliness,* p. 140.

55. Quoted in Macdonald, "The Foolish Things of the World," p. 37.
56. Day, *The Long Loneliness,* p. 255.
57. Author's interview with Peggy Brennan, October 22, 1992.
58. Harrington, *Fragments of the Century,* p. 20.
59. Troester interview with Harrington, p. 17.
60. Ibid., p. 6.
61. Author's interview with Molly Finn, September 27, 1991. Molly Finn was then married to Bill Esty. She would later marry Michael's University of Chicago classmate Jim Finn.
62. Author's interview with Betty Bartelme, March 17, 1995; author's interview with Marty Corbin, October 30, 1992.
63. Author's interview with John Stanley, July 25, 1991.
64. Author's interview with Betty Bartelme, March 17, 1995.
65. Dorothy Day, *The Long Loneliness,* p. 269.
66. Author's interview with Betty Bartelme, March 17, 1995.
67. Malcolm Cowley, *Exile's Return: A Literary Odyssey of the 1920s* (New York: Viking Press, 1951), p. 69.
68. Interview with Edmund J. Egan, October 1968, p. 15, Dorothy Day-Catholic Worker Collection. Michael recalled how "Dorothy startled me over coffee one morning when I mentioned one of my then favorite poets, Hart Crane. 'Oh that Hart,' she said. 'I used to have breakfast with him all the time when I was pregnant.'" Harrington, *Fragments of the Century,* p. 20.
69. Michael Harrington to Jim Finn, August 22, 1951, copy in author's possession.
70. Dan Wakefield's loving tributes to the White Horse fill many pages in his memoir, *New York in the 50s* (Boston: Houghton-Mifflin, 1992); see especially pp. 127–141.
71. Harrington, *Fragments of the Century,* p. 48; R. W. Tucker, *Rise and Decline Among the Reds* (Privately printed, 1991), p. 20.
72. Author's interview with Eileen Fanino-Diaz, March 16, 1995; author's interview with Betty Bartelme, March 17, 1995.
73. Troester interview with Harrington, p. 10.
74. Author's interview with Peggy Brennan Mitchell, October 22, 1992. Michael had not forgotten Peggy Brennan. She was touched many years later when he mentioned her in his memoir *The Long Distance Runner,* linking her to the most important turning point in his life. One day in the spring of 1950, he wrote, he was taking a bus to Union Square "and talking to a lovely young woman by the name of Peggy Brennan." He and Peggy "got into one of those conversations that went with our age and class: what would you do if you had a million dollars?" Michael "heard [himself] saying, 'I would give it away.'" Eight months after that "casual conversation," Michael reported, "I showed up at the Catholic Worker." Harrington, *The Long Distance Runner,* pp. 10–11.
75. Michael Harrington to Jim Finn, January 4, 1952, copy in author's possession.
76. Author's interview with Bogdan Denitch, April 6, 1991.
77. Author's interview with Roger O'Neill, April 4, 1991.
78. Troester interview with Harrington, p. 8.
79. John Cogley interview with Michael Harrington, 1965, for the Center for the Study of Democratic Institutions radio broadcast.
80. Michael Harrington, "Economics," *Catholic Worker* 18 (November 1951), p. 4. He also took issue with Buckley's views on academic freedom: "Mr. Buckley would turn the selection and discharge of teachers over to the Corporation of Yale University, a group which he feels correctly oriented toward the American economy. He finds academic freedom guilty on all counts, and would fire any professor whose political and religious beliefs are not sufficiently orthodox. Mr. Buckley is disturbed that Yale is no longer a

Christian University. In order to convert it, he would restore those economic and social doctrines which resulted in the breakdown of Christianity. If no one read this book, it would be amusing."

81. "Buckley Finds Academic Freedom A Threat to Individual Liberties—Harrington Objects," *The Vermont Cynic* 70 (December 4, 1952), p. 1.
82. Author's interview with Ned O'Gorman, May 23, 1993.
83. Michael Harrington to "Mom and Dad," n.d. [November 1952], copy of letter in author's possession.
84. Author's interview with William F. Buckley, January 6, 1992.
85. Ibid.
86. Ibid.
87. When Buckley was running for mayor of New York City in 1965, Michael paid him a backhanded personal compliment: "Buckley is honestly and sincerely innocent of the racism and viciousness of so many of his supporters." Michael Harrington, "One Vote for Lindsay," *New York Herald Tribune,* October 24, 1965, p. 8.
88. For an overview of the magazine's history, see Rodger Van Allen, *The Commonweal and American Catholicism: The Magazine, the Movement, the Meaning* (Philadelphia: Fortress Press, 1974).
89. James Finn, "American Catholics Turn Left," *Dissent* 13 (July-August 1966), p. 352. McCarthy was also opposed in the pages of the Jesuit publication *America* (although less consistently than in *Commonweal*). John Cogley, *Catholic America* (New York: Dial Press, 1973), pp. 112–113.
90. Michael Harrington, "Sanctity: The Common Bond," *Commonweal* 56 (October 3, 1952), p. 633.
91. On Michael's influence through his *Commonweal* writings on the thinking of other young Catholics in the 1950s, see Michael Novak, "Errand into the Wilderness," in *Political Passages: Journeys of Change Through Two Decades, 1968–1988,* ed. John H. Bunzel (New York: Free Press, 1988), pp. 247–248. Also see Troester, *Voices from the Catholic Worker,* pp. 30–31; Theodora Cogley Farrell, letter to the author, January 3, 1993. Cogley, *Catholic America,* pp. 177–178. For examples of Michael's contributions to the magazine in the 1950s, see Harrington, "Sanctity"; "Ballerina," *Commonweal* 57 (February 27, 1953), pp. 532–534; "Emmanuel Mounier: Tragic Optimist," *Commonweal* 60 (August 20, 1954), pp. 489–490; "The Advance of Automation," *Commonweal* 62 (May 20, 1955), pp. 175–177; "The Nature of Stalinism," *Commonweal* 63 (August 16, 1956), pp. 620–621; and "Communism's Enemy Within," *Commonweal* 67 (November 1, 1957), pp. 118–121. Michael also contributed his first piece to *Partisan Review* in these years: Harrington, "André Malraux: Metamorphosis of the Hero," *Partisan Review* 21 (November 1954), pp. 655–683.
92. Macdonald, "The Foolish Things of the World," p. 37. Macdonald's career is chronicled in Michael Wreszin, *A Rebel in Defense of Tradition: The Life and Politics of Dwight Macdonald* (New York: Basic Books, 1994). Wreszin writes that Macdonald viewed both Day and French pacifist Simone Weil, who he also profiled for the *New Yorker,* as "role models of the committed life. They took risks, they dared to fail and even to make themselves look ridiculous in their efforts. Their persona was that of a modern 'holy fool,' which Dwight may well have been crafting for himself" (p. 274). Harrington described Macdonald's reaction to Dorothy Day in a 1988 interview reprinted in Troester, *Voices from the Catholic Worker*, p. 75.
93. Wreszin, *A Rebel in Defense of Tradition,* p. 376.
94. Harrington, *Fragments of the Century,* p. 38.
95. Michael Harrington, "Five Poems," *Poetry* 80 (August 1952), pp. 256–259. In a letter to Karl Shapiro, editor of *Poetry,* on April 25, 1952, a clearly very pleased Michael Harrington thanked him twice for acceptance of his poems for publication: "It is the first I have ever had and all the more exciting." The letter can be found in the *Poetry* papers in the Department of Special Collection, Joseph Regenstein Library, University of Chicago.
96. Troester, *Voices from the Catholic Worker,* p. 128.

97. The basic source on public opinion during the Korean War is John Mueller, *Presidents and Public Opinion* (New York: Wiley, 1972), pp. 43–52.
98. On Cold War popular culture see, for example, Peter Biskind, *Seeing Is Believing: How Hollywood Taught Us to Stop Worrying and Love the Fifties* (New York: Pantheon, 1983); J. Fred MacDonald, *Television and the Red Menace: The Video Road to Vietnam* (New York: Praeger, 1985); and Tom Englelhardt, *The End of Victory Culture: Cold War America and the Disillusioning of a Generation* (New York: Basic Books, 1995), especially pages 69–171.
99. Cardinal Spellman's poem made such an impression on Michael that he quoted it years later in an article on Vatican II: Michael Harrington, "Pope John's Message Contribution to Struggle Against Nuclear War," *New America,* May 12, 1963, p. 1. For other examples of religious or pseudo-religious invocations to wage Cold War, see Marty, *Modern American Religion,* vol. 3, pp. 151, 203; Stephen J. Whitfield, *The Culture of the Cold War* (Baltimore: Johns Hopkins Press, 1991), pp. 77–89.
100. Quoted in Patricia McNeal, *Harder Than War: Catholic Peacemaking in Twentieth-Century America* (New Brunswick, N.J.: Rutgers, 1992), p. 78.
101. On pacifism during the Korean War, see Maurice Isserman, *If I Had a Hammer: The Death of the Old Left and the Birth of the New Left* (New York: Basic Books, 1987), pp. 137–140.
102. Michael Harrington, "Operation Peace," *Catholic Worker* 17 (October 1951), p. 1. Also see Harrington, "War and Arms," *Catholic Worker* 17 (December 1951), p. 3. For a discussion of the "just war" doctrine and the Catholic Worker's objections, see McNeal, *Harder Than War*, pp. 2–3, 41–42, 46–48.
103. Harrington, *Fragments of the Century,* p. 23.
104. Betty Bartelme was among those who attempted to persuade him not to go to Fort Drum. After a long argument, Michael wrote her a twenty-two-page letter (unfortunately no longer available) justifying his decision. Author's interview with Betty Bartelme, March 17, 1995.
105. Harrington, *Fragments of the Century,* pp. 23-24.
106. Michael Harrington to Jim Finn, August 22, 1951, letter in author's possession
107. Michael Harrington to Jim Finn, January 4, 1952, letter in author's possession.
108. This passage appears in Michael's FBI file, in a document dated May 11, 1964. I was able to obtain Michael's files after a six-year struggle with the bureau to secure their release. I am grateful to New York's Senator Daniel Patrick Moynihan for assisting me in this unnecessarily tedious process. I am depositing my copy of Michael's FBI files with his papers at New York University's Tamiment Library. Rather than citing these documents by the FBI's confusing internal code, I will simply give their date.
109. Michael Harrington to Jim Finn, May 5, 1953, letter in author's possession.
110. Harrington, *Fragments of the Century,* p. 24.
111. John Stanley, letter to the author, May 9, 1992.
112. Author's interview with Bill Loftus, September 27, 1991; Troester, *Voices from the Catholic Worker,* p. 128.
113. Author's interview with Eileen Fantino-Diaz, March 16, 1995.
114. Michael's military service history is recounted in his FBI files, May 11, 1964.
115. Harrington, *Fragments of the Century,* pp. 68–69. Also see Anderson, *Bayard Rustin: Trouble I've Seen* (New York: HarperCollins, 1997), pp. 137–138. This demonstration is also described in "Daily Log of Fellowship of Reconciliation Peace Training Unit," p. 11, Bayard Rustin Papers (microfilm edition), reel 4-0540.
116. Harrington, *Fragments of the Century,* pp. 68–69.
117. Farrell, *The Spirit of the Sixties,* p. 36.
118. Troester, *Voices of the Catholic Worker,* p. 126.
119. Piehl, *Breaking Bread,* pp. 160–163. Michael wrote about the history of the ACTU in his historical article "Catholics in the Labor Movement," *Labor History* 1 (Fall 1960), pp. 241–259.
120. Day, *The Long Loneliness,* p. 221.
121. John Cort, "The Catholic Worker and the Workers," *Commonweal* 55 (April 4, 1952), pp. 635–637.

122. Michael Harrington to John Randall, June 1, 1952, Dorothy Day-Catholic Worker Collection, series W-2, box 1, Marquette University Archives.
123. Michael Harrington to Jim Finn, January 4, 1952, copy in author's possession.
124. Piehl, *Breaking Bread,* p. 119.
125. Robert Ludlow, "Personalist Revolution," *Catholic Worker* 18 (November 1952), p. 1.
126. Michael Harrington, "Paths in Utopia." In a letter to Jim Finn in August, Michael noted: "My speech went rather well. will send the last issue of the cw which contains a frgment of the speech in the form of the buber review." Michael Harrington to Jim Finn, August 22, 1951, copy in author's possession.
127. Michael Harrington to Jim Finn, January 4, 1952, copy in author's possession. Despite this immersion in revolutionary theory, he did not neglect his literary interests, mentioning that he had also read "new faulkner," "new marianne moore," and had made "a rediscovery of the fact that e e cummings is best lyric poet we have produced."
128. Dan Wakefield was among Hennacy's admirers, praising his "willingness to go against the grain, to challenge the conformity of the fifties." Wakefield, *New York in the 50s,* p. 83. Also see Patrick G. Coy, "The One-Person Revolution of Ammon Hennacy," in Coy, *A Revolution of the Heart,* pp. 135, 139.
129. Piehl, *Breaking Bread,* pp. 210–213.
130. McNeal, *Harder Than War,* pp. 89–90.
131. Troester interview with Harrington, p. 19.
132. Ammon Hennacy, *The Book of Ammon* (privately published, 1965), p. 247.
133. Troester, *Voices of the Catholic Worker*, p. 109. In 1952, Hennacy actually fasted for only seven days (the number of years since the dropping of the bomb). But on other occasions, he did fast as long as forty-eight days. Coy, "The One-Person Revolution of Ammon Hennacy," pp. 156–157.
134. Author's interview with John Stanley, July 25, 1991.
135. "Anti-Franco Picket Line Demonstrates Before Spanish Consulate," *Labor Action,* March 31, 1952, p. 1.
136. Harrington, *The Long Distance Runner,* p. 22.
137. Author's interview with Bogdan Denitch, December 7, 1984; David Hacker and Patricia Friend interview with Michael Harrington, August 19, 1988.
138. Bertolt Brecht, "The Measures Taken," in *The Jewish Wife and Other Short Plays,* ed. Eric Bentley (New York: Grove Press, 1965), pp. 87, 96. Bentley, in his introduction to the play, calls it "a kind of secular, or counter-religious oratorio" (p. 8).
139. Author's interview with Bogdan Denitch, December 21, 1990.
140. Jim Finn discussed the issue of whether a Catholic could also be a socialist with Michael in the 1950s, shortly after his conversation with Murray. Author's interview with Jim Finn, September 27, 1991. On John Courtney Murray, see Cogley, *Catholic America,* pp. 121–122; Marty, *Modern American Religion,* vol. 3, pp. 169–172.
141. Harrington, *Fragments of the Century,* p. 25. The decision may have been more drawn out than Michael later recalled. Fellow Catholic Worker Marty Corbin remembered that there was a period toward the end of Michael's time at Chrystie Street when he no longer attended mass, even on Sundays. But he kept his religious doubts to himself. Author's interview with Marty Corbin, October 30, 1992.
142. Troester interview with Harrington, p. 4.
143. Nearly a year after having left the church and the Catholic Worker, Michael wrote to Jim Finn in Chicago: "can't believe in rc [Roman Catholic] church; can't unbelieve in God; certainly can't join in protestant groups who believe in God but so much nonsense to boot; man seek community (d day [Dorothy Day] right), and i can't find one." Michael Harrington to Jim Finn, November 16, 1953, copy in author's possession.
144. Troester, *Voices of the Catholic Worker,* p. 123. The way Michael told it in 1988 made a good story, and, indeed, it may have happened that way, but it does bear suspicious resemblance to an anecdote he had included in *Fragments of the Century* fifteen years earlier: "I remember being tremendously impressed when a French Left Catholic . . . told us of a

French priest who had abandoned the Church and joined the Communist Party. 'If only he had left the Church for a woman,' our French friend said. 'That the Vatican could understand.'" *Fragments of the Century*, p. 19.

Chapter Five: *Resolute Waiting, 1952–1956*

1. Daniel Bell, "Marxian Socialism in the United States," in *Socialism and American Life*, vol. I, ed. Donald Drew Egbert and Stow Persons (Princeton, N.J.: Princeton University Press, 1952), p. 217 [emphasis in original].
2. Howard Brick discusses the circumstances that led to the writing of Bell's essay in *Daniel Bell and the Decline of Intellectual Radicalism: Social Theory and Political Reconciliation in the 1940s* (Madison: University of Wisconsin Press, 1986), p. 171. The influence of Bell's "Marxian socialism" article is discussed in Michael Kazin's review article, "The Agony and Romance of the American Left," *American Historical Review* 100 (December 1995), pp. 1488–1512. Bell described his own political evolution in an oral history interview on deposit at the Columbia University Oral History Research Office. For Michael's opinion of Bell's article in the early 1950s, see his article "A Discussion: The Third-Camp Socialist as 'Witness,'" *Labor Action,* May 17, 1954, 2-C. For his mature reflection on the strengths and weaknesses of Bell's essay, see Michael Harrington, *Socialism* (New York: Saturday Review Press, 1972), pp. 93, 308–311.
3. Harry Fleischman offered an overview of the WDL's history in *Encyclopedia of the American Left,* ed. Mari Jo Buhle et al. (New York: Garland, 1990), pp. 848–849. The WDL papers, on deposit at Wayne State Archives, contain some of the correspondence that Michael handled during his time with the organization.
4. Michael Harrington to Jim Finn, May 5, 1953, copy in author's possession.
5. Marion Magid, "The Man Who Discovered Poverty," *New York Herald Tribune Magazine,* December 27, 1964, p. 8.
6. Letter to the author from Carol [Denitch] Marshall, October 22, 1996.
7. Michael Harrington to Jim Finn, May 5, 1953, copy in author's possession.
8. Michael Harrington to Jim Finn, November 16, 1953, copy in author's possession.
9. Author's interview with Jack Stuart, January 7, 1995.
10. Author's interview with Ruth Jordan, March 10, 1992. Of course, in the circles in which he traveled in the 1950s, many of the women he encountered were his equals or betters in sexual sophistication. In his book about the Living Theater, John Tytell described actress Judith Malina's affair with writer James Agee in 1953, which was briefly punctuated by a tryst with Harrington: "One night near the end of October, [Agee] asked her to meet him. Instead of waiting at the Remo, she went to the White Horse. Some people were at a table arguing about Trotsky with a tall, lanky young man with broom-straw hair, a boyish grin and a Missouri twang. After a long commentary on Ukrainian anarchism, the young man, whose name was Michael Harrington, persuaded Judith to leave with him. . . . Two hours later, she confessed that she had to leave to meet James Agee. Scandalized and offended, Harrington, who knew Agee, was innocently convinced that the writer would never deceive his wife." John Tytell, *The Living Theatre: Art, Exile, and Outrage* (New York: Grove Press, 1995), p. 101.
11. Author's interview with Molly Finn, September 27, 1991.
12. Ron Chernow, "An Irresistible Profile of Michael Harrington (You Must Be Kidding)," *Mother Jones* (July 1977), p. 40.
13. David McReynolds to "Ben," October 9, 1953, David McReynolds Papers, Swarthmore College Peace Collection, series 2, box 1.
14. Judith Malina, *The Diaries of Judith Malina, 1947–1957* (New York: Grove Press, 1984), p. 320.
15. Michael reviewed Budd Schulberg's novel *Waterfront* for the first issue of the *Village Voice,* vol. 1, no. 1 (October 26, 1955).

16. Bell, "Marxian Socialism in the United States," p. 222 n. Also see Lewis Coser, "Sects and Sectarians," *Dissent* 1 (autumn 1954), pp. 360–369.
17. Bell, "Marxian Socialism in the United States," p. 405. Three years later, historian David Shannon echoed Bell's judgment, concluding his history of the SP with the observation, "Today it seems more likely that the Know Nothing Party might arise from a century's sleep than that the Socialists might revive. See *The Socialist Party of America* (New York: Macmillan, 1955), p. 268.
18. Shannon, *The Socialist Party of America*, pp. 164–165.
19. By the end of the 1930s, the ASU had become an influential force on many campuses and was noted for its sponsorship of annual strikes against war. But yipsels in the ASU found themselves on the losing side of a power struggle with the more powerful Young Communist League (YCL), notwithstanding the fact that the group's executive secretary, Joseph P. Lash, was one of their own. The best account of the complicated ins-and-outs of radical student politics in the 1930s can be found in Robert Cohen, *When the Old Left Was Young: Student Radicals and America's First Mass Student Movement, 1929–1941* (New York: Oxford University Press, 1993). Also see Patti McGill Peterson, "The Young Socialist Movement in America from 1905 to 1940: A Study of the Young People's Socialist League," Ph.D. diss., University of Wisconsin, 1974.
20. Irving Howe, *Socialism and America* (New York: Harcourt Brace Jovanovich, 1985), p. 57.
21. "In 1933," Irving Howe would write, "it was not foolish to suppose that world capitalism had reached its final breakdown; it was only mistaken. Nor was it absurd to think we had entered a moment of historical apocalypse; we were wrong only as to its precise nature." Howe, *Socialism and America*, p. 68.
22. Quoted in ibid., p. 74.
23. For accounts of the SP's factional battles in the 1930s, see W. A. Swanberg, *Norman Thomas: The Last Idealist* (New York: Scribner, 1976), pp. 128–133, 150–151, 172–173, 194–196; Shannon, *The Socialist Party of America*, pp. 204–268.
24. Quoted in Swanberg, *Norman Thomas*, p. 193.
25. James Cannon, *The History of American Trotskyism* (New York: Pathfinder Press, 1944), pp. 251–252. Standard accounts of the Trotskyist raid on the SP include Bell, "Marxian Socialism in the United States," pp. 384–388; Shannon, *The Socialist Party of America*, pp. 251–254; and Constance Myers, *The Prophet's Army: Trotskyists in America, 1928–1941* (Westport, Conn.: Greenwood Press, 1977), pp. 123–142.
26. Before the issue was fully resolved, Trotsky himself would fall victim to Stalin's assassins. He struggled mightily in the last months of his life to persuade Shachtman, of whom he was personally fond in a way he was not of Cannon, not to split over the "Russian Question." "If I could do so," Trotsky wrote to Shachtman at the height of their disagreement, "I would immediately take an aeroplane to New York City in order to discuss with you for forty-eight or seventy-two hours uninterruptedly." Ironically, the high esteem in which Trotsky held Shachtman helped Shachtman's followers steel themselves for the otherwise unappealing prospect of a break with the great revolutionary. Isaac Deutscher, *The Prophet Outcast, Trotsky: 1929–1940*, vol. 3 (New York: Oxford University Press, 1963), pp. 476–477.
27. Jacobson quoted in Maurice Isserman, *If I Had a Hammer: The Death of the Old Left and the Birth of the New Left* (New York: Basic Books, 1987), p. 41; Irving Howe, *A Margin of Hope: An Intellectual Biography* (New York: Harcourt Brace Jovanovich, 1982), p. 40.
28. My account of Shachtman's early years is drawn from Isserman, *If I Had a Hammer*, pp. 40–41. Also see Peter Drucker, *Max Shachtman and His Left: A Socialist's Odyssey Through the "American Century"* (Atlantic Highlands, N.J.: Humanities Press, 1994), pp. 6–105.
29. For many radical intellectuals in the 1930s, Howard Brick writes, "the theory of totalitarianism suggested the breach—and closure—of history." Brick, *Daniel Bell and the Decline of Intellectual Radicalism*, p. 33. The classic statement of the theory of totalitarianism is Hannah Arendt, *The Origins of Totalitarianism* (New York: Harcourt Brace, 1951).
30. Max Shachtman, "An Epigone of Trotsky," *New International* 10 (August 1944), p. 266; Isserman, *If I Had a Hammer*, pp. 49–50.

31. Quoted in Isserman, *If I Had a Hammer,* p. 47.
32. Dwight Macdonald, "The Root Is Man," *Politics* 3 (April 1946), p. 98.
33. Ibid., pp. 56–57.
34. Minutes of YPSL NEC meeting, December 1952, microfilm reel 2080, Socialist Party Papers.
35. Letter to the author from Peter Novick, June 2, 1991.
36. I heard several versions of the same joke from different people; this rendition is from David McReynolds. Author's interview with David McReynolds, September 16, 1991.
37. Author's interviews with Bogdan Denitch, December 7, 1984; December 21, 1990.
38. Quoted in Harry Fleischman, *Norman Thomas: A Biography* (New York: Norton, 1964), p. 254. At the same time, to the further dismay of young socialists, Thomas compromised his civil libertarian credentials by offering what amounted to a tepid endorsement of the anticommunist Smith Act (under whose provisions a number of Communist leaders had recently been sentenced to prison for "conspiracy to advocate and teach the desirability of the overthrow of the U.S. Government") and by his unqualified support for firing Communist teachers from the nation's schools. Norman Thomas, *A Socialist's Faith* (New York: Norton, 1951), pp. 222–225; Swanberg, *Norman Thomas*, pp. 368, 375.
39. *Anvil* claimed a circulation of about 5,000, probably exaggerated, but the journal was influential within the small circle of actively antiwar students in the early 1950s. For Michael's first published contribution to what had by then been renamed as *Anvil and Student Partisan,* see "'Russia, What Next?'" *Anvil and Student Partisan* 5 (Fall 1953), pp. 26–27, 31.
40. Bob Bone, "SP-YPSL Tries to Prevent Anti-War Work by Socialist Pacifists," *Labor Action*, October 29, 1951, p. 5. The December 1951 convention also officially changed the name of the organization to Young Socialists (YS), but in practice all concerned continued to refer to it as YPSL. See "Young Socialist Handbook," [1952], microfilm reel 91, Socialist Party Papers.
41. Letter from Carol [Denitch] Marshall to the author, October 22, 1996. Also See Bogdan Denitch, "Report on SP-NEC meeting," December 6, 1952, microfilm reel 91, Socialist Party Papers.

    Tiny as the socialist youth movement may have been, its maneuverings and internal disputes were still of apparent interest to the guardians of national security. According to Michael's FBI records "A copy of the Winter, 1952 'Young Socialist Review,' the official organ of the Young Socialists youth session of the Socialist Party-U.S.A., was received from the office of Senator Joseph R. McCarthy. This publication contained an article entitled 'Notes on the Future of the Socialist Party and the Young Socialists' by Michael Harrington." FBI files, December 30, 1959. References to Michael's FBI files refer to those files released to the author through a Freedom of Information Act request. Copies of these files have been deposited by the author in New York University's Tamiment Library's collection of the Michael Harrington Papers. Rather than citing these documents by the FBI's confusing internal code, I will simply give their date.
42. David McReynolds, "On Cooperation with the Socialist Youth League," *Young Socialist Review*, winter 1952, p. 5.
43. For details on the emerging YPSL-SP split, see letters from Bogdan Denitch to Organizer, NY SYL, January 6, 1953, microfilm reel 91, Socialist Party Papers; and David McReynolds to Bogdan Denitch, June 1, 1953, microfilm reel 91, Socialist Party Papers.
44. "Proceedings and Minutes, 19th National Convention, Young Socialists," microfilm reel 91, Socialist Party Papers.
45. Norman Thomas to Darlington Hoopes and Robin Myers, May 4, 1953, Socialist Party Papers, microfilm reel 2057.
46. Ibid.
47. The 1953 YPSL membership figures can be found in a letter from Michael Harrington to "Paula", April 30, 1956, Max Shachtman Papers, microfilm reel 3379.

    A slightly different figure is given in Bogdan Denitch "Report of the Acting Secretary to the July NEC," [1953], microfilm reel 91, Socialist Party Papers. In either estimate, the total was less than half of the YPSL membership in good standing at the end of

1952—which suggests that, as in many left-wing factional disputes, most members chose to vote with their feet by simply abandoning the movement. See "Report of Acting National Secretary to the YS-NEC," December 27-28, 1952, microfilm reel 91, Socialist Party Papers; "Report on Meeting Between Sub-Committee of the City Committee of Local New York and the District Executive Committee of the New York YPSL," June 17, 1953, microfilm reel 91, Socialist Party Papers; "Socialist Party Suspends New York YPSL," *Labor Action,* July 13, 1953, p. 5; Bogdan Denitch, "YPSL Breaks Ties with Socialist Party," *Labor Action,* September 7, 1953, p. 3; YPSL Committee, Socialist Party to Michael Harrington, September 17, 1953, microfilm reel 91, Socialist Party Papers.

48. David McReynolds would later note: "Max couldn't resist the temptation to pick up a bone, and as a consequence, he nearly choked when he tried to swallow the larger object later, which was the party." Author's interview with David McReynolds, September 16, 1991.
49. Michael's midwestern and Catholic background made him a "good person," Debbie Meier recalled, "to present our ideas to the unwashed masses." Author's interview with Debbie Meier, April 19, 1986.
50. Author's interview with Debbie Meier, January 6, 1992.
51. FBI files, June 28, 1954. Also see "Catholic Group Hits Rosenbergs Sentence," *Daily Worker,* November 5, 1952. In a subsequent article in the *Catholic Worker,* Michael reiterated his call for commuting the Rosenbergs' sentence, while disputing Communist charges that anti-Semitism was at the bottom of the case. See Michael Harrington, "Holy Father Begs Mercy for the Rosenbergs," *Catholic Worker,* March 1953, p. 1. The Catholic Worker had been a subject of FBI interest since 1940; the onset of the Korean War, the Worker's advocacy of draft resistance, and Dorothy Day's willingness to share a platform with well-known Communists like her old friend Elizabeth Gurley Flynn led to increased surveillance in the early 1950s. No one around the Worker seemed to care very much: In the April 1952 issue of the *Catholic Worker,* Tom Sullivan noted casually, "I don't know how it is with you, but we have had a steady run of FBI agents paying us visits." Sullivan, "Chrystie Street," *Catholic Worker* 18 (April 1952), p. 2. On the FBI's long interest in the movement, see Nancy L. Roberts, *Dorothy Day and the Catholic Worker* (Albany, NY: State University of New York Press, 1984), p. 7.
52. FBI files, June 28, 1954.
53. FBI files, August 5, 1954; September 23, 1955.
54. FBI files, September 9, 1955.
55. For Michael's arrival on the FBI security index, see FBI files, September 23, 1955. In 1955 an FBI agent in the New York office proposed that someone be sent to interview Harrington "to determine the subject's present attitude and degree of cooperation. If the subject is cooperative he can supply information concerning the YSL." More experienced hands in FBI headquarters soon put a stop to that foolish idea. See FBI files, June 22, 1955; July 7, 1955; August 25, 1955.
56. Michael Harrington, *Fragments of the Century* (New York: Saturday Review Press, 1973), p. 80.
57. For the ISL/YSL's legal difficulties in the 1950s, see "State Department Denies Passport to Max Shachtman," *Labor Action*, November 2, 1953, p. 1; and Marty Oppenheimer, "Confessions of a Low-level Victim of McCarthyism," *In These Times,* November 23–December 6, 1983, p. 11.
58. "We Take Our Stand Against War," *Young Socialist Challenge,* May 24, 1954, p. 5.
59. Bogdan Denitch, "Convention to Launch New United Young Socialist League," *Labor Action,* February 8, 1954, p. 8; Tim Wohlforth, *The Prophet's Children: Travels on the American Left* (Atlantic Highlands, N.J.: Humanities Press, 1994), p. 19. Michael put the YSL's membership at eighty-three in the autumn of 1954, six months after its founding. Harrington, *Fragments of the Century,* p. 61. The Labor Youth League (LYL), the youth affiliate of the American Communist Party, had a membership probably twenty or thirty times greater than the YSL, but in Shachtmanite reasoning, LYLers, as "Stalinists," did not deserve to be included in the tally of the nation's socialist youth.

60. Author's interview with Jim Finn, September 27, 1991.
61. "With the League," *Young Socialist Challenge,* May 17, 1954, p. 3-C. Among other campuses, they visited the University of Chicago, the University of Wisconsin, and Antioch College.
62. Tim Wohlforth, who joined the YSL in 1954 and went on to a long career on the sectarian left, describes the Denitch-Arden visit to Oberlin in his memoir, *The Prophets's Children,* pp. 17–19; also see, Aaron Roth, "Oberlin Responds with Enthusiasm," *Labor Action,* April 19, 1954, p. 4-C.
63. Wohlforth, *The Prophet's Children*, pp. 24–25.
64. Irving Howe, "'Dissent' Editor Replies," *Labor Action,* May 15, 1954, p. 7. In his autobiography, Howe noted that while he was editor of *Labor Action* in 1940, he regularly wrote as much as half of the newspaper. "Prolific and cocksure, brimming with energy and persuaded I had a key to understanding the world, I needed only the reams of yellow paper on which I typed and the *New York Times,* from which to draw facts. (Blessed *New York Times*! What would radical journalism in America do without it?)" Howe, *A Margin of Hope,* p. 85.
65. See for examples, Owen Morse, "Playing and Learning at the YSL Camp," *Young Socialist Challenge,* September 6, 1954, p. 1-C; and George Rawlings (George Rawick), "At the YSL Camp and School in Wisconsin," *Young Socialist Challenge,* September 26, 1955, p. 1-C. In a somewhat heavy-handed attempt to prove that the YSLers were not all work-no play, readers of the 1954 account were informed that the campers also enjoyed "vigorous folk-dancing into the wee hours of the night, as well as the consumption of a substantial amount of beer." At the 1955 event, according to the detailed account in the *Young Socialist Challenge,* they let go with "weenie-roasting and socialist songs."
66. For example, "SDA [Students for Democratic Action] Leadership Goes in for Expulsions" led the week's breaking news in the January 16, 1956, issue of the *Young Socialist Challenge.*
67. Author's interview with Andre Schiffrin, June 19, 1983.
68. "Riverboat Slim Says He's Bored," *Labor Action,* April 6, 1953, p. 5.
69. Michael Harrington, "Young Socialists Go with the Left SP"; Edward Hill, "Students vs. Peron"; Eli Fishman, "Rector Warns of Student Disaffection," *Young Socialist Challenge,* January 30, 1956, p. 1-C.
70. Sometime after Michael left the Workers Defense League in 1954, he took a job for a few weeks in a machine shop run by two veteran ISLers, Julius Jacobsen and Herman Benson. The idea was that he would pick up the rudiments of the machinist's craft under their patient supervision and then secure a job in a larger industrial establishment, where he could join one or another of the major unions with machinist jurisdictions. Bogdan Denitch had earned his union card with just that strategy. But having seen Michael struggling to learn the basics in the Jacobsen/Benson shop, Bogdan remembered him as hopelessly mechanically inept, "all thumbs." Thus whatever potential career Michael may have had as a union activist came to an abrupt end. Author's interview with Bogdan Denitch, December 7, 1984.
71. For a more detailed presentation of this argument, see Isserman, *If I Had a Hammer,* pp. 125–169.
72. For examples of Michael's appeals for common action with pacifists, see Harrington, "An Appeal to Militant Pacifists: By a Pacifist-Socialist: For Unity," *Labor Action,* February 8, 1954, p. 8; Edward Hill [Michael Harrington], "Pacifists Join the YSL," March 1, 1954, p. 7; and Harrington, "Plenty of Common Ground!" *Young Socialist Challenge,* March 28, 1955, p. 1-C.
73. According to the records of the War Resister's League, Michael was elected to a three-year term on the group's executive committee in February 1954. He attended only three of its eight meetings that year, only a single meeting the following year, and no meetings in the final year of his term. War Resister's League papers, Swarthmore College Peace Collection, series B, box 1.

74. Malina, *The Diaries of Judith Malina,* p. 370; Tytell, *The Living Theatre,* pp. 115–116; author's interview with Eileen Fantino-Diaz, March 16, 1995; letter from John Stanley to the author, May 9, 1992. The civil defense protest received wide publicity at the time, including network television coverage, and has been described since in numerous accounts. See Isserman, *If I Had a Hammer,* p. 145; and Mel Piehl, *Breaking Bread: The Catholic Worker and the Origin of Catholic Radicalism in America* (Philadelphia: Temple University Press, 1982), p. 214.
75. Author's interview with Eileen Fantino-Diaz, March 16, 1995; author's interview with Betty Bartelme, March 17, 1995. Michael, interestingly, makes no mention of this incident in any of his published memoirs.
76. Author's interview with Jack Stuart, January 7, 1995. In his memoirs, Michael recalled the "stunned silence" that often followed when he introduced himself to the police assigned to supervise a YSL picket line. As one policeman remarked memorably, "Michael, my boy, what are you doing with *these* people?" Harrington, *Fragments of the Century,* p. 69.
77. Steven M. Gillon, *Politics and Vision: The ADA and American Liberalism, 1947–1985* (New York: Oxford University Press, 1987), p. 18.
78. See Gillon, *Politics and Vision,* p. 23, on the social make-up of ADA.
79. On SDA membership figures, see William McIntyre, "Student Movements," *Editorial Research Reports* 2 (December 11, 1957), p. 926. On Lowenstein's membership see William H. Chafe, *Never Stop Running: Allard Lowenstein and the Struggle to Save American Liberalism* (New York: Basic Books, 1993), p. 51; on Dukakis's membership, see Philip Green, "Me and Dukakis: A Sort of Memoir," *Nation,* August 29, 1987, pp. 158–162.
80. Michael Harrington, "Self-Delusions of the Liberal 'Realists,'" *Young Socialist Challenge,* April 9, 1954, p. 2-C; Edward Hill [Michael Harrington], "What Does Liberalism Offer Youth?" *Young Socialist Challenge,* October 3, 1955, p. 2-C.
81. One of the advantages of controlling the regional SDA office was that it allowed YSLers to print literature under SDA's imprimatur. See, for example, Michael Harrington, "Crisis on the Campus" (New York Region, Students for Democratic Action, n.d. [1955?]). The pamphlet carried a disclaimer—on its inside cover—noting that the "ideas expressed in this pamphlet are not necessarily those of Students for Democratic Action."
82. Harrington, *Fragments of the Century,* p. 79.
83. Quoted in Gillon, *Politics and Vision,* p. 110.
84. Ibid., pp. 107–108.
85. S.L. "SDA Leadership Goes in for Expulsions," *Young Socialist Challenge,* January 16, 1956, p. 1-C; Michael Harrington, "SDA Divides Over Fight on Democracy," June 25, 1956, p. 1-C; S.L. "Democracy Loses at the SDA Convention," *Young Socialist Challenge,* September 24, 1956, p. 1-C.
86. Author's interview with Andre Schiffrin, June 19, 1983. SDA leaders turned to Student League for Industrial Democracy (SLID) leaders like Schiffrin for advice in their battle with the YSL, since SLID had successfully beaten off the Shachtmanites earlier in the decade.
87. For accounts of the Shachtmanite efforts to infiltrate the SDA, see Jerome Breslaw, "No Unity with Young Socialist League," *Hammer and Tongs,* Spring 1958, pp. 9, 25; and Arthur Mitzman, "The Campus Radical in 1960," *Dissent* 7 (spring 1960), pp. 143–145.
88. Howe, *A Margin of Hope,* p. 42.
89. On Dwight Macdonald's "creative mistake," see Gregory D. Summer, *Dwight Macdonald and the Politics Circle: The Challenge of Cosmopolitan Democracy* (Ithaca, N.Y.: Cornell University Press, 1996), p. 42.
90. Harvey Swados, "The Myth of the Happy Worker," *Nation,* August 17, 1957, pp. 65–68. On the limits of working-class prosperity in the 1950s, see Robert H. Zieger, *American Workers, American Unions,* 2d ed. (Baltimore: Johns Hopkins University Press, 1994), pp. 138–142.
91. Zieger, *American Workers, American Unions,* p. 169; Nelson Lichtenstein, *The Most Dangerous Man in Detroit: Walter Reuther and the Fate of American Labor* (New York: Basic Books, 1995), p. 319; C. Wright Mills, *New Men of Power* (New York: Harcourt Brace,

1948), pp. 211–212. As historian David Brody concluded, "Political action, like collective bargaining, held out seemingly boundless opportunity for the exertion of labor's power at the close of World War II. It did not appear beyond reason to anticipate a role comparable to that played by the labor movement in British political life." David Brody, *Workers in Industrial America: Essays on the Twentieth Century Struggle* (New York: Oxford University Press, 1980), p. 215.

92. Michael Harrington, *The Long Distance Runner: An Autobiography* (New York: Henry Holt, 1988), p. 99; Drucker, *Max Shachtman and His Left,* p. 291.
93. Author's interview with Dorothy Tristman, July 4, 1984. Also see Isserman, *If I Had a Hammer,* p. 190.
94. Author's interview with Bogdan Denitch, December 21, 1990.
95. Michael Harrington, "A-Bombs and Socialist Policy," *Young Socialist Challenge,* May 31, 1954, p. 1C (emphasis in the original).
96. Michael Harrington, "The Ethics of Rebellion," *Commonweal* 59 (January 29, 1954), pp. 428–431.
97. Dwight Macdonald, reply to Don Calhoun, "The Political Relevance of Conscientious Objection," *Politics* 1 (July 1944), pp. 179–180.
98. Harrington, "A Discussion: The Third-Camp Socialist as 'Witness.'"
99. Michael quoted this passage in a review of a new edition of Trotsky's *The History of the Russian Revolution.* Michael Harrington, "Enduring History," *Commonweal* 67 (December 20, 1957), p. 318.

Chapter Six: *A Premature Sixties Radical, 1956-1960*

1. Michael Harrington, "The New Left, Report to YPSL," mimeo, [n.d., 1959].
2. George Rawick, "The American Student: A Profile," *Dissent* 1 (August 1954), p. 397, emphasis in original.
3. Author's interview with Deborah Meier, April 19, 1986.
4. Author's interview with Ruth Jordan, March 10, 1992. In an interview shortly before his death, Michael reflected on the YSL's "norms of debate." They "were the classic Leninist and Trotskyist ones. That is to say they were abominable. You would accuse your opponent of being an agent for the bourgeoisie if you disagreed with him or her, that sort of nonsense. And you were not supposed to take umbrage simply because somebody said you had just totally abandoned your commitment to socialism." David Hacker and Patricia Friend, interview with Michael Harrington, August 19, 1988, copy in author's possession.
5. Elisabeth Bumiller, "In School's Crisis, Union's Opportunity" *New York Times,* September 29, 1995, p. B-2.
6. One indication of the YSL's attitudes toward gays can be found in an article Michael wrote for the *Young Socialist Challenge* in 1954 noting how the hunt for political subversives had spilled over into an attack on sexual "deviants." Referring to the government's policy of firing homosexual employees for being "security risks," Michael wrote: "Why a homosexual is more open to blackmail than a philandering heterosexual is not explained." Edward Hill [Michael Harrington], "University of Chicago Administration Turns the Clock Back," *Young Socialist Challenge,* June 28, 1954, p. 1-C.
7. Author's interview with Deborah Meier, April 19, 1986.
8. FBI files, May 29, 1956, p. 8. Copies of Michael's FBI files have been deposited by the author in New York University's Tamiment Library's collection of the Michael Harrington Papers. Rather than citing these documents by the FBI's confusing internal code, I will simply give their date.
9. Author's interview with Michael Harrington, November 19, 1982.
10. Author's interview with Bogdan Denitch, December 21, 1990.
11. Author's interview with Deborah Meier, January 6, 1992; Michael Harrington, *Fragments of the Century* (New York: Saturday Review Press, 1973), p. 88.

12. Along with Virginia Brungard, the mother of Michael's childhood friend and classmate Ed Brungard, Catherine served as the cochair of Ray Tucker's successful bid for the St. Louis mayoralty in 1953. Tucker then appointed Virginia Brungard as director of public welfare for the city of St. Louis. Catherine was appointed by Tucker to fill an empty seat on the city's board of education in 1955. She also served a cochairman of the women's division for a $110,000,000 bond issue campaign in 1954, and as cochairman of the city division of the United Fund of Greater St. Louis in 1955. In 1956 she was named the *St. Louis Globe-Democrat's* "Woman of Achievement" for the year. She also was mentioned favorably as "a civic-minded housewife" and "a volunteer spark plug" in a *Saturday Evening Post* article on municipal reform in St. Louis. In 1957 she became a counselor at Harris Teacher's College and held that post until retiring in 1971. See Joe Alex Morris, "How to Rescue a City," *Saturday Evening Post,* August 18, 1956, p. 56; "Mrs. E. M. Harrington Is Excellent Organizer," *St. Louis Globe-Democrat,* December 30, 1956; and Sally Thran, "Once Known for Her Own Record, Now She Is Michael's Mother," *St. Louis Post-Dispatch*, January 20, 1971.
13. Author's interview with Jack Stuart, January 7, 1995.
14. Author's interview with Peter Novick, December 28, 1991.
15. Michael Harrington to "Joyce" [n.d., 1957], microfilm reel 91, Socialist Party Papers.
16. Michael Harrington, "Are the Campuses Awake Yet?" *Young Socialist Challenge,* December 19, 1955, p. 1-C.
17. J. M. Robertson to YSL National Secretary, May 19, 1957, microfilm reel 91, Socialist Party Papers.
18. Michael Harrington to "Ruth," October 21, 1957, microfilm reel 91, Socialist Party Papers.
19. T. Robert Yamada to "Dick" [Gilpin], November 11, 1957, microfilm reel 91, Socialist Party Papers.
20. It is not surprising that Harrington emerged as one of the heroes of Russell Jacoby's elegiac account of the decline of the public intellectual: *The Last Intellectuals: American Culture in the Age of Academe* (New York: Basic Books, 1987), pp. 9, 20, 32–33, 39, 88, 115, 123.
21. R. Fahan [Irving Howe] and H. Judd [Stanley Plastrik], "The New Labor Action," *Forum* (March 1951), p. 12. *Forum* was the internal discussion bulletin of the ISL. Also see Maurice Isserman, *If I Had a Hammer: The Death of the Old Left and the Birth of the New Left* (New York: Basic Books, 1987), p. 87.
22. "A Word to Our Readers," *Dissent* 1 (Winter 1954), p. 3.
23. "A New Forum for Socialist Views," *Young Socialist Challenge,* June 21, 1954, p. 1-C; author's interview with Michael Harrington, November 19, 1982; Isserman, *If I Had a Hammer,* p. 65.
24. Michael Harrington and George Rawlings [Rawick], "'Dissent' Holds a Conference," *Young Socialist Challenge,* March 5, 1956, p. 1-C.
25. Sidney Hook quoted in Richard Pells, *The Liberal Mind in a Conservative Age: American Intellectuals in the 1940s and 1950s* (New York: Harper & Row, 1985), p. 129.
26. On CIA funding of the Congress and its consequences, see Christopher Lasch, "The Cultural Cold War: A Short History of the Congress for Cultural Freedom," in *The Agony of the American Left* (New York: Vintage, 1969), pp. 61–114.
27. Irving Kristol quoted in Pells, *The Liberal Mind*, p. 296.
28. Michael Harrington, "The Committee for Cultural Freedom," *Dissent* 2 (spring 1955), pp. 113–122 (emphasis in original). In a subsequent article in *Dissent,* Michael again took on Hook's "Heresy, Yes—Conspiracy, No" thesis. See Michael Harrington, "The Post-McCarthy Atmosphere," *Dissent* 2 (autumn 1955), p. 291.
29. Lasch, *The Agony of the American Left,* p. 111. Michael reprinted his essay on the Committee for Cultural Freedom in a collection of his essays, *Taking Sides: The Education of a Militant Mind* (New York: Holt, Rinehart, and Winston, 1985), pp. 16, 20–33. In his memoirs, Michael insisted that "the anti-Communist Left was not at all as cowardly as some of the recent interpretations of the fifties suggest. A good number of us fought against both Stalinism and American repression and for the same democratic reasons." Harrington, *Frag-*

ments of the Century, p. 87. Victor Navasky was among the few historians of the era who gave credit where it was due to Michael and others on the anti-Stalinist Left who opposed McCarthyism: "Their journal was *Dissent,* and their message as that while Stalinism was an unqualified social evil, domestic Communists were entitled to the same rights and presumptions as the rest of our citizens." See Navasky, *Naming Names* (New York: Viking Press, 1980), pp. 43, 324.

30. Author's interview with Marty Corbin, October 30, 1992. John Cogley described hiring Michael in his memoir *A Canterbury Tale: Experiences and Reflections, 1916-1976* (New York: Seabury Press, 1976), pp. 55–56.
31. Quoted in Walter Goodman, *The Committee: The Extraordinary Career of the House Committee on Un-American Activities* (New York: Farrar, Straus and Giroux, 1968), p. 399.
32. The best sources on the Fund for the Republic are Thomas C. Reeves, *Freedom and the Foundation: The Fund for the Republic in the Era of McCarthyism* (New York: Alfred A. Knopf, 1969); Frank K. Kelly, *Court of Reason: Robert Hutchins and the Fund for the Republic* (New York: Free Press, 1981); and Harry S. Ashmore, *Unseasonable Truths: The Life of Robert Maynard Hutchins* (Boston: Little, Brown and Company, 1989). Also see Mary Ann Dzuback, *Robert M. Hutchins: Portrait of an Educator* (Chicago: University of Chicago Press, 1991), pp. 229–253. Michael described his involvement with the blacklisting study in *Fragments of the Century,* pp. 84–88.
33. Kelly, *Court of Reason,* pp. 20–21; Goodman, *The Committee,* p. 400.
34. Rodger Van Allen, *The Commonweal and American Catholicism: The Magazine, the Movement, the Meaning* (Philadelphia: Fortress Press, 1974), pp. 111–114.
35. The best source on the blacklist and its consequences is Victor Navasky, *Naming Names.* Also see Larry Ceplair and Steven Englund, *The Inquisition in Hollywood: Politics in the Film Community, 1930–1960* (Berkeley: University of California Press, 1983); and Michael Harrington, "Seeger Conviction Displays Witch-hunt at Its Lowest," *New America,* April 21, 1961, p. 2.
36. Michael Harrington to W. H. Ferry, October 29, 1954, Fund for the Republic Papers, Seeley G. Mudd Manuscript Library, Princeton University Archives.
37. Martin Gang's role in the blacklisting is described at length in Navasky, *Naming Names,* pp. 98–108, 110–111. Also see letter from Michael to Martin Gang, dated October 20, 1954, in Fund for the Republic Papers, Seeley G. Mudd Manuscript Library, Princeton University Archives.
38. Michael Harrington to John Cogley, October 6, 1954, Fund for the Republic papers, Seeley G. Mudd Manuscript Library, Princeton University Archives; Cogley, *A Canterbury Tale,* pp. 55–56.
39. Harrington, *Fragments of the Century,* p. 174; Paul Jacobs, *Is Curly Jewish?* (New York: Atheneum, 1965), pp. 185–198. Paul Jacobs's correspondence with Michael can be found in the Paul Jacobs Papers, Boston University Special Collections.
40. Michael Harrington to John Cogley, October 6, 1954, Fund for the Republic Papers, Seeley G. Mudd Manuscript Library, Princeton University Archives.
41. Harrington, *Fragments of the Century,* p. 86.
42. Among the Communists Michael met during the blacklisting study was Dorothy Healey, who was chairman of the CP's Los Angeles district. In her own memoirs, Healey recalled Michael's impact on her, when they met for the first time in 1955: "We had very freewheeling discussions. I found that I could not always answer the questions [Michael and other YSLers] posed to me about how, as a Marxist, I could justify the things going on in the Soviet Union with regard to democracy, freedom of speech, and access to information. I admitted as much to them. These meetings were a big influence on me, because they gave me an opportunity to think seriously about the Soviet Union and its problems." Dorothy Healey and Maurice Isserman, *Dorothy Healey Remembers: A Life in the American Communist Party* (New York: Oxford University Press, 1990), p. 148.
43. Michael Harrington, "Hollywood: The Bitter Town," *New America,* February 3, 1961, p. 5.
44. Harrington, *Fragments of the Century,* p. 174. The connection with the Fund for the Re-

public also provided Michael with introductions to some of the nation's leading liberal figures: At a seminar on collective bargaining held at the Fund's newly established Center for Study of Democratic Institutions in Santa Barbara in July 1960, Michael rubbed elbows with such notables as Daniel Bell, Arthur Goldberg, Clark Kerr, Leon Keyserling, Seymour Martin Lipset, and A. H. Raskin. See folder on "Collective Bargaining Conference," Paul Jacobs Papers, Boston University Special Collections.

45. John Cogley, *Report on Blacklisting,* 2 vols., (New York: Fund for the Republic, 1956).
46. John Cogley, *Report on Blacklisting,* vol. 1, *Movies;* vol. 2, *Radio-Television* (Fund for the Republic, 1956). "Here They Go Again," *Denver Post,* July 3, 1956, clipping found in the Fund for the Republic Papers, Seeley G. Mudd Manuscript Library, Princeton University Archives.
47. Shortly afterwards Michael wrote to Hutchins, offering him a "brief outline of my political record" as an anticommunist, and giving him permission to use the letter in any way he thought fit. He did confess to two political indiscretions, signing a Communist-sponsored petition seeking clemency for the Rosenbergs and signing a Catholic Worker statement opposing capital punishment both in the United States and in the Soviet Union. When the *Daily Worker* publicized the latter, while excising all criticisms of the USSR, it convinced Michael "that one could not make a single exception to the rule that democrats cannot ever cooperate with Communists or Communist fronts." Michael Harrington to Robert M. Hutchins, July 17, 1956, Fund for the Republic Papers, Seeley G. Mudd Manuscript Library, Princeton University Archives.
48. Kelly, *Court of Reason,* p. 97.
49. All quotes from Cogley's HUAC interrogation are from "Public Reaction to Report on Blacklisting," pp. 23–26, a manuscript in the Fund for the Republic Papers, Seeley G. Mudd Manuscript Library, Princeton University Archives. A transcript of the hearings can be found in the Fund for the Republic Papers, Seeley G. Mudd Manuscript Library, Princeton University Archives. Michael discussed his experience with the Fund study and with HUAC in *Fragments of the Century,* pp. 84–87, and in his review of Victor Navasky's *Naming Names,* "The Informing Heart," *Commonweal* (December 19, 1980), pp. 725–726.
50. Woltman quoted in "Public Reaction to Report on Blacklisting," p. 9. Walters quoted in Kelly, *Court of Reason,* p. 99. Also see "Witness Blasts Blacklist Use as 'Dreadful,'" *New York Post,* July 11, 1956, clipping found in the Fund for the Republic Papers, Seeley G. Mudd Manuscript Library, Princeton University Archives; Stefan Kanfer, *A Journal of the Plague Years* (New York: Atheneum, 1973), pp. 264–266; and Goodman, *The Committee,* pp. 403–404.
51. Fulton Lewis Jr., quoted in Kanfer, *Journal of the Plague Years,* p. 266; *New York Daily News,* July 11, 1956.
52. *New York Times,* August 4, 1956, p. 14.
53. "Educating Mr. Arens," *Washington Post & Times Herald,* July 13, 1956. American Committee for Cultural Freedom (ACCF) press release, July 17, 1956, in Fund for the Republic Papers, Seeley G. Mudd Manuscript Library, Princeton University Archives. Even the American Congress of Cultural Freedom, notwithstanding its own earlier attacks on Fund for being soft on communism, felt that HUAC had gone too far this time. Diana Trilling, chairman of the ACCF's board of directors, wrote to HUAC chairman Walters to protest the committee's attempts to protect its own reputation by stifling free debate. American Committee for Cultural Freedom (ACCF) press release, July 17, 1956, in Fund for the Republic Papers, Seeley G. Mudd Manuscript Library, Princeton University Archives.
54. Frederick Woltman, "House Group Investigates Republic Fund Executive," *World Telegram and Sun,* December 12, 1956, clipping found in Fund for the Republic Papers, Seeley G. Mudd Manuscript Library, Princeton University Archives.
55. FBI files, December 17, 1956.
56. HUAC continued to pressure Cogley for some time to turn over the interviews and notes gathered by the blacklisting project to their investigators, which would have re-

sulted in revealing identities of some of those interviewed confidentially. Cogley settled the issue once and for all by burning the notes in the fireplace of his Brooklyn apartment. Ashmore, *Unseasonable Truths,* p. 372.

57. Michael Harrington, "Civil Liberties—by Fiat," *Commonweal* 67 (March 28, 1958), p. 654.
58. Arthur Schlesinger Jr., *The Vital Center* (Boston: Houghton Mifflin, 1949), p. 165. Also see Pells, *The Liberal Mind in a Conservative Age,* p. 136.
59. See Taylor Branch's masterful account of Martin Luther King's rise to national prominence in *Parting the Waters, America in the King Years, 1954–1963* (New York: Simon and Schuster, 1988), p. 718.
60. Michael Harrington, *The Long Distance Runner: An Autobiography* (New York: Henry Holt, 1988), p. 40.
61. Michael provided a historical overview of socialist involvement in the civil rights struggle in "Socialists and Civil Rights," *New America,* June 30, 1961, p. 3. Also see Philip Foner, *American Socialism and Black Americans: From the Age of Jackson to World War II* (Westport, Conn.: Greenwood Press, 1977).
62. Walter A. Jackson, *Gunnar Myrdal and America's Conscience: Social Engineering and Racial Liberalism, 1938–1987* (Chapel Hill: University of North Carolina Press, 1990), pp. 327–331.
63. Harrington, *Fragments of the Century,* pp. 97–98.
64. The most complete account of Bayard Rustin's life is offered in Jervis Anderson, *Bayard Rustin: Troubles I've Seen, A Biography* (New York: Harper Collins, 1997). Also see John D'Emilio, "Reading the Silences in a Gay Life: The Case of Bayard Rustin," in *The Seductions of Biography,* ed. Mary Rhiel and David Suchoff (New York: Routledge, 1996), pp. 59–68; Milton Viorst, *Fire in the Streets: America in the 1960s* (New York: Simon and Schuster, 1979), pp. 200–212; Branch, *Parting the Waters,* pp. 171–173.
65. There are many accounts of the Montgomery Bus Boycott. See, for example, Branch, *Parting the Waters,* pp. 143–205.
66. "March on Washington," *Young Socialist Challenge,* December 12, 1955, p. 1-C.
67. Quoted in Anderson, *Bayard Rustin,* p. 195.
68. Author's interview with Michael Harrington, December 29, 1982.
69. On Rustin and Kahn's relationship, see Peter Drucker, *Max Shachtman and His Left: A Socialist's Odyssey Through the "American Century"* (Atlantic Highlands, N.J.: Humanities Press, 1994), p. 269.
70. "Youth Assembly Mobilizes for 'Pilgrimage' to Capital," *Young Socialist Challenge,* May 6, 1957, p. 1-C.
71. Nancy[?] to "Mike," April 29, 1957, microfilm reel 91, Socialist Party Papers.
72. Harrington, *Fragments of the Century,* p. 105; David Garrow, *Bearing the Cross: Martin Luther King, Jr., and the Southern Christian Leadership Conference* (New York: William Morrow, 1986), pp. 93–94; Branch, *Parting the Waters,* pp. 217–218.
73. "'March' in Capital Asks Integration," *New York Times,* October 26, 1958, p. 76.
74. Harrington, *Fragments of the Century,* pp. 105–106. Also see Michael Harrington, "Notes on the Left," *New Leader* 44 (May 22, 1961), p. 16.
75. Author's interview with Michael Harrington, November 19, 1982.
76. Quoted in Isserman, *If I Had a Hammer,* p. 30.
77. "To the Stalinist Youth in the LYL: Did a Lunatic Despot Build Your System?" *Young Socialist Challenge,* April 16, 1956, p. 1-C.
78. Author's interview with Steve Max, October 16, 1991. Also see Edward Hill [Michael Harrington], "Leader of LYL 'Explains' Attack on Stalin," *Young Socialist Challenge,* April 16, 1956, p. 1-C.
79. Michael Harrington, "Communism After Hungary: In the United States," *Commonweal* 65 (February 1, 1957), pp. 455–456.
80. Bogdan Denitch, "Gates Case Touches Off Defense of Academic Freedom," *Young Socialist Challenge,* March 25, 1957, p. 1-C. Michael debated Clark at meetings at Columbia, Brooklyn College, and City College. Bogdan Denitch, "The Campus Shows Signs of

Perking Up," *Young Socialist Challenge,* April 22, 1957, p. 1-C; "Clark in Debate on USSR Socialism," *Daily Worker,* May 17, 1957.

81. When Clark resigned from the CP in 1957, Michael wrote to him, saying that although he was "sure that you and I still disagree on a whole series of questions, especially about Russia . . . I certainly admire you for taking what must have been a very difficult step." Michael Harrington to Joseph Clark, September 10, 1957, microfilm reel 91, Socialist Party Papers.
82. Morris Stempa to David McReynolds [n.d., 1956], David McReynolds Papers, Swarthmore College Peace Collection, series 1, box 1. The SP membership figures are from a typewritten statement in the McReynolds Papers, series 3, box 1.
83. David McReynolds to Charles Curtis et al., April 30, 1956, David McReynolds Papers, Swarthmore College Peace Collection, Series 3, Box 1.
84. David Shannon, *The Socialist Party of America* (New York: Macmillan, 1955), p. 256; "Socialists Join in Convention with Segment of Social Democrats," *New York Post,* January 20, 1957, p. 8.
85. The SP-SDF merger is described in Robert J. Alexander, "Schisms and Unifications in the American Old Left, 1953–1970," *Labor History* 14 (fall 1973), pp. 540–541.
86. Quoted in Isserman, *If I Had a Hammer,* p. 67.
87. Quoted in ibid., p. 69.
88. Dave McReynolds to Carl Braden, May 21, 1957, David McReynolds Papers, Swarthmore College Peace Collection, series 1, box 2.
89. Hal Draper, "SP Left Wing Proposes Unity with ISL at Party Convention," *Labor Action,* June 25, 1956, p. 4; Dave McReynolds to "Pop," October 15, 1956, David McReynolds Papers, Swarthmore College Peace Collection, series 2, box 1.
90. Robert Alexander to the author, April 28, 1991. Also see Alexander, "Schisms and Unifications in the American Old Left," pp. 536–561.
91. Tim Wohlforth, *The Prophet's Children: Travels in the American Left* (Atlantic Highlands, N.J.: Humanities Press, 1994), pp. 51–97.
92. Quoted in Isserman, *If I Had a Hammer,* p. 71. David McReynolds remembers a meeting with Irwin Suall and Norman Thomas sometime in 1957 to discuss the possibility of merging with the Shachtmanites. In his memory, Thomas said something to the effect, "They can all come in except for Harrington and Denitch because they have lied to my face and I won't have them in the party." Author's interview with David McReynolds, July 9, 1984. ISLer Herman Benson met with SP-SDF leaders in February 1958 to discuss the possibility of unity and was asked by them if the ISL would agree to merge without bringing in two or three unnamed "detestable" individual members. H. W. Benson to ISL national committee members, March 27, 1958, Max Shachtman Papers, New York University, Tamiment Collection, microfilm reel 3370.

    But there is no surviving documentary evidence to establish whether or not Michael was one of the "detestable" members in question. To help smooth things over in preparation for the merger, Shachtman had a "fatherly talk" with Denitch and persuaded him that it would be better for the moment if he wasn't in New York. Denitch moved to Berkeley, where his name didn't stir up as many unpleasant factional memories. Author's interview with Bogdan Denitch, December 7, 1984.
93. Norman Thomas to "Dear Comrade," June 28, 1958, Julius Bernstein Papers, Spring 1958 folder, Tamiment Collection, New York University.
94. David McReynolds to "Dear Comrade," August 10, 1958, David McReynolds Papers, Swarthmore College Peace Collection, Series II, Box 27.
95. "ISL Members to Join SP-SDF," *New International* 24 (spring–summer 1958), p. 75.
96. Mel Stack, "YSL-YPSL Hold Unity Convention in New York," *Young Socialist Challenge,* September 8, 1958, p. 1-C.
97. "Eldon was not very happy" to have someone else calling the shots, as Michael himself later admitted, "and I don't blame him." David Hacker and Patricia Friend interview with Michael Harrington, August 19, 1988.

98. Ibid.
99. "National YPSL Report" from Minutes, SP-SDF National Committee meeting, February 6, 1959, David McReynolds Papers, Swarthmore College Peace Collection, series 3, box 1.
100. Charles [Curtiss] to Irwin Suall, October 6, 1958, David McReynolds Papers, Swarthmore College Peace Collection, series I, box 3.
101. "Socialist Harrington to Speak," *Daily Californian,* March 11, 1958, p. 2. In these years, the appearance of a self-professed socialist like Michael in a public forum represented in itself a small victory for civil liberties. At the University of California at Berkeley a regulation known as "Rule 17" banned "controversial" off-campus speakers from using campus facilities. The rule was finally modified in the fall of 1957 (although Communist speakers continued to be banned down through the early 1960s). On the history of "Rule 17," see Seymour Martin Lipset, "Students and Politics," in *The Berkeley Student Revolt: Facts and Interpretations,* ed. Seymour Martin Lipset and Sheldon S. Wolin (Garden City, N.Y.: Doubleday and Company, 1965), pp. 15–19.
102. Michael described his campus itinerary in *Fragments of the Century,* pp. 88–92, and also in a letter to C. D. Jackson, May 29, 1959, in C. D. Jackson Papers, box 95, "Youth Festival—Vienna (1)" folder, Eisenhower Presidential Library. Also see "Harrington Reports on Tour: Sees Basis for YSL Growth," *Young Socialist Challenge,* March 24, 1958, p. 1-C.
103. On the British New Left, see, for example, Norman Birnbaum, "British Opinion on Marchers," *Nation,* April 18, 1959, p. 339; Andrew Hacker, "The Rebelling Young Scholars," *Commentary* 30 (November 1960), pp. 409–410; and Ronald Fraser, ed., *1968, A Student Generation in Revolt* (New York: Pantheon Books, 1988), pp. 33–35. Michael described the impact of "Nouvelle Gauche" politics in France in a book review, "Yvan Craipeau's New Book 'The Coming Revolution,'" *Young Socialist Challenge,* January 27, 1958, p. 10.
104. Michael Harrington, "The New Left: The Relevance of Democratic Socialism in Contemporary America" (New York: YPSL, 1959), pp. 1, 9–10.
105. Max Shachtman, "ISL Is off the Subversive List," *Labor Action,* July 28, 1958, p. 1.
106. On the reviving fortunes of European socialism in the postwar era, see Donald Sassoon, *One Hundred Years of Socialism: The West European Left in the Twentieth Century* (New York: New Press, 1996), pp. 189–322.
107. A glowing account of the Independent Service was provided in the summer of 1959 by a young associate editor of the stridently anticommunist *New Leader* magazine, J. Kirk Sale. Sale, a personal friend of Michael's, would later become better known as Kirkpatrick Sale, author of an early and sympathetic account of the history of Students for a Democratic Society (SDS). See J. Kirk Sale, "Operation Youth Festival," *New Leader* 42 (July 20–27, 1959), p. 9. For Steinem's role in this operation, see Carolyn Heilbrun, *The Education of a Woman: The Life of Gloria Steinem* (New York: Three Dial Press, 1995), pp. 86–89.
108. Michael did suspect that some kind of government money was finding its way into the coffers of the Independent Service, but he thought it was coming through the State Department. Harrington, *Fragments of the Century,* p. 138.
109. Walter Hixson, *Parting the Curtain: Propaganda, Culture, and the Cold War, 1945–1961* (New York: St. Martin's Press, 1997), pp. 22–23.
110. Gloria Steinem to C. D. Jackson, June 1, 1959, C. D. Jackson Papers, box 95, "Youth Festival—Vienna (1)" folder, Eisenhower Presidential Library.
111. Gloria Steinem to C. D. Jackson, June 12, 1959, C. D. Jackson Papers, box 95, "Youth Festival—Vienna (1)" folder, Eisenhower Presidential Library.
112. Harrington, *Fragments of the Century,* p. 139. Also see Sydney Ladensohn Stern, *Gloria Steinem: Her Passions, Politics, and Mystique* (Seacacus, N.J.: Birch Lane Press, 1997), pp. 117–118.
113. FBI files, August 12, 1959; October 21, 1959.
114. Harrington, *Fragments of the Century,* p. 54.
115. See, for example, Michael Harrington, "The Algerian Revolution," *New International* 23(summer 1957), pp. 199–201.

116. Michael Harrington, "Old Comrades Meet," *Harper's Magazine* 254 (February 1977), p. 26. Michael's credentials for the 1959 meeting can be found in Democratic Socialists of America Papers, box 1, folder 19, Tamiment Collection, New York University.
117. Harrington, *Fragments of the Century,* p. 139.
118. Michael Harrington, "Communist Youth Festival," *Commonweal* 70 (August 28, 1959), pp. 442–444; Harrington, *Fragments of the Century,* p. 140.
119. FBI files, November 3, 1959, p. 2.
120. FBI files, October 6, 1959.
121. Harrington, *Fragments of the Century,* p. 139.
122. For the debate over "mass culture" in the United States in the 1950s, see Isserman, *If I Had a Hammer*, pp. 98–102.
123. Michael may have been influenced in his thinking by the Swedish social democrat Gunnar Myrdal, who conceded in the 1940s that America was "conservative" but noted that "the principles conserved are liberal and some, indeed, are radical." Gunnar Myrdal, *An American Dilemma* (New York: Harper and Brothers, 1944), p. 7.
124. Michael Harrington, "The Other America," *Commonweal* 72 (May 27, 1960), pp. 222–224.
125. Marty Corbin, Michael's fellow Catholic Worker, believes that Michael first got the idea of enlisting in the radical movement from his reading of Dos Passos's trilogy *USA.* Author's interview with Marty Corbin, October 30, 1992.
126. This remained a constant theme in Harrington's political writings until the end of his life. See Michael Harrington, *Socialism, Past and Future* (New York: Arcade Publishing, 1989), p. 271.

Chapter Seven: *The Man Who Discovered Poverty, 1960–1964*

1. Daniel Patrick Moynihan, "The Professors and the Poor," in *On Understanding Poverty: Perspectives from the Social Sciences,* ed. Daniel Patrick Moynihan (New York: Basic Books, 1968). This article originally appeared in the August 1968 issue of *Commentary.*
2. J. R. Goddard, "Michael Harrington: Peripatetic Ideologist Views the Unaffluent American," *Village Voice,* March 22, 1962, p. 1; Norman Thomas to Michael Harrington, December 3, 1963, Norman Thomas Papers, microfilm reel 45; James Wechsler, "Man of His Times," *New York Post,* November 19, 1964.
3. Michael Harrington, *Fragments of the Century* (New York: Saturday Review Press, 1973), pp. 92, 172. *Commentary* was then at the beginning of a sudden leftward shift in political tone. Previously, under longtime editor Elliot Cohen, the magazine downplayed any suggestion that America had domestic problems of any consequence, in line with its paramount concern of promoting the struggle against communism abroad. Cohen was incapacitated with psychiatric problems in the later 1950s, and others on the magazine's staff began to push the journal in new political directions. Cohen's successor, Norman Podhoretz, who took over in early 1960, sought to turn the journal into the voice of a "new radicalism." As a result, for the next few years, writers like Michael, Paul Goodman, and Staughton Lynd would be featured regularly in *Commentary.* On *Commentary*'s political evolution, see Norman Podhoretz's two memoirs, *Making It* (New York: Random House, 1967), pp. 288, 292, 294; and *Breaking Ranks* (New York: Harper and Row, 1979), pp. 75–76; and Richard Pells, *The Liberal Mind in a Conservative Age: American Intellectuals in the 1940s and 1950s* (New York: Harper & Row, 1985), pp. 349–350, 384–385.
4. Michael Harrington, "The Housing Scandal," *Commonweal* 60 (July 2, 1954), pp. 311–313.
5. "The State of the Union," *New Republic,* January 16, 1950, p. 14.
6. Robert Heilbroner, "Who Are the American Poor," *Harper's Magazine* 200 (June 1950), pp. 27–33.
7. Irving Howe, "America: The Country and the Myth," *Dissent* 2 (summer 1955), pp. 242–244. Notwithstanding Howe's summons to action, *Dissent* itself ran only a few articles on poverty until the late 1950s and early 1960s. See, for examples, Dan Wakefield,

"Hospital Workers Knock at the Door," *Dissent* 6 (autumn 1959); Harvey Swados, "The Miners: Men Without Work," *Dissent* 6 (autumn 1959); Herbert Hill, "Migratory Agricultural Labor—The Story of a National Crisis," *Dissent* 7 (summer 1960); H. Brand, "Poverty in the United States," *Dissent* 7 (autumn 1960); and Dorothy Day, "Poverty and Destitution," *Dissent* 8 (summer 1961).

8. Robert Heilbroner, "Who Are the American Poor," p. 27.
9. Arthur Schlesinger Jr., "The Challenge of Abundance," *The Reporter,* May 3, 1956, pp. 8-11.
10. John Kenneth Galbraith, *The Affluent Society* (Boston: Houghton Mifflin, 1958), pp. 250–258. Galbraith's experience with *The Affluent Society* was a good illustration of the rule that authors have but little control over the use to which readers will put their ideas. "Perhaps," he mused at the height of the book's popularity, "in a better day, a more courageous economist would have insisted that his publisher call the book *The Quasi-Affluent Society.*" "How Affluent Is Our Society?" *New Leader,* 42 (February 2, 1959), pp. 16–19.
11. Michael Harrington and Paul Jacobs, *Labor in a Free Society* (Berkeley: University of California Press, 1959). The book, which drew together papers presented at a conference on labor sponsored by the Fund for the Republic in 1958, attracted little notice from reviewers.
12. Leon Keyserling, "Eggheads and Politics," *New Republic,* October 27, 1958, p. 15 (emphasis in the original). Three weeks later, the *New Republic* printed yet another article on poverty, by Helen Hill Miller, which concluded, "The existence of hundreds of thousands of poor people—ill-housed, ill-clothed, ill-fed . . . is no less of a public issue, no less of a weakness in the American system because the upward movement of other incomes obscures the conditions in which they live." Helen Hill Miller, "Today's 'One Third of a Nation,'" *New Republic,* November 17, 1958, pp. 13–15.
13. James L. Sundquist, *Politics and Policy: The Eisenhower, Kennedy, and Johnson Years* (Washington, D.C.: The Brookings Institution, 1968), p. 13; Irving Bernstein, *Promises Kept: John F. Kennedy's New Frontier* (New York: Oxford University Press, 1991), p. 168.
14. Galbraith's response was also printed in *The Reporter.* He responded graciously to Douglas's critique, confessing that "the title of this book itself reflects the values and mores of Madison Avenue." "How Affluent Is Our Society?" p. 16, 19.
15. Michael Harrington, "Our Fifty Million Poor," *Commentary* 28 (July 1959), pp. 19–20.
16. Oscar Lewis, *Five Families: Mexican Case Studies in the Culture of Poverty* (New York: Basic Books, 1959), p. 2. The publication of Lewis's widely discussed *Children of Sanchez* in 1961 would further popularize the notion of the "culture of poverty." Also see Oscar Lewis, "The Culture of Poverty," in Moynihan, *On Understanding Poverty,* pp. 187–200; and Jack L. Roach and Orville R. Gursslin, "An Evaluation of the Concept 'Culture of Poverty,'" *Social Forces* 45 (March 1967), pp. 383–392.
17. Harrington, "Our Fifty Million Poor," pp. 25–27. The September issue of *Commentary* published three pages of letters responding to Michael's article. Hyman Bookbinder, AFL-CIO legislative assistant, took him to task for seeming to imply that the labor movement had been amiss in failing to do more for America's poor (not so, Michael replied; he regarded the labor movement as "the best ally of the poor"). Herman Miller of the Bureau of the Census felt that Michael had exaggerated the problem of poverty; since 1929, he pointed out, the number of families and unattached individuals with incomes under $3,000, adjusted for inflation, had declined from 67 percent to 31 percent of the total. Michael had no difficulty with this challenge. He had not denied that the United States had made significant progress against poverty since 1929, progress that could be attributed to "the striking gains of the unionization wave and other social reforms of the New Deal," as well as to wartime and postwar prosperity. But in the 1950s, progress in eliminating poverty had slowed; the remaining third of the population living in poverty was, for both cultural and structural reasons, unable to take advantage of the general prosperity. "The amazing fact remains," he concluded, that "nearly one third of the American people (or, as Mr. Miller has it, 31 per cent) live beneath the recognized standards of adequacy—and this in the most prosperous society the world has ever known." "The Statistics of Poverty," *Commentary* 18 (September 1959), pp. 259–262.

18. Michael Harrington, "Slums, Old and New," *Commentary* 30 (August 1960), pp. 118–124. For a suggestion that Michael may have painted a historically inaccurate picture of early twentieth-century slum life, see Allen Davis, *Spearheads of Reform: The Social Settlements and the Progressive Movement 1890–1914* (New York: Oxford University Press, 1967), p. xii.
19. This was, Michael recalled, "uncharacteristically stupid" advice from Shachtman. David Hacker and Patricia Friend interview with Michael Harrington, August 19, 1988, copy in author's possession.
20. Harrington, *Fragments of the Century,* p. 172. Bartelme didn't work on the project directly, but she remembered that once Michael agreed to do the book, he wrote it very quickly, and without much subsequent editing. Author's interview with Betty Bartelme, March 17, 1995.
21. See, for examples, Michael Harrington, "Harlem Today," *Dissent* 8 (summer 1961), pp. 371–377; "The Economics of Racism," *Commonweal* 74 (July 7, 1961), pp. 367–370; "Christmas on the Scrap Heap," *New America,* November 15, 1960, p. 5. Strapped for funds, as usual, Michael piggybacked a number of his research trips for *The Other America* onto the subsidized trips he took on behalf on the Fund for Republic's project on trade unionism, for which he was then consulting. Audiotape, Program #103, Michael Harrington, "The Anti-Poverty War," February 18, 1964, Center for the Study of Democratic Institutions, Santa Barbara, California.
22. Michael Harrington, "Notes on the Left," *New Leader* 44 (May 22, 1961), p. 17.
23. Michael Harrington, "The American Campus: 1962," *Dissent* 9 (spring 1962), p. 166.
24. Harrington, *Fragments of the Century,* pp. 106, 113.
25. Clayborne Carson, *In Struggle: SNCC and the Black Awakening of the 1960s* (Cambridge: Harvard University Press, 1981), pp. 9–11.
26. Harrington, *Fragments of the Century,* p. 107.
27. Ibid.
28. Clarence [Jones] to Bayard Rustin, June 21, 1960, Bayard Rustin Papers, microfilm reel 1-0571 (emphasis in original).
29. Harrington, *Fragments of the Century,* pp. 108–110.
30. "Cheers and Boos Greet Kennedy at Rights Rally," *Los Angeles Times,* June 11, 1960, p. 3.
31. Harrington, *Fragments of the Century,* pp. 114–115. Also see David Garrow, *Bearing the Cross: Martin Luther King, Jr., and the Southern Christian Leadership Conference* (New York: William Morrow, 1986), pp. 140, 382.
32. "Conference Personnel," Papers of the Student Non-Violent Coordinating Committee, microfilm reel 1.
33. Workshop information was included in a letter from Marion Berry to "Dear Friend," September 30, 1960, Papers of the Student Non-Violent Coordinating Committee, microfilm reel 1.
34. Letter from Marion Berry to George Meany, September 16, 1960, Papers of the Student Non-Violent Coordinating Committee, microfilm reel 1.
35. Michael Harrington, "Rev. King States Views on 'Time for Freedom,'" *New America,* November 1, 1960, p. 2.
36. Minutes, National Committee SP-SDF, October 22–23, 1960, David McReynolds Papers, Swarthmore College Peace Collection, series 3, box 1.
37. A. Philip Randolph, "The Cruel Deception," *New America,* September 5, 1960, p. 1.
38. Walter Bergman, "The Alabama Story," *New America,* June 2, 1961, p. 1. On Bergman's martyrdom, see John Lewis, *Walking with the Wind: A Memoir of the Movement* (New York: Simon and Schuster, 1998), pp. 137, 146–147.
39. Michael Harrington, "Blizzard Utopia," *New America,* February 24, 1961, p. 2.
40. In 1924, the Socialists had endorsed Robert M. LaFollette's independent presidential ticket. David Shannon, *The Socialist Party of America* (New York: Macmillan, 1955), p. 175. The Socialist Labor Party (SLP) and the Socialist Workers Party (SWP) were the only left-wing alternatives on the ballot in 1960, the SLP garnering 46,478 votes for its candidate Eric Hass, and the SWP garnering 39,541 votes for Farrell Dobbs.

41. "Socialists and the Election," *New America,* September 5, 1960, p. 2.
42. Michael Harrington, "Resolution on Political Action and the 1962 Elections," Proceedings, SP 1962 National Convention, June 8–10, 1962, Washington, D.C., in David McReynolds Papers, Swarthmore College Peace Collection, series 3, box 2.
43. Quoted in David Brody, *Workers in Industrial America: Essays on the Twentieth Century Struggle* (New York: Oxford University Press, 1980), p. 229.
44. "What Program for Democratic Socialits?" *Labor Action,* March 24, 1958, p. 3.
45. Quoted in Sidney Lens, *Unrepentant Radical* (Boston: Beacon Press, 1980), p. 264.
46. Michael Harrington, "Is the Restoration of Public Confidence Possible?" in *Crisis in Confidence: The Impact of Watergate,* ed. Donald W. Harward (Boston: Little, Brown and Company, 1974), p. 139; Bill McKibben, "The Other American," *Mother Jones* (July–August 1988), p. 58.
47. "City Ticket Offered by Socialist Party," *New York Times,* June 21, 1961, p. 24.
48. The tensions within the SP over realignment were battled out at the party's 1962 national convention, held in Washington, D.C. Michael wrote one of several competing resolutions presented to the delegates at the convention to set policy for the party over the next two years. Michael argued that the party should put its main emphasis upon the realignment strategy. A competing proposal, authored by William Briggs of Los Angeles, emphasized independent Socialist electoral campaigning. There was also a third resolution, which became known as "Meier/Mendelson," after authors Debbie Meier and Saul Mendelson. The two former ISLers warned that an exclusive focus on the realignment strategy would "contribute to liquidating our youth support, which is the most promising source at this time for future militant Socialist participation in all arenas of American life." After an initial vote split virtually evenly between the three perspectives, the Realignment Caucus swung behind "Meier/Mendelson," making it official SP doctrine. But the tensions between working within the Democratic Party and working in support of militant social movements for peace and civil rights were not to be easily resolved. "Political Action Is Focus of SP Convention Debate," *New America,* June 29, 1962, p. 6. Also see Sam Bottone, letter to the editor, *New America,* July 27, 1962, p. 2; Michael Shute, "45 Chapters Represented at YPSL Convention," *New America,* September 14, 1962, p. 4.
49. Cogley, along with John Courtney Murray, had provided invaluable aid to the Kennedy campaign in 1960 by defusing the religious issue. Cogley wrote the speech in which Kennedy pledged before an audience of Texas Protestant ministers to maintain a strict separation of church and state.
50. Theodore White, *The Making of the President, 1960* (Boston: Atheneum, 1961), p. 106.
51. Kennedy is quoted in Arthur Schlesinger Jr., *A Thousand Days: John F. Kennedy in the White House* (Cambridge: Houghton Mifflin, 1965), pp. 1005–1006. James N. Giglio suggested that Michael's article on "Our Fifty Million Poor" influenced Kennedy's campaign themes: see *The Presidency of John F. Kennedy* (Lawrence: University Press of Kansas, 1991), p. 117.
52. Irving Bernstein, *Promises Kept: John F. Kennedy's New Frontier* (New York: Oxford University Press, 1991), pp. 28–30, 34–35; Nicholas Lemann, *The Promised Land: The Great Migration and How It Changed America* (New York: Alfred A. Knopf, 1991), p. 145; Sundquist, *Politics and Policy,* pp. 33–34.
53. Michael Harrington, "Liberals Failure to Mobilize Threat to Kennedy Program," *New America,* February 24, 1961, p. 1; "Labor, Rights Movements Restive on New Frontier," *New America,* March 10, 1961, p. 1; "Hostile Congress Fights Weak Anti-Religious Plan," *New America,* March 24. 1961, p. 1; "Religious Issue Complicates Inadeuate School Aid Bill," *New America,* April 7, 1961, p. 1.
54. Harrington, "Resolution on Political Action and the 1962 Elections."
55. Roche is quoted in Steven M. Gillon, *Politics and Vision: The ADA and American Liberalism, 1947–1985* (New York: Oxford University Press, 1987), p. 143. Also see Allen J. Matusow, *The Unravelling of America: A History of Liberalism in the 1960s* (New York: Harper and Row, 1984), pp. 101–105.

56. Sundquist, *Politics and Policy,* pp. 92–93.
57. Irwin Unger, *The Best of Intentions: The Triumph and Failure of the Great Society under Kennedy, Johnson, and Nixon* (New York: Doubleday, 1996), pp. 30–31; Kennedy is quoted in Richard Reeves, *President Kennedy: Profile of Power* (New York: Simon and Schuster, 1994), p. 100.
58. Sundquist, *Politics and Policy,* pp. 34–40.
59. Michael Harrington, "A Reactionary Keynesianism," *Encounter* 26 (March 1966), pp. 50–52.
60. Michael Harrington, "Draft Resolution on 'The Party Under the Kennedy Administration,'" Minutes, SP-SDF National Committee, June 17–18, 1961, David McReynolds Papers, Swarthmore College Peace Collection, series 3, box 1.
61. "Binding Ties," *New America,* January 24, 1961, p. 4.
62. At a February 1961 meeting of the SP-SDF National Committee, Michael proposed a resolution declaring the SP's "emphatic" opposition to "all suggestions of American intervention, direct or indirect, against Cuba." Michael's resolution made it clear that he was not sympathetic to Castro but nonetheless regarded the deterioration of U.S.-Cuban relations as "to a considerable degree" the product of the "past American policy of supporting Latin American dictators and reactionaries like Batista." Michael's resolution was adopted by the national committee, although the minutes of the meeting interestingly noted that "Comrade Max Shachtman" asked to be recorded "as abstaining on all the votes relating to the Cuban resolution." Minutes, SP-SDF National Committee, February 11–12, 1961, pp. 9–12, David McReynolds Papers, Swarthmore College Peace Collection, series 3, box 1. On protests after the Bay of Pigs invasion, see "SP Protests Cuba Action Across U.S.," *New America,* May 19, 1961, p. 2. For a more critical interpretation of the SP's role during the Bay of Pigs, see Van Gosse, *Where the Boys Are: Cuba, Cold War America, and the Making of the New Left* (London: Verso, 1993), pp. 230–234.
63. Ann Marshall, "A Look at the Poor," *Savanah Morning News Magazine,* June 5, 1966. In contrast, in his memoirs, Michael would write that "in 1960 and 1961 . . . I had no idea that important men in Washington would be in the least interested in what I had to say." Harrington, *Fragments of the Century,* p. 179.
64. Jacob Riis, *How the Other Half Lives* (New York: Charles Scribner's Sons, 1890).
65. In *The Other America,* Michael attributed the concept of "multiproblem families" to "the language of sociology." His most likely source was Roland Warren, *Multi-Problem Families: A New Name or a New Problem* (New York: State Charities Aid Association, 1960).
66. Michael Harrington, *The Other America* (New York: Macmillan, 1962), pp. 10, 14. In choosing to describe the poor as "invisible," Michael may have been harkening back, consciously or not, to Ralph Ellison's *Invisible Man,* which he had reviewed for the *Catholic Worker* ten years earlier.
67. Harrington, *The Other America,* pp. 158–159.
68. Ibid., p. 24.
69. Ibid., p. 163.
70. Bill McKibben, "The Other American," *Mother Jones* (July–August 1988), p. 58.
71. Harrington, *The Other America,* p. 19.
72. Ibid., p. 16.
73. Ibid., pp. 133–134.
74. Ibid., p. 44.
75. Ibid., p. 12.
76. Ibid., p. 101.
77. Ibid., p. 113.
78. Ibid., p 156.
79. James Wechsler, "Harrington Explodes Affluence Myth," *New America,* February 14, 1964, p. 2. This article was reprinted from the February 11, 1964, edition of the *New York Post,* where it first appeared. Michael actually had another book published in 1962, in addition to *The Other America*, although it is unlikely that it provided him with much additional income. This was a study of the Retail Clerks union, sponsored as part of a series

on contemporary labor issues by the Fund for the Republic and the Center for the Study of Democratic Institutions. Michael thought so little of the work, that he neglected to list it among his other publications on the dust jackets of his next few books. Michael Harrington, *The Retail Clerks* (New York: John Wiley and Sons, 1962).

80. Michael Harrington, *The Long Distance Runner: An Autobiography* (New York: Henry Holt, 1988), p. 224. Maurice R. Berube was the anonymous reviewer in *Kirkus.* A veteran organizer for the Association of Catholic Trade Unionists who would join the SP for a brief period in the mid-1960s (until he left over disagreements with the party's positions on Vietnam and on community control of schools in New York City), Berube would later confess that he wished he "could now rewrite" the offending review. Maurice R. Berube, *American Presidents and Education* (Westport, Conn.: Greenwood Press, 1991), p. 65.
81. A. H. Raskin, "The Unknown and Unseen," *New York Times Book Review,* April 8, 1962, section VII, p. 5.
82. Harvey J. Bresler, "The Poor are Still With Us," *Nation*, March 24, 1962, p. 266; Robert J. Lampman, "In the Midst of Plenty," *The New Leader* 45 (December 24, 1962), p. 21.
83. Norman Thomas, "The Other America," *New America,* May 4, 1962, p. 2. A few weeks earlier Thomas described a lecture tour he had recently taken in several western states, and he reported in passing, "I was delighted in my travels to hear the good words I often heard for Mike Harrington's speeches and now his book." Norman Thomas, "Lecture Circuit," *New America,* April 20, 1962, p. 2.
84. Goddard, "Michael Harrington: Peripatetic Ideologist Views the Unaffluent American."
85. Ibid. Never one to waste a good phrase, Michael would write in his 1973 memoir that in 1962, "I felt I was becoming a socialist jukebox." Harrington, *Fragments of the Century,* p. 119.
86. Author's interview with Ned O'Gorman, May 23, 1993.
87. Author's interview with Peter Novick, December 28, 1991.
88. Michael Harrington, "Editorial Report on New America," Minutes, SP-SDF National Committee, February 17–18, 1962, David McReynolds Papers, Swarthmore College Peace Collection, series 3, box 1.
89. David Hacker and Patricia Friend interview with Michael Harrington, August 19, 1988, copy in author's possession.
90. Rob Tucker, "Rise and Decline Among the Reds," p. 20.
91. Author's interview with Arthur Moore, September 28, 1991.
92. Rob Tucker, "Rise and Decline Among the Reds," p. 20.
93. Author's interview with Stephanie Harrington, July 24, 1991. Michael described the demonstration (with no mention of the date who accompanied him) in "US and Russian Tests Flaunt World Opinion," *New America,* May 25, 1962, p. 1.
94. Author's interview with Stephanie Harrington, September 27, 1991. Among other distinctions, she contributed some of the first pieces to the *Voice* on gays in the Village. Stephanie Gervis, "Politics: A Third Party for the Third Sex?" *Village Voice,* September 27, 1962, p. 1; "The Homosexual's Labyrinth of Law and Social Custom," *Village Voice,* October 11, 1962, p. 7. The two part series prompted a letter of praise from Donald Webster Cory, the head of the board of directors of the Mattachine Society, *Village Voice,* October 25, 1962, p. 4.
95. Stephanie Gervis, "In Greenwich Village, Sex Is Where You Find It," *Village Voice,* July 26, 1962, p. 1.
96. Paul Jacobs to Michael Harrington, August 10, 1962, Paul Jacobs Papers, Boston University Special Collections.
97. Author's interview with Stephanie Harrington, September 27, 1991.
98. Michael Harrington "The New Parabolist," *The Reporter* 28 (February 14, 1963), pp. 50–52. Michael also wrote of Voznesensky's significance in a subsequent piece for *Commonweal*, "A New Soviet Man?" *Commonweal* 78 (April 5, 1963), pp. 39–42.
99. On Michael's preparations to hold his own in French, see Stephanie Gervis, "The Paris Problem," *Esquire* 61 (February 1964), p. 88.
100. Author's interview with Stephanie Harrington, September 27, 1991.

101. Author's interview with Stephanie Harrington, September 27, 1991; Stephanie Harrington, "The Last Time I Saw Paris I Fell into Deep Depression," *Village Voice,* September 26, 1963, p. 9.
102. Michael Harrington to Paul Jacobs, [n.d., April 1963], Paul Jacobs Papers, Boston University Special Collections.
103. Catherine would probably have been doubly dismayed, had she realized that she was acquiring a daughter-in-law as willful as herself. Some months after Stephanie and Michael returned to the United States, they went out to St. Louis to visit his mother. Catherine announced that she was going to have a tea party to introduce Stephanie to her friends. Stephanie informed her mother-in-law that "there was no way that I was going to go to a tea." So instead, Michael's old friend Ed Brungard threw a party for the newlyweds. Catherine came and sat moodily by herself for the whole evening. Author's interview with Stephanie Harrington, July 24, 1991.
104. "Married in Paris," *Village Voice,* June 6, 1963, p 3; "Harrington Wins Award and Wife," *New America,* July 10, 1963, p. 2; SAC, New York to FBI Director, July 18, 1963. Copies of Michael's FBI files have been deposited by the author in New York University's Tamiment Library's collection of the Michael Harrington Papers. Rather than citing these documents by the FBI's confusing internal code, I will simply give their date.
105. Michael Harrington to Paul Jacobs, [n.d., April 1963], Paul Jacobs Papers, Boston University Special Collections.
106. Harrington, "The Last Time I Saw Paris I Fell into Deep Depression." Also see Gervis, "The Paris Problem."
107. Stephanie Harrington, "Americans in Paris March on Washington—By Proxy," *Village Voice,* August 29, 1963, p. 13.
108. Michael Harrington, "de Gaulle's Popularity Frustrates French Left," *New America,* February 25, 1963, p. 3; Harrington, "The Last Time I Saw Paris I Fell into Deep Depression," *Village Voice,* September 26 1963, p. 9.
109. Rudy Pakalns, "Socialist Int'l Optimistic; Political Gains and Growth," *New America,* December 13, 1963, p. 8. Pakalns, Samuel H. Friedman, and Ernst Papanek joined Michael in Amsterdam as representatives of the SP-SDF.
110. Jacobs agreed, though he wasn't persuaded of the utility of the request: "I certainly won't arrive until around October 20th and between now and then I assume there will be a lot of fucking." Paul Jacobs to Stephanie Harrington, September 23, 1963, Paul Jacobs Papers, Boston University Special Collections. In a letter to Jacobs a week later, Stephanie wrote emphatically, "WHATEVER YOU DO, *BRING THE ENOVID* [birth control pills]!" Stephanie Harrington to Paul Jacobs, September 29, 1963, Paul Jacobs Papers, Boston University Special Collections.
111. Michael Harrington to Paul Jacobs, [n.d., September 1963], Paul Jacobs Papers, Boston University Special Collections.
112. N. Alexandrova, "The 'Invisible' America," *International Affairs* 2 (February 1963), pp. 98–100.
113. Michael Harrington, *The Vast Majority: A Journey to the World's Poor* (New York: Simon and Schuster, 1977), p. 168.
114. Michael Harrington, "What's Left?" *New Republic,* September 21, 1968, p 34.
115. Author's interview with Stephanie Harrington, August 23, 1991.
116. Author's interview with Stephanie Harrington, August 23, 1991; Eric Leif Davin and Anita Alverio, "November 22, 1963, the Day Camelot Died," *The Squirrel Hill Times* 3 (November 16, 1983), p. 1.
117. Michael Harrington, "Pragmatists and Utopians: The New Radicalism," *Commonweal* 82 (September 3, 1965), p. 626. As he wrote of Kennedy some years later, the president "never created Camelot or anything like that [but] changed the atmosphere of America. He made things possible in America. He didn't do much; he was killed before he could. He was in an extremely difficult political situation, but he changed the atmosphere." Michael Harrington, "Is the Restoration of Public Confidence Possible?" in *Crisis in*

Confidence: The Impact of Watergate, ed. Donald W. Harward (Boston: Little, Brown and Company, 1974), p. 139.

118. Letter from Theodora Cogley Farrell to author, March 11, 1993.

119. Michael Harrington, "Pope John's Message Contribution to Struggle Against Nuclear War," *New America,* May 12, 1963, p. 1; Michael Harrington, "Poverty and Politics," in *Poverty in Plenty,* ed. George M. Dunne, S.J. (New York: P. J. Kennedy & Sons, 1964), pp. 51–52; James Hennessey, S.J., *American Catholics: A History of the Roman Catholic Community in the United States* (New York: Oxford University Press, 1981), p. 311.

120. FBI files, January 15, 1964.

121. Keyserling's study of poverty, heavily statistical in content, came up with figures for the poverty population very close to Michael's own. See "Poverty and Deprivation in the U.S.: The Plight of Two-Fifths of a Nation" (Washington, D.C.: Conference on Economic Progress, April 1962).

122. Harrington, *Fragments of the Century,* p. 127; Diana Trilling interview with Michael Harrington, March 1976.

123. Michael Harrington, "The New Lost Generation: Jobless Youth," *New York Times Magazine,* May 24, 1964, p. 13; Michael Harrington, "Close-Up on Poverty," *Look* 28 (August 25, 1964), pp. 65–72.

124. Marion Magid, "The Man Who Discovered Poverty," *New York Herald Tribune Magazine,* December 27, 1964, p. 11. *Newsweek,* February 17, 1964, pp. 20–21; *Time,* February 7, 1964, p. 25; "Author of Book on Poverty Hails President's 'War' to Help Needy," *New York Times,* February 15, 1964, p. 8.

125. *Yankee Radical* 3 (March 1963), p. 1. The *Yankee Radical* was the newsletter of Local Boston of the Socialist Party. This issue can be found in the Julius Bernstein Papers, Spring 1963 folder, Tamiment Institute. Paul Jacobs wrote to Michael in Paris, mockingly imploring him "not to forget me when you get to be famous, and what with Norman Thomas touting you for the presidency of the US, this will happen very soon." Paul Jacobs to Michael Harrington, March 20, 1963, Paul Jacobs Papers, Boston University Special Collections.

126. Letter from Irwin Suall to Norman Thomas, January 9, 1964, Norman Thomas Papers, microfilm reel 46.

127. Minutes of the SP-SDF National Committee, February 22–23, 1964, David McReynolds Papers, Swarthmore College Peace Collection, series 3, box 1.

128. Michael Wreszin, *A Rebel in Defense of Tradition: The Life and Policies of Dwight Macdonald* (New York: Basic Books, 1994), p. 376. Macdonald's review, reprinted as a pamphlet by the *New Yorker,* itself sold over 18,000 copies. Dwight Macdonald, "The Now Visible Poor," in Dunne, *Poverty in Plenty,* p. 61.

129. Most accounts of the Kennedy administration and the war on poverty since the 1960s have accepted that Kennedy read *The Other America.* Arthur Schlesinger Jr. declared flatly in his 1965 history of the Kennedy administration that *The Other America* "helped crystallize [Kennedy's] determination in 1963 to accompany the tax cut by a poverty program." Schlesinger, *A Thousand Days,* pp. 1010. More recently, Nicholas Lemann, in his study of the origins of the war on poverty, offered a dissenting view. "It is part of John Kennedy's legend that *The Other America* spurred him into action against poverty, . . . but the consensus among Kennedy's aides is that he read Macdonald's review, not the book itself." Lemann, *The Promised Land,* p. 131.

130. On these early discussions, see Michael L. Gillette, ed., *Launching the War on Poverty: An Oral History* (New York: Twayne Publishers, 1996), pp. 6–13.

131. James L. Sundquist, "Origins of the War on Poverty," in Sundquist, ed., *On Fighting Poverty, Perspectives from Experience* (New York: Basic Books, 1969), p. 8. Jack Conway, a former UAW staffer working for the Kennedy administration, recalled that after reading *The Other America,* "things kind of came together and had a different meaning" for those involved in drawing up the administration's domestic legislation. The book "was 'a real blockbuster.'" Conway would later be appointed director of the Community Action Pro-

gram for the war on poverty. Quoted in Irwin Unger, *The Best of Intentions: The Triumphs and Failures of the Great Society Under Kennedy, Johnson, and Nixon* (New York: Doubleday, 1996), p. 67.

132. Johnson is quoted in John Morton Blum, *Years of Discord: American Politics and Society, 1961–1973* (New York: W. W. Norton & Co., 1991), p. 149.
133. Paul Jacobs to Michael Harrington, May 1, 1963, Paul Jacobs Papers, Boston University Special Collections.
134. "The Vicious Circle of Poverty," *Business Week,* February 1, 1964, p. 39. Also see "Poverty and Passion," *Time Magazine,* February 7, 1964, p. 28.
135. Hubert Humphrey, *War on Poverty* (New York: McGraw Hill, 1964), p. 22. In 198 pages of text, Humphrey made two direct references to *The Other America.* Humphrey was not alone in such appropriation. The 1964 Economic Report of the President of the Council of Economic Advisers, released in January, represented, in the words of one historian, a "virtual paraphrase" of portions of *The Other America.* "The poor," the CEA declared, "inhabit a world scarcely recognizable, and rarely recognized, by a majority their fellow Americans. It is a world apart, whose inhabitants are isolated from the mainstream of American life and alienated from its values." Quoted in Richard Polenberg, *One Nation Divisible; Class, Race, and Ethnicity in the United States Since 1938* (New York: Viking Press, 1980), p. 198.
136. James Q. Wilson, *The Amateur Democrat: Club Politics in Three Cities* (Chicago: University of Chicago Press, 1962), p. 3.
137. Jane Jacobs, *The Life and Death of Great American Cities* (New York: Random House, 1961); Rachel Carson, *Silent Spring* (Boston: Houghton Mifflin, 1962); Betty Friedan, *The Feminine Mystique* (New York: Norton, 1963); Ralph Nader, *Unsafe at Any Speed* (New York: Grossman, 1965).
138. Norman Podhoretz, *Breaking Ranks,* p. 76.
139. Michael Harrington, "Skirmish No War on Poverty Amidst Plenty," *New America,* January 31, 1964, p. 1.
140. Letter from Frank Mankiewicz to the author, June 16, 1992.
141. Quoted in Michael Harrington, *Towards a Democratic Left: A Radical Program for a New Majority* (New York: Macmillan, 1968), p. 8. Shriver's part of the exchange made better repartee, but Michael came away from his meetings with Shriver convinced that he, too, understood that the sums being discussed were "absolutely and utterly inadequate," and, at best, "only a beginning." Harrington, "The Anti-Poverty War."
142. Harrington, *Fragments of the Century,* pp. 174–175.
143. Paul Jacobs, "Re-Radicalizing the De-Radicalized," *New Politics* 5, no. 4 (fall 1966), p. 15.
144. Letter from James Sundquist to the author, May 6, 1998.
145. Harrington, "The Anti-Poverty War." Jacobs later offered a highly self-critical account of his and Michael's involvement with the antipoverty task force: "From the start, we had to act within the rules of the game as Shriver laid them down. This meant that although Shriver appeared to be very open to all kinds of program suggestions, it became clear very soon that they all had to be within 'acceptable' boundaries." Jacobs, "Re-Radicalizing the De-Radicalized," p. 15.
146. Author's telephone interview with Frank Mankiewicz, June 8, 1998.
147. Letter to the author from anonymous source. This may be why none of the Harrington–Jacobs February 1964 memos survived to be included in the War on Poverty Papers.
148. Quoted in Unger, *The Best of Intentions,* p. 81. Yarmolinsky's mother, the poet Babette Deutsch, had a reputation for political radicalism that marked the decidedly anticommunist Yarmolinsky as politically dangerous in the eyes of many congressmen. See Gillette, *Launching the War on Poverty,* pp. 133, 138. Also see Yarmolinsky's comments on Michael and Paul Jacobs in Gillette, p. 47.
149. Daniel Patrick Moynihan, *Maximum Feasible Misunderstanding: Community Action in the War on Poverty* (New York: Free Press, 1969), p. 84.
150. Gillette, *Launching the War on Poverty,* p. 91.

151. James T. Patterson, *Grand Expectations: The United States, 1945–1974* (New York: Oxford University Press, 1996), p. 540.
152. Sundquist, "Origins of the War on Poverty," pp. 26–27. Johnson is quoted in Lemann, *The Promised Land,* p. 149.
153. Patterson, *Grand Expectations,* p. 535.
154. Gillette, *Launching the War on Poverty,* p. 36.
155. Harrington, *The Other America,* p. 164.
156. Michael Harrington, "Poverty in Affluence," the Herbert R. Abeles Memorial Address delivered at the 33rd General Assembly, Council of Jewish Federations and Welfare Funds, St. Louis, Missouri, November 14, 1964.
157. Oscar Lewis himself strongly implied in his writings that the only real solution to the culture of poverty lay in revolutionary socialism; on a visit to Castro's Cuba in the mid-1960s, Lewis felt that the culture of poverty he had noted there on earlier visits had all but disappeared: He reported that he "was told by one Cuban official that they had practically eliminated delinquency by giving arms to the delinquents!" Oscar Lewis, "The Culture of Poverty," in Moynihan, *On Understanding Poverty,* pp. 194–195.
158. "You all know how the circle goes," photographer and reformer Lewis Hine wrote in a pamphlet for the National Child Labor Committee in 1915: "child labor, illiteracy, industrial inefficiency, low wages, long hours, low standards of living, bad housing, poor food, unemployment, intemperance, disease, poverty, child labor, illiteracy, industrial inefficiency, low wages—but we are repeating." Quoted in Alan Trachtenberg, "Ever-The Human Document," in *America & Lewis Hine* (New York: Aperture, 1977), pp. 130–131.

    In another example of the "vicious circle" argument, delivered forty years later and shortly before Michael began his own research into poverty, community organizer Saul Alinsky testified before a U.S. Senate committee in 1956 that "in the main, delinquency and crime arise out of inadequate substandard housing, disease, economic insecurity, inadequate educational facilities, discrimination, and a series of social ills which combine to foster and relate to each other in a vicious circle with each feeding into the other so that frustration, demoralization, and delinquency mounts." Quoted in Sundquist, *Politics and Policy,* p. 118.
159. Harrington, *The Other America,* p. 22.
160. Ibid., p. 105.
161. Herbert Gans has offered this critique of *The Other America*: "Harrington's 'culture of poverty' was an economic term . . . which paid little attention to 'culture' or to its transmission to later generations." Gans, *The War Against the Poor: The Underclass and Antipoverty Policy* (New York: Basic Books, 1995), p. 26. For an early critique of the ways in which the notion of the culture of poverty was being misapplied to material conditions, see Roach and Gursslin, "An Evaluation of the Concept 'Culture of Poverty,'" p. 386. Also see Polenberg *One Nation Divisible,* p. 196.
162. Michael Harrington, "Will the Real Lyndon B. Johnson Stand Up?" *New America,* May 16, 1964, p. 2.
163. Davis, *Spearheads of Reform,* p. 123.
164. Gillette, *Launching the War on Poverty*, p. xiii; Polenberg, *One Nation Divisible,* pp. 194–195. For typical coverage from the period, see, for example, the cover of the special issue of *Newsweek* devoted to exploring "Poverty USA," *Newsweek,* February 17, 1964.
165. Harry M. Caudill, *Night Comes to the Cumberlands: A Biography of a Depressed Area* (Boston: Little Brown, 1963), p. vii. On the influence of Caudill's book, see Schlesinger, *A Thousand Days,* p. 1007.
166. In March 1964 the Gallup poll asked the following question: "Which is more often to blame if a person is poor—lack of effort on his own part, or circumstances beyond his control?" Thirty-three percent of the sample responded "lack of effort," 29 percent blamed "circumstances," and 32 percent thought the two were equally important. *The Gallup Poll of Opinion, 1935–1971* (New York: Random House, 1972), p. 1870.
167. "100 Billion Advocated to Eradicate Poverty," *St. Louis Globe-Democrat,* November 16,

1964. Michael gave no source for this estimate. But it may have been based on a 1962 report from the Survey Research Center at the University of Michigan. The center had undertaken a long-range survey of American family income, a study supported by the Ford Foundation. In their 1962 report, the center's researchers concluded that the "poverty gap" in the United States could be entirely eliminated with income supplements costing "about $10 billion a year." James N. Morgan, Martin H. David, Wilbur J. Cohen, and Harvey E. Brazer, *Income and Welfare in the United States* (New York: McGraw-Hill, 1962), pp. 3, 7.

Also see James T. Patterson, *America's Struggle Against Poverty, 1900–1985*, 2d ed. (Cambridge: Harvard University Press, 1986), p. 113. In the summer of 1965, Sargent Shriver proposed spending along those lines to President Johnson, to no avail. Gillette, *Launching the War on Poverty,* p. 143, 162–163.

168. "In a letter to voters back home, Texas congressman O. C. Fisher called the antipoverty bill 'the biggest boondoggle in modern history.' It was New Deal make-work, 'leaf-raking' all over again, he wrote, and to top it all, it mandated integration. Norman Thomas, the 'veteran socialist,' Fisher claimed, 'says the bill is the biggest step we've ever taken to convert this country into a socialist welfare state.'" Unger, *The Best of Intentions,* p. 90.
169. Magid, "The Man Who Discovered Poverty."
170. Moynihan, *Maximum Feasible Misunderstanding,* p. xvii; Unger, *The Best of Intentions,* p. 100. That fall, Sargent Shriver included Michael's name on a list of suggested candidates for a "National Advisory Council" to the Office of Economic Opportunity, to be made up of prominent citizens ranging from John Kenneth Galbraith to Malcolm Forbes to Mrs. Robert S. McNamara. At the request of presidential aide Lee White, the FBI supplied the White House a summary of its files on Michael in December 1964, noting that he was "currently the subject of an FBI investigation of a security nature." When the White House released the names of the fourteen member OEO advisory council in late January 1965, Michael's was not among them. Sargent Shriver to Bill Moyers, November 23, 1964, War on Poverty Papers, microfilm reel 10, 0264; FBI document, December 18, 1964; White House press release, January 28, 1965, War on Poverty Papers, microfilm reel 10, 0249. In response to a query from the author, Bill Moyers offered an "educated guess" that "someone thought Harrington too 'radical'" and a potential "lightening rod in Congress," should he be appointed. Bill Moyers to author, July 1992. John Kenneth Galbraith, who did serve on the committee, remembered it serving mostly a "decorative" function for the war on poverty; when his own opposition to the Vietnam War grew more pronounced later in the decade, Johnson had him quietly dropped from the committee. Author's interview with John Kenneth Galbraith, May 10, 1993.
171. Michael Harrington, "Should the Left Support Johnson?" *New Politics* 3, no. 3 (summer 1964), p. 6; Harrington, "Campaign Draws Line on Vital Issues," *New America,* September 16, 1964, p. 1. The Socialist Party did not formally endorse Johnson in the 1964 election. The Realignment Caucus would have liked to have done so but was still too weak to impose its views on the rest of the party.
172. Harrington, "Campaign Draws Line on Vital Issues."
173. Norman Thomas, "Defeat Goldwaterism," *New America,* September 16, 1964, p. 2.
174. Jack Newfield, "Poverty Crusader Named Chairman of the Board," *Village Voice,* November 26, 1964, p. 3.
175. James Wechsler, "Man of His Times," *New York Post,* November 19, 1964.

Chapter Eight: *Sibling and Other Rivalries, 1960–1965*

1. Todd Gitlin, "The Sixties: Years of Hope, Days of Rage," (New York: Bantam Books, 1987), p. 117.
2. Kenneth Rexroth, "The Students Take Over," *Nation,* July 2, 1960, p. 9.
3. Karl Marx, "Theses on Feuerbach," in *The Marx-Engels Reader,* ed. Robert C. Tucker

(New York: W. W. Norton, 1978), p. 144. Michael discussed the concept of educating the educator in *Socialism* (New York: Saturday Review Press, 1972), p. 45.
4. Michael Harrington, "The American Campus: 1962," *Dissent* 9 (spring 1962), pp. 165–166.
5. Harrington, *Socialism,* p. 46.
6. Michael Harrington, *Fragments of the Century* (New York: Saturday Review Press, 1973), p. 137.
7. Dick Drinnon to Dave McReynolds, January 1, 1959, David McReynolds Papers, Swarthmore College Peace Collection, series 1, box 3.
8. For the significance of the anti-HUAC protest in San Francisco, see Maurice Isserman, *If I Had a Hammer: the Death of the Old Left and the Birth of the New Left* (New York: Basic Books, 1987), pp. 188–189.
9. Minutes, SP-SDF National Committee, June 17, 18, 1961, David McReynolds Papers, Swarthmore College Peace Collection, series 3, box 1.
10. Dale Johnson, "On the Ideology of the Campus Revolution," reprinted in Paul Jacobs and Saul Landau, eds., *The New Radicals* (New York: Vintage, 1966), p. 97.
11. Minutes, SP-SDF National Committee, February 7–8, 1959; Minutes, SP-SDF National Committee, October 22–23, 1960; Minutes, SP-SDF National Committee February 11–12, 1961; Minutes, SP-SDF National Committee December 29, 1962, David McReynolds Papers, Swarthmore College Peace Collection, series 3, box 1. SDS membership in the spring of 1962 was reported to be about "eight hundred or so" (of whom slightly more than half had actually paid dues). Kirkpatrick Sale, *SDS* (New York: Vintage, 1974), p. 46. For Jerry Rubin's affiliation with the SP-SDF, see the May 1961 letter to Dave McReynolds from Bay Area socialists, David McReynolds Papers, Swarthmore College Peace Collection, series 1, box 1. Tom Kahn's influence on Stokely Carmichael is discussed in Clayborne Carson, *In Struggle: SNCC and the Black Awakening of the 1960s* (Cambridge, Mass.: Harvard University Press, 1981), p. 163, and in Isserman, *If I Had a Hammer,* p. 187. For Mario Savio's brush with socialism in the early 1960s see Arthur Gatti, "Mario Savio's Religious Influences and Origins," *Radical History Review* 71 (spring 1998), pp. 125–127.
12. I.F. Stone, "Civil Rights Movement Moves Back Towards Socialism for Answers," *I.F. Stone's Weekly*, Septemeber 16, 1963, p. 2.
13. John Cogley interview with Michael Harrington, "Slightly Autobiographical—By Request," audiotape (Santa Barbara, CA: Center for the Study of Democratic Institutions), spring 1965.
14. Letter from Bob Ross to the author, June 4, 1991; Tom Hayden, *Reunion: A Memoir* (New York: Random House, 1988), p. 86; Hayden, "Who Are the Student Boat-Rockers?" *Mademoiselle* (August 1961), pp. 334–335.
15. Paul Cowan, *The Making of an Un-American* (New York: Viking, 1970), pp. 70–71.
16. Marion Magid, "The Man Who Discovered Poverty," *New York Herald Tribune Magazine*, December 27, 1964, p. 9.
17. On the formation of SDS, see Sale, *SDS,* pp. 15–27; James Miller, *"Democracy is in the Streets": From Port Huron to the Siege of Chicago* (New York: Simon and Schuster, 1987), pp. 33–39; and Isserman, *If I Had a Hammer,* pp. 204–205.
18. Hayden, *Reunion,* pp. 3–21; Irving Howe, *A Margin of Hope: An Intellectual Autobiography* (San Diego: Harcourt, Brace, Jovanovich, 1982), p. 293.
19. Harrington, *Fragments of the Century,* p. 140.
20. Quoted in Miller, *"Democracy is in the Streets,"* p. 54.
21. Harrington, *Fragments of the Century,* p. 144; Sale, *SDS,* p. 65.
22. Michael Harrington, "Notes on the Left," *New Leader* 44 (May 22, 1961), p. 16.
23. Ibid., p. 18.
24. Cowan, *The Making of an Un-American,* p. 8.
25. Michael would write about how he avoided the occasional violent evenings at the White Horse in *Fragments of the Century,* pp. 49–50. He would describe himself as a "physical coward" in *The Vast Majority: A Journey to the World's Poor* (New York: Simon and Schuster, 1977), p. 56.

26. Harrington, "The American Campus: 1962," p. 166; author's interview with Jack Newfield, January 6, 1992. Also see Dick Roman, "N.Y. Sit-In Diary," *New America,* June 30, 1961, p. 4; "The West 66th St. Sit-In Has its Windup in Court," *New York Post,* June 7, 1961. In his memoirs, Michael would describe the night he spent "locked in a tiny detention cell" in the police station as "devastating," *Fragments of the Century,* p. 119. But this contradicts accounts he wrote closer to the event, and the memories of those who spent the night with him, which suggest that his brief imprisonment was exhilarating if exhausting.
27. Michael's only other arrest in the 1960s came on April 22, 1964, outside the New York pavilion of the newly opened world's fair in Flushing Meadow, Queens. The demonstration, organized by CORE, demanded school integration and employment opportunities for blacks in New York City. It was designed in part to counter a threatened "stall-in" on bridges leading to the fair by a militant, dissident chapter of CORE. Three hundred of the protesters, including Michael, were arrested on disorderly conduct charges. See Stephanie Gervis Harrington, "Heigh-Ho, Come to the Fair," *Village Voice,* April 30, 1964, p. 1; and Fred Powledge, "CORE Chief Among Scores Arrested on Grounds," *New York Times,* April 23, 1964, p. 28; Harrington, *Fragments of the Century,* p. 120.
28. Ann Marshall, "A Look at the Poor," *Savannah Morning News Magazine,* June 6, 1966.
29. Richard H. Cunningham, "A Crusader Examines the Poor Among Us," *Holy Cross Crusader* [1962].
30. Harrington, "The American Campus: 1962," p. 168.
31. "Thanks to HUAC," *New America,* March 24, 1961, p. 3; Dick Roman, "The Young Fogies Boast to Defeat," *New America,* September 22, 1961, p. 1; Harrington, *Fragments of the Century,* p. 142.
32. R. W. Tucker, "Rise and Decline Among the Reds," (privately published, 1991), p. 35.
33. Buckley is quoted in John A. Andrew III, *The Other Side of the Sixties: Young Americans for Freedom and the Rise of Conservative Politics* (New Brunswick, N.J.: Rutgers University Press, 1997), p. 58.
34. Ibid., p. 167; Jack Newfield, "Liberals' Response to YAF: Picket Line and Counter Rally," *New America,* March 23, 1962, p. 1; Steven Heller, ed., *Jules Feiffer's America: From Eisenhower to Reagan* (New York: Alfred A. Knopf, 1982), p. 51.
35. "Garden Packed for Goldwater; Libs Counter with Humphrey," *Village Voice,* March 15, 1962, p. 1.
36. The main sponsor of the "Washington Action" against nuclear testing was the Student Peace Union (SPU), in whose leadership YPSL was well represented. Students for a Democratic Society (SDS) and Student SANE cosponsored the event, which attracted 5,000 student protesters, a substantial number by the standards of the time. See Isserman, *If I Had a Hammer,* pp. 196–197.
37. YPSL's organizational history in the early 1960s is summarized in Tom Kahn, "The Problem of the New Left," in *Looking Forward,* occasional paper no. 6 (New York: League for Industrial Democracy, 1966), p. 7.
38. David McReynolds to members and alternates of the SP National Committee, November 25, 1964, David McReynolds Papers, Swarthmore College Peace Center, series 3, box 2.
39. Norman Thomas to Charles Van Tassell, November 13, 1964, Norman Thomas Papers, microfilm reel 47, New York Public Library.
40. Tom Hayden to SDS executive committee [n.d., spring 1962] SDS Papers, microfilm reel 1, series 1-6.
41. Ibid.
42. Michael Harrington to John Randall, June 1, 1952, Dorothy Day-Catholic Worker Collection, series W-2, box 1, Marquette University Archives.
43. Quoted in Miller, *"Democracy is in the Streets,"* p. 112.
44. Ibid., pp. 112–113.
45. See, for example, his article "Labor in the Doldrums," *Commonweal* 71 (March 11, 1960), p. 645, in which he wrote, "Until firm action is taken, bureaucracy, racketeering, racism and all the other evils that beset the American unions, will have an easy time."

46. Michael Harrington, *The Long Distance Runner: An Autobiography* (New York: Henry Holt, 1988), p. 57.
47. Quoted in Miller, *"Democracy is in the Streets,"* p. 115.
48. Ibid., p. 116.
49. Quoted in Hayden, *Reunion,* p. 92.
50. Quoted in Gitlin, *The Sixties,* p. 115.
51. Quoted in Miller, *"Democracy is in the Streets,"* p. 120.
52. Some SDSers concluded that her concerns, and those of her fellow yipsels, were part of a plot to capture SDS. See Isserman, *If I Had a Hammer*, pp. 212–213.
53. Miller, *"Democracy is in the Streets,"* pp. 130–131. The notion that a convention should be ten days long was a capriciously arbitrary standard to apply to SDS—none of the various organizations Michael had helped form, including the YSL and YPSL, had ever spent more than a weekend in a founding convention.
54. Quoted in Jack Newfield, *A Prophetic Minority* (New York: New American Library, 1966), p. 134.
55. Harrington, *Fragments of the Century,* p. 147.
56. Author's interview with Steve Max, October 16, 1991. Not everyone was willing to forgive Michael, however. Casey Hayden told Michael, bitingly, "Well, now I know what it must have been like to be attacked by the Stalinists." Quoted in Harrington, *Fragments of the Century,* p. 148.
57. Miller, *"Democracy is in the Streets,"* pp. 126–140; Sale, *SDS,* pp. 60–68; Gitlin, *The Sixties,* pp. 116–120.
58. Harrington, *The Long Distance Runner,* p. 57.
59. Gitlin, *The Sixties,* pp. 120, 183.
60. Newfield, *Prophetic Minority,* p. 135.
61. Robert Gorman makes this mistake in his intellectual biography of Harrington, writing: "Port Huron became the central event in Harrington's life. It destroyed his reputation and credibility among heretofore sympathetic young, non-communist radicals. . . . Immediately after Port Huron, Harrington was a lonely figure on the political landscape, alienated from every major progressive constituency. . . . Almost overnight, Harrington became a rejected, isolated, aging, maverick socialist." Gorman, *Michael Harrington: Speaking American* (New York: Routledge, 1995), p. xv, 24.
62. Bob Ross to Michael Harrington, December 10, 1962, University of Michigan Library
63. On the origins of SDS's ERAP strategy, see Sale, *SDS,* pp. 95–102.
64. In 1964 Michael was one of the signatories to a statement circulated by economist Robert Theobold and the "Ad Hoc Committee on the Triple Revolution" that warned of the dire economic consequences of automation. Some of this analysis also found its way into Michael's 1965 book *The Accidental Century.* As he would later note apologetically, "If we were very wrong on the tempo of the trend (a congenital error with radicals) we did get the tendency right." Michael Harrington, "Between Generations," *Socialist Review* 93 (1987), pp. 155–156.
65. Michael described the letter in *Fragments of the Century,* p. 154, but unfortunately no copy of it has survived.
66. Harrington, *Fragments of the Century,* p. 153; E. A. Berlandt, "Harrington Urges Big Fight Against Poverty," *Daily Californian,* February 18, 1964, p. 1.
67. On Freedom Summer and the MFDP strategy, see Carson, *In Struggle,* pp. 108–109. For Michael's role in the early stages of the project, see Harrington, *Fragments of the Century,* pp. 121-122.
68. Quoted in Elizabeth Sutherland, *Letters from Mississippi* (New York: McGraw Hill, 1965), pp. 83–84.
69. "March on Conventions," *New America,* June 16, 1964, p. 2.
70. Writing about these events several years later, Michael misremembered one of the details of the compromise. In his memoirs he wrote that at Atlantic City "a compromise was offered that would have unseated the regulars and brought two honorary delegates from

the Mississippi Freedom Democratic Party to the convention floor." In reality, the regulars got to take their seats. Harrington, *Fragments of the Century,* p. 123.

71. Quoted in Carson, *In Struggle,* p. 126.
72. Quoted in Gitlin, *The Sixties,* p. 160.
73. Michael Harrington, "Should the Left Support Johnson?" *New Politics* 3, no. 3 (summer 1964), p. 6.
74. Harrington, *Fragments of the Century,* p. 124.
75. Gitlin, *The Sixties,* p. 162.
76. Ibid., p. 166.
77. Michael Harrington, "How to Start an Uprising," *New York Herald Tribune,* July 25, 1965, p. 17.
78. Feuer, a veteran of student activism at City College in the 1920s, was beginning research in the early 1960s on a comparative history of student movements; his conclusions, reinforced by the trajectory of the New Left in the later 1960s, would soon lead him in far more conservative directions. But up until the fall of 1964 he remained sympathetic to the New Left. On Feuer's later views, see his book *The Conflict of Generations: The Character and Significance of Student Movements* (New York: Basic Books, 1969). Michael described his relationship with Feuer in *Fragments of the Century,* pp. 152–153.
79. Michael Harrington, "Youth in the Sixties: Contradictions and Complexities," *Yale Review* 70 (autumn 1980), p. 27; *Fragments of the Century,* p. 153.
80. *The Gallup Poll: Public Opinion 1935-1971,* vol. 3 (New York: Random House, 1972), pp. 1933-1934.
81. Michael Harrington, "A New Populism," *New York Herald Tribune,* March 28, 1965, p. 24.
82. Quoted in John Lewis, *Walking with the Wind: A Memoir of the Movement* (New York: Simon and Schuster, 1998), p. 346.
83. Harrington, "A New Populism."
84. Alan Draper, "Labor and the 1966 Elections," *Labor History* 30 (winter 1989), p. 77.
85. Michael Harrington, "The Politics of Poverty," *Dissent* 12 (autumn 1965), p. 429.
86. Harrington, *Fragments of the Century,* p. 128.
87. Ibid., pp. 166–167.
88. Ibid., p. 170.
89. Michael Harrington, "The War on Poverty," audiotape (Santa Barbara, CA: Center for the Study of Democratic Institutions), spring, 1964. Michael discussed his finances in *Fragments of the Century,* p. 180. Further details were provided to me by Stephanie Harrington.
90. W. A. Swanberg, *Norman Thomas: The Last Idealist* (New York: Charles Scribner's Sons, 1976), p. 455.
91. On the LID donation, see letter from Tom Kahn to Norman Thomas, March 9, 1965, Norman Thomas Papers, microfilm reel 48, New York Public Library.
92. Telegram from Michael Harrington to Norman Thomas, March 16, 1965, Norman Thomas Papers, microfilm reel 48, New York Public Library.
93. Letter from Norman Thomas to Michael Harrington, March 22, 1965, Norman Thomas Papers, microfilm reel 48.
94. According to Debbie Meier: "Later on when he wrote the book and said that he had had a nervous breakdown, it was a complete surprise to me. I was not in any way aware that there was anything 'wrong' with Mike." Author's interview with Deborah Meier, January 6, 1992.
95. Harrington, *Fragments of the Century,* p. 183.
96. Ibid., p. 189.
97. Ibid., p. 194.
98. Michael Harrington to Paul Jacobs, [n.d., April 1963], Paul Jacobs Papers, Boston University Special Collections.
99. Michael Harrington, *The Accidental Century* (New York: Macmillan, 1965), pp. 15, 25.
100. Thus, Michael unearthed a rarely cited passage from Sigmund Freud's *Civilization and*

Its Discontents, in which that gloomy proponent of the repression of the deepest human instincts noted the value of freely chosen labor: "Work," Freud declared, "is no less valuable for the opportunity it and the human relations connected with it provide for a very considerable discharge of libidinal component impulses, narcissistic, aggressive and even erotic, than because it is indispensable for subsistence and justifies existence in society." Michael argued that if "all routine and repetitive chores can be done by machines," then men could freely choose to perform only those work activities that allowed the satisfactory discharge of libidinal impulse. Freud quoted in ibid., pp. 263–264.

101. William Hogan, "Harrington and the New Reality," *San Francisco Chronicle,* August 25, 1965, p. 41.
102. Bernard D. Nossiter, "Reporter on Poverty Turns to Bad Prophecy," *Life,* August 20, 1965, p. 11.
103. *Newsweek,* August 30, 1965, p. 66.
104. M. Stanton Evans, "The Education of a Socialist," *National Review* 17 (October 5, 1965), p. 878.
105. Jack Newfield, "New Styles in Leftism—Round Two," *Village Voice,* May 13, 1965, p. 9.
106. Jack Newfield, "Revolt Without Dogma: The Student Left," *Nation,*May 10, 1965, p. 494.
107. "New Look on the Left: Solidarity Forever?" *Newsweek,* May 24, 1965, p. 31.

Chapter Nine: *Socialists at War, 1965-1972*

1. David McReynolds, "A Letter to the Men of My Generation," *Village Voice,* November 30, 1967, p. 9.
2. The question of whether and when Michael came out in opposition to the war would continue to bedevil him politically for the remainder of his life. For example, in 1988, long after the two men had reconciled, Tom Hayden would list Michael as one of a group of sixties leftists who "took their militant anticommunism to such a dogmatic extreme that they supported U.S. military intervention in Vietnam." (Hayden did credit Michael with being "the first to defect from the [pro-war] consensus"—but "not until the mid-sixties." Tom Hayden, *Reunion: A Memoir* (New York: Random House, 1988), p. 92.
3. "Socialist Platform, 1964," *New America,* August 24, 1964, p. 2S. On SP involvement in early antiwar protests, see *New America,* October 21, 1963, p. 3. The same issue contained an editorial entitled "'Dirty War' in Asia," condemning American support for the South Vietnamese regime in no uncertain terms: "This is a dirty war. It is a war against students, against religious leaders, against unarmed peasants."
4. This was in a statement he cosigned with Irving Howe, Bayard Rustin, and others in *New America,* October 31, 1965, p. 5.
5. Michael Harrington, "Poverty and Viet Nam," *New York Herald Tribune,* April 4, 1965, p. 16. Michael started writing a weekly column for the *New York Herald Tribune* in February 1965, for which he was paid $60 a column. The newspaper's editorial policy was generally liberal Republican in orientation, and the editors strove for a broad range of opinion on the editorial page (Michael's column appeared on the same day each week as one by Barry Goldwater).
6. Norman Thomas to Dick Steher, February 9, 1965; and Norman Thomas to A. J. Muste, March 15, 1965, Norman Thomas Papers, microfilm reel 48, New York Public Library.
7. Quoted in James Miller, *"Democracy is in the Streets": From Port Huron to the Siege of Chicago* (New York: Simon and Schuster, 1987), p. 229. Also see Michael Harrington, *Fragments of the Century* (New York: Saturday Review Press, 1973), p. 157; and letter from Norman Thomas to C. Clark Kissinger, April 16, 1965, Norman Thomas Papers, microfilm reel 48, New York Public Library.
8. The full text of the statement was reprinted in *New America,* April 30, 1965, p. 5. For the *Post's* editorial see Thomas Powers, *The War at Home* (New York: Grossman, 1973), pp. 74–75.

9. As SDS's first historian, Kirkpatrick Sale, would note, its argument for the protest was simple: "The government of South Vietnam is a dictatorship, so naturally the majority of the people refuse to support it. . . . There was no identification with Hanoi or the NLF or 'Third World' peoples in general, just 'the people overwhelmingly want peace, self-determination, and the opportunity for development.' There was no analysis of American foreign policy as imperialist or interventionist, just 'America is committing pointless murder.' There were no attacks on the United States or the Johnson Administration or corporate liberalism, just 'this is a war never declared by Congress.'" Sale, *SDS* (New York: Random House, 1973), p. 181. For the original call, see Students for a Democratic Society, "March on Washington to End the War in Vietnam," paid advertisement, *Nation,* March 22, 1965, p. 32.
10. Quoted in Sale, *SDS,* p. 188.
11. On the change in pacifist attitudes toward Communist participation, see David McReynolds, "Pacifists and the Vietnam Antiwar Movement," in *Give Peace a Chance: Exploring the Vietnam Antiwar Movement,* ed. Melvin Small and William D. Hoover (Syracuse, N.Y.: Syracuse University Press, 1992), pp. 60–61; and Jo Ann Ooiman Robinson, *Abraham Went Out: A Biography of A. J. Muste* (Philadelphia: Temple University Press, 1981), pp. 197–200.
12. *New America* called the march a "notable achievement" for SDS: "By opposing the pressures toward conformity and unquestioning support for American foreign policy, the march made a valuable contribution toward keeping the critical spirit alive in American society." See Lucy Komisar and Paul Feldman, "Student March on Washington Calls for End to Vietnam War," *New America,* April 30, 1965, p. 1.
13. Harrington, *Fragments of the Century,* p 199.
14. Michael Harrington, "Disloyalty? Or Dissent?" *New York Herald Tribune,* October 17, 1965, p. 4.
15. For this statement, see *New America,* October 31, 1965, p.5.
16. Michael Harrington, "The American Campus: 1962," *Dissent* 9 (spring 1962), pp. 165–166.
17. Lee Webb, "Conference Working Papers and Suggested Priorities for the NC," n.d. [ca. late 1965], microfilm reel 20, series 3, SDS Papers.
18. Even Jack Newfield, who had a good deal more understanding of and sympathy for Irving Howe's political outlook than most New Leftists, criticized him for his "cool, super-rational, intellectualized style, his ego-involved over-emphasis on anti-Stalinism, his insensitivity to the personal feelings of his political enemies." Jack Newfield, "Steady Work," *Village Voice,* January 12, 1967, p. 5.
19. Stone's involvement with anti-Vietnam protest is described in Robert C. Cottrell, *Izzy: A Biography of I. F. Stone* (New Brunswick, N.J.: Rutgers University Press, 1992), pp. 238–259. One of Stone's articles that was critical of the direction taken by young radicals in the peace movement was reprinted in the Socialist Party newspaper: see I. F. Stone, "Daydreams and Suicide Tactics," *New America,* June 18, 1965, p. 5.
20. John Sibley "Clergymen Defend Right to Protest Vietnam Policy," *New York Times,* October 26, 1965, p. 4.
21. Michael Harrington, "Does the Peace Movement Need the Communists?" *Village Voice,* November 11, 1965, p. 1. This article was reprinted in Michael Harrington, *Taking Sides: The Education of a Militant Mind* (New York: Holt, Rinehart and Winston, 1985), pp. 106–115.
22. Letter to the editor from Richard Fisher, *Village Voice,* December 2, 1965, p. 4.
23. Author's interview with Carl Oglesby, April 20, 1993.
24. I owe this point to Gary Steven Stone. I am grateful to him for sending me a copy of his 1991 Columbia University master's thesis, "The Divided Center: Michael Harrington, American Social Democracy and the Vietnam War." Also see Guenter Lewy, *The Cause That Failed: Communism in American Political Life* (New York: Oxford University Press, 1990), p. 267.
25. The SP's newspaper, *New America,* practiced just such an "even-handed" approach to as-

signing war blame. North Vietnam and China, the newspaper declared in June 1965 "must bear a major share of the responsibility with the U.S. for the continuation of that bloody war and the suffering of the Vietnamese people." "Peace Mission," *New America,* June 30, 1965, p. 2.

26. Letter to the editor from Charles Hook, *Village Voice,* November 18, 1965, p. 5.
27. See, for example, Irving Howe, "Vietnam: The Costs and Lessons of Defeat," *Dissent* 12 (spring 1965), pp. 151–154.
28. Howe described his difficult relations with pacifists in *A Margin of Hope: An Intellectual Biography* (San Diego: Harcourt, Brace, Jovanovich, 1982), pp. 299–301.
29. On Rustin's severing of ties with the pacifist movement, see Jervis Anderson, *Bayard Rustin: Troubles I've Seen* (New York: HarperCollins, 1997), p. 291.
30. Michael B. Friedland, *Lift Up Your Voice Like a Trumpet: White Clergy and the Civil Rights and Antiwar Movements, 1954–1973* (Chapel Hill: University of North Carolina Press, 1998), p. 160.
31. Michael Harrington, "The Death of Roger La Porte," *New York Herald Tribune,* November 14, 1965, p. 16. Michael was also sympathetic to those who burned their draft cards to protest the war. He thought that draft-card burning was a mistaken strategy to end the war, but he still sympathized with those who placed conscience over their own freedom. As he wrote in the *New York Herald Tribune* that fall "A nation tracing its origins to the Boston Tea Party ought not to become so jittery over the possibility of a few burned [draft] cards." Michael Harrington, "Disloyalty? Or Dissent?" *New York Herald Tribune,* October 17, 1965, p. 4. The first draft-card burning took place in October 1965. David Miller, a twenty-two-year-old Catholic Worker, burned his draft card in front of the Whitehall induction center in lower Manhattan, while Dorothy Day stood beside him as a supporter. Miller had first learned of the Catholic Worker movement by reading about it in *The Other America.* He was subsequently sentenced to three years in federal prison for draft resistance. James Finn, *Protest: Pacifism and Politics* (New York: Random House, 1967), p. 188.
32. Michael Harrington, "Pragmatists and Utopians: The New Radicalism," *Commonweal* 82 (September 3, 1965), pp. 624, 627. Also see Christopher Lasch, *The New Radicalism in America, 1889–1963: The Intellectual as a Social Type* (New York: Random House, 1965).
33. Author's interview with Deborah Meier, January 6, 1992.
34. Max Shachtman, *The Bureaucratic Revolution: The Rise of the Stalinist State* (New York: Donald Press, 1962). Also see Irving Howe, "Essays on the Russian Question," *Dissent* 10 (spring 1963), pp. 191–194.
35. Peter Drucker, *Max Shachtman and His Left: A Socialist's Odyssey Through the "American Century"* (Atlantic Highlands, N.J.: Humanities Press, 1994), p. 317.
36. *New America* even managed to find an opportunity to praise Mrs. Meany when she was quoted in the *Washington Star* as calling Richard Nixon a "sneak." "Mrs. Meany," *New America,* February 22, 1972, p. 4. For a further example of the Meany cult of personality, see Midge Decter, "Organized Labor's Umbrella Keeps Its Critics Dry and Comfortable," *New America,* May 31, 1972, p. 2.
37. Rustin made his most influential statement of his new position in "From Protest to Politics," *Commentary,* February 1965, pp. 25–31. On Shachtman's influence on Rustin in this period, see Anderson, *Bayard Rustin,* pp. 283–285.
38. Drucker, *Max Shachtman and His Left,* p. 291. The greatest Shachtmanite success story came after the death of Shachtman. Sandra Feldman, a Brooklyn College YSLer in the 1950s, was appointed by Al Shanker as a UFT field representative in 1966, at the suggestion of Bayard Rustin. Twenty years later she would succeed Shanker as UFT president, before moving on to become president of the UFT's parent body, the American Federation of Teachers. M. A. Farber, "Molded in Schools, She Helps Mold Them," *New York Times,* March 7, 1991, p. B-1; "Teachers' Union Head Seizes an Opportunity," *New York Times,* September 29, 1995, p. B-2.
39. Quoted in Peter B. Levy, *The New Left and Labor in the 1960s* (Urbana: University of Illi-

nois Press, 1994), p. 48; and in Robert H. Zieger, *American Workers, American Unions, 1920–1985* (Baltimore: Johns Hopkins University Press, 1986), p. 172.

40. Drucker, *Shachtman and His Left*, pp. 280–281, 300–301.
41. When Draper and the Jacobsons broke with Shachtman, they also turned on Michael. Hal Draper, for example, would describe Michael's role with LID as the "latest in a series of attempts over the decades to create a social-democratic wing of Establishment liberalism with a 'Fabian' perspective, inoffensively socialistic in tendency and impeccably respectable in style—the 'court socialist' in the palace of power." Hal Draper, "In Defense of the 'New Radicals,'" *New Politics* 4, no. 3 (summer 1965), p. 10.
42. Drucker, *Shachtman and His Left*, p. 269.
43. Michael described the genesis of the "Freedom Budget" in Michael Harrington, *Towards a Democratic Left: A Radical Program for a New Majority* (New York: Macmillan, 1968), pp. 123–124. Also see Michael Harrington, "Common Sense," *New York Herald Tribune*, November 21, 1965, p. 14; "S.P. Calls for—Peace in Vietnam; Real Poverty War," *New America*, June 30, 1966, p. 1; Paul Feldman, "Freedom Budget Campaign," *New America*, October 31, 1966, p. 1.
44. Quoted in Gareth Davies, *From Opportunity to Entitlement: The Transformation and Decline of Great Society Liberalism* (Lawrence: University Press of Kansas, 1996), p. 105.
45. Alan Draper, "Labor and the 1966 Elections," *Labor History*, 30 (winter 1989), pp. 77–78, 91–92.
46. Quoted in Steven Kelman, "The Other New Left," *New Leader* 44 (December 19, 1966), p. 9.
47. Quoted in Stephen B. Oates, *Let the Trumpet Sound: The Life of Martin Luther King, Jr.* (New York: New American Library, 1982), pp. 433–434. Also see David Garrow, *Bearing the Cross: Martin Luther King, Jr., and the Southern Christian Leadership Conference* (New York: William Morrow, 1986), pp. 542–554.
48. Harrington, *Fragments of the Century*, p. 206.
49. Michael Harrington, "America in Vietnam: From Here to Nowhere," *Village Voice*, April 14, 1966, p. 1.
50. David Hacker and Patricia Friend interview with Michael Harrington, August 19, 1988, copy in author's possession.
51. Harrington, *Fragments of the Century*, p. 201; David Hacker and Patricia Friend interview with Michael Harrington, August 19, 1988, copy in author's possession.
52. David Hacker and Patricia Friend interview with Michael Harrington, August 19, 1988, copy in author's possession.
53. Michael himself occasionally indulged in that tactic, arguing that Negotiations Now's petition campaign "might even have more political effect than resisters pissing on the Pentagon steps." Michael Harrington, "Answering McReynolds: A Question of Philosophy, A Question of Tactics," *Village Voice*, December 7, 1967, p. 49.
54. Michael Harrington, "Ronald Radosh and Michael Harrington, An Exchange," *Partisan Review* 56 (winter 1989), p. 83. On the impact of Negotiations Now on some prominent liberals, see Tom Wells, *The War Within: America's Battle Over Vietnam* (New York: Henry Holt, 1994), pp. 135–137.
55. "YPSL: No Support to 'Mobilization,'" *New America*, March 23, 1967, p. 1.
56. Paul Feldman, "Peace Movement at Crossroads," *New America*, December 15, 1966, p. 3.
57. Donald Henderson to Norman Thomas [n.d., January 1967), microfilm reel 52, Norman Thomas Papers. Thomas forwarded a copy of Henderson's letter to Michael, asking his opinion, but no copy of a reply (if any) survives.
58. David McReynolds, "Philosophy & Tactics: Answering an Answer," *Village Voice*, December 21, 1967, p. 48.
59. Author's interview with David McReynolds, September 16, 1991.
60. McReynolds, "Letter to the Men of My Generation."
61. Harrington, "Answering McReynolds: A Question of Philosophy, A Question of Tactics," p. 5. Harrington's article was reprinted in his book *Taking Sides*, pp. 126–136.

62. McReynolds, "Philosophy and Tactics," p. 48.
63. Claudia Dreifu, letter to the editor, *Village Voice,* December 14, 1967, p. 4.
64. Figures on public opinion in 1971 are given in Wells, *The War Within,* p. 491. Also see Melvin Small, *Johnson, Nixon, and the Doves* (New Brunswick: Rutgers University Press, 1992), pp. 130, 194; and Guenter Lewy, *The Cause That Failed,* pp. 222, 245.
65. Harrington, *Towards a Democratic Left,* p. 256.
66. Quoted in Drucker, *Shachtman and His Left,* p. 298.
67. See Michael's review of *The New Industrial State,* "Liberalism According to Galbraith," *Commentary* 45 (October 1967), pp. 77–83; and his review of *Power in America,* "The New Middle Class: Whose Camp Is It In?" *Village Voice,* June 1, 1967, p. 7.
68. Harrington, "The New Middle Class," p. 7.
69. Harrington, *Towards a Democratic Left,* pp. 264, 270. Much of Chapter 10 of this book, including Michael's speculations about the rise of the conscience constituency, were drawn from his essays in the *Village Voice* the previous year.
70. Harrington, "Liberalism According to Galbraith," p. 83.
71. Milovan Djilas, *The New Class: An Analysis of the Communist System* (New York: Praeger, 1958).
72. Josh Muravchik, "Hurray! YPSL Back in Action; Student-Labor Bond," *New America,* September 30, 1966, p. 4. Also see display advertisement, *New America,* September 12, 1966, p. 6.
73. Michael Harrington, *Why I Am a Democratic Socialist* (New York: Young People's Socialist League, 1967), p. 13.
74. Eugene Kemble and Tom Milstein, "YPSL in Action," *New America,* January 15, 1967, p. 6; Carol Steinnsapir, "Year of Growth Sparks Hope at YPSL Convention," *New America,* July 29, 1968, p. 8. The estimate of Harvard-Radcliffe SDS's strength comes from Michael Kazin, who was a cochair of the chapter.
75. Michael Kazin to author, February 10, 1999.
76. For one of Michael's critiques of post-1965 New Left politics, see Harrington, "The Mystical Militants," *New Republic,* February 19, 1966, pp. 21–22. This article was reprinted in Irving Howe, ed., *Beyond the New Left* (New York: McCall Publishing Company, 1970), pp. 33–39, and in Harrington, *Taking Sides,* pp. 69–76.
77. John Leo, "Trends of New Left Alarm Intellectuals of the Old," *New York Times,* May 8, 1967, p. 33. Bayard Rustin struck a very different note at the same conference when he called for the expulsion of SANE cochairman Benjamin Spock from SANE for "'political naivete' in working along with Maoists and Trotzkyites to end the war in Vietnam."
78. Quoted in Frank Annunziata, "The New Left and the Welfare State: The Rejection of American Liberalism," *Southern Quarterly* 15, no. 1, 1976, p. 42.
79. Richard Rothstein, "Evolution of the ERAP organizers," in *The New Left: A Collection of Essays,* ed. Priscilla Long (Boston: Porter Sargent Publisher, 1969), pp. 274–278. An earlier version of this article appeared in *Radical America* in the spring of 1968. One of the radical voices criticizing the war on poverty as a fraud was, ironically, Michael's old friend Paul Jacobs, who had served with him on Sargent Shriver's antipoverty task force in 1964. Jacobs moved steadily leftwards in the 1960s, and by 1966 he was ridiculing what he described as the founding assumption of the war on poverty, namely, that "poverty will disappear once everybody in this country is properly educated, properly willing to get to work on time, and brought up in a proper family with a poppa as well as a momma to read Little Golden Books to her attentive, well-scrubbed and attractive children." Poverty was, for Jacobs, the product of power relations within capitalism and could be ended only when poor people acted collectively in their own interest, something that the war on poverty was not interested in promoting. Paul Jacobs, "Re-Radicalizing the De-Radicalized," *New Politics* 5, no. 4 (Fall 1966), pp. 17, 21.
80. Harrington, "The Mystical Militants," p. 22; "Tactics and Truths," *New York Herald Tribune,* April 17, 1966, p. 27.
81. Michael Harrington, untitled column, *New York Herald Tribune,* February 28, 1965, p. 2.

82. Michael Harrington, "Los Angeles: A City of the Deaf," *New York Herald Tribune,* August 22, 1965, p. 14.
83. Michael Harrington, "The Will to Abolish Poverty," *Saturday Review* 51 (July 27, 1968), p. 41.
84. Michael Harrington, "Yes, $100 Billion," *New York Herald Tribune,* November 28, 1965, p. 27. The Moynihan Report, along with many published reactions to it, can be found in *The Moynihan Report and the Politics of Controversy,* ed. Lee Rainwater and William L. Yancey (Cambridge, Mass.: MIT Press, 1967.)
85. Harrington, *Fragments of the Century,* p. 121.
86. Ibid., p 129.
87. Harrington, "The Will to Abolish Poverty," p. 41.
88. Michael Harrington, "Poverty in the Seventies," foreword to *The Other America,* rev. ed. (New York: Penguin, 1981), p. xix.
89. Harrington, "The Will to Abolish Poverty," p. 41.
90. Harrington, *Fragments of the Century,* p. 131.
91. For Michael's account of the controversy, see Harrington, *The Long Distance Runner: An Autobiography* (New York: Henry Holt, 1988), p. 78; and Michael Harrington, "When Ed Koch Was Still a Liberal," *Dissent* 34 (fall 1987), pp. 597–598. Also see Nat Hentoff, "Ad Hoc Committee on Confusion," *Village Voice,* September 26, 1968, p. 4; and Michael Wreszin, *A Rebel's Defense of Tradition: The Life and Politics of Dwight Macdonald* (New York: Basic Books, 1994), pp. 459–462. Maurice Berube, a veteran organizer for the Association of Catholic Trade Unionists, became assistant editor for the UFT's newspaper in the 1960s. He also joined the SP in 1964 and was part of a group of labor intellectuals with whom Michael met regularly. But in 1968, he resigned from the SP (as well as from the UFT) in opposition to the role it played in the Ocean Hill-Brownsville controversy. As he wrote to Michael in his letter of resignation, it would be "unconscionable" for him to remain in a party that was "actively promoting the temporary (I hope) racist policies of the UFT in its fight against school decentralization." Maurice R. Berube, *American School Reform: Progressive, Equity, and Excellence Movements, 1883–1993* (Westport, Conn.: Praeger, 1994), p. 82. Also see Berube's criticism of the SP's role in the controversy in his article "'Democratic Socialists' and the Schools," *New Politics* 8 (summer 1969), pp. 57–62.
92. Harrington, *Fragments of the Century,* p. 214; Harrington, "Voting the Lesser Evil," *Commentary* 45, pp. 22-30.
93. "Young People's Socialist League," *New America,* January 15, 1968, p. 4; "Local Political Activity," *New America,* April 2, 1968, p. 8.
94. Jeremy Larner, "The McCarthy Campaign," reprinted in *"Takin' it to the streets": A Sixties Reader* (New York: Oxford University Press, 1995), p. 416.
95. Michael Harrington, response to critics in "Letters from Readers," *Commentary* 46 (July 1968), p. 17.
96. Harrington, *Fragments of the Century,* p. 215.
97. Harrington, "Poverty in the Seventies," pp. xix–xx.
98. Douglas Schoen, *Pat: A Biography of Daniel Patrick Moynihan* (New York: Harper & Row, 1979), p. 143; Harrington, *Fragments of the Century,* pp. 216–217; "Poverty in the Seventies," p. xx.
99. Michael Harrington, "The Road to 1972," *Dissent* 16 (January-February 1969), p. 5.
100. Joe Flaherty, "A Concurrence of Poets and One Who Stayed Home," *Village Voice,* August 22, 1968, p. 6; Harry Gilroy, "Writers Lift Voices at Cheetah Gala for McCarthy," *New York Times,* August 15, 1968, p. 34.
101. "How Shall We Vote?" symposium in *Dissent* 15 (November–December 1968), pp. 470–471. Michael's fellow *Dissent* editor Lewis Coser disagreed. "When it comes to ending the disgraceful war in Vietnam, I see no real difference between the two candidates. Both are committed to continuing the war. And just because they both have taken this position, I cannot possibly bring myself to vote for either of them, since I believe that the war is the foremost and decisive issue that confronts us" (p. 470).

102. Donald Janson, "Rebellious Democrats Establish Coalition to Seek Party Reform," *New York Times,* October 7, 1968, p. 40. On the history of the New Democratic Coalition (NDC), see Herbert Parmet, *The Democrats* (New York: Macmillan, 1976), pp. 289–291.
103. "How Shall We Vote?" p. 471.
104. Michael last saw Norman Thomas at his eighty-fourth birthday party in late November. See Michael's obituary for Thomas, "Norman Thomas Was a Socialist," *Village Voice,* January 2, 1969, p. 13.
105. David Hacker and Patricia Friend interview with Michael Harrington, August 19, 1988, copy in author's possession.
106. Irving Howe to Tom Kahn, April 13, 1969, microfilm reel 3376, Shachtman Papers. I was alerted to the existence of this letter by reading Stone, "The Divided Center."
107. Mary Breasted, "Old Left Gives Hubert Its Academy Award," *Village Voice,* April 24, 1969, p. 3.
108. Michael Harrington, "The Vietnam Moratorium," *New America,* October 25, 1969, p. 2.
109. Michael Harrington, "Getting Out of Vietnam," *Dissent* 17 (January–February 1970), pp. 6–7.
110. Levy, *The New Left and Labor,* p. 61; Nelson Lichtenstein, *The Most Dangerous Man in Detroit: Walter Routh and the Fate of American Labor* (New York: Basic Books, 1995), pp. 426, 429.
111. Willy Brandt would later say of his silence on Vietnam, "I swallowed my grave doubts and held my tongue where it might have been better to make my opposition explicit." Quoted in Donald Sassoon, *One Hundred Years of Socialism: The West European Left in the Twentieth Century* (New York: New Press, 1996), pp. 344–345. On "Ostpolitik," see Sassoon, *One Hundred Years of Socialism,* p. 331.
112. Palme remained an outspoken critic of American policies for the remainder of the war. When Nixon launched the "Christmas bombing" of Hanoi in December 1972, the Swedish prime minister declared: "One should call things by their proper names. What is happening today in Vietnam is a form of torture." Quoted in Jonathan Schell, *The Time of Illusion* (New York: Knopf, 1976), p. 301.
113. Stephanie Harrington, "Reporting: Sweden, Alarm About America in a Neutral Democracy," *Village Voice,* June 11, 1970, p. 1. Also see Michael Harrington, "Sweden Considers New Social Goals," *New America,* June 4, 1970, p. 1.
114. See "Resolution on South-East Asia," *Hammer & Tongs,* October 9, 1970, p. 1.
115. David McReynolds, "Point of Departure," *Hammer & Tongs,* May 25, 1970, p. 22.
116. Michael Harrington, "We Socialists Are a Prophetic Minority," *Village Voice,* July 2, 1970, p. 9.
117. David McReynolds, "Socialists & Liberals: The Decline of a Party," *Village Voice,* July 9, 1970, p. 16.
118. Max Shachtman et al., "Statement on Vietnam," *Hammer & Tongs,* October 9, 1970, p. 8.
119. Michael Harrington, "Socialists and Reactionary Anti-Communism," mimeograph, n.d. [August 1970], emphasis in original.
120. Max Shachtman to Rochelle Horowitz, September 23, 1970, David McReynolds Papers, Swarthmore College Peace Center, series 3, box 2.
121. Henry Fetter and Steve Norwood to Michael Harrington, June 14, 1971, Democratic Socialists of America Papers, box 1, folder 1, Tamiment Collection, New York University.
122. Michael Harrington to Carl [Shier], June 27, 1971, Julius Bernstein Papers, SP 1971 folder, Tamiment Collection, New York University.
123. On the history of the Democratic Socialist Federation, see Robert J. Alexander, "Schisms and Unifications in the American Old Left, 1953–1970," *Labor History* 14 (fall 1973), p. 542.
124. Michael Harrington, "Draft Resolution on Socialist Unity," September 30, 1971, typescript, Julius Bernstein Papers, SP 1971 folder, Tamiment Collection, New York University.
125. Michael Harrington to "Carl and comrades," October 2, 1971, Democratic Socialists of America Papers, box 1, folder 6, Tamiment Collection.
126. Michael Harrington to Irving Howe, n.d. [fall 1971], Democratic Socialists of America

Papers, box 1, Michael Harrington correspondence, 1971, Tamiment Collection, New York University.

127. Irving Howe to Michael Harrington, July 28, 1971, Democratic Socialists of America Papers, box 1, Tamiment Collection, New York University.
128. Michael Harrington to Irving Howe, August 1, 1971, Democratic Socialists of America Papers, box 1, Tamiment Collection, New York University.
129. Harry Siitonen to Michael Harrington, February 1, 1972, Democratic Socialists of America Papers, box 1, folder 2, Tamiment Collection, New York University, emphasis in original.
130. "Rustin, Harrington and Zimmerman Head United Socialist Organization," *New America,* March 20, 1972, p. 1; Paul Feldman, "A New Day for American Socialism," *New America,* March 31, 1972, p. 1.
131. John L. Lewine to *The Yankee Radical,* July 5, 1972, Julius Bernstein Papers, spring 1972 folder, Tamiment Collection, New York University.
132. Rowland Evans and Robert Novak, "Jackson's Young Socialists," *New York Post,* August 13, 1971.
133. Joan Suall to Michael Harrington, May 11, 1972, Democratic Socialists of America Papers, box 1, Harrington correspondence, 1972, Tamiment Collection; Michael Harrington to Joan Suall, May 13, 1972, Democratic Socialists of America Papers, box 1, Harrington correspondence, 1972, Tamiment Collection, New York University.
134. Michael Harrington, "A New Ballgame," *New America,* July 3, 1972, p. 2.
135. Michael Harrington to "comrades," June 29, 1972, Democratic Socialists of America Papers, box 1, 1972 correspondence, Tamiment Collection, New York University.
136. George McGovern and Leonard F. Guttridge, *The Great Coalfield War* (Boston: Houghton Mifflin, 1972), p. v.
137. Peter B. Levy, *The New Left and Labor,* p. 181.
138. Quoted in Taylor E. Dark, *The Unions and the Democrats: An Enduring Alliance* (Ithaca, N.Y.: Cornell University Press, 1999), p. 87
139. Andrew Battista, "Political Divisions in Organized Labor, 1968–1988," *Polity* 24 (winter 1991), pp. 179–180.
140. "From the Steelworkers Convention at Las Vegas," *John Herling's Labor Letter,* September 12, 1972, p.1.
141. Max Green, "McGovern Underestimates the Communists," *New America,* July 3, 1972, p. 6; Carl Gershman, "Jewish Voters Disaffected from Democratic Ticket," *New America,* July 31, 1972, p. 4; Sidney Hook, "An Open Letter to George McGovern," *New America,* September 30, 1972, p. 4.
142. David Selden to Charles S. Zimmerman et al., September 13, 1972, Democratic Socialists of America Papers, box 1, folder 7, Tamiment Collection, New York University.
143. Michael Harrington to "comrades," October 2, 1972, Democratic Socialists of America Papers, box 1, folder 7, Tamiment Collection, New York University.
144. Michael Harrington to "Bayard and Sasha," October 14, 1972, Democratic Socialists of America Papers, box 1, folder 3, Tamiment Collection, New York University.
145. "Harrington Quits as Socialist Head," *New York Times,* October 23, 1972, p. 17. The SP-DSF responded with a resolution denouncing Michael's "irresponsible and misleading statements" to the *New York Times* and charged that they were "designed to do damage to our Socialist organization and to injure the reputations of individual members who have served it loyally." "Harrington Quits His Post: SP-DSF Disputes His Criticism," *New America,* October 25, 1972, p. 6.
146. Quoted in Michael Massing, "Trotsky's Orphans," *New Republic,* June 22, 1987, p. 22.
147. Tom Kahn, "Max Shachtman—His Ideals and His Life," *New America,* November 15, 1972, p. 4.
148. James Ring Adams, "Battle Royal Among Socialists," *Wall Street Journal,* December 8, 1972.
149. SDUSA spokesmen gave the figure of 18,000 at the December convention. "Socialist Party Now the Social Democrats, U.S.A.," *New York Times,* December 31, 1972, p. 30. Ac-

cording to a membership report of the SP dated September 1972—that is, after the SP had merged with the DSF—the actual membership was 1,601. "Membership Report, SP-DSF," September 1972, Democratic Socialists of America Papers, box 1, folder 3, Tamiment Collection. Carl Shier, analyzing membership figures for the Coalition Caucus, came up with a lower figure of 1,098. Carl Shier to "friends," November 24, 1972, Democratic Socialists of America Papers, box 1, folder 7, Tamiment Collection, New York University.

150. Harrington, *Fragments of the Century,* p. 225.
151. Harrington, *The Long Distance Runner,* p. 61.
152. Jeff Coplon, "Death of the Red Banner," *Cornell Daily Sun,* April 21, 1971.
153. Letter from Rick Hertzberg to Michael Harrington, January 12, 1972, Democratic Socialists of America Papers, box 1, Tamiment Collection, New York University.

Chapter Ten: *Starting Over, 1973-1980*

1. Irving Howe to Michael Harrington, July 13, 1973, Democratic Socialists of America Papers, box 1, folder 4, Tamiment Collection, New York University.
2. Daniel Bell to Irving Howe, April 25, 1973, Democratic Socialists of America Papers, box 1, folder 8, Tamiment Collection, New York University.
3. Michael repeatedly cited Nixon's remarks in the years to come. See, for example, Harrington, "The Big Lie About the Sixties," *New Republic,* November 29, 1975, p. 16.
4. Israel Shenker, "Ideological Labels Change with the Label-Makers," *New York Times,* November 12, 1970, p. 45.
5. Michael was widely credited with coining the term "neo-conservative," and he certainly popularized its usage. He was not so sure of his own claim to authorship, since, as he noted some years later, it was "in common use among *Dissent* editors and other associates of mine, and I do not have the least idea who was the first to use it." Michael Harrington, "An Exchange," *Partisan Review* 50 (winter 1989), p. 82; and Harrington, *The Long Distance Runner: An Autobiography* (New York: Henry Holt, 1988), p. 96. He may have first encountered the term several decades earlier in a different context. Dwight Macdonald used it in a review of William F. Buckley's *God and Man at Yale* in the *Reporter* 6 (May 27, 1952), p. 35. My attention was drawn to this earlier usage of the term by a letter from Geoffrey Wheatcroft to the *Times Literary Supplement,* December 8, 1995, p. 15.
6. Sidney Blumenthal, *The Counter-Establishment: From Conservative Ideology to Political Power* (New York: Harper and Row, 1988), pp. 160–161.
7. Banfield was not, strictly speaking, a "neo-conservative"; Michael would characterize him as a "conservative conservative who sometimes travels with the neo-conservatives." Michael Harrington, *The Twilight of Capitalism* (New York: Simon and Schuster, 1976), p. 270.
8. Edward Banfield, *The Unheavenly City: The Nature and Future of Our Urban Crisis* (Boston: Little, Brown, 1970), p. 62. Banfield's influence is discussed in Bernard R. Gifford, "War on Poverty: Assumptions, History, and Results, a Flawed but Important Effort," in *The Great Society and Its Legacy,* ed. Marshall Kaplan and Peggy L. Cuciti (Durham, N.C.: Duke University Press, 1986), pp. 69–70.
9. Nathan Glazer, "The Limits of Social Policy," *Commentary* 52 (September 1971), p. 57.
10. Michael took Glazer's article seriously enough to devote four pages in his 1973 autobiography to summarizing and refuting its argument. Harrington, *Fragments of the Century* (New York: Saturday Review Press, 1973), pp. 240–244. Glazer would soon have second thoughts about the use to which his criticisms of social welfare programs were being put. He argued in 1973 that the Great Society programs were "clearly not a uniform failure" and that many of the war on poverty programs provided "useful social services." But his second thoughts on the question were not as influential as his first. See Peter Steinfels, *The Neo-Conservatives: The Men Who Are Changing America's Politics* (New York: Simon and Schuster, 1979), p. 219; Godfrey Hodgson, *The World Turned Right Side Up: A History of the Conservative Ascendancy in America* (Boston: Houghton Mifflin, 1996), pp. 129–130.

11. Michael Harrington, "The Welfare State and Its Neoconservative Critics," *Dissent* 20 (fall 1973), p. 454.
12. Harrington, "The Welfare State and Its Neoconservative Critics," p. 438. A revised version of this article was reprinted as a chapter in Harrington's 1976 book, *The Twilight of Capitalism,* pp. 265-272. Earlier in 1973 he had sketched out some of the same ideas in a brief contribution to a symposium on welfare sponsored by *Commentary:* Michael Harrington et al., "Nixon, the Great Society, and the Future of Social Policy: A Symposium," *Commentary* 55 (May 1973), p. 39.
13. Moynihan quoted in Harrington, "The Welfare State and Its Neoconservative Critics," p. 437.
14. Harrington, "The Welfare State and Its Neoconservative Critics," p. 443. Michael did concede that the federal government's commitment to building urban high-rise public housing projects in the 1950s and 1960s, which proved to be breeding places of crime and social anomie, were "a genuine example of a liberal idea whose unintended consequences were more important than its good intentions." Ibid., p. 454.
15. Ibid., p. 440.
16. Ibid., pp. 447, 449.
17. William Schneider, "The Political Legacy of the Reagan Years," in *The Reagan Legacy,* ed. Sidney Blumenthal and Thomas Byrne Edsall (New York: Pantheon, 1988), p. 73. For comparable figures, see Kevin Phillips, *Post-Conservative America: People, Politics, and Ideology in a Time of Crisis* (New York: Vintage Books, 1982), p. 29.
18. In 1974 Michael was listed as one of the nation's seventy most influential intellectuals in Charles Kadushin's study, *The American Intellectual Elite* (Boston: Little Brown, 1974), p. 30.
19. Quoted in Robert Levey, "US Socialists Find Ripe Pickings in the Rhetoric of Reaganomics," *Boston Globe,* April 11, 1983.
20. Michael Harrington, "Say What You Mean—Socialism," *Nation,* May 25, 1974, pp. 649, 650.
21. Michael Harrington, *The Politics at God's Funeral: The Spiritual Crisis of Western Civilization* (New York: Holt, Rinehart, 1983), p. 21 (emphasis in the original).
22. Harrington, *Fragments of the Century,* p. 246.
23. Ibid., p. 245. The name "Socialist Party" did not go unclaimed for long. Over Memorial Day weekend in 1973, a group of former Debs Caucus supporters, including David McReynolds, met in Milwaukee and founded a new Socialist Party, USA. The group continues to exist and has run presidential candidates in most of the election years since its founding.
24. Deborah Meier, "Looking Backward: DSOC Marks Fifth Year," *Newsletter of the Democratic Left* 6 (October 1978), pp. 1–2, 6. Dick Wilson, an AFSCME organizer from Illinois, came up with the name DSOC.
25. Harrington, *Fragments of the Century,* p. 245.
26. Michael Harrington, "The Left Wing of Realism," *Newsletter of the Democratic Left* 1 (March 1973), p. 5.
27. "We Are Socialists of the Democratic Left" (New York: DSOC, 1973); "Toward a Socialist Presence in America," *Social Policy,* 4 (January/February 1974), p. 5.
28. "Lists of White House 'Enemies,'" *New York Times,* June 28, 1973, p. 38.
29. Jonathan Schell, *The Time of Illusion* (New York: Random House, 1975), p. 311.
30. David Broder, "Labor Exerting New Muscle in Democratic Party," *Washington Post,* September 2, 1973; Herbert S. Parmet, *The Democrats: The Years After FDR* (New York: Oxford University Press, 1977), p. 305.
31. The ADA resolution is quoted in Steven M. Gillon, *Politics and Vision: The ADA and American Liberalism* (New York: Oxford University Press, 1987), p. 229. Harrington is quoted in Ronald Radosh, "The Democratic Socialist Organizing Committee," *Socialist Revolution* (July 1973), p. 77. ADA's executive director, Leon Shull, had spoken at the February 1973 conference on the Democratic Left that launched DSOC. Shull, who had a socialist background himself, wanted Michael and his allies to join ADA instead of forming their own group. According to DSOC staffer Jack Clark, "If we had come in, it

would have been arranged for Mike to be national president of ADA in a few years." But Michael wasn't interested in the proposal. Author's interview with Jack Clark, November 23, 1991; author's interview with Patrick Lacefield, August 4, 1991.

32. Harrington, *Fragments of the Century,* p. 164.
33. Carl Shier to "Carl," May 23, 1973, Democratic Socialists of America Papers, box 1, folder 8, Tamiment Collection, New York University. Michael did not get around to resigning formally from SDUSA until after DSOC was launched in the spring of 1973. It may be that he wanted to retain membership in SDUSA just in case the new socialist group failed to get off the ground.
34. Irving Howe to Michael Harrington, July 13, 1973.
35. Ron Chernow, "An Irresistible Profile of Michael Harrington (You Must Be Kidding)," *Mother Jones* (July 1977), p. 40.
36. From the time he married until 1971, Michael had relied on Stephanie's job at the *Village Voice* for insurance coverage. When Stephanie left her job that year, the Harrington's health insurance lapsed. Harrington, *The Long Distance Runner,* p. 118.
37. "I think you ought this coming year to make a real effort to land a permanent teaching job in NYC," Howe wrote him in August 1971 and subsequently contacted Murphy. Joe Bosson, a member of the psychology department at Queens and a drinking companion of Michael's, also lobbied Murphy on his behalf. Irving Howe to Michael Harrington, August 5, 1971, Democratic Socialists of America Papers, box 1, Michael Harrington correspondence, Tamiment Collection, New York University; Harrington, *The Long Distance Runner,* p. 120; author's interview with Joe Murphy, October 16, 1991.
38. John Kenneth Galbraith to Henry W. Morton, March 19, 1974, letter attached to "Recommendation for Reappointment with Tenure," September 13, 1974. I am grateful to Joe Murphy and Marvin Taylor for making Michael's appointment records at Queens College available to me.
39. Michael Harrington, *The Next Left: The History of a Future* (New York: Henry Holt, 1986), p. 188.
40. *The Long Distance Runner,* pp. 130–132. I am grateful to two former Queens students, Neil McLaughlin and Barbara Ferman, for insights into Michael's habits as a teacher. Letter to the author from Neil McLaughlin, May 20, 1992; telephone interview with Barbara Ferman, March 27, 1992.
41. Author's interview with Jo-Ann Mort, September 26, 1991.
42. Author's interview with Stephanie Harrington, July 24, 1991.
43. Harrington, *Fragments of the Century,* pp. 233–234; *The Long Distance Runner,* p. 136.
44. Harrington, *The Long Distance Runner,* p. 85.
45. Bella Stumbo, "The Lonely Fight of Last Old Leftist," *Los Angeles Times,* April 4, 1987, p. 24; author's interview with Irving Kristol, March 21, 1991.
46. Michael Harrington to "Marty," January 3, 1979, Democratic Socialists of America Papers, box 9, Tamiment Collection, New York University. The letter is clearly misdated, since the Harringtons did not move to Larchmont until the summer of 1979.
47. Telephone conversation with Alex Harrington, June 15, 1999. In February 1940, a few months before his assassination, Trotsky sat down in his walled compound in Coyoacan to write his political testament, concluding with the passage, "I can see the bright green strip of grass beneath the wall, and the clear blue sky above the wall, and sunlight everywhere. Life is beautiful. Let the future generations cleanse it of all evil, oppression, and violence, and enjoy it to the full." Michael, noting that he had once made a pilgrimage to Trotsky's home in Coyoacan, would cite this quotation in the conclusion to his own memoirs. Harrington, *The Long Distance Runner,* pp. 6, 250.
48. Michael Harrington to "Pittsburgh friends," May 13, 1980, Democratic Socialists of America Papers, box 9, "May 1980" folder, Tamiment Collection, New York University.
49. Author's interview with Ted Harrington, February 15, 1993; Harrington, *The Long Distance Runner,* p. 9.
50. Harrington is quoted in Paul L. Montgomery, "Socialist Group Outlines Goals," *New*

York Times, October 14, 1973. Lenin is quoted in John Reed, *Ten Days That Shook the World* (New York: International Publishers, 1926), p. 126. "We . . . participated in a political culture where everyone had a working knowledge of the theory and history of the Left," Michael would write of the founders of DSOC. "A reference to a dispute between the Bolsheviks and Mensheviks in 1903, whose very terms would be incomprehensible to most of our fellow citizens, was the commonplace of our casual discussions." Harrington, *The Long Distance Runner,* pp. 19–20.

51. Ibid., p. 17.
52. In a letter to David Lewis two weeks before the DSOC convention, Bayard Rustin had accused Michael of "attempting to foster a destructive split in the united democratic socialist movement. . . . Because of its lack of real ties or involvement in the labor movement, Harrington's group has an orientation toward exacerbation of internal union disputes. His continuous ill-advised public attacks on George Meany and the AFL-CIO only further isolate him and his splinter group from the general labor movement here." Lewis, who was appalled by SDUSA's support for the American war effort in Vietnam, apparently passed the letter on to Michael. Bayard Rustin to David Lewis, October 1, 1973, Michael Harrington Papers, box 21, 10/73–10/74 folder, Tamiment Collection, New York University. Also see Paul Feldman, "Harrington Resigns: SD Replies to Attack," *New America,* July 30, 1973, p. 6; and "For the Record: The Report of Social Democrats, U.S.A. on the Resignation of Michael Harrington and His Attempt to Split the American Socialist Movement" (New York: Social Democrats, USA, 1973).
53. For the *New York Times*'s coverage, see Peter Kihss, "Socialists Plan Founding Parley," *New York Times,* September 10, 1973, p. 21; Peter Kihss, "Socialist Unit Is Founded Here," *New York Times,* October 13, 1973, p. 38; Paul L. Montgomery, "New Socialist Group Plans to Work Within Democratic Party," *New York Times,* October 14, 1973, p. 63; "Author Will Head New Socialist Unit," *New York Times,* October 15, 1973, p. 41.
54. Radosh, "The Democratic Socialist Organizing Committee," p. 79. One of the things that Radosh most admired about Michael's politics in 1973 was that he had broken with the tradition of "State Department Socialism," in which democratic socialists "supported United States policy because it is anti-Communist." What excited Radosh's admiration in 1973 elicited his scorn in 1989. See Ronald Radosh and Michael Harrington, "An Exchange," *Partisan Review* 50 (winter 1989), pp. 65–84.
55. Quoted in Peter Carroll, *It Seemed Like Nothing Happened: The Tragedy and Promise of America in the 1970s* (New York: Holt, Rinehart, 1982), p. 152.
56. Allen Matusow, *Nixon's Economy: Booms, Busts, Dollars, and Votes* (Lawrence: University Press of Kansas, 1998), p. 134; David Brody, *Workers in Industrial America: Essays on the Twentieth Century Struggle* (New York: Oxford University Press, 1980), p. 240; Hodgson, *The World Turned Right Side Up,* p. 189; Carroll, *It Seemed Like Nothing Happened,* pp. 131–132.
57. Harrington, "The Left Wing of Realism," p. 5.
58. Harrington, *The Long Distance Runner,* p. 25.
59. David Bensman, "Debate—What Do Women Want?" *New America,* December 21, 1970, p. 7.
60. As Todd Gitlin has noted of the spread of "identity politics" on the Left: "From the 1970s on, left-wing universalism was profoundly demoralized. It was an airy notion without a program, a longing without a constituency. It was scorned as nonexistent, hypothetical, nostalgic, or worse, deceptive—a mask assumed by straight white males as they tried to restore their lost dominion." Gitlin, *The Twilight of Common Dreams: Why America Is Wracked by Culture Wars* (New York: Henry Holt, 1995), p. 101.
61. Michael was taken to task in the pages of the *Nation* in 1979 for failing to support gay rights at the recent Democratic midterm convention in Memphis; he wrote a letter to the editor declaring his personal support for gay rights but defending his tactical decision not to raise the issue in Memphis. Harrington, "Indictment Denied," *Nation* 229 (October 8, 1979), p. 290.
62. In 1973, Michael would later write, feminism was something he understood only "ab-

stractly, in terms of public policy and not at all in terms of our own lives." Harrington, *The Long Distance Runner,* p. 26.

63. Ibid., p. 34.
64. Andrew Battista, "Political Divisions in Organized Labor, 1968–1988," *Polity* 34 (winter 1991), pp. 184–185.
65. Author's interview with Skip Roberts, August 6, 1991.
66. Author's interview with Joe Schwartz, August 2, 1991.
67. Author's interview with Harold Meyerson, July 27, 1990.
68. Letter from Peter Mandler to author, August 14, 1994.
69. In King's original version, it was "arm of the moral universe."
70. Sheri Farsh Blake, "Quiz 6," Michael Harrington/DSOC Papers, box 9, "Reactions to MH 'Decade of Decision'" folder, Tamiment Collection, New York University.
71. Michael Harrington, *Socialism* (New York: Saturday Review Press, 1972); *Fragments of the Century* (New York: Simon and Schuster, 1972); *The Twilight of Capitalism* (New York: Simon and Schuster, 1976); *The Vast Majority: A Journey to the World's Poor* (New York: Simon and Schuster, 1977); *Decade of Decision* (New York: Simon and Schuster, 1980); *The Next America: The Decline and Rise of the United States* (with photographs by Bob Adelman) (New York: Holt, Rinehart, 1981); *The Politics at God's Funeral: The Spiritual Crisis of Western Civilization* (New York: Holt, Rinehart, 1983); *The New American Poverty* (New York: Holt, Rinehart, 1984); *Taking Sides: The Education of a Militant Mind* (New York: Holt, Rinehart, 1985); *The Next Left: The History of a Future* (New York: Henry Holt, 1986); *The Long Distance Runner: An Autobiography* (New York: Henry Holt, 1988); and *Socialism, Past and Future* (New York: Little, Brown and Co., 1989). In addition, he authored or coauthored numerous pamphlets and a political science textbook, Michael Harrington and Harrell R. Rodgers Jr., *Unfinished Democracy: The American Political System* (Glenview, Ill.: Scott, Foresman and Co., 1981), which went through several subsequent editions.
72. Chernow, "An Irresistible Profile of Michael Harrington (You Must Be Kidding)," *Mother Jones* (July 1977), p. 40.
73. Author's interview with Irving Howe, April 26, 1991. Another close associate, Cornell West, damned Michael's later books with faint praise in an obituary for the *Nation:* "Though far from original works, these books guided and inspired many progressives in their struggles for freedom, solidarity and justice." Cornel West, "Michael Harrington, Socialist," *Nation,* January 8/15, 1990, p. 59. Michael's books are discussed at greater length by several other authors: See Garry J. Dorrien, *The Democratic Socialist Vision* (Totowa, N.J.: Rowman and Littlefield, 1986), pp. 98–135; and Robert A. Gorman, *Michael Harrington: Speaking American* (New York: Routledge, 1995).
74. e-mail communication from Jim Chapin to dsanet list, November 20, 1995.
75. Michael Harrington, "Getting Restless Again," *New Republic*, September 1, 1979, p. 13; Patrick Lacefield, "DSOC Makes Gains Among Students," *In These Times,* January 23–29, 1980, p. 6; letter from Peter Mandler to the author, August 14, 1994.
76. Author's interview with Jack Clark, November 23, 1991.
77. Steven Greenhouse, "Oil Reaps the Scorn of an Uninhibited Few," *New York Times,* April 28, 1974, sec. 3, p. 25. Also see Michael Harrington, "Capitalism, Socialism, and Energy" (New York: DSOC, 1974).
78. Harrington, *The Long Distance Runner,* p. 95.
79. Ibid., p. 91.
80. Three other DSOCers were also elected as delegates, from Massachusetts, Iowa, and Alaska. "Kansas City Clips," *Newsletter of the Democratic Left* 3 (January 1975), p. 2.
81. Michael Harrington, "Can Democrats Meet the Challenge?" *Newsletter of the Democratic Left* 2 (December 1974), pp. 1–7.
82. Taylor E. Dark, *The Unions and the Democrats: An Enduring Alliance* (New York: Cornell University Press, 1999), pp. 91–91.
83. Harrington, *The Long Distance Runner,* pp. 96–97.

84. "December 4 Meeting on American Can Project," box 12, DSOC Papers, Tamiment Collection, New York Unvirsity.
85. John Judis, "Democratic Socialists Move Left," *In These Times,* February 28, 1979, p. 4.
86. "Socialism Is No Longer a Dirty Word to Labor," *Business Week,* September 24, 1979, p. 130.
87. Author's interview with Don Stillman, March 9, 992.
88. Author's interview with Steve Silbiger, March 10, 1992.
89. Quoted in "DSOC Conference Launches '76 Project," *Newsletter of the Democratic Left* 4 (March 1976), p. 7.
90. Dark, *The Unions and the Democrats*, p. 102.
91. On Michael's view of Humphrey-Hawkins, see Harrington, "Jobs for All," *Commonweal,* January 30, 1976, p. 76; "Two Cheers for Socialism," *Harper's* (October 1976), pp. 78–79; his pamphlet "Full Employment: The Issue and the Movement" (New York: Institute for Democratic Socialism, 1977); and *The Long Distance Runner,* pp. 44–45, 104.
92. Jules Witcover, *Marathon: The Pursuit of the Presidency, 1972–1976* (New York: Viking Press, 1977), pp. 369–370.
93. Harrington, *The Long Distance Runner,* p. 104.
94. *The Lesser Evil? The Left Debates the Democratic Party and Social Change* (New York: Pathfinder Press, 1977), pp. 13, 20.
95. Michael Harrington, "Electoral Victory and Full Employment Challenge," *Newsletter of the Democratic Left* 4 (December 1976), p. 1.
96. E. J. Dionne Jr., *Why Americans Hate Politics* (New York: Simon and Schuster, 1991), p. 124; Burton I. Kaufman, *The Presidency of James Earl Carter* (Lawrence: University of Kansas Press, 1993), p. 19.
97. Leo Ribuffo, "'Malaise' Revisited: Jimmy Carter and the Crisis of Confidence," in *The Liberal Persuasion: Arthur Schlesinger, Jr. and the Challenge of the American Past,* ed. John Patrick Diggins (Princeton, N.J.: Princeton University Press, 1997), p. 166.
98. Henry Fairlie, "The Passionate Socialist," *New Republic*, March 26, 1977, p. 18.
99. Dark, *The Unions and the Democrats*, pp. 15–16.
100. Ibid., p. 109.
101. Quoted in Andrew Battista, "Labor and Coalition Politics: The Progressive Alliance," *Labor History* 32 (summer 1991), p. 402.
102. Battista, "Labor and Coalition Politics," pp. 402–403; Daniel Nelson, *Shifting Fortunes: The Rise and Decline of American Labor, from the 1820s to the Present* (Chicago: Ivan Dee, 1997), p. 153.
103. Author's interview with Skip Roberts, August 6, 1991.
104. "Democratic Agenda," *Newsletter of the Democratic Left* 7 (February 1979), p. 7. Powell was originally quoted in the *Boston Globe.*
105. Quoted in Carroll, *It Seemed Like Nothing Happened,* p. 210.
106. Adam Clymer, "Liberals Press Floor Fight Before Democratic Party," *New York Times,* December 8, 1978, p. 21; "Liberals Criticize Inflation Program," *New York Times,* December 9, 1978, p. 12; Jerome Cahill, "Liberal Dems Plan a Fight on Econ Policy," *New York Daily News,* December 8, 1978, p. 16.
107. Cahill, "Liberal Dems Plan a Fight on Econ Policy," p. 7.
108. "The Tenessee Waltz," *Nation*, December 23, 1978, p. 692.
109. Hedrick Smith, "The Message of Memphis," *New York Times,* December 11, 1978, p. 1.
110. Author's interview with Don Stillman, March 9, 1992.
111. Author's interview with Jack Clark, November 23, 1991. In the aftermath of the Memphis convention, Michael joined in another organizational effort, similar in many ways to Democratic Agenda, seeking to influence the Democratic Party. This was the Progressive Alliance, a national coalition of over a hundred labor, civil rights, environmentalist, and other liberal groups, founded at the initiative of UAW president Doug Fraser. It lasted a little more than two years; its eventual failure, in the judgment of historian Andrew Battista, was due to the fact that it pursued "a politics of organizational elites rather than of mass mobilization." Battista, "Labor and Coalition Politics," p. 421.

112. He did so with a sense of personal relief, because he had earlier agreed to run as a candidate for the Democratic nomination himself, barring the entry of a more formidable challenger to Carter. David Moberg, "Harrington for President?" *In These Times,* December 27, 1978; David Hoffman, "DSOC Convention: New Goals Set, Anti-Carter Mood," *Newsletter of the Democratic Left* 7 (March 1979), p. 1.
113. Michael's attitude toward Commoner may have been influenced by the fact that Machinist president Winpisinger walked out of the Democratic convention in July and announced his own support for the third party candidate. Michael Harrington, "Beyond November: The Democrats Remain the Real Home of the Left," *The Progressive* 44 (October 1980), p. 25.
114. Ibid., p. 26.
115. Michael Harrington, "No Time for Mourning Now," *Democratic Left*, 8 (November 1980), p. 14.

Chapter Eleven: *Coming to an End, 1981–1989*

1. Nick Salvatore, *Eugene V. Debs: Citizen and Socialist* (Champaign: University of Illinois Press, 1982), pp. 229–230.
2. Quoted in Sidney Blumenthal, "Reaganism and the Neokitsch Aesthetic," in *The Reagan Legacy,* ed. Sidney Blumenthal and Thomas Byrne Edsall (New York: Pantheon Books, 1988), p. 254.
3. On supply-side economics, see E. J. Dionne, *Why Americans Hate Politics* (New York: Simon and Schuster, 1992), pp. 242–252.
4. Michael Katz, *In The Shadow of the Poorhouse: A Social History of Welfare in America* (New York: Basic Books, 1986), pp. 285–288.
5. Tony De Paul, "Socialist Calls Reagan Policies Insane, Cruel," *Bangor Maine News,* January 21, 1983.
6. George Gilder, *Wealth and Poverty* (New York: Bantam Books, 1981), pp. 119–120.
7. Michael Harrington, "The Rich Get Richer," *Today's Education* 70 (September–October 1981), p. 25. Michael returned to the attack on Gilder in his 1986 book, *The Next Left: the History of a Future* (New York: Henry Holt, 1986), pp. 99–100.
8. Gilder, *Wealth and Poverty,* p. 108.
9. Gilder and Murray's influence over public opinion and the Reagan administration are discussed in Michael B. Katz, *The Undeserving Poor: From the War on Poverty to the War on Welfare* (New York: Pantheon Books, 1989), pp. 143–147, 151–156. Murray had written a pamphlet for the right-wing Heritage Foundation in 1982 entitled "Safety Nets and the Truly Needy." William Hammett, director of the Manhattan Institute, a conservative think tank, thought that Murray's brief argument could be fleshed out into an influential book. According to historian Robert S. McElvaine, Hammett "wanted something that could do for dismantling the welfare state what Michael Harrington's *The Other America* had done to inspire it." The Manhattan Institute provided the funding that allowed Murray to carry out this task. McElvaine, *The End of the Conservative Era: Liberalism After Reagan* (New York: Arbor House, 1987), p. 48.
10. Charles Murray, *Losing Ground: American Social Policy, 1950–1980* (New York: Basic Books, 1984), pp. 20–21, 227–228, 234 (emphasis in the original).
11. Michael Harrington, *The New American Poverty* (New York: Holt, Rinehart and Winston, 1984), pp. 12, 230.
12. Ibid., p. 145.
13. Michael Harrington, "Crunched Numbers," *New Republic,* January 28, 1985, pp. 7–10. Soon afterward the *New Republic* offered an even more damning indictment of Murray's impressionistic use of statistics. See Robert Greenstein, "Losing Faith in 'Losing Ground,'" *New Republic,* March 25, 1985, pp. 12–17. Also see Katz, *The Undeserving Poor,* pp. 153–155.
14. Harrington, *New American Poverty,* p. 3. In another difference from *The Other America, The*

New American Poverty made only a few references to the idea of a "culture of poverty," and those were couched in a curiously abstract form: "There are some who hold that poverty itself is a culture. When that is said on the left, for example by the late Oscar Lewis, the intention is to emphasize the tenacity, the institutionalization, of misery in the United States. When it is urged on the right, say by an Edward Banfield, it is a tactic for making poverty something ephemeral and individualistic, a state of the soul rather than a condition of the society" (p. 181). Someone unfamiliar with his earlier writings would have a hard time concluding from that paragraph that the "culture of poverty" was ever associated with the name Michael Harrington. Within a few years, it would be widely forgotten that the "culture of poverty" had *ever* had a left-wing slant. Thus historian Jacqueline Jones would write in 1992 that "The 'culture of poverty' thesis serves a larger political purpose, for it encourages some people to believe that the poor positively revel in their own misery, that they shun stable marriages and steady employment almost as a matter of perverse principle. According to this view, the poor live in a different country, following a way of life that is as incomprehensible as it is self-destructive." Jacqueline Jones, *The Dispossessed: America's Underclass from the Civil War to the Present* (New York: Basic Books, 1992), p. 291.

15. On the development of the concept of "underclass" and its effects on the debate over poverty's causes and cures, see Herbert Gans, *The War Against the Poor: The Underclass and Antipoverty Policy* (New York: Basic Books, 1995).
16. Michael Harrington, "No to Jelly Bean Policies," *Democratic Left* 9 (September 1981), p. 2.
17. Dionne, *Why Americans Hate Politics,* p. 138.
18. Thomas Byrne Edsall, "The Reagan Legacy," in Edsall and Blumenthal, *The Reagan Legacy,* pp. 9, 11.
19. "Homeless Crisscross U.S., Until Their Cars and Their Dreams Break Down," *New York Times,* December 14, 1982, p. 1.
20. "The Leapfrog Recession," *Wall Street Journal,* July 19, 1982.
21. It was that kind of editorial judgment that led Michael to describe the editors of the *Wall Street Journal* as being "as fervidly ideological as some youthful convert to Trotskyism who has found in Marx the answer to all problems, not excluding the common cold." Michael Harrington, "Data Versus Dogma," *New Republic,* August 29, 1983, p. 29.
22. Karen W. Arensen, "Talking Business," *New York Times,* November 10, 1981, p. D2.
23. Wendell Rawls Jr., "65,000 Demonstrate at Capitol to Halt Atomic Power Units," *New York Times,* May 7, 1979, p. 1. For Michael's somewhat ambivalent feelings about the antinuclear protests (he worried that many of the protesters were too little concerned with the jobs of nuclear industry workers), see Harrington, "Nuke Battle Needs Unity," *Newsletter of the Democratic Left* 7 (June 1979), pp. 1–2, 13; and Harrington, "Getting Restless Again," *New Republic,* September 1, 1979, pp. 12–15.
24. Patrick Lacefield, "Rally Against Registration," *Democratic Left* 8 (May 1980), p. 6.
25. For an early example, in which there were only "two Georges" (Meany and McGovern), see Michael Harrington, "Is the Restoration of Public Confidence Possible?" in *Crisis in Confidence: The Impact of Watergate,* ed. Donald W. Harward (Boston: Little, Brown, 1974), p. 138.
26. William Serrin, "After Solidarity Day: Organizers Must Set Agenda," *New York Times,* September 21, 1981, p. 13.
27. David Shribman, "A Potpourri of Protesters," *New York Times,* September 20, 1981, p. 1.
28. Serrin, "After Solidarity Day"; "Solidarity Day," *Democratic Left* 9 (October 1981), p. 4.
29. Paul L. Montgomery, "Throngs Fill Manhattan to Protest Nuclear Weapons," *New York Times,* June 13, 1982, p. 1; Michael Harrington, "Beyond the Nuclear Freeze," *Democratic Left* 10 (May 1982), p. 2. Shortly after the June 12 demonstration, Michael was one of the signatories to a letter to Soviet leader Leonid Brezhnev from prominent peace activists in the United states (including Nuclear Freeze founder Randall Forsberg and David McReynolds of the War Resisters League) protesting the detention of independent peace activists in the Soviet Union. "Appeal to Brezhnev," *Dissent* 29 (fall 1982), p. 503.
30. Kenneth R. Noble, "Rights Marchers Ask New Coalition for Social Change," *New York Times,* August 28, 1983, p. 1.

31. Patrick Farrell, "Activist Calls for Full Employment Push," *Journal Inquirer,* November 18, 1982; Leonard Bernstein, "Author Offers Alternatives to Reaganomics," *Hartford Courant,* November 18, 1982.
32. The fact that the AFL-CIO backed Manatt's maneuver, in the name of preserving party unity, made it all the harder for Michael to challenge the decision. See Michael Harrington, "Toward Solidarity Day II," *Democratic Left* 10 (September 1982), p. 4; Gina Lobaco, "The Agenda Seems the Least of Democratic Agenda's Worries," *In These Times,* April 28, 1982, p. 5; John Judis, "The Battle for the Party's Soul," *In These Times,* May 26, 1982, p. 5.
33. Author's interview with Jo-Ann Mort, September 26, 1991; Ron Chernow, "An Irresistible Profile of Michael Harrington (You Must Be Kidding)," *Mother Jones* (July 1977).
34. Harrington wrote apologetically of his role at Port Huron in his two memoirs, *Fragments of the Century* (New York: Simon and Schuster, 1973), pp. 143–150; and *The Long Distance Runner* (New York: Henry Holt and Company, 1988), pp. 57–58; as well as in his anthology *Taking Sides: The Education of a Militant Mind* (New York: Holt, Rinehart and Winston, 1985), pp. 58–60; and as part of a *Socialist Review* retrospective on the twenty-fifth anniversary of the Port Huron statement, *Socialist Review* 93 (1987), pp. 152–158. It was Steve Max who finally wrote to him in 1987 and told him "that it was the last time you should write on that subject in such an apologetic tone." Steve Max to Michael Harrington, June 1, 1987. I am grateful to Steve Max for making a copy of this letter available to me.
35. Harrington, *The Long Distance Runner,* p. 66.
36. There is no published history of NAM. But see Arnold James Oliver Jr., "American Socialist Strategy in Transition: The New American Movement and Electoral Politics, 1972–1982," Ph.D. diss., University of Colorado, 1983.
37. Roberta Lynch, "Is DSOC on the Right Foot?" *In These Times,* March 30, 1977, p. 18.
38. Irving Howe, *Socialism and America* (New York: Harcourt, Brace, 1985), p. 101.
39. Author's interview with Roberta Lynch, April 3, 1992.
40. Roberta Lynch, "The New American Movement: A Political Assessment," *Moving On* 5 (March 1982), p. 4. A minority in both organizations was opposed to the merger; those in DSOC, including Irving Howe, stayed, but the antimerger minority in NAM split off to form its own small independent organization called Solidarity.
41. John B. Judis, "Despite Growth, DSA Is Unsure of Its Political Role," *In These Times,* October 26, 1983, p. 5.
42. *Socialist Forum* 9 (spring 1986), p. 35. Also see articles in *Democratic Left* reflecting concerns of radicals turning parents, such as Maxine Phillips, "Sandbox Socialism: Can We Pass the Torch?" *Democratic Left* 14 (March–April 1986), pp. 3–5. On DSA's membership loss and growing sense of crisis in the mid-1980s, see Joan Walsh, "Democratic Socialists Seek a Role in American Politics," *In These Times,* November 20–26, 1985, p. 5.
43. Author's interview with Jim Shoch, October 23, 1992.
44. Harrington, *The Long Distance Runner,* p. 143.
45. Microfiche transcript of *CBS Sunday Morning News,* January 10, 1982. Michael would also be featured on *CBS Morning News* on October 10, 1984, and May 19, 1986.
46. Author's interview with Jo-Ann Mort, September 26, 1991.
47. David Binder, *The Other German: Willy Brandt's Life and Times* (Washington, D.C.: New Republic Books, 1975); Donald Sassoon, *One Hundred Years of Socialism: The West European Left in the Twentieth Century* (New York: New Press, 1996), p. 330. Also see Harrington, *The Long Distance Runner,* pp. 203–208.
48. Michael Harrington, "A Better World in Birth," *Democratic Left* 15 (March–April 1987), p. 10.
49. Quoted in Jack Clark, "Socialist Internationalism," *Democratic Left* 9 (February 1981), p. 5. After leaving the SI, Carlsson became UN commissioner for Namibia and was killed in the terrorist attack on Pan Am Flight 103 over Scotland in 1988. Michael wrote an anguished obituary for him. Harrington, "Lost on Flight 103: A Hero to the Wretched of the World," *Los Angeles Times,* December 26, 1988. The SI's other affiliate in the United

States, SDUSA, found the new directions taken by Brandt and Carlsson less to their taste. Rita Freedman, SDUSA's executive director, denounced the SI's "tilt toward third world totalitarian movements" in a letter to the editor of the *New Republic,* June 13, 1981, p. 7.

50. Michael's attitude toward the Sandinista government was in marked contrast to that of his one-time comrades in SDUSA. Rita Freedman, executive director of SDUSA, and yipsel alumni like Penn Kemble and Josh Muravchik were among the signers of a full-page, pro-Contra ad that appeared in the *New York Times* a few years later: "We Support Military Assistance to the Nicaraguans Fighting for Democracy," advertisement, *New York Times,* March 16, 1986, p. 26. Penn Kemble also served on the board of the pro-Contra advocacy group Prodemca, which received funding from the National Endowment for Democracy (NED), which was directed by fellow SD Carl Gershman (and on whose board sat Al Shanker). Prodemca, in turn, passed funds on to *La Prensa,* the leading anti-Sandinista publication in Nicaragua. "NED Brouhaha," *In These Times,* April 2–8, 1986, p. 4. The pro-Contra *New Republic* hailed Penn Kemble as one of "a handful of young Democratic intellectuals and activists" who have "transformed both public discussion and public policy" vis-à-vis support for the Contras. "Democrats and Comandantes," *New Republic,* July 28, 1986, p. 8.
51. Jan Pieroni interview with Pierre Schori, June 11, 1993. I am grateful to Jan Pieroni for conducting this interview on my behalf during a trip she made to Stockholm.
52. Bella Stumbo, "The Lonely Fight of Last Old Leftist," *Los Angeles Times,* April 4, 1987, p. 24.
53. See, for example, Michael Harrington, "Eurosocialism Takes Off," *New Republic,* May 30, 1981, pp. 15–18.
54. "Jimmy Higgins Reports," *Democratic Left* 9 (January 1981), p. 24.
55. Harrington, *The Long Distance Runner,* p. 195.
56. Ibid., p. 194.
57. Robert Levey, "US Socialists Find Ripe Pickings in the Rhetoric of Reaganomics," *Boston Globe,* April 11, 1983.
58. Harrington, *The Long Distance Runner,* p. 248.
59. "Michael Harrington on Tour," *Democratic Left* 11 (January 1983), p. 10.
60. "Voices from the Left," *New York Times Magazine,* June 17, 1984, pp. 52–53. Not everyone was pleased with the attention being paid to Michael and Howe's ideas. For an attack from the right, see George Will, "The Laughable Left," *Los Angeles Times,* June 21, 1984, sec. 2, p. 7. And from the sectarian Left, see Alexander Cockburn, "Beat the Devil," *Nation,* July 7–14, 1984.
61. Harrington, *The Long Distance Runner,* p. 116; author's interview with Harold Meyerson, July 27, 1990.
62. Michael Harrington, "Don't Bank on Recession," *Democratic Left* 10 (November 1982), p. 8.
63. Michael Harrington, "Facing the Future: Four More Years of What?" *Democratic Left* 12 (November–December 1984), p. 3; Harrington, "Willful Shortsightedness on Poverty," *New York Times,* September 5, 1985, p. 27.
64. Salvatore, *Eugene V. Debs*, pp. 148–149.
65. Michael Harrington, "A Socialist's Centennial," *New Republic,* January 7, 1985, p. 18.
66. Michael's mother fell sick in the spring of 1978 and soon after he had to put her in a nursing home. She died at the end of July 1980. Michael, who had seen her two weeks before her death (when "she knew me, but that was about all") flew back to St. Louis for her funeral mass at St. Roch's church on Waterman Avenue, the same church in which he had been baptized. "Catherine Harrington Dies; Was Civic Leader," *St. Louis Post-Dispatch,* July 25, 1980; Michael Harrington, *The Next America: The Decline and Rise of the United States* (New York: Henry Holt, 1981), p. 86.
67. Harrington, *The Long Distance Runner,* pp. 232–234; Dick Polman, "A Socialist Prophet With Honor," *St. Louis Post- Dispatch Magazine,* November 20, 1988, p. 26.
68. Harrington, *The Long Distance Runner,* pp. 240–241.

69. At a "New Directions" conference that DSA organized in 1986 for Democratic Party activists, Jesse Jackson gave a keynote speech, and Michael praised Jackson as someone who had "talked more ideas to the American people than anyone else in the 1984 election." Robin Toner, "1000 Meet to Fight Democratic Shift to Right," *New York Times,* May 4, 1986, p. 34; "New Directions: The Left Strikes Back," *Democratic Left* 14 (May–August 1986), p. 6.
70. William F. Buckley to Michael Harrington, January 8, 1989, Democratic Socialists of America office files.
71. Polman, "A Socialist Prophet With Honor."
72. Paula Span, "The Harrington Perspective," *Washington Post,* July 1, 1988, p. B1. Also see David Behrens, "Celebrating a Socialist Lion," *Newsday,* June 30, 1988, pt. 2, p. 3.
73. Joanne Barkan, "In Celebration of Michael Harrington," *Democratic Left* 16 (September–October 1988), pp. 13–14.
74. Quoted in "In Celebration of Michael Harrington" (Next America Foundation: 1988).
75. Quoted in Gloria Steinem, "Harrington: Even Deserts Gave Him a Sense of Hope," *Newsday,* August 2, 1989 (emphasis in original).
76. Paul Berman, "Homage to Harrington," *Village Voice,* July 12, 1988, p. 31; Polman, "A Socialist Prophet With Honor."
77. Letter from Tom Murphy to author, November 8, 1991. Letter from Tony Brown to author, November 1, 1991.
78. "Words of Inspiration from Mike," *Democratic Left* 17 (September 1989), p. 4.
79. Michael Harrington to Willy Brandt [n.d., March or April 1989], Democratic Socialists of America office files, New York City.
80. Michael's travels in the spring of 1989 are chronicled in *Democratic Left* 17 (March-April 1989), p. 12; (May-June 1989), p. 8; (July-August 1989), p. 8.
81. Michael Harrington, *Socialism: Past and Future* (New York: Arcade Publishing, 1989), p. 278.
82. Author's interview with Skip Roberts, August 6, 1991.
83. Author's interview with Dinah Leventhal, August 4, 1991.

INDEX

PUBLICAFFAIRS is a new nonfiction publishing house and a tribute to the standards, values, and flair of three persons who have served as mentors to countless reporters, writers, editors, and book people of all kinds, including me.

I.F. STONE, proprietor of *I. F. Stone's Weekly*, combined a commitment to the First Amendment with entrepreneurial zeal and reporting skill and became one of the great independent journalists in American history. At the age of eighty, Izzy published *The Trial of Socrates*, which was a national bestseller. He wrote the book after he taught himself ancient Greek.

BENJAMIN C. BRADLEE was for nearly thirty years the charismatic editorial leader of *The Washington Post*. It was Ben who gave the *Post* the range and courage to pursue such historic issues as Watergate. He supported his reporters with a tenacity that made them fearless, and it is no accident that so many became authors of influential, best-selling books.

ROBERT L. BERNSTEIN, the chief executive of Random House for more than a quarter century, guided one of the nation's premier publishing houses. Bob was personally responsible for many books of political dissent and argument that challenged tyranny around the globe. He is also the founder and was the longtime chair of Human Rights Watch, one of the most respected human rights organizations in the world.

• • •

For fifty years, the banner of Public Affairs Press was carried by its owner Morris B. Schnapper, who published Gandhi, Nasser, Toynbee, Truman, and about 1,500 other authors. In 1983, Schnapper was described by *The Washington Post* as "a redoubtable gadfly." His legacy will endure in the books to come.

Peter Osnos, *Publisher*